HOUSEHOLD HINTS
& HANDY TIPS

Reader's Digest

HOUSEHOLD
HINTS
&HANDY TIPS

The Reader's Digest Association (Canada) Ltd.
Montreal

HOUSEHOLD HINTS & HANDY TIPS

The acknowledgments that appear on pages 478–480
are hereby made a part of this copyright page.

Copyright © 1988 The Reader's Digest Association (Canada) Ltd.
Copyright © 1988 The Reader's Digest Association, Inc.
Copyright © 1988 Reader's Digest Association Far East Ltd.
Philippine Copyright 1988 Reader's Digest Association Far East Ltd.

ISBN 0-88850-155-2
88 89 90 / 5 4 3 2 1

READER'S DIGEST and the Pegasus colophon
are registered trademarks of
The Reader's Digest Association, Inc.

Printed in the United States of America

STAFF

Project Editors
Sally French
Andrew R. Byers

Project Art Director
Joel Musler

Associate Editors
Ben Etheridge
Gerald Williams
Suzanne E. Weiss

Assistant Editor
Thomas A. Ranieri

Art Associate
Perri DeFino

Research Editors
Mary Jane Hodges
Wadad Bashour

Editorial Assistant
James Beran

Copy Preparation
Joseph Marchetti

Coordinator
Susan Wong

CONTRIBUTORS

Editors
Virginia Colton
Don Earnest

Writers
Therese Hoehlein Cerbie
Michael Chotiner
Thomas Christopher
Anne Falivena
William E. Hague
Lorna B. Harris
Sherwood Harris
Susan C. Hoe
Lilla Pennant
Mort Schultz
Elizabeth Tener
Karen Theroux
John Warde
Daniel E. Weiss

Copy Editor
Elaine Andrews

Artists
Janice Belove
Louise Delorme
Joe Dyas
John Gist
Linda Gist
Hatra Inc.
David Hurley
Olena Kassian
Ed Lipinski
Max Menikoff
Angel Pellegrino
Ken Rice
John Saporito
Bill Shortridge
Ray Skibinski

Researcher
Mary Lyn Maiscott

Indexer
Sydney Wolfe Cohen

Testers
Ann Rafferty
Virginia Taylor

Consultants
Jean Anderson
Sherri Austin
Jennifer Birckmayer
Trevor Cole
John L. Costa, M.D., F.A.A.P.
Sheila Danko
Clark E. Garner
Michael Garvey, D.V.M.,
 Dip. A.C.V.I.M.
Mark Gasper
Leon Grabowski
Walter A. Grub, Jr.
George E. Harlow, Ph.D.
Sara M. Hunt, Ph.D., R.D.
Elliot Justin, M.D.
Carolyn Klass
Joseph Laquatra, Ph.D.
Walter LeStrange
Jim McCann
Jean McLean
Norman Oehlke
Mary E. Purchase, Ph.D.
Peter G. Rose
Gertrude Rowland
Victor J. Selmanowitz, M.D.
Stanley H. Smith, Ph.D.
Janis Stone, Ph.D.
Marco Polo Stufano
Michael Paul Wein, CPA
Paul Weissler, SAE
Thomas A. Wilson, D.D.S.
Gabriel S. Zatlin, M.D.

**The editors thank the
following for
their assistance:**
Herb Barndt, Ph.D.
Ted R. Peck
David M. Kopec, Ph.D.
Jack E. Masingale
Julie Pryme
Damon Sgobbo
Louis Sorkin, Ph.D.

About this book

Here is a book packed with thousands of useful hints and expert tips. You can count on it to make your life easier—whether you are an on-the-go career person, a harried homemaker, a neophyte do-it-yourselfer, or someone experienced at juggling job, home, family, and friends.

Some sections of this book—such as Keeping Records, Managing Money (p.21), and Clothing & Laundry (p.267)—suggest blueprints for turning routine chores into easy procedures.

In all sections you'll find help in dealing with specific problems, even crises. For example, what if the kitchen sink won't drain when you're expecting dinner guests? Turn to the opening page of Chapter 2 (p.70), and there, under All Around the House, you'll see listed "Unclogging drains." Then flip through the pages and scan the bold headings; you'll soon discover an illustrated step-by-step description of what to do.

But suppose you don't find the answer right away. Then look in the index under Drains (or under Plumbing) to locate the correct page. You'll find similar help for a host of other problems, including lost or stolen credit cards (p.30), a flooded basement (p.119), a stain on your clothes (pp.281–285), and abdominal pain (p.313).

In a real emergency you won't have time to look in a book, or the book may not be handy. So it's best to know in advance how to handle a situation. Right now is a good time to learn what to do if

Fat catches fire on the stove	p.106
You smell the odor of gas	p.139
Your brakes fail	p.198
A dog attacks your dog	p.251
A person faints	p.341
Someone touches a live wire	p.341
A companion is choking	p.342
Someone has a heart attack	p.343

It's also a good idea to read how you can make your home safer, and thus *prevent* emergencies. Burglarproof your home (p.128); make it safe for a child (p.225) or for an older person (p.239). Prevent accidents in the bathroom (p.113) and the workshop (p.183); know how to turn off electric power (p.163) and how to use a ladder properly (p.171). A little organization goes a long way in helping you deal with the unexpected too. Most common road emergencies, for instance, can be handled with a simple tool kit (p.200).

But this book has a purpose well beyond helping you handle or prevent drastic events. You'll find an enormous variety of hints that you'll turn to again and again for help with all the vexing and perplexing difficulties of daily life.

—*The Editors*

Contents

CHAPTER ONE

GETTING ORGANIZED

Take a look at these great ideas for organizing your household, keeping personal records, and managing money. Find out how to get the most out of storage space, and the best ways to install shelves and other storage systems.

Keeping Records, Managing Money
Page 21

Your personal records; what to keep in permanent files; developing a filing system; taking an inventory of your home; what to keep in a safe-deposit box; setting up a home business office; writing cheques and reconciling bank statements; budgeting; paying your bills; complaining effectively; lost or stolen credit cards; establishing credit; your credit rights; choosing a doctor, lawyer, and other professionals; calculating your net worth; life insurance; financial investments; tips on Social Insurance and retirement; wills.

Storing It All Away
Page 35

Storage guidelines; how to find new storage space; solving entryway, living room, and kitchen clutter; getting the most use out of your bedroom closets; remodeling a closet; ideas for storage in children's rooms, bathrooms, halls, and attics; how to build rollaway storage units; how to locate wall studs and fasten storage to them; fasteners for hollow walls and masonry; hooks and hangers and how to install them; working with pegboard; buying lumber, plywood, and other shelf materials and hardware; planning and installing shelves and their supports; wire wall systems; how to build cabinets and cases; buying nails and screws; drawer organizers and slides; rollouts and pullouts.

Organizing Your Household
Page 9

The value of making lists; a self-test of how organized you are; making an organizer with a loose-leaf binder; saving time on the telephone; simplifying errands; chores you can accomplish in a matter of minutes; handling your mail efficiently; organizing housework; what to do when company is coming; hiring outside help; how to motivate the kids to pitch in; running a successful garage sale; ways to avoid clutter and massive cleanups.

Organizing Your Household

THE FIRST STEP IS YOU

Getting organized is not an end in itself. There is no "right" way to do things—unless it's right for you. It must fit your style, your energy, and your schedule. Whatever system helps you to function most effectively is the best one for you.

Beware of the tail wagging the dog situation—in which the appointment book, the budget and expenditures records, the filing system, and the master list take more time to maintain than working out the problems they're supposed to solve.

Are you a morning person or a night person? Your efficiency may increase if you arrange your tasks as much as possible around the rhythms of your body. Try scheduling top-priority projects during your peak hours, routine work during your "low" time.

The key is to start now, no matter what! If you have a call to make, start dialing. A letter to write? Pick up a pen and start writing.

Use the salami method to reach your goal. If the size of your project overwhelms you, tackle it a piece at a time. You wouldn't eat a salami whole, would you? You'd cut it into slices. Do the same thing with your big projects.

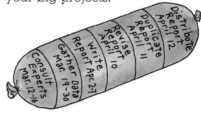

THE MASTER LIST

To organize your family's activities and to keep track of everyone's schedule, put up a large poster-sized master calendar that displays a full year. Enter all important family dates—birthdays, anniversaries, holidays—at the beginning of the year. Also enter appointments, as they are made, for everyone in your family.

Buy a notebook small enough to carry with you at all times. This notebook becomes your master list—a single continuous list that replaces those little scraps of paper. In the notebook, keep track of errands, appointments, things to do or buy, and items that will require action. As they approach, transfer dates from your master calendar to the notebook.

Shop around in stationery and office-supply stores for the notebook that best suits you. You'll probably be pleasantly surprised at the variety available these days.

9

HOW ORGANIZED ARE YOU?

1. Does it often take you more than 10 minutes to unearth a particular letter, bill, report, or other paper from your files or the top of your desk?

2. Are there loose papers on your desk, other than reference materials, that you haven't looked at for a month or more?

3. Has your electricity, gas, or telephone ever been turned off because you forgot to pay the bill?

4. Within the last 2 months, have you overlooked a scheduled appointment, an anniversary, or some other date that you wanted to acknowledge?

5. Do magazines pile up unread?

6. Do you frequently put off a work assignment for so long that it becomes an emergency or a panic situation?

7. Do you frequently misplace your keys, eyeglasses, gloves, handbag, briefcase, or other commonly carried items?

8. Do belongings gather in corners of closets, or on the floor, because you can't decide where to put them?

9. Would your storage problems be solved if only you had more space?

10. Do you want to get organized but everything is in such a mess that you don't know where to start?

11. Do your children have household jobs that they carry out willingly?

12. By the end of the average day, have you accomplished at least the most important tasks you set for yourself?

13. Are the kitchen items you use most often in the most convenient place?

14. Is your living room arranged so that family and guests can speak comfortably without raising their voices? Are there places for drinks and snacks?

Score: 1 point for each yes to questions 1–10.
1 point for each no to questions 11–14.

If your score is
1–3. Systems are under control. Some of the innovative tips in this section might make things even better.
4–7. Disorganization is troublesome. Hints in "Organizing Your Household" could help considerably.
8–10. Life must be very difficult.
11 and up. Disorganized to the point of chaos. Use the hints and ideas to change your life—and get to work immediately.

Include in your notebook all telephone numbers and details needed to accomplish a job. For example: "Call Acme customer service, 374-5000, ext. 295, re $5 overcharge on bill dated 2/4/88, acct. no. 483-456-7899."

Don't overcomplicate your notebook by listing items that are a part of your daily or weekly routine. Save the notebook for reminders and special projects.

Make a "list of lists" section in your notebook—a file of ideas. For example, set aside individual pages to list books to read, movies to rent, current movies to see, places to go when people visit, recommended restaurants, and so on.

At the start of each week—or, better yet, as the present week is ending—plan several days ahead. It gives you perspective on the week, enables you to spread out the musts, and prevents a frantic rush at week's end.

Set aside a time for fun—treat it like an important appointment. If you don't set aside a specific time for relaxation, your work and other commitments will soon take over your life.

MAKE YOUR OWN ORGANIZER

There's no need to spend a lot of money on a fancy organizer with expensive inserts that may be suited to other people's lives, but not yours. Instead, make one to suit your own personal needs.

Simply buy a small loose-leaf binder in a stationery store. Choose one with the pockets in the front and/or back to hold a small calculator and business cards. At the same time, get loose-leaf paper and dividers to fit.

Identify the categories you wish to include in your organizer—addresses and telephone numbers, errands, long-term projects, appointments, expenses, or whatever you wish. Fill in the tabs on the dividers and insert them in the binder along with an adequate amount of paper for each section.

For the appointments section, get a small calendar—perhaps the kind you get free from banks or greeting-card companies. Remove its outer cover and punch holes along the inside crease to fit the rings of the binder. Now you're ready to get organized.

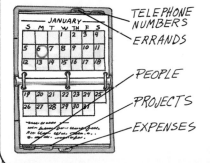

THE VALUE OF MAKING LISTS

1. Writing down activities makes them more concrete.
2. Lists enable you to consider items carefully and to give them their proper priorities.
3. Writing down activities prevents you from forgetting them. Moreover, once you start listing your activities on paper, you can also rate them in order of priority.
4. It feels good to cross items off a list once they've been accomplished.

Keep your list with you at all times. A list is worse than useless if you can't refer to it. You may think that you've disposed of a matter when in fact you haven't.

Set a goal to do one necessary chore that you really dislike each day. You'll have a sense of satisfaction each time you succeed.

Keep a second, separate notebook to cope with complex, special situations—for example, enrolling a child in college, moving to a new home, or organizing a big family holiday.

Don't be in a hurry to throw away notebook pages that have been completed. That stove part you ordered 2 months ago may be all wrong when it arrives, and you may have to call the same people all over again.

THE FAMILY MESSAGE CENTER

Establish a message center in your home. It needn't be elaborate—it can be on the refrigerator or on a bulletin board or a door. Encourage everyone in the household to use the message center to list plans, needs for the next trip to the store, and—especially important—all telephone messages.

Keep the message center current; throw away outdated notes. Take care of as many items as you can each day—or enter them in your notebook for action later.

TELEPHONE TIMESAVERS

Install telephone jacks all around the house or get a cordless phone so that you can talk wherever you are in and around your home.

Get long extension cords for your telephones so that you can move around freely while talking. Often, you can do a chore while talking on the telephone—cooking, tending plants, for example.

To save time—and frustration—whenever possible use the telephone instead of making a trip. Phone to confirm appointments, to check if a store has the item you want, to learn business hours, and so on.

Learn how to cut off time-consuming calls without hurting people's feelings. For example, it's quite all right to say, "This is a terrible time for me, may I call you back?" (Of course, do call back later.)

Sometimes a phone call is more timesaving and effective than a letter. Even a long-distance call may be cheaper, especially when you consider how long it takes to write a letter and how much your time is worth.

Resist the temptation to remove the receiver from its cradle during times when you don't want interruptions. Instead, turn down the bell. Leaving the receiver off the cradle may interrupt phone service even after you've replaced the receiver.

ERRANDS

Keep a running list of groceries and household supplies that you need. By the time you go shopping, there'll be little to add.

Group your errands so that you can accomplish several in a single trip. Try to find a convenient shopping center that has all or most of the stores, offices, and services that you need.

If possible, patronize stores and offices near your home, your work, or on the route between the two. Try to accomplish an errand on the way to something else instead of making a special trip.

If you have appointments or errands at several locations, schedule them so that you can go from one to the next with a minimum of wasted time and travel.

Eliminate additional trips by making back-to-back doctor or dentist appointments for family members (or at least for all the kids).

Ask for the first appointment in the morning so that you won't be delayed by someone ahead of you and you'll still have most of the day left when you finish.

Take your weekly list with you whenever you go out on errands. You may be able to fit in something that you scheduled for later in the week.

When shopping, buy lightweight items first and pick up heavy, cumbersome, or perishable items last. Arrange your shopping list and itinerary accordingly.

Get your family to help out with errands. If a shirt has to be returned, leave it in clear sight so that anyone going to or near that particular store can return it. To make it easy, attach a note with instructions—credit to charge account, exchange for a different size or color, or whatever.

USING BITS OF TIME

Most small chores can be accomplished in bits and pieces of time. For instance, while you're waiting in a doctor's office, you can pay bills; while riding the bus, write out your shopping list. The following lists may give you some ideas of what you can do in odd chunks of time.

What you can do in 5 minutes:
Make an appointment.
File your nails.
Water houseplants.
Make out a party guest list.
Order tickets for a concert or a ball game.
Sew back a button.

What you can do in 10 minutes:
Write a short letter or note.
Pick out a birthday card.
Repot a plant.
Hand-wash some clothes.
Straighten up your desktop.
Exercise.

What you can do in 30 minutes:
Go through backed-up magazines
    and newspapers.
Work on a crafts project.
Polish silver and brass.
Vacuum three or four rooms.
Weed a flower bed.

YOU AND YOUR MAIL

Handle most of your mail only once. Immediately discard anything that needs no action, doesn't interest you, or doesn't merit saving—a subscription request for a magazine you're already getting, for example.

If you receive an unsolicited credit card that you don't want, cut it up so that it can't be used and throw it away immediately. Do the same whenever you discard out-of-date credit cards or those you don't intend to use again.

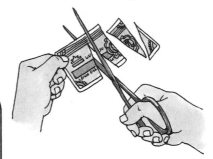

When you need a copy of your reply, make a carbon copy on the back of the sender's original letter. This way you have only one sheet to file, and the chances of mislaying the copy are greatly reduced. No need to type to get a carbon copy either. A handwritten reply done with a ball-point pen makes a perfectly legible carbon.

So that you always have greeting cards for any occasion, buy extras and file them in appropriately labeled folders (birthday, anniversary, get well).

Include on your weekly list of things to do letters that must be written, cards to be mailed, and other kinds of paperwork with deadlines—taxes, auto registrations, and so on.

ORGANIZING HOUSEWORK

Make it a habit to return everything to its proper place and remind others to do so. If you do this daily, it takes less time than waiting until the situation is out of control. An even bigger bonus is that you needn't spend time looking for out-of-place objects.

Do small chores as their need occurs so that they occupy little time. For example, laundry left until the weekend can consume the weekend; instead, start a load before breakfast, put it in the dryer after breakfast, and it's done.

In planning the week's chores, try to set aside a free day (or at least a few hours) for yourself to do whatever you want—whether it's a day out of the house or time alone to finish that book you started several months ago.

Use labor-saving gadgets or appliances whenever they'll *really* save time. But don't overdo it—chopping an onion with a knife may take no longer than using a food processor and then having to take the machine apart and wash and dry it.

Leave some slack in your day for surprises, interruptions, or emergencies. Some activities will take longer than expected, no matter how carefully you plan or allow for delays.

Think before you act—even before you do routine jobs. The way you perform simple, basic tasks is usually the result of habit, not logic. There *may* be a better way.

Why does a half-hour job often take twice as long as you thought it would? Probably because you estimated only the actual working time and didn't take into account the preparation—getting out and putting away tools, for instance.

Tackle big tasks a bit at a time. Straightening every closet in the house might take days; one closet, especially one that isn't too cluttered, may take no longer than 15 or 20 minutes.

NINETEENTH-CENTURY THOUGHTS ON HOUSEWORK

As society gradually shakes off the remnants of barbarism...a truer estimate is formed of woman's duties, and of the measure of intellect requisite for the proper discharge of them. Let any man of sense and discernment become the member of a large household, in which a well-educated and pious woman is endeavoring systematically to discharge her multiform duties; let him fully comprehend all her cares, difficulties, and perplexities; and it is probable he would coincide in the opinion that no statesman, at the head of a nation's affairs, had more frequent calls for wisdom, firmness, tact, discrimination, prudence, and versatility of talent, than such a woman.

An excerpt from *The American Woman's Home,* by Catherine E. Beecher and Harriet Beecher Stowe, published in 1869.

COMPANY'S COMING

Save time and concentrate on high-payoff cleaning—work on the most conspicuous areas, such as entrance halls and living-room rugs. Have you ever noticed how much cleaning you can do in the hour before company comes?

If company's coming and things aren't quite up to par, bring out the candles, dim the lights, and serve up good food and conversation. As long as soil and disorder don't force themselves on one's attention, no normal person will seek them out.

Once you've attended to basics, such as cleaning the bathroom, concentrate on what shows the most. Any home will pass muster if the clutter is contained, the surfaces are clean, and your best possessions are polished.

Practice cosmetic strategies that fool the eye. Keep the white chair clean, and people will assume that the black one is also clean. If you have fringed rugs, vacuum the fringe so that it lies straight and neat. Guests will assume everything else is equally orderly.

For a last-minute cleanup of the bathroom after the family has used it, go quickly over all surfaces with a spray window cleaner and a paper towel.

THE NIGHT BEFORE

Cut down the morning chaos by doing as much as you can the night before. Write absence notes, bus notes, trip permissions. Lay out clothes, fix lunches, distribute lunch money, book-order money. It doesn't take long.

While you are cleaning up the kitchen after dinner, set the table for breakfast, put out jams, cereals, and any other nonrefrigerated items; you'll have that much less to do in the morning.

MAKING LIFE EASIER

Allow time for making up the beds and tidying the kitchen before leaving the house in the morning. It makes coming home much more pleasant—and sets an example for others in the household.

Keep a bookcase near the back door. Assign each child a shelf on which to assemble lunch, homework, gym clothes, and so on. In the morning, they can pick up everything quickly as they depart; in the afternoon, they can drop their belongings there.

15

Set up a "way station" for the consolidation in one place of schoolbooks, laundered clothes, toys, mail, and other odds and ends. Once a day, have your kids pick up their belongings from the way station and take them to their rooms. Designate a chair, box, or basket for this purpose and locate it where they can't ignore it.

Designate one bookshelf specifically for library books and make sure your children return all such books to this shelf. This saves a lot of searching for library books that might get scattered around the house or mixed in with your own.

Keep a money dish handy for your small change so that you won't be caught short when someone going out the door suddenly needs last-minute funds.

SHARING THE BURDEN

Try discussing the chores each member of the family likes least and work around them accordingly. One person may hate to scrape the dishes but may not mind taking them out of the dishwasher. Rather than arguing, find something each person enjoys doing instead.

Design a revolving circular chore chart to assign mealtime chores such as setting the table and washing the dishes.

Avoid the "boss" syndrome. As soon as youngsters become proficient at a job, back away and let them be responsible for the results. Resist the temptation to keep checking up.

VARYING STANDARDS

Let family group pressure maintain standards as much as possible. When a chore isn't properly done, hold back for awhile and give others a chance to gripe and solve the problem themselves.

Be sure that you're not imposing too high a standard. When work is honestly shared, all partners are entitled to a say in how well it has to be done. If you're the only one who wants a job done better, reexamine your expectations and perhaps make some adjustments.

If your family is uncooperative, consider whether your standards are too high. If you lower your expectations somewhat, it may be easier to get chores done.

OUTSIDE HELP

If you can't get all your housework done in a reasonable amount of time, hire someone to help you. You'll be surprised at how much more you can accomplish with someone helping out just 3 hours every week!

If you can't afford professional help, be creative. Possible sources of assistance include students and neighbors who want part-time work and might be willing to take over one or two jobs, such as housecleaning, ironing, or grocery shopping—and for considerably less than it costs to hire a professional.

MOTIVATING KIDS TO HELP

Include your youngest child in the housework; it may slow progress, but it's an essential first step in helping that child feel part of the home work force.

Have your young child dust and sweep along with you at first. The youngster will feel grown up, and you may get more work done.

SOME HOUSEHOLD JOBS A 5-YEAR-OLD CAN DO

1. Make her own bed every day. It may be a little sloppy at first, but it'll improve in the course of time.
2. Put clothes back in the closet or proper dresser drawer.
3. Put toys back in the toy chest.
4. Water houseplants.
5. Feed the dog, cat, or goldfish (if she's reminded).
6. Set the table.
7. Clear the table, one thing at a time.

Teach your child step by step how to do whatever job you ask of her. Don't assume that the task will be completely learned by watching. Show, teach, train.

Once you've given your child certain definite jobs with clear-cut responsibilities, let him work without constant supervision. Check the result when he's finished and compliment him.

Clearly define the time of day when a child's job is to be completed—either before school, right after school, or by dinner. Don't let tasks hang over into the evening.

On weekends, make up a list of chores and negotiate assignments over a leisurely breakfast. Break a big job down into steps and be sure the kids' ages and abilities are equal to their assignments.

Assume that boys and girls will do the housework in equal amounts and without sex designations. Assign their chores accordingly.

Don't redo a chore that a child has just completed. If you insist that a task be done only your way, then do it and be done with it. Redoing is destructive to a child's ego. Just think back to a time when someone redid something you had just completed!

Don't expect a youngster to put in a full day's work. An hour is about all that can reasonably be expected of an 8-year-old. A 14-year-old can probably achieve almost as much as an adult, but this depends on the responsibility level of the teenager.

SOME HOUSEHOLD JOBS A TEENAGER CAN DO

In addition to the chores of a younger child (p.17):

1. Empty wastebaskets and ashtrays.
2. Carry out trash cans.
3. Vacuum rugs and floors.
4. Clean and sweep the kitchen floor.
5. Iron his own clothes and the family napkins and tablecloths.
6. Polish silver, brass, copper.
7. Carry in wood and lay fires.
8. Vacuum the inside of the car.
9. Wash the car.

YOUR CHILD'S ROOM

Remind your children that 5 or 10 minutes of effort a day will keep their rooms in pretty good shape. If they save all their straightening up for Saturday, it will take an hour or two and will surely be met with groans and complaints.

Modify children's rooms so that they can help maintain them. Supply child-sized features, such as a low dresser with nonstick drawers and a closet with hangers and hooks at a child's height.

Once you've helped put a child's room together, the room and the objects in it "belong" to the child. If you take over too much responsibility for keeping it neat, the child will feel the room belongs to you and not to her, and she may not take care of it.

A child as young as 5 can at least "spread up" a bed—it doesn't have to be perfect! Using comforters or quilts on beds will make the job a lot easier.

Ideally, older children's rooms (especially those belonging to adolescents) should be off-limits to any adult interference. Unless the room has reached a level of messiness that threatens to infect the rest of the house, the best policy is hands-off.

WHERE TO PUT THINGS

It all comes down to a place for everything and everything in its place—just as soon as it comes into the house! Otherwise, you'll put it somewhere "for now," but it will really be forever.

Before you buy something, ask yourself, "Where am I going to put it?" and make sure that you have a clearly defined place in mind.

An "I-don't-know-what-it-is" box can be a tremendous help. This is for orphan socks and gloves and all those important-looking but unidentifiable machinery parts, nuts, and bolts you find lying about. From time to time, sort the contents and dump whatever appears useless into the trash.

Keep items used together near one another—for example, tennis rackets, balls, sneakers, and other tennis equipment. Store these related items at or near the place where you use them.

FIGHTING THE "PACK RAT" SYNDROME

Go through your house periodically, eliminating items you no longer want. One possible criterion: when you no longer notice a decorative object (such as a picture), it may be time to get rid of it.

You might consider a trade-off system. Whenever you add a new item to the household inventory, discard an old one.

Caution! Do not throw out someone else's things unless they ask you to do so. Suggest and encourage, but don't take over. This applies to your parents, spouse, and any children over 4 years old.

Be ruthless with your own possessions. Discard all unused junk. When in doubt, throw it out. It takes up space, and you'll just wind up cleaning it and moving it around.

ATTACKING A MESSY CLOSET

When the enthusiasm to clean strikes, start from the outside in. Take care of the clutter scattered around the room before digging into the closet. Starting with the closet first makes a double mess.

If you're faced with an overcrowded closet, schedule an hour to work on it. Write it on your weekly list as a project. But don't try to finish the closet in one session. When the hour is up, quit. Schedule another hour and then another until the closet is done.

To keep mess to a minimum, before you begin cleaning a closet, arrange four boxes nearby to categorize those things that shouldn't go back in. Label them for "charity," "trash," "belongs elsewhere," and "decision pending."

Work on one small section of a closet at a time. Do *not* empty an entire cluttered closet at once. The resulting chaos is sure to set you back or put you off entirely.

If you absolutely can't bear the thought of throwing something away, take it to a local church or charity, the Salvation Army, a thrift shop, or a rummage sale.

KEY QUESTIONS WHEN CLEANING A CLOSET

As you weed out a closet, consider each item individually and ask yourself:

1. Have I used this item in the past year? If the answer is yes, it's worth keeping another year. If no, discard it.
2. Does it have either sentimental or monetary value to me? Yes? Then keep it.
3. Might it come in handy someday? If you answer yes but have nothing specific in mind, better put the article into a "throwaway" or "giveaway" box unless you have ample attic or basement storage space. A yes answer usually means that you're hanging onto clutter.

Have a garage sale—it's a terrific way to dispose of a lot of discardable items. If you've never had a garage sale before, ask someone who has held one to help you.

SEVEN STEPS TO A SUCCESSFUL GARAGE SALE

1. Check with your municipality to see whether you need a permit.
2. Assemble items to be sold. If you don't have enough, ask friends and neighbors to participate in the sale.
3. Run an ad in your local newspaper, giving the location, date, rain date, and time. Post notices at supermarkets and, if local regulations permit, at street corners.
4. Price goods with tags or tape (use different colors for different owners). Keep prices low.
5. Group similar items together: put clothes on racks, books in boxes, miscellaneous items on card tables.

6. Be prepared to bargain; after all, you're trying to get rid of everything. Reduce prices during the last 2 hours of the sale.
7. Give any leftovers from the sale to your favorite charity. Take down all posters.

A move to a new home is an ideal time to sort and throw out. As you do so, organize the possessions you're taking with you in cartons according to their new storage locations—attic, garage, coat closet, and so on. Using a large marker, write where they are to go on the outside of the box.

"AN OUNCE OF PREVENTION..."

Instead of spending hours a year trying to remove felt-tip marker writing and drawing from walls, spend a couple of minutes putting the markers out of reach of small children. It's also a good idea to restrict potential troublemakers, such as crayons, paints, and clay, to a specified play area.

To avoid frequent cleanups of your oven or your stove top, choose large enough pots and pans for your recipes so that the food doesn't boil or slop over.

Confine eating and drinking to certain specified areas in your home. Supply coasters for drinks and small plates for snacks. Don't fill glasses or cups to the rim. When you're entertaining guests, try not to serve crumbly or drippy finger food.

ODDS AND ENDS

To help keep clutter under control, set aside one bowl or basket in a central location to temporarily house small objects that have no current home.

Assign convenient permanent locations for small restless items that would otherwise end up on a tabletop or be mislaid: a hook near the door for keys that you always take when you go out; a small dish on the bureau top to collect loose change or earrings; a mug on the desk to hold pens and pencils.

A wastebasket in each room encourages prompt trash disposal, and laundry hampers in bedrooms and bathrooms keep dirty clothes from piling up on the floor.

Keeping Records, Managing Money

YOUR PERSONAL RECORDS

Some of the most valued "records" that you have are probably personal letters, photographs, and such mementos as newspaper clippings, diplomas, and graduation programs. Don't feel guilty about saving these, but don't be overly sentimental either—throw out the scraps that will mean little as time passes.

To protect these mementos from fire or flood—and to keep them all in one place as well—store them in a metal strongbox.

Make sure that you have copies of all birth, marriage, divorce, and death certificates. Records of births, marriages, and deaths may be obtained from your provincial government, either from the department of health or a statistics division. Divorce certificates are kept by provincial justice departments.

To get copies of a birth certificate, write to the appropriate department in the capital city of the province where the birth took place. The address will be listed in the government section of that city's telephone directory. If you wish to phone, you may also find the number under "Birth Certificates" in the government section. Get several copies of important certificates while you're at it. They'll be useful when you apply for such things as pensions, a mortgage or a passport.

YOUR PERMANENT FILE

You can set up a permanent file for your important papers on shelves or in shoe boxes but, to be really safe, a metal box or drawer cabinet is best.

Keep the deed to your home, your mortgage agreement, and other papers from the closing—such as surveys and title guarantees—in a permanent file.

If you have a cottage or a second home, maintain a permanent file of all major improvements. These documented costs can help offset capital gains tax if you sell your house at a profit later on.

Wills, powers of attorney, and life insurance policies should also be in your permanent file. Be sure to discard expired life insurance policies and superseded wills and powers of attorney.

Save all your children's report cards and school and college records in a permanent file. The kids will appreciate these later in life.

21

A FILING CHECKLIST

With this procedure, you can develop a filing system from scratch or revise an existing one that isn't working well.

1. Gather together in one place all items to be filed.

2. Have a wastebasket for trash handy, along with file folders, labels, and pens.

3. Pick up the item on the top of the pile (or the first folder if you're revising an existing file) and decide whether it has any value to you. If it doesn't, throw it away. If it does, go on to the next step.

4. If it's worth retaining, choose a folder heading for it, label the folder, and slip in the piece of paper. Some sample headings for a home file: finances, household repairs, personal letters, medical records, taxes, warranties and guarantees.

5. Pick up the next item in the stack and go through the same procedure, the only variation being that this may fit into an existing folder, rather than one with a new heading. Consolidate whenever possible.

6. Assemble your pile of folders and put them in alphabetical order.

7. Put your alphabetized folders into a file drawer or a carton that you have specially set aside for files.

8. Each time you consult a folder, riffle through it quickly and pick out and discard the deadwood. That way, your files won't become crowded.

OTHER FILES

Set up a separate file for each savings account, mutual fund, and other investments. Review their performance from time to time—at least every 3 to 6 months.

Keep canceled cheques (if your bank still returns them) in case you have a dispute about whether or not a bill has been paid.

Store bills of sale, warranties, and guarantees in a separate file so that you can quickly locate exactly what you need when equipment requires repair or replacement.

Save all receipts and sales slips so that you're able to check the accuracy of your monthly bills and in case you need to return an item or get it repaired sometime during a warranty period.

At some time or other, we all experience the panic of having lost our credit cards. You can make the replacement job easier by photocopying cards that you carry in your wallet or purse. Make a special file for the copies and put it in a safe place.

Keep a record of the numbers of your traveler's cheques and file it separately from the cheques themselves.

Store all your owner's manuals in a file folder or punch holes in them and put them in a ring binder.

If you have a lot of owner's manuals, installation diagrams, and the like, store them in a special drawer, perhaps in the kitchen.

A special file of car-repair receipts provides a record of past repairs and servicing. For easy reference, in the event of your wallet's loss or theft, keep photocopies of your driver's license and auto insurance and registration in a separate envelope in the file.

MEDICAL RECORDS

Keep all the material that you need to process medical and dental insurance claims in one file or folder—instructions, blank forms, eligible bills, birth dates and Social Insurance Numbers of all covered persons, and so on.

If you're moving or changing doctors or dentists, ask for a summary of your medical or dental records to take with you.

When an offspring leaves home for college, to live on his own, or to get married, provide him with a list of his vaccinations, X-rays, childhood illnesses, and the like. This information can come in very handy when medical attention is required.

HOME INVENTORY

For insurance purposes, take photographs of all your possessions and keep them in a metal box or in a safe-deposit box. Then, if any are lost, stolen, or destroyed, you'll have proof of having had them.

Another method of taking inventory is to have someone videotape you while you walk through your house describing and pricing (as best you can) your belongings.

HOW TO KEEP RECORDS

Tired of crossing out and erasing in your address book? Use index cards instead and store them in a file box. Write in your friends' red-letter days and the names of their children—so that you'll be reminded when you call or visit. When there are changes, you can make out a new card quickly.

Write emergency telephone numbers on a red card and put it in the front of your card file where it will be available with a minimum of fumbling.

Likewise, use blue cards (or some other distinctive color) for plumbers, electricians, babysitters, and all the other household services you use frequently.

WHERE TO KEEP RECORDS

If you have important documents or official documents that are difficult to replace—for example, marriage, birth, and death certificates, divorce papers, adoption papers, or any other court- or government-recorded papers—put them in a safe-deposit box at your bank.

It's not advisable to put life insurance policies (or wills) in a safe-deposit box. Safe-deposit boxes are often sealed by court order when the box holder dies. This may cause a delay in obtaining payment on those policies.

WHAT TO STORE IN A SAFE-DEPOSIT BOX

Because of rising crime and insurance rates, many people rent safe-deposit boxes from a bank or from a private safe-deposit company. You should put all your valuable, hard-to-replace, or irreplaceable items in one. Then keep a list of what is in your box in a safe place at home. The following are suggestions of what should be kept in the box.

A *photocopy* of your will, but *not* the original.

All stock or bond certificates or bank savings certificates (but not passbooks) that you have in your possession.

All insurance policies—*except* for life insurance policies.

Property records, such as mortgages, deeds, and titles, but *not* the deeds of burial plots.

Personal documents, such as birth certificates, marriage certificates, divorce papers, military discharge papers, passports.

An inventory of valuable items in your home, such as furs, jewelry, electronic equipment, and collectibles. List the cost and purchase date of each. If possible, include photographs of each item.

Small valuables, such as coins, jewelry, and silver.

Airline tickets bought a long time before departure.

Some files can be stored permanently out of the way on a shelf in the attic, basement, or utility room. After you've finished your taxes for the year, put away all that year's records in a single large envelope or box. At the same time, throw away the contents of the oldest envelope—if it's more than 6 years old.

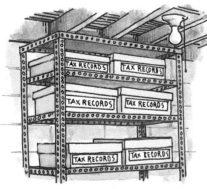

CONDUCTING BUSINESS AT HOME

Buy supplies in double quantities so that you won't have to dash out in the middle of a project to buy an item you've run out of.

To distinguish between your business and personal life, "dress" for work. Don't sit around in your bathrobe all day.

"Walk to work." Walk around the block and back home. You'll get a little morning exercise, and you'll arrive at your "office" in a more businesslike frame of mind, refreshed and ready for work.

Maybe no one will see your office, but clutter can drain your energy. Throw out dead plants, close closet doors, banish the cat from your desktop.

Be firm with people who interrupt. Because you're at home, others may not take your work as seriously as if you went to an office.

Handle interruptions just as you would at an office—tell others when you'll be free. If friends call during working hours, resist the temptation to socialize. Arrange to call them back later.

SETTING UP AN OFFICE AT HOME

Ideally, your home office should be a separate room, but if one isn't available, choose a corner that will belong to you and you alone. If necessary, invest in partitions to separate yourself psychologically from the rest of the house.

In selecting an area, consider whether there is enough space for a desk and other equipment. Is there a convenient electrical outlet and telephone jack? (If not, they can be installed.)

Your desk needn't be a "desk" at all. All you really need is a surface to write on. Whatever you choose, it should be sturdy and a comfortable height. A hollow door resting on two file cabinets provides plenty of drawer space and a good-sized desktop at just the right height.

BANKING AND BANK ACCOUNTS

Budgeting is easier if you have one bank account for paying bills. For couples, make it a joint account. Even if one person usually handles the finances, the other should be able to write cheques if circumstances require it.

If your chequing account doesn't pay interest, it might pay to convert to one that does. Shop around for the best deal. Even if the interest is small, it probably beats paying service charges.

HOW LONG DOES IT TAKE TO DOUBLE YOUR MONEY?

How many years will it take for your money to double at a given rate of interest? A simple method for calculating this is called the Rule of 72. By dividing the rate of interest into 72, you will obtain the number of years required to double your money at that rate of interest.

Rate of interest:	Years to double:
5%	72 divided by 5 = 14.4
6	72 divided by 6 = 12
7	72 divided by 7 = 10.3
8	72 divided by 8 = 9
9	72 divided by 9 = 8
10	72 divided by 10 = 7.2
11	72 divided by 11 = 6.5
12	72 divided by 12 = 6

Note: These figures are based on interest compounded annually. On interest compounded semiannually, quarterly, monthly, or daily, your money will double in a somewhat shorter time. Also, these figures do not take taxes into consideration.

Avoid carrying large balances on your cards, or using these cards for major purchases. You may pay high interest fees for this privilege. Better to take out a personal bank loan for major purchases or to consolidate any sizable credit card balances. The bank's rate of interest will probably be no more than 12 percent.

If you're having trouble selecting the best interest-bearing account from the array now available from banks and trust companies, remember that the longer a financial institution is guaranteed the use of your money, the more interest it can afford to pay you.

If you must borrow money, the best way to get the lowest possible interest rate is to offer at least as much security as the loan. Often this is the item you're planning— a new car, for example.

Disbelieve every high-rate ad until you have carefully studied all the terms. What the big black type giveth, the spidery type may taketh away.

In choosing a bank, look for one with such extra services as direct deposit of payroll cheques, direct deduction of utility payments, 24-hour teller machines, extended banking hours.

WRITING CHEQUES

Take care every time you write a cheque. Write legibly so that the bank clerk can read the name of the payee and can easily compare it with the signature of the person endorsing the cheque.

Make sure that the figures you write on the first line of the cheque agree with the amount in words on the second line—known as the "body." By law, if the figures do not agree, the written amount takes precedence over the figures. In practice, your cheque would probably be returned.

The only way to be certain your cheques are safe from alteration is to ensure that all spaces are filled or scored through. Empty spaces are an open invitation to the forger. So just draw a line before and after all your figures and letters.

BANK STATEMENTS

Balance your bank statement with your cheque-book as soon as possible after you receive it. This will help you spot a large mistake and will prevent you from writing cheques that your balance won't cover.

A little shaky about balancing your bank statements? Ask your banker for help or use the instructions on the back of your statement. If yours doesn't have any, here's a simplified form to copy and use.

BALANCING YOUR CHEQUING ACCOUNT

STEPS **YOUR FIGURES**

Cheque-book

1. List your cheque-book balance . . . . _____
2. Add earned interest (if any) . . . . _____
3. Subtract any service charges . . . . _____
4. Your new balance . . . . _____

Statement

1. List your statement balance . . . . _____
2. List cheques outstanding . . . . _____

  Cheque number   **Amount**

  _____   _____
  _____   _____
  _____   _____

  Subtract cheques outstanding . . . . _____
3. Subtotal . . . . _____
4. Add deposits not credited on statement . . . . _____
5. Your cheque-book should show this balance . . . . _____

Spare yourself the frustration of tracking down a few cents' worth of arithmetical errors. Simply add or subtract the small discrepancy and enter the correct figure in your cheque-book.

BUDGETING

Review and adjust your budget at least once a year (perhaps at tax time, when you've done a financial review) so as to take into consideration increases or decreases in income, completion of installment debts, a change in priorities. As the needs of living change, so should the budget.

If you're dissatisfied with the picture when you see your budget set out on paper, you may want to rearrange your spending priorities. This could involve cutting down on your clothing expenditures or eating out less frequently. It's easier to reduce entertainment and miscellaneous expenses.

Where to cut back is a family decision, and older children should be included in any discussion that involves belt-tightening in the home.

Set up a separate investment builder or savings account in which you accumulate funds to pay the big bills—for example, quarterly income taxes, property taxes, university tuition, vacation expenses. Total the amount needed, divide by 12, and deposit this amount every month.

Setting spending limits that are too low is a sure way to torpedo a budget. First keep track of your expenditures for a few months; then set limits you can realistically live with, allowing for inflation and overoptimism.

STEP BY STEP TO MANAGING YOUR FINANCES

1. Total your household's yearly income—family salaries, bonuses, dividends, interest, child support.
2. List expenses under two major headings: fixed expenses, such as rent or mortgage payments, taxes, or debt repayments; and flexible expenses—those over which you have some degree of control, such as food and utilities.
3. Add up amounts paid out yearly under the fixed-expenses category.
4. Add up all the flexible expenses.
5. Total the two categories of expenses. If they amount to a sum no more than the household income, congratulations—you're living within your income.
5. To arrive at a monthly spending plan, divide each category of expenses by 12.

A Monthly Budget

INCOME

Total salary	_____
Interest	_____
Dividends	_____
Other	_____
Total income	_____

EXPENSES
Major fixed expenses

Taxes	
Federal	_____
Provincial	_____
Municipal	_____
Automobile	_____
Rent or mortgage payment	_____
University tuition	_____
Insurance	
Medical	_____
Dental	_____
Life	_____
Property	_____
Automobile	_____
Debt payments	
Automobile	_____
Other	_____
Savings	_____
Total fixed expenses	_____

Flexible expenses

Food and beverages	_____
Utilities	_____
Home maintenance	_____
Furnishings and equipment	_____
Clothing	_____
Personal care	_____
Automobile upkeep, gas, oil	_____
Fares, tolls, other	_____
Medication (not reimbursed)	_____
Dental care (not reimbursed)	_____
Recreation	_____
Gifts and contributions	_____
Total flexible expenses	_____
Total expenses	_____

SUMMARY

Total income	_____
Minus total expenses	_____
Balance	_____

Budget a contingency amount for unexpected expenses. These are bound to arise, and it's impossible to predict what they'll be. They may range from a wedding gift to replacing an appliance or having dental work done.

Since you won't be making regular withdrawals from your contingency fund, consider putting it in a separate account—some kind of investment builder account—that will pay higher interest than your chequing or savings account.

LIVING WITHIN A BUDGET

Be alert for certain seasonal bargains. The best time to get a bargain on Christmas decorations and wrappings is the day after Christmas!

Seasonal sales usually offer substantial savings on merchandise that's in season. Clearance sales, held after peak demand periods, offer even larger savings.

The best shopping days of a sale are the first and the last. The first because there's usually a better selection, the last because the prices are often lowered.

Shopping from mail-order catalogs prevents the impulse purchases you might make in a store. At home you can choose thoughtfully the products that best suit your needs and budget.

Use catalogs to do research. Read up on what's available so that you'll be equipped to make comparisons as you shop around.

Make impulse purchases difficult—don't carry your cheque-book and credit cards with you *all* the time.

WHEN SALES OCCUR

Although seasonal sales still occur, it's now possible to buy almost anything at almost any time of the year. Because of the prevalence of discount stores, there are day-in and day-out sales. Increased competition among department stores has also led to more frequent discounting. It used to be predictable that linens went on sale only in January and August. But such is not the case anymore. If you're shopping for towels or sheets, you can almost always find something on sale. Should you prefer a particular model or brand, you may have to wait—but not for long. Different models and brands go on sale different months.

PAYING BILLS

Check your bills carefully for their payment-due date. To avoid a penalty, pay several days before they're due. If you pay the bills as soon as they arrive, you'll lose the use of your money and any interest that could accrue.

Instead of keeping track of a number of payment-due dates, some people find it easier to set aside two specific days of the month, a couple of weeks apart—usually near payday—to pay bills.

Pay all fixed charges, such as mortgage payments. Then check all monthly bills by matching the charges on the statement with the receipts and sales slips that you have saved.

If you can't pay a bill when it's due, telephone the credit card company before the due date and before it's referred to a collection agency. Explain your problem and state when you're likely to be able to pay at least part of the bill.

If you itemize deductions on your income tax, now's the time to sort and file receipts and statements according to their deduction categories—for example, medical expenses, charitable contributions, mortgage interest, income taxes.

After paying bills and before discarding receipts and sales checks, double-check for any that establish the purchase date for items under warranty. Put these in a separate file.

HOW TO COMPLAIN EFFECTIVELY

Question: What are my rights if I buy a defective product?
Answer: After centuries of caveat emptor (let the buyer beware), the law now offers the consumer better protection. If a product is defective, the store or the manufacturer must fix it, provided you've used it properly. If after several tries it still isn't fixed, you can expect to get a refund or an exchange.

Question: What's my best approach if I wish to make a complaint?
Answer: Start by using the phone, but use it wisely. Don't blurt out your tale of woe to the first person you talk to. This is a tactical mistake. It gives the other side the opportunity to suggest a solution that may not be fully satisfactory to you—another round of repairs, perhaps, when you want either a replacement or a refund. Instead, state your purpose: "I'm calling about that dishwasher you sold me." Ask to speak to someone who can make the decision you want made—for example, the sales manager. Describe the nature of the problem. Make your demand diplomatically, but convey the fact that you expect action. Set a time limit: "Can you send your repairman over today?" Wait for an answer. A well-timed pause can be effective in getting a satisfactory response. In extreme cases, you may have to press your point until the store agrees to make good on an item. In general, stores will meet your demand—just to retain your goodwill.

Question: What should I do if a store will not or cannot make good on an item?
Answer: Write to the consumer affairs department of the item's manufacturer. Briefly and unemotionally give all the pertinent facts: dates, an exact product description with model and serial numbers, where and when you bought the product, the nature of the problem, and your name, address, business and home telephone numbers. Send your letter by registered mail and keep several copies in case you want to contact other agencies later. Include copies of the sale slips and other relevant documents. State how you would like to see the problem remedied. If no solution is forthcoming, get in touch with a company officer—the president or vice-president. Business directories at your local library will provide the names and addresses you need.

Question: Are there agencies where I can complain about unresolved grievances?
Answer: If you get poor service from a local business or store, complain to the Better Business Bureau (BBB). Write a letter giving all details; send a copy to the dealer. Although the BBB has no enforcement power, no company wants to be on its list of those rendering poor service.

Question: Are there government agencies that can help me?
Answer: If a manufacturer ignores your complaints, contact your provincial consumer affairs department or Consumer and Corporate Affairs Canada. Provincial agencies deal with problems involving credit and contracts. Consumer and Corporate Affairs handles cases relating to advertising, packaging, and hazardous products. Call your provincial agency (see the listing of government services in your phone directory), or write to Consumer and Corporate Affairs Canada, Ottawa, Ontario, K1A 0C9.

Nondeductible bills and cheques, and receipts that have no warranty value, can be filed every month along with your balanced bank statements. The simplest way is to tuck everything for the month back into the envelope your bank statement came in; then, for ready reference, write the date of the statement on the outside.

Paying credit card charges before interest and service charges are tacked on saves money and disciplines purchasing.

LOST OR STOLEN CREDIT AND BANK CARDS

Make two photocopies of all your credit cards. Leave one at home; carry the other with you when traveling. If you lose a card, you'll know the number to report.

Notify the card issuer *immediately* when you discover you've lost a credit card. A toll-free number or some other means of contacting the company is usually printed on your monthly statement. After you have notified the company, you are no longer liable for charges made with your card.

Don't delay! You are liable for up to $50 in charges per card until you notify the card issuer.

If you use a bank's automatic teller machines, and your card is lost or stolen, your liability is limited to $50, provided you notify the bank immediately. If you fail to do so, your liability is unlimited. Once you report your loss, the bank will issue a new card.

Sign up with a credit card protection service offered through banks and credit card firms. For a small charge each year, the protection service will contact all your credit card issuers after you notify the service of a theft or loss. Also it pays any liabilities incurred after notification.

HOW TO USE CREDIT WISELY

After you've finished paying off a major loan, continue paying out the same amount to your savings account each month. You probably won't miss the money because you're used to paying it out anyway.

In the long run, you'll save money by making the largest possible down payment and repaying in the shortest possible time. And think carefully before refinancing for a longer time at higher interest rates.

How much debt is too much debt? Many professional advisers say that, exclusive of your rent or home mortgage, you should owe no more than 20 percent of your after-tax income.

Don't sign a credit contract until you have read the small print and understood every detail. If you don't understand the contract, ask questions until you're satisfied that you have been given the right answers.

ESTABLISHING CREDIT

A woman should give the creditors written notice if, when she marries, she decides to take her husband's surname, but wants to keep separate accounts.

A married woman can choose to use her maiden name (Smith); her husband's last name (Jones); or a combined last name (Smith-Jones). Just be consistent and use the same form on all accounts.

Establishing her own accounts provides a married woman with her own history of debt management if circumstances change because of widowhood or divorce.

Even though you are creditworthy—that is, you pay bills and repay loans on time—a creditor may still require your spouse to cosign contracts for major credit transactions.

Creditors cannot ask for information about your spouse or former spouse when you apply for your own credit based on your own income—unless that income is alimony, child support, or separate maintenance payments.

Creditors cannot deny you credit just because you become separated, widowed or divorced. Your creditworthiness may be called into question, however, if your finances have been changed by your new marital circumstances.

If you believe you've been discriminated against, cite the law to the lender. If the lender still says no without a sound explanation, contact the provincial agency that deals with consumer problems.

EXPERTS TO THE RESCUE

It's wise to choose a doctor before you need one. It's equally wise to choose a lawyer at leisure—before a crisis occurs.

To choose a lawyer, ask your provincial bar association for a list of local lawyers. Or get recommendations from your bank manager or accountant. You can also consult with friends and associates whose judgment you value.

If your legal affairs are simple, you might try using the student law clinic of the local law school. The clinic can inform you about the laws covering your problem.

If you need an accountant, call your local association of accountants for a list of referrals. Or ask your lawyer, bank, or employer for information about certified public accountants (CPA's) or accounting firms with whom they have had favorable dealings.

Consult your friends or business people in your community for the names of insurance brokers from whom they received good service. When you interview these people, ask them for additional references with whom you can check. It's a bad sign if they refuse to provide references.

There is really only one factor in choosing a stockbroker—will that person make money for you? Always ask for references before making a final selection. When checking them, try to get people to speak openly and specifically about the moneymaking ability of the broker. Remember, it's your money that's at risk. All the broker loses is your business.

Don't stay with any adviser you don't like. If you feel that you're not getting adequate service, take time to find someone with whom you feel secure. The relationship between client and professional should be one of compatibility and mutual respect.

NET WORTH

Calculating your net worth can be enlightening. You'll probably be amazed to find out that you're worth a lot more than you thought.

Probably the best way to get an accurate picture of how you're doing financially is to prepare a net-worth statement every year on the same date. Many advisers suggest doing this immediately before starting holiday shopping.

LIFE INSURANCE

Do you need life insurance? Its main purpose—and nothing does it better—is to create an instant estate for your family in the event of your death.

Does a single person need life insurance? Only if someone depends on you for financial support. That someone could be a child, an elderly parent, or any other family member.

HOW MUCH ARE YOU WORTH?

Net worth of (fill in name) _____

As of (fill in date) _____

Liquid assets
Cash and coins on hand _____
Chequing account _____
Savings account _____
Money market funds _____
Term deposits _____
Life insurance (cash value) _____
Government bonds (current value) _____
Municipal bonds (current value) _____
Corporate bonds (current value) _____
Stocks (current value) _____
Mutual funds (current value) _____
Prepaid taxes _____
Prepaid insurance (current value) _____
Other _____

Other assets
Private pension plan _____
Registered Retirement Saving Plan _____
Deferred profit-sharing plans _____
Home (current value) _____
Other real estate (current value) _____
Vehicles (current value) _____
Boats _____
Furnishings, large appliances _____
Personal property (value of silver and jewelry, etc.) _____
Other personal property (current value of stamp collection, coin collection, etc.) _____
Investment in antiques, art (current value) _____
Loans others owe you _____
Other _____
Total assets _____

Liabilities
Taxes due _____
Unpaid bills _____
Installment debts (balance due) on furniture, TV, appliances, car, etc. _____
Mortgage debts (home and other real estate) _____
Personal loans _____
Other _____
Total liabilities _____

NET WORTH (total assets minus total liabilities) _____

How much insurance should you have? One industry rule of thumb is that a family needs at least enough life insurance to cover four or five times its yearly income.

But that is the rule of thumb from the industry that sells life insurance. You might be better advised to think in terms of how much money you need for how long a period of time in the event of the death of the person who is being considered for insurance.

INVESTMENTS

Before you invest in anything that has the slightest risk, be sure that you have enough insurance and savings to protect yourself against an emergency. Your savings should equal about 3 months of your after-tax income.

Put aside a fixed amount of money each month and invest it regularly.

Diversify. Even if your savings are modest, spread them among different kinds of investments: savings certificates, Canada Savings Bonds, annuities, widely diversified mutual funds.

Don't wait to buy in at the very bottom of a market and don't try to sell out at the very top. *Nobody* is smart enough to do that.

SOCIAL INSURANCE

If you have any concerns about your Canada Pension Plan (CPP) or Quebec Pension Plan (QPP), check that your earnings are being correctly reported. Your CPP record is kept under your name and Social Insurance Number at the local Income Security Programs office of Health and Welfare Canada.

Applications for Old Age Security benefits should be made at least six months before your 65th birthday or whenever you become eligible. Don't forget that both your pension plan and the Old Age Security benefits are subject to income tax. If you have little or no income, you may be eligible to receive the Guaranteed Income Supplement, which is not subject to income tax.

RETIREMENT

It's too late to start preparing for your retirement on the day that you pick up your gold watch. Find out right now what your pension plan benefits will be; otherwise you may be in for a shock when you retire.

To enjoy a comfortable retirement, you should figure on needing at least 55–75 percent of your preretirement salary. To meet this goal, you'll need your pension plan benefits, both your Canada Pension Plan and Old Age Security benefits, and your own savings.

If you don't understand the provisions of your pension, discuss them with your company's employee-benefits managers. They should be willing to help you calculate your benefits.

WHAT $100 WORTH OF GOODS OR SERVICES WILL COST IN FUTURE YEARS

If you are saving or investing dollars for some future purpose—retirement, university educations, a new home—the rate of inflation is a key to whether your accumulation fund will meet your goals. The following chart shows what can happen to $100.

Annual rate of inflation	10 Years	20 Years	30 Years
2%	$122	$149	$ 181
4	148	219	324
6	179	321	574
8	216	466	1,006

WILLS

You don't have to be rich to need a will. It's the only way to be certain your property goes to those you want to have it. And only in a will can you appoint a guardian for your children.

If you don't have a will or if yours is more than five years old, you need the assistance of a lawyer (or notary, in Quebec) as soon as possible. Don't rely on stationery-store forms if you want your will to be an unequivocally valid document in the province in which you live.

In case your fortunes change, it's sensible when making bequests of money in a will to use percentages rather than dollar amounts.

Review your will every now and then, and keep it up to date. It's an especially good idea to revise your will when you retire. Also, as the tax laws change, it may be advantageous to change some of your bequests.

If you've moved, be sure that your will conforms to the laws of the province where you now live. Your will is executed according to the province of your legal residence at the time of your death.

WHAT YOU SHOULD HAVE BESIDES A WILL

In addition to your will, you should keep lists of close family members and associates and of important personal documents. This inventory should be updated at least once a year. Make enough copies so that it's readily available if an emergency occurs, and make sure that family members know where to locate a copy quickly. The inventory should include:

The names, addresses, and dates of birth of you and your immediate family.

The location of your birth certificate, citizenship papers, tax returns.

Your Social Insurance Number and the location of your card.

The location of your marriage certificate and prenuptial agreement, if any. If you were married before, your deceased or former spouse's name. If divorced, the location of your divorce papers.

The location of the original of your will.

The names and addresses of those you intend as executors, trustees, beneficiaries of your will.

The names and the addresses of your doctor, lawyer, accountant, employer, banker, insurance agent, stockbroker, and landlord.

The location of any insurance policies.

The location and enumeration of stocks, bonds, and other securities.

A complete rundown of other assets, including bank accounts, businesses, real estate, jewelry.

A complete outline of your debts and other obligations.

The location of your safe-deposit box and its key.

The funeral arrangements you prefer and any arrangements you have made.

It may also be desirable to have available a list of instructions on what is to be done immediately upon the event of your death or disability—anything from "Call my office" (give phone number) and "Stop the newspaper" (give phone number) to "Call the appraiser (give phone number) to appraise the worth of my business."

Storing It All Away

STORAGE GUIDELINES

Organize existing storage space before increasing it. New storage often creates more places for disorganized clutter and more surfaces to collect unneeded items.

To determine whether you really need more storage space, draw a floor plan and list what you want to have on hand in each room. See if something can be shifted to a room with more free space.

Strive to create "one-motion" storage. That means you can open a cabinet, closet, or drawer, reach in, and grab what you want in one motion without having to move anything out of the way.

You won't outgrow storage if it's flexible. Adjustable shelves easily adapt to changing book, music, or video collections and new electronic gear. Modular storage units can be regrouped, added to, or used separately.

FINDING NEW STORAGE SPACE

Most homes abound in overlooked storage spaces. This typical home shows just some of the possible locations you may have missed. In making your own search, look especially for places that you can use without losing too much floor space.

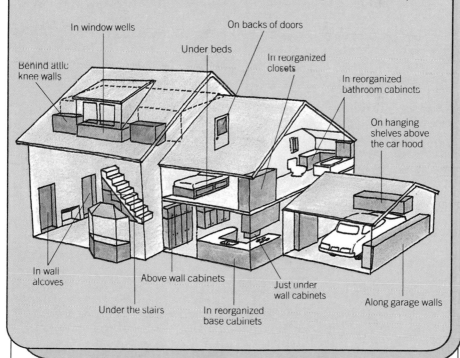

In window wells

On backs of doors

Under beds

In reorganized closets

Behind attic knee walls

In reorganized bathroom cabinets

On hanging shelves above the car hood

In wall alcoves

Above wall cabinets

Just under wall cabinets

Along garage walls

Under the stairs

In reorganized base cabinets

Keep a flexible attitude toward a storage piece's use. A chest can move from room to room, storing different materials as your needs change over time.

Having many small shelves or compartments results in neater, easier-to-use storage than having just a few large ones.

FROM THIS . . .   **TO THIS . . .**

Avoid piling. A good rule is never to stack more than three pieces that are not part of a set.

In small rooms, use open storage, such as shelves and racks. They won't make the room seem even smaller than it is.

If space is tight, make sure you really need a piece of furniture. You may not need a bureau, for example, if you substitute enough shelves, trays, and baskets.

WHERE TO STORE THINGS

Be honest with yourself about which items should go where. Just because you are fond of something, don't assume it deserves a prime location.

To find the best storage place for an item, take it to the spot where you use it most. Then determine a way to store it there or close by.

Keep frequently used items between knee level and no more than 10 inches above your head. Put items you use less regularly on higher and lower shelves.

Seldom needed lighter items

10"

Frequently needed lighter items

Frequently needed heavier items

Seldom needed heavier items

For both safety and convenience, store a heavy, regularly used article within a foot either way of waist level. Make sure that it has a sturdy support and can be removed and replaced without upsetting lighter things.

To gain more space for the things that you use every day, put rarely needed and out-of-season articles in clearly labeled boxes or bags and keep them in your home's less-accessible storage areas.

TO SPEED YOUR ENTRANCES AND EXITS

Store frequently needed gloves, scarves, and hats in a small chest of drawers by the door. Or hang small baskets for them on the back of the closet door.

Store extra outdoor accessories on an easily reached closet shelf in a box with labeled cubbyholes. A cardboard shoe-storage box from the five-and-ten is ideal.

String a clothesline with clothes-pins along the back of the coat-closet door for children's winter mittens. If you make the line low enough, the kids can learn to hang their own mittens.

Supplement your coat closet with a handsome wall rack or an old-fashioned freestanding coatrack. You'll find it's a lot more convenient for your guests' coats than squeezing them into the closet.

TO CONTROL WETNESS AND MUD AT YOUR ENTRYWAY

Keep boots and overshoes in a box or basket by the entrance. Line the bottom with a folded plastic trash bag.

Create storage for sports gear by the back door. Be sure the area includes a bench so that your family's athletes will be inspired to sit and remove their muddy shoes.

To keep water from collecting in an umbrella stand, cut a piece of sponge to fit inside the stand's bottom. Remove and squeeze the sponge dry when necessary.

IN YOUR SITTING AREA

Make your coffee table do double duty. Suspend a shelf 4 or 5 inches below the top. It's a handy place to store items ranging from magazines to games and puzzles.

For more storage space, consider using an attractive antique trunk as a coffee table or a wicker chest as an end table.

Next to your television-viewing chair, nail or hook a basket to the wall to hold mending supplies or small projects.

For the half-read newspaper or magazine, make a "pocket caddy" and attach it to your reading chair. Make a cloth envelope with a long tongue that you can secure under the seat cushion with Velcro strips. Use slipcover fabric or a compatible fabric.

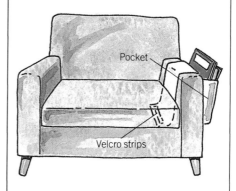

Pocket

Velcro strips

Almost any low storage unit can double as seating. A cushion can turn a storage cube into a seat. A cushion and pillows can turn a trunk into a cozy window seat.

Also consider turning a wall alcove or a window recess into a seating-storage area. Enclose the area with a plywood top and front attached to cleats on the wall. Attach the top with hinges.

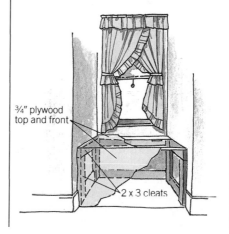

¾" plywood top and front

2 x 3 cleats

FOR YOUR AUDIOVISUAL GEAR

Don't stoop to find that album or movie. Store your records, tapes, and discs at eye level. Locate players just above waist level.

You can store audiocassettes, videotapes, and compact discs two deep on a conventional foot-deep shelf. Build a shelf insert to raise the back row up high enough to be reached easily.

1 x 6 shelf insert

Make sure that all your electronic equipment has adequate ventilation. Allow at least 2 inches of space on all sides.

Leave a 1-inch space for wires at the back of shelves that will carry electronic gear. And instead of running all the electric cords to a baseboard outlet, mount an extension strip outlet at shelf level.

KEEPING YOUR KITCHEN IN ORDER

Too much clutter? Go through each drawer and shelf, check for unnecessary duplications (do you really need three can openers?), and get rid of them.

Sort out useful, but rarely used, utensils—the egg slicer, lobster-claw crackers, Christmas-cookie cutters—and store them in an out-of-the-way drawer. Better yet, put them in a box on a top shelf.

Go to your local variety store and explore all the inexpensive storage items that might be useful in your kitchen. For example, get a wire rack for boxes of foil and plastic wrap or stacked plastic bins for potatoes and onions.

FOR KITCHEN EFFICIENCY

Whenever possible, keep toasters, mixers, and other small appliances within easy reach. If you store them away, it becomes a chore just to get them out.

To keep small appliances handy without extra clutter, put them behind small, hinged shutters or doors at the rear of the countertop.

Store cans, jars, and small boxes in single rows so that they're easy to find and reach. Consider installing narrow shelves for them along an inconspicuous wall or around a cabinet's interior.

ADDING A LAZY SUSAN TO A CUPBOARD

Revolving shelves under a counter put every item within easy reach. Making them is simpler than you might think. All you need is some ¾-inch plywood, a 4-inch bearing (stocked by auto parts suppliers), 6d finishing nails, white glue, and flexible metal countertop edging to put a lip on each shelf.

The trickiest part is cutting the plywood circles. Have your lumber dealer cut them for you unless you have a saber saw; in that case, try the technique on p.188. For a typical 24-inch-deep cupboard, you'll need circles 22 inches in diameter. But always measure your cupboard first and make sure the unit will clear all sides by at least ½ inch. One crosspiece should measure the same as the diameter of the circles. The other is actually two short pieces, each measuring half the diameter minus ⅜ inch.

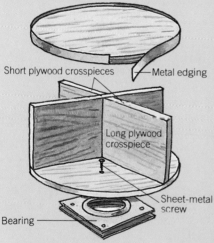

Short plywood crosspieces — Metal edging

Long plywood crosspiece

Sheet-metal screw

Bearing

To install the lazy Susan, screw the bracket to the cupboard and then attach the unit to the bracket with sheet-metal screws. Before attaching the bracket to the cupboard, however, use the tiny holes in the bracket as guides for marking and drilling screw holes in the bottom circle. Then temporarily screw the unit to the bracket to check that the sheet-metal screws are the right length.

You can make a smaller lazy Susan for a wall cupboard the same way. Just use ½-inch plywood and a 3-inch bracket.

No more misplaced rings, watches, or bracelets! Hang a cup hook near the sink to hold them while you're cooking or cleaning.

The place mats on top of the pile won't get messed up when you pull out the set below if you put sheets of cardboard between sets.

TO FREE COUNTER SPACE

Put away the clean dishes as soon as you finish washing up. This will give you a larger, clearer work area for the next round of meal preparations.

Mount items under your cabinets. You can buy fold-down racks that will hold spices, knives, and cookbooks. You can also get drawers and appliances designed to be installed under cabinets.

Fold-down rack

Install tall or bulky appliances, such as blenders and food processors, on pop-up shelves near their point of use. Get a mechanism of the appropriate size and mount it according to directions.

Pop-up mechanism

A wire dish rack that mounts directly over the sink not only frees space but also reduces moisture problems by draining your dishes directly into the sink. They're carried by kitchen speciality shops.

STORING CHINA

All china of the same pattern need not be stored together. If you have a family of four and a service for 12, move some of the place settings to a higher shelf (or even to another room).

Add a new shelf for china between existing ones. Attach it to the cabinet sides with cleats (p.64) or make an insert with legs from boards or plywood.

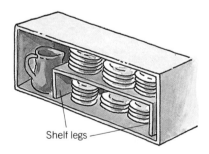

Shelf legs

Use wire racks that let you store plates, saucers, and bowls vertically. Hang cups from cup hooks or pullout cup racks.

KEEPING UTENSILS HANDY

For a simple but effective knife organizer, saw slots in a 2 x 3 about 1½ inches apart. Then glue it to the bottom of a drawer.

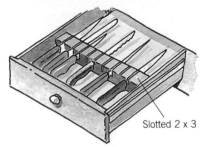

Slotted 2 x 3

Keep spatulas and other cooking utensils near your stove, and store whisks and other mixing utensils near your food-preparation area. Hang them on pegboard (p.55) or a rack with hooks.

Also consider keeping "bouquets" of small utensils in wide-mouthed jugs, or hanging steel utensils on a magnetic steel bar.

You can make almost any utensil hangable by drilling a hole in its handle. If it's too thick to fit over a hook, run a loop of cord (or a leather thong) through the hole.

To put pots and pans where you really need them, install pullout shelves or rollout bins (pp.68–69) in the cabinet next to your stove or under your built-in cooktop.

A vertical rollout with pegboard is a convenient way to store pots and pans and to take advantage of an otherwise wasted narrow space.

Run out of space in cabinets and on the wall? Hang attractive, frequently used cookware from a metal rack suspended from the ceiling. Such racks are available from restaurant suppliers.

Store baking pans, trays, and platters vertically in that hard-to-reach cabinet over the refrigerator. Make dividers from ¼-inch plywood; install them between spacers of the same material on the cabinet's top and bottom.

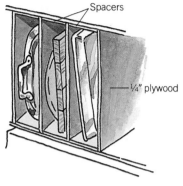

Spacers

¼" plywood

You can also create vertical dividers with wooden dowels (p.63). They're especially good for organizing pan lids.

CREATING NEW KITCHEN STORAGE

Put the inside of cabinet doors to work. Hang measuring cups and spoons and other utensils from hooks, and store spices and small packages in racks. But first make sure they won't interfere with the shelves when you close the door.

Make shallow open shelves for spices and storage jars at the rear of your countertop.

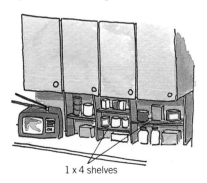

1 x 4 shelves

The narrow space next to the refrigerator may be an ideal spot for a rollout pantry, provided the refrigerator gets adequate ventilation at the top and the other side. Just mount a basic case (p.64) on two pairs of sturdy casters.

Lattice shelf lip

Make a hang-up spice rack easily with 1 x 4's and ¼-inch dowels. Clamp two 1 x 4's together and drill holes through both at once. Glue in the dowels.

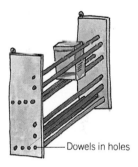

Dowels in holes

Add a bookcase to your kitchen. Use it to organize cookbooks and canisters. Convert the top into extra counter space by covering it with waterproof wallpaper.

Another helpful addition is a roll-around cart. It provides extra work and storage space that you can wheel from sink to stove to table.

To convert a cabinet into a wine cellar, replace the existing shelves with two large plywood pieces, each slotted halfway through and fitted together to form an X.

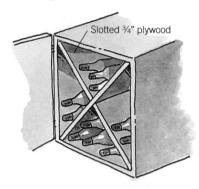

Slotted ¾" plywood

CLEANING SUPPLIES

Store your cleaning materials in a plastic carrying tray. They'll be much easier to take out and put away and to move about.

When arranging your cleaning supplies in a closet, give first consideration to making large and awkward items, such as vacuums and rolling buckets, easy to reach.

FOR THE LAUNDRY

Install a clothes rod below a high shelf in your laundry room and you'll have a handy place to hang drip-dry or freshly ironed clothes.

If you have the space, get a small sleeveboard, either loose or attachable. A sleeveboard is useful for ironing shirts and blouses.

Construct a simple cabinet with shelves or cleats to hold plastic laundry baskets. Make each family member responsible for bringing his or her own basket to the cabinet on laundry day, and for removing it—full of clean laundry—afterward.

GETTING THE MOST FROM YOUR BEDROOM CLOSET

Always hang coat hangers so that all the hooks point away from you. This makes it easy to remove several articles at once—or all of them in an emergency.

Hang all your short things at one side of the closet. Usually you'll create enough space underneath for a shoe rack, a small chest of drawers, or a second clothes rod.

Any rods that run parallel to the wall need to be about 12 inches from the wall for coat hangers to be hung at right angles to the wall. If the closet is not deep, you can hang clothes front to back on an extending rail, but they may not be easy to select.

Rub a bit of paste furniture wax on a wooden clothes rod. You'll find that hangers slide back and forth more easily.

Whenever you remove a garment from a hanger, put the hanger at the end of the rod. When you rehang the garment, you won't have to search for a hanger or create a tangle.

If you're annoyed by hangers getting tangled, remove the pole and saw shallow notches at ½-inch intervals along its top edge.

Consider storing folded clothes on shelves that pull out (pp.68–69). They are more flexible than dresser drawers, and they can be used at greater heights than drawers.

If you have a closet without a light fixture, you can get an inexpensive battery-operated light unit that mounts on the wall or ceiling.

REMODELING A CLOSET

Make the most of your bedroom closet by installing two clothes rods at different levels. In a closet used only by a man—or a child—you can devote the entire hanging space to bilevel rods, assuming coats and bathrobes are kept elsewhere. But a woman will also need a single rod at the standard 6-foot height for dresses.

In revamping a closet, first take out all the existing rods and shelves. For folded items and accessories, build a narrow case of ¾-inch plywood from floor to ceiling. Outfit it with shelves and drawers (pp.64–67). Secure it to the floor and wall studs (p.49) with L-brackets.

For clothes rods, use 1-inch wood dowels. Mount each rod in metal clothes-rod sockets on 1 x 4 cleats. Mount each socket so that its center is 11 inches from the back wall. If a shelf will rest on the cleat, put the socket near the cleat's lower edge so that you'll have space above the rod for putting in and taking out hangers. To make sure a rod is straight, mount the socket for one end; then insert the rod and place a level on the rod to determine the exact position of the other socket.

The shelves in most closets can be up to 22 inches deep. But if your closet door doesn't extend to the ceiling, shelves at higher levels may have to be shallower for you to reach them. Use ¾-inch plywood for the shelves, and mount shelves other than those above rods with 1 x 2 cleats. Secure all wall cleats to the studs. Finish plywood edges with ¼-inch-thick molding, or if you plan to paint the closet, fill the edges with wood putty.

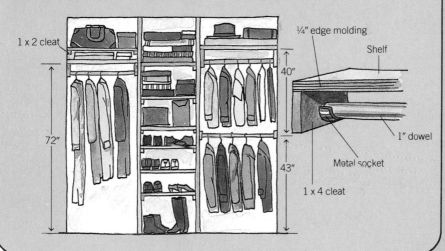

1 x 2 cleat
¼" edge molding
Shelf
40"
72"
43"
1" dowel
Metal socket
1 x 4 cleat

PLANNING NEW CLOSET SPACE

A walk-in closet is luxurious but wasteful of space; a reach-in closet uses all of its space for storage.

Unlike sliding doors, folding and accordion doors allow easy access to the full front of a closet. They also require less free space in front of the closet than a regular side-hinged door that swings out.

You can create a new closet in a deep wall alcove or across the end of a small room by simply hanging full-length folding or accordion doors from the ceiling. Equip it with shelves and clothes rods as shown in the box above.

If mildew is a problem, make sure your closet has plenty of ventilation by using wire shelving (p.63) and louvered doors. In an extreme case, insulate the back wall.

KEEPING ACCESSORIES NEAT

Golf tees make fine pegs for a belt or tie rack. Just drill rows of holes in an attractive board and glue the pointed ends of the tees into them.

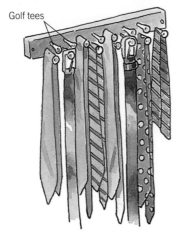

Golf tees

Shoes won't disappear into the back of the closet if you store them in wire racks or shoe bags. Or make your own simple stacking shelves for them.

Clear plastic drawers and boxes that stack on closet shelves create see-through storage that's perfect for shoes, hats, and sweaters.

If your closet lacks shelves, hang your accessories. Department stores carry hanging cases with pockets for shoes and handbags as well as special hangers for ties.

PLANNING A CHILD'S ROOM

Keep storage at your child's level. Install low horizontal shelves, cabinets, and other units instead of tall vertical ones.

If storage is flexible, it can change as your child grows. Use adjustable shelves, modular units, and easily moved chests of drawers. Avoid built-in storage units that you can't adjust.

STORING PLAYTHINGS

A very young child has trouble putting toys away precisely. Your toddler will clean up with less fuss if you provide roomy, catchall storage bins and baskets.

As your child gets older, keep playthings on shelves; they permit a toy to be found without rummaging. But use catchall units for storing quantities of related items, such as building sets.

Some playthings are unwieldy. Be sure your storage has deep shelves for storing large toys and hooks for hanging awkward ones.

For quick, inexpensive storage, cover cardboard boxes with stickon paper. Use them as bins or stack them for shelves. Replace them when they become tattered.

Modular plastic storage cases—or wooden cubes—can also serve as either bins or shelves and when empty can even be flipped over to form a stool.

Plastic dishpans and vegetable bins make handy storage drawers for toys. Mount them on cleats (p.67) or suspend them beneath a shelf from simple runners.

Mount a racing-car set on a piece of ½-inch plywood with a simple 1 x 2 frame around the edges. Add casters so that it can be rolled under the bed when not in use.

If you have two heavy, solid storage units, you can install a play table between them on adjustable tracks (p.67). This allows the table to grow with your child.

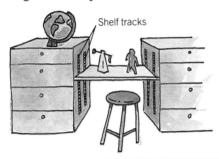

Shelf tracks

YOUR CHILD'S CLOTHING

To put your child's clothes within reach, add a second, lower rod in the closet. Install new clothes-rod sockets on a cleat (p.43). Or simply suspend the rod on chains from the higher rod. Use the upper rod for out-of-season wear.

S-hooks

AN UNDERBED CART

Just over 6 inches high, this low rollaway fits under most beds and is ideal for such items as shoes, blankets, and toys. Measure to determine the best front-to-back and side-to-side dimensions for your bed. Plan to recess the cart's front 4 to 6 inches to give you toe space under the bed. For a full-size or larger bed, make two carts, one for each side.

Cut the 1 x 6 front and back each 3 inches longer than the plywood bottom's side-to-side dimension. Cut the 1 x 4 sides and 2 x 2 cleats the same length as the bottom's front-to-back dimension.

Before assembling the unit, make sure that when the casters are screwed to the cleats, the bottom will be at least ½ inch above the floor. If not, or if your carpet has a deep pile, lower the cleats.

Assemble the unit with 2-inch No. 8 woods screws (p.66) and white glue in the sequence given below.

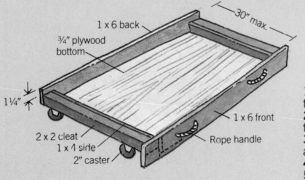

1 x 6 back
¾" plywood bottom
30" max.
1¼"
2 x 2 cleat
1 x 4 side
2" caster
1 x 6 front
Rope handle

1. Attach the cleats to the sides.
2. Attach the sides to the bottom.
3. Mount the front and back.
4. Install the casters.
5. Drill holes for handles; knot rope ends.

Shallow drawers enable a child to find socks, underwear, and shirts more easily. To prevent a deep drawer from becoming cluttered, add dividers (p.68).

Keep a clothes hamper in your child's room rather than the bathroom. It's complicated for a child to move clothes between rooms. Put it near the closet to collect dirty clothes as soon as they come off.

MAKING NEW BATHROOM STORAGE

Install a shelf just above the sink. It'll give you a handy place for cosmetics, toiletries, and grooming aids. Place the shelf high enough so that it doesn't interfere with turning the water on and off.

Fill the area below an open sink with shelf units that fit around the plumbing and open onto all the reachable sides.

Side shelf unit

Front shelf unit

If you feel more ambitious, enclose the undersink area with a cabinet version of the basic plywood case (p.64). Make it without a top or back, and attach the sides to cleats on the wall. Remove any metal legs on the sink and let the cabinet support it.

For a bath fixture that will do double duty, make a shelf unit that incorporates a towel bar. Use 1 x 6's with a 1-inch-diameter dowel. Make the hole for the dowel with a hole-saw drill attachment (p.188).

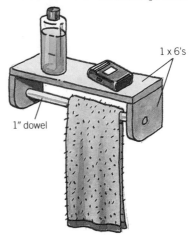

1 x 6's

1" dowel

Fill any unused space around a toilet with storage that combines shelves and towel bars in a space-saving ladder arrangement. Be sure to leave space above the tank so that you can take the top off.

Towel ladder

Protect any new wood shelf or cabinet in the bathroom with at least two coats of a urethane-based enamel or varnish.

AN UNDERSTAIRS ROLLOUT BIN

The best way to use that hard-to-reach space under the front edge of a stairway is with a rollout bin. You'll find it a perfect place to store awkward items ranging from cleaning supplies to boots and sports equipment. The bin is a simple box of ¾-inch plywood on casters. Assemble it with 2-inch and 1¼-inch No. 8 screws and white glue, reinforcing all of the cor-

ners with ¾-inch square molding (p.64).

To cut the front, back, and filler pieces at the correct angle, trace the slope of the stairs on a piece of cardboard. Then make it into a pattern for marking the plywood. The bin's front and back should clear the stairs by ¼ inch and the floor by ½ inch; the filler piece, which is nailed in place, fits flush.

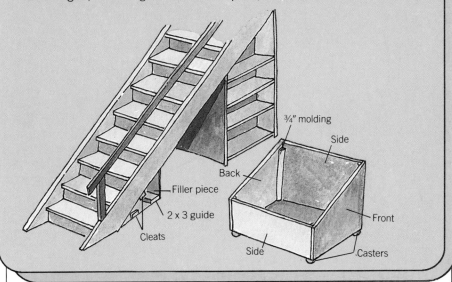

¾" molding
Side
Back
Filler piece
2 x 3 guide
Cleats
Side
Front
Casters

Don't let hair dryers, curling irons, electric shavers, and other small appliances take up precious shelf space. Hang them from a pegboard or from hooks screwed into a shelf edge or bottom. Or put them in baskets on a wire grid.
Caution: Never use or store an electric appliance where it can be dropped or pulled into a sink or tub. Always unplug it after using.

DON'T FORGET HALLS

Even a narrow hall may have space for shelves. Consider lining a wall from floor to ceiling with shallow shelves for paperbacks or for your collection of figurines or other eye-catchers.

Construct a storage loft across the end of a hall or above a stairway. Use it for luggage and other lightweight, occasionally used items.

SUMMER CLOTHES

¾" plywood
1 x 3 cleats

UNDER THE STAIRS

You'll have a much easier time dividing up the open space under stairs if you keep in mind that it's nothing more than a large triangle with a hard-to-use corner. One way to use that space is with a rollout bin (see box, p.47).

You can fill the space under stairs with shelves. Support the shelves at their stair ends with stepped vertical pieces. Use the space behind the shelves as a closet.

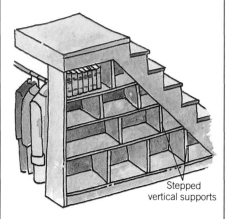

Stepped
vertical supports

IN THE ATTIC

Even if your attic is cramped and filled with cross members, you can probably find room for storage. Just cover accessible areas around the hatch with a floor of ¾-inch plywood. Don't store heavy items there if your joists are more than 16 inches apart.

If you have trouble getting plywood through the hatch to floor your attic, saw the sheets into widths that will go through. Then fit them back together in the attic.

Attic searches will be easier if you arrange items so that you can quickly survey everything from the attic hatch or doorway. Keep related articles near one another, and label cartons in large letters.

To protect attic-stored items from dust, put smaller articles in tightly closed or sealed boxes. Cover furniture and other large items with plastic drop cloths.

For storage along a gable wall, simply install shelves with brackets or with standards and brackets (p.60). Make each shelf progressively shorter to fit between the sloping sides at each end.

To make shelves under eaves, run uprights between the rafters and the joists (or floor). Then run shelf supports from the upright to the rafters. You can make shelves the same way under stairs with exposed stringers.

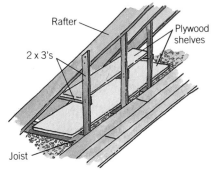

Rafter

Plywood
shelves

2 x 3's

Joist

FASTENING TO STUDS

In most homes the safest way to mount any wall storage is to attach it with screws or nails that go at least 1 inch into the studs—the wooden uprights that support the wall. The box on the facing page gives clues to help locate studs.

Another way of finding studs in plasterboard walls is to move a magnetic compass or a magnet on string back and forth and up

LOCATING WALL STUDS

In most homes the distance from the center of one wall stud to the center of the next is 16 inches. But sometimes it's 24 inches—or some other interval. In an older building the spacing may be irregular. Here are some clues for finding studs.

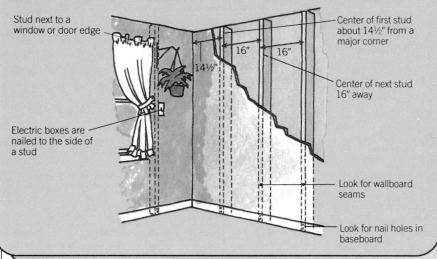

Stud next to a window or door edge

Electric boxes are nailed to the side of a stud

Center of first stud about 14½" from a major corner

16" 16"

14½"

Center of next stud 16" away

Look for wallboard seams

Look for nail holes in baseboard

and down over a wall until the compass needle or the magnet is attracted by the metal of the nails in the stud. Magnetic stud finders use the same principle.

If all else fails, you can find a stud by drilling a tiny hole angled sharply to one side. Feed a piece of coat-hanger wire into the hole until it hits a stud. Pinch the wire between your fingers; then pull the wire out and transfer the measurement to the wall. The stud's center should be only ¾ inch farther away, but drill a tiny test hole.

Whenever possible, make a stud-locating hole where the storage unit will hide it. Otherwise, drill the hole low on the wall so that it will not be very noticeable when you patch and paint it. Use a weighted plumb line to transfer the exact location of the stud to a higher position.

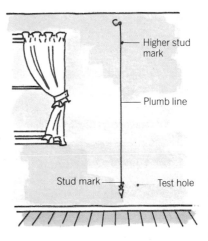

Higher stud mark

Plumb line

Stud mark — Test hole

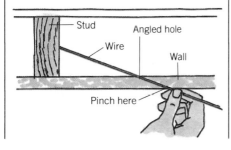

Stud — Angled hole

Wire

Wall

Pinch here

49

WHAT IS YOUR WALL MADE OF?

When you drill a test hole into . . .	You will find . . .
Wall coverings:	
Wallboard or plaster only	White dust, quick breakthrough
Thick plaster	White dust, delayed or no breakthrough
Thin plaster over wood lath	White dust, then gray, then breakthrough
Behind-wall materials:	
Wood stud	Moderate resistance, light wood shavings
Metal stud	Heavy resistance, silver shavings
Cinder block or concrete	Very heavy resistance, gray-brown dust
Brick or hollow tiles	Heavy resistance, red dust
Mortar between bricks or blocks	Moderate resistance, gray dust

Attach a heavy item, such as a cabinet, to a board screwed into the studs with lag bolts (see chart, facing page). For each lag bolt, drill a hole in the board slightly larger than the bolt's diameter; then use the hole as a guide to drill a hole into the stud that's slightly smaller than the bolt's diameter.

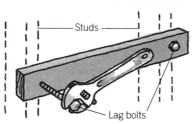

Studs

Lag bolts

You can also attach a heavy load with hanger bolts. You screw a hanger bolt into a stud, then attach an object to it with a nut. Simply drill a pilot hole and screw the bolt in using locking-grip pliers on its unthreaded midsection.

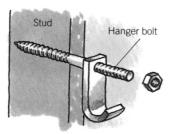

Stud

Hanger bolt

Modern buildings often have metal studs. To fasten an object to one, use a sheet-metal screw. Drill a hole until you hit the stud. Then dent the stud with a large nail and drill a hole half your screw's diameter. Use a No. 4 screw for light loads and up to a No. 8 for heavier ones. Screw sizes are the same as for wood screws (p.66).

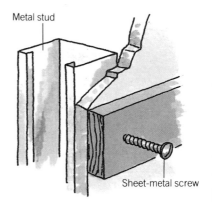

Metal stud

Sheet-metal screw

HOLLOW-WALL FASTENERS

To mount light loads between studs on a plaster or plasterboard wall, use hollow-wall anchors or toggle bolts. Reserve plastic anchors for very light loads. Putting heavy loads on these fasteners could cause the wall to give way.

WALL FASTENERS

Fastener	Use
Plastic anchor	Very light loads on hollow and masonry walls; use with a sheet-metal or round-head screw
Sheet-metal screw	Light to heavy loads on walls with metal studs; screws directly into stud
Hollow-wall anchor	Light loads on hollow walls; comes with its own bolt
Toggle bolt	Light loads on hollow walls; heavy loads on cinder-block walls; comes with its own bolt
Lag bolt	Heavy loads on walls with wood studs; screws directly into stud
Concrete nail	Light loads on concrete walls; goes through a board into wall
Masonry nail	Light loads on brick or stone walls; goes through a board into wall
Fiber plug	Light loads on masonry walls; use with wood or sheet-metal screw; also comes in plastic
Lead anchor	Medium loads on masonry walls; use with wood screws (see chart p.66)
Expansion shield	Heavy loads on masonry walls; comes with its own bolt

The more hollow-wall fasteners you use to hold an object, the lighter the load on each fastener. For all but the lightest loads, try to use at least two fasteners for each item that you put up.

The length of the hollow-wall anchors or toggle bolts you need depends on how thick the plaster or plasterboard on your wall is. To determine a wall's thickness, drill a small hole in it, then bend thin, stiff wire into a hook and curve the hook through the hole. Pull the hook against the inside of the wall and mark the wire at the point it comes out of the wall. Remove the hook and measure between the end of the hook and your mark.

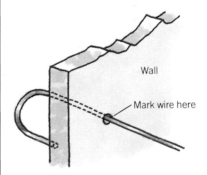

Wall

Mark wire here

To install a hollow-wall anchor, drill a hole the same size as the anchor; then insert the anchor and tighten the screw to flatten the end of the anchor against the inside of the wall. After that, you can take out and put in the screw as often as you like.

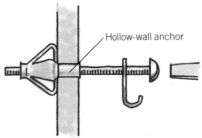

Hollow-wall anchor

51

A toggle bolt holds an object more securely than a hollow-wall anchor. But a toggle bolt is trickier to install. You must drill a hole large enough for its folded wings to pass through, and you must attach the object to the toggle bolt before you put the bolt into the wall. Once the bolt is installed, you can't remove it without losing the winged toggle inside the wall.

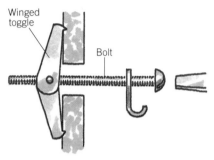

Winged toggle

Bolt

You can make a hole for a small plastic anchor in many walls by simply driving in a large common nail. Before making the hole, select a nail that is roughly the same diameter as the anchor.

Interior doors are often hollow. To attach an object to one, get a small version of the hollow-wall anchor, known as a hollow-door anchor.

If you have trouble attaching an object to a wall because the item itself is unusual or because the wall is made of an unusual material, chances are good that specialized fasteners are available. Ask for help at a building-supply or hardware store or home center.

FASTENING TO MASONRY

To secure most items to a concrete, brick, or cinder-block wall, you'll need to drill a hole and insert a wall fastener. Use lead anchors for most loads and expansion shields for exceptionally heavy ones. Use plastic anchors and fiber plugs for very light items (see chart, p.51).

To drill a hole in masonry, use a carbide-tipped bit on an electric drill, preferably a variable-speed model that will let you drill at a low speed. As you drill, move the bit in and out rather than pushing hard and continuously on it. If the drill begins to stall, release the trigger, or you'll burn out the motor. **Caution:** When drilling into masonry, always wear safety goggles and work gloves.

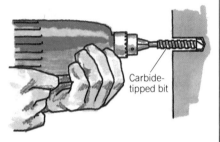

Carbide-tipped bit

If your drill lacks the power to drive a big bit into solid concrete or brick, try drilling a small hole first, then a larger one. Or rent a ½-inch variable-speed drill.

A toggle bolt is a good fastener for a cinder-block or a hollow-tile wall. Drill a hole for it with a carbide-tipped bit. Then install the fastener as you would on a hollow wall. Drill a test hole first to make sure the block's hollow interior has enough space to accommodate the bolt's wings.

You can use masonry nails (p.51) to attach boards that will carry light loads. Because these nails tend to split wood, first drill a hole in the board for each nail. Make it slightly smaller than the widest part of the nail. If a wall is very hard, drill holes for the nails in the wall too.

Masonry nails can chip a claw hammer, causing flying metal particles. Always drive these nails with a ball peen hammer or light sledgehammer. And wear safety goggles and work gloves.

If a fastener will carry a heavy load, don't install it in the mortar between masonry blocks. Under stress, the mortar is likely to crumble, and the fastener will pull out.

FAST FASTENERS

You can drive a special sharp-tipped hollow-wall anchor into plasterboard with a hammer. After that, you flatten the anchor inside the wall as you do with a regular hollow-wall anchor (p.51).

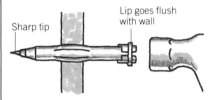

Sharp tip

Lip goes flush with wall

To put up hardware quickly, use rivetlike expanding fasteners that shoot directly into plasterboard from an inexpensive tool that you squeeze or from an attachment on a stapler. On plaster or masonry, drill a small pilot hole first.

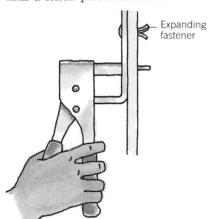

Expanding fastener

HOOKS AND HANGERS

In an open storage area, well-designed hangers can contribute nicely to the decorative scheme, especially if you coordinate their style and color. Designer hangers come in a wide variety of styles and materials.

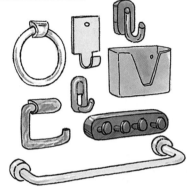

In utilitarian storage areas, it's more economical and efficient to use screw hooks, wire coat hooks, and other traditional hardware. Most have screw-in tips that are simple to install.

One especially good longtime favorite is the spring clip. A typical clip holds handles ranging from ¾ to 1¼ inches in diameter, and you put it up with a single screw. You can also get spring clips mounted on a sliding track. There are even ones that hook onto pegboard.

Spring clip

The best solution for many items that won't fit easily in regular storage areas is to hang them. An eggbeater won't take up drawer space if you hook it on a pegboard. Even a large item that's not too heavy to lift, such as a bike, can be hung from large vinyl-coated wall or ceiling hooks.

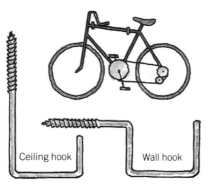

Ceiling hook   Wall hook

An easy way to make a pegboard is with wooden pegs, which you can get from woodworking supply stores. Just drill a hole in a board for the tenon and put the peg in with white glue. Mount the board with wall fasteners or with screws extending into the studs.

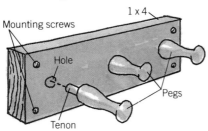

Mounting screws

Hole

1 x 4

Pegs

Tenon

The back of any door is a natural spot for hooks and pegs. Another storage device that works well there is a shoe bag. You can use its pockets for objects ranging from gloves to toiletries.

Sometimes you can also put the front of a door to work. Consider putting attractive hooks or racks there. Or cover it with pegboard.

INSTALLING HOOKS AND HANGERS

To put a hook into solid wood, first make a pilot hole. For all but the largest hooks, the quickest way to do this is with a push drill (p.184). You can make a small hole with a nail or an ice pick.

If a hook is hard to screw in, place the screwdriver through it at an angle and use the screwdriver as a lever to finish screwing it in. If the hook is too open for this to work, clamp locking-grip pliers on the hook and use them to turn it.

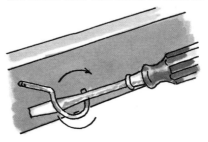

A screwdriver or locking-grip pliers can be used in the same manner to take out hooks that are locked in place by rust or paint.

If you're hanging a heavy object, make sure that your hook is long enough to screw into a wall stud (p.49). And if you want to hang anything—heavy or light—from the ceiling, use a hook that goes into a joist.

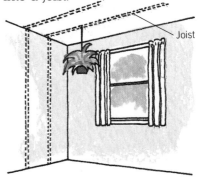

Joist

If you want to put up a hook for a light object on a plaster or plasterboard wall, use one with a screw hole so that you can put it up with an existing wall fastener (p.51). Or mount hooks with screw-in tips on a board; then attach the board with screws going into the studs.

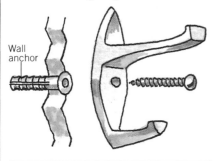

Wall anchor

PEGBOARD: A RELIABLE STANDBY

Putting up perforated hardboard, commonly known as pegboard, is still one of the easiest, fastest, and cheapest ways to create storage for flat, hangable items that you need within reach.

For hanging hand tools, kitchen utensils, and other lightweight objects, ordinary ⅛-inch-thick pegboard is fine. For heavy loads, get sturdier ¼-inch-thick pegboard. Tempered pegboard is stronger than untempered.

When selecting pegboard attachments, make sure they'll fit on your pegboard. Some can be used only on ⅛-inch pegboard and others only on ¼-inch panels. Some will fit both types.

Brownish, unpainted pegboard is a good buy for workshops and garage walls. Elsewhere you'll be better off using prepainted pegboard, available in white and many colors. Its wipe-clean factory finish is more durable than any paint you could apply.

If your decorating scheme dictates a color not available on prefinished pegboard, paint smooth, unfinished pegboard, using a urethane enamel for a hard finish. Apply it with a roller and take care not to clog the holes.

Pegboard panels come in various dimensions, up to sheets 4 feet by 8 feet for covering large wall areas. If you need a special size, look for a building-supply dealer who will cut a panel to the measurements you want.

If you cut pegboard yourself, you can prevent fraying and damage to the finish by clamping the panel between boards along the cut line and using a fine-tooth 12- or 15-point crosscut saw. Make sure the springy panel is supported evenly from below.

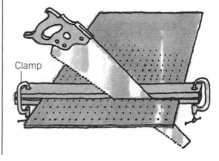

Clamp

PUTTING UP PEGBOARD

It's easy to install pegboard with plastic anchors, long screws, and ⅜-inch spacers. First mark the wall through the panel's holes. Mark at the corners and every 16 inches along the edges and at points in between. Put plastic anchors in the wall (p.51) at these points. When mounting the panel, put a screw through the pegboard hole, then through the spacer.

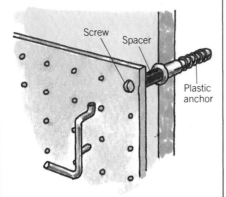

Screw Spacer Plastic anchor

If you have trouble fitting a spacer under a panel, glue it to the anchor in the wall. Use masking tape to hold it while the glue sets. Even better, look for a hardware dealer who carries a special pegboard anchor with a built-in spacer.

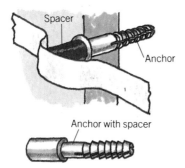

Spacer

Anchor

Anchor with spacer

Heavy-duty ¼-inch pegboard and large sheets of regular ⅛-inch pegboard require extra support. Mount them with ¾-inch furring strips instead of spacers. Nail the strips to the studs. Then screw the pegboard to them. Put strips along all the panel's edges and along every stud in the middle. Plan them so that they'll fall between rows of holes.

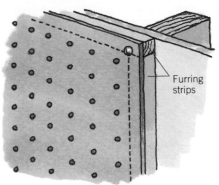

Furring strips

Furring strips are also best for mounting pegboard on rough and uneven masonry walls. Attach them with masonry nails (p.51), using scraps of wood as shims to level them.

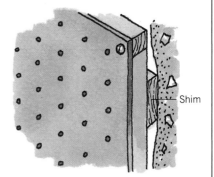

Shim

In garages and other areas with unfinished walls, screw pegboard directly to the exposed studs.

If either studs or furring strips will be visible through a panel's holes, paint them black; they won't be noticeable that way.

Put pegboard on the back of an open bookcase, and you'll have a dual-purpose room divider with shelves on one side and hooks on the other.

SHELF MATERIALS

For shelves less than a foot deep, the strongest and most rigid commonly available material is nominal 1-inch softwood lumber (see box at right). It's also easy to cut, nail, and finish.

To reduce the tendency of a wide board to curve along its length, check its growth rings and install it so that its heart side—the side that was closest to the center of the tree—faces upward. The weight of materials on the shelf will then work against the warping.

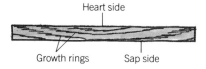

Heart side

Growth rings   Sap side

Another good shelving material is ¾-inch plywood (see box, p.58). It's ideal when you want deep shelves or shelves of a depth other than standard wood widths. It's also generally more economical for a large number of shelves.

To cut plywood most efficiently, use shelf widths that divide easily into a sheet's 48- x 96-inch dimensions, notably 8, 12, 16, 24, 32.

Plan to cut each plywood shelf ⅛ inch shorter than its potential maximum size to provide leeway for sawing. This typical plywood cutting diagram shows one way a sheet can yield 12 shelves.

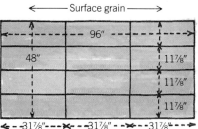

← Surface grain →

96"

48"   11⅞"

11⅞"

11⅞"

←-31⅞"-→←-31⅞"-→←-31⅞"-→

BUYING LUMBER

When buying board lumber, remember that the size you ask for isn't the size you'll get. For example, a 1 x 8 really measures ¾ inch thick by 7¼ inches wide—as the chart below shows. A board's length, however, is always exact. Most boards come in 8-foot lengths; you can get longer pieces in even-numbered feet. For an additional charge, dealers will usually cut boards to any length and width you order.

Most dealers carry one or two grades of "select" lumber—boards with few or no knots or other defects. They are ideal for highly visible shelves that will receive a natural finish. But consider a less expensive and knottier "common" grade when you're planning to paint or to put the boards in the back of a closet. Buy from a dealer who'll let you inspect the lumber. And always sight along a board's edges to make sure it's straight.

STANDARD LUMBER SIZES

Size to order	Actual size in inches
1 x 2	¾ x 1½
1 x 3	¾ x 2½
1 x 4	¾ x 3½
1 x 6	¾ x 5½
1 x 8	¾ x 7¼
1 x 10	¾ x 9¼
1 x 12	¾ x 11¼
2 x 2	1½ x 1½
2 x 3	1½ x 2½
2 x 4	1½ x 3½
2 x 6	1½ x 5½
2 x 8	1½ x 7¼
2 x 10	1½ x 9¼
2 x 12	1½ x 11¼

BUYING PLYWOOD

Plywood usually comes in sheets measuring 4 feet by 8 feet, in thicknesses of ¼, ½, or ¾ inch. Some lumber dealers sell half and quarter sheets.

Plywood is made by gluing or cementing several thin layers of wood to a central piece of veneer, particleboard, or lumber. The grain of each layer is set at right or wide angles to the next layer, creating a strong, rigid wood that does not split, chip, crumble, or crack all the way through. Plywood can be used for facing and as a substitute for lumber.

There are two main types of plywood: softwood (or construction) and hardwood (or decorative). Each type of plywood is graded by the quality of its surface. For example, softwood plywood has these grades: G2S (good on both sides); G1S (good on one side); SEL TF (select tight face, no open defects); SELECT (minor blemishes); and SHG (sheathing, obvious blemishes). G2S and G1S have sanded surfaces.

Ask your local lumber dealer which type and grade of plywood is best for your needs. Let him cut the plywood to size for you. Supply exact measurements and indicate the direction of each piece's surface grain. For strength and looks, you'll usually want this grain to run in the longer direction—along a shelf's length, for example. When you pick up your order, check each piece's dimensions.

Cover any visible plywood shelf edge with veneer tape (step 6, p.64)—or with strips of ¼-inch lumber if it will be used heavily.

For utility shelving, an inexpensive substitute is ¾-inch particleboard, which comes in sheets like plywood. But reserve this less rigid material for light loads or else support it at close intervals.

For quick shelving, prefinished shelves are a great convenience. But most have cores of particleboard and should carry only light loads or be well supported.

STRENGTHENING SHELVES

To strengthen a shelf, attach a 1 x 2 or a larger wood strip along its front edge. If the shelf's supports permit, consider putting a strip under its rear edge or providing support from below at midspan.

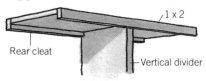

Rear cleat — 1 x 2 — Vertical divider

If you want a shelf to span a distance greater than recommended (p.60), use nominal 2-inch board lumber. Or glue two pieces of ¾-inch plywood surface to surface and glue and nail 1 x 2's on the exposed edges.

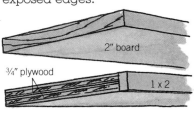

2" board — ¾" plywood — 1 x 2

SHELVES ON INDIVIDUAL BRACKETS

On shelves that will carry light loads, the brackets will be almost unnoticeable if you use large L-brackets and install them upside down so that the items you put on the shelf will hide them.

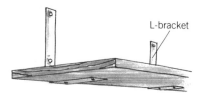

L-bracket

When installing shelf brackets right side up, always attach the longer leg to the wall. And for heavy loads use brackets with angled gussets between the legs.

SHELVES ON STANDARDS

One of the fastest, least costly ways to cover a wall with shelves is to use standards and brackets. Many versions are available, including heavy-duty metal ones and decorative wood ones. Most are installed like regular standards and brackets (p.60).

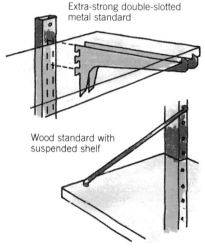

Extra-strong double-slotted metal standard

Wood standard with suspended shelf

When planning to install shelves on standards, be sure to investigate adjustable angle brackets for a magazine or book rack and long brackets for a desk or cabinet.

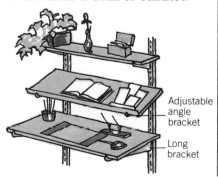

Adjustable angle bracket

Long bracket

PUTTING UP SHELF STANDARDS

If you don't have a level, you can still install a shelf standard that's perfectly vertical. Just mount it loosely from its top screw and let it swing back and forth. When it stops moving, install the bottom screw and tighten both screws.

Which end is up? If your shelf standards have no slots at one end, that end is the top. That way, the lowest shelf can be mounted at the very bottom of the standards.

On a masonry wall, it's difficult to install lead anchors that precisely match the holes on a shelf standard. It's easier to secure a 1 x 3 to the wall with cut or masonry nails and then screw the standards to it.

TYPICAL SHELF REQUIREMENTS

Kinds of objects	Depth in inches	Height in inches
Audiovisual materials		
Audiocassettes	3¼	5
Compact discs	6¼	5½
LP records	13½	13½
Videocassettes	5¾	9
Books and magazines		
Art and picture books	12	13
Novels, general books	8–12	10
Magazines	9½	12
Paperbacks	6	8
Clothing		
Men's shirts	15	10
Men's shoes	13	6
Men's sweaters	15	12
Women's blouses	14	10
Women's shoes	10½	8
Kitchen items		
Beverages	6	13
Bowls	8–12	5
Boxed foods	6–8	8–12
Canned goods	4½	5½
Cups and glasses	10	6–10
Plates (stacked)	12	5–7
Pots and pans	9–12	5–9
Trays (on edge)	11	16
Linens and bath items		
Bath towels	16–24	14
Sheets	16–24	12
Toiletries	4–8	4–10

SPACING SHELF SUPPORTS

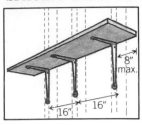

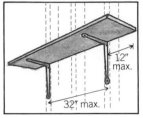

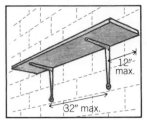

Heavy loads should have their supports held by long screws going well into the wall studs. Supports should be screwed to every stud. In most homes, the studs are spaced at 16-inch intervals (see box, p.49). Keep the overhang at each end of a shelf to 8 inches or less.

Lighter loads can be held by supports screwed into every other stud, and the overhang can extend 12 inches. But if your home has studs 24 inches apart, attach a support to each stud, whatever the load. You can attach a shelf carrying a very light load with wall fasteners (p.51).

Masonry walls call for inserting either expansion shields or lead anchors to hold the supports (p.52). For heavy loads, put supports at least every 16 inches, and keep the overhang less than 8 inches. Lighter loads need support at 32-inch intervals and an overhang of 1 foot or less.

SINGLE SHELF ON BRACKETS

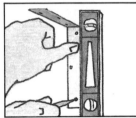

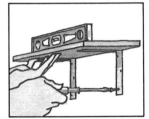

1. Position a shelf bracket on the wall. Use a level or a combination square to check that it's vertical. Mark the position of the screw holes. With a bit that's slightly smaller in diameter than the screw, drill screw holes. Screw the bracket to the wall.

2. Measure and mark the positions of both brackets on the shelf. Then drill holes and screw the other bracket to the shelf. Make sure that the bracket is square and even with the shelf's back edge. Be careful not to drill all the way through the shelf.

3. Position the shelf on the wall and check that it's level. Then attach the bracket that's on the shelf to the wall. Finally, attach the first bracket to the shelf. Each time, mark and drill holes for the screws as you did in the first two steps.

SHELVES ON STANDARDS

Awl or nail for marking

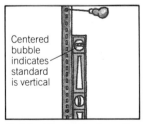

Centered bubble indicates standard is vertical

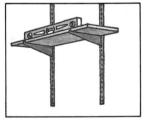

1. Position a slotted standard on the wall. Find a screw hole in the middle of the standard and mark its position. Using a bit that's slightly smaller than the screw, drill a hole at that point. Attach the standard but don't tighten the screw all the way.

2. Adjust the standard's position until the bubble in a level shows that it's perfectly vertical. Then mark and drill holes for the other screws and finish attaching the standard. If necessary, you can swing the standard out of the way while you're drilling.

3. Put a bracket on the standard and in the matching slot holes of another standard. Hold the second standard against the wall and put a shelf on the brackets. Level the shelf, then put up the standard the same way you did the first.

DISGUISING SHELF HARDWARE

Camouflage brackets for a single shelf or standards by painting them the same color as the wall.

To conceal brackets on standards, use brackets an inch or so shorter than the shelf width. Drill a hole partway into the shelf's underside for each bracket's front tip. A 1 x 2 nailed to the shelf's front edge hides the brackets even more.

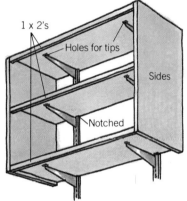

To make shelves on standards and brackets look built-in, install sides at each end. Attach them to just the top and bottom shelves so that you can still adjust the others. Notching the shelves to fit around the standards also helps.

SHELVES ON UPRIGHTS

Uprights that fit by screw or spring pressure between the ceiling and the floor provide another quick way to cover a wall or divide a room—with shelves. Poles slotted to accept brackets are available for standard 8-foot ceilings. Higher ceilings need extensions.

Install tension poles with their brackets toward the wall. This helps conceal the slots and brackets, creating a more finished look.

Whenever possible install a tension pole directly beneath a joist in the ceiling. You can usually locate joists as you do studs (p.49).

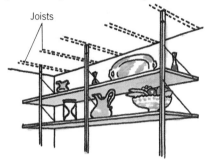

You can make your own tension poles from 2 x 4's. Cut each an inch shorter than ceiling height and screw a shelf standard to it. Then drill a hole in the top and install a screw-out furniture leveler. Put an extra nut on the leveler to lock it in place. Secure the 2 x 4 to the floor with an L-bracket.

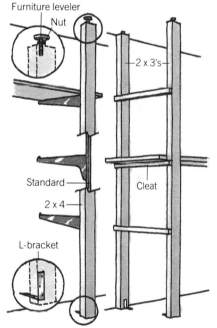

For deeper shelves, use pairs of tension poles made from 2 x 3's. Support the shelves with cleats or with clips on tracks (p.67).

If appearance doesn't matter, you can install uprights quickly with spring-loaded metal caps that top 2 x 3's. But make sure the fit between floor and ceiling is tight and that each upright is under a joist.

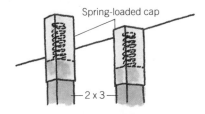
Spring-loaded cap
2 x 3

INDUSTRIAL SHELVING

Don't limit steel utility shelves to rough storage. Spray-paint a unit in a bright color and outfit it with plastic or wire bins for a bathroom. Or finish it in a subdued color and use it for large books and vases in the living room.

Industrial wire shelving may also be the answer to storage in any room—and a unit can carry a lot of weight. Many home centers carry chrome-plated units, and you can get plainer versions from commerical shelving stores.

IMPROVISED SHELVES

Create an entire storage wall by grouping together sturdy wood and plastic cartons or by combining them with boards. Keep larger and stronger cartons near the bottom, and secure higher ones to the wall and to one another. For a unified effect, paint all the containers the same color.

Bricks, cinder blocks, tile flues, wood blocks, and decorative cement blocks are all time-honored shelf spacers. Be sure to stack them straight. Locate a tall unit along a wall and secure the higher shelves to the wall.

You can make hanging shelves for light loads with rope, chain, threaded metal rods, and either woven nylon lawn-chair webbing or jute upholstery webbing. Be sure to secure the supports to ceiling joists or wall studs.

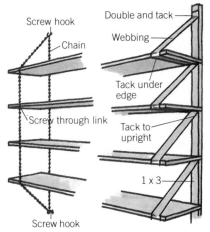
Screw hook
Double and tack
Chain
Webbing
Tack under edge
Screw through link
Tack to upright
1 x 3
Screw hook

Create a wall unit with a pair of straight ladders. Secure one side of each ladder to a stud in the wall and rest shelves on the rungs.

SHELF TIDIERS

To keep items from falling off a shelf, make shelf ends by attaching a short length of board or plywood to each end.

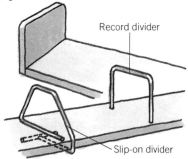
Record divider
Slip-on divider

Wire dividers that slip on and grip the shelf are a nice alternative to regular bookends. And wire LP-record dividers that fit into holes drilled in a shelf make good dividers and ends on any shelf.

Dowels make good vertical shelf dividers. To fit a dowel between two shelves, cut it ½ inch longer than the distance between the shelves. Then drill a hole ½ inch deep in the upper shelf and another hole ¼ inch deep in the lower shelf. Shove the dowel all the way into the upper hole; then drop it into the lower one.

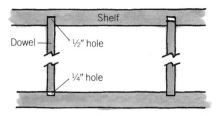

WIRE WALL SYSTEMS

Consider using a wire grid instead of pegboard. Its waterproof vinyl finish makes it especially useful in a kitchen or bath. An assortment of hooks, baskets, and other clip-ons are available.

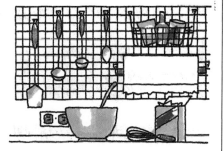

Vinyl-coated wire shelving provides a fast way to create shelves in a kitchen, bathroom, pantry, child's room, laundry room, or garage. It comes in various lengths, and you can quickly cut it to any length with a hacksaw. Mount it with the lip upward to keep items such as bottles from falling off.

You can also quickly remodel a closet with wire shelving. Get shelves with a plain rod for hanging clothing.

Install a wire system with closely spaced plastic anchors or other hollow-wall fasteners. The design of most systems requires fasteners at set intervals, usually making it impossible to fasten to studs.

CABINETS AND CASES

Before building a cabinet or case, check stores that carry unfinished furniture or prefabricated kits. A standard unit, such as a bookcase, can cost little more than the building materials.

To avoid an unpleasant surprise, plan your cabinet or bookcase on paper before sawing the pieces. Measure the space where the unit will go and make sketches with dimensions, showing front, side, and top views.

If you're fitting a cabinet in a tight space, be sure to allow enough room to get it into position. Usually a ⅛-inch clearance on each side is all you need.

If a space requires a storage unit wider than 32 inches, put in a vertical partition, or consider having two units side by side.

A BASIC PLYWOOD STORAGE UNIT

Here's an easily adaptable storage unit with a frame and shelves made of ¾-inch plywood. For the back, order a piece of ¼-inch plywood that's ¼ inch less than the unit's overall measurements from side to side and from top to bottom shelf. Get a 1 x 3 (see box, p.57) for the toeboard and ¾-inch-square molding for the cleats. Also buy white glue, 3d and 6d finishing nails, and veneer tape to cover the plywood edges.

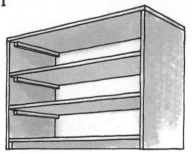

Tips on tools and wood joining appear on pp.183-192, and tips on finishing on pp.443-445.

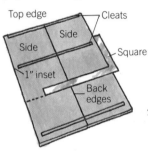

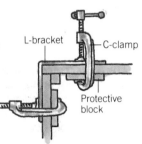

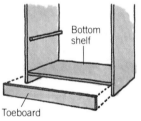

1. Align top and bottom edges of the side pieces. Mark each cleat position, making a line across both pieces at once. Make sure lowest cleat will be even with toeboard top. Cut cleats 1 inch shorter than shelf depth. Nail and glue a cleat along each line and at each side's top edge. Use 3d nails 2 inches apart.

2. Join the top and sides. At each corner apply glue and clamp the pieces together at right angles. (Here a large L-bracket was used with clamps to get a right angle; for other methods, see pp.191-192.) Secure the top to the sides with 6d nails and to the cleats with 3d nails.

3. Set the bottom shelf in place. Glue and clamp each bottom corner. Use 3d nails to secure the bottom shelf to the cleats and 6d nails to secure the sides to the shelf. Then install the toeboard, using glue and 6d nails.

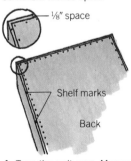

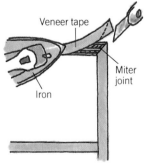

4. Turn the unit over. Measure up ⅜ inch from the top of each cleat, and make a mark across the frame's back edges to indicate where each shelf's centerline will be. Apply glue along the frame's edges. Then position the back so that it is set in ⅛ inch along all edges. Attach the back with 3d nails at 4-inch intervals.

5. Install the shelves. Put glue along each shelf's back edge and along each cleat top. Then secure the shelves to the cleats with 3d nails. Then turn the unit over. Using the marks you made earlier, draw a line across the back along each shelf's centerline. Nail the back to the shelves along the line.

6. Cover the raw plywood edges on the front of the unit with veneer tape. Use a clothing iron on a warm, nonsteam setting to smooth the tape along the entire length of an edge. Do the shelf edges first and trim the tape ends with a utility knife. Then do the sides and the top. Miter the tape at the top corners.

MAKING A CABINET

After assembling a cabinet's basic frame, measure diagonally between corners. If both measurements are exactly the same, the frame is square. If not, shift the sides until the corners are square.

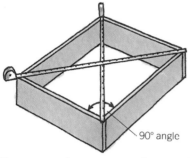

90° angle

For a case that you can dismantle and move easily, connect the four major joints with bolts and nuts. Attach the back with screws and have shelves that just lift out.

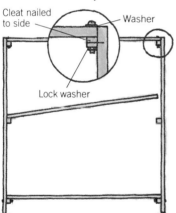

Cleat nailed to side
Washer
Lock washer

When nailing cleats to a unit's side, angle the nails downward for greater holding power.

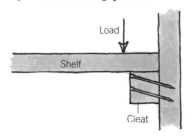

Load
Shelf
Cleat

BUYING NAILS

You can do most projects with either common nails or finishing nails. Common nails have large, flat heads and are fine for rough work. But when appearance counts, select the thinner finishing nails. You can drive a finishing nail's head below the wood's surface and fill the hole with wood putty.

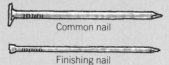

Common nail

Finishing nail

Nails are sized according to the penny system, designated by a number and a *d*. For sizes up to 10d (10 penny), you can calculate a nail's length by dividing the penny size by four, then adding ½ inch. An 8d nail, for example, is 2½ inches long. If you can, buy nails in 1-pound quantities—the cost per nail is much less than when you buy small packets.

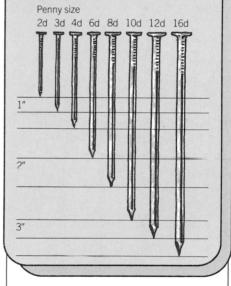

Penny size
2d 3d 4d 6d 8d 10d 12d 16d
1"
2"
3"

For stacking modular units, make the basic case (facing page) without a toeboard. Attach the bottom with corner cleats like the top.

For added strength, use 1 x 2 (or larger) cleats and attach them with glue and screws (p.66). Reinforce each shelf's edges (p.58).

To create an open shelf unit, simply nail shelves between four L-shaped corners, each made by gluing and nailing a 1 x 4 to a 1 x 3.

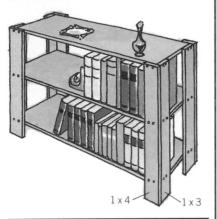

1 x 4   1 x 3

VARYING THE BASIC CABINET

Since a bookcase is narrow, you can make it from board lumber, following the steps for making a plywood case (p.64). Either 1 x 10's or 1 x 12's are good choices.

If you're building a tall bookcase, make the sides overlap the top so that the top's edge can't be seen. For added strength, nail through the sides into a middle shelf.

For a kitchen or bathroom cabinet, just make a basic case with a kick space. Notch the corners of the sides and nail a 1 x 4 toeboard over the sides.

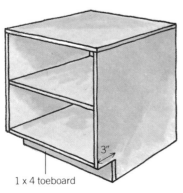

3"

1 x 4 toeboard

BUYING WOOD SCREWS

Match a screw to the type of job it will do. A flathead screw is fine for most joints. You can drive its head flush with the surface or sink it below and hide it with wood putty or a wood plug (p.190). When a screw must be exposed, an ovalhead screw is attractive and can be easily removed without marring a surface. A roundhead screw is most useful for attaching thin material, such as a metal bracket or pegboard, to wood.

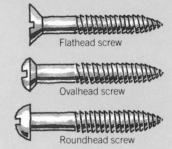

Flathead screw

Ovalhead screw

Roundhead screw

Screws usually come in lengths ranging from ¼ inch to 3 inches. Diameters are indicated by a gauge number. Many length and gauge combinations are available. When buying screws, state the length and gauge number you want—for example, a 1¼-inch, No. 7 screw. Get stainless steel or aluminum screws for a project that will be exposed to moisture and brass or bronze ones to match hardware. Otherwise, you'll save using plain, plated, or galvanized screws. Like nails, screws are most economical when you buy them in pound quantities.

Gauge number

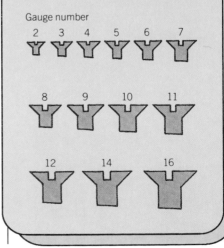

2   3   4   5   6   7

8   9   10   11

12   14   16

For a wall-hung case, replace the basic case's back with mounting boards—a 1 x 4 nailed and glued under the top and a 1 x 2 under the bottom shelf. Mount a 1 x 2 under the front of the bottom shelf too.

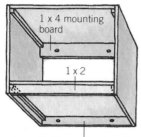

1 x 4 mounting board

1 x 2

1 x 2 mounting board

Use screw eyes to support a shelf that you may later want to move. Screw eyes are also great for adding a shelf to a finished cabinet.

For movable shelves, use metal spade pins or bracket pins that fit in rows of holes in the sides.

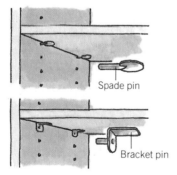

Spade pin

Bracket pin

Drill holes for pins before assembling a unit. For perfectly aligned holes, use pegboard as a guide.

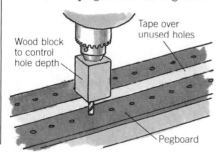

Wood block to control hole depth

Tape over unused holes

Pegboard

You can also create adjustable shelves with metal tracks and clips. Attach two tracks to each side before assembly. Notch the shelves to fit around the tracks.

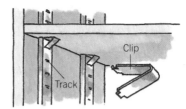

Clip

Track

Use pliers to squeeze troublesome clips into tracks.

Putting doors on a cabinet is tricky. It's easier to build the case to fit precut doors. A good choice for doors is ¾-inch-thick unfinished slat shutters. Put them between 1 x 2's nailed to the unit's front edges. Use attractive hinges.

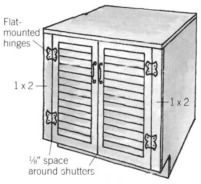

Flat-mounted hinges

1 x 2

1 x 2

⅛" space around shutters

It's also easier to build a cabinet to fit ready-made drawers. Use plastic bins and fit their rims between pairs of cleats on each side. Or use wire baskets on their own metal runners or frame.

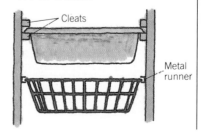

Cleats

Metal runner

To make cabinets look built in, install molding that covers the cracks along walls, ceiling, and floor and between units. Span wide gaps between units with shelves or false panels. These are great ways to adapt old or purchased units to a new space.

ORGANIZING DRAWERS

You can increase a deep drawer's usable space with a sliding tray. A simple box of ½-inch plywood on hardwood runners will do.

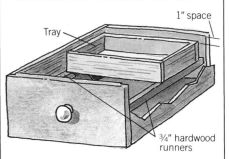

1" space
Tray
¾" hardwood runners

Make a tray half of the drawer's width or depth so that you can slide it and gain full access to the bottom. Or make it with handles so that you can easily lift it out.

Here is a versatile divider arrangement that can benefit both wide and deep drawers. Nail and glue the rear divider to the front-to-back dividers first. Then nail and glue the spacers on the drawer's front, and glue the dividers' front ends between them. Nail the rear piece through the sides.

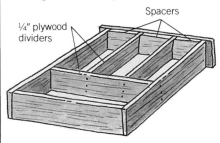

Spacers
¼" plywood dividers

To find the best arrangement for dividers, try temporary ones for a few weeks. Just use doubled-over cardboard with flaps at the bottom and ends. Use the flaps to attach the pieces to the drawer and to each other with duct tape.

Plastic trays with compartments needn't be limited to desk and kitchen drawers. Use them in any shallow drawer to organize jewelry, cosmetics, sewing supplies, tools, keys, and pocket change.

Another way to create small compartments in a shallow drawer is to notch and join strips of lattice, which you can buy at a lumberyard. Clamp the crosspieces together and cut the notches all at once so that they'll align exactly.

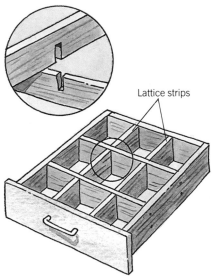

Lattice strips

ROLLOUTS AND PULLOUTS

Rollouts and pullouts are great space savers. Because you don't have to reach in, you don't have to leave room above items, and you can take out bulky items in the rear without disturbing small ones in the front.

An easy way to make a pullout shelf is to mount plywood between hardwood cleats with other pieces of cleat material on the shelf as guides. To clear your cabinet's front frame, you may have to put a spacer behind the cleats.

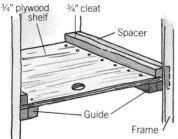

¾" plywood shelf   ¾" cleat

Spacer

Guide

Frame

For a simple rollout tray, nail and glue 1 x 4's around the edges of a piece of ¾-inch plywood. Then mount the tray to the bottom of a cabinet, using a pair of base-mounted drawer slides.

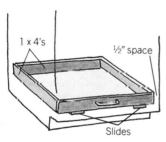

1 x 4's   ½" space

Slides

A rollout with shelves is just a simple case on drawer slides. You can build one to fit any cabinet, using ¾-inch plywood, 1 x 4's, and trim for the plywood's edges.

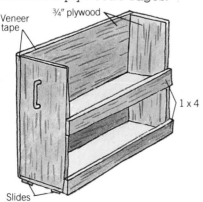

Veneer tape   ¾" plywood

1 x 4

Slides

Custom design other rollouts to fit your needs. Make a rollout with a center partition and shelves on two sides. Or, instead of shelves, install dowels like towel bars for hanging clothing or linens.

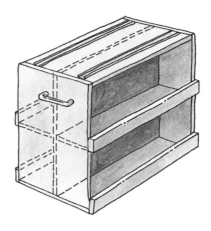

Also consider supporting a rollout from slides attached to a cabinet's top or side. If a cabinet wall is thin, mount a slide on a sturdy cleat.

SELECTING DRAWER SLIDES

After planning a rollout, show your design to a hardware dealer to find out exactly what type of drawer slides you need. If your local dealer doesn't have the kind you need, try a store specializing in cabinet hardware.

Drawer slides vary in the amount of clearance they need. Buy them *before* you cut the pieces for a rollout. They should be slightly shorter than your cabinet's depth.

Drawer slides that pull out most, but not all, of the way are less expensive and generally easier to install. But consider full-extension slides if you'll need to take heavy items out of the rear of a rollout.

CHAPTER TWO

INDOORS

Discover how to keep your entire home—from floors to ceilings and from basement to attic—sparkling clean and running smoothly. Then learn all about selecting and maintaining appliances and what to do before calling for service when a problem arises.

All Around the House

Page 71

Planning your cleaning and making it easier; how to clean in layers; choosing and using cleaning products and equipment; safety measures; washing walls and ceilings; cleaning wall coverings; treating tiles; caring for paneling; washing, waxing, and protecting floors; how to replace vinyl floor tiles; cleaning curtains; caring for window shades and venetian blinds; cleaning windows; replacing a windowpane; fixing a broken sash cord; caring for window screens; making windows energy-efficient; how to deal with a sticking door; sliding doors; fixing a door that binds; how to choose a vacuum cleaner and its attachments; vacuum maintenance, problems, and repair; cleaning and preserving carpets; patching a carpet; repairing a carpet burn; Oriental rugs; caring for your furniture and light fixtures; cleaning special objects; cleaning the fireplace; home entertainment systems; what to do before calling for a tele-

phone repairman; keeping the dining room clean; cut flowers and houseplants; bedroom upkeep; kitchen cleaning basics; kitchen safety; stove and microwave maintenance; cleaning an exhaust fan; caring for refrigerators and small appliances; clean kitchen counters; sink care; handling the garbage; unclogging drains; washing the dishes; vacuum bottles, pots, and pans; sharpening knives; safety in the bathroom; keeping a bathroom spotless; shower maintenance; toilet problems; attic hints; controlling dampness in basements and flooding; patching an inactive crack in a basement wall; leaks and seepage; fixing leaky pipes; frozen pipes; conserving energy; heating system problems; oil burner maintenance; attic and room fans; air conditioning hints; fixing a noisy air conditioner; pest control; do's and dont's of using pesticides; sorting out security systems and alarms.

Those Wonderful Appliances

Page 131

How long you will have an appliance; what to check before calling for service on an appliance; getting the most from a refrigerator and freezer; how to replace a refrigerator door gasket; selecting a stove; adjusting your oven's temperature control; what to do if you smell gas; adjusting the flame on a gas stove; selecting a dishwasher and loading it properly; getting the most from dishwasher detergent; buying and connecting your new clothes washer; saving on water-heating bills; water-heater upkeep; setting up and maintaining a new dryer; toasters and toaster ovens; cooking with a microwave; mixers, blenders, and food processors; coffee makers, percolators, and urns; caring for steam irons; humidifiers and dehumidifiers; trash compactors and garbage disposers; electric lights, plugs, and cords; testing and replacing an appliance power cord; replacing a plug; light switches; fuses and circuit breakers; shutting off electric power.

All Around the House

PLANNING YOUR CLEANING

Decide what "clean" means to you and then keep house accordingly. Clean things because they're dirty, not because it's time. If you don't notice a difference when you're cleaning something, *stop!*

It may be more practical for you to do your spring cleaning in the fall—the temperature's right for hard work, and it's more efficient to remove summer dirt that's come in through open windows before closing up the house for winter.

On the other hand, you may wish to clean and air out the house in the spring after it has been closed all winter.

Few cleaning jobs need to be done at a set time of year. Aside from cleaning screens and storm windows, and laundering summer or winter blankets, how you set up a seasonal cleaning schedule is strictly up to you. (To find out the best times for tackling exterior chores, turn to p.166.)

CLEANING IN LAYERS

When you clean according to a schedule, you build up a momentum that you don't have to break while deciding what to do next. One way to organize your cleaning schedule is to think of cleaning in layers. Adjust the following schedule to suit your specific needs, taking into account the size of your family and your home.

Layer 1 covers everyday jobs: washing the dishes, sweeping the floor, emptying the garbage, making the beds, picking up. These tasks should add up to no more than half an hour for a one-bedroom, single-level home. Add 10 minutes for each additional bedroom and level.

Layer 2 tasks are done once or twice a week: vacuuming, watering the plants, cleaning the garbage pail, wiping down the bathroom, cleaning the toilet, dusting the furniture.

Layer 3 is once-a-week deep cleaning: scrubbing the floors, polishing the furniture, cleaning the refrigerator, changing the linens. Set aside several hours to do all these jobs at once. Or add one deep-cleaning job to your list of Layer-1 tasks each day.

Layer 4 involves special projects: washing the windows and the woodwork, cleaning the oven, polishing the silver, cleaning the silver, washing summer and winter blankets, cleaning the screens and storm windows. Either choose a fixed 2 hours a week for these or add them to your Layer-3 list of things to do each week as they come up.

MAKING CLEANING EASIER

Where to begin? To see real progress fast, start with the areas that tend to go the fastest—the living and dining rooms and the halls—they're usually less cluttered and less dirty.

71

To make sure that you don't miss anything when dusting a room, start at the door and work around the room in one direction.

Eliminating clutter cuts down on the need to clean because an uncluttered home, even though not spotless, looks better than one that is dust-free but strewn with odds and ends.

Clean faster by clustering your activities; do as many tasks as you can in one place before you move on to the next area.

CHOOSING AND USING EQUIPMENT

No need to return to the cleaning closet every time you need something. Carry all your supplies from one room to the next in a "maid's basket"—a plastic bin with a handle—or a cleaning cart.

For spills and daily cleanup, install paper-towel racks in key places—the garage, workbench, baby's room, and bathroom, as well as the kitchen where they're usually kept.

Be choosy about your cleaning rags. Use cotton fabrics, such as old towels, diapers, or undershirts, and avoid cloths that contain less absorbent synthetic fibers, such as old slips.

Use clean cloths for damp or dry dusting; dirty ones will scratch surfaces.

To prevent dust from rolling out of your dustpan, dampen the pan before you start dusting.

If the edge of your dustpan becomes bent, take time to straighten it out, or you'll end up chasing dirt across the floor every time you use it.

Once you've collected the dirt and dust, you'll have to get rid of it. If you can't shake the dust mop outdoors, try shaking it into a paper or plastic bag—or try vacuuming instead of dusting.

CHOOSING CLEANING PRODUCTS

Resist the temptation to buy more types of cleaning products than you need. The more products you accumulate in your home, the greater the chance they'll be misused by children and adults.

Read all product labels before using the product. As a general rule, do not mix cleaning substances unless the directions instruct you to do so.

THE USE AND CARE OF BASIC CLEANING TOOLS

Tool	Use	Care
Dustcloths	For dry dusting of lightly soiled surfaces, use lintless cloths. Dampen absorbent terry or other cotton cloths with water or a little furniture polish to clean dust, smears, fingerprints, or soot. Follow the grain of wood surfaces	Wash in hot sudsy water after each use. Hang to dry. Cloths used for waxing and polishing should not be machine-dried because flammable fluids or fumes may remain in them
Broom	For quick, routine cleanup of hard floors. Keep broom firmly on surface and sweep slowly in one direction, collecting dirt in dustpan	Always hang to store. When soiled, dip it in hot sudsy water, rinse, and dry with rubber band around bristles to straighten them
Dust mop	For dusting bare floors between vacuum cleanings. Push across floor without raising mop, following grain of wood	Always hang to store. Shake into a large moistened bag after each use or vacuum clean. Wash in hot sudsy water, rinse, and dry in breezy, shady place. Or run through the washer and dryer in a net bag
Wet mop	For cleaning dirt and grime from washable resilient floors. Use with all-purpose cleaner or detergent and wring with wringer attached to bucket. Mop should be wet, but not sopping	Wash in hot sudsy water after each use, rinse thoroughly, shake to separate strings, and hang or turn upside down to dry (in sun if possible). Store in a cool, dry place. Never keep a damp mop on floor or in bucket
Sponge mop	For cleaning moderate-size, hard-surface floors. Soak in sudsy cleaning solution, then squeeze until just damp. Clean with firm strokes, covering no more than a 3-square-foot area at a time. Rinse, then repeat	Wash and rinse after each use, then stand upside down to dry. Moisten occasionally to keep from "drying hard." If detachable, follow care instructions for sponges
Scrub brushes	For cleaning rough surfaces, heavily soiled hard floors, and outdoor porches. Scrub with long strokes, using hot water and all-purpose cleaner	Wash in hot sudsy water after each use. Rinse in clear water; shake and let dry, bristles down. Store only when completely dry
Sponge	For all washable surfaces. Dip into hot or warm sudsy water, squeeze thoroughly, and rub with firm strokes	Clean in hot sudsy water, rinsing completely and squeezing dry. Throw in the washing machine with a general load (zip into a net bag to keep sponges from falling apart) or with a bleach load if sponges are smelly
Dry sponge	For flat-painted walls and ceilings, wallpaper, lampshades, and other areas where liquid cleaners are unsuitable. Use dry, turning and folding so that a clean part of the sponge is always in contact with the surface	Dry sponges are not reusable. Discard when saturated with dirt
Bucket	For all wet cleaning. Use two buckets — one for cleaner and one for rinse solution. Choose one with a wringer attached for wet-mopping	Rinse thoroughly after each use. Let rubber buckets air-dry; to avoid rust, dry metal buckets with paper towels after rinsing

Many people recommend making your own cleaning products. This is worthwhile only if the home-made products are much less costly and work just as safely and effectively as the commercial versions. They seldom do.

SAFETY MEASURES

Find a safe storage area for cleaning products, out of the reach of children and pets—not a cabinet where food supplies are kept. Return products to this area immediately after use. Never put a cleaning product down within a small child's reach and walk away, not even for a minute.

Always keep household cleaning products in the containers they came in. Never transfer them to containers that you normally use for food. Throw out empty cleaning-product containers immediately; they're not suitable for storing anything else.

Before throwing away a cleaning product, check the label on the container; if it has "Caution," "Warning," or "Poison" on it, follow carefully the directions for the proper disposal of the empty container.

CLEANING METHODS

Avoid extra work; follow the manufacturers' directions on cleaning supplies. If the label says use only one capful, more won't be better—it will be harder to rinse off and more expensive to use.

Cover half the holes in the top of a can of scouring powder with masking tape and the can will probably last longer.

To avoid redepositing dirt on the surface, always use a clean solution. Mix up a new bucket of cleaner and water as soon as the first bucket becomes moderately dirty.

SUBSTITUTES FOR CLEANING PRODUCTS

Ammonia, diluted with 3 parts water in an empty pump-spray bottle, can be used instead of a commercial spray to clean windows, appliances, and countertops. Use full-strength ammonia to remove wax from floors or to clean the oven (not really dirty ones, however).
Caution: Always wear rubber gloves whenever cleaning with an ammonia solution. Also, when using it full strength, make sure that the work area is well ventilated.

An excellent substitute for metal cleaner to scour copper and brass objects is ½ cup vinegar mixed with 1 tablespoon salt.

Full-strength pine oil makes quick work of cleaning and deodorizing garbage pails and bathroom and kitchen floors. If you dilute the pine oil, you won't have to rinse.

Baking soda is milder than harsh scouring powders for cleaning kitchen and bath fixtures. It also removes odors and washes stains from refrigerators and freezers, coffeepots and teapots, and thermos bottles. Try it to deodorize diaper pails and kitty litter.

A sprinkling of dry baking soda before vacuuming will freshen carpeting as well as any commercial carpet deodorizer.

WALLS AND CEILINGS

Before washing a painted surface, dust it with a broom covered with a flannel cloth. Change the cloth when it gets dirty.

To dust hard-to-reach corners, slip an old sock over a yardstick and secure it with a rubber band.

Cobwebs can be sticky and stain surfaces. Lift them away from the wall rather than push them onto the surface, using a vacuum cleaner tool or a cloth-covered broom.

When vacuuming trim, plasterwork, or woodwork, protect the surface from scratches by attaching a "bumper," a strip of foam rubber secured with a rubber band, to the head of your vacuum's crevice attachment.

WASHING WALLS

Washing painted walls is faster and cheaper than painting them. If you have your walls professionally washed, you'll probably spend a great deal less than you would for a professional paint job.

Tie a washcloth around your wrist to catch wall-washing drips. An athlete's terry cloth wristband will work well too.

Practice the two-bucket technique to make your cleaning solution last longer. Rinse and squeeze the dirt from your wall-washing sponge into a bucket of water before dipping it into the clean solution. (The two-bucket technique works well for washing floors too.)

If you start at the bottom when washing walls, the cleaning solution will drip onto the part of the wall you've just cleaned. But if you start at the top, the cleaning solution may cause permanent stains as it drips down. The best way is to work rapidly in small areas with a well-wrung-out cloth or sponge, beginning at the bottom.

Use only white, off-white, or color-fast cloths or sponges to wash walls and ceilings; some dye in colored cloths or sponges may stain the surface.

Very dirty walls may need rinsing as well. Even small fry can help with this task, bringing clean water when you need it. (Make a mark on the rinse bucket and ask the child to fill it up to the mark.)

Wiping walls dry will prevent streaking. Use terry cloth towels with a high cotton content, tumble-dried for more absorbency.

As a resting place for lint, pet hair, and other residue, baseboards are usually the dirtiest part of the room. Wash them last after you've finished washing the walls and have used cloths for wiping them. Clean the baseboards with the damp cloths; then wipe them with your sponge and a fresh towel.

WALL COVERINGS

Clean fabric wall coverings, including grass cloth, with a hand-held vacuum. Very delicate fabric wall coverings such as silk, however, may need a specialist's attention.

Transform regular wallpaper into washable wallpaper by giving it a coat of wallpaper sizing, then one of clear shellac.

Is your nonwashable wallpaper soiled? Rub it gently with an art-gum eraser, or crustless slices of fresh, "doughy" bread.

Here's a novel way to clean washable wallpaper with detergent suds. Mix ¼ cup liquid dishwashing detergent with 1 cup warm water and beat with a rotary beater into a stiff foam. Scoop up only the foam on top of the suds and apply with a cloth or sponge.

SPOTS ON WALLPAPER

Clean any spots on wallpaper as soon as possible. Blot a new grease spot with a clean paper towel. Then, holding a fresh piece of absorbent paper on the spot, press with a warm (not hot) iron. Change the paper when it becomes greasy.

Remove crayon marks on wallpaper by sponging them with dry-cleaning solvent. If the dye remains on the wall, mix 1 teaspoon liquid bleach in 1 cup water and apply to the colored stain. (Be sure to test this bleach solution on an inconspicuous spot to determine whether it will damage the pattern or the paper.)

Silver polish, applied with a clean cloth, will remove crayon marks on vinyl wall covering. Concentrated dishwashing detergent also works well.

Use chlorine bleach to remove ink spots on washable wallpaper. Pat the spots with a cloth or a cotton swab dampened with bleach, then rinse with a cloth or sponge dipped in clear water. Test this method in an inconspicuous spot first, since the bleach may remove wall covering color.

TILE TREATMENTS

Get rid of that soapy film on ceramic tile walls or floors—wipe household cleaner (either diluted or full strength) or a solution of 1 part vinegar and 4 parts water over them. Rinse thoroughly with clean water and buff tiles to prevent streaking.

For stained or mildewed grouting, apply a bleach solution (¾ cup liquid chlorine bleach to 1 gallon water) with a cloth, sponge, or toothbrush (wear rubber gloves and old clothes in case of spattering); rinse thoroughly.

Run a typewriter eraser over grouting to make it come clean.

WOOD PANELING

To clean and polish unwaxed varnished or shellacked wood paneling, apply a mixture of ½ cup turpentine, ¾ cup boiled linseed oil, and 1 tablespoon vinegar; let stand for 15 minutes, then rub until all of the cleaner is removed. To test, rub with a clean, dry finger; it should leave no smudges behind.

For surface scratches on wood paneling, apply clear wax on a damp cloth and rub the scratched area with the grain. If the paneling is dark, you may have to re- stain the scratch mark, and for a uniform appearance, you may have to wax the entire area.

To prevent paneling from developing dark spots behind a picture, place corks at the bottom corners of the frame to allow air to circulate back of it. Cut the corks so that they hold the picture parallel to the wall.

GENERAL FLOOR CARE

Before buying cleaning and waxing products, know what type of floor you're maintaining. If you can't determine it at a glance, ask your home's previous owner or a flooring expert.

After purchasing a new floor covering, keep the maintenance literature in a special file, or write instructions on an index card and tape it to the inside of your cleaning-supplies cabinet door.

Dust-mopping or vacuuming floors daily gets rid of the fine grit that grinds the shine off both waxed and no-wax floor coverings. In the long run, you're putting off the day of a major cleaning.

77

Dust mops pick up more dirt than brooms and are especially suited to the smooth, glassy finishes used on wood and no-wax floors. To make the work go faster, buy a commercial 18-inch dust mop at a home center store.

An oiled dust mop ruins a waxed surface. Use a dry dust mop or, if the room itself is very dry, one slightly dampened with water (just a few sprays will do the trick).

When dust-mopping, sweeping, or vacuuming won't do the job, damp-mopping with clear, lukewarm water is safe for all protected surfaces. (Be sure that wood floors are well sealed, however, before damp-mopping them.)

WASHING FLOORS

More floors are washed away than worn away; so wring out your mop until it's almost dry. Excess water will penetrate the seams of sheet flooring or tiles, dissolve protective coatings, and raise the grain and make wood rough.

Use your kitchen trash container as your mop bucket; this way you can clean it at the same time you wash your floors.

Keep one mop just for rinsing; it's almost impossible to get all the cleaning solution out of a mop.

WAXING FLOORS

All floors need the protection of wax or special dressing. A waxed floor is easier to clean with frequent damp-mopping and occasional washing than one that's unwaxed.

Use water-base waxes and finishes on any surface not damaged by water (just about anything except wood and cork). Solvent-base waxes can be used on most surfaces except rubber tiles.

Dampen the application pad or cloth with plain water before beginning to spread wax. This prevents excessive absorption of wax into the applicator, aids in spreading wax evenly, and makes application easier.

When a floor starts looking shabby—usually after six to eight coats of wax (or about once a year)—it's time to remove the old wax.

A squeegee (not the one you use for windows) comes in handy when removing wax. After soaking and scrubbing the floor with detergent or wax remover, squeegee the residue into an uncleaned area. Scoop it into an empty bucket with a dustpan; then damp-mop the squeegeed area with clear water.

If you're in doubt when applying fresh wax to your floors, remember that it's better to use too little than to use too much.

Avoid wax buildup on floor edges, under-furniture areas, and other light-traffic areas by only applying wax every other waxing session.

Keep track of where you do—and don't—want to wax. After you've moved the furniture and cleaned the floor, put a piece of newspaper the size of each piece of furniture on the floor where the furniture usually stands. Then wax around the newspaper.

Self-polishing floor wax hardens very quickly; wash the applicator immediately after each use.

For a quick shine between waxings, place a piece of wax paper under your mop and work around the room. (Be sure that you've dust-mopped thoroughly beforehand, since grit under the paper will scratch the waxed surface of the floor.)

To prevent worn spots on the polished floors in doorways or at the bottom of stairs, give them the following treatment once or twice a month: apply a thin coat of paste wax with a cheesecloth, allow it to dry for 15 minutes, and then polish; repeat the procedure an hour or two later.

PROTECTING FLOORS

Keep dirt from being tracked into the house by stopping it at the door. A pair of rough-textured mats— one on the outside, the other inside the entryway—will catch a lot of it.

Use area rugs to protect carpets and waxed floors where traffic is heavy—the dining area, family room, and hallways, for example.

Glue bunion pads on the feet of tables and chairs so that they can be moved without scratching the finish of the floor.

If you fear that moving heavy furniture will damage your floors, slip a piece of plush carpet, pile side down, under the furniture legs. You'll protect the floor, and the furniture will slide easier.

Before moving furniture, slip heavy socks onto the legs, or place each leg into a "shoe" made from the bottom half of a clean milk carton.

RESILIENT-FLOOR CARE

When choosing a new resilient floor, remember that solid colors are harder to maintain and to keep looking good and that patterns with grooves and indentations collect dirt.

There's no need to fill the mop bucket just to clean the bathroom floor. Simply wipe the floor with a spray disinfectant and a clean cloth or paper towels.

The natural wax color of solvent-base products may mask the true color of light-colored resilient floors. Before using a product, test it in an inconspicuous place to be sure that the resulting color is acceptable and the flooring is solvent resistant.

If your floor is in bad condition, apply two or more thin coats of a self-polishing water-base product, allowing each application to dry at least 8 hours before recoating.

Do you have a squeaky wooden floor underneath your tile flooring? You may be able to get rid of the irritating noise by pounding a hammer on the tiled area just above the squeak. To prevent any damage to the tiles, place a block of wood over them before you start pounding. The force of the hammer on the block may push any loose nails back into place.

Even though it's called a no-wax floor, it will look better if you apply a vinyl dressing made especially for no-wax finishes. To keep the product from collecting in any depressed areas of the floor, don't pour it onto the floor directly; mop it on from a shallow pan.

You may be able to remove minor burns from vinyl tiles by rubbing the surface with very fine steel wool.

Do your vinyl tiles curl up at the edges? A simple way to cure this is to warm each problem tile with an electric iron just long enough to soften the adhesive underneath. Apply fresh adhesive to the curled area, then weight down the tile until the adhesive dries.

It's easier to lay resilient floor tiles if you keep the room temperature above 70° F. Tiles are more pliable at high temperatures. Leave them in the room for at least a day before positioning them on the floor. Keep the room temperature at the same level for a week after the laying of the tiles.

REPLACING VINYL FLOOR TILES

1. Warm the old floor tile with an iron to soften the adhesive beneath, then pry out the adhesive with a putty knife, working from the crack toward the edges of the tile.

2. Scrape away the old adhesive from the floor. Check the fit of the replacement tile; if it needs trimming, cut it with a utility knife or sand it lightly. Spread fresh adhesive on the floor.

3. Warm the replacement tile with an iron to make it more flexible before setting it in the fresh adhesive, then weight it down until the adhesive sets.

REMOVING STAINS

Remove black heel marks from a resilient floor by rubbing them with a typewriter eraser.

If a throw rug leaves stains on resilient flooring, a strong solution of chlorine bleach may remove it. (Test in an inconspicuous area first.) If this doesn't work, then rub with very fine steel wool; restore the dulled area with wax.

WOOD-FLOOR CARE

To keep a rocking chair from wearing the finish off a wood floor, place a strip of adhesive tape along the bottom of each rocker.

Remove mold from wood floors with dry-cleaning fluid; if the mold is deeply embedded in the wood, use bleach or disinfectant. Rewax to restore the shine. Since mold needs a damp environment, keep it from coming back by making sure that the area is well ventilated.

Severe yellowing and darkening of older wood floors is most likely caused by the buildup of many years of varnish applications. The only way to remedy this problem is to refinish the floor (pp. 446–448).

Self-cleaning, solvent-base polishes work by removing old wax and dirt. It's important to change the applicator pad or cloth often to prevent reapplying any of the old dirt.

CLEANING WOOD FLOORS

For a quick cleanup of a wood floor, go over a small area at a time with a well-wrung-out mop, wiping dry before moving on. Instead of plain water on natural or stained dark wood, try cleaning with cold tea.

For a more thorough cleaning of wood floors, use a liquid cleaning wax containing a solvent such as turpentine or nontoxic dry-cleaning fluid. Be sure that the room is well ventilated when you do this.

REMOVING STAINS

Rub alcohol stains on a wood floor with silver polish or an ammonia-dampened cloth, then rewax floor.

Need to get rid of those white spots that can show up on wood floors after waxing? Pour liquid wax over them, rub gently with fine steel wool, following the grain, then polish the area with a clean cloth.

MASONRY-FLOOR CARE

To make cleaning easier, seal stone, brick, and concrete floors with a penetrating masonry sealer, available at hardware stores and home centers. Left unsealed, a masonry floor absorbs cleaning materials left on its surface.

Once you've sealed a masonry floor, apply several coats of a protective floor finish (a liquid acrylic finish or a paste wax) to give the floor smoothness and gloss.

Do not use harsh or abrasive cleaners on a masonry floor; it's not as durable as it seems and can be easily scratched. Clean it with water and washing soda or a mild detergent solution.

Sweep your concrete floor with industrial floor-cleaning compound (available in hardware or professional cleaning supply stores).

Wax your garage's concrete floor? Sounds crazy, but it makes sweeping easier and reduces the dust that gets tracked into the house. Be sure to seal the concrete first.

Remove grease stains on a concrete patio by wetting the stains and generously sprinkling them with dishwasher detergent. Let stand a few minutes before rinsing with boiling water.

Wet a stone floor with water before washing it with a cleaning product, then rinse well. Dried-on cleaner can cause stone surfaces to chip.

Clean brick or concrete floors with a rag mop—a sponge mop will break apart.

For stained grout between floor tiles, try rubbing the area lightly with folded sandpaper.

CLEANING CURTAINS

Wash fiberglass curtains in the bathtub. This way you don't have the unpleasant task of removing the tiny glass fibers from the washing machine, since you simply rinse them from the tub.

If just-washed curtains don't hang well, slip a curtain rod through the bottom hem of each panel and leave it there for a few days.

When you wash curtains, wash the rods as well. Then apply wax to the rods and the curtains will slip on and move more easily.

Before sending your curtains to the dry cleaner, mark the places where the hooks should be reinserted. A dab of colored nail polish on the wrong side does the job neatly.

If curtains must be rehung on specific windows, mark them with colored thread on the wrong side of the bottom hem: one stitch for the first panel; two for the second panel; and so on.

WINDOW SHADES

Clean washable window shades by spreading them unrolled on a clean flat surface and scrubbing them with detergent and hot water and a brush or cloth. Rinse with a clean damp cloth and dry them thoroughly before rerolling.

When your nonwashable shades are dirty, try rubbing them with an art-gum eraser.

If a holland blind winds up with a bang, take it down and partially unroll it, then put it back. If tension is still too great, repeat.

If a shade doesn't roll up tightly enough, remove it from its brackets and increase the spring tension by rolling up the shade by hand. Replace the shade in the brackets; if the tension is still too slack, repeat the process.

Worn or stained shades can be turned: tack the worn bottom to the top and turn a hem on the old top to make a new bottom.

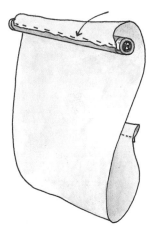

BLINDS

If you don't have a special venetian blind duster, wear thick absorbent cloth gloves and wipe the slats by hand.

Touch up soiled areas on white venetian blind tapes with liquid white shoe polish.

REPLACING VENETIAN BLIND CORDS AND TAPES

1. With the blinds drawn and the slats horizontal, remove the end caps and the metal cover from the bottom bar.
2. Unknot the cord ends and pull them out of the slats, but leave them on the pulleys. Reknot the cord ends.
3. Slide the slats out one by one.
4. Detach the tapes from their clamps on the top and bottom bars and attach new tapes of the same length.
5. Cut new cord the same length as the old. Thread it on the pulleys, following and then unthreading the old cord.
6. Put back the slats and run the new cord through the slat holes on alternate sides of the tape rungs.

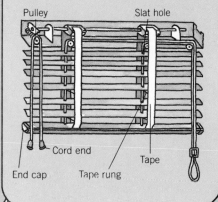

Pulley   Slat hole

Cord end

Tape

End cap   Tape rung

CLEANING VENETIAN BLINDS

There's no magic way to wash venetian blinds; to get them really clean, you must take them down and wash them in water and detergent in the bathtub. Scrub if necessary. When the blinds are clean, rinse them thoroughly with clear water and hang them over the shower-curtain rod to dry. (Protect the floor with old towels.) Shake the excess water from the blinds and let them dry thoroughly before rehanging them.

An alternative method is to lay the blinds flat on a large piece of canvas (preferably outdoors) and scrub one side at a time with a mild detergent solution. Hang the blinds on a clothesline and rinse them with the hose. Shake off the excess water and let them dry before rehanging them.

BEFORE CLEANING WINDOWS

The ideal day for window washing is one that's cloudy, but not rainy. Direct sunlight dries cleaning solutions before you can wipe them off, leaving streaks on glass.

The best time to vacuum window frames and sills is before you wash windows. Use the brush attachment of your vacuum cleaner to remove dust, soot, cobwebs, and dead insects.

If you live in an upper-story apartment or a multilevel house, consider hiring a professional window washer. Doing the job yourself may not be worth the risk.

When cleaning the outsides of double-hung windows, don't take chances sitting on windowsills. Instead, raise and lower both sashes so that you can clean each outside surface from the inside.

Cool, clear water is the choice of most professional window washers. If windows are very dirty, add 2 to 3 tablespoons of ammonia or vinegar per gallon of wash water. Choose only one; if combined, they'll neutralize each other.

Sudsy ammonia leaves streaks on windows and mirrors. Use clear ammonia instead.

One of the best window-cleaning solutions can be found right in your medicine cabinet. Pure rubbing alcohol removes dirt easily and leaves windows crystal clear.

If you do a lot of window washing, invest in a professional-quality squeegee with a brass or stainless-steel holder. When the rubber blade wears out, turn it over and use the opposite edge.

Washing small windows will be much easier if you use a squeegee that's custom-fit to the windowpane. To make one, remove the rubber blade from its holder and trim it to a length that's slightly wider than the width of the windowpane. Then use a hacksaw to cut the holder to the exact width of the windowpane.

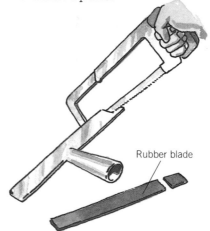

Rubber blade

WASHING AND DRYING WINDOWS

Here's an easy way to tell whether the spots you've missed are on the inside of the window or the outside. Use horizontal strokes to clean one side of the window and vertical strokes for the other.

To clean the corners of small window frames, use a cotton swab dipped in cleaning solution.

For drying windows, a wad of crumpled newspaper works just as well as expensive paper towels. Wear rubber gloves to keep your hands free of ink.

If your windows are very dirty, add a tablespoon of methylated spirits to the wash water. If the weather is very cold, the methylated spirits will stop the water from freezing on the windowpanes.

SPECIAL WINDOW PROBLEMS

Having a hard time removing dried paint from window glass? Soften the paint with soapy water or warm vinegar. Then scrape the paint off gently, using a sharp single-edge razor blade in a holder.

WASHING A WINDOW WITH A SQUEEGEE

Using a spray container, a clean sponge, or a brush with soft bristles, wet the window lightly with cleaning solution. Wipe the rubber blade of the squeegee with a damp cloth or chamois to make the blade glide smoothly across the glass.

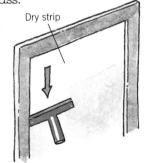
Dry strip

1. Tilting the squeegee at a 45-degree angle, press one end against a corner of the window and pull it across horizontally.

2. After wiping the blade, place the squeegee at the bottom end of the dry strip and pull it down to the bottom edge of the window.

3. Repeat across the window, slightly overlapping the adjacent dry area with each pass. Dab water drops with a dry cloth.

85

To remove oxidation deposits from the frames of aluminum windows, use a light household abrasive cleaner, a mild detergent, or fine steel wool. After cleaning, apply automobile paste wax. Reapply wax annually.

If you want to remove hard-water spots from your windows, use undiluted vinegar for the job. Scrub the spots gently, using a nonabrasive nylon pad. Afterward you can clean the window with a squeegee.

REPLACING A WINDOWPANE

Wearing heavy gloves, remove broken glass from the frame. Then scrape away old putty (soften it with a hair dryer if necessary) and remove the glazier's points with pliers. Sand all surfaces smooth. Have the new pane cut ⅛ inch smaller than the groove's length and width. Coat the groove with linseed oil or thinned alkyd (oil-base) paint to prevent absorption of oil from the glazing compound.

1. Apply a thin bed of glazing compound along all four sides to cushion the glass against stress and leakage.

Glazier's point

2. Gently press the glass against the glazing compound and tap the glazier's points halfway into the sash, 4 to 6 inches apart.

3. Form the glazing compound into a rope about ⅜ inch in diameter, and press the rope into the groove along the glass.

4. Holding the putty knife at an angle, draw it over the glazing compound to form a neat triangular strip.

5. Allow the compound to dry for about a week. Then paint it, overlapping the glass $\frac{1}{16}$ inch as a seal against moisture.

If ocean spray has deposited salt on your windows, remove the spots with denatured alcohol.

Has paint sealed a window sash to the frame? Insert a wide putty knife (never a screwdriver) between the sash and the frame and work the knife around the edge of the sash to break the bond. You may have to tap the handle with a hammer to coax the blade in.

Tap lightly

To remove dried paint from rough-textured glass, use paint stripper. Make sure the stripper doesn't drip on window sills or sashes. Clean up residue immediately.

If a double-hung window moves but doesn't slide easily, clean out the sash channels with steel wool. Then vacuum the area and lubricate the channels with hard soap, paraffin, or silicone spray.

WINDOW SCREENS

To wash window screens, lay them flat on a smooth, cloth-covered surface, such as an old sheet on a picnic table. Scrub them gently, rinse with a hose, and shake off excess water.

FIXING A BROKEN SASH CORD

By replacing a broken sash cord with a spring balance, you can eliminate the problem of broken cords or chains. Available at hardware stores, the device is inserted into the pulley hole after the old pulley mechanism has been removed. To determine which spring size is appropriate for your window, consult the chart included with the kit.

Spring balance

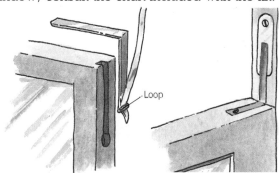

Loop

1. Insert the spring balance unit into the pulley hole and secure it with screws.

2. Attach the loop at the end of the tape to the bottom prong of the adapter.

3. Using flathead screws, attach the L-shaped arm of the adapter to the top of the window sash.

Dirty screens not only block out sunlight but cause spots on windows whenever it rains. Without removing screens, brush or vacuum them periodically.

If you find a tiny hole in a screen, there's no need to patch it. Just dab some rubber cement or clear nail polish on the opening to keep out bugs. (For other screen repair tips, see pp. 173–174.)

MAKING WINDOWS ENERGY-EFFICIENT

When the weather turns cold, allow as much sunshine as possible into the house. Remove and store window screens. On sunny days, open blinds, shutters, and shades and tie back curtains. Trim trees and shrubs that shade windows.

Light colored curtains will keep a room warmer than dark colored ones because the former reflect sunlight back into the room. Line the curtains with an acetate or acrylic fabric so that warm air doesn't pass through the curtains and out the window.

Cap curtains with an air seal by tacking or stapling a piece of fabric to the window frame, several inches above the curtain rod.

STICKING DOORS

Before trying to fix a sticking door, wait until cool, dry weather arrives. The problem may last only as long as the humidity.

If a door sticks year-round, check the screws in the hinges and the strike plate. They may need to be tightened or reinforced (p. 190).

Before repainting a door, sand its edges. This helps to prevent paint buildup, which is one of the most common causes of sticking doors.

When planing a door, always work with the grain. Plane the top or bottom of the door from the outer edge toward the center. When you finish, lay a straightedge along the surface and sand any irregularities you find.

SLIDING DOORS

Buy sliding glass doors with thermal-break aluminum frames. This type prevents cold from being conducted into the house.

If a sliding door rattles, check the bottom door guides. Replace them if they're faulty or missing.

FIXING A DOOR THAT BINDS

A door may stick because of loose or improperly mounted hinges, swelling of the wood, or even settling of the house. You can locate the points where the door binds by sliding a thin sheet of stiff cardboard between the edges of the door and the jamb while the door is closed. As a temporary measure, rub wet soap on those spots where the door sticks.

To fix an improperly mounted hinge, place a wedge under the outer edge of the door to hold it steady. If the door binds at the top, remove the screws from the jamb leaf of the bottom hinge, insert a cardboard shim under the leaf, and replace the screws. If the door binds at the bottom, remove the screws from the jamb leaf of the top hinge, insert a shim under the leaf, and replace the screws.

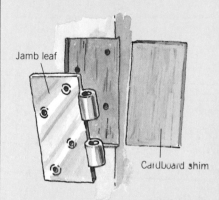

Jamb leaf

Cardboard shim

If the door still binds slightly near the top or bottom edge after either hinge has been shimmed, sand or plane a small amount of wood from the point of friction (the spot rubbed bare of its paint). If that doesn't correct the problem, your best bet is to plane the entire edge of the door.

With a hard pencil, scribe a line on the door face ⅛ inch in from the side that's binding. If the door binds near the top or along the upper edge, use a wedge to hold the door open while you plane to the line. If the door binds near the bottom or along the lower edge, remove the door from its hinges and plane to the line. In either case, prime and paint the newly bared wood to prevent the door from absorbing moisture and swelling.

Does your sliding closet door drag because it hangs crooked? Loosen the adjusting screw on the back of the roller. Then raise or lower one end of the door until it's parallel with the floor.

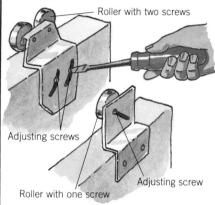

Roller with two screws

Adjusting screws

Adjusting screw

Roller with one screw

To clean sliding-door tracks, spray household cleaner on a terry cloth rag, wrap the rag around the tip of an old screwdriver, and move the padded tip along the track.

Use powdered graphite or silicone spray to lubricate the tracks of sliding glass doors. Oil attracts dirt, which makes matters worse.

SPECIAL DOOR PROBLEMS

To straighten out a door that's slightly bowed in the center, lay it on supports and place weights on top of the bulged side. Leave the weights on until the door returns to its proper shape.

To remove loose pins from their hinges, pry them up with a screwdriver and tap gently with a hammer. Remove the pin from the bottom hinge first. If a pin is rusted, apply penetrating oil.

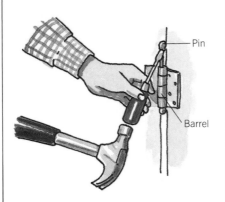

Pin

Barrel

Is that squeaky door getting on your nerves? Remove the pin from the noisy hinge, lubricate the barrel with household oil or silicone spray, and replace the pin. Move the door back and forth several times to work in the lubricant.

Here's how to fix a slightly warped door without taking it off its hinges. Add a third hinge at the spot where the door is bowed. Over time, pressure will straighten out the curve.

BUYING A VACUUM CLEANER

Before shopping for a vacuum, list the items you need to clean (carpets, hard floors, upholstered furniture, draperies). Select a model with as many appropriate accessories as possible (p.93).

CHOOSING A VACUUM CLEANER

Type	Uses	Advantages	Disadvantages
Tank/canister	Above-floor cleaning; bare floors; low-pile carpets	Provides best suction for above-floor cleaning; includes variety of attachments	Lacks agitating brush for carpet cleaning
Tank/canister with power nozzle	Above-floor cleaning; cleaning embedded dirt from carpets	Combines best suction for above-floor cleaning with carpet-cleaning ability	Attachments must be changed to suit tasks
Upright with attachments	Cleaning large carpeted areas or sturdy rugs; minor above-floor cleaning	Combines best agitation for carpet cleaning with above-floor cleaning ability; adjusts to different carpet heights	Attachments must be changed to suit tasks
Central (built-in) system	Cleaning carpets; above-floor cleaning	Quiet; no heavy equipment to carry	High-cost installation; may lack agitating brush for carpet cleaning
Wet-dry	Cleaning carpets; above-floor cleaning; cleaning liquids from leaks or spills	Versatile; includes special attachments for difficult chores	Tank must be emptied, washed, and dried after each use
Hand-held	Cleaning small, lightly soiled surfaces quickly; cleaning hard-to-reach areas	Convenient to use and store; available in cordless models	Not suitable for large surfaces or embedded dirt; cordless models require recharging after each use

To test a vacuum's efficiency, see how well it picks up a granular substance, such as sand or salt, from a carpet. Check below the carpet's pile to make sure the grains have been picked up, not just pushed down.

The more convenience features your vacuum has, the more time and effort you'll save on cleaning day. Look for a lightweight machine with a lengthy cord and easy-to-use controls, accessories, and bag-changing procedures.

Suction alone won't remove dirt that's deeply embedded in carpets; only a vacuum with rotating brushes will do the job properly.

VACUUM MAINTENANCE AND REPAIR

A full dust bag reduces a vacuum's suction power. Change or empty the bag before it's full.

Lint, hair, or thread that collects on bristles can interfere with the cleaning action of the brushes. Use the vacuum's hose to remove lint or hair. To remove threads, clip them off or unravel them after disconnecting the plug.

To patch a hole in a vacuum hose, wrap duct tape around the area. Make sure the seal is tight.

VACUUM CLEANER PROBLEMS: WHAT TO CHECK BEFORE TAKING IT IN FOR REPAIRS

Caution: Before cleaning or repairing any parts, unplug the vacuum cleaner.

Problem	Possible cause	Solution	Problem	Possible cause	Solution
Motor doesn't run	Plug not secure	Insert plug firmly into outlet	**Motor runs but suction is poor** (cont.)	Obstruction in hose, wand, or attachment	Remove the obstruction
	Power off at outlet	Replace fuse or reset circuit breaker		Leak in hose, wand, or attachment	Repair leak with duct tape or replace part
	On-Off switch broken	Replace switch		Fan obstructed	Remove the obstruction
	Power cord broken	Replace power cord (p.160)	**Vacuum blows fuses**	Too many appliances on circuit	Turn off other appliances on circuit
	Handle cord (from switch to motor) broken	Replace handle cord		Short circuit in power cord or plug	Replace power cord (p.160)
	Fan obstructed	Remove the obstruction		Short circuit in handle cord	Replace handle cord
Motor runs but suction is poor	Dust bag filled	Empty or replace dust bag	**Vacuum makes excessive noise**	Power brush loose or imbalanced	Adjust or replace parts
	Filter dirty	Clean or replace filter			
	Hose improperly connected to cleaner	Secure hose to cleaner	**Vacuum shocks user**	Power cord frayed	Replace power cord (p.160)

Bending a vacuum hose to roll it up for storage could damage its wire frame or woven shell. Instead, drape the hose over two clothing hooks in a utility closet.

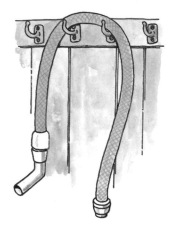

BEFORE YOU VACUUM

Pick up any small, hard objects, such as pins, buttons, coins, or plaster chips. They can easily clog the hose and filter or, even worse, damage the fan and motor.

Take chairs, footrests, and wastebaskets out of the room or set them on larger furniture to minimize furniture moving while you vacuum.

Adjust the nozzle of your upright vacuum so that it rides in close contact with the carpet's pile. If the nozzle is too low, it will make the vacuum hard to push. If the nozzle is too high, air will enter the vacuum above the carpet instead of being pulled through the carpet. Also, the brushes won't reach dirt that's embedded in the pile.

VACUUMING CARPETS

The old custom of hanging a carpet on a clothesline and beating the dirt out can break the carpet's backing. Use a vacuum instead.

Vacuum carpets at least once a week. Clean heavy-traffic areas daily with a lightweight vacuum.

To remove as much dirt as possible, move the vacuum over the carpet slowly and make several passes over each area. Work in overlapping parallel strokes.

Pay special attention to areas in front of couches and chairs. People tend to shift their feet around as they sit, loosening soil particles from their shoes and grinding them into the carpet.

VACUUM CLEANER ATTACHMENTS

No more climbing to reach ceiling dust! Use your vacuum's brush attachment and extension wands. This method gobbles up spider webs (and spiders) with no mess.

The crevice tool of your vacuum is ideal for cleaning around the legs of chairs and the bases of hard-to-move furniture.

For indoor-outdoor carpets and others with low pile, use the bare-floor brush. It's also good for sewn or braided rugs, which can be damaged by the harsh, rotating brushes of a power nozzle.

DEEP CLEANING

Save a remnant of each wall-to-wall carpet you install. When the carpet looks darker than the remnant, it's time for a deep cleaning.

If you have several dirty carpets, consider renting a steam cleaner (p.94) from your local hardware store or supermarket. It'll work better than any home vacuum and it's less expensive than a professional carpet cleaner. Prepare rooms thoroughly in advance so that you can finish the job and return the equipment in one day.

If your baby still crawls, don't deep-clean carpets until the child starts walking. Carpet-cleaning chemicals can be irritating or toxic to young children.

Wet shampoo can stain the surface of a shag or delicate carpet; use dry-foam shampoo instead.

Some professional carpet cleaners offer discounts if you're willing to move your own furniture out of the room.

Here's how to brighten a carpet that's not made of wool without shampooing it. First, vacuum the carpet. Mix ½ cup clear ammonia and 1 pint water; then test the solution on an inconspicuous part of the carpet. If there's no color change, dip a sponge mop into the solution, wring it almost dry, and run it over the surface of the carpet lightly.

If you must replace furniture on a freshly cleaned carpet before it has dried completely, place coasters under the legs to prevent stains and indentations.

VACUUM CLEANER ATTACHMENTS

Attachment	Uses	Comments
Rug-cleaning tool	Worn or low-pile carpets	Should swivel to reach under and around furniture
Bare-floor brush	Hard floors, masonry surfaces, wooden decks	Replace if worn (to prevent scratching hardwood floors)
Upholstery tool	Upholstered furniture, draperies, clothing, mattresses, automobile interiors, carpeted stairs, walls	Cover with a soft, clean cloth to dust delicate surfaces
Dusting brush	Furniture crevices, lighting fixtures, baseboards, blinds and shutters, pictures, bookcases	Cover with a soft, clean cloth to dust delicate surfaces
Crevice tool	Radiator fins, carpet edges, cushion crevices, window tracks, refrigerator grilles	Wipe clean after each use
Power nozzle	Carpets, sturdy rugs	Rotating brushes should extend to both ends of roller

SHAMPOOING CARPETS

If a carpet is small or lightly soiled, the easiest way to clean it is with an aerosol spray foam, available in supermarkets.

First, do the following: Open windows to ventilate the room and speed up drying. Remove all furniture; if a piece can't be moved, wrap aluminum foil around its legs. Vacuum the carpet thoroughly. Pretreat heavily soiled spots (see stain-removal chart on pp. 282–283).

Shake the can vigorously and apply a small amount of foam on an inconspicuous part of the carpet. If there's no color change, hold the can upside down and spray a thin, even layer of foam over the entire surface of the carpet. Let the foam dry thoroughly. Vacuum the carpet at top suction, using an empty dust bag.

93

DEEP-CLEANING METHODS FOR CARPETS

Each of the following methods has its advantages and drawbacks. The information below can help you decide which is best for a particular job. In each case, you'll have to rent equipment or buy an appropriate cleaning compound. Always vacuum before deep-cleaning, preferably with a power nozzle.

Method	Procedure	Comments
Rotary shampooing	Move unit continuously while releasing shampoo into carpet; let carpet dry for several hours; vacuum to remove released soil and shampoo residue	Rotary brushes can damage wool, cotton, or acrylic carpets and rag or braided rugs; overwetting can cause shrinkage or discoloration
Dry cleaning	Sprinkle absorbent cleaning compound on carpet and brush into fibers; wait 1 hour; vacuum thoroughly, using strong suction	Most effective on greasy soil; least effective on dry, gritty soil; easiest to use
Steam cleaning	Move unit continuously in a W pattern, releasing steam on push strokes and removing moisture on pull strokes; for heavy soil, repeat steps in opposite direction	Most effective on wool, shag, and heavily soiled carpets; water over 150° F can shrink wool fibers; overwetting can damage floors and promote mildew

SEASONAL CLEANING

Rugs will be easier to carry outdoors for an airing if you roll them up first. Delicate rugs should be rolled right side out to avoid crushing the pile; sturdy rugs can be rolled with the pile inside.

Air rugs on a flat surface, such as a wooden deck or driveway, to prevent them from being distorted. Choose a shady spot; direct sunlight could cause fading.

At least twice a year, vacuum the padding and the floor beneath an area rug. Because this can't be done under a wall-to-wall carpet, you should clean its surface frequently and thoroughly.

PRESERVING CARPETS

Turn rugs around periodically so that they wear and soil evenly.

Chemicals in some furniture polishes can destroy red carpet dyes, causing a blue or green discoloration. Before polishing furniture, cover carpet areas around legs and bases with newspaper.

Want to prevent carpet seams and edges from fraying? Brush them with a liquid resin that locks the yarns in place as it dries. It's sold at most fabric and craft shops.

The outermost braid of a braided rug usually wears out first. Save the rug from this fate by sewing a strip of bias binding around the edges of the rug.

Here's how to prolong the life of your stair carpet. When the carpet is installed, fold an extra foot of length under and against one or two risers at the top of the stairs. Periodically lift the entire carpet and shift it downward an inch or two at a time. As the excess carpet moves to the foot of the stairs, fold it under or against the lowest riser, or trim it off.

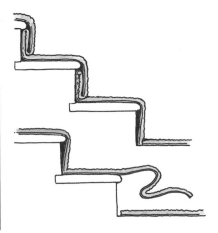

SPECIAL CARPET PROBLEMS

Always save the manufacturer's label from a new carpet. Knowing the carpet's brand name, pattern number, grade, and fiber content will help your dealer answer any questions. (For tips on carpet selection, see pp. 424–425.)

The key to preventing spills from staining carpets is to act fast. Blot the spill quickly with paper towels or a clean, white towel. Scrape away any sediment with a spoon. Cover the area with a clean, white towel and place a sheet of plastic or aluminum foil over the towel. Lay books on top. If the area is still moist the next day, repeat the process with fresh towels.

If a spill causes carpet discoloration, dip a clean, white towel into a solution of 1 tablespoon liquid hand dishwashing detergent or ½ cup white vinegar and ½ cup warm water. Alternately dab the spot and blot it with a clean, white towel. Repeat until all of the spot's color transfers to the towel. Then cover the area with a clean, white towel until it's dry. (If this method fails, consult the stain-removal chart on pp. 282–283.)

A lingering odor with no visible carpet stain can mean that furniture is hiding your pet's surprise. Check under chairs, sofas, and beds. (See p. 248 for advice on cleaning up an animal's mess.)

Scented carpet deodorizers serve a dual purpose: the rug smells better and so does the vacuum.

Repair snags and pills by holding scissors parallel to the rug's surface and snipping them off. Pulling on fibers could damage the rug's weave.

PATCHING A HOLE OR WORN SPOT IN A CARPET

1. Remove the entire damaged area by cutting out a square or rectangle with a utility knife. Make each cut with one pass of the knife, keeping the edges clean and straight. Cut through the carpet backing, but avoid cutting the padding or floor.

2. Using the damaged section as a pattern, cut a patch identical in size, design, and pile direction. (If no remnant is available, purchase one from the store where you bought the carpet.) Check the patch for fit, and trim it if necessary.

3. Spread a thin layer of carpet adhesive under the patch and the edges of both the surrounding carpet and the patch. Press the patch into place, then brush the pile with your fingertips to hide the seams. Let dry for several hours before vacuuming.

To remove deep indentations left in your carpet by furniture, lay a damp bath towel over the depression and press lightly with an iron. When the towel area is dry, the indentation will be gone.

Wrinkles in wall-to-wall carpeting have several causes. If faulty installation is to blame, ask the dealer to make adjustments. If furniture has been dragged across the carpet, lift the furniture and shift the carpet slightly from the wrinkled area to the flat area. If a carpet has been overwetted during cleaning, dampen the wrinkled area slightly and place a flat, heavy object on top of it.

A carpet treated with an antistatic agent may attract dirt easily. A better way to reduce static electricity during cold months is to place a humidifier in the room.

To prevent accidents, secure carpets and area rugs to the floor. Apply double-face carpet tape under seams and edges.

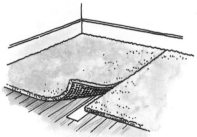

Instead of placing lamp cords under carpets, where they pose a safety hazard, run them along the wall. Hide them with electrical cord covers, available at electrical supply shops.

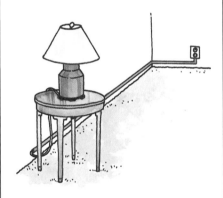

REPAIRING A CARPET BURN

1. Trim away the burned fibers with scissors, then dab rubber cement into the hole with a toothpick.

2. Cut matching tufts of carpet from an unseen area, dab their ends with rubber cement, and insert them in the hole.

3. Work the tufts upright with a pin. When dry, use the pin to blend them with the surrounding pile.

Although a vacuum with rotating brushes can be a bit unwieldy for cleaning a carpeted staircase, it's the best kind to remove ground-in dirt on the center of steps. For the corners, which don't get nearly as dirty, use a dusting brush, a hand-held vacuum, or a damp cloth.

When vacuuming the fringes of delicate rugs, use light suction and the upholstery tool. A hand-held vacuum is even better because it's gentler.

Here's how to straighten an area rug if no one is around to help you. Working from the center of the width, roll it up evenly with your hands as far apart as possible. Make sure the pad is smooth,

straight, and in the proper position. Lift and drop the rug, one end at a time so that its edges match those of the pad. Unroll the rug partially and weigh down the corners that are in the right position. Unroll the rest of the rug slowly.

ORIENTAL RUGS

If your Oriental rug needs cleaning, don't try to do the job yourself. Instead, take the rug to a professional carpet cleaner.

Trimming the untidy fringes of an Oriental rug could cause the entire rug to unravel. Instead, tie a few strands together in a single loose knot. Then tighten the knots, lining them up as you go so that they form a straight row.

Before storing a valuable rug, make sure that it's clean and dry. Then roll it up and wrap it in brown paper. Store the rug in a dark, well-ventilated place where the temperature stays between 40° F and 60° F. Otherwise, put it in professional storage.

BEGINNING TO CLEAN A ROOM

To clear out a room before you begin cleaning, carry a plastic trash bag with you to catch the contents of ashtrays and wastebaskets. Follow up with a laundry basket or carton for out-of-place items you can sort after you've finished cleaning.

Begin with dust-raising cleaning and proceed in the following order: ceiling, walls, windows, doors, blinds, draperies, lamps, radiator, shelves, upholstery, furniture surfaces, floors, carpets.

FURNITURE CARE

Arm yourself with plenty of clean, soft cloths, such as old sheets or cheesecloth, when it's time to dust your wood furniture. A dirty cloth can scratch surfaces; so turn it frequently. To hold dust on the cloth, spray it with a commercial dust-control substance.

For extra protection, wipe your wooden furniture with this finishing polish: 10 drops lemon extract mixed into 1 quart mineral oil. Apply sparingly and polish with a soft cloth. For more tips on furniture care, see pp.449–451.

Plastic furniture covers are not only cold, uncomfortable, and unattractive, they attract and show dirt much more readily than upholstery does. Protect your furniture with a chemical soil retardant instead.

Attach casters or wide-based glides to furniture legs so that you can easily move furniture to clean under it. This also prevents marring of floor coverings.

LIGHT FIXTURES

A lamp base needs only dusting or wiping with a damp sponge. Clean metal parts with the appropriate polish (p.435). Never submerge the lamp base in water—it will damage the wiring.

Wipe off light bulbs occasionally with a damp sponge to maintain maximum light. But first be sure that the bulbs are cool and that the lamp is disconnected.

To clean a glass ceiling fixture, first check that it's cool, then loosen the screws. Let the globe or lens (the glass or plastic translucent part) soak in a sink full of hot soapy water (or ammonia and water for greasy kitchen fixtures). Rinse with hot water, air-dry, and replace.

If chandelier bulbs flicker, a build-up of grime may be interfering with the flow of electricity. Turn off the power to the fixture (p.163), remove the bulbs, and, with fine sandpaper, gently sand all contacting surfaces.

CLEANING SPECIAL OBJECTS

Before you vacuum a room, use a hand-held hair dryer to blow the dust off silk or dried flowers. Use a clean, soft artist's brush to flick away stubborn dust.

Spray glazed figurines and ceramic lamps with window cleaner. Dry with paper or lintless cloth towels.

Take the risk out of vacuuming bric-a-brac. Place the foot of an old nylon stocking over the end of the vacuum cleaner nozzle—this way, only the dust will be sucked in.

Want an easy way to clean a lot of little glass and china knickknacks? Place them in the kitchen sink and spray them thoroughly with window cleaner. Move them to a towel to air-dry.

Dusting typewriter keys, louvered doors, carved furniture, or anything with nooks and crannies is easier with a clean, soft, ever so slightly dampened paintbrush.

Ashtrays—pottery, brass, or china (not glass)—are easier to keep clean if they're rubbed with liquid furniture polish before use.

PIANO CARE

To remove fingerprints from pianos and other wood surfaces with a high shine, clean with a dampened chamois. Polish dry with a second, dry chamois.

When a piano is not in use, close its top, but expose the keyboard to light. Ivory turns yellow if continuously kept from the light.

Whiten yellowed piano keys by rubbing them with a soft cloth and a tiny amount of one of the following pastes: toothpaste; 2 parts salt and 1 part lemon juice; or baking soda and water. Being careful not to get paste into the cracks between the keys, wipe off with a damp cloth, then buff with a dry cloth.

FIREPLACE CARE

Clean the fireplace and hearth at least once a week during the months that you use it. Vacuum or brush up ashes, then wipe down the hearth with a damp cloth or sponge.

Clean the walls of the firebox (where the fire is laid) with a dry bristle brush or the dusting attachment of the vacuum cleaner. (Be sure to wash and dry the attachment before using it on any other surface.) Don't scrub the firebrick or cement block with water; it may reduce heat retention.

Clean the fireplace chimney flue once a year (more often if you use it frequently). If you're adept at scaling roofs, you can do it yourself with chimney rods and brushes (available at hardware or fireplace equipment stores). Otherwise, call in a professional chimney sweep to do the job.

Dust brass and iron fireplace tools and fire screens regularly. Wash brass tools occasionally with warm sudsy water, rinse, and dry. If iron tools feel sticky, rub them with a cloth moistened with kerosene. Be sure to dry them thoroughly before placing them near the fire.

Before removing ashes, sprinkle damp tea leaves over them to keep down the dust.

Make your slate hearth gleam. Every 6 weeks or so, wash and dry it and then coat it with lemon oil.

HOME ENTERTAINMENT SYSTEMS

Unplug your TV, stereo, VCR, or home computer before cleaning it. Except for the TV screen, avoid using spray cleaners directly on the appliance—you may damage the wiring or clog the ventilation or sound-projecting holes. Instead, spray the cleaner onto your cleaning cloth.

TV, stereo, and speaker cabinets are usually made of plastic or wood veneer. Clean plastic exteriors with mild soap and warm water, using a cloth wrung nearly dry to prevent drips. Dust wood-veneer cabinets frequently with a soft, clean, slightly damp cloth.

To clean metal cabinets, chrome, or any other shiny trim on home entertainment equipment, use a soft cloth moistened with a bit of rubbing alcohol, white vinegar, or window cleaner.

ANTENNA PROBLEMS

If you have a roof antenna and your TV reception is poor, check out the problem by hooking up a set of indoor rabbit ears for comparison. If this improves reception, you'll know the roof antenna is the problem.

The lead-in wire, which connects the antenna to the TV, may be the cause of poor reception. Check connections at the TV, the signal splitter (if you have your FM radio connected to the antenna), and the antenna.

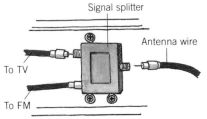

Signal splitter

Antenna wire

To TV

To FM

When the lead-in wire flaps in the wind, the TV picture flip-flops and color fades in and out. Make sure that this wire is fitted snugly to the house along its entire length.

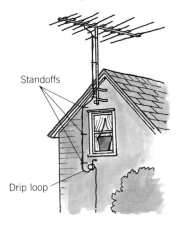

Standoffs

Drip loop

SOUND SYSTEMS

Keep your sound system looking good and operating coolly by vacuuming the ventilation louvers and speaker grilles periodically to prevent dust buildup, which can cause overheating. Cover the system when it's not in use.

When installing a stereo component system, keep all connecting wires short, direct, and neatly arranged between parts. This prevents hum and makes it easy to check connections in case there's a problem.

Staple speaker wires to the wall to prevent people from tripping over them. If you must place the speakers at a distance from the receiver, use a wire with lower resistance (14- instead of 16- or 18-gauge) for better sound.

If you don't want your sound system to bother your neighbors, place the speakers in a room with lots of padded and textile-covered surfaces. Or get a sound-dampening pad at a stereophonic equipment store.

VIDEOCASSETTE RECORDERS

VCR heads need periodic cleaning. You'll know the time has come when you can't eliminate interference on the screen with either fine tuning or VCR tracking. Refer to your owner's manual for the proper method of cleaning.

Store videocassettes away from direct sunlight, excessive heat, moisture, and the strong magnetic field that's present on top of the TV or stereo speaker.

THE DINING ROOM

To keep dining table pads clean, wipe the tops with a clean cloth soaked in warm sudsy water and wrung nearly dry. Vacuum the felt backs with the dusting or upholstery attachment, or go over them with a soft-bristle brush or a lintless cloth.

When a guest spills something on your tablecloth during a dinner party, blot up the substance as quickly as possible. As soon as your guests leave, deal with the specific stain, following the recommended method (pp. 282–283).

TELEPHONES: WHAT TO DO BEFORE CALLING FOR SERVICE

If you're having a problem with your home telephone, you may be able to locate the source of your difficulty with the following checklist.

1. Disconnect any telephone accessories, such as an answering machine, from your line. Now check to see if the cord from the phone to the wall as well as the cord from the phone to the handset are in good condition and tightly in place.
2. If you have an extension phone, try to make a call on it. If you succeed, the problem is in the other phone, not in the wire or the line.
3. If you can unplug your phone, move it to another outlet. If the phone works in the second outlet, the problem is probably in the inside wire of the first outlet.

4. If you can unplug your phone but don't have another outlet, test the phone in a neighbor's outlet. If it works there, the problem could be with the inside wire or the line.
5. If you rent your phone and the problem is in the phone or in the cord from the phone to the wall, contact the supplier. If you own your phone, check the warranty or contact the place where you bought the phone.
6. If the problem is in the line or the inside wire, contact your local telephone company's repair service.
7. If you've made all these checks and you still can't locate the trouble or you can't unplug your phone to do the tests, contact your local telephone company's repair service.

CLEANING A CHANDELIER

When you don't want to take a crystal chandelier apart, here's an easy, no-mess way to clean it. First, put a few towels on the floor under the chandelier and spread several thicknesses of newspaper over the towels. Next, to prevent any moisture from getting into the sockets, cover each bulb with a small plastic bag and secure it with a twist tie. Now, spray enough window cleaner on each pendant so that the dirt runs off onto the newspaper. The pendants can then drip-dry, or you can polish them with a soft cloth for more shine.

CANDLELIGHT DINING

Remove hardened wax from candlesticks the easy way. Place them in the freezer for an hour or so; then peel off the frozen wax, wash the candlesticks, and dry them.

If you can't wait for the wax to freeze, run the candlesticks under very hot water; then cover your finger with a soft cloth and push the wax off.

Did the candles drip onto your good wood dining table? Scrape up as much as you can with a fingernail or a plastic spatula. Rub the remaining wax into the wood with a soft, clean cloth.

When candle wax drips onto the tablecloth, rub the wax with an ice cube to harden it and then scrape off the wax with a spatula. Cover any remaining wax with paper towels under and on top of the tablecloth, and press with a warm iron, changing paper towels as the wax is absorbed. Sponge off the residue with dry-cleaning solvent, then rub gently with heavy-duty liquid detergent. Launder the tablecloth as soon as possible.

ARRANGING FLOWERS

Instead of that spongy green substance that florists use to arrange flowers, put a bunch of glass marbles into a net bag and set the bag in the bottom of a vase or bowl to hold flowers.

When arranging long-stemmed flowers in a wide-mouthed vase, crisscross strips of cellophane tape just inside the top of the vase and insert the stems into the spaces between the tape.

Anchor your flower arrangements with plastic hair rollers. Bind several together with a rubber band and place them at the bottom of a nontransparent vase.

KEEPING CUT FLOWERS FRESH LONGER

Pick flowers in the early morning or early evening. Wrap damp paper towels around their stems until you get them indoors or plunge them immediately into a container of water.

Once inside, cut the stems at an angle and put them in a pail of tepid water. (Use a sharp knife; scissors will compress the stems, keeping out the water.) Hold off arranging the flowers until the water has reached room temperature.

As you arrange the flowers in a clean container or vase, remove all leaves that will be under water.

To prevent dehydration, keep the finished arrangement away from drafts, including fans or air conditioners, and out of direct sunlight. (Sometimes wilted blooms will revive if you immerse their stems in warm water.)

HAPPY HOUSEPLANTS

Repot your root-bound plants. You can tell it's time by tapping the plant out of the pot and inspecting the root ball to see if the roots are thickly encircling it.

When repotting, transfer the plant to a clean pot only one size larger than the old one. Anything larger encourages overwatering and premature death.

Going on vacation? To keep a plant healthy for up to a month, water it well, then enclose it completely in a clear plastic bag, tying it securely at the top and bottom. Place the plant in northern light. When you return, untie the top and let the plant adjust to room air for a day before completely removing the covering.

If your hanging plant doesn't have a saucer, put a plastic shower cap across the bottom of the basket or pot while watering it, to catch the drips and protect your floor.

To keep smooth, heavy-textured leaves clean, bathe them with a dishwashing detergent solution.

If a houseplant is badly infested with bugs (p.104), your best bet is to throw it away before any other plants are affected.

HOUSEPLANT PESTS

Pest	Description	Controls	Pest	Description	Controls
Aphid	Green, black, or red $\frac{1}{16}$-inch-long insect with soft pear-shaped body and long legs	Insecticidal soap; pyrethrum or resmethrin spray; or wash with trigger sprayer	Scale insect	White, brown, or black $\frac{1}{8}$-inch-long stationary insect protected by hard covering	Resmethrin or acephate spray
Fungus gnat	Black $\frac{1}{16}$-inch-long fly	Pyrethrum spray	Slug	Yellow, orange, gray, brown, or black shell-less snail from $\frac{1}{2}$ inch to 5 inches long	Remove by hand
	Larva	Repot in sterile soil after gently rinsing all soil from roots			
Mealybug	Slow-moving $\frac{1}{4}$-inch-long insect covered with white fuzz	Insecticidal soap; resmethrin or acephate spray; remove by hand or wipe off with cotton swab saturated with alcohol	Spider mite	Barely visible black, white, or red spiderlike creature	Dicofol; resmethrin or acephate spray
			Whitefly	Flying white $\frac{1}{16}$-inch-long insect	Rotenone, resmethrin, or acephate spray; repeat 8 times at 5-day intervals

BEDROOM UPKEEP

Instead of making the bed the minute you jump out of it each morning, wait for 20 minutes. Pull the covers back to expose the sheets and to dry out the moisture absorbed from the body during the night. The body loses about 1½ pints of fluid every night.

To freshen bedspreads, blankets, and pillows, place them in the dryer with a sheet of fabric softener or a washcloth that's been soaked in a solution of water and liquid fabric softener and wrung nearly dry. Tumble on the air-only setting for about 20 minutes.

Bedmaking is easier if the bed has smooth-running casters, so that it can be pulled away from a wall or corner. If space in the bedroom permits, the bed can be moved to the center of the room, giving all-round access. If the bed cannot be moved easily, try to position it so that there is at least two feet of space on each side.

MATTRESS CARE

If a mattress or box spring becomes dirty or stained, clean it with foaming upholstery shampoo. Let it dry completely before making up the bed.

Do a good turn for your mattress. Every week or so, flip it over—side to side one time, end to end the next. This distributes wear and sag evenly.

To remove accumulated dust, go over all the mattresses in your home every now and then with the upholstery attachment of your vacuum cleaner. An occasional airing in the sun will also help keep them fresh and clean.

BED LINENS

Put linens just back from the laundry on the bottom of the pile in the linen closet. This way, as you take fresh linens from the top, sheets and pillowcases will rotate uniformly in use and wear.

Many people prefer the lightness of a thermal blanket, which, when used with a top covering, traps heat in the blanket fabric's open spaces. However, this arrangement may not be as warm as a conventional blanket with a top covering.

A good way to increase the loft of a down comforter is to tumble it with a pair of clean sneakers in the dryer (on Low).

PILLOW TALK

Choose pillows for the purpose they'll serve. For reading in bed, select a pillow with firm support; the pillow you sleep on should be much softer.

As a general rule, a pillow should be just thick enough to hold your head in the same relation to your shoulders and spine as when you are standing.

Allergy sufferers may find a bit of relief with polyester fiberfill pillows. Available in varying degrees of softness, they're not as fluffy or resilient as feather or down pillows, but they're a lot less irritating.

To revive a down or feather pillow, machine-wash it on the gentle cycle, using warm water and mild detergent (half as much as for a normal load); dry on the Low setting. Then shake the filling to one end, open the seam on the other end, and insert new feathers or down a bit at a time. Stitch the opening closed.

KITCHEN CLEANING BASICS

Soak-and-dissolve is still the easiest way, but a plastic windshield ice scraper is good for prying dried-on foods from the floor, table, and counter if you're the impatient type.

Keep sponges, plastic scrubbers, and dishmops clean and fresh smelling; every now and then, run them through a dishwasher load in the top rack.

KITCHEN SAFETY

Place a smoke detector on the same level as your kitchen, but not too near your appliances—everyday cooking can easily set it off.

Never turn off a smoke detector because you're cooking something that will cause it to sound off. It's too easy to forget to turn it back on again.

105

Don't panic if a fat fire starts in your frying pan. Just turn off the heat, stand back, and toss generous handfuls of dry baking soda at the base of the flames.
Caution: Don't try this with deep fat, however, as it could spatter the grease and spread the fire. Instead, cover the pan with a large metal lid.

If you have small children, store items that are *not* appealing to them in the cabinets over the stove. Every year hundreds of children get burned as a result of climbing onto the stove to reach treats, such as candy and cookies.

Choose flexible, round pot holders for lifting hot lids and handles; mitts or a casserole holder (a long piece with a pocket at each end) for removing pans from the oven. Square, stiff pot holders are unsafe because, when folded diagonally, they can get into the flame.

KITCHEN APPLIANCES

To keep appliances shiny, wipe them with a cloth or sponge wrung out in lukewarm sudsy water; rinse and wipe dry with a soft cloth to remove water spots. To protect the finish, apply a creamy appliance wax every now and then.

Give the chrome trim on your appliances a quick shine with a soft cloth moistened with rubbing alcohol.

Here's a remarkably easy way to remove rust from kitchen chrome. Wrap aluminum foil around your finger, shiny side out, and rub the rust until it disapears. Then wipe the surface with a damp cloth.

To clean under and behind an appliance, take your car's snow brush and whisk the dirt out in a flash. Be sure to unplug the appliance before poking around behind it.

STOVE MAINTENANCE

It's a lot easier to wipe away cooking spills and spattered grease on the stove top while the cooking surface is still warm. Use warm sudsy water and a cloth or sponge.

Heating coils on top of an electric stove usually don't need washing. Instead, turn them on *High* to burn off spills. If a spill is massive, wipe up as much as possible after the coil has cooled and let the rest burn off the next time you use the unit.

If you don't have a continuous-cleaning oven, you can still prevent grease buildup by wiping out the inside with a sudsy sponge or paper towels. Otherwise, the grease will harden and burn each time you turn on the oven.

CLEANING AN EXHAUST FAN

Covered with grease and dust, a kitchen exhaust fan may appear daunting, but it's really not difficult to tackle. For a cleaner and safer kitchen, clean your fan every 6 months or so, using the instructions that came with the appliance. If you can't find your user's guide, follow the steps below.

1. Turn the power off at the service entrance or fuse box. If the grille is removable, detach and soak it in a mild dishwashing detergent solution. If not, sponge it clean with the solution.

2. Unplug and remove the fan-and-motor unit and lay it on an old newspaper. Wipe off the heavy grease with a soft, dry cloth. (Do *not* immerse metal and electrical parts in water.)

3. Wipe out and clean the fan opening with a soft, dry cloth (do not use water), then replace the clean fan-and-motor unit and plug it in. Dry and replace the grille if you've removed it. Turn on the power.

4. If you can't remove the fan-and-motor unit — for example, in a vented range-hood exhaust — remove the grease filters. Soak them in a detergent solution. Clean the fan with the crevice tool of your vacuum. Wipe the hood with the solution before replacing the filter.

Apple pie spilled on the oven floor? Soak up the spill with a wet sponge or paper towels. Or let it cool and dry, then scrape it off with a single-edge razor blade set in a holder, being careful not to harm the surface of the oven.

Clean oven racks by placing them on an old bath towel in the bathtub and soaking them in a solution of ammonia and hot water.

Wipe off a self-cleaning oven's frame and the part of the door liner that's outside the oven seal *before* the cleaning cycle. These areas aren't reached during automatic cleaning, but they do get enough heat to bake on soil, making it harder to remove later.

To clean under an electric stove that has a storage drawer at the bottom, remove the drawer to get at the floor easily. For a gas stove with a broiler below the oven, remove the broiler drawer.

CLEANING THE BROILER AND GRILL

For easy broiler cleaning, put a few cups of water in the bottom of the pan before broiling.

To clean the broiler pan, remove it from the oven while it's still hot and pour any drippings into a grease can. Invert the grid over the pan and pour in dishwashing detergent. Then fill the pan with hot water and let it stand. Scrub later with a steel-wool soap pad.

Before your next cookout, clean the grill with a wire brush dipped in warm sudsy water or a baking-soda solution. Rinse, dry, and coat the grill with cooking oil to keep food from sticking to it.

MICROWAVE OVENS

Wipe off all spills as soon as possible, using wet paper towels to saturate dried or cooked-on food. Do not use metal tools to scrape up food because they seriously damage the interior of the microwave.

Deodorize and clean your microwave every now and then. When the oven is turned off and cold, wash its inside surfaces with a solution of 4 tablespoons baking soda per 1 quart warm water.

Two microwave cleaning don'ts: Never use commercial oven cleaners in a microwave. Never remove the cover in the top of the oven for cleaning.

REFRIGERATORS

Sticky, greasy dust on top of the refrigerator? Get after it with a heavy-duty all-purpose cleaner or a solution of 1 part ammonia to 10 parts water. Once the solution has broken down the grease, you can wipe the surface clean with paper towels. Finish up with an application of appliance wax to make cleaning easier the next time.

Remove odors and spills inside the refrigerator with a cloth wrung out in a solution of 1 tablespoon baking soda to 1 quart warm water. Rinse and wipe dry.

If your child uses your refrigerator door as a canvas for his permanent marker, you may be able to remove the artwork with lighter fluid. Then wash the door with soap and water and rinse completely.

SMALL APPLIANCES

If you use a drip coffee machine daily, you should clean it thoroughly at least once a month. Pour a solution of equal parts water and distilled vinegar into the water reservoir and run it through the brew cycle. Rinse your machine by running clean water through the cycle.

If there are any sticky crumbs left after you've shaken the toaster gently, blow compressed air (available in cans from photography supply stores) inside the appliance.

An easy way to clean your blender is to partly fill it with warm water and hand-dishwashing detergent, cover, and run for a few seconds. Empty the blender, rinse, and dry.

CLEAN KITCHEN COUNTERS

Rub countertop stains, such as mustard, tea, or fruit juice, with baking soda and a damp cloth or sponge. If the stain persists, wipe it with a cloth moistened with a little chlorine bleach.

Erase those pesky purple price marks that transfer from containers onto countertops. Rubbing alcohol gets rid of them easily.

Every few days (or immediately after cutting meat or poultry), wipe down food preparation surfaces with hot soapy water to discourage bacteria. Rinse thoroughly and wipe dry.

WOODEN SURFACES

To keep a butcher block countertop clean and fresh, scrape off all waste after each use; rub it with salt or a baking soda paste every now and then.

After cutting onions or garlic on a wooden surface, rub it with a slice of freshly cut lemon. Rinse well and wipe dry.

Tiny knife marks are sometimes considered attractive on wooden surfaces. But deep scratches should be sanded with fine sandpaper and then reoiled.

SINK CARE

To remove stains from a porcelain sink, fill it with lukewarm water, add a few ounces of chlorine bleach, and let stand for an hour or so. If stains are stubborn, line the sink with paper towels saturated with chlorine bleach and let stand 8 to 10 hours.

Do not use chlorine bleach on old, porous, or cracked porcelain surfaces. The bleach can penetrate to the iron base and cause further discoloration by rusting.

Avoid abrasive cleaners when cleaning a stainless steel sink. Instead, simply wash it with hot sudsy water and dry it (to remove finger marks and water spots).

To give a stainless steel sink extra sparkle, clean and polish it occasionally with glass cleaner or a baking soda paste.

Has your stainless steel sink become scratched or slightly pitted? Rub it gently with very fine steel wool, then buff to a sheen with a soft cloth.

109

HANDLING GARBAGE

Good garbage pail hygiene prevents odors. Line the pail with a plastic bag; drain all garbage before throwing it in the bag. Wash the pail frequently with disinfectant cleaner or hot sudsy water with a little chlorine bleach or ammonia added (do not use both). Dry in fresh air.

Eliminate odor from your garbage disposer by grinding cutup orange, grapefruit, or lemon rinds while flushing the disposer with hot water.

DEALING WITH DRAINS

Keep a drain odor-free by running very hot tap water through it after each use. About once a week, throw in a handful of baking soda, followed by hot water. Or pour in 1 cup of vinegar, let it stand for 30 minutes, then run very hot water through the drain.

It's easier to avoid a clogged drain than to clear one. Pour cooking grease into an empty can or a milk carton—never into the sink. The same applies to coffee grounds and other bits of garbage.

UNCLOGGING A DRAIN

1. Remove the sink stopper or strainer. Clean out any material stuck in the top of the drain or on the stopper. Test water flow. If there is an overflow opening, block it with a wet cloth; fill the sink about half full.

2. Place a plunger over the drain and rapidly pump it up and down 10 times, abruptly lifting it from the water on the last stroke. If the water rushes out, you've unclogged the drain. Otherwise, try several more times before giving up.

3. If the plunger fails, you'll have to get into the trap under the sink. Place a bucket beneath the trap, unscrew the plug on the bottom of the trap with a wrench, and let the water run out.

4. If there's no plug, remove the trap itself by unscrewing the two coupling nuts, beginning with the higher one. Clear the stoppage by hand or with a wire. Replace the plug or the trap.

5. If you still can't reach the clog, you'll need a snake (available at hardware stores). Twist the handle of the snake clockwise, pushing into and pulling out of the drain, until you reach the obstruction and clear it.

6. Call a plumber if all of these steps fail to clear the drain. Do not, under any circumstances, use chemical drain cleaner; it could cause serious burns to your skin and create a problem for the plumber.

To retrieve hairpins and jewelry that have slipped down the drain, go fishing. Use a magnet attached to a length of stiff twine. If your expedition fails, open the trap below the sink to clear the obstruction (see p.110).

Before using a commercial drain cleaner, try clearing a sluggish drain with a plunger. If that fails, but there is some flow of water, you can try drain cleaner. But be aware that drain cleaners are caustic and poisonous; it's important to follow the manufacturer's instructions to the letter.

DOING THE DISHES

A dishwasher is self-cleaning, except near the rim of the door opening. Wipe this area clean before starting the machine so that spills here don't become baked on.

Washing dishes by hand may not save hot water if you run it continuously. Always use a sink stopper or a dishpan and run the hot water as little as possible. Rinse the dishes in cold water.

Wash the following by hand: fine decorated china; colored anodized aluminum; wooden items; hollow-handled knives; pewter; cast iron; milk glass; some plastics. See pp.431–434 for more on caring for fine china and metals.

Remove eggs, cooked cereal, and other dried-on foods from dishes by soaking them immediately in cold water. If you don't remember to do this until later, put them in a solution of dishwasher detergent and water instead. Let the dishes stand overnight, then lift off the food with a rubber scraper.

Ugly stains on your plastic dishes or utensils? Combine ¾ cup chlorine bleach and ¾ cup baking soda and let the mixture remain on the stained utensil for 5 minutes. Wash and rinse thoroughly.

VACUUM BOTTLES

Hand-wash—but don't immerse—glass-lined vacuum bottles in dishwashing detergent and warm water. Use a bottle brush if necessary. Rinse and invert to dry.

Before filling a vacuum bottle that has absorbed beverage odors or been stored for a while, freshen it with 1 tablespoon of baking soda and warm water. Let stand 20 minutes, scrub out, rinse, and air-dry.

POTS AND PANS

Store cast-iron cookware in a dry place between paper towels, leaving lids off to prevent mustiness, moisture, and rusting.

When stirring and turning food in nonstick cookware, use only wooden or plastic utensils; avoid temperatures over 450° F.

To brighten darkened aluminum, cook an acidic substance, such as tomatoes, rhubarb, apples, or vinegar, in the pan. Try removing stains or discoloration by boiling 2 tablespoons cream of tartar in 1 quart water in the pan.

Check the manufacturer's care instructions before washing enamel cookware in the dishwasher. Use only nonabrasive cleaners to remove cooked-on food on enamel. Soak stained white enamel pans in warm water and a small amount of chlorine bleach.

Remove coffee and tea stains from glasses and glass utensils by soaking them in a solution of 2 tablespoons chlorine bleach per 1 cup water. Another method is to soak the stained cookware overnight in a solution of 2 tablespoons automatic dishwasher detergent to 1 pot warm water.

Remove stains from a pan with a nonstick surface by boiling a solution of 1 cup water and 2 tablespoons baking soda in it. Wipe the surface lightly with cooking oil or shortening before using again.

KNIFE CARE

If you have a good set of knives, don't stir hot food with them; heat damages some blades.

Unless the manufacturer specifies that cutlery is "dishwasher safe," wash all good cutlery by hand immediately after using it. Avoid soaking it in water, which can damage and loosen wooden handles. Always dry thoroughly.

Knives with serrated edges depend upon notches for their cutting ability. They should be sharpened by professionals—or not at all.

SHARPENING KNIVES

The most effective way to get a good cutting edge on a knife is to use a whetstone with a coarse and a fine side. Before using a whetstone, saturate it with vegetable oil. Sharpen a very dull knife first on the coarse side, then on the fine side; with a blade that is slightly dull, sharpen on the fine side only. Afterward, clean the stone thoroughly and wrap it in a cloth to store it.

1. Holding the knife firmly, place the blade at an angle to the stone, as shown.

2. Slide the knife firmly across the stone *away from you* from its heel to its tip. Repeat four times.

3. Turn the knife over and reverse the procedure, working *toward you*. Repeat four times.

BATHROOM SAFETY

If you must have a lock on the bathroom door, install a doorknob with an outside lock release. This will prevent children from getting locked inside accidentally.

Prevent bathroom falls by laying scatter rugs with nonskid backings and by providing tubs and showers with suction-backed rubber mats or adhesive decals.

Grab bar

Adhesive decal

Grab bar   Rubber mat

Grab bars in the bathtub or shower and next to the toilet are a help for all and a must for the elderly. Fasten the bars to wall studs.

To avoid the risk of a fatal shock, don't use electric appliances, such as heaters, hair dryers, and radios, near water. All bathroom outlets should be equipped with GFCI's (ground fault circuit interrupters). Even then, you should take the precautions mentioned.

REPAIRING A FAUCET'S LEAKING SPOUT

If your stem faucet drips when it's turned off, the washer, valve seat, or both probably need replacing. Before you begin: Turn off the stop valve under the sink; turn on the faucet; protect chrome surfaces with electrician's tape.

(If your faucet has a one-piece ball, cartridge, or valve, get replacement parts from a home center, plumbing supply store, or hardware store. Or contact the manufacturer.)

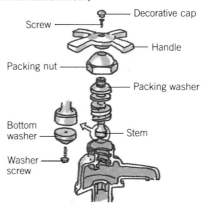

Screw — Decorative cap

Handle

Packing nut

Packing washer

Bottom washer

Stem

Washer screw

1. Pry the decorative cap from the handle, then, after removing the handle screw, lift off the handle. With an adjustable wrench, remove the packing nut. Pull out the stem, and replace the stem's bottom washer.

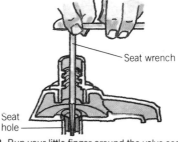

Seat wrench

Seat hole

2. Run your little finger around the valve seat to see if it's chipped or worn. If you feel any roughness, remove the seat with a seat wrench, using the taper that matches the seat's hole (hexagonal or square). Replace it with a new valve seat.

3. Before putting the faucet back together, coat all interior parts with heatproof, waterproof grease. In addition to its intended purpose, it makes for easy reassembly and a good seal.

113

To prevent hot-water burns when you take a shower or bath, always turn on the cold water first and turn off the hot water first.

Does your shower turn scalding hot when another cold water tap is turned on or a toilet is flushed? You can correct this by installing a mixing valve to automatically regulate temperature and pressure.

Mixing valve

KEEPING BATHROOMS CLEAN

Keep your bathroom sparkling clean in just 3½ minutes a day. Armed with a spray bottle of disinfectant cleaner, a sponge, and a paper towel, wipe down all bathroom surfaces. Work from the cleanest (mirror) to the dirtiest (floor), covering the sink, tub, and toilet along the way.

If you can't get around to cleaning the bathroom every day, sponge down the tub, shower, and sink with a liquid disinfectant cleaner at least once a week.

Use a cloth moistened with vinegar to rub away hard-water spots and soap scum from chrome faucet handles and drains. Dry and polish with a soft cloth.

Prevention is the best method for eliminating mildew. After showering, keep the shower curtain extended (not bunched) so it can dry thoroughly. Clean your bathroom regularly with disinfectant and keep it as dry and well ventilated as possible.

Exhaust fans (vented to the outside) and built-in heaters (in the ceiling where they won't cause burns) do a good job of removing excess moisture from the bathroom. When it's dry outside, leave the window and curtain open.

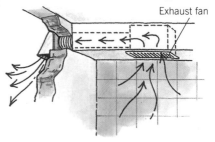

Exhaust fan

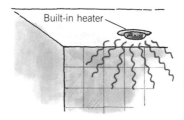

Built-in heater

Machine-wash (gentle cycle) colorfast plastic shower and window curtains in warm water. Add water conditioner to remove soap curd. Hang to dry. If the curtains are mildewed, add ¾ cup chlorine bleach to the wash cycle.

TUB AND TILE CARE

Remove mildew and stains from tub and tiles by wetting the surfaces with water then spraying them with a solution of 1 cup of bleach to 1 quart of water. Make sure that the room is well ventilated while you do the job and that bath towels and fabric shower curtains are out of spray range.

Stained tub or sink surfaces come clean with a cream of tartar-hydrogen peroxide paste. Spread the paste over the stain and scrub lightly with a brush. Let the paste dry and then wipe or rinse it off.

Wipe away soap spots or film from tile with a solution of water and water softener or a solution of 1 part vinegar to 4 parts water. Rinse then dry with a soft cloth.

Clean grungy-looking tile grout with full-strength vinegar instead of bathroom or kitchen cleaner.

The best time for bathroom cleaning? Right after taking a shower or bath, when steam has loosened the dirt. Just wipe off the damp surfaces with a paper towel.

Unsightly stains on old enameled baths—usually caused by hard water from dripping taps—can sometimes be removed with lemon juice or citric acid.

After grout has set, seal it with a commercial silicone preparation (available in hardware stores).

Before caulking cracks between the bathtub and the wall, run water into the tub to expand it. Then the seal won't crack from the water's weight when the tub's in use.

If you're tired of cleaning around nonskid decals in your porcelain tub or shower, scrape them off with a straight-edge razor blade (in a holder) dipped in soapy water. Remove adhesive residue with acetone or nail-polish remover.

Bathroom floors covered in dull, old resilient tile may need especially strong cleaning measures. Scrub with a solution of 1 part ammonia to 4 parts water, then dry with a towel. Apply a thin coat of wax, following the directions on the container.

SHOWER MAINTENANCE

A quick way to defog the bathroom mirror after a shower is to turn your hand-held hair dryer on it, using the *Low* setting. The warm air will clear the mirror.

When glass shower doors turn dull and filmy, wipe them down with a soft cloth saturated with distilled white vinegar or water softener solution, then shine with a dry cloth.

Mineral deposits frequently clog shower heads. To remedy this problem, unscrew the head, take the pieces apart, and soak them in a bowl of vinegar; brush out any stubborn sediment. Reassemble the shower head and reattach.

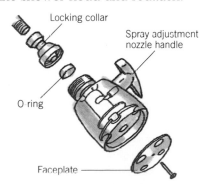

Locking collar

Spray adjustment nozzle handle

O-ring

Faceplate

Installing an inexpensive water restrictor or a water-saving shower head can cut water use in half. Follow the manufacturer's instructions; you'll need only a wrench or pliers to do the job yourself.

While you're at it, why not install a "telephone shower" for shampooing? You simply add a diverter valve between the pipe and the shower head and a hook to hold the "telephone" on the wall.

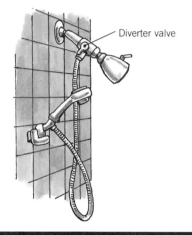

Diverter valve

TOILET TIPS

Put petroleum jelly on the lip of your plunger. It will help to stabilize its position on the drain hole.

Remember to clean under the inside rim of the toilet bowl. The holes in the rim can get clogged with lime deposits from the water; this affects the flush. Unclog each hole with the end of a coat hanger that's been bent for the job.

Undiluted chlorine bleach, allowed to stand just a few minutes, will frequently do just as good a job as commercial toilet-bowl cleaners. It will also remove mildew and surface stains (except rust) from porcelain bathroom fixtures. Use a toilet bowl cleaner to remove rust.

Retard stain buildup and remove discoloration by scrubbing the toilet bowl briskly with a bowl brush for a few seconds daily.

To remove old mineral buildup in the toilet, sprinkle 1/2 cup of water softener around the bowl (above the waterline), immediately after flushing. Really tough, old rings may require pumice or a little wet-dry sandpaper.

UNCLOGGING A TOILET

If, when you flush the toilet, the bowl fills up but won't drain, then your toilet is clogged. If the bowl is full to the brim, bail out half of it in order to prevent splashing while you work to unclog the toilet.

Place the cone of your plunger securely over the bowl's drain hole and pump the plunger up and down vigorously about a dozen times. If this doesn't dislodge the obstruction, wait for about an hour and then give it another try.

If plunging fails, aim the bent end of a closet (toilet) auger into the drain hole. Crank the auger's handle clockwise to feed its snake into the hole until it meets the obstruction. Crank the auger's handle just a bit more, then pull the auger out as you continue cranking clockwise.

If neither method works, the problem may be in the main drain; you may have to have the toilet bowl removed. The best thing to do is call a plumber.

The first rule of toilet repair: Carefully remove the breakable ceramic tank cover and set it on the floor on top of a towel, carpet remnant, or layers of newspaper before you go to work.

Here's a quick way to check for stopper-ball or stopper-valve leaks: Put a few drops of food coloring into the tank and, without flushing, see if the colored water comes into the bowl. If it does, you can assume there's a leak.

116

TOILET PROBLEMS: WHAT TO FIX

Water won't stop running: Float ball or arm; ballcock valve

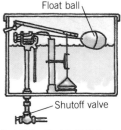

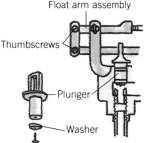

1. Lift the float ball. If the water shuts off, unscrew the ball from the float arm and shake the ball. If there's water in it, replace the float ball with a new one.

2. If there's no water in the float ball, bend the float arm slightly so that after you flush again, the water level rises no farther than 3/4 inch below the top of the overflow tube.

3. Problem persists? Close shut-off valve under tank; remove float arm assembly (turn thumbscrews) and plunger. Replace washer and, if worn, valve seat. Or replace entire system with a plastic ball-cock assembly.

Sluggish or incomplete flush: Stopper ball

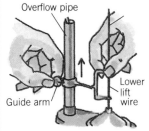

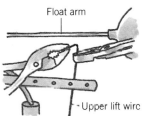

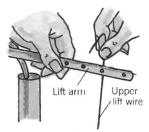

1. The stopper ball may be falling too quickly on the valve seat. Loosen the thumbscrew(s) on the guide arm. Raise the guide arm about 1/2 inch on the overflow tube so that the stopper ball will float longer.

2. To make the stopper ball rise higher, shorten the upper lift wire slightly by unhooking it from the lift arm, bending it slightly, and then rehooking it in the same hole in the lift arm.

3. If the flush is still unsatisfactory, try unhooking the upper lift wire from its hole on the lift arm and hooking it in another hole on the arm.

Gurgling, partially filled tank: Outlet valve seat

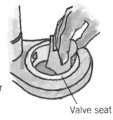

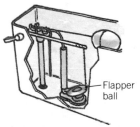

1. Check the stopper ball. If it isn't centered on the valve seat, turn off the main water valve and flush the toilet empty. Loosen the screw on the lift wire's guide arm. Move the guide arm until the stopper ball is seated properly. Then tighten the screw.

2. Inspect the valve seat with your fingertips. If it feels rough or pitted from corrosion, scour it with wet/dry sandpaper.

3. If the tank still doesn't fill and the gurgling sound persists, your best bet is to replace the stopper ball with a flapper ball, available at hardware or plumbing supply stores. Installation instructions are included.

ATTICS

Because attics are dark, damp, and secluded, they're a haven for insects and small animals. Inspect your attic periodically for nests, droppings, food scraps, and other evidence of pests. (For other pest control hints, see pp.126-128.)

When storing boxes on gable wall shelves, place them around the louvered vents, not in front of them: that way they won't block the air flow. (For other hints on attic storage, see p.48.)

Thinking of turning your attic into a rentable apartment? First check local zoning laws and building regulations. Even if the law permits you to build and rent an attic apartment, some restrictions may apply.

If there are any openings around ducts or pipes where they enter the attic floor, seal them with sheet metal or stuff them with steel wool or fireproof insulation. This will help prevent a fire from spreading upward through the house.

Good attic ventilation is the key to protecting a well-insulated home from winter moisture problems and summer heat buildup. If you have only gable vents, add vents to the roof or soffits. (For hints on attic insulation, see p.178.)

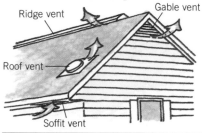

BASEMENTS

If you have small children, install vertical rails along the basement staircase to prevent falls. At each step, bolt one end of a 2 x 4 to the stair stringer and nail the other end to the handrail.

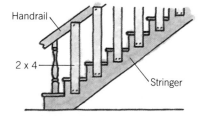

CONTROLLING DAMPNESS IN BASEMENTS

Left unchecked, dampness in a basement can rot wood, peel paint, and promote rust and mildew. Here's a simple test to determine if dampness is caused by seepage or excessive humidity. Cut several 12-inch squares of aluminum foil. Tape them to various spots on floor and walls; seal the perimeters tightly. If moisture collects between the foil and the surface after several days, waterproof the interior walls. If moisture forms on the foil's surface, take steps as follows:

Close windows on humid days.

Install a window exhaust fan.

Vent your clothes dryer to the outdoors.

Wrap cold-water pipes with fiberglass insulation or foam plastic sleeves.

Clear clogged drains and roof gutters.

Use a dehumidifier, especially during the summer months.

Treat walls with epoxy-base waterproofing paint or epoxy masonry sealer.

Cover a dirt or gravel floor with a 4-inch layer of concrete poured on top of a plastic vapor retarder.

Install a drainage system or a sump pump to combat chronic flooding.

Regrade around the house so that water will flow away from the foundation.

Keep boxes and valuables on high shelves or on 2 x 4's set on concrete blocks. The former prevents damage from floods; the latter provides ventilation around the boxes.

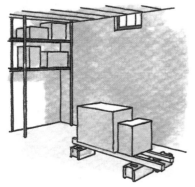

Store flammable substances, such as oil-base paint and turpentine, in metal containers well away from the heating system, the hot-water heater, or other sources of heat.

To remove a musty odor, sprinkle a hard basement floor with chlorinated lime (bleaching powder). Once the odor is gone, sweep the powder into a plastic bag, tie the bag, and dispose of it. Avoid contact with skin.

HELP! THE BASEMENT IS FLOODED

Remove water from a flooded basement as quickly as possible. If the flood was caused by a ruptured pipe, shut off the water supply. If the water is an inch or two deep, bail it out with buckets or soak it up with mops or a wet-dry vacuum.

Deeper water must be pumped out by a plumber, a waterproofing contractor, or the fire department. If no one is available, rent a submersible electric pump from a plumbing supply store. Connect the pump to a garden hose and run the hose outdoors to a storm sewer or to a spot where the runoff will flow away from the house. Then lower the pump until it rests on the basement floor. Using an extra-long heavy-duty extension cord, connect the pump to a neighbor's outlet. Keep debris away from the pump's intake. **Caution: Because water conducts electricity, have the power company turn off the electricity to your house. If you must enter a deeply flooded basement, wear high, heavy rubber boots and thick, dry rubber gloves. Standing on a wooden chair or ladder, turn off the power. Use a dry piece of wood, such as a broom handle, to flip the main switch or pull out the main fuse block. Don't touch a wall or anything else until the power is off (p.163).**

PATCHING AN INACTIVE CRACK IN A BASEMENT WALL

An active wall crack (one that continues to enlarge) may indicate a serious structural problem. Have it examined promptly by an expert. Inactive cracks (those caused by settling) can be repaired easily. To determine whether a crack is active or inactive, see p.167.

  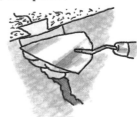

1. Using a chisel and a sledgehammer, enlarge the inactive crack so that it becomes wider at the rear than the front. Brush out any debris, vacuum the area thoroughly, then dampen it.

2. For a large crack that won't leak during repair, use a mixture of 1 part portland cement to 3 parts fine sand. For smaller cracks, use a two-part epoxy within ½ hour after mixing.

3. Apply the mortar or epoxy mix with a trowel, forcing it well into the rear of the crack. Smooth and level the mortar immediately; wait ½ hour before smoothing the epoxy with a wet trowel.

LEAKS AND SEEPAGE

Clean leaves and debris out of basement window wells periodically. If allowed to accumulate, they can cause seepage or flooding. Lay gravel at the bottom of wells to improve drainage.

If your basement floods frequently, have a plumber install an interior drainage system of pipes connected to a sump pump. The sump pit should be 1½ to 2 feet in diameter to collect sufficient water and prevent the pump from turning on and off too frequently.

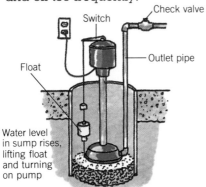

Switch
Check valve
Outlet pipe
Float
Water level in sump rises, lifting float and turning on pump

Sealing the exterior of basement walls against leaks is far more effective than sealing the interior, but it's much more costly because it requires excavating around the foundation. Use this method only as a last resort.

PLUMBING

Before making any plumbing repair, shut off the water supply at either the main valve or the valve nearest the fixture. In homes supplied by a municipal system, the main valve is the one nearest the water meter; in homes with their own wells, the main valve is near the water-storage tank.

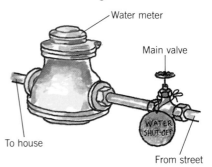

Water meter
Main valve
WATER SHUT-OFF
To house
From street

QUICK FIXES FOR LEAKY PIPES

Because dripping water can damage plaster, paint and wallpaper, and create an electrical hazard, get a plumber to repair all leaks. Until then, use one of the following methods to repair the leak temporarily. First, shut off the water supply to the pipe. Then, remove rust from the pipe with steel wool, and wipe the area clean and dry.

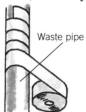

Waste pipe

Supply or waste pipe

To seal a small crack or puncture, wrap layers of electrical tape around the pipe from one side of the leak to the other.

For a small leak, wrap a rubber pad around the leak and cover it with a hose clamp. Or cut a tin can along its seam, wrap it around the rubber pad, and secure it with a C-clamp and two blocks of wood.

For a large leak, wrap a rubber pad around the leak, cover it with a pipe clamp, and bolt the clamp. Make sure the clamp is centered directly over the leak.

Hang a tag on the main shutoff valve so that family members will be able to identify it quickly and easily during an emergency.

If you hear a loud bang when a faucet is turned off abruptly, it's probably the result of pressure built up from the water flow. Because this vibration can damage pipes, install a shock-absorbing air chamber to the pipe that leads to the fixture. This hammering sound may return once the chamber becomes filled with water. If so, draining the plumbing system will readmit air to the chamber.

THAWING FROZEN PIPES

Before attempting to thaw a pipe, shut off the main water valve. This will prevent water from gushing out as soon as the pipe is thawed. Also, open the taps supplied by the pipes to reduce steam pressure, which can cause pipes to burst. Close the taps when the pipes have thawed.

If water isn't running anywhere in the house, a pipe near the water meter may be frozen. To confirm this, touch the meter and the exposed pipes adjacent to it. If they feel extremely cold, a nearby pipe probably needs thawing.

When water runs in only one part of the house, a pipe in an outside wall or uninsulated crawl space may be frozen. Turn up the heating system, then open the kitchen and bathroom sink cabinets to let in the warm air. Or heat the pipes where they emerge from the wall.

If a pipe is partly frozen, open the affected faucet all the way. Then open other hot-water faucets in the house to raise the temperature of the nearly frozen pipe. Once hot water is flowing from all the faucets, close them to a trickle. Don't turn them off completely until water is flowing freely from the faucet.

Once you've pinpointed the frozen section of a pipe, heat it slowly with a hand-held hair dryer or a heat lamp to a temperature your hand can tolerate. Work backwards from the faucet toward the frozen area.

Boiling water, propane torches, or open flames of any kind should not be used for thawing. Pipes can explode if they're heated excessively or too suddenly.

PREVENTING FROZEN PIPES

Wrap an electric heating cable around exposed metal pipes (but not plastic ones) that tend to freeze. The electric cable will keep the pipes warm when the cold weather arrives.

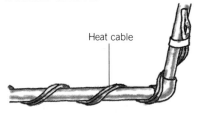

Heat cable

Taking a long winter vacation? Ask a plumber about draining the plumbing system to prevent frozen pipes and water damage.

121

ENERGY CONSERVATION

Want to cut your heating bills by 7 to 12 percent a year? Install an automatic setback thermostat. It can be programmed to lower the heat or cool the air while everyone's out during the day or when they're snug in bed at night; it turns the system on just before you get home or at daybreak.

Want a cheap heat reflector to insert behind radiators and baseboard convectors? Tape heavy-duty aluminum foil to a panel of insulation board.

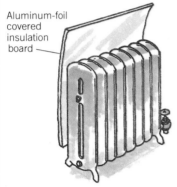

Aluminum-foil covered insulation board

Radiators or baseboard convectors not delivering heat efficiently? Dust and dirt buildup may be inhibiting heat flow. Every couple of months, turn the radiators or convectors off, let them cool down, then vacuum them with a crevice attachment and wipe them clean with a damp cloth.

Save energy dollars by wrapping insulation around the pipes leading to radiators and convectors.

Opening windows to cool rooms overheated by steam radiators wastes heat and money. Have your plumber install radiator thermostats; they maintain a set temperature. The cost varies widely; shop around for the best price.

WARM-AIR HEATING SYSTEMS

Floor-length draperies "robbing" your room of heat from warm-air registers? Install air deflectors over the registers to prevent this.

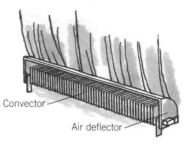

Convector

Air deflector

Cut down the amount of dust that a forced warm-air heating or central air-conditioning system brings into your rooms. Take out the grates monthly for a scrubbing in a mild detergent solution; vacuum inside the registers as far as your extension tool will reach.

How often should you change the filter to your warm-air heating system? To devise a schedule suited to your system, install a new filter and then check it every 4 weeks for dirt accumulation by holding it up to a bare light bulb. When the light shining through the filter is diffused, it's time for a new filter.

OIL BURNER MAINTENANCE

Oil bill too high? Your oil burner could be the cause. Have a service technician check its combustion efficiency by measuring the carbon dioxide (CO_2) level in the flue. If it's 10 to 13 percent, your oil burner is functioning very well; an 8 to 10 percent CO_2 level is acceptable; if the CO_2 level is less than 8 percent, the serviceperson should examine the burner's combustion chamber for air leaks, insufficient or excessive draft, and an out-of-balance air-to-fuel ratio.

WHAT TO CHECK WHEN HEAT WON'T OPERATE

At the thermostat. Set the thermostat more than 5° F above room temperature and see whether the heat goes on.

If you have an automatic day-night thermostat, make sure that the cycle hasn't been reversed.

If your thermostat's contact points are exposed to air, they may need an occasional cleaning. Turn off the power (p.163) then carefully remove the cover. Lower the setting to open the contact points, then run a business card between them. Raise the setting to close the points, then repeat the cleaning procedure. Replace the cover and restore power.

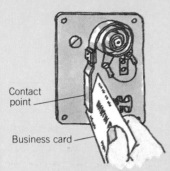

Contact point

Business card

To clean the contact points of certain round thermostats, first turn off the power, then remove the temperature setting dial. Wipe the points with a cotton swab dipped in a 50-50 vinegar-water solution.

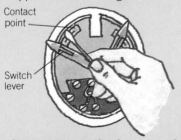

Contact point

Switch lever

At the furnace or boiler. Check the emergency switch to make sure it isn't off.

If you have an oil burner, press the overload reset button on the motor housing; then push the stack control relay switch (located on the flue or on the burner housing).

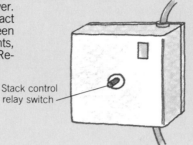

Stack control relay switch

If your oil burner is controlled by a photoelectric cell, this "seeing eye" cell could be dirty, preventing the unit from operating. First turn off the emergency switch, then unscrew the transformer from the fan housing and flip it over. You'll find the photoelectric cell on the underside of the transformer or on the housing. Gently wipe it with a clean cloth.

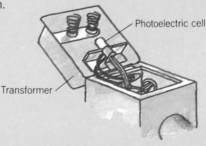

Photoelectric cell

Transformer

On your way to the furnace or boiler. Check for a blown fuse or a tripped circuit breaker (see p.163).

If you have a remote emergency switch, make sure it isn't turned off.

If you have an oil burner, check the fuel gauge on the oil tank; if there's no gauge, remove the cap of the tank-filler pipe and check the oil level with a stick.

If you have a gas burner, make sure the pilot light is on. If it isn't, relight it according to instructions in the owner's manual or on the plate mounted on the unit. If the pilot light won't stay lit, have a serviceman check the thermocouple. If your system runs but delivers inadequate heat, see p. 124.

Some oil-burner motors need their bearings lubricated; check your owner's manual. If your burner runs a warm-air system, the blower motor may need the same maintenance. Look for lube points on the motor housing.

The filter to your oil burner should be replaced twice a year—once during the annual maintenance and again midway in the heating season. Ask your oil supplier to show you how.

ATTIC AND ROOM FANS

Winter winds sneaking into your home through closed attic-fan louvers? Tape an interior (plastic) storm window over the louvers. Or cover with rigid board insulation. Both are available at hardware stores and home centers.

Run your whole-house fan efficiently: Open only the windows and doors of rooms in use while the fan is running.

HEATING SYSTEM RUNS BUT HEAT IS INADEQUATE

Hot-water system. If the water circulator pump has a reset button on it, press it.

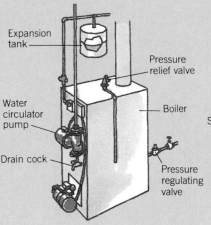

Expansion tank

Pressure relief valve

Water circulator pump

Boiler

Drain cock

Pressure regulating valve

If your system has a pressure-regulating valve to automatically maintain the correct water pressure, check the gauge on the boiler. If pressure is below the minimum mark, call for service.

If the expansion tank feels hot all over and water spurts from the pressure relief valve, the tank needs recharging with air. See owner's manual or call for service.

If some of your radiators fail to heat, they have air trapped inside. Open the valve on the end of the radiator. When water spurts out (it will be very hot), quickly close the valve.

Steam system. Check the boiler's sight glass or try cocks. Is the water level at least at the half mark? Most modern boilers have automatic water-feed mechanisms. If yours is older, use the manual water-feeding valve. Wait until the boiler cools; filling a hot boiler with cold water could cause the boiler to crack.

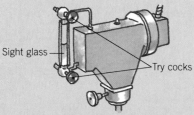

Sight glass

Try cocks

Sediment can interfere with the boiler's operation. If you haven't drained the low-water cutoff valve recently, put a pail under the drain, and open the valve. Careful, the water will be hot! Fill the pail; then refill the boiler. If the water remains dirty, add a boiler-cleaning compound.

If the boiler cycles on and off frequently and you've checked that the water level is correct, add an antisurge compound.

Warm-air system. The dust filter may be clogged, decreasing warm-air flow. Feel the ducts leading to and from the furnace; the filter is located in the one that returns cool house air. Open the panel covering the filter; if it's fiberglass, replace it; wash a plastic or aluminum filter.

AIR CONDITIONERS

Automatically timing your air conditioner saves money and prevents coming home to a hot house at the end of a workday. Set it to go off 15 minutes before you leave in the morning and to go on 15 minutes before you arrive home.

You can buy automatic timers for room air conditioners and install them yourself. Just program the timer according to instructions, plug it into a wall receptacle outlet, then plug the air conditioner into the timer.

AIR-CONDITIONING SENSE

Stop cold air leaks through floor-level openings. Close heating-system registers; tape sheets of plastic over them. Weatherstrip undersides of doors to the outside and basement.

Keep your room air conditioner working efficiently. Remove the front panel monthly and wash the filter in tepid water and mild detergent; allow it to dry thoroughly before reinstalling it. While it's out, vacuum all accessible surfaces.

Bent aluminum evaporator fins in room air conditioners obstruct efficient air transfer. Remove the front panel and filter, then straighten the fins with a plastic spatula.

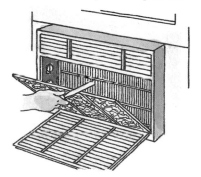

FIXING A NOISY AIR CONDITIONER

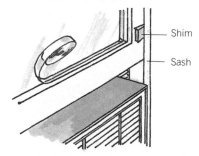

Shim

Sash

1. The unit's vibration may be the cause of noisy windows. With the unit on, press your palm against the window sash and then the glass. If the noise changes pitch in the first case, insert thin wood shims between the sash and the window frame. If the glass is the culprit, stick cellophane insulating tape tightly between the edge of the glass and the frame or reputty.

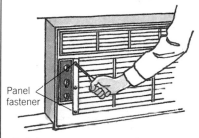

Panel fastener

2. If the unit's noise changes pitch when you press both your palms against the front panel, tighten the panel fasteners. If this doesn't work, seal the panel to the cabinet with duct tape.

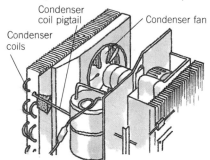

Condenser coil pigtail

Condenser fan

Condenser coils

3. Unplug the air conditioner and slide the chassis partway forward out of the housing; rest it on a stool to keep it level. If your model can be unhoused only when it's entirely out of the sleeve, have someone help you carry it onto a working surface. Spin the fan blades by hand to see if their position is uniform. If a bent blade is striking the condenser fins, straighten it. Jiggle the chassis; if the condenser coil's pigtail is striking the fan's housing, insert a foam rubber wedge between them.

125

PEST CONTROL

The key to keeping pests away is to deny them food, water, and shelter. Store food in tightly sealed glass or plastic containers. Clean up crumbs and spills immediately. Keep counters and cabinets spotless. Keep sink areas dry. Clean garbage cans regularly and secure their lids. Fill cracks and crevices. Repair torn screens. Cover chimney and flue openings with spark-arresting screening.

Electric bug zappers are ineffective on most stinging and biting insects, such as bees, wasps, and mosquitoes. However, they do draw other flying insects away from pool, patio, and picnic areas at night.

A chemically treated pest strip should not be placed in a room with an infant, a pet, or someone who is ill or elderly. Also, avoid hanging a pest strip in an area where food is prepared or where people stay for prolonged periods.

COMMON HOUSEHOLD PESTS   (not shown lifesize)

Pest	Habitat	Comments	Controls
Carpenter ant	Nests in moist or decaying wood	Can cause severe structural damage	Treat nest area with a household formulation of diazinon or propoxur
Household ant	Attracted from outdoor colonies by sweet or greasy food	Can be found by following ants' path from food supply to nest	Form insecticide barrier across path; treat window frames, baseboards, and cracks with a household formulation of diazinon or propoxur
Bedbug	Mattresses, box springs, floor and wall cracks, furniture, wallpaper	Feeds on human blood; appears flat and brown when empty, round and red when full; nocturnal	Treat with a household formulation of malathion labeled safe for bedding; let bedding dry completely before replacing sheets; for serious infestations, call an exterminator
Book louse	Warm, humid areas	Feeds on microscopic molds that form on moist surfaces; transparent	Ventilate and dry infested areas; remove food packages and utensils; treat shelves with a household formulation of malathion; replace shelf paper
Carpet beetle	Carpets, feathers, furs, hair, silk, upholstery, wool	Feeds on lint and dead insects	Treat carpet edges and empty clothes closets with a household formulation of diazinon or malathion labeled safe for carpet, upholstery, and fabric; vacuum dust- and lint-prone areas frequently (empty infested contents immediately); remove dead insects; repel with mothballs or moth crystals
Cockroach	Moist, warm, dark areas	Feeds on glue, starch, food, and garbage; nocturnal	Treat cracks and crevices with a household formulation of chlorpyrifos, diazinon, or propoxur; set feeding traps containing amidinohydrazone; sprinkle boric acid powder in kitchen and bathroom cabinets out of reach of children and pets; for serious infestations, call an exterminator

To stop ants from invading the house, sprinkle a few crumbled bay leaves on windowsills. If ants flock to your flour and sugar bins, place a couple of bay leaves inside. Replace them every month.

Avoid using so-called all-purpose pesticides. They may lack the ingredient needed to kill a specific insect. Get advice about the right pesticide from a horticultural center or the local branch of your provincial agriculture department.

If there's no bug spray on hand when a flying insect attacks, use hair spray as a substitute. It immobilizes the bug's wings, making the target easier to swat.

COMMON HOUSEHOLD PESTS		(not shown lifesize)	
Pest	**Habitat**	**Comments**	**Controls**
Flour beetle and flour moth Larvae (wormlike)	Flour, grain, bird seed, pet food	Throw away all infested foods; store fresh supplies in tightly closed plastic or metal containers	Clean shelves thoroughly; remove food packages and utensils; brush or spray corners and crevices with a household formulation of diazinon, malathion, or propoxur
Housefly	Food, garbage, and decaying organic matter, such as manure or cut grass	Spreads diseases harmful to humans and animals	Treat with space spray containing pyrethrum or resmethrin; hang chemically treated pest strips indoors (follow package directions); use fly swatter; screen doors and windows; seal garbage containers
Mosquito	Stagnant water	Adult females feed on human and animal blood; some types transmit disease	Treat with space spray containing pyrethrum; hang chemically treated pest strips indoors (follow package directions); drain stagnant water; apply insect repellent to skin; screen doors and windows
Silverfish	Cool, damp areas, such as basements	Feeds on starches, including glue and paste; nocturnal	Treat cracks and openings around wall pipes with a household formulation of diazinon, malathion, or propoxur
Spider	Spins webs in corners and crevices	Feeds on insects; harmless, except for black widow and brown recluse varieties	Remove webs and spiders with broom or vacuum with dusting brush attachment; treat with a household formulation of diazinon, malathion, or propoxur
Wasp, hornet	Attics, porch ceilings, roof overhangs, trees; mud tubes on siding; holes in ground	Hazardous to humans allergic to their sting	Treat outdoor nests at night during cool weather with a commercial wasp and hornet spray or a household formulation of carbaryl, malathion, or propoxur; hang chemically treated pest strips in enclosed spaces (follow package directions)

Ticks can easily fall off your pet and hide in the crevices and baseboards of your house. If you suspect this has happened, spray the area with a household formulation of malathion or diazinon.

To discourage bats from entering the house, screen all openings larger than ¼ inch in diameter and sprinkle naphthalene flakes in confined areas. If a bat has entered a room, open the windows and any doors to the outside just before dark; then turn out all the house lights. Once the bat exits, close windows and doors.

If a chipmunk or squirrel strays into the house, set up a live-animal trap baited with dry peanuts. Release the captured animal into the woods.

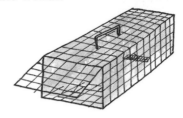

To keep mice from becoming trap shy, bait unset traps for 2 or 3 days, using bacon fat, peanut butter, raisins, or cheese. Secure them with thread or wire. Then, to avoid catching your fingers, use a pencil to move the set, freshly baited traps near the wall.

SECURING YOUR HOME

The view afforded by your door's peephole should be as wide as possible. Install a model with a 180-degree fish-eye lens. Or attach a curved mirror to a wall or tree opposite the peephole.

Locks are only as strong as the material they're attached to. Replace hollow exterior doors with solid-core or metal doors. When installing locks on window frames, use screws long enough to penetrate the studs behind the frames.

Because basement windows are often obscured by shrubbery and because they lead to an area of the house that's seldom occupied, they're a favorite access point for burglars. Keep these windows locked whenever possible.

Burglaries committed in occupied homes are not as rare as you might expect. Keep your doors locked even when you're home.

WHEN USING PESTICIDES

DO

Read and follow package directions and warnings carefully.

Mix pesticides in a well-ventilated area.

Wear rubber gloves.

Keep pesticides in original containers that are tightly closed and clearly labeled.

Store pesticides in a locked, well-ventilated area, away from heat and direct sunlight.

Wrap empty containers in thick layers of newspaper before discarding them.

Exhaust all gas from pressurized cans before disposing of them.

Remove food, utensils, pets, and their dishes before spraying indoors.

DON'T

Use pesticides near children or domestic animals.

Smoke, eat, drink, or chew gum.

Inhale sprays, dusts, or vapors.

Store pesticides near food.

Dump pesticides in places where they could endanger fish or wildlife or contaminate water.

Reenter a treated room for ½ hour after it has been sprayed.

For greater security and convenience, equip each exterior door with one or two high-quality, pick-resistant locks rather than a series of standard or cheap ones.

If you are worried about break-ins, install locks on doors leading to the basement, garage, and storage room. Secure the doors with a dead bolt lock rather than a latch lock. The dead bolt should be 1 inch thick and have a throw of 1 inch.

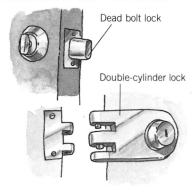

Dead bolt lock

Double-cylinder lock

For doors with a window or a mail slot, use a double-cylinder lock that requires a key to unlock the door from either side.

The lock on the outside door of your garage or porch should be as sturdy as the one on your front door. If a burglar gains access to either one of these areas, he'll be well out of view, and free to take his time breaking into the house.

To prevent sliding glass doors from being lifted out, insert spacers or protruding screwheads in the top grooves. Place a length of pipe or a cut broom handle in the inside bottom track to prevent the door from being moved sideways.

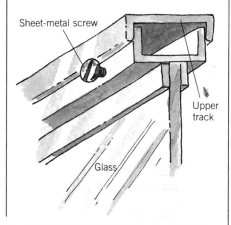

Sheet-metal screw

Upper track

Glass

SORTING OUT SECURITY SYSTEMS AND ALARMS

Even the most sophisticated electronic security system can give a false alarm, be bypassed by an expert burglar, or become worthless in a home where other precautions aren't taken. Yet of all the security measures you can take, installing an alarm system is the most effective. To determine which system is best suited for your home, ask your local police department to conduct a free survey of your property.

Type	How it works	Advantages	Disadvantages
System			
Perimeter (protects boundaries)	Alarm is activated by a break in an electric circuit that connects all windows and doors	Inexpensive; easy to install; visible deterrent	Easily penetrated by an expert burglar
Motion detectors (protects interior)	Alarm is activated by motion registered by infrared beams, ultrasonic waves, sensitive microphones, or pressure-sensitive mats	Difficult to spot and elude	Easily activated by pets, children, or air conditioners
Alarm			
Local	On-site alarm and flashing lights are activated	Sudden, conspicuous noise and light deter intruder	Ineffective if no one is nearby; often goes off when no intruder is present
Central	Switchboard operator is alerted to call home, office, or police	Reduces false alarms	Provides extended time for intruder to act and escape
Police hookup	Police switchboard operator is alerted to dispatch unit	Provides fast assistance	Frequent false alarms may incur fines

Here's how to make a double-hung window extra-secure. With the window closed tightly, drill a hole through the top of the lower sash into the bottom of the upper sash. Insert a nail whose shank is long enough to penetrate the entire thickness, but narrow enough to remove easily when you wish to open the window.

TAKING PRECAUTIONS

Before you move into a new house or apartment, have the cylinders of each door lock changed.

Overgrown shrubbery and high hedges provide as much privacy for burglars as they do for you. Trim foliage often so that it can't camouflage a burglar's activities.

Prune tree branches and remove trellises if they provide access to second-floor windows.

In an apartment building, lock any windows or doors that lead to balconies, fire escapes, or rooftops. If you live on the first or second floor, lock all windows when you're not home.

Make your valuables harder for thieves to sell, and easier for police to find, by engraving your Social Insurance Number on them. You can borrow an engraving tool from a local police department.

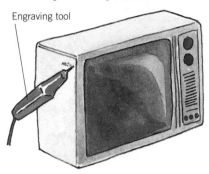

Engraving tool

If you have a telephone answering machine, don't reveal your name, whereabouts, or any other personal information on the recorded message. Say simply that you can't come to the phone right now, but will return the call as soon as possible.

A family dog is one of the best burglar alarms you can have. The sound of loud, frantic barking is often all that's needed to discourage a would-be intruder and alert family members and neighbors.

Whether you're planning an evening out or an extended vacation, invest in an automatic timer to create the illusion that someone is home. Use it to activate those items, such as lamps, TV's, and radios, that will make the house appear occupied.

When leaving town for an extended absence, ask a friend, neighbor, or relative to park a car in the driveway, mow the grass, shovel snow, and put out garbage on pickup days. Also, arrange to have mail and newspaper deliveries halted until you return.

Those Wonderful Appliances

SELECTING A REFRIGERATOR OR FREEZER

How large should your refrigerator be? Plan on 8 cubic feet for two people plus 1 cubic foot for each additional person in your household. Add 2 more cubic feet if you do a lot of entertaining.

Before buying a refrigerator, check the shelving and its organization. Glass shelves are easy to clean but breakable; wire-grille types are durable, but let food fall through. Half-width shelves make it easier to store awkward items.

A refrigerator with a freezer and main compartment that are side by side usually provides more freezer space than a unit with a freezer at the top. But a side-by-side's narrow shelves can be a problem if you have to store large or bulky items. Also, it uses about 15 to 20 percent more energy.

Confused by the various defrosting claims? With cycle defrosting, the refrigerator compartment defrosts itself, but you have to defrost the freezer. On a frost-free model, both compartments defrost themselves. However, these units, also called no-front, frostless, or fully automatic, use more electricity.

Which freezer style is best? Depends on your needs. A chest uses less energy because its cold air, which is heavier than warm air, stays inside when you open the top. But an upright takes up less floor space. And since its contents are easier to reach, you probably won't keep the door open as long when you look for food.

HOW LONG WILL YOU HAVE AN APPLIANCE?

Knowing how many years you're likely to keep an appliance helps you to compare models more accurately than if you base your purchasing decision on just the initial cost. With a major appliance, first find the estimated yearly cost on the appliance's energy guide label, then multiply that yearly cost by the appliance's estimated life. Add the result to the purchase price and you will have a good approximation of the appliance's true cost.

Average first-use life of appliance in years

Blender	8	Dishwasher	11	Mixer	9
Broiler oven	9	Food processor	8	Stove (electric or gas)	15
Clothes dryer (electric)	13	Freezer	15	Refrigerator	13
Clothes dryer (gas)	14	Garbage disposer	10	Toaster	8
Clothes washer	12	Humidifier	8	Garbage compactor	10
Coffee maker (drip)	3	Iron	9	Water heater (electric)	12
Coffee maker (percolator)	6	Microwave oven	11	Water heater (gas)	10

INSTALLING AND MOVING A REFRIGERATOR OR FREEZER

Consider a refrigerator with casters. You'll find that rolling it rather than pushing it to clean underneath is much easier on you and the kitchen floor. But don't get casters if you have a soft vinyl floor covering; they'll leave imprints on the vinyl.

Locate your refrigerator or freezer away from direct sunlight or from a heat source, such as a stove, dishwasher, or heating vent.

Don't put your refrigerator in an unheated space either. At room temperatures below 60° F a unit won't run often enough to keep food properly cold.

Don't blow a fuse or trip a circuit breaker and end up with spoiled food. Always plug a refrigerator or freezer into a 15-ampere circuit with nothing else on it. The outlet should accept a grounded three-prong plug. If you must use an extension cord, it should be a heavy-duty three-wire cord.

Lay a carpenter's level on top of a a new or relocated unit to make sure that it's level. If it isn't, tilt the unit back and prop it with a wood block. Then screw the leveling legs in or out a few turns, remove the block, and check again. Consult your owner's manual to adjust casters or a different type of legs.

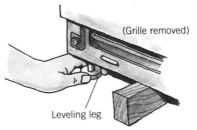

(Grille removed)

Leveling leg

When you open a refrigerator door to a 45-degree angle and let go, it should shut itself. If it doesn't, adjust its legs so that the refrigerator tilts back slightly.

Before transporting a refrigerator or a freezer, turn it off for a day. Take out all removable parts. Secure the doors with rope. Move it upright; not on its side or back.

To move a refrigerator without casters, tilt it and slip pieces of carpet scrap, pile side down, under the front and back legs.

Carpet scrap

If your refrigerator has an automatic ice maker, the water tube attached to it limits how far you can pull the unit from the wall.

When discarding an old refrigerator or freezer, remove the doors to prevent a child from crawling in and getting trapped.

When storing a freezer or refrigerator, secure the door with strong tape or rope. To prevent mildew, however, use a wood block to keep the door open a crack.

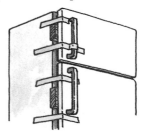

GET THE MOST FROM YOUR REFRIGERATOR AND FREEZER

A refrigerator or freezer operates most efficiently when fully loaded, but be sure to leave enough space between items for air to circulate. In a refrigerator's freezer compartment, take care not to cover any vents that send cold air to the refrigerator compartment.

Keep a refrigerator between 34° F and 40° F. Keep a freezer close to 0° F. To check a refrigerator's setting, leave a refrigerator-freezer thermometer in a glass of water overnight. To check a freezer, stick the thermometer in ice cream or between frozen-food packages.

Refrigerator-freezer
thermometer

Here's a more casual way to check that all's well: Your milk is cold without crystals and ice cream is firmly solid but not brick-hard.

Is sweat forming on the outside of your freezer? You may have set the unit at an unnecessarily low temperature; 0° F is adequate. If conditions are humid, try blowing a small fan across the surface. If the problem occurs in a chronically damp place, such as a basement, a dehumidifier will help.

A power-saver switch on a refrigerator saves energy when it's off. It controls small electric heaters that keep the outside of the cabinet from sweating. Turn it on during humid periods, but keep it on *Off* during dry weather.

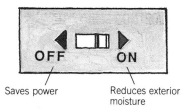

Saves power   Reduces exterior
                     moisture

STORING FOOD CORRECTLY

Control refrigerator odor! To prevent odors from spreading, make sure all food is wrapped, covered, or bagged in plastic. The only exception is the fruits and vegetables stored in crisper drawers. And in a frost-free, bag those too; otherwise they'll dry out.

Before refrigerating any liquid, put it in a tightly sealed container. Moisture that evaporates inside a refrigerator just makes the unit work harder.

To cool food quickly before freezing (and to reduce energy costs), set hot pans in ice water. Wrap the food and freeze it at once.

When stocking an empty freezer, add 3 pounds or less of unfrozen food per cubic foot of space each day until the freezer is full. This will allow the food to freeze quickly and thoroughly, retarding the growth of bacteria.

Keep a freezer inventory list. It cuts the time you keep the freezer door open looking for food and helps you use older items first. For freezer storage times, see p.358.

DEFROSTING

Defrost a refrigerator or a freezer when the frost is ¼ inch thick.

Scraping frost with a sharp utensil can cause serious damage. Use a dull plastic scraper instead and don't scrape against metal parts.

After defrosting, dip a cloth in glycerin and wipe the freezer coils with it. The frost will come off more easily next defrosting.

To free a stuck ice-cube tray, apply a towel soaked in hot water to its edges for a few seconds.

REFRIGERATOR TROUBLES

Is your door's gasket tight? To check, put a 150-watt outdoor flood lamp inside and aim the light at one side at a time with the cord coming out the other. With the kitchen lights off, close the door and look for light leaks.

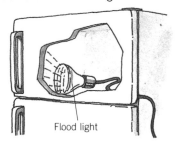

Flood light

REPLACING A REFRIGERATOR DOOR GASKET

If the rubber gasket on a refrigerator door is torn or badly worn and doesn't seal tightly, you should replace it. This can be tricky because the screws that hold the gasket also hold the door's inner panel and insulation in place. To avoid having the door come apart, work on one section at a time and loosen the screws only partway. If the door does becomes misaligned, you may have to repeat Step 3 below a few times to straighten it.

Get a new gasket that fits your door's exact size from an appliance dealer. Or get replacement gaskets in L-shaped sections at a hardware store; you cut these to size and install the magnet strips from the old gasket in them. Soak the gasket in hot tap water for a few minutes to make it pliable and to remove the crimps.

The gasket shown is the most common type. If yours differs, consult your dealer about the replacement procedure. Most gaskets are held on by hex-head screws that you remove with a nut driver of the appropriate size.

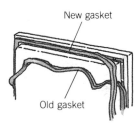

New gasket

Old gasket

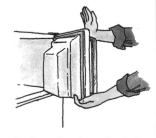

1. Starting at a top corner, fold out the old gasket and loosen the screws along half of the top and half of the side. Loosen the screws only as much as you need to pull the gasket from under the metal retainer strip.

2. Pull the old gasket out of the way. Then attach the new one by pushing its lip under the metal retainer and retightening the screws. Replace the other top corner section and then each bottom one in the same way.

3. Close the door. Check for gaps between the gasket and the frame, indicating door warp. If necessary, reloosen screws and straighten the door by pushing at the top and pulling at the bottom, or vice versa.

A poor gasket seal can often be corrected by simply adjusting the refrigerator's leveling legs (p. 132).

Are there black specks in the cubes made by an automatic ice maker? They indicate that the coating on the tray that molds the cubes is disintegrating and needs to be replaced. Hard water is probably the culprit.

If you find discolored water in your frost-free's drain pan, don't worry. A spill was probably washed into the pan by defrost water.

To fix a sagging door, loosen the hinge screws at the top of the door, using a nut driver. Then lift the door into position and retighten the hinge screws.

REFRIGERATORS: WHAT TO CHECK BEFORE CALLING FOR SERVICE

Problem	Possible cause	Possible solution
Unit doesn't run; light inside is off	Power cord disconnected	Plug in cord
	Tripped circuit breaker or blown fuse	Check that no other appliance is operating on same circuit. Then reset circuit breaker or replace fuse
	Faulty power cord	Unplug. Remove back panel and check all of cord. If needed, remove screws holding cord and test it (Step 2, p.160). If faulty, install an exact replacement. Be sure to connect grounding wire
Unit doesn't run; light inside goes on	Temperature control turned off	Check control and reset it
Noisy operation	Loose shelf; touching food containers hitting one another	Open door and wait for unit to turn on. Listen and look for noisy items
	Rattling defrost drain pan	Remove base grille. Reglue any felt pads that have fallen off. Make sure pan rests securely on its tracks
	Refrigerator not level	Test with a level; adjust legs (p.132)
	Paper caught in condenser fan blade	Disconnect power and remove paper
Unit runs longer than usual	Hot, humid weather; large amounts of warm food in unit	It's normal for a unit to run longer under these conditions
	Door opened frequently	Plan ahead; open door once to remove all the items for a meal
	Condenser coils under refrigerator clogged with dust	Vacuum the coils
	Door gasket not sealing	Replace gasket (see facing page)
	Light stays on when door is shut	Open door and press door switch. If light stays on, remove bulb until you can get switch replaced
Unit not cold enough	Temperature control not set properly	Reset. Consult instructions on unit or in owner's manual
	Not enough air circulating to coils on back of unit	Make sure unit is 4 inches from wall; remove any paper or other items caught in coils

NOTE: Any cause that makes a unit run longer can also keep it from cooling properly

If water puddles under your frost-free's vegetable and meat drawers, the drain may be clogged. If there's a drain cup, remove and wash it. Then use a meat baster to shoot hot water through the drain tube into the drain pan.

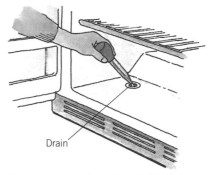

Drain

Frost in your frost-free? Check the defrost timer behind the grille. With the refrigerator running, use a screwdriver to turn the slotted knob slowly clockwise until you hear a click and the refrigerator goes off. Wait 5 minutes for defrost water to appear in the drain pan. If the frost doesn't melt or if the problem recurs, call for service.

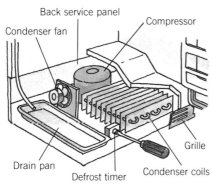

Back service panel
Compressor
Condenser fan
Grille
Drain pan
Defrost timer
Condenser coils

SELECTING A STOVE

Gas or electric? Generally a gas stove costs less to operate, has fewer breakdowns, and allows faster control of the top burners' heat. An electric stove usually operates more cleanly and efficiently, giving off less waste heat.

A freestanding stove or built-ins? A model that stands alone is cheaper to install and easier to move. A separate built-in cooktop and oven allows greater flexibility in planning a kitchen, but requires all new cabinetry.

Look for features that will avoid or aid cleanups. Among them are a lipped cooktop that stops spills from running down the front and sides of the stove, and a lift-up or removable top that allows below-surface access for easy cleaning.

Depending on whether you use them or not, some features may be an added convenience or an unnecessary expense. These include a clock, extra indicator lights, oven window, and griddle, grill, and rotisserie accessories.

Whenever possible, get a stove hood with a multispeed fan that blows fumes and other cooking odors outdoors through a vent. If you can only have a nonvented hood, get one with a charcoal filter. Replace the filter each year.

Ever heard of a downdraft cooktop? It has a built-in venting system that draws smoke downward before expelling it outdoors. It's a wise choice for a kitchen where you can't easily install a hood.

CONTINUOUS-CLEANING OR SELF-CLEANING OVEN?

Both of these automatic oven-cleaning systems can relieve you of a thankless, messy task on either a gas or electric stove, but each does it in a different way. A continuous-cleaning (catalytic) oven has a special rough-textured porcelain lining. Spills and splatters spread over this material and gradually burn off as you use the oven. The lining's speckled appearance helps hide the soil while it burns off, but the oven may not always look as clean as you would like.

A continuous-cleaning oven costs only slightly more to buy than a regular oven. And because it cleans while you use the oven, it costs nothing more to operate. It consumes extra energy only when heavy baked-on deposits must be burned off at 400° F or more with the oven empty. But you can often eliminate this by always wiping up large spills as soon as the oven cools. Starchy and sugary spills especially need to be wiped up; the system doesn't remove them as well as it does greasy soil. Because scrubbing the spe-

cial lining or applying oven cleaner to it will damage it, many stoves have a standard porcelain finish on the oven floor and door so that such spills can be cleaned in the normal fashion.

A self-cleaning (pyrolytic) oven has a special cleaning cycle. It lasts about 1½ hours and raises the temperature to nearly 900° F, incinerating spills and splatters. Before next using the oven, you just run a damp cloth over the oven floor to collect the fine gray ash that remains. On some models you can also put the reflector or burner bowls from the cooktop in the oven and clean them too.

Surprisingly, an oven that self-cleans doesn't use a lot of energy, because it's heavily insulated. Indeed, a cleaning cycle costs less than the chemical oven cleaner that you'd need for a standard oven. The insulation saves energy during cooking and lets you bake or roast without overheating the kitchen, but it does reduce oven size. You can't use an oven during the self-cleaning process.

GAS STOVE CONSIDERATIONS

A pilotless electric ignition system uses a spark or a red-hot coil to ignite the gas when you turn on a burner. It uses 30 percent less energy than a pilot light.

If you're moving to an area without natural gas, bear in mind that a service technician can convert almost any gas stove to burn LPG (liquefied petroleum gas).

When you're shopping for a gas stove, check whether the oven floor is removable. It'll be a lot easier to clean if it is.

If you make soups and stews often, look for a thermostatically controlled burner. It controls the flame precisely for a perfect simmer.

ELECTRIC STOVE CONSIDERATIONS

On an electric stove, check that the cooktop elements plug in (so that you can remove them for cleaning) and that the bake element in the oven bottom lifts up (so that you can wipe up spills).

Do you do a lot of baking and need a steady temperature? Consider an electronic temperature control. It keeps an oven within 5° F of the setting; a regular thermostat may allow up to 25° F variation.

For the most even baking, get a convection oven. It has a fan that circulates heated air, which eliminates any hot and cold spots. This usually speeds up cooking too, so be sure to follow the baking times given in the owner's guide.

137

SAVING ENERGY ON YOUR COOKTOP

Adjust a gas burner's flame so that it just touches or is lower than a pot's bottom. A flame that curls around a pot wastes energy.

On an electric stove, put a pan on a cooking element that's the same size or slightly smaller than the utensil's bottom. Make sure the bottom is absolutely flat so that it's in full contact with the element.

Put your burner or element control on a high setting when you begin cooking a dish; then turn it lower to finish. In fact, turn off an electric element a minute or two before the food is done and let the residual heat complete the cooking.

On an electric stove, the oven vent is usually under a burner. Use that burner to keep a dish warm when the oven is on. You can locate the vent by the heat it gives off when the oven is hot.

Use a pressure cooker. It cuts cooking time on the stove top by almost two-thirds, and it beats a microwave at cooking tough cuts of meat and large quantities of food. It's especially good if you live at a high altitude and have to extend cooking times to make up for lower boiling temperatures.

SAVING ENERGY IN AN OVEN

Arrange racks in an oven before you turn it on. It not only saves heat; it's a whole lot safer.

If a roast or a casserole will cook for more than an hour, start it in a cold oven and cook it for the prescribed time. If the time is under an hour, extend it slightly. Reserve preheating for baking.

Cook small quantities of food in a microwave oven rather than in an electric oven. A microwave can use one-third to one-half as much energy as an electric oven. But always use a stove oven for large quantities of food.

ADJUSTING YOUR OVEN'S TEMPERATURE CONTROL

To test your oven, place an oven thermometer in its center, set the oven for 350° F, and run it for 20 minutes. To get the most accurate readings, use an oven thermometer with a mercury-filled column. They are stocked by kitchen specialty shops and are great baking aids too.

To adjust the thermostat on many ovens, pull off the temperature control knob and look on its underside. Loosen any screws (or clips) and adjust the disc. A notch usually represents 10 degrees. If you have to move more than two notches, have the thermostat replaced.

For other ovens, pull off the temperature control knob and turn the screw inside the knob's hollow shaft. Turning it clockwise lowers the setting; counterclockwise raises it. If it requires an adjustment of more than 25 degrees, about an eighth of a turn, have the thermostat replaced.

Put as many dishes in an oven at once as you can. If the recipe temperatures differ, just adjust their times. If you have three dishes that require 325° F, 350° F, and 375° F, set the oven for 350° F. Then cut a few minutes from the 325° F dish and add a few to the 375° F dish. Leave 1 or 2 inches of space around each dish.

If you have dishes, such as several sheets of cookies, that you can't bake at the same time, do them in quick succession.

Keep track of cooking time with a timer. Don't keep peeking into an oven. Each peek can cost as much as 25° F; it can also affect browning and baking.

If possible, start the self-cleaning cycle of an oven while it's still warm from cooking.

COOKING SAFELY

Use only dry pot holders. A damp pot holder transmits heat. Also avoid using dish towels. They're not thick enough to protect you.

Dress safely when you cook. A loose sleeve could hook a pot handle, or a dangling scarf could brush a burner. Wear close-fitting clothes or an apron.

Turn pot and pan handles so that they are over the center or sides of the stove. Don't place handles over an adjacent burner where they can get hot and burn you or over the front where someone can bump into them.

IF YOU SMELL GAS

If you smell a heavy gas odor, immediately turn off any flames, open the windows and doors, and get everyone out of the house. If your stove's shutoff valve isn't within easy reach, turn off your home's main gas shutoff valve at the meter or liquefied petroleum gas tank. Do not touch a light switch, pick up a telephone, or make any electrical connection that could create a spark. If you need light, use a flashlight. Report the leak to your gas company or your gas supplier from a neighbor's telephone.

The shutoff valve on a gas stove or oven is located near the point where the gas line enters—usually under the cooktop. If yours isn't there, consult your owner's manual or call your appliance dealer. On some models it's under the broiler drawer.

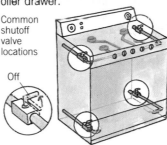

Common shutoff valve locations

Off

If you notice a faint scent of gas, check for a burner flame or a pilot light that has blown out. Check the oven also. If you're not cooking, perhaps a pilot light has gone out. Turn off any flames and air out the room. Relight the burner or pilot only after all gas odor is gone. If any odor persists after you've aired out the room, turn off the gas at your home's main shutoff valve and call the gas company.

When ventilating a room, keep in mind that natural gas is lighter than air and collects in the upper part of the room; liquefied petroleum gas sinks to the floor.

For your kitchen, get a dry chemical or foam fire extinguisher approved for fires ranked Class B (grease and other flammable liquids) and Class C (electrical).

STOVE PROBLEMS

Before repairing an electric stove turn off the power at the fuse box or circuit breaker (p.163).

To remove a cooktop element, lift the edge just enough to clear the reflector. Then pull it straight out.

Always open and close an electric stove's lift-up cooktop carefully to avoid pulling or crimping wires that carry current to the elements.

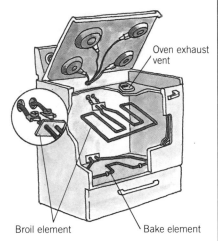

Oven exhaust vent

Broil element   Bake element

To replace a broil or bake element, turn off the power (p.163), and remove the screws holding its front and rear brackets. (For some bake elements you needn't detach the front bracket.) Then carefully pull the element forward and unscrew the wires leading to it.

ELECTRIC STOVES: WHAT TO CHECK BEFORE CALLING FOR SERVICE

Caution: Before making any repair to a stove, shut off the power to it by removing the fuse or turning off the circuit breaker (p.163). Let a heat element cool completely before touching it.

Problem	Possible cause	Possible solution
No cooktop or oven elements will go on; lights and timers are out	No power to stove	Check for a blown fuse or a tripped circuit breaker (p.163)
One cooktop element won't go on	Burned-out element	Before replacing element, try it in receptacle for a same-size element or have repair shop test it
	Faulty receptacle for element	Remove element; clean contacts if dark and corroded. Check receptacle with a flashlight; if blackened and corroded, have it replaced
One oven element goes on; the other doesn't	Burned-out element	Remove element (see above); have repair shop test it
Oven won't go on	Oven set to come on automatically at a specific time	Switch the automatic-manual control to *Manual*
Oven dishes are burned or undercooked	Temperature control set too high or low	Recheck recipe temperatures and times
	Temperature control incorrect	Readjust temperature control (p.138)
	Food dishes blocking air circulation	Space dishes at least 1 in. apart

GAS RANGES: WHAT TO CHECK BEFORE CALLING FOR SERVICE

Problem	Possible cause	Possible solution
Cooktop burner won't light	Pilot light out	Relight pilot (see below); stop any drafts that may have blown it out
	Gas supply off	If other burners and gas appliances won't light, call your utility company
	Dirty spark igniter	Clean igniter (see owner's manual)
Burner flames are uneven	Clogged burner	Clean holes in burner (see below)
Yellow burner flame, soot on pot bottoms	Not enough air in gas-air mixture	Open the air shutter as needed (see below)
High, hissing burner flame	Too much air in gas-air mixture	Close the air shutter as needed (see below)
Oven won't light; top burners work	Pilot light out	Relight pilot following directions in owner's manual
	Electric ignition not working	Make sure power to range is on
	Oven set to come on automatically at a specific time	Switch automatic-manual control to *Manual*

If a spot on an electric cooktop element glows brighter than the rest of it, the element may be failing. Replace it before overheating at the bright spot damages your pots. The same is true of a broil or bake element in the oven.

If the holes in a gas burner become clogged, clean them with a straight pin or pipe cleaner. Avoid toothpicks, which may break off and plug the hole.

If a power failure knocks out your gas stove's electric igniter, start a burner by holding a match to it and turning the control to *High*.

If a knob won't pull off, just slip a piece of cloth under the bottom edge and pull.

Does oil collect on one side of the frying pan? Do cakes rise unevenly? Your stove is probably not level. Check it with a spirit level. You can level an electric stove as you would a refrigerator (p. 132), but a gas stove should be leveled by a service technician.

FLAME ADJUSTMENT ON A GAS STOVE

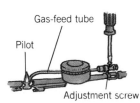

Gas-feed tube
Pilot
Adjustment screw

Air-shutter screw
Shutter

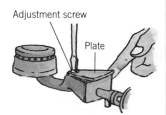

Adjustment screw
Plate

To relight a pilot, turn the screw on its gas-feed tube counterclockwise slightly. Hold a match to the pilot, and turn the screw clockwise until the flame is ¼ inch high. A pilot that's too high can damage the cooktop.

To regulate a burner on a range that has a barrel-shaped chamber for mixing air with the gas going to the burner, loosen the air-shutter screw. Then open or close the shutter by rotating it. Retighten the screw.

On other ranges the mixing chamber is triangular shaped and covered by a flat plate. To regulate the burner, loosen the screw holding the plate and pivot the plate from side to side. Then retighten the screw.

SELECTING A DISHWASHER

If buying and installing a built-in dishwasher is too expensive, consider a portable. It can be almost as easy to use, especially if you have a convenient place to store it between uses. And like all portable appliances, it can go with you if you move.

Are you delaying purchasing a dishwasher until you remodel or move? Get a convertible model, which you can use as a portable now and later have built in.

To save energy, get a dishwasher with a booster heater that automatically heats hot water from your water heater to the temperature required to clean dishes. It saves energy by letting you keep the water heater at a lower temperature. It's also your best bet if you live in an apartment and can't control water temperature.

LOADING A DISHWASHER

Don't bother to rinse dishes before loading them. The machine's water system pulverizes and flushes away food particles. But it's not a waste disposer; scrape off bones and large quantities of food. Just empty glasses and cups.

Put pots and baking dishes with heavy or encrusted residue in the lower rack facing down toward the spray arm. Make sure pot handles are secure and can't drop down and block the spray arm.

Put large platters or cookie sheets in the back or on the sides. In the front, they can keep water from reaching the detergent dispenser and the silverware basket.

A dishwasher can't clean everything. If a pot has burned-on or charred food, the only way to get it clean is to wash it by hand.

Use the top rack for smaller and lighter items, including plastics rated dishwasher-safe. Put cups and glasses between or over the prongs; don't let them hang loosely on prongs. Never wash glasses or fragile glassware in the bottom.

To keep lightweight items, such as plastic cups, from flipping over, put them in the top rack's corners where the water spray is weakest. Sometimes you can anchor them between heavier objects or fit them snugly over two prongs.

Silverware cleans best when you put it in the basket with the handles downward. But for safety point sharp knives down. Just be careful not to let a thin knife stick through the basket bottom and stop the spray arm.

SAVING ENERGY WITH YOUR DISHWASHER

Always wash full loads. A dishwasher uses the same amount of hot water and energy whether it's half-filled or fully loaded. Use the rinse-and-hold cycle when you don't have a full load.

Let your dishes air-dry. If your machine doesn't have an *Energy Saver* switch to stop heated drying, just wait for the final rinse to end, then release the door latch and turn the control knob to *Off*. Wait a few minutes for the steam inside to subside, then open the door and pull the top rack out partway to hold it open.

GETTING THE MOST FROM DISHWATER DETERGENT

Fill a detergent dispenser just before washing. Left standing, detergent absorbs moisture, cakes, and loses its cleaning power.

Are you wasting detergent? Experiment to see how much you really need to get dishes clean. Try filling the dispenser only halfway if you live in a soft-water area and three-quarters in an area with moderately hard water. Use a full dispenser only in a hardwater region. For more on hard water, see p.281.

DISHES NOT GETTING CLEAN?

Make sure your water is hot. Put a glass in the sink and run hot water into it for a few minutes. Then put a candy or meat thermometer in it. If the temperature is not between 140° F and 160° F, adjust your water heater.

If your water heater is not near your kitchen, run the hot-water tap in the sink until the water is hot before starting the dishwasher.

Do your dishes seem less clean in cold weather? The water temperature may be dropping as it flows from the water heater. Insulate exposed pipes and turn up the water heater in winter.

Taking a shower, running a load of clothes, or watering the lawn while using the dishwasher can also result in uncleaned dishes. When the water pressure drops too low, the dishwasher doesn't get enough water during the time allotted to filling.

SPOTS AND STAINS

Black marks on china are probably the result of metal utensils rubbing on the china. Separate metal items from china. Secure lightweight aluminum pans between heavier pans so that they can't bounce around.

Is there a film on your dishes? Check that the water is hot. Also try using more detergent or a new brand. To remove the film, open the dishwasher after the rinse phase, remove all metal items, and set a bowl containing 2 cups of white vinegar on the bottom rack. Then wash and rinse again.

If your glassware has become etched with a film that you can't rub off, the damage is permanent. To avoid the etching of other glasses, try using less detergent and loading fewer dishes. Another possible cause is low water pressure, which prevents the machine from filling completely.

To prevent pitting on silverware, rinse it before you put it in the machine whenever you're going to delay washing. Don't sprinkle detergent on silver.

Find water spots on your dishes? Use a rinse agent. It causes water to flow off the dishes in sheets. If your unit doesn't have a dispenser for liquid rinse agent, get a rinse agent in a solid bar that hooks onto the upper rack.

A DISHWASHER IN DISTRESS

Yellow or brown stains on your machine's interior (and on dishes) indicate iron in the water. To remove stains, stop the machine after it fills for the wash and add ½ cup citric acid crystals. Or try a compound that appliance dealers sell to remove rust from a water softener's resin and follow directions. To stop staining, install an iron filter in your water supply.

DISHWASHERS: WHAT TO CHECK BEFORE CALLING FOR SERVICE

Problem	Possible cause	Possible solution
Dishwasher won't run	No power to unit	Check for blown fuse or tripped circuit breaker (p.163); check that portable unit is plugged in
	Door not latched	Make sure door is fully latched
	Jammed or stiff door latch is not engaging door switch	Try opening and closing door a few times
	Cycle-selecting button not depressed	Push button all the way in
Dishwasher doesn't fill	Water cutoff valve closed	Open the valve located under sink on the water line going to the dishwasher
	Float stuck in up position	Clear obstructions under the float
Dishwasher doesn't drain	Clogged filter screen	Clean filter screen (p.145)
Dishes aren't completely clean	Water not hot enough	Test water temperature (p.143) and reset water heater's thermostat
	Clogged spray arm or filter screen	Clean spray arm and filter screen (p.145)
	Detergent dispenser not dumping	Move any dish or pan obstructing dispenser operation. Open front panel of door (see owner's manual) and check dispenser mechanism for a broken spring or lever or for corrosion
Dishes don't dry	Water not hot enough	Test water temperature (p.143) and reset water heater's thermostat
	Water not draining	Check for a clogged filter screen (p.145)
Dishwasher leaks from door vent	Improperly loaded dishes deflecting water through vent	Reload dishes following instructions in owner's manual
Dishwasher leaks from bottom of door	Oversudsing	Don't use a nondishwasher detergent. Don't prerinse dishes in liquid detergent
	Door gasket is worn or cracked	Replace gasket; some pop in, others are held by screws or clips (see owner's manual)
Dishwasher is noisy	Spray arm hitting dishes	Reload so that spray arm can rotate freely; check loading guidelines in owner's manual
	Low water pressure prevents machine from filling completely	Don't use house water supply while dishwasher is filling
	Silverware or broken dishware in bottom of tub	Remove piece; let heating element cool completely before reaching in tub
	Dishes bouncing around	When loading dishes, make sure lightweight items are held firmly in place

Is there a chalky deposit in your dishwasher? Start the machine without dishes or detergent on a rinse-and-hold cycle. During the fill, add 1 cup white vinegar and let the machine finish the cycle. Then add detergent and run the empty machine through a cycle.

If a dish rack sticks, its rollers may be jammed. Turn them by hand to loosen them. If they are worn and no longer round, replace them. Some can be removed by taking out screws; most simply pull off.

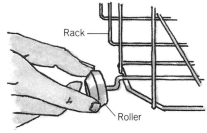
Rack
Roller

If a rack sticks because it's bent, replace it. On many machines, you lift out a rack simply by pulling and tilting it. On others, you have to take out the pins that hold it to its slides.

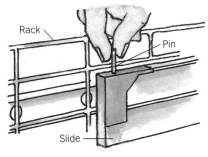
Rack
Pin
Slide

Are the prongs on a rack chipped? Appliance parts dealers stock repair kits containing rubber tips that glue over the damaged ends.

To tell whether a spray arm is rotating, note its position and start the washer. Then stop the machine and see if it has moved.

To clean a spray arm, remove the racks, unscrew the hub cap holding the arm, and lift it off. Unclog the holes with stiff wire. Flush out the arm under a running faucet.

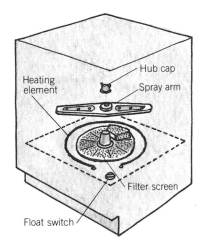
Heating element
Hub cap
Spray arm
Filter screen
Float switch

If a filter screen is clogged, remove the spray arm and any clips securing the screen. Then wash the screen under running water with a stiff brush.

GETTING A NEW CLOTHES WASHER

If you don't have space for a washer and dryer next to each other, buy units that stack or get a combination machine, which does both washing and drying.

A front-loading washer is a space saver; its top is free for work space. Also, instead of agitating, a front-loader tumbles clothes like a dryer, making it gentler on clothes and less wobbly when spinning. But most models have less capacity than a top-loader and can't clean ground-in dirt as well.

Give your washer room to vibrate. Make sure the space where you plan to put it is an inch wider all around than the machine.

If your washer's power cord won't reach an outlet, move the outlet or install a longer power cord. **Caution:** Don't use an extension cord. If water touches the connection between it and the power cord, you could be electrocuted.

Don't install a washer in an unheated garage or utility room. It can be damaged if water trapped inside freezes. A washer in an unheated vacation home should be drained completely by a service technican at summer's end.

KEEPING YOUR WASHER PROPERLY CONNECTED

A burst washer hose can flood your house. Always turn off the faucets when you finish washing. If household members tend to forget, put up a sign to remind them. Leaving the house while a washer is running invites a disaster.

Every month or so, turn the water on and run your hand over the washer hoses. Replace both hoses if you feel a bulge in either.

Hoses made by a washer's manufacturer usually resist pressure and heat better than brandless bargain replacements.

The screens that filter water going into a washer need cleaning occasionally. On some washers, just unscrew the hoses from the faucets and take them out. On others, unscrew the hoses from the washer and use a screwdriver or long-nose pliers to take them out of the washer's inlet ports. Scrub them with a toothbrush under a faucet.

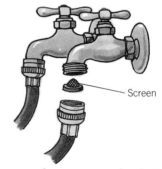

Screen

When replacing a washer's drain hose, you'll find it easier to put on the new hose if you replace the spring hose clamps with worm-drive hose clamps. Just be careful not to overtighten the new clamp.

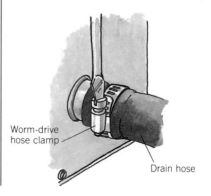

Worm-drive hose clamp

Drain hose

CONTROLLING WASHER NOISE AND VIBRATION

Does your washer wobble excessively when spinning? The cause may be an unevenly distributed load, often a large item that has wadded up to one side. Just stop the washer and redistribute the clothes for better balance.

Ordinary washer vibration can cause a machine to move and become unlevel and noisy. Periodically stop the water while the machine is filling and see if the water is even with a row of holes around the tub diameter. You can level most washers as you do refrigerators (p. 132).

If a washer that's level produces excess vibration and noise, open the top of washer and check the snubber assembly, a device that absorbs vibration. Look for a loose or broken spring. Clean and lightly sand the friction pad if the snubber sticks to the pad's surface. If necessary, replace the pad.
Caution: Unplug your washer before attempting to make any repair. Disconnect hoses if you have to move the washer.

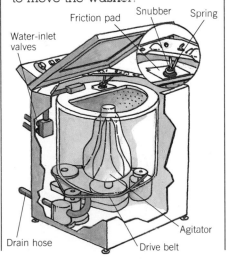
Friction pad · Snubber · Spring · Water-inlet valves · Drain hose · Agitator · Drive belt

To open the top on most washers, cover a putty knife blade with masking tape and slide it into the joint between the top and the cabinet about 2½ inches in from the edge. Then push to release a clip while pulling up on the corner. Repeat at the other corner.

Clip

When opening the top of a washer, be careful to release any hoses that are attached to the top.

OTHER WASHER PROBLEMS

Agitation or spinning problems may be caused by a loose drive belt. To test a drive belt, remove the washer's rear access panel and press the belt in. If it deflects more than ¾ inch, tighten it or, if worn, have it replaced.

To tighten a loose belt on a top-loading washer, simply loosen the motor's mounting nut and move the motor along the slotted opening, increasing tension on the belt. Then retighten the nut.

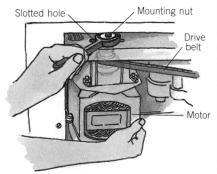
Slotted hole · Mounting nut · Drive belt · Motor

If your machine leaks, check first to see if it's a simple hose problem you can fix yourself. Run the unloaded washer through a cycle. Look for a damaged inlet hose during the fill and for a loose drain hose during the spin.

If tears or snags appear in clothes after washing, wrap an old nylon stocking around your hand and slowly rub it around the washer tub and agitator to find any sharp edges or rough spots. Smooth them with fine sandpaper.

Did you find a cracked or broken vane on an agitator? Replace the agitator or it'll tear your clothes. A loose, worn agitator can also produce tears on your clothes.

To remove a washer's agitator, take off any softener dispenser and unscrew the agitator cap. If the agitator won't lift off easily, fill the tub with hot water. If it still won't come off, place a block of wood next to it and tap it gently with a hammer to loosen it.

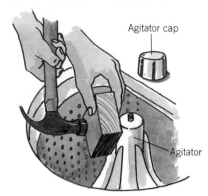

Agitator cap

Agitator

CLOTHES WASHERS: WHAT TO CHECK BEFORE CALLING FOR SERVICE

Problem	Possible cause	Possible solution
Machine won't turn on	No power to machine	Check for unplugged power cord, blown fuse, or tripped circuit breaker (p.163)
	Overload has tripped automatic safety switch	Reduce load; then reset switch (see owner's manual)
Machine won't fill or fills slowly	Water faucets closed	Turn on faucets
	Clogged filter screens on water hoses	Clean filter screens (p.146)
	Kinked or pinched water hoses	Straighten hoses; replace hoses if kinks have hardened
Water isn't hot	Hot-water faucet off	Turn on faucet
	Inlet hoses are reversed	Check hose connections; correct if necessary
	Clogged filter screen on hot-water inlet hose	Clean filter screen (p.146)
	Hot-water supply exhausted or water heater set too low	Check water heater; set thermostat higher if necessary
Motor runs but machine doesn't agitate	Loose drive belt	Tighten drive belt (p.147)
Machine spins but clothes remain wet	Oversudsing is slowing spin	Add cold water to reduce suds. Use less detergent in future
	Clogged or kinked drain hose	Clear obstruction or straighten hose; replace hose if kink has hardened
Machine doesn't spin or spins slowly	Overload or unbalanced load has tripped automatic safety switch	Reduce or redistribute load; reset switch (see owner's manual)
	Overload or unbalanced load keeps basket from reaching proper speed	Reduce or redistribute load
	Loose drive belt	Tighten drive belt (p.147)

SAVING ON WATER-HEATING BILLS

Except for heating and cooling units, the water heater is your home's largest energy user. Unless you need a higher temperature for a dishwasher (p.143), set your unit for 120° F. Turn it off when you go away for more than a few days.

Does your water heater feel warm when you touch it? It's losing heat. Wrap it with an insulating fiberglass blanket sold in a kit. Take care not to block controls. Don't cover a gas unit's top or block the air flow to the burner at bottom.

If you're buying a new water heater, get a superinsulated energy-saving model. Putting extra insulation on one won't save much.

WATER-HEATER UPKEEP

If your plumbing is noisy only when the hot water is running, the water temperature may be too high, creating steam in the pipes. Try lowering the temperature.

Is your hot water dirty? Does it take a long time to reheat after the tank is exhausted? Both indicate sediment in your water heater's tank.

No hot water from your electric-powered water heater? If a tripped circuit breaker or a blown fuse isn't the cause, turn off power (p.163), remove the access panel over the upper heating element, and press the reset button. Replace the access panel; then restore power and test.

To clear sediment from a tank, turn off the gas or power and the cold-water inlet valve. Open an upstairs hot-water faucet. Then attach a garden hose to the drain valve and drain the tank through the hose into a floor drain. This may take a few hours. Reopen the cold-water valve and let water run through the empty tank until the water drains clear.

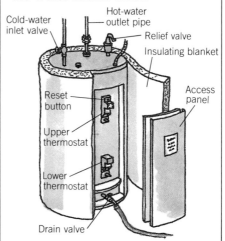

Cold-water inlet valve

Hot-water outlet pipe

Relief valve

Insulating blanket

Reset button

Access panel

Upper thermostat

Lower thermostat

Drain valve

It's easy to prevent a sediment buildup. Drain the tank into a pail (or through a hose) until the water is clear two to four times a year, or monthly for very hard water.

To find out how quickly your water heater recovers, look for a plate on it that notes how many gallons it can heat in an hour.

If your tank-type heater runs out of hot water often, you may be doing too many tasks that consume lots of hot water in too short a time span. Few realize how little hot water a heater contains. Only 70 percent of the water in the tank reaches the desired temperature—roughly 30 percent at the bottom remains cooler. A 40-gallon tank, therefore, has only 28 gallons of hot water— enough to fill a bathtub to about 5½ inches deep. Once you've exhausted this supply, you may wait an hour before the tank reheats.

SETTING UP A NEW DRYER

Plan to locate a dryer in a place where the surrounding temperature stays above 45° F; the higher the better to cut drying time.

Before buying a dryer, check the location of its exhaust hole. Then check the spot where you plan to put the dryer to make sure that you can run a vent hose from the exhaust hole to the outdoors. Depending on the dryer, you may be able to vent out to the back, to either side, or through the floor.

Never vent a dryer into a chimney, crawl space, or attic. Lint from the dryer is combustible.

Plastic vinyl hose is not very effective for venting a dryer. Get either rigid or flexible metal ducting instead. Exterior vent hoods that open a full 4 inches are more efficient than ones that open less.

If a dryer's vent hose is too long, it will greatly increase your clothes' drying time. Keep the length from the dryer to the outside vent hood to 25 feet or less. Deduct 5 feet from this length for each elbow, except for the elbow at the dryer.

FOR DRYER EFFICIENCY:

Clean the lint filter after each use.

Dry light and heavy fabrics separately.

Avoid overloading and underloading a dryer; both waste energy.

Don't add wet items to a load that's already partly dry.

When drying more than one load, dry them one immediately after another to utilize the heat in the dryer from the previous load.

DRYER MAINTENANCE

Is a lint-clogged venting system keeping your clothes from drying completely? Go outside and hold your hand under the vent hood while the dryer is running. If it's venting properly, you should feel a strong flow of air.

To prevent a lint buildup in your dryer's vent duct, clean it once a year. Remove the duct and shake it out. If necessary, run a wadded cloth through it. Be sure to reseal joints with fresh duct tape.

Outdoors, clean the damper and its hinge by inserting a length of straightened coat hanger into the vent hood.

Make sure that your vent duct is straight. Dips and kinks collect water and lint, blocking air flow. If the duct runs through an unheated area such as a crawl space, cold can aggrevate the problem.

To shut off all the power to an electric dryer, you have to remove two fuses or flip two circuit breakers in your home's main electric service panel (p. 163). Both together control the power to the heating element and one also controls the power to the motor.

Is your dryer making unusual noises? Rotate the drum by hand. A slow thump that varies with the speed that you turn the drum probably indicates a worn drive belt that needs replacing.

If you hear many thumps each time you rotate the drum, it indicates a worn support roller. To replace it, consult your service manual or have a service technician make the repair.

Is a leaky door seal the cause of long drying times? Check for moisture on the door. Also move a piece of tissue paper around the door's edge while the dryer is running. If the paper is drawn in, the seal needs to be replaced.

If a door seal is just glued to the door or jamb, you can replace it by pulling off the old seal and gluing on a new one. Get a special nonflammable adhesive at the appliance parts store when you buy the new seal. Have a seal that mounts between the cabinet and drum opening serviced.

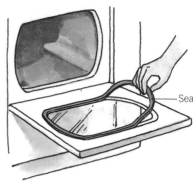

Seal

DRYERS: WHAT TO CHECK BEFORE CALLING FOR SERVICE

Problem	Possible cause	Possible solution
Dryer won't run	No power to dryer	Check for unplugged power cord, blown fuse, or tripped circuit breaker (p.163)
	Dryer door is not fully closed	Shut door firmly
	Drying cycle selector may not be set	Set control to drying position
	Start button has not been pressed	Press start button
Clothes take too long to dry	Dryer is overloaded	Reduce amount of clothing
	Incorrect drying cycle selected	Consult owner's manual to determine correct cycle
	Dryer venting system is clogged	Clean the lint filter, vent duct, and vent hood (facing page)
	Final washing machine rinses are being done with cold water	Expect longer drying times than when using warm rinses
	Clothes were too wet when put in	Make sure washing machine isn't being overloaded and is draining and spinning properly
	Leaky door seal	Test door seal (see above); if necessary, replace or have serviced
Dryer doesn't produce heat	One of the fuses or circuit breakers that controls heating element on electric dryer is blown	Replace fuse or reset breaker (p.163)
	Temperature selector set for air cycle rather than heat cycle	Reset control
Dryer makes noise	Foreign object is stuck in drum hole	Use a flashlight to look for nail, screw, curtain hook caught in a drum hole; remove object with pliers if necessary
	Hard objects on clothes such as buttons and zippers are hitting drum	Noise is normal
	Loose trim and exterior panels rattling	Tighten all visible screws

151

If you have a dryer that turns off automatically when the clothes reach the desired degree of dryness, use fabric softeners labeled safe for this type of dryer. Some softeners can coat the moisture sensors and prevent them from turning the dryer off.

If you suspect that your dryer's moisture sensors are coated with softener, wash them with warm, soapy water. You'll find them just inside the door or on the drum's baffles (see your owner's manual).

TOASTERS AND TOASTER OVENS

Toast always getting stuck? Get wooden toast tongs from a kitchen speciality shop. When faced with a slice that's reluctant to leave the toaster, unplug the toaster, gently work the tongs around the bread, and pull it out. Be careful not to damage the heat elements.

A toaster oven has no equal in toasting split muffins or bagels. But a toaster produces better toast. In a toaster oven, slices of bread tend to dry out before getting brown. If you like toasted thick-sliced bread, consider a toaster with an extra wide opening.

Want a warm dish for your food? Put an ovenproof plate on top of the toaster oven while your food cooks.

Keeping your toaster oven sparkling clean inside and out will extend its life. But cleaning the heat elements can cause them to fail prematurely. They self-clean by burning off spills.

Is the door of your toaster oven or broiler oven difficult to open? Unplug the unit and wash the pivots and hinge rods with a cotton swab dipped in water mixed with liquid dishwashing detergent. When the parts dry, use another swab to apply a light coating of a heat-resistant silicone lubricant. Then open and close the door a few times to spread the lubricant.

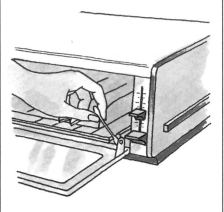

TOASTING SAFELY

Get yourself and your family in the habit of unplugging a toaster oven or broiler oven after each use. This will decrease the odds that someone may accidentally leave the switch on after baking or broiling, causing it to overheat and start a fire.

Be careful not to let a metal pan or an aluminum container touch a top heating element in a toaster oven. This can create a short and burn out the element. If you are touching the metal, you could get shocked or even electrocuted.

WHAT TO LOOK FOR IN A MICROWAVE OVEN

Programmable electronic controls let you set a series of different power levels for different lengths of time. For example, you can set the controls to defrost and cook a dish, then keep it warm. It's also handy to have a turntable that rotates food for even cooking and a door release that you can operate with an elbow.

Another useful microwave feature is a temperature probe. You insert it into the food as you would a meat thermometer. When your food reaches the desired temperature, the oven sounds a signal. Some models automatically shut off but still keep the food warm.

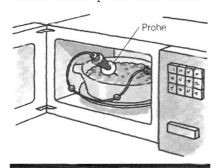

Probe

MAKING ROOM FOR A MICROWAVE

What's the best height for a wall-mounted microwave? Position the oven so that it's at the chest level of the shortest adult who's going to be using it.

Want to build your microwave into a cabinet or mount it beneath? To make sure it's safe, check the model number with your dealer or the manufacturer. Also ask about a kit for trimming your model's edges (if you build it in) or a bracket for under-cabinet mounting. Be careful not to block any vents.

Putting a microwave above your stove isn't a good idea because of the heat, grease, and steam a stove produces and because you have to reach over a hot surface. If you have no other convenient place to put a microwave, get a special over-stove unit with a stove hood on the bottom.

USING THAT MIRACULOUS MICROWAVE

For the best results, follow the cooking times in the recipe book that comes with your microwave. The times in most cookbooks and magazines are for an average 600- to 700-watt microwave. To produce the desired result, a compact 400-watt microwave will take more time, and a large 1,000-watt one will take less. Also, the various power-level ratings, such as *High* or *Medium*, are not standardized.

Even if you have a turntable to rotate food in your microwave, it's a good idea to stir such dishes as stews and vegetables to ensure that all ingredients get fully and evenly heated.

Sparks or flashes in a microwave indicate a dish containing metal, which shouldn't be used for microwave cooking. Remove the dish, and transfer the food to a container that's microwave-safe.

Avoid using brown paper bags and overcooking popcorn in a microwave. And keep an eye on dishes with lots of sugar. All are common causes of flare-ups.

If a fire develops in a microwave, keep the door closed and unplug the unit. Let the fire extinguish itself before opening the door.

MICROWAVE COOKWARE

Not sure if a dish is suitable for the microwave? Put the empty dish and a glass measuring cup half filled with water in the oven and set it on full power for 1 minute. Then gingerly touch the dish and the water. If the water is hot and the dish cool, the dish is OK to use.

Some surprising items can be used as microwave cookware. Try warming leftovers on a paper plate, cooking bacon on paper towels, and heating rolls wrapped in a napkin in a straw basket.

In a microwave, food in a round dish cooks more evenly. A shallow dish also cooks more evenly than a deep one. And any dish cooks slower in the center than at the edges. Give preference to dishes with straight rather than sloping sides.

Before putting food in the microwave, cover the dish with plastic wrap or a glass lid. (Don't let the plastic touch the food.) Your meal will heat faster and more evenly.

Don't rush out to buy special cookware for your new microwave. Most of your present ceramic and glass casserole and baking dishes are microwave-safe.

Save the microwave-safe plastic containers that some frozen foods come in. They're great for heating individual portions of any food in the microwave, and you can put them in the dishwasher.

Select plastic microwave cookware that can also be used for freezer storage so that precooked portions can go directly from the freezer into the microwave.

MIXER MASTERY

If you use a mixer just for whipping cream and beating eggs, a hand-held model is fine. But if you plan to do demanding tasks, such as kneading dough, consider a heavy-duty pedestal model, preferably with a set of metal bowls.

Are the beaters on your mixer difficult to remove? Try putting a drop of light household oil into each beater's sleeve.

To straighten a bent beater blade, lay the damaged portion on a cutting board and press on it with the bottom of a teaspoon.

Is your pedestal mixer's bowl not turning? Swing up or lift off the top housing and adjust the beater height by turning the screw on the pedestal's top (or housing's bottom). The beaters should just clear the bowl. But if one beater has a plastic disc on the bottom, the disc should touch the bowl.

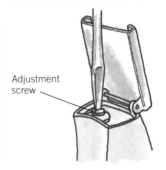

Adjustment screw

KEEPING YOUR BLENDER WHIRLING

How many speeds should your new blender have? Four or five will probably fill your needs nicely; any more will just raise the appliance's cost unnecessarily.

A switch that lets you "pulse" a blender on and off is a handy feature. Pulsing promotes even blending because the food redistributes itself between pulses. If your blender doesn't have a *Pulse* switch, you can get the same effect by just alternately pressing one of the speed-control buttons and the *Off* button.

If a blender push button doesn't work, get a can of electrical contact cleaner from an appliance parts store. With the blender unplugged, spray a little of the cleaner on each side of the button and let it seep in. Then press the button on and off several times.

If a blender's motor labors while you're processing a heavy mixture, soften the food with some water. Or divide the mixture into smaller quantities before blending.

Let very hot liquids cool for a while before putting them in the blender. Otherwise, trapped steam and moisture may erupt when you open the blender while processing the food.

THAT FABULOUS FOOD PROCESSOR

Look for a food processor with a built-in circuit breaker that will shut off the motor when jammed food or an unusually heavy load strains it. Any food processor with a motor that's guaranteed for as long as you own the unit is likely to have this feature.

If your food processor stops suddenly, an overload may have tripped its built-in circuit breaker. Turn the machine off and correct the problem. Wait 5 minutes before starting it again.

Does the noise that your food processor makes drive you crazy? Put the unit on a thick pad of rubbery plastic, sold in large stationery shops for keeping office machines quiet. It's a good idea to test the noise level of a food processor in the store before buying it.

Ever wondered about the large holes on your food processor's discs? They let you pick up the discs without touching the sharp edges that cut and grate.

CLOGGED COFFEE MAKERS

You pour 2 cups of water in your gravity-feed drip coffee maker but only 1 cup comes out! Check the drain hole in the water tank. If it's clogged, poke it open with a thin wire. If the bimetallic bar under the drain hole is corroded or broken, replace the water tank with a duplicate from the manufacturer.

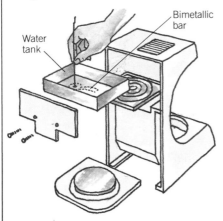

Bimetallic bar

Water tank

Spout clean and still no drip from your pump valve coffee maker? Mineral deposits may be clogging the valve. Unplug the machine, unscrew the baseplate, and remove the rubber elbow from the reservoir. Remove the valve and scrub it in detergent and warm water. Replace it; it should now move up and down freely. (For a thorough cleaning, see p.108).

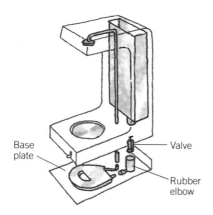

Base plate

Valve

Rubber elbow

PERCOLATORS AND URNS

If you get hot water, not coffee, from a percolator, check that the tube is firmly seated in the center well. Try brewing another potful. If you again get only hot water, replace the tube.

Water leaking from around the faucet of a large coffee urn? When the percolator is empty, remove the nut holding the faucet. Pull the faucet out of the hole, reverse the washer, and replace it on the faucet. Reinstall the faucet and tighten the nut. If reversing the washer doesn't stop the leak, you'll have to replace the washer.

STEAM IRONS

If your iron doesn't steam as it should, minerals are clogging the steam ports. Try reaming them out with the end of a straightened paper clip or bobby pin, after the unplugged iron has cooled.

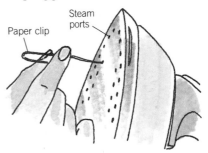

Steam ports

Paper clip

If the above doesn't help, fill the tank with a solution of half white vinegar, half water. Turn the iron on to the steam setting and, holding it horizontal, operate the spray and let it steam until the liquid is gone. More than one treatment may be necessary.

Although some makers say that it's OK to use tap water in a steam iron, why chance it? Instead, try demineralized water, which you can buy from a drugstore or supermarket. Or melt frost from your freezer to get distilled water. Or run tap water through a special filter, available in hardware stores.

CARE AND REPAIR

Does your iron stick to your clothes and stain them? Unplug the iron and let it cool. Clean the soleplate with a cloth dampened with rubbing alcohol, buff it with extra fine steel wool, and wipe it with a soft cloth. If, however, your iron is coated with a nonstick substance, rub wadded waxed paper over the soleplate (warm) or buff it very gently with extra fine steel wool.

You can replace a steam iron's frayed power cord if there's a screw-on cover over the terminal housing. Disconnect the iron, remove the screw and housing cover, and detach the faulty power cord from its terminals. Install a duplicate cord, tighten the terminals well, and reattach the cover.

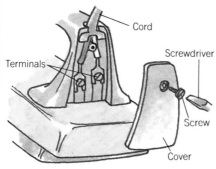

Cord

Screwdriver

Terminals

Screw

Cover

USEFUL HUMIDITY

Do you get an electrostatic shock whenever you touch someone or something in your home? Is your skin often dry, your nasal passages parched? If so, a humidifier will benefit you, your pets, plants, and furniture.

A humidifier works best if your house's insulation has a vapor barrier (pp. 176, 178). Without one, moisture seeping into the walls can render the insulation less effective and cause wood in the walls to swell and decay. In an uninsulated house, moisture within the walls can eventually cause wood to rot.

If you have a warm-air heating system, you can eventually humidify the whole house: Attach the warm-air heating system to a self-filling humidifier that is connected to a water supply pipe. Do it yourself only if the furnace manual or your heating contractor recommends it.

Portable or movable humidifiers are the only alternative if you have baseboard heating or radiators. Ultrasonic portables are safer, quieter, and more efficient than the evaporative kind.

Buy a portable humidifier with a wide-mouth tank; they're easier to clean and refill. Daily rinsing (1 tablespoon chlorine bleach per pint of water) prevents bacteria and mold growth. These microbes can be harmful to anyone with respiratory problems or allergies.

Distribute moisture evenly: Place a humidifier as near the center of a room as possible, and direct the nozzle toward open space.

ULTRASONIC HUMIDIFIERS

The white dust from a humidifier can cause electronic equipment to malfunction. Place the humidifier as far as possible from your TV, home computer, and VCR. Or fill the tank with distilled water, available at supermarkets.

Notice a decrease in your humidifier's mist output? The nebulizer (a vibrating mist-creating disc) may be clogged with mineral deposits. Clean it with a small paint brush dipped in white vinegar or in a commercial solvent recommended by the manufacturer.

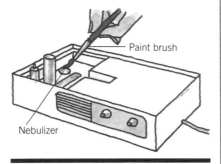

Paint brush

Nebulizer

EVAPORATIVE HUMIDIFIERS

Mineral buildup on an evaporative humidifier's belt, rollers, or padded drum reduces the machine's output. Remove and clean these parts with a solution of half white vinegar, half water. Replace them if they become difficult to clean. Always unplug your humidifier first.

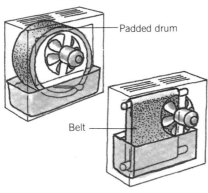

Padded drum

Belt

If after a good cleaning, your humidifier still doesn't work, check the drive belt. It should deflect ½ to ¾ inch under thumb pressure. If it doesn't, adjust it according to instructions in the owner's manual. If the belt is worn or broken, replace it.

DEHUMIDIFIERS

When purchasing a dehumidifier, check that it has automatic defrosting (to avoid frost buildup on evaporator coils), an automatic shut-off switch (to prevent water overflow), and a humidistat control (so that it runs only when the surrounding air is humid).

Your dehumidifier can do an optimum job only if you keep doors and windows closed in the area being dehumidified.

Dirt buildup can cause a dehumidifier's refrigeration system to work inefficiently. Unplug your unit each season (or oftener) and let moisture on evaporator coils dry. Then remove the dehumidifier's back cover (or the entire housing if necessary) and, with a vacuum cleaner's crevice attachment, vacuum all accessible surfaces.

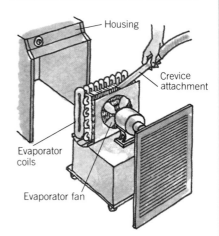

Housing

Crevice attachment

Evaporator coils

Evaporator fan

Tired of emptying your dehumidifier's drain bucket every day? If so, remove the drain bucket and place the dehumidifier right over the basement floor drain. Or run a garden hose from the dehumidifier's hose connection to the floor drain or into a sink (after placing the unit higher than the sink).

GARBAGE COMPACTORS

Avoid problems with your garbage compactor: place glass bottles on their sides and don't put aerosol cans in it at all.

Even an in-compactor deodorizer can't combat the stench of tuna and sardine cans and of melon rinds. Rinse the cans well before putting them in the compactor. In addition, line the compactor's bottom with newspaper. As waste compacts, the newspaper will absorb smelly liquids (and protect the bottom from shattered glass and jagged can tops).

Garbage compactor won't run? Maybe you can fix it without going to too much trouble. Open the drawer and shove it shut to ensure it latches; the latch should engage the switch that operates the motor. If your compactor still won't work, check it with a carpenter's level— a tilt may be preventing the drawer from latching. If neither of these helps, phone for professional assistance.

To prevent compactor odor, clean the ram weekly. Unplug the unit, and then open the drawer and lift it off its tracks. Using a scrub brush, wash the bottom of the ram with detergent and hot water. Finish the job with a disinfectant spray if you wish.

GARBAGE DISPOSERS

Thinking of buying a garbage disposer? Before you do, find out whether your municipality allows them and if the model you want can handle heavy food waste (corncobs, bones). If you have a septic tank, consider that it will need more frequent pumping out.

When a garbage disposer jams, switch off the unit, insert a dowel or the handle of a wooden spoon, and, pushing it against a flyweight, rotate the flywheel counterclockwise. If a small L- or Z-shaped wrench came with the unit, use it to clear a jam, following the owner's manual.

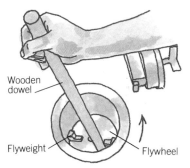

Wooden dowel

Flyweight   Flywheel

Garbage disposer clogged with greasy food? Try throwing ice cubes into the unit and running it. The ice should congeal the fat, allowing the unit to grind the fat into disposable bits.

ELECTRIC LIGHTS, PLUGS, AND CORDS

Light bulb broken off at the socket? Unplug the lamp or turn off the circuit that the light fixture is on (p. 163). Then, wearing a heavy glove, take a wad of newspaper and press down and twist counterclockwise on the top of the socket.

To replace a three-prong plug on a heavy-duty cord, trim the end and insert it in the plug; then strip off the outer and inner insulation and twist the wire strands (Steps 1, 2, and 4, facing page). Then just stick the wire ends under metal tabs or into holes and tighten the screws. Tighten the clamp screws to keep the cord from pulling out.

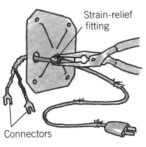

Green screw

Prong assembly   Clamp

On flat, lightweight lamp cord, use a self-connecting flat-wire plug, which can be put on quickly without stripping wires. When you clamp the plug onto a cord, small points on the prongs penetrate the insulation and make contact with the wires.

Prongs

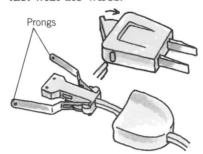

TESTING AND REPLACING AN APPLIANCE POWER CORD

You can often tell that a power cord is defective by just examining it for frayed insulation, a bare wire, or a damaged plug. To test a cord, buy a continuity tester, an inexpensive, battery-operated tool. If a cord passes the tests in Step 2, the appliance itself has a defect.

When replacing a cord, get an exact match from the manufacturer or from an appliance parts store; install it in the reverse order from which you took it off. If you must make a new cord, take the old cord to the store with you and get a cord, a plug, and connectors that match. Make sure that the cord has the same current capacity and insulation. You may also need a stripping and crimping tool.

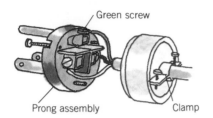

Strain-relief fitting

Connectors

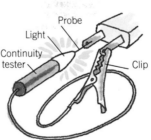

Probe
Light
Continuity tester
Clip

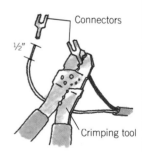

Connectors
½"
Crimping tool

1. To remove a cord, unplug the appliance and open it as the owner's manual directs. Then release the strain-relief fitting that secures the cord to the appliance. Use pliers to squeeze a typical fitting, rotate it a quarter turn, and pull it out. Then unscrew or unclip the cord from the appliance.

2. To test the cord, attach a continuity tester's clip to one plug prong; then touch the tester's probe to the other prong. If the tester lights, the cord has a short. Next attach the clip to one of the cord's connectors (or wires) and touch the probe to the corresponding prong. Then test the other wire. If the tester doesn't light either time, there's a break in the wire.

3. To make a new cord, put a round-cord or three-prong plug on one end (see above). If the old cord's bare wires were attached to terminal screws, strip and attach the new cord the same way. If wires had connectors, strip ½ inch of insulation from the wires and twist the wire strands; then attach new connectors by slipping their sleeves over the wires and squeezing them with a crimping tool.

REPLACING A PLUG ON A POWER CORD

Always replace a plug with one compatible with the cord. The steps below show how to replace the plug on a round cord, used for small appliances and medium-weight extension cords. The plug shown is a "dead-front" plug, which puts a solid barrier between you and the bare wires inside. Even when the plug you're replacing has a cardboard insulator, use this safer type of plug.

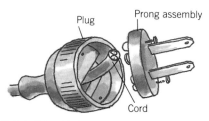

Plug
Prong assembly
Cord

1. Cut off the old plug and any damaged wire with heavy-duty scissors or wire-cutting pliers. Then unscrew and remove the prong assembly on the new plug and slip the cord through the plug.

2. Remove 1½ inches of outer covering from the cord. Use a utility knife or a sharp pocket knife to cut around the covering; then pull it off. Slit the covering lengthwise if it won't pull off easily. Be careful not to cut the wires inside. If you do, cut off the damaged section and try again.

Underwriters knot

3. Tie the two wires in an Underwriters knot: Loop one wire clockwise; then loop the other wire over the first wire and pass the end through the loop in the first wire. Pull the knot tight. This keeps the cord from slipping from the terminal screws.

4. Remove ½ inch of insulation from the end of each wire. Use a wire stripping tool or cut around the insulation with a knife and pull it off. Take care not to cut off any of the wire strands. Then twist the wire strands together in a clockwise direction.

Chrome screw

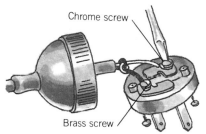

Brass screw

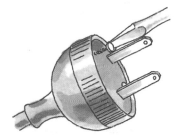

5. Loosen the terminal screws on the prong assembly. Loop the white cord clockwise around the chrome screw. Make sure that the bare wire fits all the way around and that the insulation comes up to the screw but doesn't go under it. Then tighten the screw. Attach the other wire to the brass screw. If both screws are brass, attach the white cord to the screw for the wider prong.

6. Pull the cord so that the knot is firmly seated in the plug. Then push the prong assembly onto the plug and screw it in place. To replace plugs on other kinds of cords, see the hints at the top of the facing page.

161

LIGHT SWITCHES

Do you have to grope in the dark to find a light switch? Replace the switch with an illuminated one. It has a tiny light inside the switch lever; you locate it by its glow.

If you have to feel your way out in the dark after turning off the light, put in a time-delay switch. It keeps the light on for about 45 seconds after you turn off the switch.

Do you always have your hands full when coming into or leaving the kitchen, nursery, or laundry room and can't reach the light switch? Install a switch with a large rocker lever that you can operate with your elbow.

FUSES AND CIRCUIT BREAKERS

Does an air conditioner or another appliance regularly blow a fuse when it turns on? Substitute a time-delay fuse. It withstands the temporary power surge that occurs when an appliance starts, but it'll blow if there's a short circuit or if the overload lasts longer than a few seconds.

Always replace a fuse with one of the same amperage. If you use one with a larger capacity, the circuit could become overloaded and cause a fire.

Like many people, you may be puzzled by the different kinds of fuses that are available for use in your home. The three CSA-certified types are "C," "P" and "D." The "C" type is an ordinary link fuse. But "P" and "D" types are heat-sensitive fuses that will blow before the temperature reaches 200°C. The "D" type can also handle short-term increases in high current that may be caused by air conditioners, refrigerators, freezers, dryers and other household appliances. Although "P" and "D" fuses are expensive, they provide extra protection against possible fire hazards.

You'll never have to change a fuse again if you put screw-in circuit breakers in your fuse box. When one trips, a button pops up. After correcting the cause of the trip, you push it in to restart the power. Before installing screw-in breakers, however, make sure your local electrical code permits them.

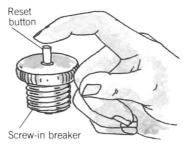

Reset button

Screw-in breaker

A close look at a fuse may reveal why it has blown. A clear fuse window with a broken metal strip inside is usually from an overload. A clouded or smudged window usually indicates a short circuit.

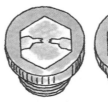

Overloaded fuse   Shorted fuse

SHUTTING OFF ELECTRIC POWER

Your home's main electrical service panel is usually located in the basement, the garage, or a utility room near the point where the power line enters. Four common types are shown below. When you turn off a circuit, always test to make sure that it's really off. Plug a lamp that you know works into an outlet on that circuit and make sure the light won't turn on. Flip a switch on and off to check that a light fixture it controls is really off. **Caution:** It's dangerous to touch your home's main electrical service panel when water is present. If the floor is damp, stand on a dry board. If the wiring may be wet, have the power company or an electrician turn off the electricity. In an emergency, use a dry wood pole to turn off the main switches.

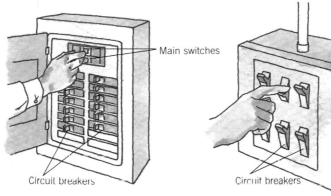

On a circuit breaker panel with one or two main switches, flip those switches to shut off all the power. To shut off power to a circuit, flip the circuit breaker that controls the circuit. When turning on a circuit breaker switch that has tripped, press down the *Off* side to reset it before flipping it on.

On other circuit breaker panels flip all of the switches to *Off* to shut off all the power. To shut off power to an individual circuit, flip the circuit breaker that controls that circuit. When you turn on a circuit breaker switch that has tripped, first press down the *Off* side to reset it; then flip it on.

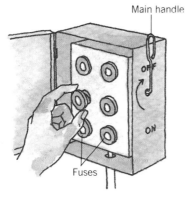

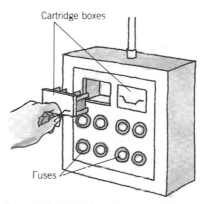

On a fuse box shift the handle to the *Off* position to shut off all the power. To shut off the power to a circuit, just unscrew the fuse controlling that circuit. Whenever you take out or put in a fuse, first turn off all the power with the handle.

On a cartridge-type fuse box pull out the boxes holding the cartridge fuses to shut off all power. To shut off power to a circuit, unscrew the fuse controlling that circuit. Whenever you take out or put in a fuse, pull out the cartridge boxes first.

CHAPTER THREE

OUTDOORS

Keep the exterior of your house shipshape, from rooftop to foundation. Learn how to paint like a pro. Organize your workshop so that it works for you. Tools and techniques for building and fixing. Automobile tips for emergency repairs and routine maintenance. Enhance your home with a lovely landscape. Find out how to make trees, flowers, lawn, and vegetables flourish.

The Exterior of the House
Page 165

Checking troublespots on your home's exterior; cleaning and repairing stucco and sidings; spotting signs of termite activity; preserving porches and decks; cleaning gutters and downspouts; buying ladders wisely and using them safely; repairing a roof and knowing when to replace one; replacing screening in metal- and wood-frames; fixing storm doors; selecting the right caulk for the job and applying it properly; how to install weather stripping on doors and windows; questions and answers about home insulation; painting the house to give it a fresh face; choosing between latex and alkyd paint; creative color combinations for your house; preparing surfaces; when, where, and how to apply paint; putting the final touches on trim.

Workshop
Page 183

Planning your workshop; a basic household tool kit; using your tools safely and effectively; storing tools and supplies; marking and measuring made easy; checking for surface irregularities; sawing a board; driving and removing nails; drilling holes in wood and metal; driving screws; how to tighten loose screws; choosing the right glue for the job; improvising clamps.

Garage & Car Maintenance
Page 193

Washing and waxing; when to service your car; rust prevention and removal; replacing an oil filter; fuel-saving tips; coping with road emergencies; replacing spark plugs; changing a tire; overheating and stalling; driving in snow, rain, or fog; frozen locks; storing snow tires.

Yard & Garden
Page 203

Designing a landscape for your home; getting rid of poison ivy and poison oak; planning for seasonal variety; stretching the visual boundaries of your property; protecting valuable trees while landscaping; testing your soil's pH; deciding which trees and plants are ideal for your yard; the correct way to plant young trees; providing shrubs and trees with the right amount of water and the best fertilizer; tips on pruning trees; protecting plants and shrubs from wildlife; retraining overgrown hedges; lawn maintenance; getting rid of lawn weeds; patching a lawn; enriching garden soil; double-digging; how to make a compost heap; flower beds; planting bulbs; building raised beds; transplanting seedlings; roses— buying, planting, and maintaining them; increasing perennials; vegetables and fruits; choosing mulches; pest control in the garden; care and storage of garden tools and outdoor furniture.

The Exterior of the House

MAINTAINING SIDING

Before rushing to brighten dingy siding with paint, try washing it. Washing is the first step to a lasting paint job anyway.

A yearly washing helps preserve siding and its finish. For painted wood siding and aluminum siding, use a solution of 1 cup detergent and 1 quart chlorine bleach in 3 gallons of water. Use an extra-strength detergent sold by paint and hardware stores. Wear rubber gloves, safety goggles, and protective garments. Rinse the siding thoroughly.

To spruce up vinyl siding, hose it down; then sponge it with a mild liquid detergent. Rinse with spray from a hose.

Surprisingly, it's best to wash siding from bottom to top. The siding soaks up less detergent and, as a result, is less likely to streak.

WHAT TO CHECK FOR ON YOUR HOME'S EXTERIOR

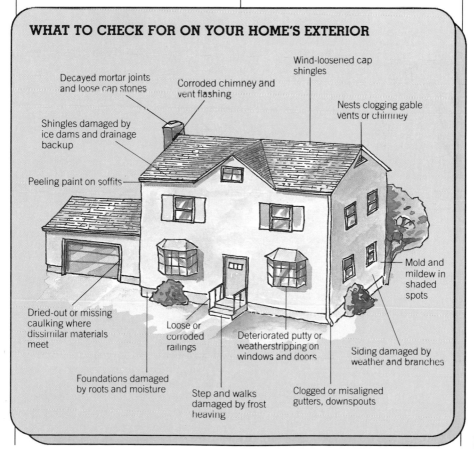

Decayed mortar joints and loose cap stones

Corroded chimney and vent flashing

Wind-loosened cap shingles

Shingles damaged by ice dams and drainage backup

Nests clogging gable vents or chimney

Peeling paint on soffits

Mold and mildew in shaded spots

Dried-out or missing caulking where dissimilar materials meet

Loose or corroded railings

Deteriorated putty or weatherstripping on windows and doors

Siding damaged by weather and branches

Foundations damaged by roots and moisture

Step and walks damaged by frost heaving

Clogged or misaligned gutters, downspouts

A great tool for washing siding is a long car-wash brush on a hose.

STAINS ON SIDING

Bleach away green copper stains with a solution of ¾ pound oxalic acid crystals in 1 gallon hot water. Sponge on and wait 5 minutes, then rub with a cloth. Repeat until the stain lightens.

Caution: Always wear rubber gloves, safety goggles, and protective clothing when mixing and using solutions of oxalic acid, muriatic acid, chlorine bleach, or other stain-removing compounds.

Lighten rust stains with a solution of 1 part sodium citrate crystals to 6 parts water. Dip a cloth in it; then stick the wet cloth on the siding, covering the stain for 15 minutes.

If you're going to paint, sand rusty nailheads and surrounding stains with a medium-grit sandpaper to take off as much rust as possible. Cover a recessed nailhead with caulk (p. 175). Then prime the area with a rust-inhibiting paint.

If you're not sure whether a stain is soil or mildew, dab at it with a bleach-soaked rag. If particles begin to fall off, it's mildew.

EXTERIOR MAINTENANCE CALENDAR

In most parts of the country, spring and fall are the seasons for making the majority of exterior repairs. In the spring, fix damage caused by cold weather and moisture and prepare for the coming hot season. In the fall, get the exterior in shape for winter's return.

Spring
Roofing: Repair damaged shingles and flashing

Gutters, downspouts, and drains: Clear debris and flush with water. Straighten and correct the pitch of misaligned gutters. Reset downspouts and tighten fasteners

Siding and trim: Renail loose pieces. Caulk. Touch up damaged paint. Wash all exterior surfaces

Masonry: Repair cracks and seams. Clean crumbling mortar from joints; remortar

Windows: Remove storm sashes; repair and clean before storing. Clean and unstick sashes; repair damaged putty (p.86, Steps 3-5). Install screens in windows used for ventilation and put up shading devices on south-facing windows

Ironwork: Remove rust and paint as necessary

Pests: Check foundations for termite tunnels. Check vent louvers, chimneys, and other protected nooks and crannies for bird and insect nests

Chimneys: Clean and inspect flues when seasonal use ends

Summer
Driveways: Repair holes and cracks in asphalt drives; protect the blacktop by applying asphalt sealant

Gutters, downspouts, and drains: Clear debris at midseason

Fall
Gutters, downspouts, and drains: Clear debris and flush with water

Outdoor water supply: In frost-prone areas, shut off supply, drain lines, and leave valves open

Siding, trim, and foundation: Patch and seal open cracks. Seal openings where animals may take refuge. Close vents of unheated crawl spaces

Windows and doors: Put storm sashes in place. Clean and repair screens; spray with protective coating. Inspect and fortify weatherstripping. Clear debris from basement window wells

Winter
Chimneys: Clean and inspect flues in midseason if you use a wood stove or fireplace frequently

Gutters, downspouts, and drains: Keep clear of ice

To remove a white crusty or powdery buildup on brick or concrete, scrub with a solution of 1 part muriatic acid to 10 parts water. For heavy buildups, use a stronger solution, from 1 to 2 parts. Rinse the surface thoroughly.

SIDING REPAIRS

If a siding board is warped, try inserting 2-inch wood screws to pull it in flat against the sheathing under it. Drill pilot and countersink holes (p.191) and cover the recessed screwheads with wood putty or caulking compound.

To fix siding that's split along the grain, pry open the crack and coat both edges with waterproof resorcinol glue (p.192). Then push the pieces together and nail along the siding's lower edge.

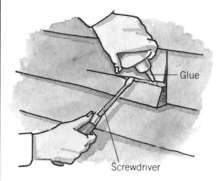

Glue

Screwdriver

When repairing siding, use hot-dipped galvanized or aluminum nails to prevent rust stains.

In stucco, fill a small crack with a latex caulk, then coat the caulk with latex paint. Chisel out all loose stucco in a larger crack and fill it with vinyl-concrete patching cement. This material adheres better than regular sand-concrete mix and doesn't have to be kept wet for days afterward.

To fix a dent in aluminum siding, drill a small hole in the dent's center. Thread in a sheet-metal screw a few turns and pull out the dent. Then remove the screw and fill the hole with plastic-aluminum filler compound. After it hardens, sand and paint the spot.

FOR FIRM FOUNDATIONS

To determine if a crack in masonry is active and indicates a structural problem, bridge over the crack's surface with a layer of plaster of Paris. Wait several months. If the plaster cracks, consult a builder.

To get from the soil to your home, termites build mud tubes. Check for them regularly on foundation walls. Look especially at the spots where pipes and conduits enter.

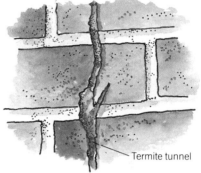

Termite tunnel

Another sign of termite activity is accumulations of translucent ½-inch wings near your foundation walls. If you spot these in early spring, call an exterminator.

If you're not sure whether winged insects are termites or ants, keep in mind that termites have thick midbodies and four wings of the same size. Ants have pinched waists and pairs of smaller and larger wings.

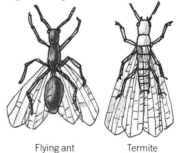

Flying ant   Termite

(greatly enlarged)

In some areas, carpenter ants are as much a threat to your home as termites. Get professional help if you find unexplained sawdust on the ground, wall, or floor, or spot ½-inch-long black ants, especially near wood exposed to wetness.

PORCHES AND DECKS

Most porch problems are caused by moisture from the ground below. To control moisture, cover the ground with overlapped strips of polyethylene sheeting or roofing felt. Then top this vapor barrier with 2 inches of sand.

If paint on your porch or deck is always peeling, moisture is probably entering the boards from below and causing the paint to lift off. Either install a vapor barrier or paint the underside with the same deck enamel you use on top.

If your porch is small and light, you may be able to raise a sagging joist with a support post. Establish a solid footing for the post. Then cut a 4 x 4 to fit between the footing and a joist's lower edge, adding the amount you want to raise the floor. Then force the post under the joist.

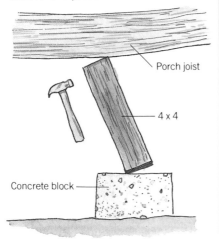

Porch joist

4 x 4

Concrete block

To reinforce a sagging, weak joist, first straighten it with a 4 x 4 post or a jack. Then nail to it a new joist of the same length and lumber size.

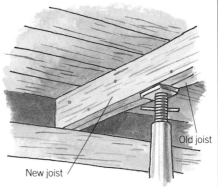

Old joist

New joist

If wooden stair treads are badly worn, carefully take them off and reattach them with their bottom sides facing upward.

Tread

To remove a stair tread, strike the underside with a hammer. Then strike the top of the tread to drive it back down. This should pop the nailheads, making it easy to grab them with a hammer claw.

GUTTERS AND DOWNSPOUTS

A depression in the ground just under a gutter is a sure sign that the gutter isn't working properly. Clean the downspouts and check the gutter's pitch.

Icicles forming along an eave are another sign of a malfunctioning gutter that needs attention.

To check a gutter, run water from a garden hose into it. If pools of water form, look for and fix damaged hangers or brackets that allow the gutter to sag. Sight along the gutter to make sure it maintains an even downward slope.

Stablizer

Leaning a ladder on an aluminum gutter is unsafe and can damage the gutter. Instead, use a tall stepladder or add a stablizer to your extension ladder to hold it out from the wall.

When adjusting the pitch of a strap-supported gutter, you can raise areas just by twisting the straps with pliers.

If you can't unplug a downspout with water pressure from a hose, try reaming it out with a plumber's snake and flushing again.

SELECTING LADDERS

A typical house needs two ladders—a stepladder and an extension ladder. A fold-up stepladder is essential indoors and useful outdoors as well. For most homes, a 5- or 6-foot stepladder is fine. But make sure you can reach your ceiling while standing two steps down from the ladder's top.

If your house is low, you may be able to do all exterior jobs with a regular straight ladder. But most houses need an extension ladder, which has two sliding sections. Check an extension ladder's label for its "maximum working length"—its length when fully extended. This is less than its nominal length because, for safety, the two sections must overlap by 3 feet or more. Thus a 20-foot extension ladder has a 17-foot usable length. A ladder's maximum working length should be 3 to 4 feet greater than the highest level at which you'll be working.

You can get wood or aluminum ladders. An aluminum ladder is lighter in weight and less prone to decay. But a metal ladder isn't safe to use when making electrical repairs, and when on it, you should use only power tools that are double insulated and grounded. Outdoors, you must always look up to avoid touching power lines. Touching one causes a lethal shock. The same precautions apply to a wet wooden ladder.

In any ladder, look for overall sturdy construction. Check a wooden ladder for cracks, knots, and other imperfections; check an aluminum one for bends, dents, and rough edges. On a stepladder, look for grooved treads, nonslip safety shoes, and angled metal braces on the lowest tread. On a wooden one, also look for metal rods reinforcing every tread. To test a stepladder's sturdiness, open it, stand on the lowest tread, and shake it from side to side.

An extension ladder should have pivoting safety shoes, a bottom rung with braces or a reinforcing rod, and a mechanism that locks the sections together securely. A pulley and rope for extending the ladder is a great convenience. Always buy a ladder rated Type I (heavy duty) or Type II (medium duty); they're sturdier and safer than Type III (light duty).

For tips on how to use your ladders safely, see p.171.

To prevent basement dampness and damage to your foundation walls, make sure the runoff from your gutters flows away from the house. If necesssary, install splash blocks under the downspouts.

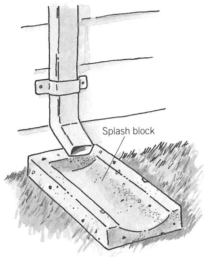

Splash block

Using wire-mesh screens to keep leaves out of gutters may seem a great idea. But they can be difficult to remove when you clear away other debris. A more practical solution is to put a leaf strainer in the top of each downspout.

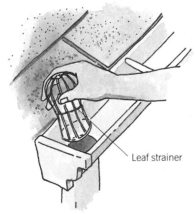

Leaf strainer

For a gutter patch that will last, get a fiberglass patching kit and apply it according to directions. Make sure the area is clean and dry so that the resin will bond well.

Is a gutter leaking at the joint where two sections meet? Apply silicone sealant to the joint's inside seams. Smooth the sealer's edges so that it won't collect debris.

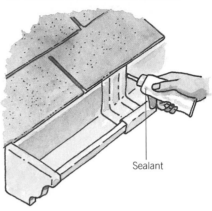

Sealant

DO YOU NEED A NEW ROOF?

Even if a roof leaks, it may not need to be replaced. If the roofing is less than 15 years old, just find the leak and patch it.

Check the condition of asphalt shingles on a warm day. Gently bend a few shingles back. If they aren't flexible or if they crumble easily, consider reroofing.

If the black mat of your asphalt shingles shows through the colored surface granules, chances are good that it's time to reroof.

If your roof's ridge isn't horizontal or if the plane of each roof section isn't flat, you've got a structural problem that needs professional evaluation—and repair.

Before reroofing with asphalt shingles, gently lift a shingle that's a couple of rows in from the edge and see if there's another layer of shingles below. If there is, you'll need to rip off all the old shingles and start from scratch.

USING A LADDER SAFELY

Inspect a ladder before climbing it; look for cracks, bends, and wobbling. Tighten the nuts on the reinforcing rods if a ladder feels shaky. Make sure an extension ladder's safety feet pivot freely. On uneven ground, put a firm, flat block under a ladder's lower foot. On soft ground, place a wide board under both of a ladder's feet.

To set up a long straight ladder, brace its feet against the wall and walk it upright, grabbing the rungs hand over hand.

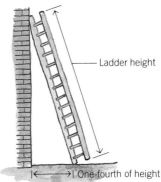

Position a straight ladder so that the distance between the wall and the base of the ladder equals one-fourth of the ladder's height.

When climbing up and down, always face the ladder and use both hands. Carry tools on a belt or haul them up with a line after you're set.

When climbing onto a roof, make sure that the ladder extends 3 feet or more above the roof edge. Don't climb onto a roof from a gable end.

When working on a ladder, keep your hips within the span of the ladder's side rails. Don't lean to the side or reach out too far.

Open a stepladder fully and lock its braces. Climb no higher than the second step from the top. Standing on the top invites an accident.

FINDING ROOF LEAKS

When a roof leaks, the culprit may not be the roofing material. First, check the flashing in roof valleys and around chimneys, dormers, vent pipes, and other objects that project through the roof.

Flashing

Don't risk life and limb to inspect your roof's flashings and shingles. Get a close view with binoculars.

Leaks are rarely located directly above the water spot on the ceiling. While it's still raining, check under the roof deck for a drip trail starting at a higher point.

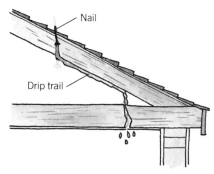

Nail

Drip trail

When you find a leak in the attic, push a nail or wire through it to help you locate it outside.

To spot roof leak sites, go to the attic on a bright day and turn off any lights. After your eyes adjust, examine the roof's undersides for telltale pinpoints of light.

On a wood shingle roof, light showing through the underside doesn't necessarily signify a leak. Wood shingles have cracks between them when they're dry, but the wood expands and seals the cracks as it absorbs moisture.

ROOF REPAIRS

You can patch any hole in roofing or flashing up to the size of a nickel by simply covering it with a layer of roof cement.

To patch an asphalt shingle, cut a rectangle of sheet copper or aluminum, coat one side with roof cement, and slip it, cement side down, under the shingle. Then put roof cement on top of the patch and press the shingle to it.

Metal patch

If a wooden roofing shingle is split but is otherwise in good shape, coat the edges of the split with roof cement, butt them tightly together, and secure them with galvanized or aluminum roofing nails. Cover the nailheads with roof cement.

Roof cement is one of the stickiest and messiest materials invented by man. When making extensive repairs with it, wear clothing and shoes that you won't mind throwing away afterward.

To clean roof cement from your skin, clothing, and tools, wipe them with a rag moistened with paint thinner. Don't use kerosene.

SCREENS AND STORM DOORS

When taking down screens or storm windows, write a number in a hidden spot on each window frame and on its screen or storm window. Put each window's hardware in a bag marked with the number. For a neat job on wooden storm windows, use small metal numbers that hammer in place.

Metal screens can last almost indefinitely. Just apply a light coat of thinned spar varnish each year. Be sure to clean the screens first (p.87); let them dry thoroughly.

To fix a hole in a screen, patch it with a square of screening. Unravel a few wires along each edge of the patch and bend the remaining wire ends at right angles. Then shove the ends through the screen and turn them down on the other side.

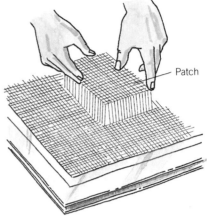

Patch

Keep the drain holes in the bottom of your storm windows clear to prevent condensation from rotting your sills. If your storm windows don't have these holes, drill them. Three ⅛ inch holes will do.

REPLACING A METAL-FRAME SCREEN

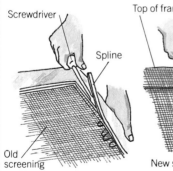

Screwdriver

Spline

Old screening

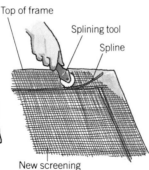

Top of frame

Splining tool

Spline

New screening

Utility knife

Spline

1. Remove old screening by prying out the splines that hold the screen in place. Start at a corner and use a screwdriver to lift each spline out of its groove. If the spline is still flexible, you can use it again. Replace metal splines or hardened plastic splines with new plastic splines.

2. Cut new screening the same size as the frame's outer dimensions. Trim the corners at a 45-degree angle. Then attach the screening at one end. Start at a corner and use a splining tool to force the spline in with short, firm strokes. Or put a wood block over the spline and hammer it in.

3. Pulling the screening taut, attach the spline at the other end; then attach the spline along each side. Finish by trimming off the excess screening along the edges with a utility knife.

173

When a screen door or storm door begins to sag, use wire cables and a turnbuckle to give it a lift. Run the support diagonally from the top corner on the hinge side to the lower outside corner, making the wires as taut as you can by hand. Then tighten the turnbuckle.

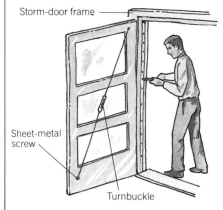

Storm-door frame

Sheet-metal screw

Turnbuckle

If your aluminum storm door won't close because it's hitting its frame, try to realign the metal frame by tightening the screws that hold it to the jamb on the hinge side.

If your storm door won't close and it's not hitting the frame, try adjusting the air-intake screw and the hold-open washer on the door's tubular pneumatic closer device. If necessary, replace it.

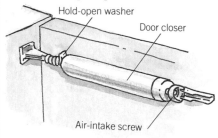

Hold-open washer

Door closer

Air-intake screw

Fix wooden screen frames when you put in new screens. After removing the old screening, reglue any corner and center joints that are loose and reinforce them with metal mending plates or long wood screws inserted from the side. Then repaint the frames.

When fixing screens, don't forget to check for loose mounting brackets on the window frame.

REPLACING A WOOD-FRAME SCREEN

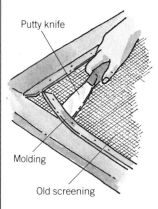

Putty knife

Molding

Old screening

New screening

C-clamp

Wood strips

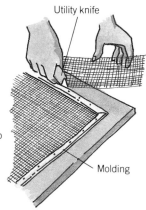

Utility knife

Molding

1. To remove old screening, pry off the moldings. Then use pliers to pull out tacks or staples holding the screening. You can reuse intact molding, but if it breaks, replace it. Using strong scissors, cut new screening 2 inches larger all around than the opening.

2. Staple the new screening along the top. Then bow the frame by putting a wood strip under each end and clamping it to a work surface at the center. Pulling the screening taut, fasten it along the bottom. Remove the clamps from the frame.

3. Staple the screening to the center rail and then along each side, starting from the center and working toward the ends. Then renail the molding. With a utility knife, trim off the excess screening that's left outside the molding's edge.

Condensation on windows? If it's inside the inner windows, caulk storm windows outside and inner windows inside. Also weatherstrip cracks between sashes. If that fails, cover inside windows with plastic or interior storm windows; ventilate bathrooms and kitchens. If moisture is between storm and inner windows, weatherstrip and caulk inner windows.

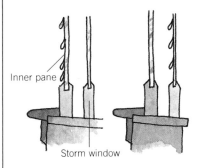

Inner pane

Storm window

SELECTING CAULK

Confused by all the caulks that are available? Silicones adhere best and last longest. Butyls bond well to metals. Latex caulks are fine for narrow cracks. Inexpensive oil-base caulks are short-lived.

Paint won't adhere to pure silicone caulk. Choose clear or a color that goes with the color of your house. If you insist on a paintable caulk and want durability, use siliconized acrylic caulk.

USING CAULK

Where should you caulk? Wherever two dissimilar building materials abut, most notably where siding meets foundation, decks, steps, pipes, chimneys, and corner, window, and door trim.

Loading a caulking gun is simple. Just pull the plunger all the way back and slip in the tube of caulk-

ing. Push in the plunger and twist it to engage the ratchet. Then cut the tube's tip at a 45-degree angle and push a long nail down the spout to puncture the inner seal.

To apply caulking, squeeze the trigger slowly and draw the tip along the seam you want to fill. Work at a slow, even pace, filling the joint completely.

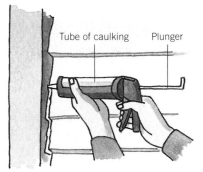

Tube of caulking   Plunger

Want to be sure a joint is filled with caulk? Push the tube along the seam instead of pulling it.

Does your caulking gun's tip leak when you pause between seams? Each time you pause, turn the gun's plunger to disengage the ratchet and relieve the pressure.

Weather affects how caulk goes on. Caulk on a mild, dry day when it's over 50° F. On a hot day, refrigerate caulk for an hour or two to keep it from running.

Keep unfinished tubes of caulk fresh. Plug the hole in the tip with a 10d common nail.

WEATHERSTRIPPING

Even in air-conditioning season, your windows should be weatherstripped and storm-sashed. Sealing windows can cut heat gain almost as much as it reduces heat loss in winter.

When you apply weatherstripping, lay a bead of caulking first. It acts as an adhesive and stops drafts from surface irregularities.

Tired of self-adhesive weatherstripping always peeling off? The next time you put some up, use tacks or staples for reinforcement.

It takes no time to weatherproof a door. Just tack metal-backed door weatherstrips along the stops on the jamb. Then screw a door bottom strip with a sweep onto the door. Cut both with a hacksaw. Make sure they fit snugly.

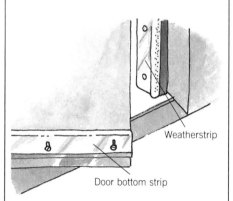

Weatherstrip

Door bottom strip

KEEPING YOUR HOME SNUGLY INSULATED

Reviewing your insulation needs? Don't overlook a wall or floor that separates your living space from an unheated garage, basement, or crawl space. Insulation at such a juncture is almost as vital as it is on ceilings and exterior walls.

Don't let condensation make your insulation wet and useless. Install it with a vapor barrier facing inward, toward the heated space.

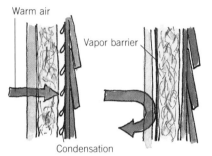

Warm air

Vapor barrier

Condensation

If you're having insulation blown into walls as a retrofit installation, coat the interior walls with a special moistureproofing paint to create a vapor barrier.

WEATHERSTRIPPING WINDOWS

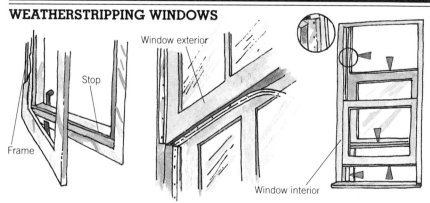

Window exterior

Stop

Frame

Window interior

Felt or foam strips are most useful on casement windows. Nail or glue them to the frame on the hinge side. Fasten them to the stop molding on the other three sides.

Vinyl gaskets are inexpensive and easy to install. Mount them on the window's exterior so that they aren't visible inside. Staple or tack vertical pieces to the stops and horizontal pieces to the window sashes as shown.

Spring-metal strips seal tightest, last longest, and show least. With the nail edge inward, install vertical strips in window channels, sliding them under the sashes' sides. Install horizontal strips on the sashes as shown.

YOUR HOME'S INSULATION NEEDS

Question: What are RSI and R values?
Answer: The quality of insulation depends on its RSI value—its resistance to the passage of heat. RSI per centimeter of thickness is stamped on the cover of most insulation. You may find, however, that some insulation is also marked with R values (per inch), which were used when only imperial measurements were in force. The higher the RSI or R number, the less heat is likely to escape from your house.

Zone A
Zone B
Zone C
Zone D

Question: How can I find out which RSI values are suitable for my home's insulation needs?
Answer: The map above, which was prepared by Energy, Mines and Resources Canada, shows the four climate zones of our country. For each climate zone, there are government-recommended insulation levels for ceilings, roofs, walls, and floors. In zone B, for example, a ceiling should have insulation rated at RSI 5.6, and floors (over unheated spaces) should be insulated at RSI 4.7.

Question: How can I determine the thickness of insulation that would be right for my home?
Answer: Just divide the RSI values recommended for your climate zone by the RSI value of the insulation you propose to install. Say, for example, that your roof space needs RSI 5 insulation. Then, if you buy mineral wool with an RSI value of 0.5 per centimeter, you will need a layer of wool 10 centimeters deep (5 divided by 0.5).

Question: How do I measure insulation my house already has?
Answer: In an unfinished attic, simply measure the thickness of the insulation. In a floored attic, you may have to pull up a floor board. In a finished one, drill a hole in the attic's ceiling.

Question: How do I measure insulation inside the walls?
Answer: Turn off the power going to an electric receptacle or switch (p.163); then remove its cover plate and measure the insulation next to it. Cut away some of the plaster or wallboard if necessary.

Question: What about measuring my house's floor insulation?
Answer: Above an open crawl space or an unheated basement, look for blankets or batts between floor joists. In an enclosed crawl space, the insulation is usually inside the foundation walls, running from the sill to the ground. Aboveground walls in a heated basement should also have insulation.

Question: What are some of the insulation materials that are available to me?
Answer: Glass- or mineral-fiber batts are the commonest types of insulation and the easiest to install. Both have an RSI value of 0.5 per centimeter. Loose fill—mineral, glass or cellulose fiber, vermiculite, polystyrene—is poured or blown into uninsulated spaces. The RSI values vary from 0.36 (vermiculite) to 0.6 (cellulose fiber). Rigid board—polyurethane and polystyrene panels—have high RSI values.

If you live in a humid region that requires more air conditioning than heating each year, the main problem is outside moisture condensing. Reverse the standard rule and put the vapor barrier facing toward the exterior wall.

Fiberglass insulation is extremely irritating. When working with it, wear a dust mask, goggles, work gloves, and clothing with tight-fitting openings. Coat exposed skin with petroleum jelly.

For a fast, neat job, cut batts of insulation with hedge trimmers or a serrated kitchen knife.

To insulate a floor over an unheated crawl space, garage, or basement, push the batts or blankets, vapor barrier up, between the floor joists. Support them by stapling chicken wire to the joists.

ATTIC INSULATION

If snow on a roof melts in one spot before others, it's a sign of missing or damaged attic insulation.

An often overlooked source of heat loss is the attic hatch. Make sure yours is well insulated and weatherstripped.

When insulating an attic floor for the first time, lay polyethylene sheeting as a vapor barrier between the joists before installing loose wool or unfaced blankets and batts as insulation.

To add more attic insulation, just put a layer of unfaced batts or blankets on top of the insulation that's there. The second layer shouldn't have an effective vapor barrier. If it has a foil face, slash the foil diagonally every foot.

If your present attic insulation is already level with the joist tops and you want to add more, increase the value of the second layer by installing it at right angles to the joists.

New insulation

Joists

Present insulation

In an unfinished attic, lay boards across the joists to walk and kneel on when installing insulation. A couple of 1 x 6's or some ¾-inch plywood will do.

When you install attic insulation, work from the eaves toward the center. This way you can do any cutting and fitting in the area with the most headroom.

PAINTING: GIVE YOUR HOUSE A MAKE-OVER

To make a low house look more gracefully proportioned, emphasize its verticals. Paint elements such as doors, shutters, and corner trim in a color that contrasts with the siding.

Accentuate horizontals on a high house. Use a contrasting trim color on parts such as windowsills, flower boxes, foundation walls, and fascia boards and gutters at the roof edge.

178

COLOR COMBINATIONS THAT WORK

When selecting exterior paint colors, first consider the color of the roof and coordinate with it. The roof color is the hardest to change. Even with this limitation, there is still a wide range of harmonious color combinations for you to choose from.

Roof	Siding	Trim
BLACK OR GRAY	Cream-yellow	Bright red, tile red, bright yellow, dark green, gray-green, white
	Pale green	Tile red, bright yellow, green, dark green, gray-green, white
	Dark green	Pink, cream, bright yellow, light green, white
	Putty	Red-orange, tile red, dark green, gray-green, dark blue, blue-gray, brown
	Dull red	Pink, cream, light green, blue-gray, white
	Gray	Pink, bright yellow, white, all reds, all greens, all blues
	White	Pink, cream, bright yellow, all reds, all greens, all blues
GREEN	Cream-yellow	Bright red, tile red, light green, dark green, gray-green, brown, white
	Pale green	Red-orange, tile red, bright yellow, dark green, white
	Dark green	Pink, red-orange, cream, bright yellow, light green, white
	Beige	Tile red, dark green, gray-green, blue-green, dark blue, blue-gray
	Brown	Pink, cream, bright yellow, light green, white
	Dull red	Cream, light green, gray-green, white
	Gray	Red-orange, cream, bright yellow, light green, white
	White	Pink, cream, bright yellow, brown, all reds, all greens, all blues
RED	Cream-yellow	Bright red, tile red, blue-green, dark blue, blue-gray
	Pale green	Bright red, tile red, white
	Dull red	Cream, light green, gray-green, blue-green, white
	Light gray	Bright red, tile red, dark green, white
	White	Bright red, tile red, dark green, blue-gray
BROWN	Buff	Tile red, dark green, gray-green, blue-green, brown
	Pink-beige	Tile red, dark green, gray-green, brown, white
	Cream-yellow	Tile red, dark green, gray-green, blue green, brown
	Pale green	Dark green, gray-green, brown
	Brown	Red-orange, cream, bright yellow, white
	White	Red-orange, tile red, bright yellow, dark blue, blue-gray, brown, all greens
BLUE	Cream-yellow	Red-orange, tile red, dark blue, blue-gray
	Blue	Red-orange, cream, bright yellow, light blue, white
	Gray	Red-orange, cream, light blue, dark blue, white
	White	Red-orange, tile red, bright yellow, light blue, dark blue

You can also make a house look lower by painting it a dark color, provided the roof is dark too. A light color, on the other hand, will help your house look larger.

For a coordinated look, paint your garage, toolshed, playhouse, and other outbuildings with the same color combination as your house. Use the trim color on wood fences and lampposts.

If your house is a hodgepodge of conflicting textures—vertical siding, shingles, and brick, for example—effect a peaceful reconciliation. Paint them all the same color or two related shades of the same color. Overall dark tones especially disguise architectural flaws.

Painting metal roof flashing the same color as the roof will make it less noticeable.

SELECTING HOUSE PAINT

Latex is almost everyone's first choice for exterior paint because it is easy to apply, cleans up with water, and dries quickly. On top of that, it's long-lasting.

If you don't know what you're painting over, choose alkyd paint. Alkyd will adhere to most surfaces, including chalking ones; latex is more finicky about what old paints it will bond with.

Is it always damp around your house? Choose a latex paint or stain. Porous latex breathes and lets moisture escape. Moreover, it doesn't contain vegetable oils that encourage mildew by feeding it.

Latex is also great for most masonry and can usually be applied without a primer. It bonds best when the surface is slightly damp.

For cinder blocks, get a solvent-thinned rubber-base paint. The water in latex can penetrate into the blocks, causing embedded iron particles to rust and stain your fresh paint job.

Before choosing a stain color or blend, test the color on an inconspicuous spot on your siding. Display samples can be misleading.

You can revive faded aluminum siding with any standard topcoat. But first you must sand the problem areas, wash the surface well, and coat any bare metal with a zinc-base primer.

For doors, windows, and other places where durability is a concern, pick a glossy paint. It contains more of the resins that give a paint body and hardness.

PREPARING SURFACES FOR PAINT

If your house's exterior is badly soiled, rent power washing equipment. The high-pressure jet of water it emits will blast away flaking paint as well as dirt.

Scraping off loose flaking paint is an important part of preparation. But don't overdo it. There's no need to scrape off any paint that's firmly stuck to the surface.

For heavy scraping, a pull scraper is better than a flat blade scraper. Be sure to keep replacement blades for the pull scraper handy.

Keep a beer can opener handy when you're preparing a surface. It's perfect for scraping old paint, caulk, and putty from hard-to-reach cracks and crannies.

Areas where you've scraped off flakes and blisters will be less noticeable after the final paint job if you smooth the sharp edges of the old paint with sandpaper.

WHEN TO PAINT?

For best results, paint when the temperature is from 50° F to 90° F. With alkyd paint, pick a warm, nonhumid day to cut drying time between coats. (Latex dries in a few hours in any weather.)

Spring and fall are the best seasons for painting. Besides moderate weather, nearby leaf-bearing shrubs are usually bare.

Don't be an early bird when painting! Let the dew evaporate before starting. In the evening, stop before dampness sets in.

To prevent a sunstroke for yourself and a paint problem for your house, avoid working in direct sunlight. Do your house's west side in the morning and its east side in the afternoon. Paint the south side when it's most shaded.

When painting, try to time your breaks to occur where siding and trim meet or at some other visual transition point. This prevents lap marks and disguises subtle color differences that may occur when you start again.

PAINTING TECHNIQUES

With alkyd paint, two thin coats are better than one thick one. But with latex, apply a heavy coat, even when you plan another.

Even if you buy a standard color, ask your paint dealer to shake the cans on his automatic mixing machine. It'll reduce the amount you have to stir.

Working from a full paint can invites spills and dripping. Pour half of the paint into an extra can or bucket and use that for painting. Seal the original can until you need more paint.

Avoid paint-can mess! Punch a series of holes in the rim groove; the paint that collects there will drain back into the can. Tape or glue a drip-catching paper plate to the can's bottom.

Loop of masking tape

PAINTING SIDING

Paint a wall from the top down. Work your way across its entire width, painting areas about 3-feet wide and five boards deep. After finishing an area, skip ahead the same distance and then paint back toward the area that you've just completed. This procedure can be used with most types of sidings. If a siding has grooves or recesses, paint them first. On vertical siding, paint boards from top to bottom.

1. Paint the bottom edge of the board. Work paint into the crevice with the brush tip.

2. Apply three or four short dabs of paint across the main surface of the top board.

3. Smooth the paint across with long, even strokes. Finish the other boards the same way.

For easier stirring and better mixing, drill a few ¼-inch holes in your stirring paddle.

You won't have a messy can or brush if you load the brush properly. Dip only the bottom third of the bristles in the paint. Then gently tap the brush on both sides of the can and lift it out without wiping it against the can's edge. This makes cleanup easier too.

Don't try to break up lumps in old paint; you'll just end up brushing the pieces on your job. Instead, strain the paint through window screening into another container.

TACKLING TRIM

When doing the trim, wrap cloth around your ladder tops to avoid marring the newly painted siding. For ladder safety tips, see p.171.

On panel doors, start by outlining each panel edge. Then fill in the panel. Finish by painting the rails and stiles. Start at the top of the door and work downward.

Rail

Stile

Don't forget to do a door's edges. They need to be protected by weather-resistant exterior paint. To reach the bottom edge, you may find it necessary to take the door off its hinges.

To avoid getting trim paint on the siding, keep your brush's bristles pointing toward the edge that you must cut cleanly.

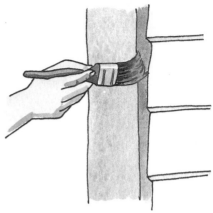

When painting a circular object, such as a drain pipe, you'll get better coverage if you work diagonally around it first and then make long strokes along its length.

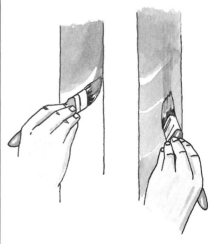

Need to use the stairs while you're painting them? Paint every other step. Let them dry thoroughly before painting the skipped steps.

Make quick work of railings and openwork with a sprayer. Just be sure to put cardboard or some other shield behind them to block the overspray.

Workshop

PLANNING A WORKSHOP

If a workbench requires more space than you have, build a fold-down unit in your garage. Use a solid-core door for the benchtop; fasten it to a wall, using a piano hinge. Legs should also be attached with hinges.

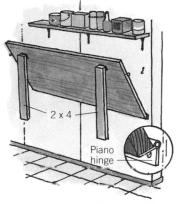

For most people, the ideal height for a workbench is 34 to 36 inches. If you need a shorter or taller surface, choose a height midway between your waist and your hips.

Because concrete is hard on the feet and damages tools that are dropped accidentally, cushion the workshop floor with old sheets of plywood, carpet, or even unfolded, flattened cardboard boxes.

IMPROVING SAFETY AND EFFICIENCY

When working with any power tool—whether it's large or small, stationary or portable—use only a heavy-duty, grounded (three-prong) extension cord that is 14-gauge or larger.

Short of space in your workshop? A back-of-the-door tool rack with a built-in drawer is ideal for storing small tools and supplies. Mount the rack to a solid-core door, or to the internal cross rails of a hollow-core door.

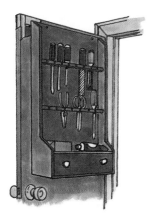

To keep power-tool cords out of the way as you work, hook the slack on a long spring screwed into the ceiling above your workbench.

Make sure you have good lighting in your workshop. If you intend to spend long hours there, install an overhead track or "lighting duct." But avoid glare; no part of your workshop should be more than three times as bright as any other.

183

A BASIC HOUSEHOLD TOOL KIT

You don't need an arsenal of tools to be prepared for emergency repairs and routine maintenance, but your tools should be the best quality you can afford. Except for doing specialized chores, most householders can get by with the following hand and power tools:

Tool and use	Tool and use

Crosscut saw
(with 6 to 8 points per inch)
Cutting wood to length

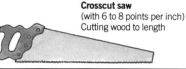

Flat file
Smoothing metal edges or surfaces

16-ounce claw hammer
Driving or removing nails; prying wood

Block plane
Trimming wood, particularly end grain

Nail set
Driving nailheads below wood surfaces

Wood chisel
(½-inch)
Trimming or shaping wood

Screwdrivers
(regular and Phillips)
Driving or removing screws

Utility knife
Cutting or trimming wood, veneer, hardboard, particleboard, cardboard, or plastic

Slip-joint pliers
Gripping or turning metal pieces

Putty knives
(1- and 3-inch)
Spreading or smoothing putty or plaster

Needle-nose pliers
Gripping or turning small objects in confined spaces

10-foot steel tape measure
Measuring dimensions

Wrench
(adjustable to 1¼ inches)
Tightening or loosening nuts or bolts

Carpenter's level
Checking vertical or horizontal surfaces

Push drill
Drilling small holes in wood or plastic

Pairs of C-clamps
(2-, 4-, and 6-inch)
Clamping wood or metal pieces for cutting, drilling, or gluing

Portable electric drill and bits
Drilling holes; driving or removing screws; sanding or buffing (with attachments)

Safety goggles
Protecting eyes against flying particles or harmful liquids

Because linseed oil is prone to spontaneous combustion, even in cold weather, quickly discard any rag used on linseed oil or a product that contains linseed oil.

STORING TOOLS

To help yourself identify your own tools from those you may have borrowed, paint your initials on them.

If you store tools on wall hooks, paint the outline of each tool on the wall to remind you and others where to replace a tool.

If you have small children, store all tools in locked cabinets or drawers. As the children grow up, introduce them gradually to the safe use of hand tools; continue to lock up power tools.

To make a handy rack for screwdrivers and other small tools, drill a series of ½- to 2-inch holes through a 1 x 3. Mount the rack on the wall with angle brackets.

Need a storage receptacle for sharp or pointed tools? Cut a block of plastic foam from the lining material in an appliance carton.

Do your tool drawers slip off their glides and spill their contents? Screw an oblong stop to the inside of the drawer's back panel. Fasten the stop with a pivot, which can be turned to a horizontal position if the drawer needs to be removed.

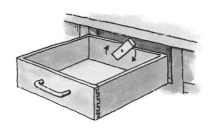

To protect the teeth of a small circular-saw blade, cut an old automobile-tire inner tube and stretch it around the blade. For a handsaw blade, use a slit length of old garden hose.

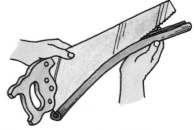

To prevent metal tools from rusting, store them in sealed wooden bins with camphor and sawdust.

STORING SUPPLIES

In a garage, you can store lumber and pipe on exposed ceiling joists. Screw cross members to the bottom edges of joists to support materials you wish to tuck up and out of the way.

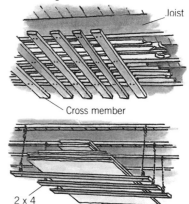

Joist

Cross member

2 x 4

Here's a simple assembly you can make for off-the-floor storage for plywood and other sheet materials. Insert screw eyes into 5-foot lengths of 2 x 4's. Using S-hooks, fasten a heavy chain to each screw eye. Suspend chains from ceiling joists. For adequate support, use three 5-foot lengths.

Looking for convenient, out-of-the-way storage space? Use the unfinished stud spaces of your workshop walls. To make shelves, nail old boards horizontally between the studs.

A good way to organize washers and nuts is to hang them according to size on large safety pins or on wire coat hangers whose necks have been untwisted.

Jars with screw tops are ideal for storing small items, such as nails, screws, nuts, and bolts. You can double your shelf capacity by screwing the lids to the underside of shelves. Place a lock washer under the head of the screw so that the lid won't turn when you unscrew the jar.

If you need a rack to store abrasive discs, cut off one-third to one-half of an aluminum pie plate and fasten it to the wall bottom side out.

A good way to monitor your supply of paints, glues, and other liquids in opaque containers is to wrap a rubber band around each container at the level of its contents. Remember to adjust the rubber band as the level changes.

MARKING AND MEASURING

Always read a rule straight on, with your eyes directly in front of or above the point being read. If you're off to one side, your reading will be distorted.

For more accurate marking and measuring, hold a ruler on its edge rather than flat against the surface. Mark points at the tip of a V so that they'll be easier to spot.

Here's a quick, easy way to make a long, straight line. Pin two points of a carpenter's chalk line to the surface. Lift the taut line at an intermediate point and allow it to snap back quickly. The result will be a straight chalk line.

To duplicate an irregular line or edge, hold the pivot of a compass on the line or against the edge to be duplicated and move both points evenly as you scribe.

If you know the span of your hand, you can approximate measurements when you don't have a ruler. With your fingers spread out as widely as possible, measure the distance between the tips of your thumb and your pinky. To measure a distance, "walk" your hand along the surface, counting the "steps"; then multiply by your hand span. For short distances, use a finger segment that approximates 1 inch.

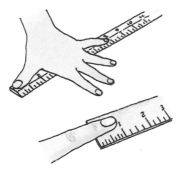

To divide a board into equal sections, lay a rule at an angle across the board. Align the end of the rule with one edge of the board. At the other edge, position an inch mark that is evenly divisible by the number of sections you want. Mark the appropriate intervals along the rule.

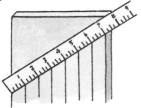

SAWING AND CUTTING

Save elbow grease by using soap. Rub your handsaw blade with a bar of dry soap to reduce friction.

To reduce splintering when crosscutting, place the board so that the growth rings arc downward.

SAWING A BOARD

1. Using a sharp pencil and a combination square, mark the cutting line across the top edge of the board.

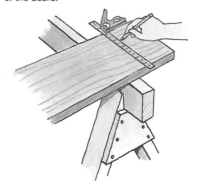

2. Set the board on sawhorses, with the waste section on the outside. Allow several inches of clearance for the saw.

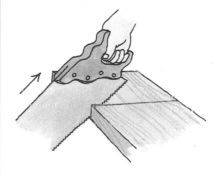

3. Place the end of the blade nearest the handle just outside the pencil line. Begin the cut with a few short pull strokes toward you.

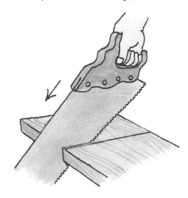

4. Once a groove has been formed, use longer strokes, pressing down on push strokes and relaxing on pull strokes.

Here's a crosscutting guide that keeps a handsaw cutting straight and at the correct angle. Rest the jig on the work and let its face guide your saw blade.

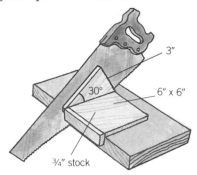

To hand-saw a thin slice from the end of a board, clamp a longer piece of scrap wood underneath it and cut through both pieces. This will make the task much easier.

If your handsaw begins to bind as you cut with the grain, insert a screwdriver into the end of the kerf (the channel made by the blade) to hold it open.

Here's how to prevent a saber saw blade from breaking when you cut a circle out of plywood. Make straight cuts from the edges of the wood to the circumference. Space the cuts about 30 degrees apart, in alignment with the diameter. The waste will fall off in sections as you cut the circumference, relieving stress on the blade.

Having a hard time starting a hacksaw in metal? Nick the edge of the material with a file.

When using a hole-saw drill attachment, avoid tearing the back surface of the wood. Drill about halfway through the wood, until the tip of the bit pierces the back surface. Then insert the bit into the opening on the reverse side and complete the hole.

To make it easier to cut through knots in wood, rock your saw to change the angle of the stroke.

When using a combination or try square to check that a surface is regular or a corner is right-angled, position the square against the work and hold both up to the light. If light is visible between the square and the work, correct the irregularity by planing or sanding the work's edge.

DRIVING NAILS

To get full advantage of the weight of a hammer's head, hold the handle as far from the head as possible without sacrificing a firm grip. After the nail is started, swing the hammer from your elbow.

In general, nails should be approximately the same length as the combined thickness of the stock that's being fastened.

If a nail is too small to hold with your fingers, use a bobby pin or a pair of needle-nose pliers to hold it in place as you hammer.

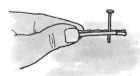

For starting brads or tacks that are shorter than 1 inch, use a magnetized tack hammer.

When starting a nail, hold it between your index and middle fingers with your palm up. If you accidentally miss the head, you'll strike the fleshy part of your fingers, which hurts a lot less than hitting your thumb or fingernail.

An easy way to avoid splitting wood is to blunt the sharp points of nails. Tap them with a hammer.

Here's how to conceal a nailhead. Chisel a shaving parallel to the wood grain, leaving the shaving attached to the surface. Drive in the nail. Glue the shaving back in place over the nailhead.

When fastening moldings with finishing nails, use a strip of pegboard scrap to shield the wood. Drive nails through one of the holes as far as possible, then set the heads with a nail set.

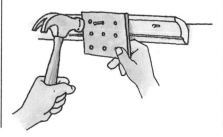

To remove a nail whose head is below the wood surface, place the hammer claw slightly in front of the nail with the tapered ends on the wood. Strike the hammer face with a rubber mallet to drive the claws into the wood surface.

Cutting pliers are ideal for removing nails with narrow or broken heads. Rock the pliers back and forth gently to ease the nail out.

DRILLING HOLES

Although a single-speed, ¼-inch drill is adequate for drilling holes in wood, a variable-speed, ⅜-inch model with reversing capability is more versatile. It will drill holes in masonry, drive and remove screws, and accept attachments for sanding, wire-brushing, and polishing.

To increase precision and reduce bit breakage, hold a drill with your palm high up on the handle, directly behind the chuck. Extend your index finger along the drill's body and use your second or third finger to operate the trigger.

If you lubricate drill bits with silicone spray before using them, they'll break less easily and stay sharp longer.

To prevent a drill bit from wandering as you start a hole, use a nail set to make an indentation where the hole's center will be.

Need more light on the spot you're drilling? Tape a penlight to the casing of your drill.

To make depth stops for your drill bits, drill undersize holes through the center of corks. Each cork should fit its bit snugly so that when you drill a hole to the proper depth, the cork doesn't move up on the bit.

When drilling smooth sheet metal, stick a piece of masking tape where the hole's center will be. This prevents the bit from wandering.

Here's how to avoid splintering the back surface of wood every time the tip of the bit emerges. Place a block of scrap wood under the piece. The bit won't tear the wood as it breaks through.

A portable electric drill can be used for more tasks than boring holes. Accessories are available so that it can be used as a disc sander, polisher, power wire-brush, and power screwdriver.

DRIVING SCREWS

The tip of a screwdriver should match the screw slot's length and width as closely as possible. A tip that's too narrow can damage the slot; one that's too large can mar the surface of the wood.

When working on the surface of wood, use a screwdriver with a winged blade. For work below the surface, the wingless type is better because it won't mar the wood as the screw is tightened.

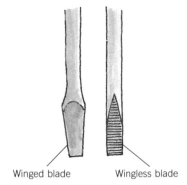

Winged blade   Wingless blade

To start a screw in a hard-to-reach spot, push the screw through a slit strip of masking tape (adhesive side up). Place the screwdriver tip into the screw slot and fold the tape ends to secure the screw to the screwdriver. Remove the tape after the screw has been started.

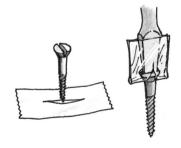

If screws are hard to turn or tighten, try rubbing their threads with soap or paraffin.

Unable to tighten a loose screw? Replace it with one that's larger in diameter, or insert wooden toothpicks to give the threads something to grip. If these fail, insert a plastic plug of the correct size into the screw hole, or squeeze wood filler into the hole and drive the screw while the filler is still wet.

Because a screw can only enter wood at the rate its thread cuts the wood, applying more pressure to a hard-to-turn screw is *not* the answer. What does help is to use a large-handled screwdriver with a blade as wide as the screw's slot.

To increase torque (turning force), use a wrench in conjunction with a large-handled, square-shanked screwdriver.

Want to conceal the head of a screw? First drill a pilot hole. Then drill a countersink hole with a bit that's the same size as the screw head. Insert the screw below the wood's surface. Fill the hole with a plug cut from the same wood or with wood putty.

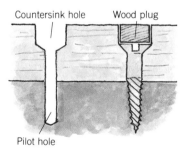

Countersink hole   Wood plug

Pilot hole

GLUING AND CLAMPING

If you're about to spread glue on a joint's surfaces, stop! First do a dry run-through with the clamps you plan to use.

If your C-clamps are too small for a particular job, place the stationary jaws of two clamps against one another to form an S, then tighten the screws onto the work.

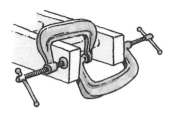

Two C-clamps and a length of braided wire cable can be used to make a clamp of any capacity. Loop the ends of the cable around the stationary jaws of the clamps, then tighten the adjustable screw pads around the work.

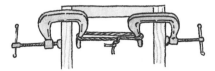

If you have any old thread spools, don't throw them away; they can be used to make a clamp. Find a bolt long and narrow enough to fit through two spools and the workpiece. Then insert the bolt through the spool holes, and tighten a wing nut to close the "jaws."

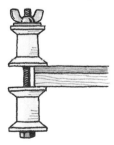

When applying wood glue, keep in mind that less is more. Apply thin, even coats of glue on mating surfaces; then clamp them together tightly for the correct length of time (p. 192).

To prevent glue squeeze-out from staining the area around a joint, apply masking tape to adjacent surfaces. Peel off the tape after the clamps have been removed and the glue has dried.

You'll know that clamps are sufficiently tight when a thin line of glue appears along the entire joint. Avoid overtightening; this can distort the work and weaken the joint by squeezing out too much of the glue.

Wood blocks taped to the jaws of clamps serve two purposes: they protect surfaces of the work from being marred or stained, and they distribute pressure more evenly, resulting in stronger glue joints.

Nothing's worse than finishing a gluing job only to find that the clamps or wood blocks are stuck to the wood. Avoid this by placing sheets of wax paper between surfaces and clamps.

To improvise a benchtop clamp for a large frame or other workpiece, secure stops to a benchtop and use paired wedges to hold work between them.

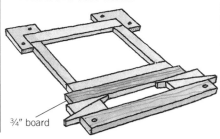

¾" board

WHICH GLUE FOR THE JOB?

Material	Adhesive type	Instructions	Comments
Wood to wood (indoors)	Polyvinyl acetate (white glue) or aliphatic resin (yellow carpenter's glue)	Ready to use; apply sparingly to both mating surfaces; clamp for 1½ to 4 hours; let dry for 24 hours at 70° F or above	Clamp polyvinyl acetate within 15 minutes of application, aliphatic resin within 5 minutes; dries clear or yellow; nonwaterproof; for cleanup, use soap and warm water
Wood to wood (outdoors)	Resorcinol	Mix components in a disposable container; apply to both mating surfaces; let set for 5 minutes; clamp for 16 hours; let dry for 24 hours at 70° F or above	Clamp within 1 hour of application; dries brown; waterproof; for cleanup, use cool water while wet
Laminate, veneer, or fabric to wood or wood products	Contact cement	Ready to use; apply to both mating surfaces and let dry; position material on underlayer, using brown paper to separate glued surfaces; when ready, remove brown paper and burnish top layer to underlayer with roller or wood block; no clamping necessary; let dry for 24 hours at 70° F or above	Join mating surfaces after application has dried on both surfaces; dries amber; water-resistant; for cleanup, see container for appropriate thinner
Metal to metal	Epoxy	Mix components in a disposable container; apply to both mating surfaces; clamp for 8 hours; let dry for 24 hours at 70° F or above	Clamp immediately after application; dries clear, white, or gray; water-resistant; for cleanup, use acetone while wet
Nonporous surfaces (metal, rubber, plastic, ceramic, and glass)	Cyanoacrylate (instant glue)	Ready to use; apply sparingly to one mating surface; press mating surfaces together, exerting pressure for 10 to 30 seconds; no clamping necessary; let dry for 12 hours at 70° F or above	Join mating surfaces immediately after application; dries clear; water-resistant; for cleanup, see container for appropriate thinner

Caution: The fumes from some glues are dangerous; therefore, always use glue in a well-ventilated area and never near an open flame. Cyanoacrylates bond to the skin; wear rubber gloves to prevent contact

Garage & Car Maintenance

ORGANIZING THE GARAGE OR CARPORT

Attach mirrors in the front and rear corners of your garage or carport. Install them at a height at which you can see if your car lights are working as you back out.

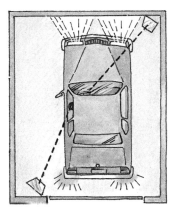

Hang an old worn-out tire from a garage or carport rafter, positioning it so that it rests against the back wall. If you happen to enter the area too fast, or if your brakes don't stop the car in time, the car's nose will hit soft rubber instead of a hard wall.

To make your garage or carport look neater, paint boundary lines on the floor to keep cars, bikes, lawn mowers, and other vehicles in their assigned spots.

Make a permanent hanger for an extension cord by tying rawhide or heavy twine behind the plug. After rolling up the cord, wrap the rawhide or twine around it, tie a bow, and use one of the bow loops to hang up the cord.

KEEPING THE FLOOR CLEAN

Kitty litter does a good job sopping up oil and other auto fluids. When there's a leak, place paper towels under your car until you can have repairs made.

To remove oil from a concrete driveway or garage floor, pour paint thinner over the affected area and cover with kitty litter. Leaving the garage door open, give the litter time to absorb the oil; then sweep up.

Caution: When using paint thinner, make sure that nobody smokes or strikes matches in the vicinity and that the working area is well ventilated.

A push broom makes the best garage floor sweeper. To keep the handle from loosening, reinforce it by screwing lengths of ⅛-inch-thick wire or a wire hanger between the pole and the broom head.

CLEANING THE WINDSHIELD

Moisten a rag or sponge with rubbing alcohol or mineral spirits to wipe away any windshield spots that resist store-bought window cleaners.

Are your car's windshield wipers smearing the windshield? Clean the windshield *and* the wiper blades with rubbing alcohol. If this doesn't work, scrub the windshield with a low-abrasion scouring powder to remove possible waxy buildup.

Sponge the inside of windows with vinegar to remove haze from plastic fumes in a new car. Rinse with water and wipe dry.

WASHING AND WAXING

Wash your car with a solution of dishwashing detergent and water. Starting with the roof, wash and rinse in sections so that the soap doesn't dry on the car. Dry with an old bath towel; then for a supershine, finish off with a good-quality chamois.

After a car has been thoroughly washed and waxed, spruce it up every now and then by hosing it down and wiping it dry with clean cloths or a sponge.

Shine up your car with the right kind of product. If your car is new, buy one designed specifically for new cars. If your car is older, however, you'll need a cleaner-polish with a light abrasive; severely weathered cars require an even more abrasive product.

WHEN TO SERVICE YOUR CAR

In addition to the regularly scheduled maintenance services outlined for your car by the manufacturer in the owner's manual, the following recommendations will help you keep your car trouble-free

While driving, be alert to the onset of any of the following; report it to a mechanic as soon as possible:

Slower-than-normal cranking

Vibration

Brake-pedal softness or hardness; brake noise

Steering-wheel pull

Unfamiliar engine noise

Automatic-transmission noise; slipping; erratic or rough shifting

Engine roughness and loss of power

Hard starting

Deterioration in ride and handling

Clutch chatter or slipping

Exhaust-system roar

No horn

Windshield-wiper streaking

Gasoline or other unusual odor

A dashboard warning light that comes on

A gauge that shows an abnormal reading

When filling the fuel tank:

Check engine oil level

Check coolant level

Once a month and before a long drive:

Check tire pressure (including that of the spare); examine tires for cuts and abnormal wear

Once a month (contd.)

Be sure that all lights work

Check ground beneath parked car for fluid leaks

Check automatic-transmission fluid level

Twice yearly (usually spring and fall):

Check power-steering, brake, and manual-transmission fluid levels

Check fluid level of hydraulically operated clutch

Check fluid level in rear axle

Check temperature protection strength of coolant

Inspect drive belts

Check radiator, heater, and air-conditioner hoses

Inspect exhaust-system components for signs of rust-through; retighten clamps

Rotate tires if mileage traveled since last rotation conforms with tire maker's rotation recommendation

Check front-wheel-drive axle boots for cracks and leaks

Examine battery-cable terminals for corrosion

Yearly:

Inspect brake lines for cracks; inspect brake pads and linings for wear (do this twice a year if most of your driving is stop-and-go)

Lubricate lock cylinders, body points, door hinges, hood hinges and latches, trunk hinges and latches, fuel-door hinges; check door weatherstripping

Test ability of parking brake and *Park* position of automatic transmission to hold

Make your whitewall tires sparkling clean. Apply undiluted liquid laundry detergent to wet tires with a scrub brush, then rinse.

ELIMINATING RUST

Apply a thin layer of clear silicone rubber sealant along the tops of body moldings to keep water from getting behind the moldings. Water trapped there can cause rust.

An electric hand grinder with a conical stone removes dime-size rust spots without damaging the surrounding paint. Use it carefully to avoid penetrating the metal. Follow with primer and paint.

Get rid of rust in hard-to-reach corners with a gasket scraper (available at auto parts stores). Brush with a small wire brush, then prime and paint.

CAR PROBLEMS

When a mechanic is working on your drum brakes, make sure he returns the plugs to the inspection holes in the backing plates. If he fails to reinstall these plugs, road grit will enter the brake housing and cause excessive wear.

It is important to check the brake fluid every 20,000 miles to see that it is no more than ½ inch below the top of the reservoir. If it is, have a mechanic check for a leak in the system.

CHANGING AN AIR FILTER

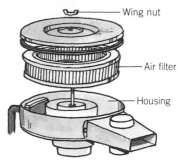

Wing nut
Air filter
Housing

1. The air filter is usually located in the housing at the top of the carburetor. Remove its cover by undoing the wing nut, clips, or nuts holding it in place. Disconnect any hose that's in the way. Lift out the filter.

2. Examine the filter for dirt, tears, or damage. Tap it against a solid surface to dislodge dirt and dust. Hold a light inside the filter as you revolve the filter around it. If you see light and the element is not coated with oil, you need not replace the filter.

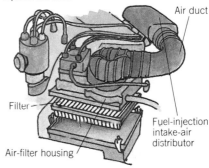

Air duct
Filter
Fuel-injection intake-air distributor
Air-filter housing

3. In some cars the air filter is hard to find. To locate it, trace the large air duct from the carburetor or from the intake-air distributor to its end. Undo the fasteners and proceed as explained. To reinstall the old filter or install a new one, reverse the procedure and secure the cover.

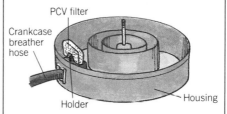

PCV filter
Crankcase breather hose
Holder
Housing

4. If your car has a positive-crankcase-ventilation (PCV) filter, inspect it as well. With the air-cleaner cover off, simply pull the PCV intake air filter out of its holder. (You needn't remove the clip and the holder or disconnect the hose.) Examine the filter; if it's dirty, clogged, or oil-soaked, replace it.

Spray belt dressing on the fan belt while the engine is running to tell at once if a squeal is caused by the belt. If the noise disappears, replace the fan belt. If it doesn't, look elsewhere for the problem.

If your car surges when you drive with the cruise control engaged, check for a bad speedometer cable or a clogged cruise-control vacuum hose. (Note: Add-on cruise controls don't have vacuum hoses.)

Are you suddenly feeling steering-wheel vibration in your front-wheel-drive car? Put your car on jack stands or have it lifted. Then squeeze the boot over the inner tie-rod socket on each side of the vehicle as you turn the wheel to the left and right. If parts inside the boot feel loose, replace both sockets to avoid losing your steering.

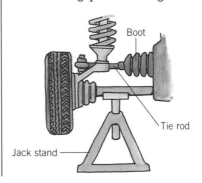

Boot

Tie rod

Jack stand

CHANGING THE OIL AND THE OIL FILTER

Band wrench

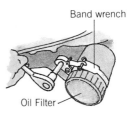

Oil Filter

1. Warm the car's engine; unless there is adequate working space beneath the car, raise and support the front of the car on jack stands or on ramps. (It's unsafe to work under a car supported only by the jack that comes with the car.) Place a pan beneath the drain plug.

2. Loosen the plug with a wrench; then turn by hand. Pull the plug away quickly to avoid hot oil. Drainage is complete when drips are 15 seconds apart. Clean the drain plug and drain hole with a soft rag or paper towel. Replace and tighten the plug by hand; then give it a half-turn with a wrench.

3. Although automobile manufacturers specify a new oil filter every other oil change, ideally, you should change the oil filter every time you change the oil. Move the pan beneath the filter. With a filter wrench, loosen the filter counterclockwise; then unscrew it by hand.

4. Wipe clean the mating surfaces of the filter and the engine. Coat the gasket of the new filter with clean engine oil; thread the filter clockwise onto the mounting stud, hand-tighten until the filter gasket makes light contact with the base; then turn 180 degrees with a filter wrench.

5. Lower the car. Wipe the oil-filler area clean and add the quantity and type of oil your owner's manual calls for. Run the engine for about a minute; then turn it off. Check for leaks at the plug and filter; then, with the dipstick, check the oil level and add more oil if necessary.

6. Pour the old oil into a plastic container with a top and dispose of it properly by taking it to a service station with a used-oil holding tank.

MAINTENANCE MISCELLANY

A thin coating of silicone dielectric grease (sold in hardware stores) or petroleum jelly will help prevent battery-terminal corrosion.

To loosen an oil filter that won't budge, buy a filter wrench or chain-type locking pliers that can grasp the filter close to the base, minimizing the twisting force.

Don't wait for radiator hoses to burst and leave you stranded. At least once a year feel the hoses. If they're spongy, disconnect them; push a rag into each hose, then pull it out. If flakes of rubber come out with the rag, replace the hose—it's starting to deteriorate.

To prevent excess wear on your tires, never turn the steering wheel while the car is standing still.

To see at a glance whether vehicle vibration has caused loosening of the nuts and bolts on wheels, put a dot of paint on each fastener as well as dots on adjacent parts. If side-by-side dots go out of line, you'll know the fastener needs retightening.

FUEL ECONOMY

Unless your owner's manual specifically recommends premium gasoline, don't buy it because you think it will provide greater fuel economy or more power. It doesn't—except in high-performance turbocharged engines. The only reason to switch from regular gasoline to premium is to rid an engine of a ping; but first see if a different brand of regular will do the job.

Don't top off a fuel tank in hot weather. Heat increases the pressure in a tank so that the fuel rises and overflows—an unnecessary waste.

Suspect a fuel leak if your fuel economy drops or you smell gasoline. If no fuel is leaking, try replacing the filter in the base of the evaporative emissions charcoal canister. (If there is no filter, replace the canister.) After 30,000 miles, this part can clog and cause these conditions.

Neither a dawdler nor a racer be. To attain maximum fuel economy when starting a car from a standstill, reach your desired speed quickly and smoothly. *Smoothly* is the key word.

OTHER ECONOMY MEASURES

Instead of replacing a coolant overflow tank that's leaking, insert a heavy-duty plastic freezer bag in the tank to hold the coolant.

Be safe and save money—replace shock absorbers in pairs. If only one shock is leaking or worn out, replace the other shock on the same axle even if the latter is all right; otherwise, vehicle stability will be affected.

197

ROAD EMERGENCIES

Getting stuck is no fun; it's also dangerous. Warn motorists by doing all of the following: open the hood; turn on the hazard-warning flashers; tie a distress flag to the door handle or to the antenna; and place warning flares 10 and 300 feet to the rear of the car and 100 feet to the front.

If the accelerator jams, tap it lightly; then lift up on it with your toe. If this doesn't free it, quickly shift into *Neutral*, apply the brakes to stop the car, then turn off the ignition.

To stop a car when the brakes fail, try pumping the brakes rapidly and repeatedly. If that doesn't slow the car, shift into low gear and gradually apply the parking brake.

REPLACING SPARK PLUGS

For peak ignition-system performance, inspect your car's spark plugs annually, or at least every 10,000 miles. If they appear worn or fouled, replace them—usually every 2 years or 20,000 miles. Any major brand of spark plug should perform properly in your engine if you use the part number for your make, model, and engine as listed in the plug manufacturer's catalog and install it correctly.

1. Let the engine cool, and label spark plug cables according to their location before removing them. Twist the boot to free the cable, then blow debris out of the plug port with compressed air. Fit a spark plug socket over the plug and apply pressure counterclockwise with a ratchet wrench to remove the plug. For hard-to-remove plugs, use a ratchet wrench and a U-joint.

2. As you take out each plug, wrap it with masking tape and note its engine location and whether it has deposits, oil, or carbon on its tips so that you can tell a mechanic later.

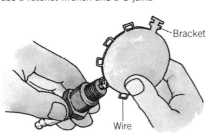

Bracket

Wire

3. Using a spark plug gauge, set the gap on the new plugs according to the specifications printed in the owner's manual or on a sticker under the car's hood. The specified thickness gauge should just slide through the gap between the electrodes (not easily and not with great force). Fit the gauge wire snugly in the gap. Use the gauge's bracket to bend the L-shaped side electrode to adjust the gap. Recheck with the wire.

4. Apply a coat of antiseize compound to the plug threads before installation in an aluminum cylinder head. Insert the plugs and screw them carefully into the engine (don't cross threads) until finger-tight. Using the ratchet wrench, turn the plugs with a gasket a quarter to a half turn; others a sixteenth. Apply silicone dielectric grease to the inside of the rubber nipple before reconnecting the cables to the plugs.

If dashboard lights or an accessory stops working, check for a blown fuse. If there is none, grasp the fuse controlling the device with a fuse puller. Move the fuse in and out. If the accessory works, pull the fuse. With an emery board, sand the contacts of the fuse and the holder to remove corrosion. Reinsert fuse.

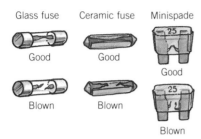

Glass fuse   Ceramic fuse   Minispade

Good   Good   Good

Blown   Blown

Blown

FLAT TIRES

Keep both your hands free for changing a flat tire at night— buy a magnetized battery-operated light or make a flashlight holder using a suction cup and a swivel clamp (available in hardware or photography stores).

If penetrating oil or rust remover isn't available to loosen frozen nuts and bolts, pour cola on them and let it penetrate.

OVERHEATING

If the temperature warning light glows or the temperature gauge nears the overheat mark while you're in traffic, turn the heater and the fan on at high speed, and drive to a garage as quickly as possible.

CHANGING A TIRE

1. Turn on the hazard warning flashers. Shift an automatic transmission into *Park*, a manual transmission into *Reverse*. Set the parking brake and turn off the ignition.

2. Check that the spare is inflated; if it's not, you'll have to pay for emergency road service. If the spare is adequate, block the tire that's diagonally opposite the flat tire with a chock or a large rock. Pry off the wheel cover and loosen each lug nut with one turn of the wrench.

3. Follow the instructions in the owner's manual or glued in the jack compartment, and jack the car up to raise the tire approximately 3 inches off the ground. (If you've parked the car on a soft surface, place a board under the jack to serve as a firm base.)

4. Remove the lug nuts, the wheel, and the tire; put on the spare. Reinstall the nuts by hand, tapered end first. Tighten the nuts with a wrench in the crisscross pattern shown. (Improperly tightened, they cause unequal pressure that can distort a wheel.) Lower the car and remove the jack and chock. Wrench-tighten all the nuts again in the correct sequence and tap the wheel cover into place.

To prevent road breakdowns, replace all hoses and belts every 4 years or 50,000 miles.

BATTERY PROBLEMS

If you have to jump-start a battery, make sure that both batteries are of the same voltage. Wear goggles to protect your eyes. Connect and disconnect cables in the order illustrated below.

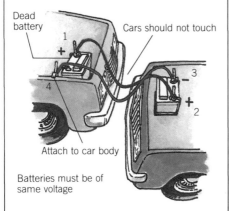

Dead battery

Cars should not touch

Attach to car body

Batteries must be of same voltage

If your battery has to be recharged every few weeks, check your car's interior lights. First push the switch button on the glove compartment to see if the light goes out, then open the hood and the trunk just a crack to see if either light is on. If so, remove the bulb until you can have repairs made.

COLD WEATHER

A car kept in a cold garage during subzero weather will start much more quickly in the morning if you buy a battery warmer, a low-wattage heating element in a blanket of insulation. It even helps a little when not plugged in because the insulation holds in heat.

If you park your car outdoors overnight in cold weather, position it so that the morning sun will hit the hood; if you're parking the car for the whole day, position it for the

A TOOL KIT FOR ROAD EMERGENCIES

Keep the following tools and supplies in your car to handle common emergencies. Wrap metal tools in cloths to prevent rattling. Keep all small items in an old suitcase or duffel bag. (For a winter emergency kit, see p.201.)

General equipment
Flashlight and spare batteries
Light that plugs into the cigarette lighter or clips to the car battery
Emergency flares and distress flag
Work gloves

Supplies
Squeeze-type siphon to pump gas from a fellow motorist's tank to yours
Gallon plastic jug to hold water or gas
Quart of engine oil
Board (2 feet by 1 foot) to serve as a base for a jack
Wheel chock (or use a roadside stone to chock the wheel)
Penetrating oil
Tire sealant-inflator
Jumper cables

Spare fuse kit and fuse puller
Scrap electrical wire for lashing down a sprung trunk lid or hood or for tying up a dropped tail pipe
Duct tape
Spare radiator hose
Spare fan belt
Spare clamp

Tools
Adjustable wrench
Insulated slip-joint, needle-nose, and locking pliers
Insulated screwdrivers: one Phillips head, one standard
Utility knife
Jack
Lug wrench; 2- to 3-foot length of pipe that fits over the end of the wrench

afternoon sun. The warmth from the sun may make the difference between starting and not starting.

If your car keeps stalling after you start it and before it warms up, the thermostatically controlled valve in the air-cleaner housing may be stuck. To check, reach with your hand or a screwdriver into the air-cleaner snorkel while the engine is running (cold). If the plate isn't closed to begin with and doesn't open gradually as the engine warms up, see an auto mechanic.

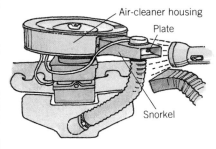

Air-cleaner housing
Plate
Snorkel

On cars that have carburetors, a malfunctioning choke vacuum break (also called a vacuum pull) may cause repeated stalling before the engine warms up in winter. Ask an auto mechanic to test this part.

If, on a mild winter day, you've flooded the engine from excessive pumping of the accelerator (you may smell gas) and your car has a carburetor, push the accelerator to the floor and keep it there for 15 seconds as you crank the engine. If the car still doesn't start, turn off the ignition for about a minute; then repeat the procedure.

DRIVING IN SNOW

Put snow tires on the front wheels of vehicles with front-drive axles and on the rear wheels of those with rear-drive axles.

PREPARING FOR WINTER

To get you and your car safely through the winter, have the following done before the onset of cold weather:

1. Ask a mechanic to test and replace the battery if it doesn't deliver current according to its cold-cranking amperage rating.
2. Tune the ignition and fuel systems. If necessary, install new spark plugs, test spark plug cables, adjust ignition timing, have cylinder performance tested, replace air and fuel filters, adjust slow and fast idle speeds, test the automatic choke, see that the carburetor's thermostatic air cleaner is working properly, inspect for vacuum leaks, inspect the distributor cap and rotor, and check the manifold heat control valve (if your car has one).
3. Drain, flush, and fill the cooling system with a mixture of antifreeze and water, in a concentration of 50 to 70 percent antifreeze. If the solution presently in the cooling system is less than 2 years old, you need only test it with a hydrometer to determine if it provides the necessary protection. If not, add more antifreeze.
4. Mount snow tires; make sure that all the tires (including the spare) are properly inflated and have adequate tread.
5. Test the heater, windshield defroster, and rear-window deicer/defogger.
6. Replace worn windshield wiper-blade squeegees.
7. See that the reservoir is filled with wintertime windshield-washer fluid.
8. Test all lights and flashers.
9. Add a scraper and brush to your emergency tool kit (p.200).
10. If you travel in areas where heavy snows are possible, gather emergency equipment: blankets or sleeping bags, a shovel, bags of sand, candles, matches, canned goods, plastic eating utensils, an empty 2-pound coffee can (to hold water or candles), and plastic bags.

Even in heavy snow country, keep your tires inflated at the pressure recommended by your owner's manual. Lowering the pressure won't give you better traction—it will only cause the outer parts of the tread to wear more rapidly.

For extra traction, place four 50-pound sacks of sand in the trunk of your car. (If necessary, you can spread this sand around the tires to help you out of a snowdrift or off a patch of ice.)

FROZEN LOCKS

If the door or trunk lock freezes, heat its key with a match; then quickly put the key into the cylinder and turn. To prevent burned fingers, wear gloves.

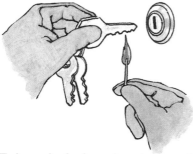

To keep locks from freezing, squirt some graphite lubricant (never oil) into the cylinders; then open and close the lock several times.

RUST

Salt splashed into the wheel wells can cause rust; be sure to hose away salt at the end of winter and at least once before then.

At the beginning of spring, rid the bottom of your car of all rust-causing agents. Park the car over a lawn-soaker hose and turn on the water for at least 20 minutes.

To prevent rust, most car doors have underside drain holes so that water can escape and moisture can dry. These holes eventually get plugged. At least once a year, probe them with a small screwdriver or a wire coat hanger to unclog them.

RAIN AND FOG

After driving through a deep puddle, test the brakes to make sure that they hold. If they're wet and don't hold, drop your speed to about 20 miles an hour and put your left foot lightly on the brake pedal. Driving like this for about a quarter of a mile will generate enough heat to dry the linings.

For maximum visibility in fog, a combination of fog lights and low headlight beams works best. Next best are the low beams by themselves. High beams provide minimum visibility.

If you pull over to the side of the road in fog, remember to turn on your hazard-warning flashers. A steady glow from parking lights may make a driver behind you think that you're driving too—and he may plow right into you.

SUMMERTIME

Before storing snow tires for the summer, spray them with silicone (never a petroleum product) to keep the rubber from drying. Do the same for conventional tires that you store for the winter. Lay stored tires flat, not on edge.

If your car begins to stall or hesitate in summer, switch to a different brand of gasoline. Alcohol blended into some brands can lead to problems in hot weather.

Yard & Garden

PLANNING FOR GARDEN ENJOYMENT

Beautifying your yard is satisfying—and even profitable. Well-placed trees, shrubs, flowering plants, and an attractive lawn can increase your property's value by as much as 10 percent.

Before drawing up a plan, call your municipality's building department. Ask about zoning and building regulations and laws that concern digging for any purpose other than tilling the soil.

It's best to live with a new garden a year before starting to plan. In that period, you can establish traffic patterns and snowdrift areas.

A detailed landscaping plan will help you visualize your future yard and give an idea of how to program the project in stages.

For accuracy, base your landscape plan on the property dimensions given in your property survey. If you don't have a survey, ask city or municipal authorities where you can get one.

MAKING A PLAN FOR LANDSCAPING YOUR YARD

Tape a sheet of graph paper to a work surface. Then, referring to your property survey, draw the outlines of features such as the house, garage, shed, driveway, existing trees, shrubs, and rock outcroppings. Mark the locations of drains, sewers, telephone, electric, and gas lines to avoid damage while landscaping. Indicate wind and sun directions to help you decide where to put trees, shrubs, hedges, beds, and fencing. Show areas of poor drainage, which you may want to correct. Identify house windows and all views: those you wish to keep and those you want to camouflage. Tape a sheet of tracing paper over this plan to draft your landscape design. Replace it with another sheet for changes.

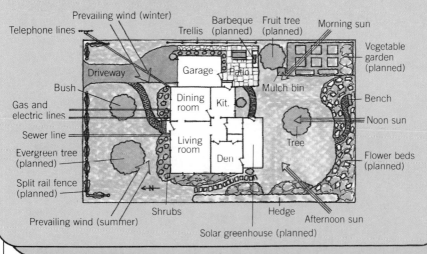

Prevailing wind (winter) — Telephone lines — Trellis — Barbeque (planned) — Fruit tree (planned) — Morning sun — Vegetable garden (planned) — Driveway — Garage — Patio — Mulch bin — Bench — Bush — Dining room — Kit. — Gas and electric lines — Noon sun — Sewer line — Living room — Den — Tree — Evergreen tree (planned) — Flower beds (planned) — Split rail fence (planned) — Shrubs — Hedge — Afternoon sun — Prevailing wind (summer) — Solar greenhouse (planned)

For quick and easy landscape plans, project photo slides of your yard onto large pieces of paper. After you trace the outlines of existing elements, sketch in your changes or additions. You'll see right away how the landscaping will look.

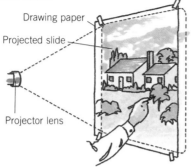

Drawing paper

Projected slide

Projector lens

On a windless day, two weeks before spring planting, spray poison ivy and poison oak with glyphosphates. Wear heavy-duty cotton gardening gloves when you spray and also when you cut off the dead plants. Double-bag the plants for disposal or for burying.

Keep your goal in mind when planning the placement of shade trees. If you want afternoon shade on a southwest-facing patio, for instance, plant a small tree no more than 15 feet south and west of it. For a tree that will grow to be very large, you must increase these distances accordingly.

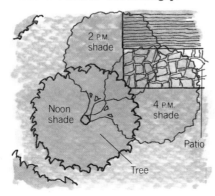

2 P.M. shade

Noon shade

4 P.M. shade

Patio

Tree

Plan your planting for a brilliant fall-foliage display. Ash, ginkgo trees, smoke trees, birches, witch hazels, sugar maples, and poplars provide brilliant yellows; red oaks, red maples, juneberry, arrowwoods, and winged euonymuses furnish gorgeous reds and oranges.

Avoid planting trees or shrubs over or near drains, waterlines, and septic fields. Their extensive root systems—particularly those of such water-loving species as willows and poplars—can cause damage by cracking and clogging the tile or pipe.

If you find that you have to run a sewer, gas, or drain line under a tree, aiming the trench under the trunk's center may avoid extreme root damage.

Lateral planting beds will make your yard look longer and deeper, if you angle their inside borders toward each other from the front to the rear of the yard.

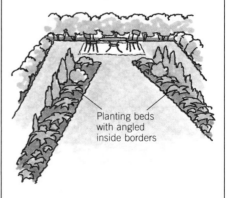

Planting beds with angled inside borders

GARDEN STRUCTURES

If your property's grade must be raised because of construction, protect your valuable trees with a drainage and air circulation system so they won't suffocate. Consult a landscaper for this task.

Highlight garden features at night with spotlights and floodlights. You can plan the effect of their placement by positioning a high-powered flashlight in various locations. Well-lit paths and entrances promote safety and help discourage burglars.

Spotlight
Floodlight

Creosote-treated lumber greatly prolongs the life of fences and retaining walls, but it can also be toxic to plants. Lumber treated with copper-based preservatives is safer.

To help fence posts shed rain water effectively, saw off their tops at an angle or cover them with sloping metal caps (available at most lumberyards).

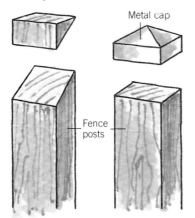
Metal cap
Fence posts

YOUR SOIL'S pH FACTOR

Before you landscape, test your soil's alkalinity and acidity. Because do-it-yourself soil-test kits aren't completely reliable, let your nearest agricultural college or your province's agricultural experimental station do the job. Dig up soil samples from different parts of your garden. Dry them and seal them in plastic bags before you have them tested. For a moderate fee, the agricultural experts will analyze your soil, tell you how it can best be used, and suggest how it can be improved. A landscape gardener will also test your soil for a fee.

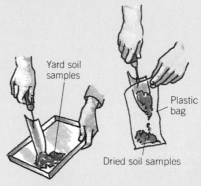
Yard soil samples
Plastic bag
Dried soil samples

Test results will reveal your soil's pH. The pH scale ranges from 1 to 14, indicating whether the soil is sweet (alkaline) or sour (acid). Most plants flourish in neutral soils (pH 6.5 to 8); some, however, require distinctly acid (pH 4 to 6) or alkaline soils (pH 8 or higher). The test results will indicate which trees and plants are right for your yard. If, after testing, you still want to plant species that are not suited to your soil, you'll need to alter the soil.

Acid-favoring trees: Fir, flowering dogwood, hemlock, hickory, oak, pine, red maple, spruce.

Acid-favoring shrubs: Azalea, bog rosemary, cistus, heather, holly, mountain laurel, rhododendron.

Alkaline-favoring trees: Black locust, juniper, sugar maple.

Alkaline-favoring shrubs: Bamboo, boxwood, butterfly bush, cotoneaster, forsythia, lilac, mock orange.

TREES AND SHRUBS

Are chilling winds inflating your home heating bill? If so, shield the windy side of your house with a staggered double row of evergreen trees, cutting heating costs.

Staggered double row

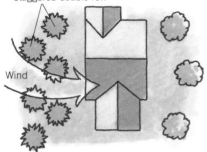

Wind

If you want a fast-growing protective barrier against the wind, plant a row of poplars on the windward side of the evergreens. The poplars will act as "nurse" trees and should be removed once the evergreens are fully grown.

Let deciduous trees and shrubs help regulate your home's temperature. In summer their sun-blocking leaves help keep the house cool; in winter their bare branches let the sunshine in.

When shrub branches are split or broken, it's better to prune them back than to try mending them with a splint.

BUYING AND PLANTING

Don't buy a burlapped evergreen that has a cracked, loose soil ball. Its leaves may wilt or curl after you have planted it. Or, after a brief healthy period, its leaves may fall off and it will die.

If you're a bargain hunter, bare-root trees and shrubs may be for you. They're often less than half the price of balled-and-burlapped specimens, and if watered properly, they have a very high survival rate.

You can successfully plant many trees in early fall, but some, such as birches, red and silver maples, are better off being planted in the early spring.

When you have to transplant a large shrub, put it on a snow shovel and slide it across the lawn.

FERTILIZING AND WATERING

Feed tree roots in late fall when the ground is moist; use a fertilizer of medium nitrogen content: 2 pounds per trunk-diameter-inch at breast height. Pour it in evenly spaced holes, 2 feet deep, from the trunk to a few feet beyond the drip line. Or use micropore release packets. Their fertilizer is slowly released over 3 to 8 years.

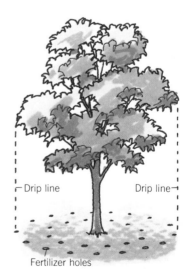
Drip line   Drip line

Fertilizer holes

American beech and crab apple trees are especially sensitive to fertilizer. When treating them, reduce the usual dosage by half.

Spray your shrubs for quick results. Liquid fertilizer sprayed onto the leaves is absorbed by plant tissues in minutes.

If your shrubs' yellowing leaves result from iron-poor soil, use an iron-mixture spray: 1 teaspoon chelated iron to 1 gallon water.

Water your evergreens, rhododendrons, laurels, and hollies in early November if the soil is dry. Because their leaves give off moisture, they need those extra showers before winter begins.

PRUNING

Your maples, elms, dogwoods, birches, and yellowwoods won't "bleed" if you prune them in late summer or early fall.

For cleaner, faster healing cuts, use a bypass (hook-and-blade) pruner on branches.

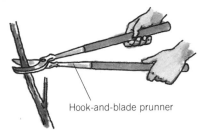

Hook-and-blade prunner

Prune trees in winter when they're dormant. Less trauma for them and no leaf-raking for you.

Prune forsythia and honeysuckle, as well as other spring-flowering shrubs, after they bloom; shrubs that flower in summer (rose of Sharon, for example) should be pruned in early spring.

PLANTING A YOUNG TREE

The best time to plant a young tree is on a cool, windless, and overcast day in early spring or early fall. You'll need a shovel, long-nose pliers, a hammer, a garden hose, two 6-foot wooden stakes, two 6-inch rubber buffers (from an old hose), 24 feet of heavy-gauge wire, and soil nutrients (those indicated by a soil test) plus peat moss or compost. Water the tree's root ball well before you begin the task.

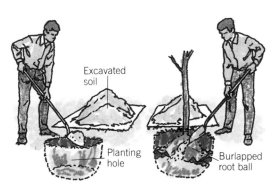

Excavated soil

Planting hole

Burlapped root ball

Buffers

Wire

Stakes

"Dish"

1. Dig a hole that's roughly twice the diameter of your tree's root ball and 1½ times as deep. Crumble the soil you've dug up together with the peat moss or compost and the added nutrients. Make your mix 1 part additive, 2 parts soil.

2. Refill the hole until the tree can sit with its crown at the same level as the surrounding ground. Untie the ball's burlap casing. Roll down the casing carefully so that the soil ball remains intact. Finish refilling.

3. Tamp the soil around the tree into a dishlike depression. Fill it with water and let it soak in. Beyond the tree's roots, drive stakes 2 feet into the wet soil. Wrap the wired buffers around the trunk as you anchor the tree to the stakes. Leave some slack.

Avoid collar damage when pruning a damaged limb by stub-cutting it first and then sawing off the stub where the collar ends. This promotes quick healing and lessens the chance of decay.

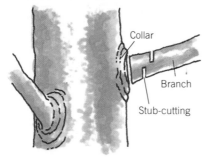

It's better to let tree cuts heal on their own rather than treat them with wound dressing. By keeping the wood damp, wound dressing encourages decay.

Don't give apple trees a heavy trimming in summer. If you cut off a lot of foliage, you expose their delicate bark to the hot sun, which can cause scorching.

PROTECTION FROM WILDLIFE

Safeguard saplings from rabbits and mice: Wrap their trunks with strips of fiberglass insulation.

You can protect bushes and trees against rabbits by surrounding the trunks with plastic guards (available at hardware stores) or spraying them with rodent repellent.

To protect your shrubs from hungry deer, suspend a bar of Ivory soap wrapped in netting from the shrubs' branches.

CUTTING BACK AND RETRAINING OVERGROWN HEDGES

Some hedge plants, such as privet, prunus, and honeysuckle, react well to drastic pruning. Cut them back to 6-inch stumps and they'll quickly sprout new growth. Forsythia, rugosa roses, and barberry also may regain vigor after you've cut back their old branches to ground level. Such drastic pruning must be done in early spring and you must give the plants extra fertilizer and regular waterings.

Most hedge plants, however, require more gradual training and should be cut back in stages over a 3-year period. Here's how:

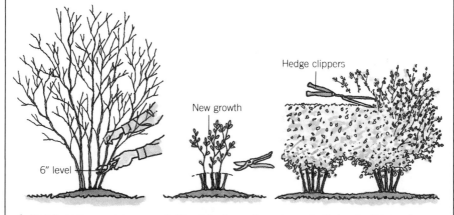

1. In early spring, reach in near the center of the shrub and cut back two or three of the oldest branches to 6-inch stumps.

2. The following spring, when you see new growth sprouting from these stumps, prune the other large branches.

3. During the third spring, cut back the youngest branches to reduce the hedge to the desired height and width.

Have squirrels been harvesting your apples before you've had a chance to do the job? Puncture a hole in a dozen aluminum pie plates; tie them singly with twine to the low branches of your fruit trees. The clanging will frighten the squirrels away.

Aluminum pie plates

LAWN PROBLEMS

If a soil test shows that your soil needs lime, apply it in early fall and thereafter no oftener than every 3 years. If you've already limed too much and your soil suffers from calcium excess, treat it with elemental sulphur: 5 pounds per 1,000 square feet.

If moles are tunneling your lawn, there are grubs in it. Treat the lawn with an insecticide (diazinon or chlorpyrifos) to rid it of grubs, and the moles will depart.

Patches of turf mysteriously torn up overnight? Quite likely the work of insect-seeking raccoons or skunks. A sprinkling of moth crystals may help to persuade them to dine elsewhere.

LAWN MAINTENANCE

Question: With all the different brands of turf fertilizer on the market, how can I choose the one that is best for my lawn?
Answer: Shop by formula, not by brand. The three numbers on the product's label — 10–6–4, for example — stand for the percentages of major nutrients it contains — nitrogen, phosphorus, and potassium, in that order. The high nitrogen content of 10–6–4 (10 percent) makes this an ideal spring-feeding formula, one that encourages leaf growth. Switch to 5–10–5 in fall when the high phosphorus content (10 percent) benefits the roots.

Question: My neighbor spreads lime on his lawn every spring. Is that necessary?
Answer: Only if a soil test (p.205) shows that your lawn's pH needs adjusting. Too much lime encourages crabgrass.

Question: How can I tell when my lawn needs watering?
Answer: If your footprints stay on the lawn, it needs water. Well-watered turf springs back; dry grass doesn't.

Question: How often should I water my lawn, and how much water does it need?
Answer: In general, you should water twice a week, 1/2 inch of water each time; if the soil is sandy, 1/2 inch three times weekly. To gauge the amount, place measure-marked containers within the sprinkler's range.

Question: How often should I mow?
Answer: A weekly light mowing is good for most lawns. Never cut more than 40 percent of the leaf blades; a close cut weakens turf and causes browning.

Question: Is there any way to make leaf removal easier?
Answer: Rent an industrial-grade leaf blower. It will make a clean sweep in a short time. Or let gravity work for you: rake leaves down a slope. Bag them for disposal or run them through a shredder for mulch or compost.

Question: My turf fertilizer contains synthetic nitrogen. Is organic better?
Answer: Because organics release their nutrients more slowly, their benefits last longer than those of synthetics.

Moss on your lawn may result from poor drainage and compacted soil. A cheap remedy is gypsum, spread at the rate of 40 pounds per 1,000 square feet.

Rake up grass clippings from the lawn regularly. Without a grass catcher, clippings accumulate faster than they decompose, forming a thick covering of thatch, which can prevent water and fertilizer from penetrating a lawn.

If your lawn gets heavy traffic, you can increase its resilience by encouraging strong root growth. Apply superphosphate: 10 pounds per 100 square feet annually.

Accumulations of leaves left on the lawn will smother the grass. Rake them away promptly before they form a blanket.

CUTTING THE GRASS

If grass tips turn white after you've mowed, your mower blades probably need to be sharpened. Rotary blades should be honed monthly, reel types annually.

To prevent the soil beneath your lawn from becoming compacted, use a garden fork to loosen and aerate it once a year. All you need to do is thrust the fork into the soil and wiggle it back and forth. Or, if you prefer, wait until you've mowed the lawn and then rent a mechanical aerator for the job.

Swiftly turning mower-blade tips can turn sticks and stones into dangerous missiles. Use a rear-mounted grass-collection system to prevent accidents caused by flying objects.

GETTING RID OF LAWN WEEDS

Know your enemy well! Accurate identification is the key to weed control; different weed types need different treatments.

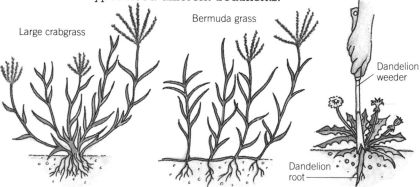

Large crabgrass

Bermuda grass

Dandelion weeder

Dandelion root

Annual grasses. In spring, crabgrass and other annual weed grasses sprout. As they grow, they tend to crowd out the turf grasses. About the time crocuses start to blossom, you can eliminate the annual weed grasses with a preemergent herbicide that won't harm turf grasses. These include DCPA, amitrole, siduron, and bensulide.

Perennial grasses. Many coarse grasses are unsuitable for lawns because they form tufts. Equally unsuitable are fine-leafed bent grasses, which turn brown with heat and close-mowing. Preemergent chemicals won't control perennial weed grasses. Instead, spray isolated clumps with glyphosphate. For widespread infestations, kill the entire lawn with glyphosphate, then reseed.

Broadleaf weeds. You can uproot some of these perennials (plantain and other fibrous-root species) with a trowel; tap-rooted species must be levered out with a dandelion weeder. Certain weeds with tenacious roots are easier to eliminate by treating them with 2,4-D, or some other chemical, in spring or fall.

Tractor wheels won't compact the soil if you vary your mowing pattern weekly.

When mowing without a grasscatcher, mow inward and counterclockwise from the lawn's outer perimeter. Clippings won't pile up on uncut turf and clog your mower; they'll be blown outward.

Prevent houseflies from breeding in grass clippings matted on mower parts. Clean the clippings off before putting your mower away.

PATCHING OR STARTING A LAWN

Renovate your lawn in early spring before the weather gets hot. Or, if you wish, renovate during late summer to give the grass a chance to become well established before the winter comes.

Replace small bare patches on your lawn by cutting in new sod. Remove the soil to a depth of ¾ inches, cut the edges of the exposed area square, and fit the sod into place.

Buy only "certified" grass seed. This label means that the container has been federally inspected for purity and quality. Certified grass seed also contains less weed seed than non-certified types.

Be sure to specify "fertile loam" when buying topsoil to supplement existing soil; if you say just "topsoil," you may wind up with a poor, worthless soil.

When spreading seed or fertilizer, ensure even coverage by working in a crisscross pattern. Spread one half moving from north to south; the other half from east to west.

Lightly rake the soil to bury grass seed for germination. Or drag the bottom end of a chain link fence section across the seeded patch.

Salt hay makes an ideal light mulch for newly seeded lawns. Available at most garden centers, it's cheap and free of weed seeds, and it decomposes rapidly.

To keep seed from being washed off a steep slope, peg cheesecloth over it. Grass will grow right through the porous cloth, which can be removed later.

Water a newly sown seedbed daily (twice a day when the weather is sunny or windy). Keep the soil moist but not flooded.

When rototilling for a new lawn, break up clods that are larger than golf balls, but don't reduce the soil to powder—powder eliminates the surface crevices where seeds find shelter from the drying wind and sun.

IMPROVING GARDEN SOIL

Leave healthy topsoil alone. Tilling or spading yearly only destroys soil structure and curbs fertility. If you want to give your soil extra enrichment, use an organic mulch; it not only controls weeds, it breaks down into humus.

Coffee grounds are good for your garden. Sprinkle them around melons and carrots, for instance. As they decompose, they supply the soil with nutrients.

You can still grow flowers and vegetables even if your soil turns out to be infertile, stony, and poorly drained. Solve the problem by building framed raised beds and filling them with enriched soil. See the box on the next page.

A cheap and nutritious mulch for your flower beds? Try autumn leaves. Run your power mower over them to chop them up.

DOUBLE DIGGING

To keep your flower bed in the best condition, or to prepare the ground for deep-rooted plants, work the soil deeply by making trenches or double digging.

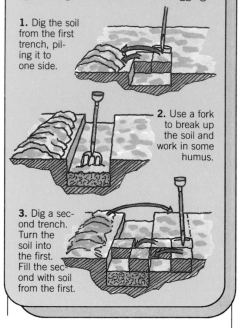

1. Dig the soil from the first trench, piling it to one side.

2. Use a fork to break up the soil and work in some humus.

3. Dig a second trench. Turn the soil into the first. Fill the second with soil from the first.

COMPOSTING THE EASY WAY

Choose an isolated corner of your yard—a shady or sunny, well-drained, slightly sloping spot—for your compost heap. You can build a compost bin of wire mesh or wooden slats (one side removable) or leave your compost pile freestanding. In hot weather, compost may be garden-ready in roughly 6 weeks.

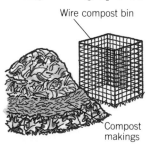

Wire compost bin / Compost makings

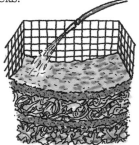

Garden-ready compost

1. Pile compost makings near the bin: dead leaves, grass clippings, weeds, and such kitchen waste as coffee grounds and fruit and vegetable peelings (no meat or dairy foods).

2. Stack the mixture in the bin in concave layers 5 to 10 inches deep. Wet each layer thoroughly. Sprinkle the makings with handfuls of 10-10-10 fertilizer or with horse manure, and add 2 inches of rich garden soil.

3. Turn the pile with a fork every other week (or be lazy and don't, if you can wait a year for results). Keep the pile wet. When the compost pile becomes crumbly brown, it's garden-ready.

PLANNING AND PLANTING FLOWER BEDS

Keep your flower border to a reasonable width—5 to 6 feet is the best. Arrange to have a narrow path at the back of the bed to make weeding easier.

For a beautiful, stronger display, plant flowers in groups of at least three of the same type and color. Larger groupings or drifts are even more dramatic.

If you have a shady garden, think of it as a challenge instead of a limitation. Many beautiful flowering plants can tolerate shade in partial or full doses: coralbells, meadow rue, goatsbeard, daylily, and Solomon's seal are just a few.

BULBS

Plant bulbs at a depth two and a half times their diameter. A daffodil bulb with a diameter of 3 inches should be planted approximately 7½ inches deep.

If deer are a problem in your area, plant daffodils and forget about tulips. Deer relish tulip flowers but won't touch daffodils.

Fertilize your tulips with a commercial bulb food in early spring before their tips appear. Spread it over the bed, rake it lightly into the soil, and let spring showers take care of the rest.

Do you want your spring bulbs to have bigger, longer-lasting blossoms? Save the potash-rich wood ashes from your stove or fireplace and sprinkle them over the soil at the start of the growing season. Remember, however, that wood ashes increase soil alkalinity.

BUILDING A RAISED BED

Raised beds provide many advantages, such as warmer planting soil, easier weeding, and minimal soil erosion; they're good-looking structures too.

You can build an 8- by 12-foot, two-tier, raised bed in a few days. You'll need 10 used 8-foot railway ties (two sawn in half), 12 3-foot, ⅜-inch reinforcing bars (rebars), a dozen 12-inch galvanized spikes, a shovel, and a 6-pound mallet. If you want a raised bed higher than 3 feet, check local building codes to see if this is allowed.

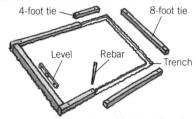

1. Choose a site, then lay the first tier (four 8-footers and two halves) in an 8- by 12-foot rectangle; where the ends meet, leave space for drainage. Mark the tier's outline with a shovel blade; then remove the ties and dig out a level trench 2 inches deep. About 6 inches from the ends of each tie, drill a ¾-inch hole.

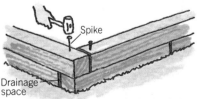

2. Reposition the ties in the trench, check them with a level, then nail them to the ground with the rebars. Position the second-level ties so that they overlap the ends of those beneath. This will stengthen the frame. Spike the two levels together.

3. Fill the frame with topsoil mixed with well-rotted compost, stable manure, or decomposed leaves. The total amount of topsoil and organic materials required to fill an 8- by 12-foot raised bed is about 3½ cubic feet. Organic materials should comprise about a quarter of the volume.

To hide daffodils that have flowered, gather the foliage into bunches, bend them over, and put a rubber band around each bunch. Interplant with annuals, which soon grow and hide the foliage.

Bound foliage   Annual

Allow bulb foliage on your lawn to die back before you mow. It's a source of nourishment for next year's flowers.

Spring flowering bulbs must be planted in the fall. If you are given some daffodil or tulip bulbs in the late fall, get them into the ground as quickly as possible. If you simply store them, they will not survive the winter.

Plant tulips 8 to 10 inches deep in the ground. If you plant the bulbs above this level, they will divide into numerous small bulblets the following spring. Unfortunately, bulblets produce leaves but no flowers.

If you want more daffodils and grape hyacinths, simply make use of their bulblets. In early summer, when the foliage is brown, excavate the bulbs, pry off the bulblets, and then replant them all. It'll be 1 to 2 years before grape hyacinths produce blooms; 2 to 3 years for daffodils.

TRANSPLANTING YOUNG PLANTS

Bulblets

Before transplanting young plants in your garden, take two weeks to ready them for change by gradually exposing them to sunshine and outdoor conditions. Place their flats in a cold frame that can be covered during the night. Increase the daily dose of sunlight by leaving the flats uncovered for longer periods. If you have no cold frame, place the flats out during the day and bring them in later each night. Continue this process until the plants have been out all night—just before planting. Transplant when all danger of frost is past and the soil is warm. Perform this task on a cloudy day or a windless afternoon or evening.

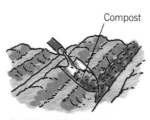

Compost

Cardboard strip

1. With a trowel dig a furrow or individual holes deep enough to accommodate the plants at the same level at which they've been growing. Mix compost with the soil at the bottom, or work in 1 teaspoon 5-10-10 fertilizer (per plant) in the holes or furrow and cover with 2 inches of soil to prevent contact with the plants' roots. Fill with water and let it soak in.

2. Water the flats well a day before you transplant. Carefully work your trowel into the soil under a plant; use your hand for added support as you lift it out of the flat. Keep the soil-covered roots intact as much as possible.

3. Wrap a 2-inch strip of cardboard or tarpaper around the stem of each vegetable transplant to protect it from cutworms; better still, collar it with a bottomless styrofoam cup. Place plants in the furrow or holes; fill in and firm soil around each stem. Half of the collar should be visible. Water generously; keep moist until the plants are well established and show signs of growth.

When forcing crocus or hyacinth bulbs, add charcoal to the water to avoid unsightly algae growth.

Continue to water and feed forced bulbs after they have finished blooming. Once the foliage dies down, they can be dried off for fall planting.

CHOOSING ROSES

For free advice on planning or planting a rose garden, write to the Canadian Rose Society, 686 Pharmacy Avenue, Scarborough, Ont. M1L 3H8. It will put you in touch with expert rose growers in your area.

Price isn't always a guide to rose quality. No. 1 roses (the finest) usually cost more than nos. ½ and 2. But tried-and-true classics (more plentiful) are often cheaper than the latest prizewinners.

Shrub roses are the modern counterpart of the old-fashioned garden roses. In general, they bloom intermittently and need little pruning. Older canes from established bushes should be removed in early spring. Shrub roses vary greatly in hardiness. Some types thrive only in coastal British Columbia; varieties that grow on the Prairies need protection. Consult your local nursery for the varieties that are suitable for your area.

Thorny Scotch roses form a highly effective barrier against animals and they also tolerate poor soil.

Rugged rugosa roses are an ideal choice for cold-climate or seaside plantings. These attractive shrubs will survive salt spray, prolonged drought, and temperatures as low as −30° F. They grow into dense hedges which, like all hedges, must be controlled by pruning.

Climbing roses make a beautiful ground cover. Just peg their canes to the ground with wire hoops.

HOW TO CONTROL AND INCREASE YOUR PERENNIALS

Many perennials grow outward, dying at the center. This can give your flower bed or border a ragged, unhealthy appearance. If you have overgrown perennials, rejuvenate them by dividing each one into many plants. Water them first, then, a couple of days later, dig them up and divide them. Although most perennials can be divided in either spring or fall, there are exceptions, such as peonies (late summer) and chrysanthemums and shasta daisies (spring).

1. Cut your perennials back to a height of 6 inches so that you can easily choose those that need dividing. After you've selected one, dig out the entire clump, being careful to keep the roots as intact as possible.

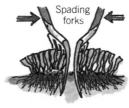

2. Take two spading forks and insert them back-to-back into the clump. Press their handles together and pry the plant apart slowly. If it has a dead center, divide the living portion into smaller clumps for replanting.

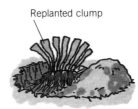

3. Enrich the soil in the hole with humus and a nitrogen-free fertilizer such as 0-10-10. Replant one clump in the old hole and the others elsewhere in the flower bed or border.

ROSE CLASSES: THEIR CARE AND CHARACTERISTICS

Feed your roses a balanced fertilizer (5-10-5) or prepared rose food in spring when the buds swell; when one blooming period ends (to encourage another); and in mid-to-late summer for a fall flowering. Roses should not be fed during the first year after planting.

The majority of roses fall into one of the following classes:

Hybrid tea rose. They bloom continuously from late spring until frost and display large, bright, double flowers (usually one per stem) with conical centers. The canes should be cut back in early spring. They make excellent cut roses. With sufficient protection, they can thrive even on the Prairies.

Antique rose. This class includes China, tea, and noisette roses, all of which are found in British Columbia. Other types, such as hybrid perpetuals, bourbons, or gallicas, and roses introduced before the hybrid tea's first appearance (1864), grow in colder parts of Canada. China, tea, and noisette roses require relatively little pruning or spraying. The other types benefit from spring pruning of no more than one third of each cane and another similar pruning after the first flush of flowers.

Floribunda. They bloom heavily throughout the growing season, displaying clusters of saucer-shaped flowers. Although hardier and more disease resistant than hybrid teas, they require the same treatment. They make an excellent flowering hedge.

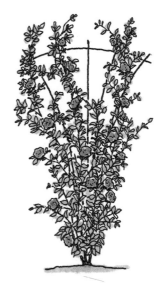

Grandiflora. These tall, stately bushes bloom much like floribundas, combining that class's free-flowering, hardy habits with the blossoms of the hybrid tea. They require the same care as the hybrid tea.

Climber. This class includes everbloomers and once-blooming roses. Prune everblooming types in early spring. Remove dead and diseased stems; retain new canes. When blossoms fade, cut back the side branches for new flower growth: ¼ inch above the second of five-leaflet leaves. Prune ramblers and other once-blooming types after flowering; remove dead canes. In most areas of Canada, climbers require winter protection.

MAINTAINING ROSES

When pruning roses, start by removing the three D's: dead, damaged, and diseased wood. Finish by getting rid of all crossing and weak branches.

If your roses' leaves develop sooty spots and then fall off prematurely, the bush is probably suffering from black spot, a fungus disease. Give the plant weekly treatments with benomyl spray.

Would you like your hybrid tea roses to bear larger flowers? With your fingertips, carefully nip off the tiny side buds below the central terminal bud.

VEGETABLES AND FRUITS

Lick weed problems before starting a new garden: Plant buckwheat in the spring. Thick growing, it smothers weeds and adds humus to the soil. Be sure to turn this crop under before it sets seed.

Radishes can serve several purposes when you sow them along with slow starters such as carrots. Quick sprouters, they make good row markers; they also loosen the soil as they push up and as you harvest them.

If you're saddled with a space problem in your yard, consider planting dwarf fruit trees. Many bear fruit earlier than standard varieties, and you'll never need a ladder to prune, spray, or harvest.

INCREASING CROPS

Make the most of your garden space by planting lettuce seedlings between slow-maturing vegetables (broccoli, cabbage).

You can increase the productivity of a small garden by planting fruits and vegetables among flowers. Strawberries, parsley, and chives make neat borders; carrot and asparagus fronds are attractive among perennials.

PLANTING BARE-ROOT ROSES

You can order bare-root roses by mail or buy them from a local nursery. You should plant them only in early spring or late fall, depending on your climate zone. Reliable suppliers will schedule their delivery to arrive at the correct planting time in your area.

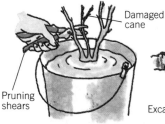
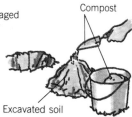
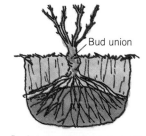

1. Unpack bare-root plants as soon as they arrive and immerse them—roots and stems—in a pail of water for 24 hours. Cut back broken roots and damaged canes before planting.

2. Dig a hole that will accommodate the roots without crowding. Add compost, peat moss, or well-rotted manure to the excavated soil, increasing the soil's volume one third.

3. Set the plant on a small mound at the bottom of the hole; spread its roots out evenly. Its bud union should be below the level of the surrounding bed. Fill the hole three-quarters full, and then fill with water. After it drains, finish filling the hole.

Reap several harvests from your spinach, lettuce, and chard: Cut them back to 2 inches instead of uprooting the plant. They'll grow back again and again.

Harvest several cabbages from one plant. When spring-planted cabbages are somewhat larger than baseballs, cut them off, but leave four outer leaves on each stalk. In autumn, there'll be a small, delicious cabbage for each outer leaf.

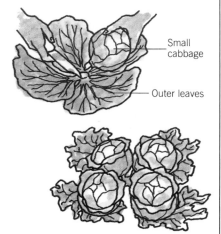

Small cabbage

Outer leaves

After harvesting your peas, cut off the plants for your compost heap and leave the roots in the ground; they're a rich source of nitrogen. Plant green beans several inches away from these roots so that they can benefit from them. Leave green bean roots in the ground after harvest; they're nitrogen-rich too. You can plant other crops in this area next season without using a nitrogen fertilizer.

ENCOURAGING GROWTH

Want a two-week head start on melons? Bottomless plastic milk jugs set over the seedlings make effective miniature greenhouses. On sunny days, remove the caps for ventilation.

Did you know that 6 to 7 pounds of human hair contain as much nitrogen as 200 pounds of manure? Get clippings from a local barbershop, but use them sparingly.

MULCHES

Make your newspapers do double duty: use them for mulch after you've read them. A layer, several sheets thick and anchored with rocks, makes a cheap, water-conserving, biodegradable mulch. Avoid pages with colored ink; they may contain lead.

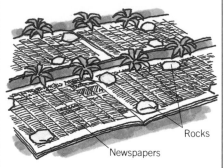

Rocks

Newspapers

Get earlier, heftier tomato crops by mulching with black plastic. An efficient solar collector, this material warms the soil and increases yields. To achieve even greater growth, set large waxed cardboard containers (used for fruit juice or milk) around tomato transplants. These cardboard chimneys vent the plastic's heat up around the plants.

While your watermelons grow, their vines can act as a living mulch around root crops such as onions, carrots, and beets. Plant root crops in rows 8 feet apart, with hills of watermelons running down the center.

When preparing your strawberry garden for winter, apply mulch only after the ground freezes. If you do it before, the mulch might stimulate root growth and jeopardize the plants when sub-zero temperatures do arrive.

CHOOSING MULCHES

Mulches protect and improve the soil they cover by conserving moisture, keeping soil temperature uniform, and reducing weed problems. Many kinds of materials, each with advantages and drawbacks, make good mulches.

Organic mulches. These include such materials as buckwheat, ground corncobs, cocoa-bean hulls, grass clippings, old hay, shredded leaves, pine needles, and shredded or chipped bark. Because many of these materials are agricultural by-products, they may be quite inexpensive locally. Organic mulches add humus and nutrients to the soil as they decompose. They also serve as insulation, keeping the soil cool in hot weather. Apply a 2- to 4-inch layer in midspring; turn over with a spading fork in late fall to evict overwintering insects and rodents.

Inert mulches. Crushed stone, pebbles, gravel chips, fiberglass insulation, black plastic film, and plastic fabric (spunbonded polypropylene) are among the inert mulches. Because these materials don't decompose, they last longer than the organics but lack their soil-building qualities. Plastic mulches are especially effective at curbing weed growth and warming the soil to speed the growth of heat-loving crops such as peppers, tomatoes, and eggplant. Roll up and store plastic mulches during winter. None of the inert-mulch materials harbor insect and animal pests.

Double your yields of squash, cucumbers, and corn by using sheets of aluminum-foil mulch. The reflected light repels insects while enhancing plant growth.

Not all leaves are suitable for mulch. The decomposing leaves of cedar, juniper, and walnut, for example, release chemicals that are toxic to plants. Oak leaves decompose very slowly.

Looking for cheap or free mulch sources? Check out what's available locally: spent mushroom compost, seaweed, cocoa-bean hulls, spent hops, and tobacco stems are all good.

DEALING WITH PESTS

Garlic is said to ward off aphids, snails, and caterpillars. Toss 3 garlic heads and 6 tablespoons mineral oil into a blender and mix until smooth. Let the mixture stand at room temperature for 48 hours; then add it to a solution of 1 pint hot water and 1 tablespoon oil-base soap. Pour into screw-top jars and refrigerate. Gardeners who concoct this brew claim that 2 tablespoons added to 4 pints of water make a potent spray.

If you're tired of dealing with garden pests and disease-prone vegetables, plant a crop of kohlrabi. It's virtually pest- and disease-free, and if you plant this hardy vegetable in late summer, you can harvest even past frost.

Planting marigolds among your beans, spinach, tomatoes, and celery may help protect these vegetables from root nematodes and other insects. The roots of marigolds produce a chemical in the soil that kills nematodes.

Drape old sheer curtains over your fruit vines and berry bushes to frustrate hungry birds and other animals. The material won't harm plants or animals.

Are earwigs the cause of your young plants dying or vanishing overnight? Dampen newspaper, roll it into a tight cylinder, then place it near the scene of the crime. It should be full of earwigs the next morning when you unroll it. Burn it up or bag it well. Continue doing this until the morning the newspaper is empty.

Dampened newspaper

Earwig

Take careful note of signal words on the labels of pesticides; someone's life may depend on it. "Caution," means misuse may cause illness; "Warning," misuse could mean injury or illness, and "Danger," misuse could be fatal. Lock up pesticides and pesticide equipment out of children's reach. Use only government-approved pesticides.

Store all pesticides and pesticide equipment in a separate, well-ventilated, locked cabinet marked "Danger — Pesticides." This cabinet should be kept in an area that's free from excessive cold, moisture, and heat.

GARDEN TOOLS AND FURNITURE: CARE AND STORAGE

Use a reel-on-wheels to keep your garden hose unsnarled and transportable. Store it in the garage or shed. Vinyl hoses, in particular, should be sheltered from the sun's ultraviolet rays, which cause vinyl to deteriorate.

Is your hose leaking—spouting water from pin-sized holes? Seal them carefully with the glowing point of a heated ice pick.

Ice pick

If you have a sink in your potting shed, mount a hose reel on the wall next to it for ready connection. Run the hose from the door or window into the garden.

Be sure to sharpen your hoe on the right side—the inside edge—so that you can pull it through the ground with considerable ease.

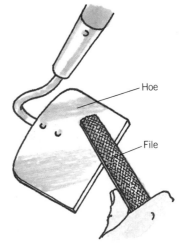

Hoe

File

RUST PREVENTION

Clean and lubricate your digging tools in a sand–motor oil mixture. Keep a tub of it (1 quart old motor oil to 40 pounds sand) in your tool shed. Just plunge the blades into the mix several times after use.

Protect the moving parts of gardening machinery, such as mower blades, and keep your tools rust- and corrosion-free with WD-40 and other moisture-displacing spray lubricants.

Stubborn rust on your tools? Rub them with a soap-filled steel wool pad dipped in kerosene or turpentine. Finish them off with a brisk rub on wadded aluminum foil.

EQUIPMENT ECONOMIES

Looking for garden equipment at low prices? Garage sales are often good sources for big items such as lawn mowers and wheelbarrows.

Adapt broom handles, hockey sticks, scrap wood, or prunings from old trees for staking peas, beans, and tomatoes. Use rags and yarn to tie the plants to the stakes.

Have you ever thought of recycling an old baby carriage or a child's wagon for use as a wheelbarrow?

Make your own seed-starting kits with egg cartons and potting soil.

STORAGE SOLUTIONS

Time to put away lightweight, fold-up patio furniture and your basement is cluttered? Make use of the joists. Equip them with ¾-inch dowels inserted and glued in predrilled holes. Hang your furniture on the dowels.

Do you need more space for tool storage? Hang them on the exterior walls of your shed if there's an overhanging roof. Protect your tools' metal parts with taped plastic sheeting.

Store your long-handled gardening tools on hooks on the wall instead of leaning them against the wall. They'll take less space, be easier to select, and you won't trip over them.

Garage rafter space should not be overlooked. It's ideal for storing tools and outdoor furniture.

CLEANING JOBS

Are the aluminum parts of your patio furniture looking worn and dingy? Spruce them up with a detergent-and-water scrub. Wipe dry with a soft absorbent cloth, then weatherproof the parts with a coat of car wax.

Scrub mildew from your wooden patio furniture with a solution made of 1 cup ammonia, ½ cup vinegar, ¼ cup baking soda, and 1 gallon water. Wipe it off with an absorbent cloth. When the furniture is completely dry, coat each piece with mildew-resistant paint, available at hardware stores. If the wood is unpainted, coat it with a latex primer. Make sure it dries completely before you treat it with mildew-resistant paint.

CHAPTER FOUR

YOU & YOURS

Establish a harmonious household for the young and old; learn to care for the pet in your life; the best ways to buy, clean, and store clothes; secrets of personal grooming; plus scores of effective first-aid tips.

Family Life
Page 223

Caring for the newborn; older child's relationship to the baby; childproofing the home; safety measures; time to go to school; reasons to keep a child out of school; reading and learning during the growing years; tips for older children; helping with homework; baby-sitter guidelines; social graces and sportsmanship; traveling and eating out; allowances and money; hints for teenagers; working parents and latchkey child; single parent strategies; when parents remarry; safety and health for aging parents; finding the right nursing home.

The Pet in Your Life
Page 241

To own or not to own a pet; choosing a pet; coping with the extra upkeep; helping the pet adjust to its new home; teaching children to handle a dog; grooming; fleas, ticks, other parasites; daily care; accident prevention; first aid; poisoning; feeding time; housebreaking; dog obedience training; dog and cat behavioral problems; aggressiveness in dogs; teaching a dog tricks; problems with cats; other pets.

Personal Grooming
Page 253

Shampooing and conditioning your hair; setting, styling, cutting hair; permanent waves; special hair treatments; what to do for thinning hair; beards, mustaches, and shaving; taking care of your skin; special facial treatments; tips to keep your skin young looking; applying foundation, blushers, powder, and eye makeup; lip, mouth, and denture care; hints for hands, nails, and feet; dressing your best by choosing the right colors of clothes and cosmetics; the most flattering styles for your figure.

Clothing & Laundry
Page 267

Before shopping for clothes; properties of fabric fibers and finishes; caring for and storing clothes; moths and mothballs; dry cleaning; washday wisdom; laundry products: detergents, bleaches, and fabric softeners; stain removal do's and don't's; some special laundry problems; ways to dry clothes; preparing to iron; pressing particular fabrics and items; sewing equipment and sewing machines; attaching hooks and eyes; how to hem and mend; fur and jewelry care.

First Aid & Family Health
Page 306

When there's an emergency; a first-aid kit; checking temperature and pulse; taking medication; advice to the elderly; colds and flu; using ear, nose, and eye drops; headaches; menstrual and abdominal cramps; causes and treatment of vomiting and diarrhea; fever in children and adults; nosebleeds; toothaches, backaches, blisters, bruises, and cuts; how to stop severe bleeding; sprains and fractures; making slings and splints; insect and snake bites; caring for burns; internal poisoning; treating skin poisoning; aid for someone in shock; how to help a person who is choking.

Family Life

NEW BABY

If your baby is cranky during the day, strap it into a front-pack carrier next to your body and take a walk around the house.

A fussy baby can often be lulled to sleep by taking the tot around the block in the carriage or for a ride in the car.

When feeding your newborn at night, put a warm heating pad in the crib. Remove the heating pad when you put the baby down. Because the crib won't be cold, he will settle down more quickly.

If your baby has a diaper rash caused by strong urine or stools and if it does not clear with diaper creams, try rubbing a liquid antacid, such as milk of magnesia, onto the rash with each diaper change. This may neutralize the acidity of the urine or stools. If the rash persists, call your doctor.

YOUR OLDER CHILD'S RELATIONSHIP TO THE BABY

If your older children haven't seen you since you went into the hospital, they'll be eager to welcome you with hugs when you get home. Have your husband hold the baby while you greet them.

Don't be surprised if an older child is cool to the new baby. Imagine how you would feel if your spouse brought home a new husband or a new wife and tried to convince you what a good idea it was!

Let the older tot be actively involved in the care of the baby. Try to fit your newborn into the household routine rather than change the routine to suit the baby. This will help to avoid jealousy in the older child.

Ask a brother or sister to teach the baby to smile. When the baby finally smiles back, the older child will probably be thrilled. Praise the older child for teaching the baby something so important.

Emphasize an older child's "seniority" by awarding new privileges: a larger bed, dining with parents, the responsibility for setting the table (make a sample setting to be imitated), or the use of the phone (with help).

TODDLERS

Make it a habit to name things when you and your preschooler encounter them—it's a good way to enrich a child's vocabulary.

The silent signs—a hug for no apparent reason, a touch on the arm when you're correcting or criticizing, a back rub while sitting together anywhere, a smile from across the room—can mean a lot more to your child than the most effusive compliments.

Try not to ask a 2-year-old if he wants to do something. The answer will be no. Instead, say, "Shall we go out of the house to the store through the back door or the front door?"

Have a toddler put several favorite toys to bed, one by one. The child is last and stays up the latest.

Remember, if you give kids a choice of two things, they'll probably pick the second one simply because it's mentioned last. If you have a preference, it's wise to put it last.

SHADOWS IN THE NIGHT

When nighttime shadows take on frightening forms, take your child on a daytime walk and look at the shadows you make and those made by trees and other things outdoors. Experiment with daytime shadows and have a shadow puppet show at home.

All you need for shadow puppets is a strong direct light and a pair of hands. Think back to your childhood and use your imagination to create a variety of shadow forms.

A good way to shampoo hair: lean your child back in the bathtub, supporting the head with your arm and holding the shoulders; this keeps water out of the face and makes the child feel more secure. Tell the child that you remember this was the way he *loved* to be shampooed as a baby.

Let your child sort the laundry with you. This will help the youngster learn the names of colors as you sort the lights and the darks.

MEAL AND SNACK TIMES

A nice aftermeal routine. First wipe your child's hands. Say, "Hands in the air, please," and wipe the child's mouth and the tray. Then ask him to lower his arms around your neck for a big hug—and a kiss.

Your children should be encouraged to eat everything on their plates before getting seconds. But don't overload the plate with food. A general rule of thumb is a tablespoon of food for each year the child is old. For example, a 2-year-old child might have 2 tablespoons each of meat loaf and mashed potatoes and 2 slices of apple for dessert.

To keep children from pestering you for candy and cookies when you shop, give them apples, yogurt, or another nutritious snack.

TOILET TRAINING

Older children are terrific role models for toilet training younger ones. Three-, four-, and five-year-olds are proud of their accomplishments and, if invited, will be delighted to show a little brother or sister how to use the toilet.

The prospect of wearing fancy underwear instead of diapers can be a great incentive for toilet training. When you think your child is physically ready (usually between the ages of 2½ and 3), point out that neighbor Jimmy wears baseball-player underwear because he goes to the toilet by himself or that cousin Kate can wear frilly underpants because she doesn't get them wet.

SAFETY MEASURES

Tie knots in plastic dry-cleaner bags before throwing them out in the garbage. Children have suffocated from playfully putting these bags over their heads.

Never leave children alone in a car. They seem to know almost instinctively how to release the emergency brake.

CHILDPROOFING A HOME

When you buy toxic products, look at them the way a child would. Is the package attractive? Does it have an inviting look, touch, or smell? If so, consider purchasing an alternate product that is less appealing.

Store all substances that might be harmful if swallowed or dangerous to eyes and skin in cabinets that can be locked and are beyond a toddler's reach. These substances include all types of medications; bleaches, detergents, ammonia, spot removers, and other cleaning materials; paint removers and thinners, kerosene, gasoline; pesticides and herbicides; and some cosmetics.

Install safety latches on all cabinets and drawers containing dangerous objects and materials, delicate glassware, or bric-a-brac. Safety latches are specially designed to hinder small children from opening drawers and cabinets. They are easy to install and are available at most hardware and home-products stores.

Discard all your old drugs. All remaining medications should be locked away. Vitamins should also be kept out of a child's reach.

Keep knives, scissors, and other sharp objects in drawers that are out of reach.

Look around for easily breakable objects on coffee tables, sideboards, and other easy-to-reach places. If you don't want them broken, put them away!

Buy safety caps for electrical outlets to prevent small children from poking objects into them.

Put all matches and lighters out of reach. A drawer with a safety latch is best.

Select your household plants carefully. Many household plants are poisonous—the leaves, stems, and blooms of philodendrons, poinsettias, foxglove, and purple nightshade, for example. Do not grow them if you have children.

If you refrigerate flower or plant bulbs, be sure to keep them away from children; the bulbs of many household plants, such as daffodils and autumn crocuses, are also poisonous.

Keep attics, basements, and other storage areas locked.

If your windows are double hung, locate your screens in the upper part for ventilation. If this is impossible, upper-story screened windows should be closed when your child is up and about.

Store lawn mowers, axes, hedge trimmers, and other sharp-edged garden tools and equipment in a locked area.

Always check inside the oven and broiler before you turn either one on, if they're within a toddler's reach. You just never know what might have been placed in there for "safekeeping." It's also smart to cook on the back burners whenever possible and to turn pot handles toward the rear of the stove.

After you've put the kids in the car and fastened their seat belts, have them put their hands on the tops of their heads. You will know just where their fingers are when you shut the car door.

Put red paint or nail polish on all hot-water faucets and teach your child not to turn them on. At the same time, paint cold-water faucets green; your young one will learn about traffic lights as well as sink safety.

DRESSING

Have your child watch as you put his shoes together, and make a mark on the inside edge of each one. Then tell the child that when the marks are next to each other, the shoes will always be on the correct feet.

Children's rubber boots a tug-of-war to get off and on? Spray the boots' insides with silicone. (Works for grown-ups too.)

Sew on Velcro strips to replace the fasteners on overalls or anything else your child may have difficulty fastening.

Your child can zip up his clothes much more easily if you attach a key ring to the end of the zipper.

LEARNING TO PUT ON A COAT

Use the time-tested nursery school method to teach your young child how to put on a coat. Once children learn to put a coat on all by themselves, they feel superindependent.

1. Lay the coat on the floor on its back, with the arms and neck at the child's feet.

2. The child sticks both arms in the sleeves and flips the coat over her head.

3. Be sure there is lots of clear space in which to do this. Zippers and buttons can hurt if they accidentally strike somebody as the coat is flipped.

TOYS

Put all the odd pieces of toys in one box. Then there's only one place to look for a missing part.

Ask a preschooler to pick up five toys during cleanup time. You do the rest, but increase the number daily as cooperation increases.

Teach your children to store large toys on shelves whenever possible. Small items can be placed in bags or boxes. Explain that one is for blocks, one for dolls, and so on. The children can draw pictures on the outside of the bags or boxes. When pickup time comes, let them sort the toys into their proper categories and put them away.

SIBLINGS

Do a special project with each child or take each one someplace alone. It's good to do things together, but an occasional outing alone makes each child feel important.

If there's any dispute about the last portion of food, have one child divide it in half and the other child choose the portion she wants. The division will be equal.

Use a kitchen timer to time turns when children are sharing something. They tend not to resent a timer; it's a neutral referee.

When arguments persist, separate the children for a cooling-off period. The buzz of a timer can signal the end of the period.

OFF TO SCHOOL

Walk with your child to school or to the bus stop at least once before the school year starts. Be sure the child understands any special arrangements you have made for his going to school and returning home. Practice proper street crossing at every opportunity.

Be sure your child has seen and used a public toilet or urinal, as the case may be, so that the school bathrooms won't seem strange. And teach him or her to use the correct words to ask to "go to the bathroom" or to "use the toilet." Emphasize the need to wash hands even when grown-ups are not around with reminders.

If your child will be eating lunch in the school, visit the cafeteria together so that the procedures will be familiar. Let your child practice at home carrying a loaded tray or using a lunchbox.

It is important for your child to know his or her full name, address, phone number, and your work number. (One way to teach these is to set them to the tune of a nursery rhyme, such as "Jack and Jill.") Give the school the name and number of a parent substitute to call if you're not available in an emergency.

Make a safe place to keep any notes to and from the teacher by inserting a manila envelope with holes punched on one side in your child's loose-leaf notebook. The notes won't fall out.

227

Invite your children to make their own lunch according to a set of menus you have drawn up together. Whenever they do, let them pocket all or part of the price of a school lunch.

What if your child consistently misses the bus? (1) Tell the child to walk, if that's possible, and be tardy. (2) Let the child stay home, but don't let it be fun—no TV, no friends over after school. (3) Drive your child to school, noting how long it takes. The child can do chores for that amount of time after school.

SICK DAYS

Too sick to go to school? Talk to your child; listen carefully. The problem may not be stated in words but instead may be buried beneath several seemingly unrelated statements. If you decide to allow your child a day off, have a long, quiet talk and accompany it with lots of tender loving care.

If your child has too many pleas for sick days, consider causes other than illness, such as being teased, frightened, fearful of parental separation, and so on. If you elect to keep your child home from school and in your judgment the child is not truly ill, staying home should not be fun. Put the child to bed for the day to "get well." If his pleas persist, call your doctor for further advice.

THE SHY CHILD

A shy child is likely to retreat further into himself in a group of several boisterous children. Being paired for play on a one-to-one basis improves the shy child's social skills when the other child is of the same age. When the playmate is *younger*, the effect may be even greater.

A shy child usually has a hard time with surprises. Give plenty of notice if you expect guests or if you plan to visit others.

Help a shy, soft-spoken child prepare for reading aloud or for oral testing by having the youngster read aloud to you. Sit a bit farther apart each time so that the child has to raise her voice and learn to speak up.

Share your child's concerns over his shyness, and don't laugh them off. Diminishing the problem diminishes the child.

REASONS TO KEEP A CHILD HOME FROM SCHOOL

A fever of 101° F or greater.

Nausea and/or vomiting.

Abdominal cramps.

Diarrhea.

A cold, when it is associated with a fever, frequent coughing, or heavy nasal congestion.

A cough, when its symptoms aren't due to an allergy or the aftereffects of a recent illness.

A sore throat, with fever.

An unidentified rash, which should be checked by your doctor for the possibility of measles, chicken pox, or other infectious disease (see pp.317–318).

Any infectious disease that your doctor has diagnosed.

An earache.

Conjunctivitis (pinkeye).

Your own visual test or gut feeling that tells you your child really isn't well.

Your child is overly tired or emotional.

THE GROWING YEARS

Put a door knocker or a "Please Knock" sign on each child's bedroom door as a reminder to everyone to knock before entering and to reinforce respect for privacy.

Encourage your child to start a collection. It might consist of rocks, postcards, fingerprints, keys, insects, bottle caps, corks, buttons, coins, shells, or stamps. Keep the collection in a personal museum.

Encourage the development of the skills in which your child shows some ability—even when they are not necessarily the skills you would choose.

The examples set by you and others in the family determine the values a child will grow up with. What must a child think if he hears such comments as "I got the wrong change, but I kept it"?

READING AND LEARNING

If a child has trouble sitting still, allow doodling while you read aloud. And remember that your child's favorite doll or stuffed animal may like to hear the story too.

Reward reading. For example, delay the lights-out time by allowing quiet reading alone in bed for a few extra minutes. Try to use a "time bank" to balance reading and television time.

Ignore your child's reading level sometimes. If a youngster is fascinated by dinosaurs or insects, get every book and magazine you can find on the subject; it's not necessary that every thought or word be fully understood. Likewise, let your child read "baby" books occasionally, just for fun.

Assign each child a shelf or two in a bookcase for his or her favorite books, and make it a family tradition to add a special book at each gift-giving occasion.

Take dictation from a child who can't write yet, or write out a story the child tells you. Label any pictures she draws with her own description of them.

Above all, when you read your child's writing, enjoy the creativity, and don't focus on errors.

Leave an old typewriter out permanently for your family to type on. Even the child who hasn't learned to read and write can create "words," and the one who can will pour out his or her imaginings freely and happily.

MUSIC APPRECIATION

Listen to classical music with your child. Play an imagination game. Ask, "What do you think is happening in this music?" You may be surprised at the answers.

Expose your child to music of all kinds. Play favorite music to get going in the morning; substitute a quiet listening period for reading time some nights.

HOMEWORK

Make a special long-term homework project a recurring topic at family dinners. This helps the child feel that the project is important, and the discussion leads to thinking out what has to be done and how to do it. Other family members will become interested and contribute too.

Help your child think of the study area as the "office," with office supplies, reference books (dictionaries are often more helpful than encyclopedias for children), and if at all possible, a typewriter and personal computer at hand.

Save some paperwork from the office or the household and work along with your child while she studies. The child will recognize that she is not the only one with "homework" that must be done—and also should a question arise, there's advice nearby.

Help your child set up a notebook for assignments and a chart to check them off as they're done. This will provide a sense of accomplishment.

Be sure to tell your child's teacher of any unusual circumstances at home—for instance, a death in the family, the loss of a job, the separation of the parents, or even a difficult relationship with a sibling. Such situations may cause problems at school, and the teacher may be able to help.

TELEVISION

Watch television with your child as often as possible. Explain and comment on what you see, including the news and the commercials. Even very young children can learn to be critical of what they see and hear; otherwise they may passively accept everything on TV as the truth.

Set up regular hours for TV viewing. When your child does watch television, try to be there and discuss the program that's on. When you can't be there, ask the child to relate the story of the program to you. This will not only help you monitor the programs but will also help the child mentally organize sequences of events and make the television an educational tool.

Take advantage of your TV-viewing time together to snuggle and rub backs.

Combat sexism by pointing out characters on TV who are competent in a variety of jobs and who are shown as individuals, not male or female stereotypes. Also, point out characters who care about others or who embody the ideals of different cultures and ethnic groups.

BABYSITTERS

Call your local high school and talk with the guidance counselors. They may be able to suggest dependable students who babysit.

BABYSITTER CHECKLIST

Where parents can be reached:_____

When parents will return:_____

Names and nicknames of children: ___
_____

Telephone number of neighbor(s) who
can help: _____

Location of flashlights, clothing, toys,
diapers, and other special equipment:
_____

Favorite stories or activities:_____

Where children play: _____

Dangerous or off-limits areas in the
house: _____

TV rules: _____

Meal (or snack) times:_____

Bedtimes and sleeping arrangements:
_____

Sitter privileges:_____

Special health or safety precautions:
_____

FAMILY DOCTOR:_____

POISON INFORMATION: _____

FIRE DEPARTMENT: _____

POLICE DEPARTMENT: _____

DIRECTIONS TO YOUR HOUSE (be
sure to include your address and the
best way to get there so that sitter can
direct others there in case of an emergency):_____
_____

Arrange the checklist to fit on one 8½-
inch by 11-inch sheet of paper. Fill in the
information that does not change and
photocopy an ample supply of forms.
Then, each time you get ready to go out,
fill in the blanks that remain for that
particular occasion.

Talk to neighbors whose opinions you respect for the names of baby-sitters they use. Also, some of your neighbors may have teen-aged children who babysit. Consider asking elderly neighbors to sit; they may enjoy being with children and like a bit of extra money.

By the age of 12 or so, most children can be allowed to stay home by themselves for an hour or two in the daytime while you run an errand nearby.

If you have several children, consider putting the oldest in charge of the others. Or, if you prefer, make each one responsible for any duties you assign.

Set up rules and instructions as carefully for your children as you would for a hired sitter. Write them down, or have the children use the same babysitter checklist you already have.

FAMILY SQUABBLES

Tell children they can use words to tell you how angry they feel, but they cannot hurt living creatures or damage property. They can hit a punching bag if it helps them feel better.

231

An angry child? Count to 10 so that the youngster can cool off a little. The same goes for the parents.

For a screaming child, try whispering. It's hard to hear someone who is whispering a secret in your ear while you're yelling.

Hugs are great for breaking up fights. They also break the ice and help your child talk about what is bothering him.

Don't get involved in an argument about when it's time for a playmate to leave. When the playmate arrives, agree upon a departure time, set the alarm clock, and you'll save a lot of bickering.

Don't embarrass your child with reprimands in front of other people. Also, don't seek revenge by choosing public times to recount past misbehaviors or to correct bad habits.

BAD LANGUAGE

Make up a substitute word or phrase that any member of the family can use to vent anger and other profanity-provoking emotions. This innocuous expression will then become the official family "profanity" instead of less socially acceptable language.

Don't overreact to foul language by attaching more importance to it than it deserves. Remember that young children are probably just trying to get your attention. Older children may want to test your reaction.

Insist that so-called bathroom humor be confined to the bathroom. It's not much fun to be shocking all by yourself.

SOME SOCIAL GRACES

Try to get your children to make eye contact and smile when they talk to others.

Impress on your children that they are entitled to their own feelings, but they are *not* entitled to act them out to the point where someone else is hurt.

Encourage your children to be hospitable to others, but tell them to ask you in private if they want to invite a friend to stay for dinner or overnight.

Children love to form clubs, and friendships developed in this way may turn into lifelong relationships. Encourage "open membership," but don't fret if a club is "for boys" or "for girls" only.

Provide a place for "secret meetings"—perhaps a ventilated closet or the space under the basement stairway.

SLUMBER PARTIES

Make it clear from the beginning that sleep-overs and slumber parties are strictly for weekends and vacations, not for school nights.

Limit the size of a slumber party to five or six. Otherwise, the children may separate into groups and start squabbling.

If the children are sleeping in a tent in the backyard, don't be surprised if this "wonderful" experience ends with them coming inside, especially if they're early elementary school age.

Expect a "secret" raid on your refrigerator. Stock it with foods you'd like to have the kids eat.

Set the curfew for being bedded down for an hour before you actually expect the children to go to sleep. (And don't expect to get a good night's sleep yourself!)

SPORTS AND SPORTSMANSHIP

Encourage such lifetime interests as tennis, golf, or swimming, as well as team sports, which, in most cases, are played only while an individual is in school.

Don't worry if your child picks an interest—such as a sport or a musical instrument—that neither of you knows much about. The two of you can learn about it together by reading books and specialized periodicals and by attending special events together.

If your child takes up a sport, stress that fun and the satisfaction of teamwork and of one's increased individual skill are the goals of sports, no matter whether the team wins or loses.

Don't deny the "agony of defeat" when your child's team loses the game; let the youngster express frustration and grief.

TRAVELING

The best time for trips is when your child is under 6 months of age. Try to take advantage of those long naps a baby requires.

Buy your youngster a small duffel bag, and make sure that it is light enough for the child to carry without help. Let him or her pack appropriate clothes and a few special toys in it—only what will fit easily in the bag. Small duffel bags fit easily into a crowded car or under the seat of a plane.

When you visit friends or relatives, a sleeping bag is a convenient take-along bed for an older child in case there's a shortage of sleeping accommodation.

Going on an overnight trip with your child? Take along a favorite stuffed animal or blanket. It will be a familiar and comforting sight for the child.

With a toddler, if you have a choice, set out on a long car trip about an hour or two before his naptime or bedtime. Then, just about the time the child gets fussy, he will probably fall asleep. To avoid further upset, dress the child in his nightclothes before setting out on your trip so that you need not awaken him upon reaching your destination.

Stop at a playground or a park for your travel break so that your child can work off all of her pent-up energy.

Play Simon Says in the car. Simon says, "Smile," Simon says, "Wiggle your toes," and so on. This keeps children busy and uses up excess energy.

Try not to go anywhere if your child is tired. Even if you plan to buy only a few things at the supermarket, it's best to wait and let your child nap first. It's easier to deal with a crowd of shoppers when your child is rested.

If your child must take an airplane trip alone, prepare for it by approaching the trip as an adventure. Explain the whole trip, including details about how the flight attendant will help him and how he will be met at the other end. Coach him on things that might be unexpected, such as airsickness or ear pain on takeoff or landing. Supply gum or hard candy to ease ascent and descent.

EATING OUT

In preparation for meals eaten outside the home, practice conversations at the dinner table in "restaurant" voices. (This is also good practice for church, movies, and other places where children should lower their voices.)

When eating out, choose a restaurant that serves familiar food; save fancy restaurants for those evenings when you have a sitter. Go to the restaurant *before* your child is really hungry, or provide a snack to make the child more patient while you are waiting to be served your meal.

MOVING

If a family move is coming up, hold a good-bye party and let your child invite all her special friends. Exchange small remembrance gifts and addresses and telephone numbers to assure your child that she will not be completely cut off from old friends.

Load your child's belongings onto the moving van last so that they will be unpacked first.

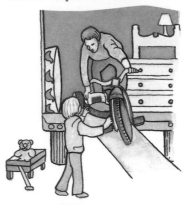

ALLOWANCES AND MONEY

A child's behavior should not determine whether he gets an allowance. If your spouse is the family's main breadwinner, would it be fair for you not to have the money to cover household expenses because you had a fight or an automobile accident?

It is reasonable to expect that some chores will be done without regard to allowance. This should be worked out in advance and those chores understood by all. As a child grows older and can help more around the house, let him know that his list of responsibilities will grow as well. Each year might involve a bit of renegotiation.

Pay your child's allowance regularly and consistently, once or even twice weekly for a young child whose sense of time is not well developed. An older child can adjust to payment once or twice a month, perhaps on an adult's payday.

Review your child's allowance regularly, perhaps at the beginning of the school year.

What is the right amount? Take into account what others your child's age are getting for an allowance. It's as bad to give far too much money as it is to be miserly. Some parents believe that children learn from working out how to make ends meet.

Let your child see you handle real money—pay cash for some purchases. Cheques and credit cards make spending look free.

Encourage your child to save but not to hoard. Help the child set small savings goals—college is too far into the future; a new baseball mitt or bicycle is a more immediate need.

Don't allow a child to use money to play off one parent against the other, especially when the parents are divorced. The parent with whom the child is living should be the one to give the allowance.

TEEN TIPS

For better communications ask your teenager to repeat instructions or rules. If misunderstandings occur frequently, be sure a third party is present.

Encourage a teenager to get more work experience, whether paid or volunteer. If money is earned, it can be kept in addition to the regular allowance and used for personal needs. The rewards of volunteering should be discussed.

Chequing and savings accounts will help teens manage their money better, especially if they are earning extra money from part-time jobs. Start them early, help them cope with bank statements— and be patient.

KEEPING IN TOUCH WITH ONE ANOTHER

Make it a family tradition—especially as the children get older and begin to leave home—that everyone knows how to reach everyone else at all times.

Insist that all members of the family leave numbers where they can be reached whenever they go out. A good place to attach the notes is the refrigerator door, using magnets. Or post a corkboard or blackboard near the phone.

Keep a list of family and emergency phone numbers posted by the telephone at all times.

In trouble while out at night? Encourage your teenager to call home anytime, no matter what. A caring family takes care of its own and will rescue the one in trouble and sort out the problems later.

DISCIPLINE

Both parents should agree on a course of action in disciplinary matters and support each other. If at all possible, use logical consequences instead of punishment. If a teen comes home past curfew, it makes more sense to require her to come home early next time than to deprive her of TV.

Don't make extra chores as punishment for unrelated behavior. For example, don't make your child wash the car because he didn't walk the dog. Some extra dog walking might be in order, however.

When teens are under peer pressure to do something they don't want to do, tell them to say, "My parents won't let me!" Peers will accept stern parents as a reason.

WORKING PARENTS

Expect the unexpected, and prepare to be flexible at all times! The best-planned schedules can be upset by the washer that breaks down, the unexpected guests who drop in, or the car that won't start.

Plan *carefully* for some time to yourself and some to spend alone with your spouse, even if it's only a weekly lunch together.

Let your child have friends in to play while you unwind from work and get dinner. Spend time together as a family later, when you're refreshed.

Compensate for a time away from the family due to job-related travel or a busy work period by throwing your schedule to the winds and doing something satisfying to all—and totally unexpected.

LATCHKEY CHILDREN

Be sure that your children are mature enough to be left alone after school before you allow them to become latchkey children. If possible, work with schools, community groups, and neighbors to provide afterschool supervision and care for children who need it.

If your child must be unsupervised, make it a rule that she telephone you as soon as she gets home. The call needn't be long, but you need to know that the child is safely home and what her plans are for the remainder of the afternoon.

Let your child pick out his or her own key ring and the place where it is to be hidden. Make having the house key an important event. Label it with your pet's name or a favorite fictional character. Don't use your address—in case it's lost and found by someone you don't want to have it.

Post all important numbers in a prominent place near the phone: parents' work, the poison information center, fire and police, a neighbor who has agreed to be available in an emergency, and any others you think necessary.

Also post your address and the *best* route to your home, in case your child must call for emergency help. Practice handling such calls properly, and warn your child never to hang up before all necessary information is given.

Try to be home when you say you will be; a few extra minutes can seem like a very long time to a waiting child. Call if you're going to be late.

Plan for your child to play at a friend's home some days after school. If you don't want visitors in your house while you're gone, you might arrange to have the visits returned on weekends.

SINGLE-PARENT STRATEGIES

During a separation or divorce, be prepared for your child to hope that you'll reunite. It's a common fantasy that can last for years. Don't get angry; just be consistent and nonemotional while explaining that it's unlikely to happen.

Don't make your child act as a messenger between you and your former spouse. It's unfair and sets the child up as a mediator, a situation you must avoid.

Let your child go to the departing parent's new home as soon as he wants to, perhaps to help with unpacking and settling in. The child may wish to save the first visit for a little later. At least be sure plans have been made for a visit in the near future.

Change the dinnertime routine if it's a meal you normally shared— eat at a different hour, in a different room, or occasionally at a restaurant. Don't have a conspicuously empty place at the table.

Recognize that no joint custody is perfect. But if yours works for your child, make it work for you, even though it will be difficult as you routinely make the switch from single parent to single person.

Let school officials know that both parents must be informed of activities and of any problems that arise, especially if the child will be moving from one home to the other frequently.

Don't rule out having other individuals present during your visits—it's a good idea to get to know your child's friends—but don't *always* include another person; you and your child need some time alone together.

Aim to keep visiting schedules somewhat flexible to avoid disappointments and uncertainty. Give full, honest explanations to your child if you must cancel or postpone a visit.

REMARRIAGE

Set up the first meeting with a prospective stepchild on neutral territory—a restaurant or park, perhaps—and plan a specific activity. Making conversation may be difficult; doing something fun probably won't be.

Start your new family in a new house or apartment if it's at all possible—especially if more than one set of children is involved—in order to cut down on feelings involved with territory.

Provide for some time alone for the visiting child and his natural parent. Occasionally, this may actually involve a stepparent going away for a few hours or days.

Let the biological parent do as much of the disciplining of a child as possible at first—the stepparent should assume it very gradually. This is an especially tricky challenge for a stepmother, who may spend more time with a child than a father does.

Include the visiting child in household chores and projects as well as in excursions and play, to help the youngster feel a part of family life and to make the other children accept the visitor as a member of the family.

Try to create some new family rituals or traditions—for example, candles on the dinner table, pancakes for a weekend breakfast, Friday dinners at a restaurant.

AS YOUR PARENTS GROW OLDER

Never forget birthdays, anniversaries, and events of importance to your parents.

Losing the ability to drive is a devastating loss of independence. Don't be in too big a hurry to help them sell the car.

When your parents can no longer drive, set up weekly trip schedules for all regular events—shopping, visits to the doctor, barber, hairdresser, and the like. This will be less disruptive to your life and easier for your parents to cope with than spur-of-the-moment trips.

Encourage a grandchild of driving age to help drive her grandparents around. Most teens take pride in this kind of responsibility, and the grandparents will enjoy the opportunity of having their grandchild all to themselves.

HEARING LOSS— WHAT DOES IT MEAN?

As people reach their seventies and eighties, they often lose their ability to clearly hear certain spoken sounds—particularly ch, f, s, and th. A person with a moderate degree of old-age hearing loss will hear something like this: "Plea ange an annel in a ba o of a week tart at ha pa ta evan" instead of "Please change the channel since the best show of the week starts at half past seven."

You can partly overcome this hearing disability by speaking slowly, clearly, and close to the older person's better ear. A well-adjusted hearing aid may help, but frequently it simply makes the sounds louder but no less distorted.

Picking up part or all of an ongoing expense is often a more tactful way of helping out financially than giving cash. You might also consider giving your parents a contribution in kind: a favorite (but possibly unaffordable) food, a new television set, clothes, a vacation—almost anything they might want or need.

Just because your father retires doesn't mean your mother will. She'll still have a house to keep and meals to cook. Be alert for ways to help her get some time off too (perhaps by suggesting to your father that he share some of the household chores).

Be sympathetic if your parents discover it's not always comfortable to be together 24 hours a day.

Frustrated about all those wonderful family photographs that have never been sorted and put in albums? Ask an elderly relative to do it. He will be able to supply names for many of the faces you don't know.

Ask your parents to compile a family genealogy. Some elderly people will relish it; others may have trouble writing. If so, get them to talk about the family and record the conversation on tape. You can transcribe it later.

If aging parents have difficulty reading, investigate the large-type reading selections available through your local library. Many publications, such as the *Reader's Digest* and Reader's Digest Condensed Books, are also available in large type. In addition, books on cassettes can be borrowed from most libraries or can be rented or purchased from your local branch of the Canadian Institute for the Blind.

YOUR PARENTS' SAFETY

Check that stairways are well lit and that switches are easy to find at the top and bottom of the stairs. If any risers are a different height than the others, mark them clearly. Be sure the handrail is sturdy and comfortable and runs the entire length of the stairs.

Replace worn stair treads. Secure the carpeting to all the steps. Replace worn carpeting and avoid deep-pile or dark-colored carpeting that makes it difficult to see the edges of the steps.

See to it that an elderly person's slippers and shoes are in good repair, are well fitting, and have nonskid soles.

Be sure your parents have a telephone that they can reach while in bed. Also leave a bell or whistle beside the bed and in the bathrooms in case they need to get emergency help.

Make sure that you childproof (p.225) your parents' home before you bring young grandchildren to visit. You can temporarily secure cabinets that don't have safety latches by tying the knobs with heavy-duty rubber bands.

While you're at it, you can also check for hazards to your parents: lamp cords that cross traffic lanes or are near water, an absence of handrails, or a lack of antiskid strips in the bathtub or grab bars on the bathroom walls.

Consider a safety frame and a raised seat for the toilet, to ease getting on and off.

Throw rugs on slippery floors are an invitation to disaster. Ask your parents if you can get rid of the rugs or nail them down.

To prevent scalds—and save energy as well—help your parents reset their water heater to 120° F.

If your parents do not have smoke detectors or fire extinguishers, buy some for a birthday or other gift-giving occasion—and help them put them up. Install smoke detectors at the top of the stairway, one in the bedroom hallway, and in other places where heat or smoke would be a hazard. Do not put one near a stove or a fireplace, where it would go off instantly.

NURSING HOME CHECKLIST

When looking for a nursing home, use this checklist to satisfy yourself that the patient will receive good care.

Does the home have a current license from the province to operate?

Is regular medical attention available, and a physician on call in emergencies?

Does the home provide special services that the patient may need, such as individualized diet and physical therapy?

Is the location of the home convenient for the patient, his or her doctor, and family and friends?

Are there handrails in hallways and grab bars in bathrooms?

Are all exits and paths to these exits clearly marked and unobstructed? Are the doors unlocked from the inside? Are all stairways enclosed?

Do all the bedrooms open onto a corridor and have a window?

Do you smell heavy, unpleasant odors?

Are the hallways wide enough to accommodate two wheelchairs to pass with ease? Are there handgrips on each side? Are the walls decorated with colorful paint and pictures?

In the kitchen, are the food preparation, garbage, and dishwashing areas all separated from one another?

Are toilet facilities designed to accommodate wheelchair residents?

Are residents encouraged to go outside?

Does the dining room look attractive? Is it furnished with comfortable chairs and tables that can be moved easily to accommodate residents in wheelchairs?

Does the home have an activity room? Are the residents, who are able, involved in some activity like reading, craft work, or playing cards?

Is the staff friendly and caring? Are they pleasant and accommodating to residents and visitors?

Is there an active resident council or a resident participation program? Do the residents have a role in recommending changes within the home?

Place fire extinguishers near the stove, furnace, fireplace, and other possibly hazardous locations. The extinguishers should be able to control paper, electrical, and oil fires, and be easy for an elderly person to handle.

YOUR PARENTS' HEALTH

Having trouble keeping track of pills? Using egg cartons, number the cups with the hours of the day from rising to bedtime. Place the dosage for each hour in the correctly numbered cup.

Check that there is good lighting surrounding the medicine cabinet. Mark medicines and household chemicals clearly.

If your parents have trouble cooking for themselves, investigate the Meals-on-Wheels program or its equivalent in your community.

People on restricted diets need lots of support. Don't eat a sticky, frosted pecan bun while they are nibbling on a piece of dry toast!

DISTANT PARENTS

If you can't visit your aging parents regularly—or have them visit you—make an *extra* effort to stay in contact. Call them frequently with all the news of the family.

Write as frequently as you can. Many short notes are better than fewer long ones. Include newspaper clippings of interest and discount coupons for things they like.

Send them surprise packages: little gifts on occasions other than birthdays and Christmas or even on nonoccasions. That way they'll know you're thinking about them.

The Pet in Your Life

IS OWNING A PET FOR YOU?

In deciding whether or not to get a puppy, keep in mind that in order to be socialized, a pup needs company. If someone won't be home most of each day, consider a cat or a mature dog.

If you already own a dog when a baby arrives, be sure to give your pet its own special time with you each day so that it knows it hasn't lost your affection.

If you're thinking of giving a child a pet, remember that although a 3- or 4-year-old can love and play with a pet, it's usually only a 10-year-old who can take over a pet's feeding and exercise.

Many elderly and homebound people find that caring for a pet helps them to hold onto the world of reality and of strong emotional relationships.

CHOOSING A PET

Acquire a puppy when it's 6 to 10 weeks of age. Left any longer in a kennel or with only other dogs for company, a puppy has a harder adjustment to its human family.

For a household with small children, a large, docile dog may be best, but always check out the individual animal. Avoid a small, fragile dog; it could be seriously injured by active children.
Caution: It's not safe to leave a small child alone with even the gentlest of dogs.

When choosing a puppy, look for one that approaches you confidently but unaggressively. Avoid the undersized, shy puppy.

KEEPING DOWN THE UPKEEP

A certain amount of dirt goes with pets, but much of it can be prevented.

Tuck a small towel in your pocket on rainy or snowy walks and mop up the animal before it tracks in moisture and mud. When bathing must be in the bathroom, cover the floor with towels. Towel the dog at least partly dry—and don't open the bathroom door until it has shaken off all the water it can.

All animals slop water and food. To trap the drips and simplify disposal, cover a generous eating area with newspaper. Except for that area, don't leave newspapers around while you're paper-training a puppy; it can't tell papers apart.

If a pet carries food away from its usual eating spot, keep moving the food back until the animal gets the idea.

As for shedding, you can roll up the hairs on furniture and clothes with a damp sponge or with masking tape wrapped around your hand. For the fine fuzz on baseboards and the edges of furniture, try dampened paper towels.

A dog need not be vicious to protect you. A small, yappy dog is fine burglar protection. A big dog that scares people on sight is the best defense against street crime.

THE NEW PET AT HOME

In a new home a cat will often "disappear." In fact, it's just hiding in a dark corner until it feels safe. If the home is quiet and unthreatening, the cat will soon emerge.

As soon as possible, take your new pet to a veterinarian to get the necessary shots and to learn what is the best diet for it.

Have a male cat neutered between 8 and 10 months of age. Unless you plan to breed a female cat or dog, have it spayed (its ovaries removed) when it's about 6 months old.

TEACHING CHILDREN HOW TO TREAT DOGS

Unless children know how to approach a dog, their enthusiasm and curiosity may provoke growls or bites on the dog's part. Teach your children to:

Stay away from strange animals unless an owner is present.

Be especially wary of dogs raised in homes where there are no children.

Keep children's faces well away from an animal's face or claws.

Enter a home where a dog lives only if someone who can control it is there.

Make a fist and let the dog sniff it before petting the dog.

Leave a dog alone while it's eating or sleeping and never take away its food.

Forbear tugging a dog's tail or ears, teasing it, or squeezing it too hard.

To help a puppy adjust to being away from its old home and littermates, put something warm and comforting—a piece of your old clothing or a hot-water bottle—in its crate. Or leave a radio playing softly nearby to soothe it to sleep.

Introduce a new pet to an old one by stages. Confine the old pet to one room and let the newcomer become accustomed to the other's smell. Then let them meet through a child's gate or a screen door.

When picking up a puppy, always put one hand underneath to support its weight.

If you give a puppy an old shoe to play with, you are teaching it that shoes are fair game. It will probably chew new shoes too. Give it toys of hard rubber with no loose parts that might be swallowed.

Observe what interests a puppy and figure out ingenious ways to make toys for it. For example, a vacuum-cleaner belt is cheap, almost indestructible, and great for a game of tug-of-war.

You'll save your upholstery if you provide a new kitten or cat with a scratching post. It should be at least 12 inches tall (taller for a mature cat) and on a sturdy, non-tipping base. Cover the post with carpeting, place it near the kitten's sleeping quarters and, if necessary, show the kitten how to use it.

GROOMING

Regular grooming improves your pet's coat. At the same time, inspect for fleas (tiny reddish-brown insects that jump) or the tiny black specks that are their droppings, and lice (blue-gray or light brown insects that cling to the hairs and don't jump). If you find fleas or lice, call your veterinarian.

A puppy accustomed to grooming when it's young will endure it patiently always. Feel your puppy all over, inspect its teeth and ears, pick up its feet, talking constantly. When it can sit still for a while, start brushing with a soft brush.

Most dogs' nails need clipping. Start this early too. Use dog nail clippers from a pet store. Avoid cutting back to the quick—visible

as a thin pink line if the dog's nails are light in color. If they're dark, clip off just to where the nail begins to curve downward.

Long-haired cats (some dogs too) brushed daily are less prone to hair balls forming in the stomach, causing the animal to retch. If a cat has this problem, try giving it ½ teaspoon of petroleum jelly in its food once a week.

For brushing a cat, a woman's hairbrush with round-tipped plastic or rubber bristles is better than the brushes sold for cats. The latter are usually too soft to do the job — and they're expensive.

Some dogs and cats don't mind being vacuumed; others find the noise frightening. It's an easy way to get rid of loose hair if your pet will adjust to it. Be careful around the face and ears.

FLEAS, TICKS, AND OTHER PARASITES

Because fleas live much of their cycle off the pet—in bedding, rugs, and crevices—killing those on the pet isn't enough. Consult your veterinarian about effective sprays and defoggers to eliminate them from the house.

Embedded ticks must be removed head and all. To be sure of getting out every last bit, dab on alcohol, then pull the tick straight out with tweezers; don't twist it.

If a cat or dog rubs its ears often, it may have ear mites—a serious problem. Other signs are bad odor or dark discharge from the ears. Have a vet check them.

Bells on a cat or dog collar will prevent the animal capturing wild prey. Birds, rabbits, and rodents carry parasites that can be transmitted to a pet.

Have a newly acquired puppy or kitten checked for worms. Thereafter, have it checked once a year when it gets its shots or whenever it has repeated problems with loose bowel movements.

If mosquitoes are prevalent in your area, have your dog tested yearly in spring for heartworm, a parasite that can kill. The preventive medicine that your vet prescribes should be used as long as mosquitoes are active.

DAILY CARE

Get to know the feel of your pet's coat, the color of its gums, and the look of its nose. Observe its eating, drinking, and elimination habits. A change in any of these may be an early warning of illness.

Wipe a dog's eyes daily with a dampened cotton pad so that secretions don't become encrusted.

To clean a dog's ears, put drops of mineral oil in them; let the oil warm 10 minutes; then wipe the ears with a cotton swab. Don't let the swab get into the ear canal.

When it's hot and humid, exercise your dog in the cool hours of early morning or late evening.

If your pet's foot pads become cracked, rub some petroleum jelly on them.

Dog bothered by salt on streets or by ice balls forming between its pads when it walks in the snow? Make dog boots out of golf-club covers, baby booties, or small socks. Sew leather or vinyl on the bottoms. Your dog will enjoy its winter walks.

If you leave your dog outside on a running wire, install a stop on the wire so that the dog can't wrap its chain around the tree or post. Also, check that the swivel on the chain works, and have a doghouse within reach for shelter.

If your pet is lame, has a stiff neck, is reluctant to get up or lie down, or has tense abdominal muscles, take the animal to a veterinarian as soon as possible. All of these are signs of pain and illness.

PREVENTING ACCIDENTS

When your dog is in the car, take off its leash. It could get caught on something in the car. Better yet, have your dog ride in a carrier or, if it's large, behind a grill in the rear of the car.

Many cats are injured and killed in falls from open windows. To be sure your cat is safe, screen all windows that are ever opened and that are more than 5 feet off the ground.

Puppies and kittens are just like children: everything gets tested in the mouth. For either, "childproof" your home (see p. 225). On streets watch for broken glass, animal bones, and animal feces; try to steer your puppy clear of them.

Prevent pets from chewing electric cords by rubbing the cords with a bar of strong laundry soap.

COPING WITH EMERGENCIES

Be prepared! Take two good color photos of your pet and make a note of particular markings. It is hard to provide exact details after a pet has disappeared.

You can capture a cat by tossing a towel over it. If the cat is injured, wrap the towel around it and carry it, supporting its hindquarters, abdomen, and chest with one arm, its head and neck with the other hand.

When a cat is "marooned" in a tree, forget about rescuing it. The cat climbed up; when it's ready, it can and will climb down.

If your pet is sprayed by a skunk, saturate the sprayed area with straight tomato juice or with equal parts vinegar and water. Rub in, then wash off with soap and water. This won't get rid of the odor completely but will reduce it to a more tolerable level.

ACCIDENTS

If you find a dog or cat that can't get up after an accident, slip it

very gently onto a stiff board or a blanket or even a coat held taut as a stretcher and take it immediately to a veterinarian.

Before handling an injured dog, muzzle it with gauze, a handkerchief, or whatever's handy. Release the muzzle at once if the animal appears to be vomiting.

If an animal is bleeding severely, put sterile gauze pads or clean cloths over the wound and apply continuous, firm pressure. Tie the pads in place securely while you take the animal to a veterinarian. If the pads become soaked with blood, tie more over them.

After any fall or accident, have your pet checked by a veterinarian. Watch for at least 48 hours for signs of shock—shallow breathing, a glassy gaze, or very pale gums. If any of these appear, confer with your vet.

POISONING

Animal poisoning is particularly dangerous because it is often unclear what's wrong or why. Vomiting, labored breathing, abdominal pain, shivering, convulsions, or spontaneous bleeding are all symptoms of poisoning. Call your veterinarian at such signs.

Pesticides for ants, roaches, and rodents are, unfortunately, attractive to pets too. Place them only where there's no chance of your pet's chewing or licking them.

Pellets that kill garden slugs look like dog biscuits. Don't use them in any area accessible to dogs, either yours or your neighbors'.

To discourage a cat from eating indoor and outdoor plants, grow a 4-inch pot of wheat or oat grass for it to nibble. Start a new pot every 2 or 3 weeks and keep it from the cat until the grass is 4 inches high.

Car antifreeze tastes delicious to dogs and cats and is usually fatal. Store antifreeze in sturdy closed containers and, if it spills, wipe up every bit and hose the area.

FEEDING YOUR PET WISELY

Base a pet's meals on any good commercial pet food. If you wish, supplement it with no more than 10 percent table scraps—eggs, chicken, meat, or vegetables.

A dog will happily and healthily eat the same food day after day. Cats like and need variety, easily supplied by varying their food's dominant flavor—meat, poultry, fish, liver—often.

In your zeal to have your dog or cat eat well, avoid overfeeding. An overweight animal is prone to heart, lung, and joint ailments and will have a shorter life than a pet with normal weight.

Adequate fresh water, vital with any food, is especially important with dry food. Wash your pet's bowl often and fill it twice daily. Some pets respond to a reminder to drink: try splashing the water with your fingers.

Most dogs love eggs and can be fed a cooked one once or twice a week. But don't feed eggs to cats.

Avoid feeding a pet raw or undercooked meat; it can introduce parasites into an animal's system. Also, spoiled food can be as harmful to a pet as to a human.

A dog's system adjusts slowly to new foods. To change a dog's food, gradually mix the old and new, increasing the proportion of new over several days. An abrupt change may cause diarrhea.

Should you give your dog a bone? If you feel you must, buy a rawhide bone. However, watch out if your dog bites off and swallows large chunks; they can block the digestive system.

In choosing food and water dishes, consider shape as well as capacity: shallow for a snub-nosed cat or dog, narrow at the top to keep long ears out of food. The dishes should be heavy enough so that they don't tip or slide.

Beware of plastic dishes; if not washed thoroughly, bacteria lingers in their porous surfaces.

Kittens, puppies, and pregnant or lactating females need more calories per pound of body weight than normal adults. Give small, frequent feedings, adding up to more than an adult gets. An elderly pet can be fed similarly, but the food should amount to less than the animal ate in its prime.

Unless a pet is on a self-feeding regimen, give it a reasonable time to eat, then pick up the remains. Moist foods spoil especially rapidly.

Empty soft-margarine tubs make fine containers for storing uneaten food in the refrigerator.

TRAVEL AND EXERCISE

When traveling with a pet, take along its usual food. Familiar food relieves the stress of being in an unfamiliar place and prevents diarrhea that often results from sudden diet change.

Withhold food for 2 to 3 hours just before a car trip. After the journey or after any strenuous exercise, let your pet rest at least half an hour before feeding it.

When a dog is working or playing hard, give it many chances to drink *small* amounts of water.

THE WELL-BEHAVED PET

Always praise good behavior—coming when called, sitting, or following any other command—no matter how reluctantly the pet does it. A pet won't understand if you reprimand it for slowness.

A well-treated dog (a cat too, once it trusts you) is eager to please. Use this natural desire; if training is going badly, rethink your method and proceed more slowly.

HOUSEBREAKING

Puppies and kittens have tiny bladders and can't wait patiently for hours or even minutes as a mature pet can. If a pup whimpers, walks in a circle, or sits beside the door, get it outside—fast.

HOW TO HOUSEBREAK A PUPPY OR KITTEN

The moment you bring a new puppy home, take it directly to the place that's to be its "bathroom." If other dogs use the same area, this will help the puppy understand what's expected. When the puppy performs, point to what it has produced and praise it warmly.

Crate training. Most professionals recommend keeping a puppy in an open-sided wire crate whenever it's not being supervised, played with, fed, watered, or exercised. If the puppy's bed is kept small, leaving just enough room for the puppy to turn around, it will try hard to keep its new nest clean.

Paper training. In an apartment, you may want to begin this way: liberally cover a small tiled or vinyl floor area with newspapers. Confine the puppy there with its bed whenever you are going out and at night; take it there whenever it starts to circle or squat. When it uses the papers, praise it warmly. Gradually reduce the papered area until it is very small.

If you are not crate training, you'll have to watch almost constantly for restlessness and circling. Take the pup outside or to the papers every 2 hours during the day, on demand at night, upon awakening, and after any activity, including eating. Shower it with praise whenever it performs in the proper place.

Training a cat. Cats are naturally fastidious and, consequently, they're easier to housebreak than dogs. Usually it is enough to introduce a kitten to a shallow, accessible litter tray, perhaps scratching the litter with one of its paws. If the kitten uses another part of the floor, take up the deposit or puddle and place it in the tray to show the kitten where to go the next time. For a tiny kitten, put many shallow trays around, gradually reducing them to the one it prefers.

A calm, secure puppy is easier to housebreak than a nervous one. Because anxiety and fear contribute to bad behavior, resolve never to hit or holler at your puppy or "rub his nose in it."

A dirty litter box disgusts a cat too. If you fail to keep its box clean, the cat will soon make some cleaner place its bathroom.

To remove a dog or cat mess, scoop up any solids and blot as much liquid as possible. Apply vinegar or lemon juice, then scrub with warm, sudsy water. Sponge dry and repeat. Finish by wiping the area with a cloth moistened in ammonia to neutralize any remaining odor. See p. 282 for removing stains.

Once a cat has used an area as its bathroom, it may repeat the misdeed unless you prohibit its access to the area, feed it at that spot, or cover the area with aluminum foil. Gradually reduce the size of the foil over a period of weeks until only a small piece is left.

Another trick that may get a cat back to its proper bathroom area is to move the litter box to the offending spot. Then gradually, a little each day, move the box back to its original place.

DOG OBEDIENCE TRAINING

From its old pack instincts, a dog expects either to lead or to follow. To train a dog well, you must always be the leader, the dog the obedient follower.

In training a dog, try using three different voice levels: high voice (almost baby talk) for praise; normal voice and authoritative tone for commands; and a quick, low, and controlled voice when you make corrections.

To teach a dog to come on command, start as soon as you get it home. Call "Come!" and reward the right response with lots of praise, even a biscuit.

Be sure your dog masters each command before going on to the next. Use the same commands consistently: come, sit, stay, down (for lie down), heel, stand. Dogs don't understand sentences.

To teach your dog to sit, gently pull up on its collar while tucking its hind legs underneath. Praise the dog as soon as it sits.

To train your dog to stand on command, hold it gently in position and praise it for holding the position for even a second or two.

To teach walking to heel, first coax your dog toward the heel position beside your left leg. Then say "Heel," start to walk, and praise it. If it pulls ahead, give a short, sharp correction with the lead and bring it back to heel.

When training your dog to heel, keep it guessing by altering your direction frequently, but don't follow a consistent pattern.

Half the secret of good walking to heel is attention. Keep up a steady stream of chitchat and your dog's attention won't stray.

Accustom your dog to lying beside you for long periods before training it to stay in place while you leave it. Practice while you read, eat, or watch television.

If you expect to tie your dog outside stores, start when it is young. Check that its collar is tight and securely fastened; a determined dog can slip a loose collar.

Some dogs, particularly sporting and working breeds, respond well to training; others, such as terriers, can test the skill and patience of professional trainers.

DOG BEHAVIOR PROBLEMS

Experts agree that the best way to handle a dog's misbehavior is to prevent it by proper training from puppyhood on. Corrective training builds on the basic commands that every dog should learn and respond to immediately.

Look beyond any annoying behavior to the root cause—loneliness, insecurity, strange people in the house, or change in routine—and try to correct it.

When your dog misbehaves, say "No" in a loud firm voice. As soon as it obeys, shower it with praise and affection.

If a dog jumps up at you, give it a sharp blow in the stomach with your knee. It should be so quick that the dog doesn't know where the blow came from.

A dog that slips its leash may run off and refuse to come when called. Don't chase it! Sit down and try to coax it to you in a pleasant voice. Or walk briskly away from the dog, calling it to heel. Reward it with praise and a biscuit when it comes.

Have a friend help you train your dog how to behave when you open your door. If the dog is barking, stop it. Go to the door with the dog and place it beside you; tell it to lie down. Now open the door; the dog is in position to protect you if necessary. Dogs with a strong guard instinct may need leashing.

For a dog that barks or cries continuously while you're gone, try leaving a radio on softly or putting a ticking clock wrapped in a blanket in the dog's quarters.

Be firm when your dog greets you by jumping up, no matter how joyful it is to see you. Command it to sit; then pet and praise it. This conditions it to receive all its affection on the ground.

If your dog is truly incorrigible, have a trainer observe it; a professional can tell an unbalanced animal from one that will respond to corrective training.

AGGRESSIVENESS IN DOGS

The safe way to stop a dogfight is to prevent it by leashing your dog in public. If you see signs of antagonism toward another dog—rising hackles, a stiffened gait—say "No" and move rapidly away.

If another dog threatens you or your dog, a loud, firm "Go home" will often send it away. Failing that, pick up a stone or a large stick; even the gesture of bending down when no implement is there will often turn a dog away.

If a dogfight breaks out, it's safer to let the dogs settle it themselves unless one dog is in danger.

If you must stop a fight, try a loud distraction to make the dogs release their grip—except shouting, which may excite them. Then, with one person to each dog, pull the dogs apart by their hind legs.

TEACHING A DOG TRICKS

Tricks can entertain both you and your dog. They give your dog a chance to show off and to earn the praise and attention that all dogs thrive on.

The go-and-find trick uses a dog's acute sense of smell. Tell your dog "Sit" and "Stay." Put a biscuit a few feet away on the ground, then say, "O.K. Find it." Make sure the dog doesn't eat it except on cue. Move the biscuit farther and farther away until it's in the next room and half hidden.

In all dog training, replace food with praise as soon as you can. A dog trained only with food has its mind on that rather than on what it's supposed to be doing.

PROBLEMS WITH CATS

When you expect bad manners and contrariness from a cat, quite often that's exactly what you'll get.

A cat cannot be trained by threats or punishment. Instead, use gentle persuasion and, if possible, remove the source of temptation until better habits are formed.

When talking to your cat, use a high voice. Cats associate a loud voice with scolding.

An angry reaction to a cat's aggression will only agitate the cat more. Be gentle, say "No" firmly, and try to interest it in a toy.

If your cat chases and bites your ankles, it may need more play. Get several objects that amuse the cat: a ball suspended in a doorway, a rubber mouse, balled-up aluminum foil, even another cat.

If a cat bites, scratches, or growls, you can correct it with a swat of a rolled newspaper; this resembles the way another cat retaliates and will be accepted by the cat.

For other types of misbehavior, try a squirt from a water pistol (not in the cat's face, though) or a loud noise, preferably so that the cat doesn't see you do it.

To discourage a cat from jumping onto the kitchen counter, leave several aluminum baking pans near the edge so that they'll clatter when the cat lands.

Can't keep the family cat off the furniture? A sprinkling of moth flakes beneath the cushions will deter it.
Caution: Moth flakes are poisonous to animals and humans. Don't use this method when small children are around.

To attract a cat to a scratching post and away from your furniture, try rubbing a little catnip on the post. Or secure a toy to a string and hang it alongside the post.

Most cats regard food left out in plain sight as theirs. If you leave tantalizing food in a room with a cat, you're inviting undesirable behavior.

To give fair warning to neighborhood birds, attach a small bell to your cat's collar. However, don't be surprised if the cat learns to move silently with the bell.

To stop your cat from jumping on furniture, tie some small, inflated balloons to the furniture. Cats hate loud noises.

To discourage bird chasing, hide behind a bush until your cat starts after a bird, then give it a good squirt with a water pistol. Repeat as many times as necessary. If your cat is skilled at finding baby birds, keep it indoors during the hatching season.

OTHER PETS

To catch a loose bird, throw a light cloth over it and pick it up ever so gently. The slightest pressure is enough to break a bird's bones.

If your hamster gets loose, make a baited trap out of a lidded box. Cut a hole big enough for the hamster, put a paper towel over the hole and sprinkle the towel with food.

While you're cleaning your gerbil's cage, put the animal in the bathtub. It can't scramble up the tub's slippery sides.

Personal Grooming

SHAMPOOING YOUR HAIR

Lather hair twice only if it is very oily or very dirty. Otherwise you'll strip your hair of natural oils.

Don't be surprised if your favorite shampoo seems to leave your hair less bouncy after months of satisfactory performance. No one is exactly sure why, but "shampoo fatigue" may be due to a buildup of proteins or other conditioning ingredients. Many people switch brands, only to perceive a drop in performance with the new shampoo within several months. Try switching back to the old one.

When you need a dry shampoo, try bran, dry oatmeal, baby powder, or cornstarch. Use a large-holed shaker or an empty baby-powder container to apply. Work through hair with your fingers and brush out thoroughly.

CONDITIONING YOUR HAIR

If you have an oily scalp, but dry or damaged hair, condition hair *before* you shampoo. Wet hair, towel it dry, and apply conditioner, starting an inch from your scalp. Work conditioner through your hair, wait 5 minutes, and rinse. Then shampoo as usual.

To revitalize and give luster to all types of hair: beat 3 eggs; add 2 tablespoons olive or safflower oil and 1 teaspoon vinegar. Apply mixture to hair and cover with plastic wrap. Wait half an hour and then shampoo well.

A hair conditioner that is bound to draw raves! Combine ¾ cup olive oil, ½ cup honey, and the juice of 1 lemon and set aside. Rinse hair with water and towel dry. Work in a small amount of conditioner (store leftovers in the refrigerator), comb to distribute evenly, and cover with a plastic bag or plastic wrap for ½ hour. Shampoo and rinse thoroughly.

When swimming daily in chlorinated or salt water, alternate hair care, using shampoo one day and conditioner the next.

SETTING AND STYLING HAIR

Never use a hard-bristled brush on your hair when it's wet—wet hair is weak hair. It stretches more easily when wet, and it can stretch only so far before it snaps and breaks. If you really must, use a plastic-bristled brush.

For a permed look without the perm, try pipe cleaners for quick volume and texture. Bend a pipe cleaner into a U shape. Section hair in thin strands, and weave each strand in and out around the pipe cleaner. Twist the ends of the pipe cleaner to secure. Let dry.

253

An easy way to make your hair wavy or curly: apply a small amount of setting gel or lotion, comb through hair, and use your fingers to "scrunch up" hair all over while drying.

To tame flyaway hair caused by static electricity and dryness, apply a cream rinse or rub a fabric-softener sheet over your hair.

Another way to deal with static electricity—apply hair spray to the palm of your hand and, after each brush stroke, run your open palm over your hair. Reapply spray to your hand as necessary.

HAIRCUTS AND TRIMS

When trimming bangs, use a spray bottle to keep hair damp.

For better looking bangs, bring down a fine layer of fringe first. Holding your comb just above the length you want, trim off the excess hair. Keep bringing down layers, using a comb and fingers, trimming each layer as you go.

For a neat, turned-under look for long hair, part the hair across the head from ear to ear, clip up the top section, and trim the lower section first. Then cut the top portion about ½ inch longer than the lower portion.

SPECIAL HAIR TREATMENTS

Remove dandruff easily—shake 1 tablespoon of table salt into dry hair. Massage gently into your hair before shampooing.
Caution: Do not use this treatment if you have any cuts or abrasions on your scalp.

To keep your hair bouncy in damp weather, try one of these. For light hair, mix 1 teaspoon nonfat dry milk in ½ cup warm water and apply to the hair. For dark hair, simmer a handful of dried rosemary leaves in 1 cup water for 5 to 10 minutes. Remove from heat, and steep until warm; strain and apply to the hair.
Caution: Rosemary occasionally causes an allergic reaction, so administer a patch test (p. 256) before using this treatment.

A home highlighter for dark hair: simmer 1 teaspoon allspice, 1 teaspoon crushed cinnamon, and ½ teaspoon cloves in 1 cup water. Strain, cool, and pour over freshly shampooed hair. Rinse off with clear water.
Caution: Cinnamon occasionally causes an allergic reaction, so administer a patch test (p. 256) before using this treatment.

To highlight red hair: brew a cup of orange tea, or dilute strained beet juice. Pour the cooled liquid through freshly shampooed hair; let it sit for 5 minutes; rinse well with clear water.

For brunettes or redheads: add highlights to dull hair with a coffee rinse after your shampoo. (Use only black coffee, of course.) Rinse off with clear water.

PERMANENT WAVES

A perm for "thicker" hair? Yes, permanents make hair feel slightly thicker because its surface texture is changed and wavier hair has more bulk.

Permanent waves or curls can be fragile when new, so let your hair dry naturally the first time you shampoo it after a perm. Blow-drying too soon can relax the waves and curls.

If a new permanent is too tight, blow it dry. (The highest setting straightens best but may damage your hair.) And wait—you'll have a calmer perm in 4 to 6 weeks.

THINNING HAIR

To give thinning hair more fullness, texture, and body, apply some styling mousse while your hair is still wet; then blow-dry. Thin, fine hair will look better if you use a mousse rather than a gel; gels tend to plaster down hair and make it look greasy.

Don't let the sides grow long if you're losing hair on top of your head—it only looks scraggly and clownish. Keep the sides short to balance what you've got on top. Also, you might consider a body wave or partial permanent for the thinning hair on top—it may help add body to your whole "look."

Thin-hair help: color it a lighter shade. Lighter hair blends better with the scalp and isn't so obvious.

BEARDS AND MUSTACHES

Make your facial hair work for you. A mustache directs attention away from a low hairline, a large nose, or a broad face. A full, neat beard camouflages an irregular nose, a receding hairline, or a narrow face.

Facial hair requires care. Shampoo and condition your beard daily; use an antidandruff shampoo if it itches. Trim your beard and mustache weekly to avoid that unkempt look.

If a beard or mustache appears unruly, try using a hair-styling gel or mousse that is meant for the hair on your head. Work the product into your beard, arranging and smoothing with your fingers.

SHAVING AND OTHER HAIR-REMOVAL TECHNIQUES

To raise whiskers, smooth on the shaving cream against the grain of hair growth. Leave the lather on for 2 minutes or so before beginning to shave.

If you nick your skin while shaving, take a small piece of toilet paper, put it over the nick, and apply pressure for 90 seconds. You shouldn't have any swelling, and the nick won't be noticeable.

Another way to stop the bleeding from a shaving nick is to wet a tea bag with cold water and press it on the cut.

For painless eyebrow tweezing, pack a gauze or plastic bag full of crushed ice. Apply on brow until the cold becomes uncomfortable. Your skin will be numb enough now not to feel the tweezing.

SKIN PRODUCTS

A patch test for skin-care products: if you suspect you may be allergic to any substance, put a dab of it inside your wrist or elbow; cover with an adhesive bandage; leave it on for 24 hours. If no redness or irritation is evident, the product is probably safe. Because you can become allergic to something you have used regularly, repeat this test whenever you haven't used a substance in several weeks.

Change brands if you are experiencing a rash or lesions or other serious allergic reactions. Contact your dermatologist and the manufacturer and also notify the nearest office of the health protection branch of Health and Welfare Canada.

CLEANSING THE SKIN

Don't worry if your forehead, nose, and chin are oily, but your cheeks are dry. Washing with a thick washcloth removes dead cells and stimulates circulation, whatever your skin type.

When choosing a soap or cleanser, smell the product before you buy it. Some overly scented products irritate the skin and may not clean as well as those with little fragrance.

Excessive stinging or drying are signs that your toner, astringent, or aftershave lotion is too strong. Change brands or add 1 teaspoon of mineral water to each ounce of the product.

Hot-weather tip: for a cool skin treat refrigerate your facial toner, freshener, or astringent.

BATHING

In winter, your bath or shower water should be tepid, not hot, since hot water inflames the skin and increases moisture loss afterward. Apply a moisturizing lotion right after bathing while your skin is still damp.

A simple but effective way to relieve dry skin and winter itch: completely dissolve 1 cup of salt in a tub of water and bathe as usual. Bathing in salt often works better than using expensive bath oils, but if you really want to use oil, a plain mineral oil will generally fulfill your needs.

MOISTURIZING YOUR SKIN

Always apply a moisturizer right after cleansing to prevent the surface moisture from evaporating. Moisturizers should last about 10 hours. If your face feels tight before then, freshen it with a toner and reapply your moisturizer. You may need a richer moisturizer.

Change your moisturizer with the seasons. In winter, when skin is exposed to dry air, use a creamier moisturizer. In warm weather, a lighter-textured lotion is best for the skin.

To avoid that cracked, flaky look on your elbows, make it a habit to pay special attention to them at the same time you lubricate the rest of your body.

If you are getting lines around your eyes and want to make them less obvious, rub eye cream between your fingers to warm it before patting it around the eyes—this makes it easier for the skin to absorb the cream. Do not pull or stretch the skin around the eyes.

SUN PROTECTION

Give your skin time to absorb a sunblock's ingredients before you need them. Apply a half hour before you go outdoors; reapply if you swim or perspire heavily.

Take a long lunch hour from outdoor exposure. The sun is highest in the sky and is most intense between the hours of 10 in the morning and 2 in the afternoon.

If you're planning on spending some time outdoors, use a moisturizing sunblock or sunscreen along with your regular moisturiz-er. Choose a sunblock with an SPF (sun protection factor) keyed to your skin's response to the sun's rays. Sun protection factors range from 2 to 20. The low-factor sunblocks are suitable for dark-skinned individuals; the high-factor sunblocks are meant for the fair-skinned.

SPECIAL FACIAL TREATMENTS

To cleanse your face thoroughly, try the following method. Fill a clean sink with warm water; dip facial soap into the water and rub the bar over your face. Dip the soap back into the water and make a lather in your hands. Massage this lather over your face. Rinse 15 to 20 times with the soapy water. Then rinse 10 times in warm running water. Finish off with several cold-water rinses. Blot your face dry with a towel.

For a deep-cleansing mask, stroke milk of magnesia on your face with cotton balls, avoiding the eye area. Leave the mask on for 10 minutes. Remove with a warm washcloth and apply moisturizer.

A good mask for dry skin: mix 1 egg yolk, 1 teaspoon honey, and 2 tablespoons sour cream. Apply to clean skin with cotton balls, being careful to avoid the eye area. Leave on for 15 minutes; then rinse thoroughly.

An oily-skin mask: make a paste of honey, oatmeal, and lemon juice. Apply to face; leave on for 10 minutes. Rinse with warm water.

For a normal-skin mask, make a paste of 1/3 cup finely ground almonds and enough witch hazel to moisten. Apply to face, being careful to avoid the eye area; leave on for 15 minutes. Wipe off with tissues; then rinse face with warm water.

MAKEUP FOUNDATION

If you never seem to buy the right shade of foundation, try it on just under the jawline rather than on the wrist. It should be just slightly lighter than your skin tone.

To deemphasize puffiness under the eyes, apply concealer below the puffy area and blend. (Applying concealer on the puffy area would only emphasize it.)

CAN YOU AGEPROOF YOUR SKIN?

Question: Why do some people seem to age faster than others?
Answer: A varying combination of factors is at work: heredity, general health and environment, color of complexion, and exposure to the elements—especially the sun—make people of the same age appear younger or older looking than their peers.

Question: What's the simplest way to prevent wrinkles?
Answer: Stay out of the sun. It's the most effective advice so far. Always use a sunblock or sunscreen on exposed areas whenever you must be outdoors in the sun. You should protect yourself as early in life as possible, even during childhood.

Question: How else can a person prevent premature wrinkling?
Answer: Stop smoking! Studies have shown that people who smoke may develop deeper and sharper wrinkles at the outer corners of their eyes and mouth than those who do not smoke.

Question: Can moisturizers help?
Answer: Moisturizers won't prevent wrinkles, but they can have a positive effect on the way skin looks. When given moisture, the surface of the outer layer of skin "plumps up." The skin appears smoother, and minor wrinkles are temporarily softened. The skin feels better, too.

Question: What about wrinkle creams?
Answer: Many wrinkle creams are formulations designed to help "fill in" wrinkles.

They work only on the surface layer, so their effect is temporary. Other than that, many creams are excellent moisturizers containing ingredients that actually help to trap moisture within the layers of the skin. Since moisturized skin generally looks younger, these products help, but they won't prevent or "cure" wrinkles.

Question: Is petroleum jelly just as effective as expensive wrinkle creams?
Answer: Petroleum jelly will prevent loss of moisture and protect the skin, but it won't reduce surface wrinkles. It also may encourage blackhead and whitehead formation—even in elderly skin. A better remedy would be a noncomedogenic lubricant—a moisturizer that does not encourage the development of blemishes. Your dermatologist can give you the name of several products.

Question: Is there any advantage to using wrinkle creams on younger skin?
Answer: Since wrinkles can't be prevented, it's probably futile to use wrinkle creams at a young age. Some products contain oils that could cause breakouts on younger skin or could worsen already present acne.

Question: Will facial exercises help?
Answer: Facial exercises will not prevent wrinkles and, in fact, can do more harm than good. Your face is constantly in motion when you eat, speak, and otherwise exercise your face in the normal routine of living; it's precisely because of repeated motion that lines are formed.

To transform a heavy, oil-based foundation into one that glides on more smoothly, add a bit of moisturizer or salt-free mineral water to the foundation. Use your palm or a small dish—not the makeup container—to do the mixing.

BLUSHERS AND POWDERS

For those "gray" days, mix a drop of liquid blusher with your foundation. Spread this instant "glow" all over your skin.

When you're feeling tired and dragged out, use blusher very lightly around the entire outer contour of your face, from the hairline to the chin, blending with a cosmetic sponge. It will give you a wonderful glow.

Under fluorescent lights, which destroy the rosy tones in the skin and give a yellowish look, apply your blusher a little darker and use a little deeper-colored lipstick.

Store loose powder in an old salt or pepper shaker so that you can shake it into your palm. Then dip a makeup brush or puff into the powder and dust it on.

EYE MAKEUP

Makeup—especially eye makeup—is perishable. Bacteria from your eyes can be introduced to the product and vice versa. Wash applicators frequently or use cotton swabs. Also, label shadows, pencils, and mascaras with their purchase dates. Replace your shadows and pencils every 6 months, your mascara every 3 months.

If you use liquid eyeliner, try dotting it on along the lash line. It will look less harsh than a solid line.

To get a sharp point to your eyebrow, eyeliner, and lip pencils, put them in the freezer for an hour before sharpening.

Tame unruly brows with a little bit of styling gel or mousse applied with an eyebrow brush.

LIP CARE

Your lipstick will stay on much longer if you use the following method. Layer on in this order: face powder, lipstick, powder, lipstick. Wipe off excess powder with a damp washcloth or a tissue.

To repair a broken lipstick: use a cigarette lighter or long fireplace match to melt (slightly) the bottom of the broken piece and the piece it must adhere to. Attach the two pieces and seal the edge of the break with a clean match or toothpick. Place in the refrigerator until completely cooled.

HOW TO APPLY MAKEUP—STEP BY STEP

Always start with clean skin and clean hands. Wash your hands during the application of makeup as well; dirty hands can contaminate any makeup that you apply with the tips of your fingers, possibly causing your skin to break out. Begin your makeup by cleansing, toning, and moisturizing your face.

1. Put dots of concealer on undereye circles and on blemishes. (Some makeup experts advise using concealer after foundation. You may want to experiment with both techniques.)

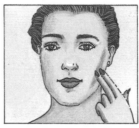

2. Apply foundation in long sweeping strokes over the face down to the jawline. (Do not put on eyelids.) Blend with a non-rubber cosmetic sponge using short quick strokes.

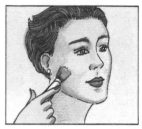

3. When foundation has had a chance to dry, lightly dust on translucent powder with a big brush. This helps to "set" the makeup you've just applied.

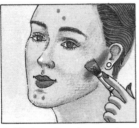

4. Next, apply a deep shade of powder blusher from the middle of the cheek to the hairline and a cream rouge on the cheekbone. Dot cream rouge on chin and forehead. Blend with sponge. Go over cream rouge with similar shade of powder blusher.

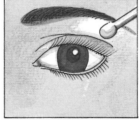

5. Apply a neutral shade of eye shadow to the lids as a foundation or base color. Highlight just under the brow with a white or light shade. Use a muted shade on the lids themselves. Take care that eye-shadow colors don't make you look tired.

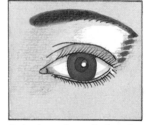

6. Apply another color from the outer corner of the eye up to the brow bone. Use tiny brush strokes as shown. The base color in the inner corner of the eye will brighten your eyes. Blend edges well with a sponge.

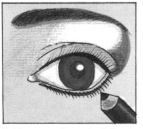

7. Use an eyeliner pencil directly on top of the upper lashes and just below the lower lashes. If you line the inside of the lower lid with color, it will make the whites of the eyes appear whiter, but it will also make the eyes look smaller.

8. Apply mascara with a brush or wand. For a heavier appearance, try using translucent powder on lashes between mascara applications.

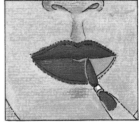

9. Using a lip pencil, draw a line just outside your natural lip line if you feel they're too thin; just inside if you feel your lips are too full. Use a lip brush to apply lip color. Dip it into clear gloss first, then into lipstick. Blend the lip color and lip-pencil line.

To prevent feathering and bleeding of lip color, use a lip base under your lipstick, and outline lips with a lip liner.

REMOVING MAKEUP

Always make sure that you have removed every trace of makeup from your face before you go to sleep. Habitually sleeping with a layer of cosmetics, dirt, and dead skin cells stuck to your face will leave your complexion looking muddy and dull.

When you're removing mascara, if it seems to get all over your face, wrap a tissue around your index finger and hold it just under the lower lashes. Remove eye makeup as usual with the other hand.

PERSPIRATION

Tired of commercial deodorants? Apply a thin layer of antibacterial cream on underarms instead; ask your druggist to recommend one. Bacteria cause the offending odor, and this will reduce their numbers considerably.

If underarm deodorants tend to irritate your skin, try applying hand cream before the deodorant. If the irritation persists, you may be suffering an allergic reaction; stop using the deodorant, and consider consulting a dermatologist about the problem.

For relief of those embarrassing sweaty palms, try massaging an antiperspirant into the palms of your hands.

Shoes in need of deodorizing? Sprinkle their insides with baking soda. (Be sure to shake the powder out before wearing the shoes.)

FRAGRANCES

New places for perfume: put a few drops on cotton and tuck inside your bra; place some on light bulbs before you turn them on to delightfully scent your home.

Avoid wearing perfume in the sun; the oils it contains can cause brown spots on the skin.

In the sink, mix cologne with warm water and, using a washcloth, freshen up all over with a perfume sponge bath.

MOUTH CARE

The best toothbrush is one with soft, rounded, nylon bristles. Replace it every 3 or 4 months. Frayed or bent bristles don't remove plaque effectively and can damage your gums.

The best time to use dental floss is *before* you brush. That way you can brush away the plaque and fragments of food with your toothbrush and rinse. If you floss after brushing, the loosened particles may remain in your mouth.

Flossing made easy (especially for children): tie a length of dental floss (about 10 inches) into a loop. Wrap the loop around your index fingers and thumbs, leaving approximately an inch of floss between them. Use a gentle sawing motion to get the floss between your teeth.

DENTURE CARE

It's not enough to simply soak your dentures; you should brush them as well. Soaking provides gentle, nonabrasive cleaning; brushing removes the sticky plaque from dentures.

For denture cleanup away from home, use a small piece of nylon net for a quick scrub without having to remove the dentures.

A solution of 1 tablespoon household bleach and 1 teaspoon water softener, such as Calgon, in ½ cup water makes an excellent homemade denture cleaner.

FOR FRESHER BREATH

Carry mint tea bags for an afterdinner mouth freshener when you are not able to brush your teeth. Mint tea is a sweet-smelling alternative to coffee.

To avoid bad breath, eat regular meals. When you skip meals, bacteria build up on the tongue, causing odor.

For sweeter breath, brush *all* of the inside of your mouth, including your tongue — not just your teeth. Otherwise, the odor-causing bacteria linger in your mouth.

HAND CARE

To help heal chapped or cracked skin on hands, apply cream, oil, or petroleum jelly; then cover with cotton gloves. Wear rubber gloves over all for dish washing. The double layers are especially good for working in hot water.

Moisturize hands the right way: dab some hand cream or lotion on the back of one hand, and massage with the back of the other for a few seconds. Then, to distribute the cream evenly, rub both hands together all over. The backs of the hands need the most moisturizing because the skin there can be very dry.

To lighten dark spots on your hands, apply an over-the-counter bleaching cream twice a day after washing your hands, as well as a sunblock before going outdoors. If this treatment doesn't work after several months, ask your dermatologist to prescribe a stronger bleaching cream.

Caution: Some people are allergic to bleaching creams, so it is wise to administer a patch test before application (p. 256).

NAIL CARE

Insert your fingertips in half a lemon and twist your fingers back and forth to clean your cuticles and nails before a manicure.

To help your nail polish last longer, apply a top coat of clear enamel. To keep the nails shiny and looking freshly polished, apply a top coat every day. This also cuts down on chipping.

If you mess up a nail, you don't have to take off all the polish. Instead, dampen the pad of your opposite index finger with nail-polish remover and pat the remover over the offending nail. The polish will smooth out sufficiently so you can let it dry and polish right over it.

Never peel off nail polish. Along with it, you'll peel off the thin, protective, topmost layer of your nails, weakening them.

Choose pale or neutral shades of polish, especially if your fingernails are short. With light nail polish, slight nicks will be barely noticeable, and quick touch-ups will be easier than if you wear dark shades of polish.

FOOT CARE

To prevent calf muscles from permanently shortening and tightening, alternate high heels with low heels or with flats from day to day. Also, slip into lower heels for a while before going barefoot to give your calf muscles a chance to lengthen and relax, preventing calf pain.

Give your feet a rest while you're relaxing around your home. If they're swollen, elevate them as much as possible. In warm weather, wear flat sandals; in cold weather, a heavy knit sock with leather sewn on the foot for a sole.

If you like to paint your toenails—and not your toes—cut a sponge into triangular shapes and use to keep the toes separate.

If your toes, nails, or the skin on your feet are discolored, rub the discolored areas with half a lemon. For extra bleaching and softening, cup the lemon on your heels for 15 minutes. Be sure to moisturize afterward.

DRESSING YOUR BEST

Slenderizing fabrics are those that are medium in weight and texture. Patterns on fabrics should be medium in size or in proportion to your height.

Women with shorter haircuts may need softer lines, softer colors, or ruffles rather than man-tailored looks. Try shawl-collared blouses and jackets. Use pastels to your best advantage.

If dark tones make you feel drab, but you wear them frequently to look slim, wear another flattering color close to your face (pp. 264-265). A brightly colored blouse under a dark jacket or sweater, or a pretty scarf at the neck can really make a difference.

If you travel a great deal, pale, neutral colors travel the best to the most places. Include off-white, pale gray, beige, camel, and tan in your wardrobe—they're nondescript colors. Add variety with texture or bright accessories.

DISCOVERING YOUR BEST COLORS

The latest colors may not always be right for you. The best guides for choosing the colors of your clothes and cosmetics are the natural colors of your hair, skin, and eyes. Of these, your *natural* hair color is the most important. To look your most attractive, you should wear your best colors. Use the palette below as a guide when buying clothing and makeup.

PALE BLONDS

Core colors: Suits, coats, dresses, etc.

Accent colors: Sweaters, shirts, scarves, ties, etc.

Natural hair color:
Platinum and light blond to brownish blond; always has ash tones.
Skin:
Pale or translucent.
Eyes:
Light blue, light gray, or blue-green.

Foundation:
Flesh tone, beige, rose-beige, rose-brown.
Blusher:
Dusty rose, tawny pink, raspberry.
Eye shadow:
Gray, blue-gray, pink, taupe, soft gray-brown, teal, mauve.
Eye liner:
Taupe, gray, gray-blue, mauve.
Mascara:
Brown, mauve, dark blue.
Lip and nail color:
Dusty rose, plum-pink, bright pink, blue-red.

GOLDEN BLONDS

Core colors: Suits, coats, dresses, etc.

Accent colors: Sweaters, shirts, scarves, ties, etc.

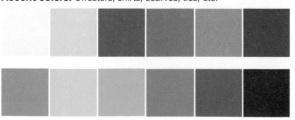

Natural hair color:
Light golden brown to strawberry blond; no ash tones.
Skin:
Peach or ivory.
Eyes:
Crystal blue, blue with brown flecks, blue-green, or golden brown.

Foundation:
Ivory to peach tones, warm beige, mocha tan.
Blusher:
Peach, coral, ginger.
Eye shadow:
Smudgy brown, russet, golden tones, aqua tints, and smoky blue to violet.
Eye liner:
Smudgy brown, smoky blue.
Mascara:
Brown, electric blue.
Lip and nail color:
Peach, pinky coral, ginger-brown, mocha, orange-red.

BRUNETTES

Core colors: Suits, coats, dresses, etc.

Accent colors: Sweaters, shirts, scarves, ties, etc.

Natural hair color:
Medium to dark brown and black.

Eyes:
Light to dark brown, black, green, gray, and light or deep blue.

Skin:
Porcelain, beige with a hint of pink, ivory, light or dark olive, and light or dark black.

Foundation:
Rose-beige, medium beige, light beige, cocoa, rose-brown, dark bronze. *Amber, dark honey, copper-tan, beige-tan.*

Blusher:
Blue-pink, rose-brown, rose-wine. *Bright red, plum, orchid, amber-rose, pink or red cheek gloss.*

Eye shadow:
Plum, taupe, blue, gray, gray-green, mauve. *Shades of rose, plum, teal, mid to navy blue, smoky violet, taupe, blue-black.*

Eye liner:
Charcoal, taupe. *Electric blue, mauve, brown-black.*

Mascara:
Brown-black, electric blue. *Brown-black, purple.*

Lip and nail color:
Bright red, cherry-red, pink-plum, bright burgundy, fuchsia. *Rose-red, brilliant red, plum, raspberry, mocha-red.*

Colors for dark-skinned brunettes are in italics.

REDHEADS

Core colors: Suits, coats, dresses, etc.

Accent colors: Sweaters, shirts, scarves, ties, etc.

Natural hair color:
Light red to dark auburn or brown with definite red or auburn tones.

Skin:
Fair or reddish.

Eyes:
Turquoise, green, blue, brown, or hazel.

Foundation:
Golden beige, cream-beige, peach-beige.

Blusher:
Tawny, peach, apricot, coral.

Eye shadow:
Russet, teal, golden copper, olive green.

Eye liner:
Moss green, charcoal, brown.

Mascara:
Dark brown, green.

Lip and nail color:
Brick red, coral, peach.

A man who regularly carries a wallet in his jacket or trousers should include it while trying on new clothes to check for tightness or pulling over it.

For women who carry a briefcase: get a small handbag that fits inside. Don't let too many bags—or oversized bags—overpower you.

An easy way to remove "pills" from a sweater: run a medium-grade sandpaper across the garment's surface. Remove the pills from the sandpaper, and you can reuse it.

If you have little occasion to wear a "good" dress or formal outfit, keep the color and style discreet. Distinctive colors and bold prints are a bit too memorable. A simple outfit or dress lends itself to more creative accessorizing.

QUICK CHANGES FOR CLOTHES AND ACCESSORIES

Wear cotton T-shirts under wool sweaters that feel itchy.

Need a choker-length necklace? Add clasps to inexpensive costume beads that are long enough to double up into a choker length but won't go over your head twice. You can find jewelry clasps in crafts and department stores.

Make a pin or tie tack from a beautiful old button. You can find pin makings at a crafts store, or you can glue a safety pin to the back of the button.

Old clip-on earrings can perk up plain pumps. To avoid marring the shoe's outer surface, you can use floral clay to stick the clip to the inside of the pump.

WHICH IS YOUR MOST FLATTERING STYLE?

Small bust? Details such as gathers, tucks, ruffles, or shirring amplify a small bust. So do cardigans, cable-knit sweater, notched jacket lapels, Empire waistlines, and wide, cinched belts. Avoid clinging garments.

Large bust or broad shoulders? Look for dolman sleeves, blouson sweaters, small collars, vertical necklines, narrow lapels, and wrap fronts in nonclinging fabrics. Avoid wide necklines, puffed sleeves, ruffles, gathers, padded shoulders, wide belts, and Empire waistlines. Be sure garments don't pull across the bustline or shoulder blades.

Short waist? Shop for overblouses, tunics, Empire-waisted dresses, and pullovers with dropped waistlines that will elongate your torso. So will a long scarf worn as an accessory. Avoid belted waistlines, which will cut you in half visually and will shorten your torso.

Large abdomen? Buy pants in woven fabrics (poplin, gabardine, or wool flannel) that hang straight from a tailored waistband. Avoid jersey or polyester knits and elasticized waistbands; they accentuate bulges. Wear unbelted dresses; avoid fitted midriffs. Wear control-top panty hose for additional support.

Heavy thighs or hips? Choose softly gathered skirts, straight skirts with small slits or kick pleats, or dresses in an A-line or slightly flared silhouette. Jackets with epaulets or padded shoulders and wide lapels can help to balance your upper torso with your hips. Try to avoid pleated skirts or pants with patch pockets at the hips.

Short legs? Select skirts with hems that fall below your knees. Team them with color-coordinated hosiery and shoes. If you wear boots, be sure your hem covers the tops. Choose shirtwaist dresses or coatdresses that have vertical seams from neckline to hemline. Wear tapered pants, without cuffs. Avoid above-the-knee hemlines, wide, cuffed pants, as well as boots that reach midcalf or just above the ankle.

Clothing & Laundry

BEFORE SHOPPING FOR CLOTHES

Plan your wardrobe around one or two color groups (pp.264–265). Choose basic styles that can be dressed up or down. Know which items you already have and buy separate items and accessories to spruce them up.

If you have a hard time remembering your family's clothing sizes when you go shopping, record them in a small notebook. It will also come in handy for holding fabric swatches from articles you want to coordinate.

When you shop for clothing, wear the following: garments that are easy to remove; the same type of shoes and undergarments you intend to wear with your new item; a minimum of makeup and jewelry.

To find the best values, do your shopping at a variety of places: factory outlets, department stores, thrift shops, mail-order houses, and garage sales.

BUYING CLOTHES

To get the best clothing for your dollar, look for quality and buy as expensively as you can afford. Signs of quality include:

Clean, odor-free fabric that doesn't hold wrinkles after being crushed by hand.

Fabric cut on straight grain (or on bias if that's the style of the garment).

Straight grain   Off-grain

Linings that are smooth and invisible from the right side.

Plaids, stripes, and cross seams that match evenly.

Flat, smooth seams with finished edges.

Straight, smooth, unbroken stitches.

Hems and seams that are even in width and adequate for alterations.

Collars and lapels that have even points and do not roll upward.

Zippers that lie flat and work smoothly.

Securely held trims, pockets, buttons, and fasteners.

BEFORE BUYING CLOTHES

Before buying a garment, read its care label (p.274) to determine how much time and money is required to keep it clean; its fiber-content label (p.268) to determine how much comfort and durability it provides; and its size label to make sure it fits properly.

FABRIC FIBERS: PROPERTIES TO CONSIDER WHEN SHOPPING

Fiber	Characteristics	Care
Cotton	Strong; soft; very absorbent; shrinks and wrinkles easily unless treated; damaged by mildew, perspiration, and chlorine bleach	Hand- or machine-wash (normal cycle) colorfast cottons in warm water, others in cold water; use any detergent; tumble-dry at permanent-press setting; iron at hot setting while damp
Linen	Strong; crisp; very absorbent; shrinks, stretches, and wrinkles easily unless treated; damaged by mildew, perspiration, and chlorine bleach	Dry-clean to retain crisp texture; if softness is preferred, hand- or machine-wash (normal cycle) in warm or cool water; use any detergent; dry by any method; iron at hot setting while damp
Silk	Strong; smooth; absorbent; resists wrinkling and mildew; water-spots easily; damaged by perspiration and chlorine bleach	Dry-clean; if labeled "Washable," hand-wash in warm or cool water, using mild detergent; drip-dry; iron at cool setting, using damp press cloth
Wool	Weak but durable; soft and warm; very absorbent; resists wrinkling; shrinks unless treated; damaged by moths and chlorine bleach	Dry-clean; if labeled "Washable," hand-wash in tepid or cool water, using mild detergent; dry flat; iron at cool setting, using damp press cloth
Nylon and polyester	Strong; not absorbent; resist wrinkling, shrinking, moths, and mildew; damaged by heat and sulfuric acid (in polluted air); prone to static electricity, pilling, and greasy stains	Hand- or machine-wash (gentle cycle) in warm water, using any detergent (add fabric softener to reduce static electricity); tumble-dry or drip-dry; for touch-ups, iron nylon at cool setting, polyester at warm
Rayon	Weak when wet; soft; absorbent; shrinks, stretches, and wrinkles easily unless treated; damaged by mildew, perspiration, and chlorine bleach	Dry-clean; if labeled "Washable," machine-wash (gentle cycle) in warm water; use any detergent; tumble-dry at low setting; iron at warm setting while damp
Acetate	Weak; smooth; slightly absorbent; wrinkles and stretches easily; resists shrinking, pilling, moths, and mildew; damaged by heat, perspiration, nail polish remover, and perfumes with organic solvents; prone to static electricity	Dry-clean; if labeled "Washable," hand- or machine-wash (gentle cycle) in warm water, using any detergent; tumble-dry at low setting; iron at cool setting
Triacetate	Weak; smooth; slightly absorbent; resists wrinkling, shrinking, moths, mildew, and fading from polluted air and perspiration; damaged by heat, nail polish remover, and perfumes with organic solvents	Hand- or machine-wash (normal cycle) in warm water, using any detergent; drip-dry pleated garments, tumble-dry others; little or no ironing needed
Acrylic	Strong; soft; not absorbent; resists wrinkling, shrinking, moths, and mildew; damaged by heat and perspiration; prone to pilling, static electricity, and greasy stains	Machine-wash (normal cycle) in warm water, using any detergent; tumble-dry (add fabric softener to reduce static electricity); little or no ironing needed
Modacrylic	Strong; soft; not absorbent; resists wrinkling, shrinking, moths, and mildew; flame retardant; damaged by heat; prone to pilling, static electricity, and greasy stains	Dry-clean; if labeled "Washable," follow care-label instructions; do not iron

Items marked "Irregular" may not be perfect in size or color but are free of substantial damage. However, those marked "Seconds" often have serious flaws.

How well a garment "breathes" depends not only on the absorbency of the fabric, but on its fiber content, construction, thickness, and finish. When shopping for clothes, keep in mind that some synthetic fibers (such as those used in sportswear) are as cool as natural fibers.

When shopping for knits, look for even, circular loops in the fabric; reinforced shoulders and buttonholes; lined skirts and pants.

FABRIC FINISHES

Finish	Purpose	Comments
Mercerizing	Increases strength, luster, color brightness, and wrinkle resistance of cotton	Follow care-label instructions
Crisp finish	Gives sheer cotton a starched appearance	Follow care-label instructions; starch may be needed after first washing
Permanent press	Reduces need for ironing after washing	Follow care-label instructions; chlorine bleach weakens fabric; some finishes turn yellow
Stain resistant	Provides stain and soil resistance	Follow care-label instructions; blot up spills as soon as possible
Shrink resistant	Helps garment retain its original size and shape after washing	Follow care-label instructions; read garment label for amount of expected shrinkage (2% or less is acceptable)
Water repellent	Provides resistance to water, but is not waterproof	Follow care-label instructions; finish becomes less effective if not dry-cleaned properly; finish can be restored by dry cleaner
Waterproof	Prevents water from penetrating fabric	Follow care-label instructions; finish usually does not allow air to pass through fabric
Flame retardant	Provides fire resistance	Follow care-label instructions; some fabrics become less effective when washed with soap or nonphosphate detergent, particularly in areas with hard water

When choosing rainwear, look for a fabric labeled "Water Resistant" (or "Water Repellent") and "Soil Resistant"; double layers of cloth over the shoulders; and a lining that can be removed.

BEFORE YOU WEAR A NEW GARMENT

Most new clothes can stand a bit of reinforcing even before you wear them. First, check the stitching. If any loose thread ends are visible, fasten them or pull them to the wrong side and secure them.

Turn the garment inside out and look closely at the seams for loose, broken, or skipped stitches, and repair them. Are the seam allowances finished? Do their edges show signs of fraying? If the seam allowance is unfinished and the fabric has begun to fray, sew a row of straight or zigzag stitches along the raw edges of the seam allowance.

If your new garment has set-in sleeves, secure them with a second line of stitching ⅛ inch to ¼ inch away from the original armhole line in the seam allowance.

No more torn pockets! Before you wear a garment with patch pockets, reinforce them by stitching a tiny triangle at each top corner.

In a slim skirt, the stitching often comes apart at the top of the kick pleat. If the pleat hangs for the full length of the skirt, turn the skirt to the inside and stitch from the top of the pleat opening to the folded pleat edge. This shifts the strain at the point where the skirt ordinarily rips.

269

Reinforce slits at the bottom of close-fitting pants and at the wrists and side seams of a blouse or shirt. Sew a bar tack across the top of the slit on the wrong side through the seam allowance only.

PROMOTING LONGER WEAR

Iron-on patches applied to the inside of the knees of jeans will make them last longer. Also apply patches to the inside of elbows of shirts or jackets that get a lot of rough use.

To strengthen the elbow area of a sweater, weave a length of similar yarn perpendicularly through the sweater knit. Work from the wrong side, splitting the original yarns as you pass through them.

To keep the cuffs of sweaters and mittens from stretching, weave several rounds of elastic through the underside of the cuffs.

Protect your favorite dress from perspiration stains by inserting underarm shields, preferably the cotton type. They can be tacked on or attached with snaps.

Before you wear a new garment, resew any fasteners, such as buttons, hooks, eyes, or snaps, that are loosely sewn to the garment.

The fabric area surrounding gripper snaps often tears from the pull of constant use. To alleviate the strain, machine-stitch along each side of the gripper parts.

REMOVING LINT AND WRINKLES

To remove lint from clothing, use a damp sponge or a clothes brush. Or wrap masking tape around your hand, adhesive side up, and brush the garment gently.

To remove wrinkles from clothing, especially when traveling, hang garments in the bathroom while you take a hot shower. Close the bathroom door and window to hold in the steam. Let the garment air-dry before wearing it.

Another fast fix for wrinkles is to place the item in the dryer with a damp towel and run the dryer for about 10 minutes.

HANGING UP CLOTHES

When you take off your clothes, look for any stains, rips, tears, or loose buttons. Clean or repair them before they get worse.

Because wire hangers from dry cleaners may rust or distort clothing, use plastic or wooden hangers instead.

Garments will retain their shape better if you close their top fasteners before they're hung.

Hang garments on suitable hangers. For shirts, blouses, jackets, and coats, use shaped or padded hangers; for skirts and pants, use skirt and pants hangers.

Want to keep a soft roll to the collar of a shirt or blouse? Slip a twisted piece of tissue paper underneath.

Dresses with narrow straps won't slip off their hangers if you wrap a rubber band around each end.

Let your clothes air out or dry before you put them away. Don't wear the same items day after day; allow at least 24 hours for moisture to evaporate.

If your slacks are damp from the rain, hang them up by the cuffs or lower hem.

STORING CLOTHES FLAT

Some garments should be folded and stored flat rather than hung up. In general, the looser, softer, or finer the fabric, the more likely it will benefit from flat storage.

Knits, unless they're tightly constructed, should be stored flat. If you must hang up a knitted garment, drape it lengthwise over the padded bar of the hanger.

To prevent a garment made of very thin fabric from creasing, stuff it loosely with tissue paper before folding it for storage.

To minimize creasing of folded garments, put lighter items at the top of the stack.

CLOSETS AND DRESSERS

To keep closets smelling fresh, try the following: clean clothes before putting them away; leave the door slightly ajar to allow air to circulate; put a box of baking soda in the closet to absorb odors; hang a pomander ball (p.272) or sweet-smelling sachet in the closet.

To reduce dampness in closets, wrap 12 pieces of chalk together and hang them up.

FIGHTING MILDEW

To prevent mildew from forming on stored clothes:

Don't put garments away if they're still damp; let them air-dry or iron them at the highest temperature safe for the fabric.

Avoid storing clothes in plastic bags or boxes, which can trap moisture.

Ventilate storage areas when the weather is dry and cool.

Pack storage areas loosely so that air can circulate around clothes.

Don't use starch or fabric finish on items to be stored.

When storing clothes, use a chemical desiccant such as silica gel or calcium chloride, but don't let it touch garments.

Place paradichlorobenzene mothballs or crystals inside closets and drawers; they prevent mildew and absorb moisture.

To protect garments from snags, and possibly acid damage from wood, line your dresser drawers with quilted fabric or good quality shelf paper that is ungummed. (Gummed paper attracts insects and is hard to remove.)

For sweet-smelling clothes, put unwrapped bars of scented soap, empty perfume bottles, or fabric-softener sheets into drawers.

As a safety precaution, make sure that closets can be opened from the inside.

SEASONAL STORAGE

Consider professional cold storage if you have any of the following: furs or fur-trimmed clothes; a climate that is very hot or humid; inadequate storage space; chronic problems with carpet beetles, silverfish, moths, or mildew.

MAKING A POMANDER BALL

To give your closet a nice, spicy fragrance, try this recipe for a pomander ball: Completely cover an orange, lemon, or lime by sticking whole cloves into the skin. If the fruit is small, mix 1 teaspoon of cinnamon and 1 tablespoon of orrisroot powder (available in most herb stores or mail-order catalogs); if it's large, double the ingredients. Place fruit and mixture in a plastic bag and shake until fruit is coated. Store fruit in tissue paper in a dry place for about 2 weeks. Remove fruit and hang it in the closet.

Before you put clothes in storage, make sure they've been cleaned thoroughly; insects are attracted by dirt, especially from perspiration, food, and beverages.

Storage areas should be clean, dry, free of insects, and away from light, which can fade some colors (especially blues and greens) and promote hatching of insect eggs.

To wrap folded garments and to line dresser drawers, use white tissue paper or washed muslin; at least once a year, replace the tissue paper and wash the muslin.

Store clothing in places that have moderate temperature or humidity; avoid extremes, such as a hot attic or a damp basement.

Because garments made of natural fibers (cotton, wool, silk, and linen) need to breathe, store them in a well-ventilated area in containers with ventilation holes.

When you take your clothes out of storage, put them in the dryer for about 10 minutes on the air-only cycle (no heat). This will help get rid of wrinkles.

STORING SPECIAL FABRICS

Furs: If garment is small, store at home in a cold, dry place. Cover with cloth or washed muslin. Otherwise, use professional cold storage.

Leather and suede: Store in a cool, well-ventilated closet. Cover with cloth or washed muslin. For soft leather, pad with white tissue paper and fold flat.

Linen: Roll if possible. If you must fold, refold periodically to avoid creases. Cover with cloth or washed muslin.

Metallics: Roll with white tissue paper or washed muslin to separate each layer. If you must fold, place white tissue paper between each layer and refold periodically to avoid creases. Cover with cloth or washed muslin.

Quilts: Fold and store flat. Cover with cloth or washed muslin.

Rayon: Store flat. If you must hang garment, pad it well with white tissue paper. Cover with cloth or washed muslin.

Silk: For sheer or knitted silks, store flat. If you must hang garment, pad it well with white tissue paper. Cover with cloth or washed muslin.

Velvet: Pad with white tissue paper and hang on a padded hanger, supporting skirt area from loops attached at waist. Cover with cloth or washed muslin.

Wool: Clean thoroughly, pad with paper, fold, then wrap in white tissue paper. Add mothballs to storage area.

MOTHS AND MOTHBALLS

Mothballs and crystals won't kill those moth eggs that are already present in clothing when it's stored. Clean clothing thoroughly before you put it away.

Because mothballs and crystals emit a vapor which is heavier than air, suspend them in containers above clothing. Keep them away from children and pets (they are poisonous if eaten).

Old stockings or socks make good bags for mothballs. If you're using moth crystals, sprinkle them on the adhesive side of masking tape and hang them up.

To dispel mothball odor, add a pomander or an herbal potpourri to the storage area. Either suspend it or pack it in a small sack. A very simple herbal is five or six bay leaves strung together.

To protect stored clothing from moths, a cedar chest must be made of cedar heartwood at least ¾ inch thick. It should also have felt gaskets to make it airtight.

Although cedar will kill newly hatched or young worms, it won't kill eggs, half-grown worms, the pupae or chrysalises, or moths.

PRESERVING YOUR CLOTHES

If you wipe away body oils at your neck and wrists with witch hazel before getting dressed, you'll save on dry-cleaning bills.

To extend the life of your more expensive clothing, change into a casual outfit as soon as you get home from work.

Avoid getting a shiny seat on your pants; sit on fabric-covered seats or seat pads rather than those made of leather or plastic.

SPECIAL CLOTHING-CARE PROBLEMS

If you find a snag in a garment, don't cut it. Instead, pull it to the inside of the garment, using a fine crochet hook or the head of a flathead straight pin.

Are your brassiere straps constantly falling off your shoulders? Try sewing thin elastic between them in the back.

SPECIAL CARE LABELS

When the label reads...	It means...	When the label reads...	It means...
Washing		**Washer cycle** (cont.)	
Machine-wash	Wash by any customary method, including commercial laundering. If no bleach statement is made, use any bleach; if no temperature is given, use hot water (up to 150° F)	Durable-press or permanent-press cycle	Cool down or cold rinse before short spin cycle
		Drying	
		Tumble-dry	Use machine dryer. (If no temperature is given, hot setting can be used.)
Warm wash Warm rinse	Use warm water or warm machine setting (90° F to 110° F)		
Cold wash Cold rinse	Use cold tap water or cold machine setting (up to 85° F)	No wring No twist	Handle gently to prevent wrinkles and distortion
Hand-wash	Launder by hand. If no bleach statement is made, use any bleach; if no temperature is given, use hand-comfortable hot water (90° F to 110° F)	Drip-dry	Hang dripping wet with or without hand-shaping and -smoothing
		Line-dry	Hang damp and allow to dry
		Dry flat	Lay garment on flat surface
Wash separately	Wash alone or with like colors	Block to dry	Reshape to original dimensions while drying
Rinse thoroughly	Rinse several times to remove detergent, soap, and bleach	**Ironing**	
Do not launder commercially	Use laundering methods designed for home use or wash in a laundromat	Do not iron	Don't iron or press with heat
		Steam iron	Use iron at steam setting
		Iron damp	Dampen garment before ironing
Bleaching		Cool iron	Use lowest setting
Bleach when needed	All bleaches can be used	Warm iron	Use medium setting
Do not bleach	No bleaches should be used	Hot iron	Use highest setting
Only nonchlorine bleach when needed	Chlorine bleach should not be used. Use oxygen bleach	Steam only	Don't let iron touch fabric
		Use press cloth	Place dry or damp cloth between iron and fabric
Washer cycle		**Dry cleaning**	
No spin	Remove wash load before final spin cycle	Dry-clean	Dry-clean commercially or in a coin-operated machine
Delicate cycle Gentle cycle	Use slow agitation and reduced time	Dry-clean professionally	Have dry cleaner follow care-label instructions

Because garments made of fluffy wool and blended materials shed easily, store them separately or in tissue or paper bags.

Do the hems of your blue jeans turn up when you wash them? Apply a strip of iron-on mending fabric to the inside. Avoid machine-drying; heat will melt the fabric's adhesive.

If a collar button won't close because its buttonhole is too stiff from starch, loosen it by moistening with warm water.

WHAT TO DRY-CLEAN

In general, dry-clean an item if it is:

Labeled "Dry-clean Only."

Soiled with difficult or large stains.

Tailored—for example, a lined jacket or beaded evening gown.

Constructed with two or more fabrics.

Made of sheer or delicate fabrics or trim.

Composed of fabrics with crimped or bouclé yarns.

Unlabeled, but seems to contain wool.

The following symbols are used to indicate the proper care required for a garment. "Stop" symbols appear in red, "Be careful" symbols appear in yellow, and "Go ahead" symbols appear in green.

	Stop	Be careful	Go ahead
Washing	Do not wash	Hand wash in lukewarm water 40°C Machine wash in lukewarm water at a gentle setting—reduced agitation 50°C Machine wash in warm water at a gentle setting—reduced agitation	50°C Machine wash in warm water at a normal setting 70°C Machine wash in hot water at a normal setting
Chlorine Bleaching	Cl Do not use chlorine bleach	Cl Use chlorine bleach as directed	
Drying		— Dry flat Tumble dry at low temperature	Tumble dry at medium to high temperature Hang to dry Drip dry
Ironing	Do not iron	110°C or Iron at low setting 150°C or Iron at medium setting	200°C or Iron at high setting
Dry Cleaning	Do not dry clean	Dry clean—tumble dry at low temperature	Dry clean

DRY CLEANING

If a coordinated outfit needs to be dry-cleaned, clean all parts at the same time; any color change that occurs will be uniform.

Dry-clean a garment as soon as possible after it becomes stained; the longer a stain remains, the more difficult it is to remove. If you can, identify the source of the stain to the dry cleaner; it will help him select the best cleaning method.

Consider using a coin-operated dry-cleaning machine if clothes are sturdy, not heavily soiled, and require little pressing. This is an economical way to ready clothes for long-term storage.

When you bring clothing home from the dry cleaner, remove the plastic bag so that the fabric can breathe. If you have children, guard against accidental suffocation by tying the bag in several places before throwing it away.

NINE BASIC STEPS TO TROUBLE-FREE LAUNDERING

1. Sort clothes carefully (p.277).
2. Pretreat spots and stains.
3. Mix large and small items together in the same load.
4. Use the correct water temperature.
5. Use the appropriate kind and amount of laundry product.
6. Select the right washing action.
7. Rinse items thoroughly.
8. Dry clothes at the proper setting.
9. Hang clothes promptly after removing them from the dryer.

BEFORE LAUNDERING YOUR CLOTHES

It seems too obvious to say, but many's the shrunken garment that could have been saved if only the owner had read the care label before washing the item (p.274).

Turn pockets inside out and brush them free of lint and dirt. This helps prevent staining and protects garments from damage by foreign objects.

If other household members need help with the laundry, write simplified instructions on an index card, cover it with clear plastic, and tape it near the washer.

Because white nylon and nylon-blend fabrics are notorious color scavengers, wash them separately to prevent color transfer.

WASHDAY WISDOM

Detergents can only hold soil in suspension for a limited time before finer particles that are much harder to remove settle on clothes. To avoid this, wash garments no longer than necessary; 10 to 12 minutes for cottons, 7 to 9 minutes for synthetics, and 3 to 4 minutes for delicate fabrics or wool.

Washing tips: Don't overload or underload the washer. Choose the correct setting and time for the items being washed; use higher spin speeds to remove more water and reduce drying time. Use cold-water rinses.

Set a kitchen timer to time wash cycles. Carry it with you when you go to another part of the house.

Fabrics that are cooled before the final rinse will have fewer wrinkles (the permanent-press cycle does this for you automatically).

PRETREATING SPOTS

To use heavy-duty liquid detergent as a prewash treatment, try applying it with a toothbrush or a small, clean paintbrush.

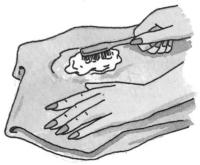

To clean ring-around-the-collar, rub some heavy-duty liquid detergent into it or use a pretreatment spray. Then wash as usual.

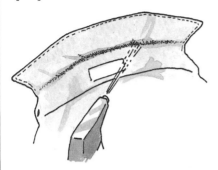

HOW TO SORT LAUNDRY

The purpose of sorting clothes is to separate those items which could damage others. Sort your laundry according to the following: color, the type and amount of soil, the construction of the fabric and garment, and the texture of the fabric. All items in a load of laundry should require the same water temperature, agitation speed, wash time, and use of bleach.

Color groupings: Whites, pastels, and white background prints that are colorfast. Colorfast colors. Noncolorfast colors of similar color.

Soil groupings: Lightly soiled. Heavily soiled or greasy.

Fabric and garment groupings: Moderate to sturdy. Delicate.

Texture groupings: Lint producers (terry cloth, chenille, and flannel, for example). Lint receivers (such as permanent press, cotton-polyester blends, corduroy, velveteen, and synthetics).

While sorting:
Remove unwashable belts and trims.

Close zippers and fasteners so that they won't snag other garments.

Tie sashes and strings to avoid tangling.

Empty pockets.

Brush loose dirt from pockets and cuffs.

Mend rips and tears.

Treat spots and stains (pp.282–283).

Because solvent-based prewash products work quickly, add the treated item to the wash water before the solvent evaporates.

When you use prewash sprays, avoid getting them on the washer or dryer. Some of the ingredients can damage the plastic and painted finishes of your appliances.

When you pretreat spots with liquid detergent, it's easier to control the amount of detergent if you pour it from an old squeeze bottle.

If you're pretreating clothes with a bar of laundry soap, wrap it in nylon netting to provide some abrasion.

PREPARING A LOAD

Protect small or delicate items by putting them in a pillowcase. Tie the pillowcase with a cord.

Before washing a knitted, permanent-press, napped, quilted, or highly textured fabric, turn the garment inside out. This helps to prevent wear, fading, or pilling.

To help prevent tangling in the machine, button shirt and blouse sleeves to front buttons.

Washing an item with a draw-string? Tie both ends together so that the drawstring won't slip out of its casing.

Polyester fabrics pick up grease and oil easily. If you can't avoid washing these fabrics with items that have greasy or oily stains, pretreat the stains with an aerosol pretreatment spray.

LAUNDRY PRODUCTS

Using too much of a laundry product can be just as bad as using too little. Read the package instructions to determine how much to use and when to use it.

Remember that nearly all laundry products are toxic and should be stored out of reach of children.

LAUNDRY PRODUCTS

Product	Purpose	Comments
Detergents		
Heavy duty (all-purpose), granules	For laundering washable fabrics	
Heavy duty (all-purpose), liquids	For laundering washable fabrics; pretreating spots and stains	Especially good for removing oily soils
Light duty, granules	For delicate fabrics and baby clothes	
Light duty, liquids	For hand-washing	Because of high sudsing qualities, do not use in automatic washers
Soaps*		
Light duty, granules	For lightly soiled items, delicate fabrics, and baby clothes	If used in hard water, will form a sticky white or yellow residue on clothes and washer
Light duty, bars	For pretreating heavy soils and stains; hand-washing lingerie and hosiery	If used in hard water, will form a sticky white or yellow residue on clothes and washer
Bleaches		
Chlorine (liquid and dry)	For whitening and brightening fabrics; removing soil and stains; and disinfecting and deodorizing	Do not use on noncolorfast fabrics, wool, silk, mohair, spandex, and leather. Before using on a colored fabric, make sure fabric is bleachsafe. Add near end of wash cycle to avoid deactivating enzyme products
Oxygen (liquid and dry)	For whitening and brightening fabrics; removing soil and stains	Before using on a colored fabric, make sure fabric is bleachsafe
Enzyme products (detergent boosters and presoaks)	For improving detergent performance; removing heavy soils and stains	Good for removing body oil, perspiration, urine, and protein stains such as blood, baby formula, grass, and many foods. Because skin is protein, wear gloves while using enzyme products
Prewash soil and stain removers (aerosol, pump spray, liquid)	For pretreating heavy soils and stains	Especially good for removing oil-based soils and stains, particularly on synthetic and permanent-press fabrics
Fabric softeners	For softening all washable fabrics; reducing static cling, drying time, and wrinkling	Overuse may cause clothes to look dingy or feel greasy. Skip softener every few washings
Water softeners (precipitating and nonprecipitating)	For reducing water hardness; improving detergent performance	Because precipitating water softeners can leave a chalky residue on fabrics and washer parts, use a nonprecipitating product
Starches, fabric finishes, and sizings	For adding body to fabrics; improving soil resistance; and facilitating stain removal	Starch is most effective on cotton fabrics. Fabric finishes and sizings work better on synthetics

*May set certain tannin stains (p. 282)

Keep a graduated measuring cup in the laundry and use it to make sure you're adding the correct amounts of laundry products. Rinse the cup after each use.

Don't mix chlorine bleach with ammonia, cleaning fluids, rust removers, vinegar, or other acids. When combined, these chemicals can produce toxic gases.

DETERGENTS

When deciding how much detergent to use, keep in mind that amounts suggested on packages are based on average washing conditions: a 5- to 7-pound load, moderate soil, moderate water hardness (p.281), and average water volume.

More than the usual recommended amount of detergent will be needed when washing under the following conditions: cold water, very hard water (p.281), very dirty clothes, a large load, or extra water volume in large-capacity washers.

Under the following conditions, less than the usual recommended amount of detergent may be used: hot water, very soft water (p.281), reduced water volume in the washer, very light soil, or a small load.

Don't dump detergents on top of your clothing as the washer fills with water. This can cause some dyes to fade.

With granular detergent and cold water, dissolve detergent by adding it as the washer fills; then add the clothing. Or dissolve the detergent in hot water first, add it to the wash water, then add clothing.

BLEACHES

To avoid damage from bleach, don't allow undiluted bleach to come in contact with any fabric. Follow the instructions for bleach-safe testing given on the bleaching product package, measure the amount of bleach carefully, and use the bleach dispenser if your machine has one.

Although liquid oxygen bleach is gentler than chlorine bleach, it's slower acting and must be used in warm (preferably hot) water for good results.

If you have no liquid oxygen bleach, substitute hydrogen peroxide (antiseptic, not hair bleach), available in most drugstores.

FABRIC SOFTENERS

Always dilute fabric softener before adding it to the wash; otherwise it can cause greasy looking stains on fabrics. To remove these stains, pretreat them with a paste of water and detergent or with a prewash stain remover.

Use fabric-softener sheets twice, then store them in a jar with liquid softener. When drying a load of clothes, pull out a sheet, squeeze out the excess solution, and toss it in the dryer.

HOMEMADE LAUNDRY PRODUCTS

Have a delicate item that must be handwashed? Try this soft, gentle soap: mix ¼ cup soap flakes and ¼ cup borax in a saucepan with 1 cup water. Simmer, while stirring, to a uniform consistency; strain solution into a container.

To make your own prewash solution, mix 1 teaspoon liquid detergent and 2 tablespoons household ammonia with 1 pint warm water; pour into a clean spray bottle. Apply to stains and let stand for 15 minutes. Then wash as usual.

For white silk and other delicate fabrics that require a very gentle bleach, mix 1 part hydrogen peroxide to 8 parts water. Immerse the garment in the solution for 5 to 30 minutes, as necessary. Rinse in clear water.

HAND-WASHING

To hand-wash articles, pretreat spots and stains. Dissolve detergent in water before adding laundry. Let soak for 15 minutes; swish items through solution rather than twisting and wringing. Rinse at least twice with cool water.

When you soak items, use a small, plastic bucket that can be removed easily if someone needs to use the sink.

Wash delicate items by shaking them in a jar filled with warm, mild, soapy water.

If your white handkerchiefs have become gray or dingy, they'll look much brighter if you soak them in a solution of cold water and 1 teaspoon of cream of tartar.

Washing a wool sweater? First lay it flat on a sheet of clean paper and draw its outline. After washing and rolling in a towel to absorb most of the moisture, lay the sweater down on the paper and gently stretch it to fit the outline. Then lay the sweater flat to dry.

Make sweaters soft by adding a capful of cream hair rinse to the rinse water.

WASHING OVERSIZED ITEMS

Before laundering a washable electric blanket, protect the plug by tucking it into a corner of the blanket and pinning it in place.

Before washing feather pillows, repair weak seams or holes, then put the pillows in cases. Fill the washer with warm water and push pillows in until soaked (wash two pillows at a time for a balanced load). Use the gentle cycle, but halfway through, turn the machine off and turn the pillows over. When they're done, put them in the dryer with a clean sneaker to ensure even drying.

To wash a down sleeping bag, put it in the tub in warm water and mild detergent. Let it soak for about 30 minutes, squish the suds through it, then rinse it 3 times. Avoid twisting the bag; let it drip over the tub on a line for 1 hour, squeezing out as much water as you can. Put in the dryer at a low setting; add a clean pair of sneakers to ensure even drying.

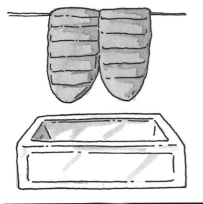

DEALING WITH HARD WATER

Don't know if your water is hard? Some telltale signs are bathtub rings; crusty deposits on faucets and shower heads; streaked or cloudy china and glassware; and the need for extra soap or detergent to produce adequate suds.

To find out if you have hard water, ask your public utility company or have a water-treatment company analyze your water supply. Your provincial ministry for health and the environment may also be prepared to carry out a test. Consider softening water of more than 3 grains of hardness.

How much nonprecipitating water softener (p.278) you'll need depends on the hardness of the water and the amount of water and detergent used. If water feels slippery between your fingers,

you're probably using the correct amount of water softener.

You can make your water soft by installing an ion exchange softening tank in your home water supply. This device replaces calcium and magnesium ions with sodium ions. However, it is recommended that you not drink or cook with softened water, particularly if you're on a low-salt diet.

REMOVING STAINS

To remind yourself that a garment is stained and needs pretreating, tie a loose knot in its sleeve or leg before tossing it into the hamper. Remember, though, that the longer a stain remains, the more difficult it is to remove.

If you can't identify the stain in a washable fabric, soak the item in cold water and rub it together at the stained area. If the stain remains, rub heavy-duty liquid detergent into it, then rinse thoroughly. If the stain persists, use a bleach solution safe for the fabric, then wash normally.

When no spot remover is available, try using automatic dishwashing detergent. Apply a paste of it with an old toothbrush, then rinse thoroughly.

STAIN REMOVAL   Read pp. 284 and 285 before attempting to remove any stain

Type	Washable fabrics	Nonwashable fabrics
Dyes Beets, bluing, carrots, cherries, color bleeding, grass, green vegetables, soft drinks containing food dye, tempera paint	Rub liquid detergent gently into stain. Rinse thoroughly. Soak in solution of all-fabric powdered bleach and water. If stain remains, try liquid chlorine bleach solution, if safe for fabric. Wash normally	Sponge with water. With absorbent pad, apply a solution of mild detergent and a few drops of vinegar. Flush with water. Blot and dry.* Sponge with water. With absorbent pad, apply solution of mild detergent and a few drops of ammonia. Flush with water. Blot and dry.* To remove traces of stain, apply bleach solution, if safe for fabric, with medicine dropper. Flush with water after each bleach application. Apply vinegar solution to remove excess bleach. Flush with water. Blot and dry.* Have garment dry-cleaned
Oils Automotive oil, bacon fat, body oil, butter, cooking oil, face cream, grease, hair lotion, hand lotion, lard, margarine, mayonnaise, ointment, colorless salad dressing, suntan lotion	Rub heavy-duty liquid detergent gently into stain. Rinse thoroughly. Wash in hot water	Sponge with dry-cleaning solvent. With absorbent pad, apply dry spotter or paint-oil-and-grease remover. Keep stain moist with spotter or remover, blotting occasionally with absorbent material. Flush with dry-cleaning solvent. Except for initial sponging, repeat until no more stain comes out. Blot and air-dry. With medicine dropper, apply several drops of detergent solution and then a few drops of ammonia. Work into stain. Continue until no more stain comes out. Flush with water. Blot and dry.* Have garment dry-cleaned
Proteins Baby formula, baby food, blood, cheese sauce, cream, egg, feces, gelatin, ice cream, milk, mud, mucus, pudding, school paste, urine, vomit	DON'T use hot water (it sets stain). Soak and rub in cold water. Wash in warm water. If stain is old, treat with detergent or enzyme presoak	Blot to remove stain. Apply pad moistened with enzyme product over stain. If fabric is strong, press down lightly with spoon. Flush with water, then ammonia solution, and water again. Blot. Flush with vinegar solution, then water. Blot and dry.* Dry-clean
Tannins Alcoholic beverages, beer, berries, coffee, cola drinks, fruit juices, preserves, jellies, soft drinks without dye, tea, tomato juice, washable ink, wine	DON'T use soap bars or flakes (they set stain). Wash normally, using detergent. If you can't wash immediately, blot up as much stain as possible. Sponge with water. Wipe with dry cloth	Sponge with water. With absorbent pad, apply detergent solution and a few drops of vinegar. Cover with pad moistened with detergent and vinegar. If fabric is strong, press down lightly with spoon. Flush with water. Blot and dry.* Have dry-cleaned
Combination stains (oil and dye; wax and dye) **Group A** Ballpoint pen ink, candle wax, carbon paper, carbon typewriter ribbon, crayon, eye makeup, floor wax, furniture polish, lipstick, pine resin, shoe polish, tar	To remove oily or waxy part of stain, spray or sponge with dry-cleaning solvent, then rub gently with heavy-duty liquid detergent. Treat dye part with bleach solution, if safe for fabric. Wash normally	Spray or sponge with dry-cleaning solvent. Blot to remove excess dye. Continue using dry-cleaning solvent until no more stain comes out. Then sponge with detergent solution. Flush with water. Blot and dry.* If stain remains, apply bleach solution, if safe for fabric, with medicine dropper. Flush with water. Blot and dry.* Have garment dry-cleaned
Group B Barbecue sauce, ketchup, chocolate, cocoa, face makeup, gravy, hair spray, salad dressing containing food dye, tomato sauce	To remove oily or waxy part of stain, rub gently with heavy-duty liquid detergent. Treat dye part with bleach solution, if safe for fabric. Wash normally	Follow instructions for Group A
Chewing gum	Apply ice to harden gum. Scrape off excess. Rub heavy-duty liquid detergent into stain. Rinse with hot water. Wash normally	Apply dry-cleaning solvent with absorbent pad. Peel off excess gum. Cover stain with pad moistened with solvent. Change pad often. Flush with solvent. Blot and air-dry. Have dry-cleaned

STAIN REMOVAL   Read pp. 284 and 285 before attempting to remove any stain

Type	Washable fabrics	Nonwashable fabrics
Coffee or tea with cream or milk	Soak in cold water. Wash normally, using detergent, not soap	Sponge or spray with dry-cleaning solvent. Apply warm water and vinegar. To remove traces, use an oxygen bleach, if safe for fabric. Flush with water. Blot and dry.* Have garment dry-cleaned
Deodorant	Apply heavy-duty liquid detergent. Wash in warm water. (Buildup of aluminum or zinc salts may be impossible to remove.)	Sponge with warm water combined with a few drops of mild detergent and a few drops of vinegar. Flush with water. Blot and dry*
Felt-tip pen ink	Follow instructions for dye stains	Follow instructions for *Combination stains,* Group A
Lead pencil	Use art-gum eraser to lift off excess, but avoid hard rubbing. Spray with prewash aerosol product, rub with heavy-duty liquid detergent, and rinse in warm water. Wash normally	Use art-gum eraser to lift off excess but avoid hard rubbing. Flush with dry-cleaning solvent. Blot and air-dry. Have garment dry-cleaned
Mildew WARNING: Mildew causes permanent damage. Avoid storing clothes in damp, dark, warm places	Shake or brush garment outdoors. Pretreat darkest stains with heavy-duty liquid detergent. Wash in hot water with heavy-duty detergent and bleach	Do not treat. Have garment dry-cleaned if it is salvageable (ask dry cleaner)
Mustard	Follow instructions for dye stains	If stain has dried, brush off excess. Sponge on dry-cleaning solvent, then detergent solution combined with a few drops of vinegar. Apply hydrogen peroxide (3%) with medicine dropper, if safe for fabric. Flush well with water. Blot and dry.* Have dry-cleaned
Paint, alkyd (oil base) WARNING: If paint has dried, removal may be impossible	Treat while wet. Rub paint thinner into stain until paint is softened. Wash, using heavy-duty detergent	Treat while wet by flushing well with paint thinner. Blot and air-dry. If paint has dried, have garment dry-cleaned
Paint, latex (water base) WARNING: If paint has dried, removal may be impossible	Treat while wet. Soak in cold water. Wash in cool water with heavy-duty detergent. If paint has been allowed to dry 6 or more hours, follow instructions for *Combination stains,* Group A. Wash in hot water; rinse; repeat treatment	Treat while wet. Flush well with warm water. Blot and dry.* If paint has dried, have garment professionally spot-cleaned and dry-cleaned
Perspiration	Apply heavy-duty liquid detergent or soak in warm water with presoak product 15 to 30 minutes. Wash	Sponge with detergent solution. Flush with water. Blot and dry.* Have garment dry-cleaned
Rust	Use a commercial rust remover. WARNING: Rust removers are highly toxic and can damage the finish on appliances. Wear rubber gloves, and rinse garment before washing. Do not use on metallic or glass fabrics	Do not treat. Have garment dry-cleaned
Scorch WARNING: Scorched fabrics may be weakened, and stain-removal treatment may cause further damage	If fabric is thick and fuzzy, brush to remove charring. *Gently* rub heavy-duty liquid detergent (if fabric is delicate, use mild detergent) into stain. If stain remains, use all-fabric bleach. Wash normally	Using medicine dropper, apply hydrogen peroxide (3%) to stain. Flush well with water. Blot and dry.* Have garment dry-cleaned

*With hair dryer on low, hold dryer 12 inches from fabric and move it constantly

NOTE: Because of dyes, invisible finishes, or previous stain treatments, these methods may not work perfectly or completely. If garment will be dry-cleaned right away, let the cleaner remove the stain

BEFORE ATTEMPTING TO REMOVE A STAIN

DO'S

Read care labels (p.274).

Treat stains immediately; then launder or dry-clean as quickly as possible. If the fabric is nonwashable, blot the stain and take it to a dry cleaner immediately.

Use stain-removing techniques only in emergencies.

Pretest all stain-removal agents, including ammonia and vinegar. Apply several drops of the recommended remover to a hidden part of the garment, such as a seam. Rub gently with a white towel. If color transfers to the towel, or if a color change occurs, do not use the remover. Consult a dry cleaner.

Test fabric before using a bleach solution. Put a drop of the solution on a hidden part. Let stand for 5 to 10 minutes. Blot dry. If a color change occurs, don't use bleach on the fabric.

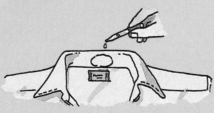

When using a bleach treatment, watch the stain; as soon as it disappears, flush with water. Even if the stain remains, flush with water after 15 minutes.

Use stain removers only in a well-ventilated room far away from electric or gas appliances or any open flame. Avoid spilling on skin or clothes; if you do spill a solvent, wash it off immediately.

Wear rubber gloves when you're working with enzyme products.

Washables
Use spot treatment for washable fabrics too delicate for rubbing. Place aluminum foil and then clean white cloths or paper towels on a work surface. Put the garment stain side down on the padded surface. Use a white cloth dampened with the recommended remover to blot the stained area. Feather the edges of the stain, working from the outside toward the center of the stain to avoid a ring. Repeat the recommended treatment until the stain disappears.

With washable fabrics, once you've finished the treatment and laundered a garment, recheck the stain to be sure no trace remains. If it shows, repeat the stain-removal procedure before putting the garment into the dryer.

Nonwashables
Before treating stains on nonwashable items, put an absorbent pad under the stained area (with a layer of aluminum foil between the pad and the work surface).

With nonwashable fabrics, if the stain disappears after any of the steps in the stain-removal procedure, stop treatment after flushing and then drying the spot as directed. Have garment dry-cleaned.

When you take a garment to a professional dry cleaner, explain what the stain is and what you've already used on it.

DON'TS

Don't allow a nonwashable garment—especially one made of cotton, rayon, or linen—to remain wet for more than 3 to 4 minutes.

Don't treat silk, except to blot up as much of the stain as possible. Take the item to a professional dry cleaner.

Don't use chlorine bleach, including solution, on silk, wool, spandex, polyurethane foam, or garments containing rubber.

Don't use metal spoons or containers when working with bleaches.

Don't overwet; use solvents sparingly.

Don't combine chlorine bleach with ammonia or rust removers. The mixture may produce fatal toxic gases.

Don't smoke when using solvents.

Don't use ammonia, chlorine bleach, or heavy-duty detergent on wool stains.

Even colorless substances such as perspiration, body oil, unsaturated cooking oil, alcoholic beverages, soft drinks, juices, syrup, and candy can cause "invisible stains." If not treated immediately, these stains can become permanent. To remove invisible stains from washable fabrics, pretreat them with heavy-duty liquid detergent and soak before washing; if the fabric is nonwashable, identify the source and location of the stain to the dry cleaner.

All dressed and ready to go when you find a spot on your white garment? Mask it by rubbing in some baby powder.

If you spill something on your clothes while eating out, dip a clean, white cloth napkin or handkerchief into a glass of club soda and sponge the spot.

To remove a wet red-wine stain, quickly sprinkle salt on it. Then put the item in cold water and try to rub out the stain before washing the fabric.

Try this to remove red-wine stains from white table linens: Fill a tub with tepid water, add a very small amount of liquid bleach, and dip the spotted portion in the solution. Rub gently with fingers until stain dissolves. Rinse thoroughly.

STAIN-REMOVAL SUPPLIES

Absorbent materials
Clean white cloths

Cotton balls

White or neutral sponges

White paper towels

Acids and alkalies
Ammonia — household ammonia without added color, fragrance, or suds

Ammonia solution: 1 tablespoon ammonia in ½ cup water, or add ammonia to detergent solution (see below)

White vinegar

Vinegar solution: 2 tablespoons white vinegar in 1 cup water, or add vinegar to detergent solution (see below)

Bleaches
All-fabric powdered bleach

Hydrogen peroxide — 3 percent, sold as antiseptic (not hair-bleaching peroxide)

Liquid chlorine bleach

Bleach solution: for washable fabrics, 1 tablespoon liquid chlorine bleach in ¼ cup water; for nonwashable fabrics, 1 teaspoon bleach in 1 tablespoon water

Detergents
Heavy-duty liquid laundry detergent

Mild liquid detergent — hand dishwashing type

Detergent solution: 1 teaspoon mild liquid detergent in 1 cup warm water

Enzyme products
Enzyme-containing laundry detergent

Enzyme presoak

Enzyme solution: ½ teaspoon enzyme product in ½ cup warm water

Lubricants
Dry spotter: 1 part coconut oil or mineral oil to 8 parts dry-cleaning solvent

Solvents
Acetone

Amyl acetate (banana oil)

Dry-cleaning solvent: perchloroethylene, trichloroethane, or a commercial spot cleaner (don't use gasoline or lighter fluid as solvents)

Paint-oil-and-grease remover

Prewash stain remover

Commercial rust remover

Hair spray removes a ballpoint-ink stain, but on silk or acetate test-spray a hidden area for bleeding dye. Afterwards, flush with water; wash or dry-clean garment.

LAUNDRY PROBLEMS

Problem	Possible causes	Action/Prevention
Grayness	Insufficient detergent	Increase detergent and/or use a detergent booster or bleach
	Low wash-water temperature	Wash in hottest water safe for fabric
	Transfer of soil due to incorrect sorting	Rewash with sufficient detergent and hottest water safe for fabric. In future, sort by soil
	Transfer of color due to incorrect sorting	Do not dry items. Quickly rewash with detergent and a bleach safe for fabric
Yellowing	Insufficient detergent	Increase detergent; use bleach or enzyme
	Low wash-water temperature	Increase temperature
	Machine-washing synthetic fabrics with short, gentle, cool washes, or hand-washing them with mild detergent	Wash in hot water, using permanent-press cycle. Increase detergent and/or use a detergent booster or a bleach safe for fabric
	Use of chlorine bleach on silk, wool, or spandex	Irreversible condition
Poor soil removal	Insufficient detergent	Rewash, increasing detergent
	Low wash-water temperature	Rewash in hottest water safe for fabric
	Overloaded washer	Wash fewer items; use proper water level
Stiff, harsh, or faded fabrics	In hard water, nonphosphate granular detergents may combine with minerals to form residue	Add 1 cup white vinegar to 1 gallon warm water; soak items and rinse. In future, use liquid laundry detergent or a non-precipitating water softener
Lint	Improper sorting: washing lint producers (sweaters, towels, flannels) with receivers (synthetics, corduroys, velours)	Hand-pat dried items with masking tape. Rewash with detergent, using fabric softener in final rinse. Dryer dry. In future, sort carefully
	Tissues in pockets	Hand-pat dried items with masking tape. In future, check pockets before laundering
	Overloaded washer or dryer	Wash and dry fewer items in a load
	Insufficient detergent	Rewash, increasing detergent
	Static electricity due to overdrying	Rewash, using fabric softener. In future, remove items while slightly damp
	Full dryer lint screen	Rewash clothes; clean dryer lint screen
	Clogged washer lint filter	Clean washer lint filter after each use
Wrinkles in synthetic or permanent-press fabrics	Incorrect cycle	Use permanent-press cycle on washer and dryer, if available. If not, use warm water, cold rinse, and a slower or shorter spin speed for the washer, and a high-temperature dryer setting followed by 10 minutes of air drying
	Overdrying	Rewash, then dry at permanent-press cycle. In future, remove items as soon as dryer stops
	Overloaded washer or dryer	Allow wash load to move freely in washer and dryer. In future, avoid overloading
Shrinking	Overdrying	Irreversible condition. In future, reduce drying time and remove clothes while slightly damp
	Residual shrinkage	Irreversible condition. When purchasing knit and woven fabrics, allow for shrinkage
	Agitation of wool items	Irreversible condition. In future, keep agitation in both wash and rinse cycles at minimum
Pilling	Abrasion from normal wear	In future, use a fabric softener in washer or dryer. When ironing, use spray starch or fabric finish on collars and cuffs

SPECIAL LAUNDRY PROBLEMS

If your cloth-covered buttons are still dirty after laundering, brush them with mild liquid detergent and a soft toothbrush.

To soften new jeans, wash them several times. Or soak them for 12 hours in a small tub filled with cold water and plenty of fabric softener. Then wash as usual.

To prevent jeans from streaking, turn them inside out before washing. Do the same for corduroys to keep the nap up.

To remove scum and mildew from plastic shower curtains, wash in the machine with detergent; add a few cloth towels to act as buffers.

If perspiration odor remains after laundering, try this: Sponge the area with a mixture of 1 teaspoon white vinegar and 1 cup water, then rinse. If the odor persists, work a paste of enzyme or other presoak product into the area, keep moist for 20 minutes, then rinse thoroughly.

Too many suds? Get rid of them by sprinkling them with table salt from a shaker. Next time reduce the amount of detergent or use a low-suds product.

To remove detergent scum from your washing machine and hoses, fill the machine with warm water, add 1 gallon of white vinegar, and run the solution through an entire cycle.

Had a close encounter with a skunk? Don't bury your clothes; soak them for several hours in a solution of ½ cup baking soda and 1 gallon water before washing.

If your washer drains into a sink, you can prevent lint from clogging the drain by filtering dirty water with an old nylon stocking; fasten it with a rubber band. Clean or replace the stocking periodically.

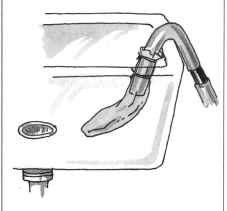

LINE-DRYING

To save space on the clothesline, hang small items on a multitiered hanger secured to the line.

Hang bias, full, or pleated skirts from the waistband to avoid wrinkling the body of the skirt. Clip a spring-type clothespin to the bottom of each pleat so that they'll dry in place and need little ironing.

Hang drip-dry items by their hems to distribute weight evenly and avoid clothespin marks.

An ideal place for drying clothes is a screened porch with a southern exposure. For even faster drying, use a portable fan; direct its air flow along the length of the line.

If you're hanging sheer curtains out on a windy day, weigh them down every few feet with a spring-type clothespin.

When hanging dark or brightly colored items outdoors, put them in a shady area or turn them inside out to prevent the sun from fading them.

An easy way to hang sheets is to fold them in half and hang them by the hems. If you want them to dry faster, drape them from two parallel lines.

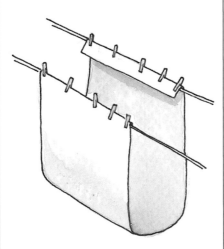

To remove frozen clothes from the line, lift them gently and bring them inside the house to thaw. Crumpling or folding them while they're frozen can break the fibers of the fabric.

Use an old baby stroller, child's wagon, or grocery cart to hold laundry while hanging clothes on the line.

SPEEDING UP DRYING

If you must dry just a few items, add a few clean towels of comparable color to the dryer to absorb moisture.

Pull trouser pockets inside out so that they'll dry faster.

If you need to dry panty hose in a hurry, hang them on a line and blow-dry them with a hair dryer.

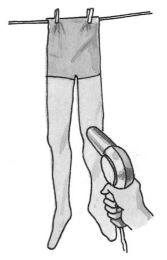

HOUSEHOLD DRYING AIDS

For indoor clothes drying, use an adjustable tension rod over the bathtub or shower instead of a clothesline.

For quick indoor line-drying, put a fan on a table about 3 feet from the end of the clothesline. Turn the fan on high and let the air flow along the center of the clothing.

To dry sweaters and other items that must be flat-dried, spread them out on a hammock; make sure they're out of the sun.

The skeleton of an old umbrella makes a great indoor drying rack. Hang it upside down by its handle from a sturdy, horizontal support.

CLOTHESPINS AND CLOTHESLINES

Try using a plastic, hanging-plant pot as a clothespin container; rainwater will drain from the bottom. If you want something portable, use an old shoulder bag.

To clean a nylon clothesline, use a household spray cleaner; wash a cotton line with soap and water. Either kind can be put in a pillowcase and cleaned in the washer.

Does your clothesline sag? Tie a short length of chain to one end of the line, then attach to the metal hook whichever link provides the best tension.

SPECIAL DRYING PROBLEMS

To prevent fabric harshness, wrinkling, shrinkage, or puckering, machine-dry clothes only as long as necessary. If an item is accidentally overdried, dampen it to restore its original moisture, then air-dry it.

Before drying overalls, insert the buckles in a pocket and pin them in place. This will prevent them from banging against the inside of the dryer, which could damage the enamel finish of the drum.

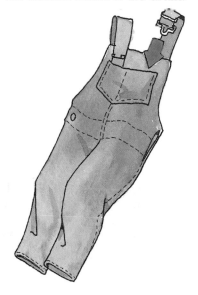

Clothes taking too long to dry? Is there damp lint in or around the lint filter? Your dryer's exhaust system or lint screen may be clogged. If so, clean them according to the maker's instructions. (See p. 150 for dryer maintenance tips.)

PRESSING AND IRONING

Pressing requires lifting and lowering the iron with a light touch. Ironing requires sliding the iron back and forth in the direction of the fabric grain. Pressing is a more precise technique; ironing can stretch and distort the fabric. Here are some pointers:

Set the iron for the correct temperature for the fabric. For a blended fabric, use the temperature that's suitable for the most heat-sensitive fiber in the fabric.

On an inconspicuous part of the garment, test the temperature and the amount of steam necessary, if any.

When ironing your clothes, begin with those that require the lowest temperature and work your way up to the highest temperature.

In general, press the small areas of an item first, then iron the larger ones.

Iron a garment on its reverse side; if you must iron the right side, use an appropriate press cloth.

Avoid overpressing; use a light touch.

Before putting clothes away, let them cool and dry.

DAMPENING CLOTHES

Does anyone still dampen clothes instead of using a steam iron? You bet! Clothes that are dampened before they're ironed come out smoother. They also hold their press longer.

Your clothes will dampen faster and more evenly if you use warm rather than cold water. Spray it from a plant mister or spray bottle.

If you're not ready to iron dampened items, put them in a plastic bag and keep it in the refrigerator until you catch up.

Set your dryer for a timed cycle so that clothes are just damp enough for ironing; you won't have to sprinkle them, and there will be fewer wrinkles to iron out.

IRONS, IRONING BOARDS, AND PRESS CLOTHS

When ironing an abrasive surface, use a press cloth to protect the soleplate of your iron from being scratched.

Use a clean mustard or ketchup squeeze bottle to fill your steam iron. (See pp. 156-157 for cleaning and maintenance tips.)

Try to keep your ironing-board cover clean. If it's washable, put it on the board while still damp so that it will fit snugly when dry.

Use only white or neutral-colored fabrics as press cloths: cheesecloth or handkerchiefs are great for lightweight fabrics; a clean, flat diaper or old cotton sheet for medium-weight fabrics; canvas or wool for heavy-weight fabrics.

SPECIAL IRONING PROBLEMS

When ironing large items, use the wide end of the ironing board. To help keep the item clean, lay a plastic tablecloth on the floor beneath the board.

To press fabric with a raised, embroidered design, lay it right side down on terry cloth, and press. For velvets and embossed fabrics, use a needleboard.

To reduce fabric shine caused by overpressing or wear, try this: Soak a press cloth in 1 cup of water; then wring it out. Place the damp press cloth on top of the shiny surface and steam-press; repeat several times. Press the area almost dry. Using a soft brush, raise the nap of the fabric.

PRESSING SPECIFIC ITEMS

Belts. Press wrong side, then right side.

Buttons. If they are delicate, cover them with the bowl of a spoon while ironing the surrounding fabric.

Collars. Press underside, then topside, working from each point to the center.

Cuffs. Press inside, moving from the edges to the seam; then press outside.

Dresses. Iron as a shirt (p.292), but do the skirt area first.

Gathers and ruffles. Press on wrong side from outer edge toward gathers.

Handkerchiefs. Press in layers of two.

Hems. Press inside of garment; then, if necessary, press outside lightly.

Pleats. Press inside from top to hem, then outside. If necessary, pin pleats to the ironing board at top and bottom; don't iron over pins.

Seams. Smooth seams flat; press inside length of seam, then press outside.

Zippers. First close the zipper and, with the garment inside out, press the inside flaps, using the tip of the iron. Then open the zipper and press lightly along the fabric in which it's set. Close it again and press on outside. Don't let the iron touch the teeth of plastic, nylon, or polyester zippers; heat will melt them.

PRESSING PARTICULAR FABRICS

Corduroy and velveteen. Place facedown on thickly padded surface, and steam-press without pressure.

Cotton. Iron right side with steam or dry iron; for dark, solid colors, use press cloth or turn inside out.

Embroidery and lace. Place facedown on terry cloth; steam without pressure.

Furs and fake furs. Get expert care.

Knits. Press and lift the iron.

Leather and suede. Place facedown over brown paper. Press with dry iron at low setting, using a press cloth.

Metallics. Press very lightly with cool iron, using a thin press cloth.

Nylon. Little or no ironing necessary; use a steam iron for touch-ups.

Pile and nap. Place facedown on a padded surface and steam without pressure; shake or brush pile or nap slightly.

Polyester. Little or no ironing necessary; use a steam iron for touch-ups.

Silk. With dry iron at low setting, press wrong side lightly, using a press cloth.

Wool. With steam iron, press wrong side, using a press cloth.

PRESSING SHIRTS

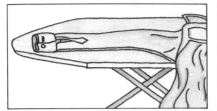

1. Start with the cuffs. Iron the insides first, then the outsides. Iron the body of each sleeve, first the cuff-opening side, then the reverse side.

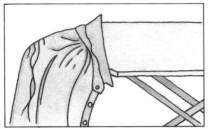

2. Slip one shoulder over the narrow end of the board and iron the yoke, moving from the shoulder to the center of the back. Do the same on the other side of the yoke.

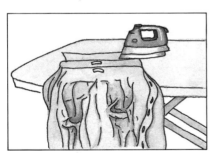

3. Iron the collar—underside first, then topside— working from each point to the center.

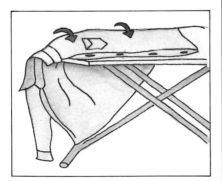

4. Iron the body of the shirt, beginning with one front panel and continuing to the other.

PRESSING PANTS

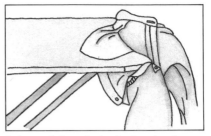

1. Lay pockets on the ironing board and press.

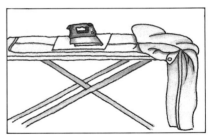

2. Fit the waistline around the ironing board and press the top of the pants, rotating the garment away from your body.

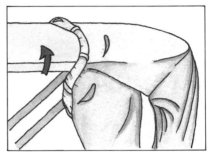

3. Lay pants flat, legs on top of each other, with the sides and inseams aligned. Fold back the top leg and press the inside of the bottom leg, using a dampened press cloth. Turn the pants over and press the inside of the other leg.

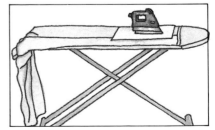

4. Press the outside of each leg, setting the creases (to the seat in back, to 6 inches below the waistband in front).

PUTTING LAUNDRY AWAY

Give each family member a different color laundry basket so that each can put away his or her own clothes. To separate items that need to be hung up, place each person's laundry on a different arm of a floor-to-ceiling plant pole.

Having a hard time telling everyone's clothing apart? Using an indelible pen or laundry marker, identify each garment with its owner's first initial.

Sorting linens after washing will be easier if you use whites, colors, and prints to help you distinguish twin, regular, and queen sizes.

Hang similar garments together—skirts in one place, blouses in another, and so on—to speed up your selection of clothes.

RECYCLING OLD CLOTHES

If your pullover sweater has become a bit tight, transform it into a cardigan. Measure the exact center of the front, mark it, and machine-stitch down either side. Slit between the lines of stitching. Finish the edges with ribbon or decorative tape.

Revive a classic floor-length dress or skirt by shortening it to the current street length.

Do you have a favorite dress whose style is outdated but whose fabric you love? Cut off the top and turn it into a blouse, or turn the bottom half into a skirt.

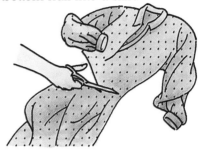

Turn an old dress into a jumper by removing its sleeves. Cut away the collar or reshape the neckline by cutting out a V shape. Be sure to cut the armholes slightly larger to accommodate a blouse underneath. (Cut armhole and neckline facings from discarded sleeves, or face with bias binding.)

Turn a worn-out full slip into a serviceable half-slip. Cut off the bodice and add a length of elastic around the waist. Stitch in a hem on the remaining top and you'll have a useful camisole.

Don't discard that old half-slip. Instead, cut off the elastic waistband and use the slip as a lining for a wool skirt.

Remove buttons, snaps, and zippers from garments destined for the trash or being made into rags (but *not* those you're giving to the thrift shop). These notions may come in handy for repairs.

SEWING EQUIPMENT

If hand-sewing strains your back, put a sofa cushion on your lap. You won't have to bend over as far to work on the material.

Sharp, small-pointed scissors are a must. For quick and ready access when sewing, hang them from your neck with a loop of tape. For protection when storing them, cover their points with rubber knitting-needle tips or stick a cork over the points. You can also store scissors in an unused eyeglass case.

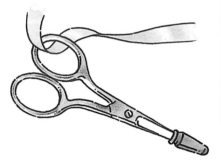

To give new life to an old cloth tape measure, place it between two sheets of wax paper, cover with a paper towel, and press with a hot iron.

Use a magnet to retrieve fallen pins and needles, a damp sponge to pick up threads from the floor or carpet.

NEEDLES

A quick way to sharpen your pins and needles—rub them with an emery board.

Once you remove needles from their packages, it's very hard to tell a sharp point from a ball point. Help distinguish them by painting a little colored nail polish on top of the needle shank.

For smoother hand-sewing, insert the point of the needle into a bar of soap every now and then as you work.

If you have difficulty penetrating heavy fabric with your needle, rub a bar of soap over the fabric before you begin stitching.

When stitching plastic fabric, rub talcum powder on the needle to avoid sticking.

THREAD

To keep a spool of thread neat, tape the thread end down or place a rubber band around the spool. Or stick a thumbtack into the spool and wrap the thread end around the tack.

Be sure you keep a spool of clear thread in your sewing box for mending any hard-to-match fabrics.

Cut thread at an angle; never break or bite it. Thread the needle with the cut end and knot the same end.

Do you have trouble threading a needle? Try holding the needle against a background that contrasts with the thread you're planning to use.

You can also stiffen the thread end by dipping it into clear nail polish or applying a little hair spray.

To keep thread from snarling, rub some beeswax, soap, paraffin, or a sheet of fabric softener along the length of the thread.

Avoid static electricity when you sew with synthetic thread—plan ahead and store it in the refrigerator for a few hours beforehand so that it will collect humidity and thus reduce clinging.

You don't always have to use commercial thread. You can use a 6- or 10-pound fishing line to sew buttons on heavy clothing, and if the thread color doesn't matter, you can also use dental floss.

THIMBLES

A thimble saves wear and tear on your finger when you're stitching heavy, stiff, or multilayered fabrics. Choose one that fits snugly over your middle finger.

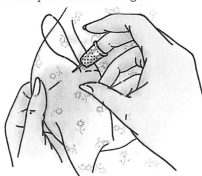

If your thimble's too loose, insert thin strips of adhesive tape on the inside until it fits snugly.

If wearing a thimble bothers you, protect your fingertip with an adhesive bandage instead.

ZIPPERS

To make a zipper slide more easily, rub the teeth with paraffin or soap, being careful to remove the excess. Rubbing the zipper teeth with graphite from a lead pencil also works.

If the pull tab on a zipper comes off, replace it with a small paper clip; wind thread or fine yarn around the clip in a color to match the garment fabric.

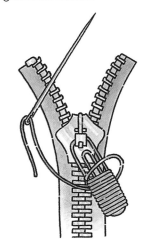

BUTTONS

Organize your button box: string same-size buttons on dental floss and tie its ends. You can also store buttons on a large safety pin or slip them on a hairpin and twist the ends together.

Thread your needle with doubled thread so that you're sewing with four strands. You'll need fewer stitches to secure a button.

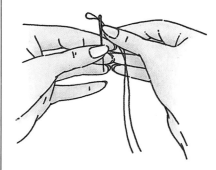

To make a skirt or pants more comfortable, try sewing on a waistline button with elastic thread.

For a slightly different look, work the thread through the buttonholes to form a cross, a square, an arrow, or two parallel lines.

For a quick emergency repair, use the wire from a twist tie to reattach a button.

If you're sewing on several buttons by machine, save time by taping each in place with a small piece of double-sided tape.

Buttons always coming off no matter how often you sew them back on? Dab the button thread with a bit of clear nail polish every now and then, and the button will stay put longer.

Add new life and gloss to pearl buttons by covering them with a coat of clear nail polish.

Before buying new buttons, measure the existing buttonhole; then choose a button that is about ⅛ inch less in diameter than the length of the buttonhole. If the button is chunky, add the button diameter to its thickness to determine the button measurement.

To avoid cutting fabric when removing a button, slide a comb under the button; then cut through the thread with a razor.

HOW TO SEW BUTTONS ON SECURELY

1. With a double strand of thread, take two small stitches at the button location. For a sew-through button, bring the thread up through one hole. Center the button over the stitches; place a toothpick between the button and the fabric. Stitch through each pair of holes at least four more times.

2. Bring the needle and thread out between the button and the fabric and remove the toothpick. Wind the thread several times around the attaching threads, and take a few small stitches in the fabric. Fasten the stitches on the wrong side of the garment.

3. For a shank button, begin as for a sew-through button. If the shank is adequate, take about six to eight stitches through the hole; then finish as with a sew-through button. If the shank is too short for the fabric's thickness, place a toothpick beneath it and proceed as with a sew-through button.

SEWING MACHINES

For easier cleanup, tape a small paper bag to the edge of your machine table to catch scraps of fabric and thread while sewing.

Attach a rubber suction cup or a piece of foam rubber under the foot pedal of your sewing machine to keep it from creeping across the floor as you sew.

No more hunting around for your tape measure. For convenience sake, lay a spare one along the front edge of your sewing machine and attach it with double-sided tape.

If the thread on your sewing machine unwinds at high speed, attach a small rubber faucet washer to the top of the spool.

MEASURING HEMS

Avoid extra stooping. When you mark a hem on a child's skirt or pants, ask the child to stand on a table while you pin. Of course, make sure the table is sturdy.

ATTACHING SNAPS, HOOKS, AND EYES

Snaps

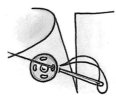

1. Position the ball half of the snap on the wrong side of the garment's overlap section at least ¼ inch from the edge. Make a single stitch under the snap, then insert the needle into the fabric and one hole of the snap.

2. Take five stitches in each hole. When all holes have been stitched, secure the thread with a small knot in the fabric.

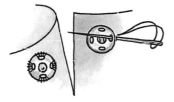

3. Rub the ball half with chalk and press against the underlap section of the garment to mark the position of the socket half; attach as described for the ball half.

Hooks and eyes

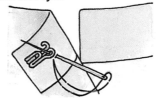

1. Position the hook on the wrong side of the garment ⅛ inch from the edge. Make a single stitch under the hook, then insert the needle into the fabric and one hole of the hook. Take five or six stitches in each hole.

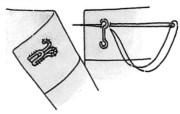

2. Pass the needle inside the fabric to the end of the hook, take five stitches, and secure the thread. Mark the eye placement on the underlap and attach as described for the hook.

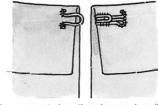

3. On a garment where the edges meet, position the two edges so they're even, mark the placement of the eye on the wrong side of the edge, and attach.

Avoid eyestrain when measuring a hem with a yardstick. Place a rubber band around it at the desired height; you'll be able to locate the right measurement at a glance as you go around the hemline.

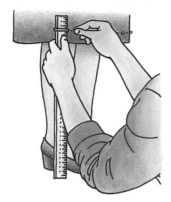

If you don't have marking chalk to mark the width of a hem, use white soap on washable fabrics.

To measure a hem's width, mark the desired width on a piece of cardboard. Then notch the spot with scissors. Use as a guide while pinning the hem.

When hemming a loosely woven fabric, use clothespins to hold the hem in place; they'll stay in better than straight pins, which can easily slip out.

HEMMING

To avoid knots when doing a small repair, use a short length of thread—no more than 18 inches.

For a temporary repair to a hem that comes unsewn, hold the broken section in place with transparent tape.

If your jeans need a quick fix, use silver-colored duct tape to hold up the hem. It will even last through several washings.

CHANGING A HEMLINE

1. Using small-pointed scissors, remove the old hem. Press the fabric flat.

2. With pins or tailor's chalk, measure and mark the desired length at a uniform distance from the floor. It's best to ask someone else to do this while you're dressed in the garment and the shoes and undergarments you plan to wear with it.

3. Fold up the fabric on the pin line; then pin the hem to the garment halfway between the hem's upper and lower edges.

4. Remove the first set of marking pins and lightly press the hemline.

5. Put the garment on to check for length and evenness. Correct if necessary.

6. Take off the garment; trim the hem allowance to an even width, as close to the original width as possible.

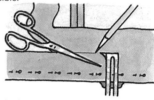

7. If the fabric ravels, finish the edge of the hem by folding it over and machine-stitching it or by edging it with seam tape. If the fabric doesn't ravel, a line of machine-stitching will suffice.

8. Sew the hem into place, using one of the stitches shown. Space them ¼ to ½ inch apart. Don't pull the thread so tight that the fabric puckers. Remove pins when finished.

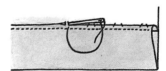

Slipstitch for lightweight fabrics

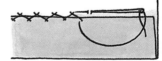

Catch stitch for stretchy knits, lightweight wools, raw silk

Blindstitch for heavy fabrics

9. Press the hem fold from the wrong side. To touch up the right side, use a press cloth.

MENDING SEAMS, HOLES, AND TEARS

Broken seams

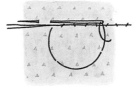

1. To machine-stitch a broken seam, turn the garment inside out. Stitch along the seamline, overlapping the old stitches at each end of the break.

2. If you choose to hand-sew a broken seam, make small backstitches along the seamline. When you reach the end of the break, secure the stitches with several small backstitches one on top of the other.

3. If you can't work from the inside of a garment, use slip-stitches on the outside to repair a break. Secure the thread's end with backstitches.

Darning

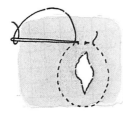

1. Repair small holes or frays by filling in the area with stitches; this reweaving of fabric is known as darning. Starting ¼ inch from the tear on the wrong side of the garment, make rows of tiny running stitches around the hole.

2. Then, working parallel to the fabric grain, fill in the hole with side-by-side stitches.

3. Next, weave across these stitches at right angles, keeping the stitches loose enough so that the darned area does not have a tight, pulled-in appearance. Secure the thread with a backstitch on the wrong side of the fabric.

Patching

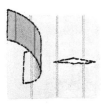
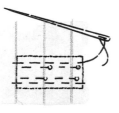

Multizag stitching

1. Strengthen a fabric tear or a wear spot with a patch. Make the patch slightly larger than the tear and place it under the tear, making sure that the grain lines match and that the nap in both fabrics runs in the same direction.

2. Pull the edges of the tear together; pin and then baste them to the patch. Remove the pins.

3. With the tear facing upward, machine-stitch over the edges of the tear, using zigzag or multizag stitches. For hand-sewing, use tiny, inconspicuous stitches, and stitch back and forth over the edges of the tear.

299

Don't cut off material to shorten a child's garment. Make a hem-tuck instead to allow for growth. Mark where the hem should be, then make a tuck between this point and the existing hem. Sew the tuck by hand or with a long machine-stitch. Press toward the hemline. Later, when more length is needed, remove the stitches.

ELIMINATING CREASES

To get rid of a hemline crease, press out the crease, then sponge a soap and water solution along the line before steam-pressing again.

If the crease can't be removed to your satisfaction, try camouflaging it with decorative stitching or with a trim applied after you've rehemmed the garment.

Spray starch can work wonders on stubborn wrinkles or creases in newly purchased clothes. If the fabric is washable, apply a little spray starch over the problem area and then iron dry.

To remove a white crease line from blue jeans, mix permanent blue ink with water until you get the right shade; then apply this mixture over the crease with a small brush. Be sure to allow the ink to dry.

PATCHING

To hold a patch in place while stitching it, secure it with transparent tape or apply a little household glue beneath the patch. (The glue will wash right out the first time you launder the garment.)

To get a sturdier bond, pink the edges of an iron-on patch before pressing it in place.

To remove an old worn-out iron-on patch, press with a hot iron. The patch should peel right off.

When applying an iron-on patch, put a piece of aluminum foil under the hole in the garment so that the patch won't stick to the ironing board.

BELTS

Need a convenient place to store your belts or purses? Attach a row of cup hooks to the bottom of a wooden hanger, or slip several shower-curtain hooks over your closet rod.

To keep belt buckles shiny, cover them with four coats of clear nail polish, allowing each coat to dry before applying the next one.

FOOTWEAR

Don't buy shoes strictly by size. Walk around in them for several minutes before making a final decision. Shoe sizes can vary, depending on the style and manufacturer, and your feet can swell up to a half size larger if you've been walking a lot.

Resist the temptation to wear your new shoes until you have polished them first with a stain-repellent product or plain shoe polish. (These products tend to darken the color of leather shoes.)

Don't slip and slide with your new shoes; before wearing them, sandpaper the soles or rub them across a rough sidewalk.

Make your own boot trees. Tie two or three paper-towel cylinders together, or use large soda bottles or even rolled-up newspaper.

Shoes a bit tight? To temporarily solve the problem, saturate a cotton ball with rubbing alcohol and rub it inside the shoes at the tight spot. Then put your shoes on and walk around for a while.

A more permanent way to solve the problem of tight shoes is to rub alcohol on their insides and put them on shoe stretchers (shoe trees will do in a pinch) for at least 2 days.

Shoelaces constantly coming undone? Dampen them before you tie them.

Don't wear the same shoes two days in a row. Give them time to recover their shape and get rid of accumulated odors.

Stuff your wet shoes with crushed newspaper and allow them to dry away from heat and sunlight. When they're thoroughly dry, rub them with a leather conditioner.

To waterproof shoes, polish them first, then apply a light coat of floor wax. Or spray them with silicone.

CLEANING SHOES

To remove salt stains from shoes and winter boots, wipe them with a solution of 1 cup water and 1 tablespoon vinegar.

To cover ugly scuff marks, use a matching color in acrylic paint, indelible felt marker, or crayon.

Typewriter correction fluid makes a great cover-up for scuff marks on white shoes; try a bit of India ink on black shoes.

Remove light scuff marks with an art-gum eraser.

To remove tar and grease stains from white shoes, try a little nail-polish remover.

Recycle your old flannel shirts and nightgowns, socks, or terry-cloth towels into first-rate shoe buffers.

For a speedy clean and shine on patent leather, rub a minute amount of petroleum jelly over your shoes, and buff. Or use a spray-on glass cleaner.

If shoe polish has hardened, soften it by heating its metal container in a bowl of hot water.

For a quick shine, rub a dab of hand cream over your shoes and then buff.

Avoid messy shoe-polish stains when cleaning sandals; slip the hand holding the sandal into a small plastic bag.

Give your wooden shoe heels a high shine with an application of lemon oil or furniture wax.

SUEDE SHOES

A good way to raise the nap is to rub a dry sponge or a stiff upholstery brush over suede shoes after each wearing.

Rub a very fine sandpaper over suede shoes to remove stubborn scuff marks.

To steam-clean suede shoes, hold them over a pan of boiling water. Once the steam raises the nap, stroke the suede with a soft brush in one direction only. Allow shoes to dry before wearing them.

CANVAS AND ATHLETIC SHOES

Spray a fabric protector or starch over new canvas shoes to keep them looking clean.

Help your canvas tennis shoes keep their shape and wear longer. After washing and drying, stuff them with paper towels, cover with liquid starch, and let dry.

Clean cloth sneakers quickly with a spray-on carpet cleaner. Scrub with a toothbrush, let dry, then brush with a dry brush.

HOSIERY

Your panty hose will last longer if you freeze them when they're brand new. After wetting them thoroughly and wringing them out, store them in the freezer in a plastic bag. When you need a pair, thaw and let dry.

Panty hose will resist runs much better and go on more easily if you starch them very lightly.

To stop a run in hose, rub it with wet soap, spray it with hair spray, or dab on colorless nail polish.

HANDBAGS AND PURSES

To maintain the shape of your leather bags, stuff them with tissue or plastic bags. Then, to keep them from sticking together when you store them, place each in a flannel bag or a pillowcase.

To brighten a patent-leather bag, spray on a little glass cleaner; then wipe with a paper towel.

Keep the metal trim on your bag from tarnishing—apply a coat of clear nail polish over it.

Every now and then, it's a good idea to clean and condition your leather purses. Wipe them with a damp cloth and mild soap, or apply a colorless leather conditioner with a dry cloth.

Replace a broken strap on a purse with a heavy chain necklace.

GLOVES

When trying on a new pair of gloves, clench your fist and see how comfortable the glove feels. Make sure the glove opening falls right at your wrist and palm joint and the seams are well sewn.

To keep gloves looking as good as new, always pull them back into shape right after removing them.

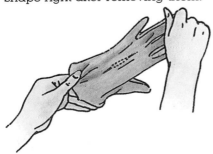

Remove stains on leather gloves by rubbing an art-gum eraser or white cornmeal on them.

Oily stains on leather gloves? Dust them with cornstarch and leave it on overnight before brushing off the residue.

HATS

Brush inside leather hatbands with a little melted paraffin to prevent oil and dirt from accumulating.

Brush and sponge a straw hat regularly. If it's especially dirty, run a hand vacuum over it.

To add sheen to a dull straw hat, apply a light coating of glycerin or hair spray.

Reshape an old straw hat—soak it in salt water, then contour it by hand and let it dry.

Keep your beret from shrinking after laundering; slip it over a dinner plate as it dries. (Be sure you use a plate that's the same size as the hat.)

To keep felt hats fresh looking, brush them with a soft brush after each use and store in plastic bags.

Caught in the rain wearing your good felt hat? Blot the drops of water with an absorbent tissue; then rub over the rain spots with a wad of tissue paper, using a smooth circular motion.

Refresh your tired felt hat. Hold it over steaming water for a second or two and brush with the nap.

An empty coffee can makes a convenient hat stand.

TIES

Tired-looking silk tie? Refresh it with a little steam. Hang the tie in a steamy bathroom. Or wrap a damp piece of cloth over the sole-plate of your iron and pass the steaming iron over the tie.

If you get a water spot on a silk tie, let the spot dry, then take a hidden part of the tie and rub the spotted area vigorously. More often than not, the spot will disappear.

FURS

When buying a fur coat, look for sheen, luster, uniform markings, and bright color. Ask if the coat is made of full or partial skins; full skins are usually more expensive.

A fur coat should fit well (it's a long-term investment), feel light on the shoulders, and be roomy enough to be worn over sweaters and jackets.

Hang your fur coat on a broad shoulder hanger and don't crowd it into a closet; fur needs air circulating around it.

Never cover fur with a plastic bag; use a cloth cover instead.

Exposing fur to direct sunlight and heat can cause it to change color and dry out.

If a fur coat gets wet, shake it out immediately and hang it to dry in a well-ventilated area, away from a heat source and out of the sun.

Furs easily absorb odors, so don't use mothballs or chemical sprays anywhere near them.

Avoid wearing heavy jewelry that constantly rubs over one area of the fur garment.

Since cleaning may eventually dry the pelt, clean most furs only every 2 years. However, long-hair furs, such as beaver, raccoon, and fox, should be cleaned every year to prevent matting.

JEWELRY CARE

To restore its natural sparkle and beauty, it's wise to treat your jewelry to a good cleaning every now and then. A word of warning if you're doing your cleaning in the sink—keep the drain tightly closed and covered with a washcloth.

Amber. Put 2 drops of linseed oil on a cotton ball and rub into the amber; remove oily residue.

Amethysts, aquamarines, emeralds, garnets, jades, sapphires, rubies, topaz, tourmaline. Add 1 tablespoon ammonia to ½ cup warm water; immerse jewelry and scrub with a soft toothbrush. Rinse in clear water and dry on a lint-free cloth.

Diamonds. Mix I cup hot water with ¼ cup ammonia and 1 tablespoon detergent. Soak diamonds in this mixture for 20 minutes; scrub firmly but slowly with a toothbrush. Rinse in hot water, then dip in rubbing alcohol and air-dry or dry with a lint-free cloth (do not rinse off alcohol).

Gold. Mix 1 cup warm water with ½ cup ammonia. Soak jewelry in this mixture for 10 to 15 minutes; gently scrub with a soft toothbrush, then rinse in warm water. Let dry on an absorbent towel.

Ivory. Rub ivory with denatured alcohol; then for extra shine, rub with a drop of lemon oil.

Lapis lazuli, malachite, turquoise. Use detergent (not soap) in cool (never hot) water and clean with a soft brush.

Opals. Clean with detergent (not soap) and water; handle carefully since opal is very fragile. When not worn, opals should be immersed occasionally in water to prevent the development of cracks.

Pearls. Soak pearls in warm water and a few drops of diswashing liquid. Rinse and buff with a flannel cloth. For greater luster, wear pearls often so that they absorb natural skin oils. For the same effect, rub a little olive oil over pearls and wipe dry with a chamois cloth. Store pearls in a bin of rice.

Silver. Rub silver with silver polish, toothpaste, or a dry cloth dipped in baking soda; use a toothbrush to get into holes or crevices. Then rinse and towel-dry. For a quick clean, rub dry ashes over silver.

JEWELRY

Gold chain in a knot again? Dust it with a little talcum powder and then try to unknot it. If the knot is really stubborn, place a drop of baby oil on a sheet of waxed paper. Lay the knot in the oil and work it out with two pins; then clean the chain in ammonia or warm, sudsy water.

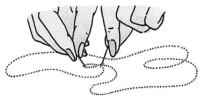

Don't swim in a chlorinated pool while wearing gold jewelry—chlorine can eat away at gold.

Plastic ice-cube trays make terrific organizers for rings and earrings.

Keep track of your pierced earrings. Fasten them through the holes of small buttons. Or line a section of your jewelry box with foam rubber and stick the earring posts into it.

When giving jewelry a final rinse, use the jet spray on your oral-hygiene appliance.

To avoid getting the green residue from tarnished costume jewelry on your skin, clean the jewelry thoroughly. Then apply a coat of clear nail polish to the part of the jewelry that comes in contact with your skin.

Apply makeup and cologne *before* putting on your jewelry.

First Aid & Family Health

EMERGENCY CALLS

If you call an emergency number, don't hang up until after you've given your name, your location (and directions on how to get there), your phone number, and the nature of the emergency.

EMERGENCY NUMBERS

Keep these vital telephone numbers near your phone at all times.

1. Many areas of Canada are now served by the toll-free 911 emergency number. This connects with the local ambulance service, poison control center, and the local fire and police departments. These emergency services are listed separately in areas not served by the 911 number.
2. Your physician.
3. Your local hospital emergency department.
4. The local poison information center. If there is none, dial the regional number, listed with the area code, or the local hospital emergency department.

CALLING THE PEDIATRICIAN

Before you telephone your child's doctor, write down his temperature, symptoms, and the type of first aid you have already given him. When you call:

1. Describe your child's condition as you have written it down.
2. Write down the doctor's instructions and read them back.
3. Ask what course might be expected with the child's condition.
4. Ask when you should call again or when to take the child to see the doctor.
5. Double-check where you should pick up a prescription if one is prescribed.
6. If the doctor is not in, leave a brief but clear message.

Don't call an emergency number or a doctor with a crying baby in your arms. Neither you nor the other party will be able to hear very well.

Whenever possible, have the victim speak directly to the doctor or other party. The victim can best answer the questions the medical personnel will need to ask.

Do as you're told. If an ambulance is coming to you, stay where you are. The driver can travel faster than you, and the emergency professionals have the training to administer first aid immediately.

If you're being rushed to hospital, ask someone to phone your physician. He may be able to expedite your admission and may even meet you in the emergency room.

USING A THERMOMETER

Do not take a temperature immediately after a person has been very active, had a bath, a full meal, a hot or cold drink, or a cigarette because you may then get a false reading.

If your child is old enough to understand how to hold a thermometer in his mouth without biting it, you can take the temperature orally; otherwise take it rectally.

Never leave a young child alone with a glass thermometer, since both the glass and the mercury can be harmful if the thermometer is broken.

THE BASIC HOUSEHOLD FIRST-AID KIT

You can buy an already assembled first-aid kit at a drugstore or medical supply store, or you can gather together the following supplies in a childproof box, such as a toolbox or fishing tackle box.

Tools
Oral and rectal thermometers
Flashlight and extra batteries
Dosage spoon or eyedropper
Hot-water bottle and ice bag
Blunt-end scissors
Tweezers
Packet of needles
Tongue depressors or frozen-ice sticks for splints
Cotton swabs
Safety matches

Dressings
Adhesive bandages in assorted sizes
Rolls of 2- and 4-inch gauze bandages
Box of 4- by 4-inch gauze pads

Tape emergency numbers (p.306) to the lid. Don't forget to include a first-aid manual. Keep the kit out of the reach of children, but make sure that all the older members of the family know where it is.

Roll of 1-inch adhesive tape
Large triangular bandage and large safety pins for a sling
Elastic bandage
Roll of absorbent cotton

Other supplies
Aspirin or acetaminophen
Ipecac syrup
3% hydrogen peroxide solution
An antibiotic ointment
Antacid
Powdered activated charcoal (for swallowed poisons)
An antihistamine/decongestant
An antivomiting compound
Eye pads

TAKING A TEMPERATURE

Hold the thermometer at the end, away from the bulb. Give it a few sharp snaps with your wrist to force the mercury toward the bulb. The thermometer should read no higher than 97° F (36° C) when you insert it.

With the patient sitting or lying down, put the bulb end under his tongue. Leave the thermometer in the mouth for at least 3 minutes.

Take a young child's temperature rectally. Shake the thermometer and lubricate the bulb end with petroleum jelly. Lay the child facedown across your lap or on his side. Spread his buttocks and gently insert the bulb into the rectum until the mercury tip is no longer visible, but no farther than 2 inches. If the child is uncomfortable, lay him on his side. Remove the thermometer after 3 minutes.

To read a mercury thermometer, rotate it so that the white surface is away from you. Adjust it until you see the silver or red line. The temperature is indicated at the end of this line. Frequently, there is an arrow marking 98.6° F (37° C), the average normal temperature.

A rectal thermometer can be used to take temperatures in the mouth if it has been thoroughly cleaned in an antiseptic solution for at least 10 to 15 minutes or with soap and water. In no situation, however, should an oral thermometer be used rectally.

Temperatures will differ depending on the method used. A rectal reading will be 1° F higher than an oral one. On the other hand, an axillary (armpit) temperature is usually 1° F lower than an oral one. Be sure to tell your physician how a temperature was taken.

MEASURING PULSE

A quick way to measure pulse: count the number of beats for 15 seconds and multiply the result by 4. Twenty beats counted would mean a pulse of 80.

TAKING A PULSE

The usual place to take a pulse is in the wrist. Hold the hand palm up. Feel where the base of the thumb meets the wrist; press your index and middle fingertips about 2 inches up the arm from that point. Adjust pressure until you feel a pulse. Then count the beats as you watch a clock's hand measure 1 minute.

A pulse can also be taken on the neck, under the jawbone, and alongside the windpipe. This pulse is stronger than the wrist pulse. When taking a neck pulse, don't press too hard—it can slow the heartbeat.
Caution: Do not press simultaneously on both neck pulses.

The normal resting pulse for an adult is 60 to 80 beats. Children's rates can be higher—around 80 to 90 for a 10-year-old, up to 140 for a newborn baby. Exercise, excitement, anxiety, and fever will all raise the pulse.

TAKING MEDICINE

Check the expiration dates of your medicines frequently and get rid of those that have expired. Make sure that you replace all essential medications, such as ipecac syrup, which induces vomiting in the event of poisoning.

Drugs do *not* belong in the bathroom—dampness, light, and heat can speed their deterioration. The best place is outside the bathroom in a separate small cabinet or closet that can be securely locked; those that say so on the label belong in the refrigerator.

Do *not* tell children that medicine tastes good or is "candy." They may think all medicines are candy

and seek them out when you're not looking. Accidental poisonings can result. Be honest about the taste. Give children a little juice or a cracker before and after they down medicine.

BEFORE YOU TAKE ANY MEDICATION...

To get the most out of your medicine—whether over-the-counter or prescription—you should ask your doctor or pharmacist the following questions:

1. What is the name of the medicine?
2. What is the medicine supposed to do?
3. What side effects may occur?
4. How many times a day should you take the medicine; before or after meals?
5. How long should you take the medicine? Should you continue to take it after you're feeling better but while there's some still left in the bottle?
6. Are there other medicines you should not take while you are taking this one?
7. Are there any foods or beverages you should avoid?
8. Should you avoid alcoholic beverages while taking the medicine?
9. Can the prescription be refilled without an appointment?

The best way to swallow a tablet or capsule: place it in your mouth with a small amount of water, tilt your head backward, and you can swallow readily; follow with more water.

If medicine must be taken at certain times, and you're afraid that you won't know when it's time to take it, set your alarm watch or clock for the correct interval of time between dosages and just listen for the alarm to ring.

When pouring out bottled medicines, keep the label side facing up. This way, any drips or spills will not ooze over the label and make the directions hard to read.

If you have to give liquid medicine to an infant, put the prescribed amount in a nipple, then give it to the baby just before feeding time. She'll be so hungry she'll hardly realize she has swallowed the medicine.

Another way to give medicine is with a plastic dropper placed against the baby's inner middle cheek. Squeeze the dropper slowly; the infant will begin to suck automatically.

When giving a liquid medicine to a child, hold a small paper cup under her chin. Whatever dribbles into the cup can be mixed with a little water, and she can drink the rest down.

SICKROOM TIPS

If your patient is nauseous, put a garbage-bag liner in the wastebasket and keep it near him at all times. When the bag has served its purpose, you have neat, instant, and odorless disposal.

When the patient needs a bedpan, rinse it in hot water first—to take the chill off it.

No hot-water bottle? Fill a heavy-duty rubber glove with hot water. Close it tightly with a strong rubber band and wrap it in a towel. A plastic bottle with a tight-fitting lid will also serve as a substitute hot-water bottle.

To prevent bedside-table crowding, hang a multipocketed shoe bag by the bed. This makes a handy holder for tissues, eyeglasses, combs, and all the other little things that a bedridden patient may need.

ARTHRITIC AIDS

Painful arthritic knees? The answer to your problem may be ice. Fill small plastic bags with ice and seal them. Hold or secure one over and one under each knee. Do this several times a day, for 15 or 20 minutes at a time.

Hug shopping bags rather than carry them by the handles. Or try carrying your groceries in a small backpack.

Sleeping under an electric blanket or atop an electric mattress pad can be helpful for arthritic and other aches. Hot-water bottles cool quickly; heating pads on too high a setting may burn the skin.

Wear stretch gloves at night to reduce or eliminate morning arthritic pain, stiffness, and joint swelling.

If you have arthritis and have difficulty holding a pen, push the pen through a small rubber ball. Or wrap masking tape around and around until it's large enough for you to hold.

ADVICE TO THE ELDERLY

If a person is too weak or feeble to bathe, set a lawn chair in the tub and turn the shower on. If you think the chair may slip, put a towel under it. (The towel will also prevent marks in the tub.)

If you have difficulty getting out of a bathtub, turn over onto your hands and knees and push yourself up—*slowly*.

Trouble getting out of bed in the morning? Tie a piece of rope to the bedpost or to the side of the mattress frame, also tying knots at intervals so that you can get a good grip. Pin the rope to the sheet or blanket at night so that it's handy come morning. Then grab the rope and pull yourself up!

Are the covers too heavy on your feet in bed? Get a large cardboard box and cut out two opposite sides; place the box at the foot of the bed between the bed and the heavy covers. Slip your feet in the box opening, and the covers won't crush your feet.

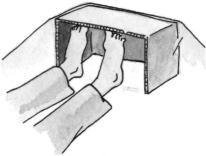

COLDS AND FLU

Give plenty of fluids to anyone with the flu—water, juices, soups, caffeine-free soda pop. If at all possible, try serving something different every hour or so. For a child who resists, try half juice, half ginger ale.

During the cold and flu season, freeze different kinds of fruit juices on wooden sticks. When a child refuses to drink juice from a glass, an iced fruit treat may prove tempting. (It's also good for soothing bumped and bruised lips.)

If you get the flu, attempt to minimize your contacts with others. Wash your hands often and avoid touching others' food and utensils. Discard used tissues in a paper bag and dispose of it daily.

NASAL CONGESTION

To relieve nasal congestion, buy a room humidifier. Change the water in it daily and follow the manufacturer's cleaning schedule to prevent the growth of bacteria.

DIAGNOSING COLDS AND INFLUENZA

The common cold and influenza, or flu, are both viral diseases. A cold causes fatigue, a scratchy or sore throat, hoarseness, coughing, sneezing, a runny or stuffy nose, watering eyes, and headaches, but it usually does not cause a fever over 100° F (37.7° C). Cold symptoms usually last from 5 to 7 days.

Flu symptoms are initially the same as those of a cold, but they become more severe, causing fever in adults, and even higher fever in children. Flu sufferers also experience pain in their muscles and joints, weakness, and loss of appetite. Flu symptoms may disappear in 1 to 2 weeks, but full recovery can take from 2 to 3 weeks.

There are no cures for cold or flu infections, but you can relieve some of the symptoms.

Those in the high-risk groups—for example, the elderly and those with chronic cardiac or respiratory conditions—should be immunized against the flu, since it is far more dangerous for these people.

Be sure you don't mistake cold and flu symptoms for those of another disease or condition. Contact your physician if you perceive any of these symptoms:

1. An earache or blurry vision.
2. Wheezing or hard and rapid breathing with flared nostrils.
3. A heavy, prolonged cough, one with cloudy mucus, or one that lasts more than a week.
4. A fever that does not come down with treatment (p.317) in 2 or 3 days.
5. A sore throat with swollen glands and fever over 100.5° F (38° C) that doesn't improve within 2 to 3 days.
6. A fever of 102° F (38.9° C) for 24 hours or longer.
7. A stiff neck or a rash.
8. Severe abdominal pain or moderate abdominal pain that lasts longer than 4 to 6 hours.
9. Chest pain or shortness of breath for more than 10 minutes.
10. Disorientation or loss of coordination or consciousness.
11. Excessive sleepiness.
If the patient is under 2½ years old and is running a fever over 102° F (38.9° C) at any time, contact the doctor immediately.

Adults and adolescents can use nose sprays more effectively with this technique: spray each nostril once and wait for 5 to 10 minutes; then spray once more in each nostril. The first spray will shrink the membranes in the front part of the nose, allowing the second spray to penetrate deeply to the back of the nose.

Don't use commercial decongestants for more than 2 or 3 days at a time. They should not be used by young children at all without a doctor's permission.

To make saline nose drops in a hurry, mix ¼ teaspoon table salt in 1 cup water. With a dropper, place 2 or 3 drops in each nostril ½ hour before meals and at bedtime—more often if it is helpful.

Draw mucus from an infant's nose with a plastic bulb syringe. Most babies will cry because they dislike the sensation, but there is no pain.

COUGHS

For home-brewed cough medicine that helps dissolve mucus in the throat: mix 1 teaspoon honey and 1 teaspoon lemon juice in a glass of warm water.

Put a dab of honey on the back of the tongue to bring relief from a nagging cough.

SORE THROATS

Sore throats caused by drinking, smoking, or shouting will respond to rest. Gargling with warm salt water, sucking throat lozenges, and limiting yourself to soft (nonspicy, nonsalty) foods may help in these situations.

A sore throat that accompanies a cold, the flu, or other respiratory ailments usually clears up when the ailment does. In the meantime, gargling, drinking warm liquids, and sucking hard candies or medicated lozenges may soothe your throat. A humidifier or vaporizer may help as well.

Caution: A very young child may choke on candy or lozenges.

If a sore throat lasts longer than 48 hours, call a physician. And contact a physician if any sore throat is accompanied by the following symptoms: white spots on the ton-

sils, fever, swollen or tender neck glands, skin rash, persistent headache, foul breath, stiff neck, or pain that interferes with swallowing. If the sore throat develops after exposure to someone with strep throat, see a physician.

CROUP

If your child awakens with a sudden barking cough or a crowing sound when inhaling, you should suspect croup. Carry the youngster into the bathroom, turn on a hot shower (to increase the humidity, let the water remain in the

USING DROPS PROPERLY

Whether you are using ear drops, nose drops, or eye drops, there are several steps you should always take before you insert them:
1. Wash your hands thoroughly.
2. Warm the drops to near body temperature by holding the bottle

in your hand for several minutes.
3. If the drops are a cloudy suspension, shake the bottle well.
4. Draw medicine into dropper.
5. After using the drops, replace the dropper in the bottle right away and wash your hands.

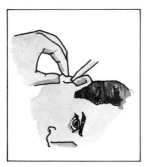 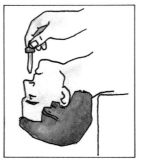 

EAR DROPS
Note: Having someone else insert the ear drops may be easier.
1. Tilt the affected ear up or lie on your side.
2. To allow the drops to run in: Adult — Hold the earlobe up and back.
Child — Hold the earlobe down and back.
3. Place the prescribed amount of drops into the ear. (Do not insert the dropper into the ear.)
4. Keep the ear tilted up for a few minutes, or else insert a soft cotton plug, whichever has been recommended.

NOSE DROPS
1. Blow your nose gently before washing your hands.
2. Lie down on a flat surface, such as a bed; hang your head over the edge and tilt your head back as far as is comfortable.
3. Place the prescribed number of drops into the nose.
4. To allow the medication to spread in the nose, remain in this position for a few minutes.

EYE DROPS
1. Pull the lower lid away from the eye at a right angle, forming a pouch. Drop the medication into the pouch.
2. Immediately look down, close the eye, and keep it closed for a minute or two. Have a tissue handy to press on eyes if needed or to wipe off excess.
3. For easy eye-drop application in a child's eyes, have her lie down and close her eyes; then place the eye drops in the corner of each eye. As she opens her eyes, the drops spread gently throughout.

tub), and sit in the steamy room with the child on your lap. The steam and the upright posture should help relieve the cough. When you return the child to bed after breathing becomes easier, place a vaporizer in the bedroom.

Call your doctor immediately if there are no rest periods between the coughing episodes, if the lips or face turns blue, or if the breastbone is sucked in deeply with each inspiration; or the child cannot speak.

HEADACHES

Ease a tension headache with a gentle massage of the facial muscles or by applying a heating pad or hot compress to the forehead and the base of the skull. Aspirin or its substitutes may also reduce the pain. The ultimate solution to a tension headache, of course, is avoiding the source of the tension.

A migraine headache is a severe, recurring condition, often accompanied by vomiting and visual disturbances. If you suspect your headaches are migraines, seek the help of a physician.

You may get temporary relief from a migraine headache by using cold packs or by pressing on the bulging artery in front of the ear on the painful side of the head.

Regular exercise, such as swimming or yoga, may help to prevent migraine headaches by relaxing the body. Some migraine sufferers find that meditation also helps.

A migraine attack can often be aborted just by exhaling into and rebreathing from a paper bag placed over the nose and mouth.

See a physician if a headache is sudden and crushingly painful, sudden and caused by an accident, accompanied by a stiff neck and fever, confined to an ear or an eye or to one side of the head, accompanied by nausea or vomiting, or part of a pattern of headaches of increasing severity and frequency.

MENSTRUAL PAIN

Exercise regularly to relieve menstrual cramps. If this doesn't work, heat may soothe the pain, either in the form of a heating pad, a warm bath, or a cup of tea.

Contact a gynecologist if you are experiencing pain after years of pain-free menstruation, if the pain is more severe than usual, if you have been dizzy or have lost consciousness, if you have pain in your shoulders, if you have increased bleeding or abnormal vaginal discharge.

ABDOMINAL PAIN

The next time you feel overstuffed after a meal, try placing a cold cloth over your ear for relief. This stimulates a branch of a nerve that also runs through the digestive tract. Stimulating the nerve in the ear may relieve that uncomfortable bloated feeling.

If your abdominal pain is just below the center of the rib cage, take an antacid, then lie or sit in a comfortable position and eat or drink nothing. If the pain doesn't subside in 2 to 4 hours, or if it gets worse, contact a physician.

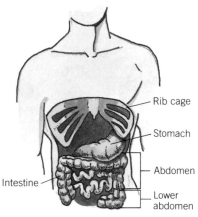

Rib cage
Stomach
Abdomen
Intestine
Lower abdomen

Pain in the lower abdomen cannot be alleviated with antacids; don't take them. Rest in a comfortable position and do not eat or drink. If the pain intensifies, or doesn't diminish after 2 or 3 hours or is accompanied by vomiting, contact a physician.

Contact a physician if you have abdominal pain and the abdomen is tender to the touch, if the abdomen is rigid, if there is vomiting of blood, if there is severe pain in one section of the abdomen, if there is passage of dark stools, if there is fever accompanied by bloody diarrhea, if there is dizziness or decreased consciousness.

Choose antacids containing magnesium or aluminum rather than sodium bicarbonate or calcium carbonate. Sodium bicarbonate has too much salt, and calcium carbonate causes acidity.

Liquid antacids may be more effective than tablets. Tablets must be chewed thoroughly in order to be effective. Whichever type you choose, don't use them for more than 2 weeks at a time.

For acute gas, gently massage the abdomen and apply a hot-water bottle or heating pad to the area. Or walk around the house slowly for 15 to 20 minutes.

HELPS FOR HEARTBURN

Tight garments and belts increase pressure on the abdomen. Avoid wearing them or at least loosen them after meals.

It takes several hours for the stomach to empty its contents into the intestine. If you eat a meal and lie down afterward, regurgitation and heartburn may occur. Don't eat near bedtime—for the same reason.

Try not to consume effervescent substances, such as soda water, that cause belching. These allow acid from the stomach to flow back into the esophagus.

Avoid bending over soon after meals; that can cause the stomach contents to back up into the esophagus.

At times when you think you might regurgitate, take an antacid an hour after meals and just before going to bed to help neutralize stomach acid.

Obesity increases pressure on the abdomen. Losing weight may help heartburn.

VOMITING AND DIARRHEA

When an infant 6 months of age or younger is vomiting, give half-strength formula. Return to full-strength formula as soon as vomiting has ceased.

Give a child with diarrhea half-strength skim milk, decarbonated soda pop, weak tea, clear soup, gelatin, rice cereal, bananas, yogurt, toast, and crackers. Withhold solids if a child is vomiting.

THE CAUSES AND DANGER SIGNS OF VOMITING AND DIARRHEA

Vomiting and diarrhea have a variety of causes—contaminated food, infections, an intestinal virus, and so on. Vomiting usually lasts 24 to 48 hours, although diarrhea may persist for several more days. An intestinal virus may start with vomiting for 24 to 48 hours, followed by diarrhea, with or without fever; it may take from 2 to 7 days to run its course.

You should call your doctor if the following conditions exist:

1. Constant or severe abdominal pain.
2. Vomiting and diarrhea are accompanied by a fever of 101° F (38.3° C) or over.
3. There is blood in vomit or stools.

4. Vomiting is unusually severe and lasts longer than 24 hours.
5. A child is less than 6 months old, and vomiting does not lessen or stop within 12 hours.
6. A child is less than 1 year old, and diarrhea does not improve within 24 hours.
7. An adult or a child more than 1 year old has diarrhea for more than 3 days.
8. A child refuses to take fluids, has diminished urine output, or has a dry mouth.
Caution: Vomiting and diarrhea can lead to dehydration, a potentially life-threatening condition. To prevent it, provide water, fruit juices, or liquid gelatin.

For 12 to 24 hours after vomiting, take only clear fluids, such as diluted apple juice, weak tea, broth, or decarbonated soda pop.

Older children and adults can slowly resume solid foods on the second day after vomiting. The best foods to start with are rice, other cooked cereals (with a small amount of milk and sugar), bananas, soda crackers, plain bread or toast, yogurt, baked potatoes, or lean white meat. Continue with plenty of clear fluids.

Prevent traveler's diarrhea by adhering to the old adage: If you can't peel it, boil it, or otherwise cook it, forget it.

CONSTIPATION

Proper diet can prevent much constipation. Eat fibrous foods, such as whole-grain breads, bran cereals, fresh fruit, and leafy vegetables, and stay away from dairy products. Avoid the routine use of laxatives and enemas—they only make the problem worse.

Walking and other types of exercise—done on a regular basis—will do a lot to keep your digestive system working smoothly.

Nervous tension can cause constipation. Try to reduce stress by taking up a sport, pursuing a hobby, talking out problems, meditating, or doing whatever it is that most relaxes you.

Consider yourself constipated only if your normal pattern changes. But if you have had no bowel movements for more than 5 days and get no relief from a laxative, contact your physician.

RECTAL BLEEDING

For itching hemorrhoids, sit in a warm bath 2 or 3 times a day and apply soothing witch hazel compresses. Try not to sit or stand for any extended time.

For bleeding hemorrhoids, take warm baths 4 to 6 times a day, drink extra fluids, and take a bran-type stool softener.

See your physician if you develop bright-red rectal bleeding, if you have black, tarlike bowel movements, or if you have severe rectal pain. Rectal bleeding can originate higher in the intestinal tract and be caused by tumors, ulcers, or inflammations.

HANGOVERS

You can reduce the morning-after effects of too much alcohol by drinking two or three glasses of water before you retire for the night.

If you feel hung over when you wake in the morning, drink several glasses of water and have a bland breakfast without coffee or tea.

Forego coffee, if you're feeling queasy from a hangover. Excessive alcoholic consumption can cause dehydration and stomach irritation. Coffee, which acts as a diuretic, can lead to further fluid loss, postponing recovery.

To hasten the body's return to normal metabolism, drink lots of fruit juice; besides providing fluids, it adds calories—both things the body desperately needs.

JET LAG

Eat cautiously before and during a flight. Avoid difficult-to-digest, heavy, or exotic dishes.

Eat only when your stomach says it's time—you can always refuse the meal that the airline offers.

Make an effort to consume extra liquids, even if you don't feel thirsty; the air in planes is very dehydrating.

MOTION SICKNESS

Try candied ginger as an alternative to commercial motion-sickness drugs—it has no adverse side effects like drowsiness, dry mouth, or blurry vision.

Do not travel on an empty stomach—have a light, bland meal an hour before leaving. Do not drink alcohol before or during the trip. Don't allow smoking in the car—it can trigger motion sickness.

Sit in the most stable parts of the vehicle you're traveling in (usually in the front of the vehicle, not over the wheels) and concentrate on looking at the horizon.

CHILDHOOD DISEASES

If your child has a fever, discuss the symptoms with your physician. Because some researchers have linked aspirin, given when chicken pox or flu are present, to Reye's syndrome (an inflammation of the brain), the doctor may recommend an aspirin substitute.

Provide a variety of liquids, but do not force your child to eat solid food or to stay in bed. Encourage rest or light activity, such as reading, coloring, doing puzzles, or watching TV.

FEVER

A fever—an oral temperature above 100° F (37.7° C) or a rectal temperature above 101° F (38.3° C)—is not a disease, but rather a symptom. It is the body's response to infection. A person with a fever often experiences chills, headaches, or a "feverish feeling."

Adults may get relief from a fever by taking aspirin or an aspirin substitute. They should also drink ample fluids and get lots of rest.

If a child has a fever, give her extra fluids. Dress her in light clothing to let the heat dissipate. If your doctor recommends it, give her aspirin or acetaminophen to reduce the fever.

If the child does not feel more comfortable with this treatment, call your physician. If the fever is extremely high, he may suggest that you give the child a sponge bath. Sit the child in a tub or on a waterproof surface and sponge her with lukewarm water. Do *not* use cold water or alcohol, which will only make her shiver or vomit, and thus raise her temperature. Continue for 15 to 30 minutes and repeat as often as necessary to get the desired effect. If she struggles or begins to shiver, discontinue.

Occasionally, a high fever can cause a child to have convulsions. Although a simple febrile seizure is not dangerous, convulsions can be frightening. Do not panic. This type of convulsion will not harm your child. If one occurs, try to keep the child cool (by removing her clothing and sponging her with tepid water) and, since vomiting may occur, lay her on her side to prevent her swallowing her vomit. Once you have the situation under control, call your doctor for further advice.

Call your physician in the following situations:

1. A rectal temperature of 100° F (37.7° C) in an infant less than 6 weeks of age.
2. A child's fever that remains over 101° F (38.3° C) for 2 days.
3. A child who does not look or act well, regardless of the degree of the fever.
4. An adult's fever over 102° F (38.9° C) that lasts longer than 2 days.
5. In an adult, a fever with chest pains, shortness of breath, cough, production of sputum, headache, earache, stiff neck, abdominal pain, or confusion.

When a child has German measles—a disease that is dangerous to the unborn—keep the child away from pregnant women. If a pregnant woman has been exposed to a child with the rash or has had contact with the child within 1 week of the rash, she should contact her physician.

If your child is healthy, he should have the following vaccinations:
DTP—diphtheria, tetanus, pertussis (whooping cough)
Polio—oral (OPV) or injection (IPV)
MMR—measles, mumps, rubella (German measles)
Hib—Haemophilus influenza type B
TD—tetanus, diphtheria
You should also ask your physician about the advisability of a tuberculosis test.

IMMUNIZING YOUR CHILD	
Age	**Vaccine**
2 months	DTP and polio
4 months	DTP and polio
6 months	DTP, polio (if oral used)
12 months or after	MMR
18 months	DTP, polio
2 years	Hib
4 to 6 years, or before school	DTP, polio
14 to 16 years, and every 10 years thereafter	TD

There is no general vaccine available for chicken pox, a very contagious childhood disease. Chicken pox's telltale spots can be extremely itchy, mostly during the healing stage. Encourage your child *not* to scratch them, since they can become infected or leave scars. To relieve the irritation, apply calamine lotion to the affected area. A cool alcohol rubdown or tepid oatmeal or baking soda baths may help. Also try an oral antihistamine to relieve the itch.

No vaccination is available yet for scarlet fever. Its symptoms include a sore throat, a rash resembling prickly heat, and a fever. If you suspect that your child has scarlet fever, see your physician right away. He will prescribe an antibiotic, which should be taken exactly as directed.

NOSEBLEEDS

One technique for stopping nosebleeds is to pinch the nose and apply cold compresses or an ice pack to the back of the neck, to contract the blood vessels.

If a child's nose bleeds frequently, daub a bit of petroleum jelly into each of his nostrils once or twice a day. It's also a good idea to run a humidifier in the bedroom while the child is asleep.

EAR PROBLEMS

A child will complain if he has a pain in his ear. Since an infant cannot complain, however, you must watch very carefully for special signs: he may pull on his ears, have cold symptoms, lose his appetite, run a fever, be irritable, or occasionally, have a discharge from the ears.

If your child has an earache, call your physician. Should the doctor prescribe a medication, be sure that the child takes it for the prescribed time—even after symptoms disappear.

Never put your infant or young child to bed with a bottle of milk, juice, or soda pop. If he insists upon sleeping with a bottle, fill it with water.

TREATING A NOSEBLEED

If a nosebleed is the result of a head injury and you suspect a fractured skull, do *not* try to stop the bleeding. Call an ambulance or get to a hospital immediately. If bleeding follows a nose injury, apply an ice pack and go to the hospital. Contact a physician right away if there is uncontrolled bleeding and/or the victim has a bleeding disorder or high blood pressure.

1. To stop a simple nosebleed, have the victim sit up unless he feels dizzy. Ask him to lean his head forward and to breathe through his mouth. Pinch the sides of the nose firmly just below the cartilage. Hold for 10 minutes—do not keep checking to see whether bleeding has stopped. After 10 minutes, if the nose is still bleeding, continue for another 10 minutes.

2. The simple pinching technique will stop most nosebleeds, but if you do not succeed, hold an ice bag or a cold compress over the victim's nose for another 10 minutes. At the same time, continue to apply pressure to the nostrils.

3. If this also fails, soak a piece of cotton gauze or a cotton ball with phenylephrine, an over-the-counter liquid nasal decongestant, or in water. Put the cotton into the nostril and apply gentle pressure over it. After 10 minutes, gently pull out the cotton. If the bleeding still hasn't stopped, contact a physician or go to a hospital emergency room.

Never put anything smaller than a washcloth in a child's ear. If there is constant wax buildup in the ear, discuss with your doctor how it should be treated.

Itchy ears? Here's a simple but effective treatment. Make certain any soap is removed by rinsing your ears with a mild saltwater solution and then tilting your head to let it run out. Apply an emollient such as baby oil or glycerine, using your little finger (*not* a cotton-tipped applicator).

Insect in your ear? Suffocate the insect by filling the ear canal with vegetable oil. Then see a doctor to have the insect removed.

HICCUPS

To stop hiccups, hold your breath as long as you can and then exhale slowly. Slow, deep breathing may also solve the problem.

Try sipping a glass of warm water slowly. If this doesn't work, drink the water out of the opposite side of the glass.

Nibbling on a teaspoon of granulated sugar may cure hiccups.

Some people favor putting a paper bag over the nose and mouth and inhaling from it and exhaling into it repeatedly.

If you have recurring attacks of hiccups, or if an attack lasts longer than 3 hours, see a doctor.

MOUTH PAIN

See a dentist about any toothache, however mild. If you have extreme pain or swelling, call a dentist immediately.

WHEN YOU CAN'T CALL THE DENTIST

To deal with a middle-of-the-night toothache, try the following measures. You may only need to use one of them before feeling results. But even if the pain goes away, call the dentist in the morning.

1. Floss between the aching tooth and its neighbors—sometimes impacted food can set up the pain. Rest an ice bag or a cold compress on the jaw of the affected side. If cold applications don't help, try heat—apply a hot-water bottle or a warm compress.

2. If you see a cavity, clean it out gently, using sterile cotton on the end of a toothpick; then saturate another bit of cotton with oil of cloves and pack it gently into the cavity with a toothpick.

3. Apply ice to the web of skin between the thumb and index finger on the same side of the body as the toothache. (How this works is unknown, but it often does, and it is the site where acupuncturists insert needles to relieve tooth pain.)

If the pain is mild, try to ease it by taking aspirin or an aspirin substitute. Rinse your mouth periodically with a solution of baking soda and warm water.

To relieve temporary swelling and irritation of the gums, eat pineapple sherbet. It tastes good, the cold acts like an ice pack to reduce the swelling, and according to some studies, the pineapple has curative properties.

After oral surgery, you may be able to control bleeding by placing a small piece of folded gauze or a tea bag over the wound and exerting pressure, either with a finger or by closing the opposite jaw over the gauze or tea bag for 20 minutes or so.

Treat a simple canker sore by touching it with the tip of a styptic pencil. Or rinse it with a mild solution of baking soda and water.

BACKACHE

For mild backache pain, soak in a warm bath for half an hour. Then lie on a firm mattress with a heating pad beneath the painful area. (Complete bed rest for 24 to 72 hours would be ideal.) Simple painkillers, such as aspirin or acetaminophen, may also relieve the pain.

When lying in bed, you'll be most comfortable with a small pillow under your head and a large pillow under your knees.

If yours is a sedentary life, spend more time walking or undertake an exercise program to strengthen your abdominal and back muscles. Bicycling works wonders on those muscles.

Avoid housework-related lower-back pain. When doing dishes, open the cupboard door below the sink and keep one leg elevated on the cupboard ledge. When ironing, rest one foot on a box or a step stool. If you're vacuuming, for example, bend your knees and move your feet slowly rather than jerking them forward and back.

If backache pain is severe or recurring, or if it follows an accident, contact your physician. If the pain radiates into the hip or leg, or if it is associated with bowel or urinary problems, you should see a physician as soon as possible.

STIFF NECK

Relieve a stiff neck by wearing a soft cervical collar for 48 hours. Or roll up a Turkish towel and fasten it around your neck with a pin.

A heating pad or a hot-water bottle and aspirin or acetaminophen will help ease the discomfort of a stiff neck.

PREVENTING BACK PAIN

Sit in a firm chair with a supportive back. Never sit in very deep or overstuffed chairs or sofas.

When sitting, keep your knees ½ to 1 inch above your hips. A small footstool can provide this lift.

Try not to sit in one position for long. Get up and move around at least once every half hour.

If you must stand in one position for a long time, shift your weight from one foot to the other or elevate one foot on a small stool or ledge.

Push large objects, don't pull them.

Stand on a step stool when reaching for high objects.

Sleep on a mattress that is very firm. Consider using a bed board.

When a stiff neck is accompanied by fever, nausea, headache, pain radiating into the arm, or weakness or numbness in the head, see your doctor. And, of course, see your doctor about neck pain that results from injury.

BLISTERS

Never pop a blister—just cleanse the skin and cover it with a sterile gauze pad and adhesive tape.

If rubbing is unavoidable, protect the blister with adhesive cushioning. Cut out a hole to fit the blister and secure the cushioning with strips of adhesive tape.

If a blister breaks, which most do in 3 to 5 days, carefully peel away the dead covering skin, preferably with sterilized tweezers (p. 323), and cut it off with cuticle scissors. Wash the affected area with soap and water and cover it with a sterile gauze pad attached with adhesive tape.

If you have large or extensive blisters, see a physician. Ruptured blisters frequently become infected. Should you notice any of the signs of infection (p.322), see a physician.

BRUISES

To reduce pain and swelling, cover a new bruise with a cold pack or an ice bag for several hours. Elevate the bruised area as much as you can.

Need an emergency cold pack? Use a plastic bag of frozen vegetables from your freezer. Just tap the bag on a hard surface to loosen and separate the frozen vegetable pieces; then lay the bag on the affected area. The bag easily conforms to the contours of your body.

For child-size cold packs, cut up a sponge, soak it in water, and freeze it.

If a large bruise occurs between your heart and any rings or tight bracelets, remove them to prevent a stoppage of circulation.

Bruises that appear without an apparent cause, such as an accidental bump, should be evaluated by a physician. They may be signs of a bleeding disorder.

See a physician if a bruise is very large or if it swells a great deal; if it is on the head or face and there is headache, difficulty seeing, neck pain, or shortness of breath; if it is on the chest and there is a deeper chest pain; if it is over the kidneys (on the sides of the midback below the ribs); if there is persistent abdominal pain; or if there is reduced sensation or difficulty moving the bruised limb.

CUTS AND SCRAPES

Wash a scrape with lukewarm, soapy water, then hold it under cold running water for 5 minutes. Be sure all dirt, grit, and other foreign material is flushed out—

use a cotton swab if necessary. If there is swelling, hold an ice pack over the wound for 20 to 60 minutes and elevate it. If the scrape is large, contact a physician.

Clean a child's cut or scrape with a damp red or other dark-colored washcloth. The blood won't show, and the child won't be scared.

When your child gets hurt, make an effort to remain calm; it will help him stay calm.

Cover a scrape only if it's likely to get dirty or if it will hurt when it rubs against clothing. In that case, spray on a nonadherent dressing; then cover the scrape with an adhesive bandage or with sterile gauze and adhesive tape.

The first step in treating any cut is to cleanse it thoroughly. Using warm, sudsy water, wash in and

THE SIGNS OF INFECTION

All injuries that break the skin—lacerations, punctures, bites, stings, burns, and so on—present a danger of infection. In the hours and days that follow an injury, you should watch carefully for the signs of infection—it can be far more dangerous than the original injury. The signs of infection are:

1. Swelling of the affected part.
2. Throbbing pain.
3. Tenderness.
4. Pus—a white, yellow, or green discharge from the wound.
5. Red streaks radiating from the wound.
6. A sensation of heat.
7. Inflammation—any more than a red rim just around the wound.
8. Fever that has no other obvious cause, such as a flu or other illness.
9. Swollen, tender lymph glands—in the groin (leg and lower torso infection), armpit (arm and upper torso infection), neck (head and upper torso infection).

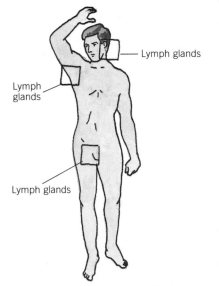

If these signs develop following an injury, contact a physician immediately.

around the wound. If, after washing and rinsing for 10 minutes, any foreign matter remains in the wound, try to remove it carefully with sterile gauze, cotton swabs, or sterile tweezers (see below). Blot the wound dry with sterile gauze. Apply direct pressure with a clean dressing for 10 to 15 minutes and, if it is possible, elevate the wound above the level of the heart. After the blood flow stops— a little oozing is normal—bandage the wound.

Sterilize tweezers by placing them in boiling water for 10 minutes or by holding them over a gas flame until the tips glow. You can also use a match or candle flame, but be sure to wipe the carbon from the tweezer tips with a sterile gauze pad. Let the tweezers cool before you use them.

Use a butterfly bandage to close up a small cut. Apply one side of the butterfly; tug gently as you apply the second side, checking to be sure the edges of the cut meet and align. The cut should be closed, but don't let its edges curl inward or overlap.

If you don't have a butterfly bandage on hand, you can make one very easily from a regular adhesive bandage.

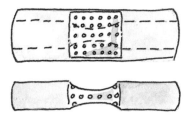

With any wound—but especially with dirty or extensive wounds— there is a danger of tetanus. If the victim hasn't had a tetanus shot within 10 years—5 years if the wound is seriously contaminated by dirt—call a physician. If untreated, tetanus is frequently a fatal disease.

Watch carefully for infection (p. 322); it may not appear for several days. If infection is apparent, or if the wound is very contaminated, see a physician.

A cut should be seen by a physician if it is more than 1 inch in length; if it is on the face or over a joint; or if there is difficulty moving or feeling the wounded part.

PUNCTURES

If a small, pointed object, such as a nail or pencil, punctures the skin, pull the object out. To remove trapped bacteria, wash the wound carefully with soap and water and hold it under running lukewarm water for 10 minutes. If there is swelling, put an ice pack over the wound and elevate it for 15 to 30 minutes. Then spray the wound with a nonadherent dressing and cover it with sterile gauze attached with adhesive tape.

If a puncture is caused by a large object, or if it is very deep, call a physician. You may be told not to remove the object, but rather to hurry to a hospital emergency room because removing it yourself might cause severe bleeding. For the trip to the hospital, the object should be secured with a dressing and a cup.

STOPPING SEVERE BLEEDING

If someone is bleeding profusely, have him lie down to prevent fainting. If he has already fainted, raise his legs higher than his head.

Unless you suspect a broken bone, elevate the wounded limb, and with a pad of cloth or a sterile dressing, apply direct pressure to the wound. Most bleeding will stop in a few minutes; don't lift the pad until you're sure it has.

If bleeding from an arm or a leg is severe and doesn't stop after several minutes, you can try to diminish the blood flow in the artery that supplies the limb. Apply pressure with your hand or fingers to the artery in the arm or groin while continuing pressure directly on the wound. (Do *not* apply pressure to arteries of the head or neck to control bleeding.) When the bleeding stops, tie a dressing firmly over the pad. Get medical attention for the victim promptly.

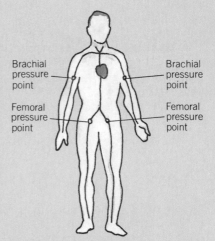

Brachial pressure point

Brachial pressure point

Femoral pressure point

Femoral pressure point

Caution: Tourniquets should only be used in critical emergencies and only by experienced personnel. They generally do more harm than good.

See a doctor if a puncture contains foreign matter; has entered a joint, an eye, or any part of the airway; or is in the chest or abdomen.

BANDAGES

If commercial bandage strips irritate your skin, use a sterile gauze pad and paper tape instead.

To make adhesive tape stick better and increase its durability, rub a moist bar of soap across the edges of the tape. As the soap dries, it will harden and seal the tape, preventing premature loosening.

Don't apply salve or liquid antiseptic directly to a cut. It's less traumatic if it's put on the bandage before securing it to the skin.

To ease the pain of your child's cut, draw a funny design on the adhesive bandage with a brightly colored felt-tip marker.

EVERYDAY ITEMS FOR USE IN EMERGENCIES

You may not realize it, but certain items in your home that you don't ordinarily associate with first aid are suitable for emergency use. Here are just a few—why not look around your home for more?

Disposable or regular diapers: compresses to control heavy bleeding; bandages; padding for splints.

Sanitary napkins: same as above.

Towels, sheets, linens: same as above.

Diaper pins: pins for bandages or slings.

Blankets: to keep victim warm.

Magazines, newspapers, umbrellas, pillows: splints for broken bones.

Table leaf, old door: stretcher for head, neck, and back injuries.

Fans: to cool heatstroke victim.

Large scarves or handkerchiefs: eye bandages or slings.

Tap water: to irrigate burns and eyes.

Wrapping tape: to secure bandages and apply pressure.

To lessen the pain when removing a bandage, apply a warm compress or a cotton ball soaked in vegetable oil over the bandage.

If the wound shouldn't get wet, blow hot air from a hair dryer on the tape for a few seconds to soften the adhesive and make bandage removal easier.

FRACTURES

After an injury, take RICE (Rest, Ice, Compression, and Elevation). This means you should stop using the injured part and wrap it in ice. Then secure an elastic bandage tightly over the ice and position the injured part so that it is above the level of your heart.

To cover an ugly white arm cast, get a supply of different-colored tube socks. Select a sock to go with your outfit of the day, cut off the toe, and slide it on for a color-coordinated look. For a leg cast, try leg warmers.

Try to prop up a broken leg in a cast as much as possible to help the circulation. If you're on crutches, you can turn the crutch upside down and rest your foot on the hand grip.

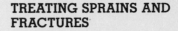

TREATING SPRAINS AND FRACTURES

If a person complains of pain and tenderness in an injured area or the loss of normal use of an extremity, immobilize the area with a simple splint or sling, and see a physician or go to a hospital emergency room for treatment.

In many cases it is impossible to distinguish between a sprain and a fracture without an X ray. A sprain is an injury to the ligaments and tendons around a joint. A fracture, on the other hand, is a break in the bone: a complete fracture is one in which the break is total and the two broken parts separate from one another; an incomplete fracture is more like a crack and does not extend all the way across the bone.

If the victim has very minor symptoms and you suspect it's just a mild sprain, call a physician for advice. Usually, aspirin or an aspirin substitute, rest, elevation of the affected extremity, and ice packs are the suggested treatments for the first 24 hours. On the days following the injury, hot moist packs and warm baths are often helpful. Resting the limb will speed recovery; using it will prolong it.

When you think that there are several broken bones, or when the skull, neck, back, pelvis, or thigh may be broken, call an ambulance service to transport the victim to the hospital. In the meantime, move him as little as possible. If there is bleeding, elevate the injured limb above the level of his heart, using a sling or pillows; and apply ice packs to areas of swelling. If there are open wounds, cover them with sterile or clean dressings. If bone has broken through the skin, do *not* try to push it back in; this could cause a severe infection. If there is deformity, immobilize the extremity in the position it is found.

If you're not sure about the nature of the injury, call a physician or go to a hospital emergency room in the following situations: if there is pain localized to a particular joint or bone; if there is deformity around the injured area (compare it with the other side of the body); if there is black and blue discoloration, swelling, or tenderness over the bone or joint; if the victim is unable to move, use, or feel the part or if he is trying to protect it.

SLINGS AND SPLINTS

Slings and splints are used to immobilize an injured bone or joint so as to prevent further damage and to relieve pain. The idea is to secure the injured part to a firm object. The ends of the splint should extend beyond the injured area, to immobilize the joints above and below the injury.

ARM SLING

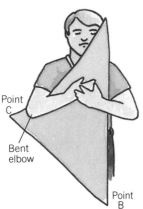

Point C

Bent elbow

Point B

1. Make a triangular piece of cloth with two sides measuring 36 to 40 inches and one side about 55 inches. (Sling cloths can also be purchased.) Place arm on cloth as shown above.

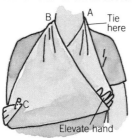

B A Tie here

B C

Elevate hand

2. Tie and pin the sling as illustrated above, making sure that the hand is elevated.

FINGER

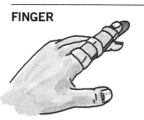

Use a flat piece of wood, such as a wooden coffee stirrer or tongue depressor, as a splint. Secure the splint to the finger with strips of cloth or tape.

FOREARM OR WRIST

1. Make a splint of a section of newspaper, a piece of wood, or any stiff object that's handy. Pad it with a towel. Place forearm or wrist at a slight right angle across the person's chest, with the palm facing toward the chest and the thumb pointing upward.

2. Tie the splint in place with strips of cloth above and below the break. Support the injury with a sling tied around the neck so that the fingers are slightly higher than the elbow.

ANKLE OR FOOT

Remove the victim's shoe. Mold a pillow or rolled blanket around the leg from the calf to the foot. Secure the pillow or blanket with strips of cloth.

UPPER ARM

1. Put some light padding in the victim's armpit. Place the victim's arm at his side with his lower arm at a right angle across his chest. Attach a splint to the outside of the upper arm with strips of cloth, tying it in place above and below the break.

2. Support the lower arm with a sling tied around the neck, and bind the upper arm to the victim's chest, tying the binding in place under his opposite arm.

LEG

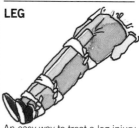

An easy way to treat a leg injury is to splint the injured leg to the uninjured leg. Immobilize the injured leg in the position in which it is found and place padding between it and the other leg. Tie the injured leg to the other leg in several places, but not directly over the break.

To get relief from the terrible itching beneath a cast, blow air or baby powder down inside it with a hair dryer. Do not stick pencils or coat hangers down the cast. Your skin is very sensitive and can easily become infected.

SPRAINS AND STRAINS

You can easily tell the difference between a sprain and a strain by looking for swelling and discoloration. A sprain will have both.

To reduce the pain and swelling of a sprain or strain, apply an ice pack. Then support the injured area with a bandage and try not to use it for a day or two.

PREVENTING INSECT BITES AND STINGS

Most mosquitoes bite early in the morning and 1 to 2 hours after sunset. Stay inside or use the suggested precautions at those times.

Apply insect repellent before going into a mosquito-infested area. Head for a breezy spot—it's much harder for mosquitoes to find you when the wind is blowing.

If you're the person mosquitoes seek out in a crowd, even when you're wearing insect repellent, it could be because of something else on your skin. Suntan products, perfumes, and colognes, as well as scented soaps, lotions, and shampoos, all increase your chances of being bitten. Some products—for example, deodorants, shaving lotions, and hair sprays—may actually *attract* the pesky insects.

Favor light colors such as white, light green, tan, and khaki.

Wear long sleeves and pants and socks and shoes outdoors—and, as much as possible, keep from looking or smelling like a flower to insects. That is, make every effort not to wear floral prints, bright colors, or scented products. Also avoid floppy clothing, which may entangle insects.

INSECT STINGS

Remove a stinger with tweezers or scrape across the skin with a knife or razor blade. Try not to squeeze or press down against the stinger, which will expel more venom into the victim. Wash the area with soap and cold water; then cover it with sterile gauze and attach it with adhesive tape.

If there is swelling, apply ice or a cold compress. Keep the stung area elevated above the heart, using a sling for a hand or forearm or a pillow for a foot or leg. Some redness and swelling around the sting is normal and should begin to diminish within a few days.

Insect stings become dangerous when the victim has an allergic reaction. The symptoms of such a reaction are headache, weakness, general itching, hives, wheezing, difficulty in breathing, or loss of consciousness. If any of these develop, or if the victim has had a serious reaction in the past, call 911, if your area is served by this emergency number, an ambulance, or get the victim to a hospital.

If you encounter a bee or some other stinging insect, don't swat at it—just try to move away slowly and calmly. Striking out at the insect in alarm may simply excite its attack.

If an insect gets trapped in the car, stop the car and open the windows and doors so that the insect can fly out.

ALLERGIC REACTIONS

Insect bites and stings may cause serious allergic reactions. If you or someone in your family is subject to them, have your physician prescribe an insect-bite medicine and carry it with you at all times.

If you have had a serious reaction to an insect sting, ask your doctor about desensitization treatments. They can substantially decrease your risk.

There's always a first, unexpected time, so if you do get an allergic reaction to a bite—for example, difficulty in breathing, hives, or perhaps a brief loss of consciousness—call a doctor or the local emergency medical service immediately or go to the hospital.

RELIEVING DISCOMFORT

No matter which biting insect—mosquito, blackfly, horsefly, and so on—has bitten you, wash the affected area with soap and cold water. Cold compresses and elevation will ease the swelling; calamine lotion or an anesthetic ointment will relieve the itching.

Scratching an itchy bite can lead to infection. If you have a number of bites and feel general discomfort, contact a physician.

To ease the stinging discomfort, make a paste of ¼ tablespoon meat tenderizer and 1 to 2 teaspoons water. Rub the paste into the stung area as soon as possible after the sting. Repeat in an hour if it still stings. The tenderizer contains papase, an enzyme that can break down insect venoms, making them harmless.

An often effective, inexpensive remedy for itchy mosquito bites is a dab of ammonia or vinegar.

TICKS

Do not handle a tick with bare hands; shield them with rubber gloves, a tissue, or paper towel.

Contrary to folk wisdom, a red-hot match won't help loosen the grip of a tick. This tiny parasite fastens itself to the skin by its teeth and, with a probe, sucks blood into its body. To remove it, grasp the tick's mouth parts or head region as close to the skin as possible with curved forceps or tweezers. Pull steadily; avoid jerking or twisting the tick, and make sure that none of its parts remain in the skin.

After the tick has been removed, disinfect the bite with alcohol and wash your hands carefully with soap and warm water. In the next few days, watch for signs of infection (see p.322).

If you succeed in removing the body but not the head of the tick, see a physician as soon as possible; he may have to remove the head with a small incision.

Do not crush the tick. Its body fluids may contain infectious materials. Put it in a container of alcohol or flush it down the toilet.

If the victim develops a fever, rash, stiff neck, or pain or swelling in the joints, contact a physician.

ANIMAL BITES

A pet whose immunizations are up to date is unlikely to have rabies. However, if it bites someone, and the attack was unprovoked, arrange for the animal to be observed for the next 10 days to make sure that it doesn't develop rabies.

If the bite was by a dog or a cat, if the animal is being reliably observed for sickness by its owner, and if its immunizations are up to date, antirabies injections won't be needed by the victim as long as the animal stays healthy.

Any bite by an animal other than a pet dog or cat requires consultation with a physician or the local health department as to whether or not the use of antirabies vaccine will be required.

POISONOUS SNAKES

Learn beforehand if poisonous snakes live in areas where you travel. Show your children pictures of them so that they can identify and avoid them.

The snake-bite kits sold in camping stores are for wilderness travel and other situations where medical help can't reach the victim in an hour or two. Use them only under such circumstances. If you carry one, read the instructions before you begin a trip.

TREATING ANIMAL AND HUMAN BITES

Treat all bites, regardless of source, very carefully—there is always the danger that they will become infected. (Human bites are among the worst.)

Hold the bite under cool or tepid running water for 5 to 10 minutes. Then wash the bite carefully with soap and water and rinse. Pat it gently but firmly with a sterile gauze pad to remove any remaining debris. If there are other particles in the wound, remove them with sterile tweezers (see p.323) or a cotton swab. Run water over the bite for another 5 minutes; then dry the area. If the bleeding still hasn't stopped, apply direct pressure to the bite and elevate it. Then spray it with a nonadherent dressing and

apply a sterile gauze pad attached with adhesive tape. Elevate the bite above the level of the heart for about 8 hours.

Check if the victim has had a tetanus shot within the last 10 years. If not, or in any of the following circumstances, see a physician: if the tissue below the skin has been exposed by the bite; if the bite is over a joint; if you spot any of the signs of infection (see p.322); or if it was a wild-animal bite.

If you suspect that a rabid animal made a bite, go immediately to a hospital for treatment—home cleansing of the wound, no matter how thorough, will not protect against rabies. If untreated, rabies is usually fatal.

TREATING SNAKE BITES

If there are poisonous snakes in an area, and someone is bitten by a snake, first get him away from the snake so that he is not bitten again. If a long stick is handy, kill the snake with a blow to the head; keep the carcass for identification. But don't waste time chasing it if you fail to kill it.

Assume that the snake is venomous unless you are absolutely certain that it isn't. Keep the victim calm and still, either sitting or lying down. Remove all bracelets and rings close to the bite. Run water over the bite and immobilize the bitten area by splinting it (p.326). If possible, pack the bite in ice to delay the spread of the venom. Call 911 if the area has this number. Otherwise call a doctor or get the victim to a hospital immediately. If the bite is on the foot, carry the victim if possible—he shouldn't put weight on a bitten foot unless it is unavoidable.

If you think that it will be a couple of hours before you can get help, place a constricting band of cloth or rope 2 inches above the fang mark—that is, be-tween the heart and the fang mark—or 2 inches above the swelling if it has begun. Do not make the band tight—you should be able to slip one finger between it and the skin. If the flesh swells, keep moving the band so that it stays 2 inches above the swelling. If there is no swelling, loosen and then retighten the band every 15 to 30 minutes. Meanwhile, give the victim fluids to drink, but no alcohol.

If the snake is poisonous and did in fact deliver venom, obvious symptoms will usually develop: pain; bruising and swelling around the bite; difficulty in swallowing; blurry vision; nausea, vomiting, and diarrhea, seizures or convulsions; slurred speech; bizarre behavior. If you haven't taken the victim to a hospital, these are signals to do so immediately.

If you have killed the snake, bring it with you for identification. Be careful; even a dead snake can bite from reflex.

If you're certain that the bite was delivered by a nonvenomous snake, treat it as described on pp.322–323.

IDENTIFYING POISONOUS AND NONPOISONOUS SNAKES

Most of the poisonous snakes in North America are pit vipers. There are only three Canadian types—massasauga, prairie and timber rattlesnakes. In the United States, the group includes rattlesnakes, cottonmouths, and copperheads. All these snakes have arrow-shaped heads and indentations between their slitlike eyes. Of course, rattlesnakes also have a rattle at the tip of their tails.

The deadliest American snakes are coral snakes, which are prevalent from North Carolina to California. They have wide bands of red and black separated by narrow rings of bright yellow encircling their bodies. Coral snakes have blunt heads with round eyes and black snouts; they have nonvenomous imitators. Nonpoisonous snakes generally have egg-shaped heads and round pupils.

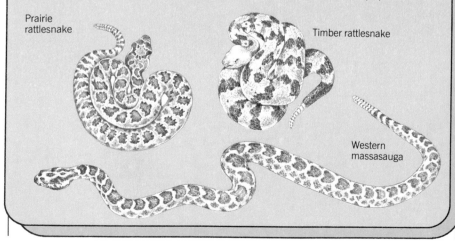

Prairie rattlesnake

Timber rattlesnake

Western massasauga

If you're walking in an area infested by poisonous snakes, wear heavy, high-topped hiking boots, long pants, and leather gloves. In rocky terrain, be on the watch for rock ledges above and below your path where snakes may lie sunning themselves. Make it a rule never to put a hand or a foot on a surface you can't see.

SUNBURN

When skin turns red or brown, it's a clear sign of damage by the sun's radiation. Excessive tanning leads to degeneration of the skin and may cause skin cancer. Weigh these effects against the cosmetic benefits.

If you must tan, do it slowly. A half an hour before you go into the sun, apply a sunscreen; check its sun protection factor (SPF) on the label—the higher the number, the more protection you'll get. A warm shower and vigorous drying with a towel before application will aid penetration through the skin's pores.

Avoid being in the sun from 10 in the morning to 2 in the afternoon (11 to 3 during daylight saving time) when the ultraviolet rays—the ones that do the most damage—are the strongest.

To get relief from a sunburn, apply compresses of ice-cold water, milk and water, or Burow's solution for 10 minutes every few hours. To reduce inflammation and itching, use an anti-inflammatory cream after the compresses. Aspirin or a similar painkiller may also help somewhat. A doctor may prescribe stronger medication for a bad burn. If your arms or legs are swollen, elevate them. If any of the signs of infection develop (see p.322), call a physician.

For a severe sunburn, apply ice-cold water compresses frequently for the first 6 to 10 hours, take aspirin or a similar painkiller to relieve pain and inhibit inflammation, and consult a physician.

After the sunburn pain is gone and dryness and itching develop, use a moisturizing cream or lotion or apply an anti-inflammatory cream after bathing. Stay out of the sun until all evidence of the burn, including peeling and flaking, has disappeared. When returning to the sun, apply a strong sunblock (SPF 15 or higher).

BURNS

When someone's clothing or hair catches fire, smother the flames with whatever is at hand. If this doesn't work, roll the victim on the floor or the ground. Do not let him run. If you catch fire, wrap yourself in a blanket or coat or roll on the floor or the ground.

FIRST-, SECOND-, AND THIRD-DEGREE BURNS

The key to initially treating a burn is determining its degree of severity.

1. A first-degree burn is red and hot. There are no blisters, but there may be slight swelling because of the accumulation of fluid beneath the skin. The burn is very painful, which is a good sign because it indicates that the burn is superficial and the nerves are not damaged. First-degree burns heal on their own. (An ordinary sunburn is a first-degree burn.)

2. A second-degree burn is more severe and is also painful. It is red and blotchy. The skin is moist, swollen, and probably blistered. The blisters should *not* be popped. (A bad sunburn is a second-degree burn.)

3. A third-degree burn is the most severe. It is deep, involving the full thickness of the skin. The skin may be from white to black in color, or it may be charred; it may appear waxy and stiff. The victim usually has no feeling at all in the burned area.

TREATING A FIRST- OR SECOND-DEGREE BURN

If the burn is caused by a chemical, see p.339. If not, hold the burn under cold running water for 15 to 30 minutes or immerse the burned area in a basin of very cold water (*not* ice water) for the same amount of time. Gently wash it with a mild soap and rinse it thoroughly. After cleansing, try to keep the burn site elevated above the level of the heart.

You can leave the burn site uncovered unless it's likely to get dirty or cause pain when it rubs against clothing. In that case, spray on a nonadherent dressing and cover with a sterile nonadherent pad attached with tape. Change the dressing daily. Keep the burn site elevated when possible. If there's pain, aspirin or a similar painkiller may help.

Don't pop the blisters; burn blisters will burst on their own in a few days. Remove the dead skin with a clean washcloth and soap or with sterilized tweezers (p.323) and cuticle scissors.

Watch for signs of infection (see p.322). If one develops, contact a doctor. If the burn becomes encrusted, it may be infected.

Extensive blistering should be seen by a physician. Also see the doctor if the burn is more than 2 to 3 inches in diameter; the burn is on the face; there is evidence of burning around the mouth or nose, such as singed beard, nasal hairs, or eyelashes; the victim is coughing sooty or bloody sputum; the victim is hoarse or is having trouble breathing; the burn is over a joint; the burn is in, on, or around the armpits, groin, rectum, or between the fingers and toes. Check if the victim has had a tetanus shot in the last 10 years. All burns caused by electricity, including lightning, need evaluation by a physician.

TREATING A THIRD-DEGREE BURN

Cover the burn with a dry, sterile dressing or with a clean sheet or towel, a sanitary pad, or a diaper. Do *not* hold the burn under cold or icy water. Call your doctor or take the victim to a hospital immediately.

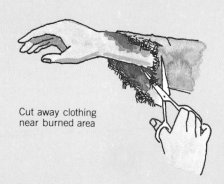

Cut away clothing near burned area

Hold burn under cold running water

Lightly bandage burned area

Do not remove dry, burned clothing or any clothing that is stuck to a burn. Remove clothing that has been soaked in hot fat or boiling water immediately.

Take off all rings, bracelets, or any unburned clothing that could impede circulation to or away from the burned tissue.

Do not apply ointments, such as petroleum jelly, butter, or anything gooey to a burn. Do not cover it with anything fluffy such as cotton that will stick to it.

To reduce the inflammation and pain resulting from a mild burn, apply *very* cold water, but not icy, compresses immediately and frequently. Follow with applications of an over-the-counter anti-inflammatory cream. If there is any infection, consult a physician.

Any second-degree burn that involves more than 2 or 3 inches of skin is extensive and should be seen by a physician. Also any second degree burn on the face or hands should be seen by a physician to ensure there is no disfigurement or loss of function.

If you burn your tongue with a hot drink or food, a few grains of sugar sprinkled on the site can sweetly undo the misery. Icy cold water works too.

Avoid exposing burned areas to the sun. If the area is not easily covered, apply a strong sunblock (SPF 15).

HEAT EMERGENCIES

Make every effort to avoid overexertion in hot, humid weather. If you must work in heat, take frequent breaks out of the sun and drink lots of water and other non-alcoholic liquids.

Wear light clothes in hot weather and a lightweight hat when you are in the sun. Try to avoid being in the direct sun.

If your vision becomes blurry or you feel dizzy, nauseous, or weak, lie down in the shade right away and drink cool fruit juices or plain water (*not* coffee, tea, or alcoholic beverages).

You are more susceptible to heat emergencies if you are obese; have heart disease, diabetes, or a central nervous system disorder; are taking certain types of medications (ask your doctor or pharmacist about them); are healthy but fatigued.

COLD TEMPERATURES

In cold weather, someone who has had a major accident loses body heat quickly. Keep the victim well covered and place an insulating material beneath him.

Don't stay outdoors until you become numb. (Victims of hypothermia may not even notice the symptoms.) Remember that wind and water only enhance the cold.

When you drive in bad weather, carry protective clothing, sand (for traction), and a shovel. For a long trip, add sleeping bags, a flashlight, emergency food and water.

When going out in the cold, wear a hat and gloves and several layers of clothing, since air caught between the layers acts as insulation. Change out of wet clothing as soon as possible.

If you are going outside for any length of time, wear thermal underwear and two pairs of socks (at least one pair woolen); make sure your boots cover your ankles; wear mittens over light gloves and a ski mask to protect your face from the wind.

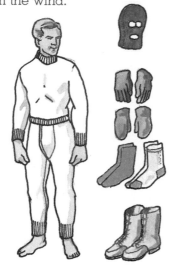

Fuel your body with food, especially carbohydrates, and don't drink alcohol; it dilates blood vessels and leads to a loss of heat. And don't smoke; smoking decreases the flow of blood to the extremities, where you often feel the cold the most.

Measures you should *not* take for frostbite: never rub or massage a frostbitten area; never rub frostbite with snow or ice; never cover the area with ointment or anything gooey. If you are outdoors and sense frostbite developing in a foot or leg, avoid walking on it if you can. If you suspect you have frostbite, don't smoke.

EYE INJURY

If you receive a blow that gives you a black eye, cover your eye with a cold compress and make

REMOVING A FOREIGN BODY FROM THE EYE

If you can't remove a foreign body from the eye easily, call a doctor. If you have succeeded in removing the object but you then experience blurred vision, discomfort, or pain, by all means call a doctor. Keep your eye closed until you get to the doctor; this will minimize discomfort and prevent additional damage to the eye.

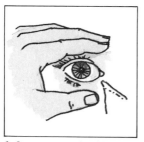

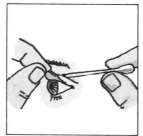

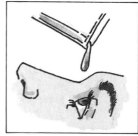

1. Suppose your daughter complains of something in her eye. Ask her to sit under a good light. While you gently pull the lower lid, have her look straight up, then as far to the left as she can, then as far to the right. If there's a foreign body—and there isn't always—you should be able to see it. Remove it with the corner of a clean cloth or tissue.

2. Sometimes the foreign body catches under the upper eyelid. Hold a cotton swab or similar object on the lid and roll the lid up over it. If you can see the particle in the eye or on the upper lid, gently remove it with a cotton swab or the tip of a piece of clean cloth or tissue. Proceed very cautiously.

3. Another way to remove the foreign body is to hold a large glass of tepid water a few inches above the eye and slowly pour the water over the eye. Or fill a medicine dropper with water and squeeze the dropper over the eye to flush out the object from the eye.

an appointment with a physician so that he can determine if there's further damage.

If a splinter or some other sharp object pierces an eye—a very rare occurrence—don't pull it out. Cover the eye and the object with a paper cup, or bend a piece of sturdy paper into a cone; tape this protective covering in place. Then take the victim to a hospital emergency room.

If someone gets a poison or a chemical in his eye, flush it out immediately. Either hold his head under running lukewarm water or fill a pitcher with lukewarm water, hold it a few inches above the eye and pour continuously for 15 minutes, refilling the pitcher as necessary. *Then* call 911, if available in your area, or a physician. Do not call before you irrigate; permanent damage can be done in the time it takes to make the call.

REMOVAL OF FOREIGN OBJECTS

Obey this principle—don't try to remove an object from an ear or the nose on your own if you can't see it. Now's the time to seek medical attention.

If your child sticks a bean or a bead into his ear or nose, don't try to remove it. Take the child to a physician right away.

REMOVING RINGS FROM FINGERS

If a ring is stuck on a finger, place your ring hand in a bowl of ice water. Soak your hand until the chill of the water contracts the ring finger enough so that the ring slips off.

Another method is to apply ice to the finger for 10 to 15 minutes and elevate it above the level of the heart. Then massage the finger, working from the tip to the hand, trying to push the fluid from the finger back into your hand.

If ice fails, slip one end of a 3-foot piece of string or waxed dental floss under the ring. You may need a toothpick to help get the string under the ring. Leave the end of the string lying loose on the back of the hand. Wrap the remaining string tightly around the finger on the other side of the ring until you reach the nail. Then pull the loose end of the string toward the fingertip. As you pull, the string will unwind. It should have compressed your finger so that the ring will slide off easily.

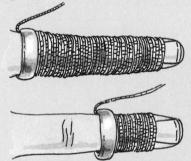

Caution: The tight string can stop circulation to your finger if the string is left in place for more than just a few seconds.

When using tweezers to remove an object from ear or nose, push the tips only as far as you can see. Otherwise, you could push the object in deeper, damage unseen tissue, or puncture the eardrum.

Don't try to remove an object by blowing your nose vigorously. If the object can't be withdrawn easily, see a physician.

If a child gets a hand stuck in a glass jar, a safe way to free it is to wrap cloth or cardboard around the child's wrist for protection, then submerge the hand and jar in a bucket of water. Using a hammer you can easily control, tap the jar smartly above its base. Because glass will break but not shatter under water, you should be able to remove the jar without injuring the child.

REMOVING A FISHHOOK

If a fishhook is implanted but the barb is still showing, pull it out the way it went in.

If the hook is near the surface of the skin and the barb is implanted, you still may be able to gently rotate it back.

If that doesn't work, rub ice over the spot where the hook is caught until sensation dulls. Then push the hook so that the barb pops up through the skin. Cut the barb with wire cutters and pull the shank out the other way.

Cleanse the area carefully with soap and water and hold the wound under cool running water for 5 to 10 minutes. Apply an antiseptic such as hydrogen peroxide. If the wound continues to bleed, apply pressure to the area with a clean cloth and elevate it. When the bleeding stops, bandage the wound. Check to see if the victim has had a tetanus shot in the last 10 years. In the days following the injury, watch for signs of infection (see p.322).

If a hook is deeply embedded, or if it catches an eye or some other sensitive part of the body, do not treat it yourself. Go to a hospital emergency room.

SPLINTERS

When you know that you have a splinter but you can't see it, place a piece of adhesive tape over the sore spot; then pull up straight and sideways to lift the splinter out. This simple technique won't always work, but it's worth a try.

If no part of the splinter projects from the skin, put an ice cube over the area to anesthetize it. Then wash the skin with soap and water. Using a flame-sterilized pin or needle, slit the skin just over the end of the splinter and lift it up; then pull the splinter out with clean tweezers or your fingernails. Wash the wound again and cover it with a sterile bandage.

Look carefully at the wound. If you think that any part of the splinter remains lodged deep in the skin, have a physician look at it.

SWALLOWED POISON

Be prepared for poisoning—keep on hand ipecac syrup (a safe, effective vomiting inducer) and the phone number of the nearest hospital emergency department or poison information center.

CALLING THE POISON INFORMATION CENTER

If someone has swallowed poison, immediately take the first-aid measures described below. Then call the poison information center nearest you. In many areas you can do so simply by dialing 911. Be prepared to provide these details:

1. If the victim is a child, his age and weight.

2. What the victim swallowed. Look around for spilled liquids, an open pill bottle, parts of a plant. Keep anything you find for analysis by medical personnel.

3. If you know what the poison is, take the container to the phone. How much did the victim take? It's often hard to be sure about this, but the center will suggest ways.

4. An estimate of how long ago he swallowed the poison.

5. The symptoms. If he is old enough to talk, ask him how he feels. Ask where it hurts. Look for signs of headache, a weak pulse, difficulty in seeing, rapid swallowing, abnormal breathing, vomiting or diarrhea, chest or abdominal pain, a rash or spots on the skin, hot skin or dry mouth, restlessness, weakness, a lack of response when you talk to or touch him, irritability, euphoria, or excitation. Corrosive chemicals burn the lips. Petroleum products can be identified by smell. If he vomits, look for pill fragments. Note the color of the vomit; look for blood in it. If there is a bowel movement, note its color.

This isn't the time to be squeamish—a life could be at stake. The poison information center will give you instructions. Follow them exactly.

Keep all products in their original containers (never transfer inedibles, such as household cleaning products, into food or beverage containers), and store all inedibles, such as cleaning products, out of sight and out of reach of children. Secure all medicines in a locked cabinet.

It's best not to use over-the-counter antidotes. They may be ineffective or harmful. If an antidote is necessary, follow the instructions of your local poison information center or hospital emergency department.

Do not take medicine while your children are watching; they love to imitate their parents. If you discuss medicine with children, be honest as to its purpose. Never refer to children's medicines (or any medicines for that matter) as candy and avoid giving candy-flavored children's medications, such as vitamins or aspirin, whenever possible.

ORAL POISONING

If a person who has swallowed poison is unconscious, has no pulse, or is not breathing, call 911 or the nearest hospital emergency department immediately. If you're trained, begin cardiopulmonary resuscitation (CPR) right away. If the person has a pulse but is not breathing, which often is the case after an overdose, give mouth-to-mouth resuscitation.

In all other cases, call the poison information center right away, if possible by dialing 911. The center may tell you to induce vomiting. Induce vomiting only if you are told to do so, since in some cases, it could be dangerous. This is best done with ipecac syrup. Give the prescribed dosage: usually 1 tablespoon for a child, 2 for an adult. Then have the victim drink several glasses of water. If possible, have him walk around the room. Keep a basin handy or have him stay near a bathroom. If the victim doesn't vomit within 15 to 20 minutes, put your finger in his mouth and touch the back of his throat. If this doesn't induce vomiting, give him more ipecac syrup and repeat the procedure.

If the poison information professionals have told you to handle the poisoning at home, someone will usually call back later to check on the victim. You can ask follow-up questions then.

FOOD POISONING

Contaminated food can cause nausea, vomiting, and diarrhea. This so-called food poisoning will usually resolve itself spontaneously within 24 hours without medical treatment. It's important not to become dehydrated during that time; make an effort to drink lots of fluids, beginning with water and noncaffeinated sodas for the first 12 hours and gradually adding juices, broth, and bland solid foods over the next day or so.

Call your doctor if food poisoning occurs in a child younger than 3, if it lasts longer than 2 days, if watery diarrhea occurs every 10 to 15 minutes, if it contains blood or mucus, or if abdominal pain or fever is constant.

To prevent food poisoning, it is wise to take the following precautions.

1. Wash your hands thoroughly before handling food.

2. Cook food to 212° F to kill most surface bacteria.

3. Thaw frozen meat before you cook it, especially chicken and turkey. Once meat has thawed, don't refreeze it.

4. Serve cooked food immediately or else refrigerate it.

5. On picnics, avoid foods that nourish bacteria, such as custards, cream fillings, mayonnaise, and bologna.

6. Smell the food first—if it doesn't smell right, don't eat it.

7. When canning foods, follow the instructions to the letter.

If you find medicine in an unmarked container, discard it immediately by flushing the contents down the toilet.

When taking medicine during the night, always turn on the light so that you can read the label and be certain you're taking the right medicine and dosage.

If you are interrupted while taking medicine, take it with you or put it away. It only takes a child seconds to get into it.

POISONOUS PLANTS

When walking or working near an area where you suspect poisonous plants grow, wear boots, long pants, and a long-sleeved shirt. Wear work gloves if you're weeding, pruning, clearing, or cutting wood in such areas.

Learn to recognize—and avoid—the three most common poisonous plants: poison ivy, poison oak,

and poison sumac. If you are allergic to any one of them—and most people are—the slightest contact can cause an itchy, oozing rash, which can easily spread when scratched. The streaky red, bumpy rash generally appears within the first few days after exposure.

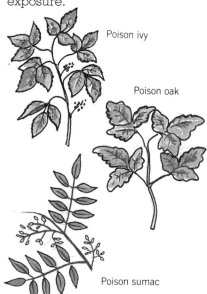

Poison ivy

Poison oak

Poison sumac

If you are sensitive to poison ivy and poison oak, you *may* avoid becoming affected by them if, within 1 to 3 minutes of exposure, you remove the irritating oil by washing the affected area with rubbing alcohol, or, if none is available, lots of water.

If you make contact with one of these plants, and such early washing is not feasible, then as soon as possible flood the site of exposure as well as its surrounding area with rubbing alcohol. Follow with a shower. Pat on calamine lotion to soothe the itch.

If your clothing or equipment has touched these plants, clean them as soon as possible with alcohol and then soap and water. Also, if your pets have been among these plants, clean them as well, since it is possible for them to carry the irritant and pass it along to you.

To relieve the burning and itching, apply cold-water or, preferably, cold Burow's solution compresses, for 10 minutes every few hours. After the compresses have air dried, apply calamine lotion. If these don't work, ask a physician for other recommendations.
Caution: Avoid lotions containing diphenhydramine hydrochloride, an antihistamine, and benzocaine, a topical anesthetic.

It goes without saying that you shouldn't scratch the itchy site. But you may not know that you should also avoid using hot water on the affected areas.

Rubbing the crushed leaves and stems of the orange- or yellow-flowered jewelweed over poison-ivy inflammation provides emergency relief in the woods.

Don't pop the blisters—the top of the blister serves as a sterile dressing. Open blisters are open wounds that are more susceptible to infection.

If a rash is extensive or very painful, call a physician. Watch out for any sign of infection (p.322).

SKIN POISONING

Certain household chemicals can be absorbed through the skin; among them are insecticides, weed killers, solvents, and strong cleaning agents.

If any of these get on your skin, immediately hold the affected area under lukewarm running water for 10 minutes. If poison has spilled on your clothing, remove the clothing before you do this.

Wash the area with soap and water and rinse thoroughly. Then call 911 or the poison information center. Follow the directions you are given. Do not try to neutralize acids by applying alkalis, or vice versa. This can lead to dangerous chemical reactions and severe burns.

INHALED POISON PRECAUTIONS

Protect yourself when using insect poisons, weed killers, solvents, and cleaning agents. Use liquids and sprays in well-ventilated areas. When spraying paints, pesticides, and similar preparations, wear a mask over your mouth and nose. It's also wise to cover your skin and wear goggles.

TREATING A VICTIM OF INHALED POISON

Before entering a poisoned atmosphere to rescue a person who has inhaled gas, fumes, or smoke, inhale and exhale two or three times; then take a deep breath and hold it. Carry or drag the victim out into the fresh air. Don't have the victim exert himself and don't stay for any length of time in the poisoned atmosphere yourself. After reaching the fresh air, call 911 or the nearest poison information center or a doctor and follow the advice given. Administer cardiopulmonary resuscitation (CPR) if you're trained and if it's needed. After recovery, make sure that the victim goes to a hospital for evaluation.

The most commonly inhaled poison is carbon monoxide, which is odorless and colorless. Suspect it if the victim is in a confined, semi-airtight space with automobile or other combustion fumes. The symptoms of carbon monoxide poisoning include headache, shortness of breath, nausea, vomiting, irritability, blurry vision, dizziness, odd behavior, and chest pain.

Don't mix the remains of different kinds of cleaning products or use two products simultaneously. The combination of chemicals, when inhaled, can be dangerous.

To prevent noxious gases from spreading throughout the house, have a warm-air heating system checked annually for leaks and blockages.

Vent fuel-burning space heaters to the outside, just as you would furnaces and wood stoves, to prevent carbon monoxide poisoning. In no circumstances should you use them in a closed room.

If you begin to feel headachy and drowsy while driving, pull over to the side of the road and stop the car. Get out and breathe fresh air. If you must continue driving, open a window. Have your exhaust system checked by a mechanic as soon as possible.

LOSS OF CONSCIOUSNESS AND THE RECOVERY POSITION

People who are unconscious or are losing consciousness need immediate medical help.

First, check to see if the victim is breathing and has a pulse (p.328). If not, begin cardiopulmonary resuscitation (CPR) immediately. Have someone call 911 and ask for an ambulance. If the person is a victim of a motor-vehicle accident, or if you suspect the victim has a head or neck injury, do not move him unless he vomits.

If or when the victim is breathing normally, loosen any tight clothing around his neck and chest and move him into the recovery position shown below. After treating an unconscious person, stay with him until medical help arrives.

1. Cross the victim's far arm over his chest and the far leg over his near one at the knee.

2. Grasp the victim's clothing and pull his body toward you.

3. Draw up and bend the upper arm and thigh as shown. Tilt the victim's head up. Lift the near arm up over the head.

FAINTING

If you feel faint, lie down flat with your legs raised. This is better than sitting and lowering your head between your knees. The feeling should pass quickly. If it doesn't, seek medical attention right away.

After a fainter revives, raise him very gradually to prevent another faint. Anyone who has recently fainted should see a doctor as soon as possible.

WATER ACCIDENTS

No matter how proficient you are, don't swim alone, especially in unknown waters. Make sure someone is nearby to help.

Never leave a small child alone in a bathtub or a wading pool— even for a few seconds.

Time is essential. Don't waste it by clearing water from a drowning victim's lungs. Provide mouth-to-mouth resuscitation right away.

ELECTRIC SHOCK

Before giving first aid, switch off the current at the breaker panel or fuse box or separate the victim from the current, using a clean, dry, nonconducting object such as a wooden broom handle. The rescuer must be on dry ground and should not touch the victim until the victim is free of the current.

If struck by lightning, a person is not "live" and can be given first aid immediately. The first thing to do is to check for pulse and breathing and to give cardiopulmonary resuscitation (CPR) if it is needed and if you are trained.

SHOCK CAUSED BY TRAUMA

Always suspect shock after any serious injury, especially if it's a major burn, a bleeding wound, or a fracture. A person in shock usually has pale, cold, and moist skin and a weak, rapid pulse. Her breathing may be shallow, and she may be thirsty. She may be anxious and may become drowsy, confused, and eventually unconscious. Someone in shock requires immediate medical attention.

To prevent or at least to minimize shock, take the following measures after all serious injuries.

1. Unless the victim is vomiting, lay her down and raise her legs about 1 foot above her head.

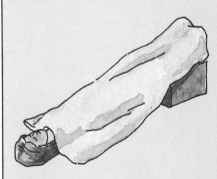

2. Loosen any tight clothing and wrap the victim in a coat or blanket.

3. Do not give the victim anything to eat or drink unless it will be several hours before medical help can reach you. In that case, give a conscious person water or lightly salted water, and reassure her that help is on the way.

AIDING A CHOKING PERSON

1. If a choking person's cough is weak, if he cannot speak and makes a high-pitched crowing sound when inhaling, there is a serious obstruction. Treat this like a total obstruction, which prevents all speech and breathing and makes the victim turn pale and then bluish around the mouth.

2. If the victim is standing, move behind him and wrap your arms around his waist. Make a fist with one hand, pressing your thumb knuckles against the victim's stomach. Grasp the fist with your other hand. Press your hands above the victim's navel, well below the ribs and the breastbone. Press your fist inward and upward with a quick thrust. Repeat this motion continuously until the foreign body is expelled or the victim becomes unconscious. If unconscious, repeat thrust 6 to 10 times, then check for the foreign body.

3. If an unconscious victim's airway still isn't open, reach into his mouth with one finger. Start along the cheek and sweep across the back of the mouth to see if you can dislodge the object. If you can, pull it out. If the airway remains blocked, give mouth-to-mouth resuscitation and repeat the 6 to 10 thrusts.

4. If the victim is seated, move behind his chair and wrap your arms around him and the chair. Apply the thrusts as described.

5. Thrusts to a pregnant woman or to someone who is obese, are delivered to the chest. Stand behind the choking victim with your arms directly under her armpits. Then clasp your hands, as described above, and press them to the middle of her breastbone. Deliver the same number of chest thrusts as you would abdominal thrusts.

6. If you start to choke and no one is around to help you, administer abdominal thrusts to yourself. Make a fist and place your other hand over it, as if you

were aiding someone else. Press your fist above the navel but below the breastbone. Thrust inward and upward toward your diaphragm with a quick motion, using both hands. Repeat until

the obstruction is cleared. Or use the edge of a firm object instead of your hands. Position yourself over a chair back, table, or something similar. Press your abdomen against it sharply so that the edge thrusts in and up toward the diaphragm.

7. For a child over 2 years old, give abdominal thrusts, as described. Modify the force of the thrusts according to the child's size. (In cases of severe or total obstruction, do not probe a child's mouth with your finger or turn him upside down and strike him on the back.)

8. Treat a child under 2 years old more cautiously. Drape the child over your arm or thigh (depending on his size); his abdomen should rest on your arm or thigh, while you support his head with your hand. Deliver four blows between the shoulder blades with the heel of your other hand.

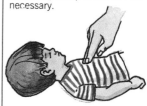

9. If this fails, hold him in your lap or have him lie on his back. Place two fingers on the breastbone and quickly press straight down. Repeat up to four times if necessary.

10. Look in the child's mouth and, if you see the obstruction, sweep it out. Then give mouth-to-mouth resuscitation.
Caution: Anyone who has received abdominal thrusts as a choking victim should see a physician as soon as possible.

CHOKING PRECAUTIONS

If you see someone choking, ask "Are you choking?" If the person can talk, or is able to cough forcefully, the obstruction is partial. Do not interfere; let him dislodge it himself by coughing.

When you're choking, you aren't able to speak. To alert others to help you, reach for your throat, around the voice box, with thumb and forefinger. This is the universal choking sign. Teach your children to use it.

If you are choking, stay with your companions so that they can assist you. If a dining companion is choking, don't let him leave the room. Many choking victims die in restaurant rest rooms.

Insist that a child stay still while eating. Running around with food or other objects in his mouth invites choking.

Keep swallowable objects away from the reach of small children and babies. Think like a child; look around your home for things that seem inviting to be put in the mouth, such as coins, bottle caps, and detachable parts of toys. Place them where they are inaccessible to children.

CARDIOPULMONARY ARREST

Cardiopulmonary arrest—when both the heart and lungs stop working—is the most life threatening of all emergencies. If a person's heartbeat and breathing don't restart within just a few minutes, the brain suffers permanent damage and death occurs.

Cardiopulmonary resuscitation (CPR) is a technique that can sometimes save the life of a person in cardiopulmonary arrest. The procedures involved are easy to learn. Instruction is available through the local branch of the St. John Ambulance. If you want to learn this vital skill, contact this organization.

THE SIGNS AND SYMPTOMS OF A HEART ATTACK

One of the first signs of a heart attack is a viselike pain in the middle of the chest. The pain may get worse and spread through the whole chest and down the left arm. The pain may also spread to both arms, shoulders, the back, neck, or jaw. A squeezing sensation in the abdomen may even be mistaken for indigestion. Pain may occur in any one or a combination of these areas. It could even go away and return later. Sweating, nausea, vomiting, or shortness of breath often accompany the pain.

Call 911 or a doctor at the first sign of any of these symptoms or go to an emergency room.

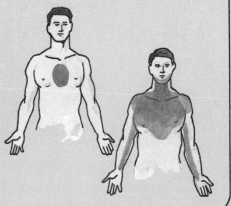

CHAPTER FIVE

FOOD & NUTRITION

Discover the secrets of eating wisely with these helpful meal-planning basics. And learn how to make life easier in the kitchen and your parties more enjoyable. . . .60 pages of invaluable food tips!

Healthy Eating
Page 345

Obtaining the basic nutrients through proper meal planning; ways to perk up meals; vitamins and minerals (their best sources and what they can do for you); staying thin; the best sources of starch and fiber; eating less cholesterol, fat, salt, and sugar; obtaining your daily protein requirements without meat; hints for the elderly.

Buying Food
Page 351

Getting organized before you go shopping; tips on couponing (plus pitfalls you should look out for); how supermarkets encourage you to buy; smart shopping; understanding food labels (comparing the ingredients, cost, and quality); buying fruits and vegetables in season when they are better tasting, more nutritious, and cheaper; buying fish and meat.

Storing Food
Page 355

Best ways of storing foods to avoid waste and maintain their quality; how to keep frozen food safe during a power outage or a freezer breakdown; useful storage-time charts for the refrigerator and freezer.

Preparing Food
Page 360

Hints to save you preparation time; step-by-step illustrations for cutting up chicken; filleting fish; kitchen utensils; weights and measures (with metrics); on-hand mixes for spur-of-the-moment main courses (hamburger-noodle skillet, chili con carne, pizza); breads (baking powder drop biscuits and pancakes); cakes (spice cake and chocolate cake).

Cooking
Page 376

Emergency substitutions when a recipe catches you short; instructions for making yogurt; how long to steam vegetables; enhancing food with the right herbs; roasting times for chicken and turkey; cooking times for the broiling, braising, and roasting of meats; step-by-step illustrations for carving meats and poultry; making a lattice-top pie; equivalents and yields for common ingredients; cooking during a power failure; quick, thrifty recipes.

Entertaining Tips & Etiquette
Page 392

Writing invitations; renting and borrowing equipment and furniture; hiring help; cocktail parties and easy hors d'oeuvres; handling the problem drinker; how to tell your guests when it's time to leave; party countdown (geting started weeks ahead); centerpieces and other decorations; how to arrange a buffet —plus menus; a formal place setting—plus menus; how to write place cards and menu cards; easy and attractive garnishes; party protocol for informal and formal affairs; special types of parties; parties and games for children.

Healthy Eating

GETTING THE NUTRIENTS

Eating a wide variety of foods daily from each of the Basic Four Food Groups—fruits and vegetables (4 servings); cereals, breads, and other grains (4 servings); milk and milk products (2 servings); and poultry, meat, fish, and eggs (2 servings)—will virtually ensure that your body gets the nutrients it needs. The key is in varying your food choices.

A small amount of protein goes a long way. For example, a 3-ounce pork chop, ½ cup cottage cheese, and 3 ounces of tuna (a total of 61 grams of protein) will supply a 170-pound man's daily need.

GUIDE TO VITAMIN-RICH FOODS

Vitamin	Function	Sources	Vitamin	Function	Sources
Vitamin A (Retinol)	Keeps skin and mucous membranes healthy and resistant to infection; prevents night blindness	Liver; eggs; cheese; butter; milk; yellow, orange, and dark-green vegetables (e.g. squash, carrots, spinach)	**Folacin (Folic acid)**	Helps form body proteins, genetic material, and red blood cells	Liver; kidneys; dark-green leafy vegetables; wheat germ; brewer's yeast; whole grains; enriched breads and cereals
B₁ (Thiamin)	Maintains appetite, digestive system, and nervous system; helps convert food to energy	Pork; liver; oysters; whole-grain and enriched breads; cereals; pasta; wheat germ; brewer's yeast	**Biotin**	Promotes fatty acid formation; releases energy from carbohydrates	Egg yolk; liver; kidneys; dark-green vegetables; milk; whole-grain breads and cereals. Made in intestinal tract
B₂ (Riboflavin)	Helps cells to use oxygen; keeps vision clear and skin smooth	Liver; kidneys; enriched breads; cereals; milk; dark-green leafy vegetables	**Vitamin C (Ascorbic acid)**	Maintains bones, teeth, blood vessels; forms collagen, which supports body structure	Citrus fruits; tomatoes; strawberries; melons; green peppers; potatoes; dark-green vegetables; cauliflower
Niacin	Maintains health of skin, digestive tract, and nervous system	Liver; poultry; meat; tuna; whole grains; enriched breads and cereals; nuts; legumes	**Vitamin D (Calciferol)**	Builds and maintains strong bones and teeth	Milk; egg yolk; liver; tuna; salmon. Made on skin in sunlight
B₆ (Pyridoxine)	Enables body to use proteins and fats; maintains red blood cells	Whole-grain cereals and breads; liver; legumes; wheat germ	**Vitamin E (Tocopherol)**	Prevents breakdown of cells and vitamins A and D	Vegetable oils; margarine; whole-grain cereals; bread; wheat germ; liver; dried beans; green leafy vegetables
B₁₂ (Cobalamin)	Builds genetic material, forms red blood cells, and operates nervous system	Liver; kidneys; meat; fish; eggs; milk; oysters	**Vitamin K**	Helps blood to clot normally	Green leafy vegetables; vegetables in cabbage family; milk. Made in intestinal tract
Pantothenic acid	Regulates energy metabolism	Liver; kidneys; whole grains; nuts; eggs; dark-green vegetables; yeast; many other foods			

A 60-pound child can obtain the daily requirement of protein with 2 cups of milk, 1 ounce of cheese, two slices of bread, and a baked potato (a total of 33 grams).

Four servings of grain products a day sounds like a lot? Try this: cereal for breakfast, a slice of bread with lunch, rice with dinner, and 3 rye wafers for a snack. Put two 1-inch cubes of hard cheese on those wafers for a serving of milk products.

To get four servings of fruits and vegetables, snack between meals on fresh fruit, raw vegetables, or juice; they're nonfattening too.

Choose whole-grain cereals and breads rather than refined ones. You'll get more fiber as well as B vitamins and minerals.

Cook vitamin-C-rich vegetables in as little water as possible or eat them raw—vitamin C is easily destroyed by cooking.

Romaine lettuce is greener than iceberg lettuce and has about three times as much vitamin C and about six times as much vitamin A as iceberg lettuce. A good point to remember is that the greener the vegetable, the higher it is in vitamins and minerals.

Potatoes boiled or baked whole in their skins retain nearly all their vitamins and minerals. Halving or peeling causes nutrient loss.

MINERALS YOUR BODY NEEDS

Minerals	Function	Sources
Calcium	Builds bones and teeth; helps blood to clot and nerves and muscles to act normal	Milk; cheese; dark-green vegetables; sardines; oysters; clams
Chromium	Works with insulin to metabolize glucose	Meats; whole-grain cereals
Copper	Works with iron to form hemoglobin	Liver; kidneys; shellfish; whole grains; legumes; nuts
Fluoride (Fluorine)	Helps maintain bone and tooth structure	Some drinking water; seafood; tea; milk; eggs
Iodine	Regulates growth and rate of metabolism; helps prevent goiter	Seafood; iodized salt
Iron	Maintains red-cell count in blood; carries oxygen from lungs to other parts of body	Liver; lean meats; legumes; whole grains; dark-green leafy vegetables; dark molasses; shrimp; oysters; dried fruits
Magnesium	Needed for bone structure, nerve and muscle activity, and energy release; regulates body temperature	Whole-grain cereals; green leafy vegetables; nuts; legumes, including soybeans
Manganese	Needed for normal bone structure, reproduction, and growth	Legumes; nuts; whole-grain cereals
Phosphorus	Builds bones and teeth	Milk; cheese; meat; liver; fish; poultry; grains; legumes; corn; nuts
Potassium	Regulates acid-base balance, body-water balance, and nerve function	Meat; milk; many fruits; cereals; legumes; vegetables
Sodium	Helps regulate acid-base balance, nerve functions, and water balance	Most foods except fruit
Zinc	Maintains growth, appetite, and digestion	Seafood (especially oysters); wheat germ

When cooking vegetables in water, leave them whole; they'll retain more vitamins and minerals. And they're much easier to chop or slice after they're cooked.

Almonds are good for you; 1 cup of them contains more calcium than 1 cup of skim milk. And they are high in fiber, too.

COMMON CALCIUM SOURCES*

Food	Amount of food	% of Recommended Nutrient Intake
Cheese, Swiss	45 g	54
Sardines, with bones, canned, drained	90 g	49
Cheese, cheddar	45 g	40.5
Skim milk	250 mL	39.5
Buttermilk	250 mL	37.5
Mozzarella	45 g	29
Yogurt, from partially skimmed milk	125 g	25
Spinach, cooked	125 g	22
Cheese, cottage, low-fat	250 mL	20
Ice cream, soft type	125 mL	18.5
Broccoli, cooked	250 mL	18
Turnips, cooked	250 ml	16
Rhubarb, cooked, sugar added	250 mL	13
Salmon, canned	100 mL	12.5
Ice cream, hard	125 mL	11.5

*Listed in descending order of calcium content. Recommended daily calcium intake is 800 mg.

People who regularly substitute caffeine-type beverages, such as coffee, tea, and cola, for milk are not only limiting their intake of calcium, they may be *losing* calcium as well. For example, the caffeine in 1 cup of coffee can cause 6 milligrams of calcium loss through the urine beyond the amount the body normally loses.

Although eggs contain a good deal of iron, this iron is poorly absorbed by the body and may interfere with the absorption of iron from other sources.

Cooking acidic foods, such as rhubarb, cranberries, tomato sauce, or applesauce made from Granny Smith or green apples in a cast-iron pot will add iron to that food, making it more nutritious.

PLANNING MEALS

Turn menu planning into a family project. Ask family members to list their favorite dishes, then compile menus using them. When given a chance to participate, people enjoy their meals more.

Perk up your dinners by serving your family a new dish each week if possible. Exchange recipes with your friends and neighbors; check food sections of magazines and newspapers. Try unfamiliar fruits and vegetables.

Change your meal pattern: instead of the same old routine—meat, potatoes, and vegetable for dinner every day—serve a hearty soup, an unusual casserole, or a main-dish salad.

Notice what your family enjoys at restaurants. Consult your cookbooks and try to duplicate the dishes at home.

Vary the shapes, colors, and textures of vegetables. For example, mashed potatoes make a nice contrast to Brussels sprouts, or green beans to carrots.

To add interest to a soft-textured meal, serve a crunchy vegetable salad or crisp bread.

Serve something other than rice or potatoes to accompany gravies and sauces. Try barley, bulgur (cracked wheat), or pasta in unusual shapes.

When serving leftover meat or fish, don't just reheat it. Instead, prepare it in a different form. For example, grind it and shape it into patties, dice it for casseroles, or slice it thin and add it to stir-fry dishes or to a white sauce.

KEEPING TRIM

Use cooked fruit or a thin smear of jam rather than syrup to sweeten pancakes and French toast.

Sautéed diced vegetables make a delicious low-calorie topping for pasta, baked potatoes, or rice.

Puréed vegetables make excellent low-fat sauces for fish, poultry, pasta, or vegetables.

Mix powdered salad dressings into plain yogurt instead of oil or sour cream. Or add buttermilk, cottage cheese, or tomato juice to the dressings. Use yogurt instead of sour cream for dips.

If you like your yogurt sweet, buy plain yogurt and add a teaspoon or two of preserves (now available without sugar or artificial sweeteners). You'll get fewer calories than in the sweetened commercial yogurts.

Pie lovers can save approximately 150 calories per serving by eating single-crust fruit cobblers instead of two-crust pies.

Eat slowly. Taste your food. Put down your knife and fork after every two or three bites. Make each meal last 20 or 30 minutes.

Postpone that second helping for about 20 minutes. You'll realize you don't need it, and you'll feel less hungry too.

Serve yourself on a small plate so that smaller portions will not look so skimpy.

THE LOW-FAT WAY

Your body needs only 1 tablespoon of dietary fat a day, but most people eat far more. Much of it is hidden in meats, cold cuts, pastries, other commercial baked goods, and such prepared foods as potato chips, French-fried potatoes, and frozen dinners.

To avoid saturated fats (the kind that clog your arteries), buy margarine that lists liquid oil as its first ingredient. The second ingredient should be partially hydrogenated vegetable oil.

Because they help to reduce the cholesterol levels in your blood, polyunsaturated or monounsaturated oils are the best choice for salads and for cooking. Safflower oil is the most polyunsaturated. Others in descending order are sunflower, soybean, corn, and sesame oil. Olive and peanut oils are monounsaturated.

Bottled salad dressings may be loaded with saturated oils and preservatives. Make your own by mixing 3 or 4 parts polyunsaturated vegetable oil, olive oil, yogurt, or buttermilk with 1 part vinegar or lemon juice, and seasonings.

Instead of frying, use low-fat cooking methods such as poaching, steaming, roasting, and broiling. After cooking, drain off as much fat as possible.

In place of high-fat gravy, serve broth. Instead of butter, season foods with lemon or lime juice, vinegar, spices, or herbs.

Because the yolk of one large egg contains a day's quota of cholesterol, limit yolks to three or four a week, including those in prepared and processed foods. However, you can only guess how much egg yolk is in such foods.

Eat as many egg whites as you wish. They're a fine low-calorie source of protein. Omit the yolks of hard-boiled eggs in salads.

In preparing eggs, give every other yolk to your dog. In other words, make your omelet with two whites and one yolk. Do the same with pancakes or French toast. You won't notice the difference and, if you do it occasionally, your dog will develop a beautiful, shiny coat.

SWEETS IN FOODS

Buy unsweetened cereals and add sliced fruit or raisins, instead of sugar. Although raisins have some sugar, they also provide vitamins, minerals and fiber.

Get in the habit of serving fruit—preferably fresh fruit—for dessert. A fresh fruit cup can't be beat for appearance and taste. If you must rely on canned or frozen fruit, look for brands packaged in water instead of sweetened syrup.

Read food labels for clues on sugar content. If the word *sugar, sucrose, glucose, maltose, dextrose, lactose, fructose,* or *syrup* appears first on the label, then sugar is the ingredient used in greatest quantity in this product.

Instead of buying cakes, pies, or cookies, make your own and cut the sugar in the recipe by a third or even a half.

Try satisfying your sweet tooth with dessert breads containing relatively little sugar. Add nourishing ingredients such as whole-wheat flour, oatmeal, nuts, raisins, and a fruit or a vegetable such as pumpkin, zucchini, cranberries, or carrots.

EATING ADEQUATE STARCH AND FIBER

Starchy foods are good sources of protein, vitamins, and minerals. Those at the top of the list are grains (wheat, oats, corn, and rice), products made from grains (flour, pasta, such as macaroni and noodles, bread, and breakfast cereals), potatoes, and dry beans and dry peas.

COMPLEMENTARY VEGETABLE PROTEINS: NUTRITIOUS COMBINATIONS

If you combine vegetable proteins in the same meal in any of the ways suggested below, you will obtain complete protein.

Rice with one or more of these:	Legumes* Soybeans Sesame seeds
Wheat with one or more of these:	Legumes* Soybeans Soybeans and sesame seeds or sunflower seeds
Legumes* with one or more of these:	Grains: Corn Rice Wheat Barley Oats Seeds, specifically: Sesame seeds Sunflower seeds

*Legumes include peanuts and all dried beans and peas. Beans and peas most commonly consumed are soybeans, black-eyed peas, kidney beans, navy beans, pinto beans, lima beans, and chick-peas.

Oatmeal made from steel-cut or rolled oats (not the instant variety) leads the pack in food value for hot cereals because oats contain the most protein of any of the commonly eaten grains.

349

When cooking a hot cereal, use skim milk as part or all of the liquid, and you'll greatly improve the nutritional value.

Raw fruits and vegetables have more useful fiber than those that have been peeled, cooked, puréed, or processed.

Drink lots of liquids when you eat foods containing fiber, or the fiber may be constipating instead of stimulating to your bowels.

Generally, coarse fiber is more effective than the same fiber finely ground. Look for the words *whole grain*, *whole wheat*, or *whole oats* when you buy breads, cereals, and crackers.

BEST SOURCES OF DIETARY FIBER

Food	% Fiber
Wheat bran	42.4
Bran cereal, 100%	30.1
Bran cereal, with raisins	20.5
Figs, dried	18.5
Wheat cereal, puffed	16.6
Popcorn, popped	16.5
Prunes, dried	16.1
Almonds	14.3
Wheat cereal, shredded	13.3
Crackers, rye	11.7
Crackers, whole wheat	11.1
Beans, kidney, cooked	10.4
Crackers, graham	10.1
Wheat germ	9.5
Beans, lima, cooked	9.3
Peanuts, roasted	9.3
Brazil nuts	9.0
Beans, white, cooked	8.8
Dates, dried	8.7
Peanut butter, smooth	7.6
Raspberries, red, raw	7.4
Pecans	7.2
Raisins, dried	6.8
Spinach, cooked	6.3
Blackberries, raw	6.2
Chick-peas, cooked	6.0
Bread, pumpernickel	5.8
Corn, sweet, cooked	5.7
Muffins, whole wheat	5.4
Walnuts	5.2
Peas, green, cooked	5.1
Bread, whole wheat	5.1
Cranberries, raw	4.2
Yams, cooked	3.9
Broccoli, cooked	3.8

SHAKING THE SALT HABIT

Go easy on such salty foods as potato chips, pretzels, salted nuts, popcorn, snack crackers, commercial frozen dinners, pickled foods, cured meats, canned tuna or crab, sauerkraut, steak sauce, soy sauce, and garlic salt.

Read labels on processed foods; often such foods contain sodium in forms other than table salt. Be aware of these ingredients: sodium nitrate, sodium bicarbonate (baking soda), monosodium glutamate (MSG), sodium benzoate, and sodium phosphate.

THE LATER YEARS

Although the elderly are less active and need less energy from food than young adults, their nutrient requirement is just as important. The one exception is iron: an elderly woman needs less than a young adult woman.

Select whitefish or white meat of poultry. Darker fish and the dark meat of poultry are much higher in fat. When eating red meat, be sure you trim the fat. Choose packages of ground meat that are marked "extra lean."

Drink skim milk often. The calcium and high-quality protein in milk are extremely beneficial. Even though bones may have stopped growing, the body needs calcium to prevent bone deterioration.

Eat high-fiber foods. If your teeth won't allow you to chew raw vegetables, eat generously of cooked ones. Many raw fruits, such as prunes and berries, are high in fiber and are still tender enough to chew easily.

Buying Food

GETTING ORGANIZED

You can save a lot of wandering up and down the aisles by organizing your shopping list according to the way the store is organized. Arrange your route so that you pick out fresh vegetables and fruits last; they won't be crushed by other items in the grocery cart.

Self-stick notepads, posted in your kitchen, make handy shopping reminders. Peel off the back paper from the pad, press the pad onto the wall at a convenient height, and hang a pencil or pen nearby. Peel off the sheets one by one when they're filled and take them to the store with you.

The back of an envelope is also a good place for jotting down what you need at the store. You'll have a handy pocket for redeemable coupons, receipts, and notes.

Check your local newspaper advertisements for special offers around which you can plan a meal. Not all of the items advertised as specials are good buys; when possible, it's a good idea to comparison shop among the ads.

Limit your food shopping to one trip per week if possible. The less time spent in the market, the less money you'll spend.

Don't make that one trip a week just before a meal, when you're feeling hungry. Everything you see will look good, and you'll end up buying unnecessary items.

COUPONING

A good way to accumulate a coupon inventory is to go through newspapers and store circulars and to check your pantry, utility closet, and medicine cabinet for products with coupons printed on boxes and labels. Clip every coupon you find, even those you don't intend to use; swap the unwanted ones to friends.

PITFALLS OF COUPONING

Redeeming coupons can slice big dollars from your grocery bills. But if you aren't careful, it can cost you money. Here's what to look out for.

1. Think twice before switching brands. There may be a significant saving between the new brand and your regular one, but your family may not like the product. Result? A waste of money.

2. Occasionally, you'll see coupons offering large deductions, say $1 off the regular price. Generally, these coupons are for an expensive food, such as an elaborate dessert. However, it may not be an item you would normally buy, especially if you have a large family to feed. Also, even with the coupon, it may cost more than your homemade cake.

3. Many foods that offer coupons are highly processed, expensive, and low in nutrients. You may pay a fancy price for foods that don't provide good nutrition.

4. Don't forget to look at the cost of the store brands. Even with price reductions by coupons, brand-name items may be more expensive than store brands.

5. Sometimes a tie-in offer gives you an item free or at a bargain price if you stock up on another product at a regular price. If the freebie isn't *exactly* what you want, it can take a large bite out of your week's budget, and it may never be used.

Take a few minutes to examine the packaging of various items on your shopping list. Whenever possible, select items that include coupons you can cut out and use later.

Always verify that your coupons are valid for Canada and show a Canadian redemption date.

A convenient system for organizing your coupons is to arrange them by product category, such as canned goods, cleaning products, and then alphabetize them in an accordion-fold check file. Another method is to sort them by expiration date instead of by category.

To ensure that your coupons will always be with you when needed, keep them in a small change purse that you can fit easily in your handbag or the car glove compartment.

Buying large quantities of an item is usually thrifty, but by using coupons, you may be able to get a better deal on the smaller size. When this is true, if you have more than one coupon, purchase several smaller packages rather than one large size.

To help speed things up at the checkout counter, use bright ink to underline the expiration dates on your coupons so that the cashier can find them easily.

SUPERMARKET STRATEGY

Try to leave the children at home. Many foods, such as candy, that appeal to children are placed on the shelves at their eye level.

Whenever possible, shop alone or entrust the task to the family member who is least likely to stray from your shopping list.

Try to avoid shopping when stores are crowded (just before weekends, for example). Stocks are often low at busy times and you have less chance to compare prices or read product labels.

If you need only a single item, get that item and head for the checkout counter. (The milk and meat departments are often toward the rear of the stores to tempt you into selecting many other items along your way.)

Be aware that the crackers and cookies at the ends of aisles and magazines, candy, and chewing gum at the checkout counters are there to tempt shoppers to make impulse purchases.

Look for less-known brands; they are often cheaper than the nationally advertised ones. The latter are usually shelved at an adult's eye level, the cheaper brands above and below them.

Look behind newly marked, higher-priced items at the front of a shelf. You may find a few of them still marked at the old price.

Reweigh marked items of produce and meat. If there is a discrepancy, point it out to the manager.

Try to unload your grocery cart completely before the checker starts totaling your bill. Watch the checkout process carefully for inadvertent errors. At home, review the register tape. If you find mistakes, save the tape and call the mistakes to the manager's attention the next time you're in the store.

CHOOSING WISELY

Do not buy damaged cans; their contents may be spoiled. When you choose packaged goods, be sure that any seal has not been opened or tampered with.

Don't throw away a spoiled product that you have just bought. Return it to the store for a refund.

Check the dates on perishable foods carefully and note that the

SEASONAL BUYING GUIDE

Fruits	Peak Season
Apples	September – March
Apricots	August – September
Blackberries	August – September
Blueberries	May – July
Cantaloupes	June – August
Cherries, sweet	June – July
Cranberries	September – December
Figs	June – October
Grapefruit	October – May (peak)
Melons	June – October
Nectarines	July – September
Peaches	July – September
Pears, Anjou	October – March
Pears, Bartlett	July – October
Persimmons	October – January
Pineapple	April – June (peak)
Plums	June – September
Pomegranates	September – November
Quinces	July – October
Raspberries	June – October
Rhubarb	February – July
Strawberries	May – July
Tangerines	November – March
Watermelons	June – September

Vegetables

Artichokes, globe	March – May
Asparagus	April – June
Beets	June – October
Broccoli	October – May
Brussels sprouts	September – November
Cauliflower	August – October
Celeriac	October – April
Corn	July – September
Endive, Belgian	November – April
Fennel	October – April
Kale	June – July
Leeks	July – December
Mustard greens	October – April
Okra	June – August
Parsnips	October – April
Peas	June – September
Radishes	March – July
Tomatoes	May – September

fresher ones usually are toward the back of the case.

RICE

Although converted rice is more expensive than polished white rice, the former contains more nutrients. Brown rice, which hasn't been processed, is even more nutritious but it takes longer to cook.

Don't waste money on packages of seasoned rice. Cook plain rice and add your own choice of herbs and spices.

DAIRY PRODUCTS

Save on cheese for grating and for use in recipes by asking for the low-priced ends at the delicatessen counter.

Use eggs within three weeks of purchase. Keep them refrigerated with the large end up, away from strongly flavored food.

Did you know that large, medium, and small eggs vary in price according to how plentiful they are? Generally, if there is no more than a 7-cent price spread per dozen eggs between one size and the next smaller size in the same grade, you'll get more for your money by buying the larger size.

To save money, buy plain cottage cheese and plain, unflavored yogurt and add fresh cut-up fruit or vegetables at home.

FISH

When purchasing fresh fish, make sure that the eyes are as clear and as bright as those of a live fish. Also, if the gills don't smell fresh, decomposition is well on its way.

FOOD LABELS AND WHAT THEY MEAN

Knowing how to read food labels, you can compare foods for ingredients, price, quality, and nutritive value and purchase the ones that best suit your needs.

All package labels must have the name of the foods, the weight of the content, and the name and address of the manufacturer, packer, or distributor.

According to Canadian law, the customer must be informed about the contents of food products. All processed foods containing two ingredients or more, either man-made or natural, must list the names on the label in descending order of predominance by weight. A single ingredient—for example, frozen vegetables or coffee beans—is exempt from this regulation.

For computerized checkout systems, many labels include a Universal Product Code symbol. This symbol of numbers and lines of varying widths and lengths registers the price of the food and updates the inventory of the stock.

Other symbols may also appear on the food label. An *R* means that the name adjoining it is a registered trademark. The letter *C* means that the label has been copyrighted. *K* or *U* inside a circle signifies that the food was prepared according to kosher standards. *Pareve*, a Yiddish term, assures the consumer that neither milk nor meat was used in the preparation of the food.

Two other markings that may appear on foods are grade marks (denoting the quality of the product, such as Canada A for eggs, and Canada 1 for butter and cheddar cheese), and a health inspection stamp (indicating that the food was wholesome and was slaughtered, packed, or processed under sanitary conditions).

Try cheaper kinds of fish fillets, such as pollock, ocean perch, or whiting. They are often good substitutes for the more expensive fillet of sole.

When buying frozen fish in plastic wrap, look for the ice glaze that should cover the fish. If it's dented or cracked, the glaze is no longer protecting the fish from losing moisture—and quality.

MEAT

Bologna, salami, and other processed meats purchased in bulk and sliced at home are less expensive than packaged meats.

If you need just a little ham for a recipe, ask for inexpensive ham ends at the delicatessen counter.

Canned hams that require refrigeration are more flavorful than canned hams labeled "needs no refrigeration."

The most tender pork chops are those with pink rather than red meat. Chops with red meat are from older, tougher hogs.

For the best value in a porterhouse steak, buy the one with the largest tenderloin part and the smallest tail.

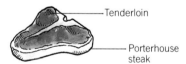

Tenderloin

Porterhouse steak

To select the most tender sirloin steak, look for the cut that most closely resembles the shape of a porterhouse steak.

Flat-bone sirloin steak

Which chickens are better—yellow- or white-skinned? It doesn't matter as long as the bird is labeled Grade A and is young.

Storing Food

FRUITS AND VEGETABLES

Berries will keep several days if stored, unwashed, in a colander in the refrigerator.

To freeze berries without having them turn to mush, place them on a cookie sheet, freeze, and then pack the berries in airtight containers. Return them to the freezer.

If you have too much fruit to process for jelly at one time, cook and strain the juice and freeze it until you have time to make the jelly.

Mash overripe bananas or push them through a sieve, add a little lemon juice to keep them from turning brown, and freeze. Thaw for use in cakes or breads.

When you chop onions and green peppers, make several cups more than you need. Freeze the vegetables in plastic bags for use in soups, sauces, and casseroles.

To keep asparagus fresh for a day or more, cut a small amount off the bottom of each stalk. Stand the stalks upright in a container in a small amount of water. Cover with a plastic bag and refrigerate.

Before you store beets, carrots, turnips, and other root vegetables, cut off their leafy green tops to prevent the tops from extracting nutrients from the roots.

To store watercress, wash it, then stand it upright in an inch of cold water in a glass. Cover the glass and watercress with a plastic bag and refrigerate. If the watercress was fresh when bought, it should keep for about a week. Store parsley, basil, dill, and coriander this way too.

If you have trouble getting a head of lettuce or some other vegetable into a plastic bag, place your hand in the bag, grasp the lettuce through the bag, then pull the bag over the lettuce.

To prevent pimientos from spoiling once you have opened the jar, cover the remaining pimientos with vinegar and store them in the refrigerator.

Save any leftover vegetables as well as the cooking water from these vegetables and add them to a container in your freezer. When the container is full, use the contents for making nutritious soups. Or try freezing the vegetables and water separately, and use the water in place of chicken or beef broth in recipes.

Tomato paste in a tube is a convenient product available at many speciality stores. It will keep for months in the refrigerator after opening, and you can squeeze out only the amount you need.

If you use vegetable oils infrequently, you should refrigerate an opened container to keep the oil from turning rancid.

BAKED GOODS AND GRAINS

Before freezing a pie, let it cool to room temperature; then place an aluminum-foil pie plate atop the pie and tape the top plate to the bottom one. Label and freeze.

You can freeze part or all of a batch of bread dough. Just mix the dough, wrap, and freeze it. Or let it rise once, punch it down, wrap, and freeze. When it thaws, put it in the bread pans for its second rise.

Keep whole-grain flours in a cool, dry place or, better yet, in the refrigerator.

Refrigerate any leftover pasta and sauté it in butter the next day. It tastes really terrific. If you wish, add a bit of garlic powder.

DAIRY PRODUCTS

Cottage cheese will keep fresh longer if it's refrigerated upside down in its original carton.

Although cottage cheese breaks down when frozen and thawed, it can be used in cooking. After thawing, just whip until creamy.

Some small cheeses (1 pound or less and not more than 1 inch thick) can be frozen for 6 months. Good candidates are brick, cheddar, Camembert, Edam, Gouda, mozzarella, Muenster, Port Salut, provolone, and Swiss.

A firm or semifirm cheese will stay moist better if it's wrapped in a cloth dampened with water or with a mild brine solution: ½ cup water, ½ teaspoon salt, and 1 teaspoon vinegar.

Store dry milk in tightly closed containers. If it's nonfat, keep it at room temperature. If it's not, refrigerate it.

Whipped cream can be made well in advance without separating. Sprinkle ½ teaspoon unflavored gelatin over 1 tablespoon of cold water in a custard cup, then set the cup over simmering water to melt the gelatin. Whip 1 cup of heavy cream until almost stiff. Add the gelatin mixture, and whip until stiff. Cover and refrigerate as long as 3 days.

Before returning an opened carton of ice cream to the freezer, press plastic wrap onto the surface of the ice cream to prevent ice crystals from forming.

If you're in doubt about the freshness of an egg, put it in a deep container of cold water. If it floats to the top, it's too old to use.

Freeze leftover egg whites as individual cubes in a plastic ice-cube tray. Once they're frozen, pop them into a plastic bag and store in the freezer. Use for making angel food cake and meringues.

To freeze egg yolks, mix them with a little sugar or salt to prevent coagulation.

Because eggs are porous and will absorb odors from the refrigerator, they should be stored in their original carton, not in the refrigerator door compartment.

FISH, MEAT, AND POULTRY

To prepare raw hamburger patties for freezing: separate them with small plastic coffee-can tops, stack them in a pile, place them in a plastic bag, and seal.

Poultry and meat will keep fresh longer if you remove the original wrapping and wrap the meat loosely in wax paper to allow air to circulate around the flesh.

POWER FAILURES AND FREEZER BREAKDOWNS

Question: How long will food keep in the freezer if the power goes out?
Answer: If the freezer is full and packed tightly and the door is kept closed, food should stay frozen for 48 hours. Food in a partly filled freezer may keep 24 hours.

Question: I'm thinking of buying a freezer. What kind operates best during a power failure?
Answer: Chest-type freezers are not only more energy efficient than uprights, but retain the cold better when power failures occur.

Question: I've heard that dry ice will keep food frozen while the freezer is off. Is this true? And where can I buy dry ice?
Answer: Dry ice (frozen carbon dioxide) will indeed keep frozen food from thawing—its temperature is −109° F. Most large towns and cities have one or more suppliers of dry-ice blocks and pellets. Check your local yellow pages for the phone number and address of the nearest dry-ice maker. During a power failure, you may find dry ice hard to come by because others are likely to be looking for it too.

Caution: Don't let dry ice touch your skin or the food; keep it in cardboard containers; and wear heavy gloves when handling the cardboard. Make sure the room is well ventilated.

Question: I live in a rural area that is subject to periodic power failures. Is there anything I can do in advance to prevent spoilage during a failure?
Answer: (1) Keep your freezer loaded and packed tight. Fill any empty spaces with reusable ice containers. Or fill empty milk containers about 4/5 of the way with water, cap the containers loosely, and freeze. 2) Make sure the freezer-door gasket forms a tight seal. It should hold a piece of paper snugly around the entire perimeter of the door.

Question: How can I tell if my frozen food has gone bad?
Answer: "If in doubt, throw it out." Specifically, if something has an off-color or off-odor, get rid of it. Ice cream, cream-filled cakes, and cooked food that have thawed should be thrown away. Uncooked food that still has ice crystals on it or is still cold (40° F or below) can be safely refrozen.

REFRIGERATOR AND FREEZER STORAGE TIMES

To maintain the best quality and prevent spoilage, foods should be refrigerated at 34° F to 40° F and frozen at 0° F or lower. Some foods may keep longer than the storage times listed in the columns below, but they will gradually begin to lose their texture, flavor, and food value.

Food	Refrigerator (34° F to 40° F)	Freezer (0° F or lower)
DAIRY PRODUCTS		
Butter, margarine	1–2 weeks	6–8 months
Cheese, cottage	5 days	Do not freeze
hard (cheddar, Edam, Swiss)	3–4 months	6 months
soft (Brie, blue, Camembert)	2 weeks	4 months
Eggs, hard-boiled	1 week	Do not freeze
in shell	1–2 weeks	Do not freeze
Whites, uncooked	1 week	12 months
Milk	1 week	1 month
Yogurt	7–10 days	Do not freeze
FISH AND SHELLFISH		
Lean fish fillets and steaks (cod, flounder, halibut, sole)	1 day	6 months
Oily fish fillets and steaks (bluefish, mackerel, salmon)	1 day	3 months
POULTRY AND MEATS		
Bacon	5–7 days	1 month
Beef roasts, steaks	2–4 days	6–12 months
Chicken or turkey, whole or pieces	1–2 days	6–7 months
Cooked meats	2–4 days	2–3 months
Ground beef, veal, lamb	1–2 days	3–4 months
Ground pork	1 day	1–3 months
Lamb, veal roasts	2–4 days	6–9 months
Pork roasts, chops	2–4 days	3–6 months
Sausage	2–4 days	2 months
Smoked ham, whole	5 days	2 months
Variety meats	1–2 days	2–3 months

Food	Refrigerator (34° F to 40° F)	Freezer (0° F or lower)
PIES AND CAKES		
Pies, unbaked fruit	1 day	6–8 months
baked fruit	3 days	2–4 months
custard and cream	3–5 days	Do not freeze
Cakes, unfrosted	—	6–8 months
frosted	—	2–4 months
FRUIT		
Apples, citrus fruit, cranberries	1–2 weeks	
Apricots, ripe bananas (skin will darken), berries, cherries	2–3 days	Commercially frozen: 12 months. Home frozen: 8–12 months
Avocados, melons, nectarines, peaches, pears, plums	3–5 days	
VEGETABLES		
Artichokes, broccoli, cauliflower, collards, green beans, eggplant, lima beans, peas, peppers, radishes, spinach, turnip greens	3–5 days	Commercially frozen: 8 months. Home frozen: 8–12 months
Asparagus, cooked vegetables	2–3 days	
Beets, green and red cabbage, carrots, turnips, squash	1 week	
Corn	1 day	
Lettuce, tomatoes, celery	1 week	Do not freeze

When rewrapping prepackaged meat for freezing, cut the label from the original wrapping and tape it to the new package. You'll have a record of the cut of meat, its weight, and the date of purchase.

To cook bacon in advance, arrange the slices side by side on a rack in a baking pan. Bake at 400° F for 12 minutes or until crisp. Cool, stack the slices, wrap in foil, and freeze. Reheat the amount you need in a skillet over low heat.

Freeze raw or cooked meatballs on a cookie sheet, then transfer them to a container, seal, and freeze. They'll stay separate, and you can use as many as you want when you need them.

When you are planning to freeze a casserole, line the dish with aluminum foil; then fill, cook, and freeze. When frozen, remove the casserole, foil and all, and store it in the freezer. The dish is now free for other uses.

Freeze beef and chicken broth in ice-cube trays; store the frozen cubes in plastic bags.

Cook enough food for several meals. Place the food (meat, vegetables, and dessert) in leftover TV trays. Wrap, label, and freeze. When ready to serve, just pop the tray in the oven to heat.

Fresh-caught uncooked fish retains its flavor best if frozen in clean milk cartons filled with water. (After thawing, use the water to fertilize house plants.)

HERBS AND SPICES

Keep ground ginger, chili powder, and paprika in the refrigerator. Once opened, these spices loose their flavor quickly.

Place fresh ginger root in a plastic bag and store in the freezer. It will keep for months. Just grate the amount you need and return it to the freezer.

So that you can find herbs and spices quickly, organize them in alphabetical order on one or more plastic revolving trays available in hardware stores.

Parsley freezes especiallly well. Wash it, shake, then pat dry with paper towels. Mince it and freeze in a plastic container. Chives and basil can be kept the same way.

To preserve fresh herbs, chop them, then place them in ice-cube trays, add a little water, and freeze. Transfer the frozen cubes to a plastic bag and return to the freezer. Drop into soups, spaghetti sauce, and stews.

DESSERTS

Save the liquids from canned fruits and thicken them with cornstarch; heat and serve as sauce over cake or pudding.

Want fresh fruit pies all year? Prepare several pie fillings and freeze them in pie plates lined with aluminum foil. When frozen, remove the fillings, transfer them to plastic bags, and return to the freezer. Anytime you want a pie, just bake a crust, put a frozen filling in it, and thaw.

Freeze a frosted cake, then wrap it. The wrapping won't stick to the frosting. Remove the wrapping before thawing the cake.

Drop dollops of whipped cream onto a cookie sheet and freeze. Transfer them to plastic bags and return to the freezer. They'll thaw in 20 minutes.

Don't throw out empty potato-chip cylinders. Decorate them and use them as boxes for gifts of cookies and candy.

BEVERAGES

Coffee beans and ground coffee retain their strong flavor longer if kept in the freezer.

To keep loose tea and tea bags fresh, store them in air-tight containers in a cool, dark place away from strong-flavored foods.

Preparing Foods

FRUITS

Avocados slow to ripen? Arrange them in a bowl with other fruit, such as apples, pears, and bananas. Or place them in a paper bag for 2 days or more.

You can peel oranges quickly and separate the sections cleanly if you cover them with boiling water. Let them stand for 5 minutes. Then drain, cool, and peel.

Before squeezing a lemon, submerge it in hot water for 15 minutes. You'll get more juice from it.

Don't discard the rind of lemons, grapefruit, or oranges. They make excellent flavorings for muffins, cakes, and frostings. Grate the rinds, and store in the freezer.

If you are preparing pineapple rings or cubes and have difficulty peeling the fruit, cut it into discs, then peel and core each disc.

You can prevent a pound of freshly cut fruit from discoloring by tossing the mixture in the juice of half a lemon.

Candied fruits and figs will be less sticky if you freeze them before chopping or cutting them. Cutting will be easier still if you keep dipping the knife in hot water.

NUTS

To skin almonds, put them in a pot of boiling water. Remove from the heat, let stand for 2 minutes and drain. Press each nut between your thumb and index finger, popping the nut out of its skin.

Shelling Brazil nuts is much easier if they've been frozen. The shells become brittle, and the nuts will come out whole.

Roasting chestnuts in the oven or fireplace can be risky unless you create an escape for the steam that builds up. To do this, place the nut on a potholder or towel to keep it from slipping, then cut a cross through the flat side of the shell with a sharp paring knife. This also makes peeling easier after they're cooked.

To open a coconut, first pierce the two eyes with an awl or an ice pick. Drain and reserve the liquid for another use. (It makes a delicious drink.) Bake the coconut in a 325° F oven for 20 minutes. If the shell doesn't crack in this time, wrap the nut in a towel or newspaper and give it a few hearty blows with a hammer.

Shelled nuts are easier to chop or sliver if they are heated for 5 minutes in a 350° F oven.

When you want freshly grated coconut, peel the brown skin from the coconut meat with a potato peeler; then cut the meat into small pieces and drop them into a blender or food processor. This is a lot easier than grating the meat by hand.

VEGETABLES

Don't throw away the tough lower stalks of fresh asparagus. Peel the stalks with a potato peeler until you reach the soft interior. Cook as usual; the stalks will be as tender as the tips.

Always wash the top of a can with soap and water before opening it. Many stores spray their shelves with insecticides. Better yet, open the can from the bottom; it's still a good idea to wash the bottom.

You can avoid damaging the delicate tips of canned asparagus if you open the can from the bottom. Hold the lid gently over the asparagus, drain, then carefully empty the asparagus onto a plate.

A quick way to mash an avocado is to put it through a potato ricer. This gives it a uniform consistency. Mix in a few drops of lemon juice to prevent darkening.

The quickest and most thorough way to rid a celery stalk of strings is to peel it with a potato peeler.

Here's a faster way than overnight soaking (which may cause a slight fermentation in the beans) to soften dried beans. Place the beans in a saucepan, and cover with about 2 inches of cold water. Bring to a boil over high heat, reduce the heat, and boil the beans gently for 2 minutes. Remove from heat, cover the pan, and let the beans stand for about 1 hour. They'll be ready for cooking.

Although flatulence from beans is due primarily to their high fiber content, you may be able to decrease the amount of gas a bit by throwing out the water they're soaked in.

Brussels sprouts will cook more evenly and quicker, too, if you cut a cross into the stem end. Don't overcook; they taste better when crisp-tender.

To break off cabbage leaves for stuffed cabbage without tearing them, remove the core of the cabbage with a sharp knife; then submerge the cabbage head in boiling water and let stand in the water for 5 minutes. Cool the cabbage in a bowl of cold water.

The easiest technique for removing corn silk from an ear of corn is to rub it with a vegetable brush under running water.

To get popcorn to pop more easily, sprinkle it with warm water an hour before popping.

Large cucumbers are more appealing if you remove their seeds. Peel them (if they are waxed) and cut them in half lengthwise. Scoop out the seeds by running the tip of a teaspoon down the center of each cucumber half.

To peel garlic in seconds, put the clove on a chopping board, then place the flat side of a wide, heavy knife on top of the clove. Firmly press the side of the knife with the heel of your hand. The skin will come right off.

You'll shed fewer tears when peeling and chopping onions if you chill them thoroughly in the refrigerator beforehand.

The fastest way to peel an onion is to cut off both ends, slice the onion in half crosswise, and then peel each half. Small white onions to be cooked whole can be blanched for about 30 seconds in boiling water. Place them in cold water to cool. Then cut off the ends and the skins will slip right off.

Small white onions won't "telescope" (the center slip out) if you cut a small cross ¼ inch deep into each of the stem ends before cooking the onions.

When boiling potatoes in their skins, peel a ½-inch band of skin around the center of the potatoes. The skins won't burst and you'll have more attractive potatoes.

Beat cooked, mashed pumpkin with an electric mixer to remove the coarse strings; they'll adhere to the beaters.

Select slender young carrots for eating raw. Those with tops will be fresher and more nutritious than those with tops removed. But never store with the leaves attached.

Sweet potatoes decay easily, so should be stored in the refrigerator, and used within four days of purchase.

Corn will store longer if refrigerated in the husks, stem-end-down in a little water. When buying corn, tear back the husks slightly to examine the kernels. Large, dark-yellow kernels mean the corn is past its prime; small white ones, that the corn is too young to have developed much sweetness.

The heavier eggplants are meatiest; the smaller ones are sweetest. While eggplants vary from egg-shaped to globular, the best buy is pear-shaped and between 3 and 6 inches in diameter.

SALAD HINTS

If you mix the oil and vinegar into a salad separately, add the oil first. If you reverse the order, the oil just slides off the wet leaves.

Slice tomatoes vertically rather than horizontally. The slices will stay firmer in your salad and they'll help keep the salad dressing from getting watery.

An aspic or gelatin salad or dessert will set quickly if you put it in the freezer for 25 minutes. Then remove it and refrigerate.

Another fast way to get a salad or dessert to gel is to dissolve the gelatin in a cup of boiling water. Substitute 10 ice cubes for the cold water or liquid, stir until the mixture is syrupy, and remove any ice. Mix in fruit or other ingredients and refrigerate.

Old spice jars are perfect one-shot salad dressing containers to take along with a salad lunch. Pour your choice of dressing into the jar and place it with the salad. No wilted lettuce or leakage.

Chop parsley quickly by gathering as much as you need into a tight ball and slicing it as thin as possible with a sharp knife.

If you soak onion rings in cold water for about an hour, they'll taste milder in your salad.

CREAM

Heavy cream will whip faster if you chill the bowl and the beaters in the freezer until they're very cold. Avoid using the ultrapasteurized variety of heavy cream; it takes much longer to whip.

When you want to whip a small amount of cream, put the cream in a cup and use only one whisk of the electric beater.

If you like whipped cream sweetened, it will be fluffier and less likely to separate when made ahead if you use confectioner's instead of granulated sugar.

To whip evaporated milk (it has a lot less cholesterol than heavy cream), pour it into an ice-cube tray and freeze for about ½ hour or until ice begins to form around the edges. Remove the tray from the freezer, pour the milk into a chilled bowl, and whip it with a chilled electric beater until it thickens.

If you run out of fresh milk for your tea or coffee, use powdered milk instead of coffee whitener. Although relatively low in calories, coffee whitener contains saturated fats and sugar.

BUTTER

Need a stick of butter softened in a hurry? A few seconds in your microwave oven will do the job.

Run out of butter? Whirl a cup of heavy cream and a few ice cubes in your food processor. This process churns the cream, separating out the butterfat and creating a batch of white, unsalted butter. Strain off the liquid and the butter is ready to use.

CHEESE

To grate cheese neatly, place the grater inside a plastic bag and insert a wedge of cheese in the bag. Grasp the cheese through the bag, then grate. No mess.

Most cheeses taste best when they're at room temperature. A serving portion heated on medium in a microwave oven will be just right in about 15 seconds.

EGGS

You can test an egg's freshness without breaking it. Place it in a pan or bowl of cool water. If the egg floats, throw it out. If the egg sinks to the bottom and rests on its side, it's very fresh.

How do you halve an egg? In most cases, it doesn't matter; just use the whole egg. However, if you think it's critical to the success of a recipe, beat the egg slightly in a small bowl, measure it in a cup, and use half of the beaten egg.

If you need eggs at room temperature and have forgotten to remove them from the refrigerator, put them in a bowl of warm water for about 10 minutes.

It's easier to separate egg whites from yolks if the eggs are cold, so leave them in the refrigerator until you are ready to crack them.

A small funnel is a handy utensil for separating egg whites. Carefully open the egg over the funnel; the white will run through and the yolk will remain.

If possible, put off beating egg whites on a muggy or damp day. Moisture-laden air partially collapses the beaten egg whites.

The bowl and beaters should be spotlessly clean when you beat egg whites. Any grease will keep the whites from mounting properly. Be sure, too, that there is not even the tiniest bit of egg yolk in the whites.

You'll get more volume from egg whites by letting them stand at room temperature to warm up for about a half an hour or more before you beat them.

Stiffly beaten egg whites will have more body if you whip in the sugar after you've beaten the egg whites until soft peaks form. Then whip in the sugar gradually. If you add sugar too soon, or too much at any one time, you'll get a marshmallowy sauce that won't stiffen.

To prevent an egg from cracking when it's placed in boiling water, pierce the broader end about ¼ inch deep with a sharp needle.

To tell the raw eggs from the hard-boiled ones stored in your refrigerator, mark the hard-boiled eggs with a pencil. Another way is to spin an egg on its side. If it wobbles, its uncooked. A cooked egg will spin smoothly. And here's a third method—add about ½ teaspoon of turmeric to the cooking water to color the eggshells.

Hard-boiled eggs will peel more easily if, immediately after cooking, you plunge them into a bowl of cold water. Then crack the eggs gently all over and let them remain in the water until cooled.

A quick way to stuff hard-boiled eggs is to place the stuffing in a pastry bag and squeeze away.

MEAT AND POULTRY

To form meatballs or hamburger patties quickly, shape the meat or meat mixture into a log and slice into sections. Roll the slices into balls or shape into patties.

Beef, lamb, or pork is easier to cut into thin slices for stir-fried dishes if the meat is partially frozen.

Before sautéing meats, pat them dry with paper towels. Otherwise, the moisture will prevent successful browning and searing.

Slash the edges of fat on steaks and chops at 1-inch intervals to keep the meat from curling while it's cooking.

When preparing a leg of lamb for roasting, make about a half dozen ½-inch-deep incisions here and there into the fat. Into each incision, insert small slivers of garlic and, if you wish, a small pinch of rosemary or thyme.

A marinade helps tenderize tough meats and also adds flavor. Here's one for beef, lamb, pork, or venison. In a glass bowl, mix 1 cup vegetable oil with ½ cup dry red wine. Add 1 onion, minced; salt; pepper; and thyme or rosemary to taste. Add meat and roll it over in the marinade. Cover and refrigerate overnight.

CUTTING UP A CHICKEN

1. Pull one leg away from the body and cut through the skin to expose the hip joint. Bend the leg bone back until the hip joint pops out of its socket. Cut through the joint. Repeat with the other leg.

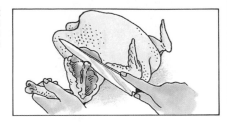

2. Bend the drumstick toward the thigh to expose the knee joint and cut through the joint into two pieces. Repeat with the other leg.

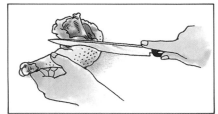

3. Pull the wing away from the body and cut through the joint, removing some of the breast along with the wing. Repeat with the other wing.

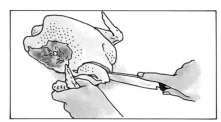

4. Cut along the natural break in the rib cage to remove the top of the breast from the lower carcass. Pry open until the back cracks.

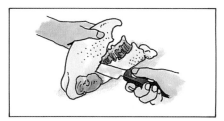

5. Cut down through the bones to detach the breast from the back. Cut the back into two pieces, if desired.

6. Cut the breast in half, not through the bone, but along one side of the breastbone.

Before opening a canned ham, run hot tap water over the can for a few minutes. The gelatin around the ham will melt enough so that the ham will slide right out.

Save on boneless chicken breasts by doing the boning yourself with a sharp knife. It's a lot easier if you freeze the breasts slightly before you begin.

You don't need a special mallet to flatten chicken breasts or other thin pieces of meat. Place the meat between sheets of plastic wrap and pound with the underside of a small, heavy frying pan or a saucepan.

When you cut up a chicken, always save the back, neck, and gizzard. Freeze them, along with roast chicken and turkey carcasses. When you have enough, use them to make delicious broth for soups or other uses.

To get a crisper coating on fried chicken, mix cornstarch well into the flour (about 2 teaspoons of cornstarch to ½ cup flour). For additional flavor, season the flour with salt, pepper, and paprika.

The day before roasting a chicken, season it with salt and pepper and, if you like, tarragon, rosemary, or other herbs, and a little lemon juice. The dish will be much more flavorful. Remove the bird from the refrigerator at least an hour before cooking.

If time allows, the easiest and most thorough method of removing fat from a broth is to refrigerate the broth until the fat hardens on the surface. The fat will lift right off.

There's no need to thaw frozen stock before using it. Just drop the frozen stock into a saucepan and heat gently until you have melted as much stock as you need. Then refrigerate the remainder.

SEAFOOD

Use a beer-can opener to open oysters. Work the point under the hinge on the top side (the darker, flatter side) of the oyster and push down hard. This is easier and safer than using an oyster knife.

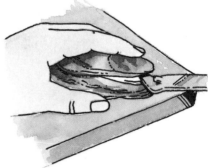

If you are going to use cooked clams or oysters in a recipe, you can open them easily by placing them in one layer on a baking pan and heating them in a preheated 450° F oven for 3 to 5 minutes or until the shells open. Save the juices for your recipe.

Hard-shell clams can be opened more easily if you first drop them on their sides on a hard surface, such as the kitchen floor.

You can remove sand from clams by sprinkling them with a handful of cornmeal, then covering them with cold water and letting them stand for about 3 hours. The clams will eat the cornmeal and disgorge the sand.

Scales are more easily removed from a fish if you wet it first. Run cold water over the fish just before you begin.

A whole fish will have a better taste if you remove the gills before poaching or baking the fish.

QUICK BREADS

For the lightest pancakes and waffles ever, replace the liquid in the batter with club soda. But you can't store the batter. Use up all of it as soon as it's made.

If you have trouble getting muffins out of the pan, place the bottom of the hot pan on a wet towel for about 30 seconds. Or cook the muffins in paper baking cups.

FILLETING ROUND FISH The fish does not have to be gutted before filleting.

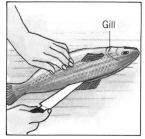

1. Hold the fish steady with one hand and cut from head to tail to expose the backbone.

2. Cut the flesh crosswise directly behind the gill, then cut parallel along the ribs to the tail.

3. Cut crosswise directly behind the gill on the other side. Hold up the exposed backbone at the center and make a parallel cut along the ribs to the tail. Cut off the tail.

FILLETING FLATFISH The fish does not have to be gutted before filleting.

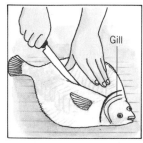
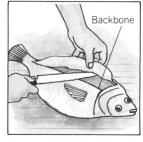

1. Cut down the center of the fish along the backbone from head to tail. Make a semicircular cut directly behind the head and halfway through the thickness of the fish.

2. Cut parallel along the ribs from head to tail while holding the flesh away from the ribs with your other hand.

3. Cut just above the tail to remove the fillet. Repeat with the other side of the fish.

You can easily determine whether you need a fresh supply of baking powder by pouring ¼ cup of hot tap water over ½ teaspoon of baking powder. If the mixture doesn't bubble actively, it's too old.

Baking powder biscuits (pancakes and muffins, too) will be tough if you overmix after adding the liquid. Stir just long enough to dampen the dry ingredients; don't worry if there are a few lumps.

To make baking powder biscuits so that they split neatly for buttering, roll out the dough about ¼-inch thick on a floured board, fold half of the dough over onto the other half, and cut into biscuits. If you like a richer biscuit, lightly brush the dough with melted butter or margarine before you fold it.

In a hurry when preparing biscuits? Roll out the dough and cut it into squares. There'll be no scraps left to roll out and cut again.

Your nut bread won't crumble as much when you cut it if you let it cool, then refrigerate it, covered, overnight. Use a knife with a serrated edge to cut the cold bread.

YEAST BREADS

One of the secrets to making good yeast bread is to use as little flour as possible and still be able to handle the dough. The dough should be quite moist. Adding flour beyond this point will make the dough heavy and tough.

If your yeast dough springs back constantly while you're trying to roll it out, it needs to relax a bit. Cover it with a dish towel to keep it from drying out and let it rest for about 10 minutes.

If your yeast dough doesn't rise, two things to look out for are old yeast (check the expiration date) and the temperature of the liquid. Dissolve fresh compressed yeast in liquids that are not more than 85° F; active dry yeast in liquids not more than 115° F. Check it with a candy thermometer.

Out of bread crumbs? You can use many kinds of dry cereals as crumbs if you put them through a blender or food processor. They're excellent in meat loaf and hamburger. They're also good added to yeast bread dough.

To keep dinner rolls piping hot, wrap a hot ceramic tile in a napkin, and place it in the bottom of the serving basket. Be sure to place the basket on a trivet to protect the table.

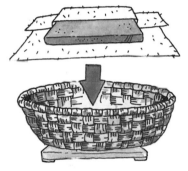

Stale rolls can be revived if you spray them lightly with cold water, place them in a paper bag or wrap in foil, and warm in a 375° F oven for about 5 minutes.

Lunchbox sandwiches won't get soggy if you spread the mayonnaise and other moist condiments between the meat or cheese and lettuce layers instead of directly on the bread. Another trick: pack lettuce, tomato, and pickles in a separate plastic bag and add them to sandwiches just before eating.

PIES

Place a damp dish towel under your pastry board so that it won't slide around when you roll out biscuits or pie dough or when you knead bread dough.

Before you sift flour onto wax paper, always crease the paper down the center. This creates a handy pouring spout.

Sprinkle your pastry board with about 4 tablespoons of quick-cooking rolled oats before rolling out your dough. This gives the crust a nutty flavor and extra nutrients.

For better piecrusts, have all ingredients very cold before combining them; mix only until the ingredients are blended. Chill the dough before rolling it out.

To add flavor to piecrusts, replace ¼ cup of the flour with whole wheat, oat, soy, or millet flour or quick-cooking oatmeal.

For a flakier piecrust, just brush the top crust lightly with cold water before baking.

Save leftover pie dough, wrap in aluminum foil, and freeze. When you need an instant topping for a baked fruit dish, grate the frozen dough over the top.

For a meringue that won't stick when it's cut, sift a little granulated sugar over as it browns at a low temperature. Or, butter the knife first or dip it in boiling water before cutting the pie.

CAKES AND FROSTINGS

When you're using eggs and oil in baking, crack your eggs in a measuring cup first, and then pour them into your mixing bowl. The eggs coat the cup so that when you measure the oil, it will slide out easily.

To keep your mixing bowl from slipping on the counter, place a pot holder under it.

Always sift confectioner's sugar when you make a frosting and you'll never have lumps.

Make a heart for your valentine: bake a round cake and a square cake. Cut the round cake in half, then turn the square cake so that the corners face you in a diamond shape. Place each half of the round cake on two sides of the diamond. Frost and serve.

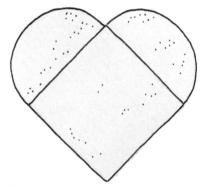

You can make your own pastry bag. Cut a small hole in one corner of a heavy plastic bag, fill with whipped cream or other mixtures, and pipe away.

An easy way to fill a pastry bag is to place the bag inside a large jar for support, turn the top of the bag down over the top of the jar rim, and fill.

When frosting a cake, put narrow strips of wax paper under the bottom of the cake. When you've finished frosting, pull each of the pieces of paper gently and slightly sideways from under the cake. The cake plate will be clean with no smudges.

If you're going to cut just a couple of servings from a cake and store the rest for a while, cut the cake in half and take a portion from the middle. Then press the 2 halves together. The cake will stay moist.

For a fast, attractive topping for unfrosted cakes, place a paper doily with a large design on top of the cake, and dust confectioner's sugar over it lightly. Gently lift the doily from the cake.

COOKIES

Oatmeal cookies will taste better if you toast the oatmeal first. Sprinkle it evenly in a jellyroll pan and bake it in a 300° F oven for about 10 or 12 minutes.

When using your hands to shape cookies, especially if the dough contains a lot of shortening, wet your hands with cold water from time to time and the dough won't stick to your palms.

Roll cookie dough between sheets of wax paper; you can avoid adding too much flour, and the dough won't stick to the rolling pin.

A quick way to put a nice topping on cookies without making frosting is to cover the cookies with a thin layer of jelly or preserves before you bake them. When cool, the cookies will have a tasty glaze.

When cutting bar cookies, use a pizza cutter. It makes nice, smooth squares. Good also for cutting out strips of dough for lattice-top pies (see p.389).

If you have no cookie sheet or you need extras, turn a roasting pan upside down and use the bottom as the baking surface.

OTHER DESSERT TIPS

You can prevent "skin" from forming on puddings and custards by resting plastic wrap on their surface before they cool.

Before unmolding a gelatin dessert or a gelatin salad, sprinkle the platter lightly with water. Then you'll be able to slide the gelatin to center it on the platter.

A simple way to unmold gelatin desserts and salads, rather than dipping the mold in hot water, is to soak a towel in hot water, wring it out slightly, and wrap it around the mold for about 15 seconds. Then with both hands, unmold with a quick downward snap of the wrists onto a plate.

If you're out of superfine sugar, you can make it by refining granulated sugar in your blender. Pour the sugar (a few batches at a time) into the blender and run it at high speed. Great when making meringue; it dissolves quickly and prevents "tears" from forming on top of the meringue (see p.389).

Soften hardened brown sugar by sprinkling it with water and placing it in a shallow pan, uncovered, in a 200° F oven. When the sugar becomes soft, crumble it with a fork or whirl it in the container of an electric blender or food processor.

If honey crystallizes, stand the jar in a pan of hot water or place the opened jar in a 250° F oven until the honey liquefies.

AROUND THE KITCHEN

Don't have a flour sifter? You really don't need one. Sift the flour through a kitchen sieve.

You can make your own temporary funnel for dry goods by clipping the corner of a small paper bag. For cool liquids, cut off the corner of a heavy plastic bag.

Need a sturdy funnel? No need to buy one. You can make one easily. Just cut a plastic, ½- or 1-gallon bottle in half with a sharp, heavy knife. Use the half containing the spout for your funnel. Remember to wash the funnel thoroughly with hot, soapy water before you use it.

LIQUID CAPACITY

Spoons, cups, pints, quarts, gallons	Equivalent measure & fluid ounces	Approximate metric equivalent
Pinch or dash	Less than ⅛ tsp.	
1 tsp.	⅙ fl. oz.	5 mL
1 T.	3 tsp., or ½ fl. oz.	15 mL
2 T.	6 tsp., or 1 fl. oz.	30 mL
¼ c.	4 T., or 2 fl. oz.	60 mL
⅓ c.	5 T. plus 1 tsp., or 2⅔ fl. oz.	90 mL
½ c.	8 T., or 4 fl. oz.	125 mL
½ pt.	1 c., or 8 fl. oz.	250 mL
1 pt.	2 c., or 16 fl. oz.	500 mL
1 qt.	2 pt., or 32 fl. oz.	1,000 mL or 1 L
1 gal.	4 qt., or 128 fl. oz.	4 L

Approximate conversion formulas:
To convert ounces to milliliters, multiply the ounces by 30 (e.g. 100 oz. × 30 = 3,000 mL)
To convert milliliters to ounces, multiply the milliliters by 0.03 (e.g. 3,000 mL × 0.03 = 90 oz.)

A saltshaker that delivers salt too fast can be easily remedied by plugging some of the holes. Wash the shaker top to remove all salt, and dry thoroughly. Use colorless fingernail polish to stop up the desired number of holes.

Make it a habit to sharpen a knife with a butcher's steel each time you use it. Ten or so strokes should be adequate. Your knives will stay sharp much longer.

Eventually, your knives will need more attention. Ask the butcher at your supermarket where he sends his knives to be sharpened or look in the Yellow Pages of your phone book for "Sharpening Services."

A plastic chopping board is preferable to a wooden board for several reasons. First, it won't warp; also it can be scrubbed with soap and hot water or cleaned in your dishwasher. If it becomes stained, moisten it with full-strength household bleach, wait a few minutes, and wash thoroughly.

Make excellent pot holders from old bath towels or mattress pads. Cut an 8- by 15-inch rectangle from the fabric. Ideally, one of the long sides should be a selvage or other finished edge. Fold the rectangle in half, right sides together. Stitch along the two unfinished edges. Turn right side out and stitch the opening.

WRONG SIDE

WEIGHTS & METRIC EQUIVALENTS

Ounces & pounds	Grams
¼ oz.	7.5 g
½ oz.	15 g
1 oz.	30 g
2 oz.	60 g
4 oz. (¼ lb.)	120 g
8 oz. (½ lb.)	240 g
16 oz. (1 lb.)	480 g

Approximate conversion formulas:
To convert ounces into grams, multiply the ounces by 30.
To convert grams into ounces, multiply the grams by 0.03.

Create extra counter space when preparing for a crowd or when baking for a holiday by placing large trays or cookie sheets across pulled-out drawers. If you are really in a pinch for space, set up your ironing board.

Here's another way to increase your counter space. Get a wooden board that will fit over the sink. If you cut a 2-inch hole near one corner of the board, you can push peelings directly into the sink. When it's not in use, you can tuck it alongside the refrigerator.

A food grinder or pasta maker that won't stay firmly in place is a nuisance. Place a small piece of folded sandpaper, rough side out, between the clamp and the table.

For a cookout, pack charcoal briquettes in cardboard egg cartons and tie shut. There's no mess, and you can ignite them right in the carton at the picnic site.

To prevent ice-cube trays from sticking to the freezer shelf, line the shelf with wax paper.

To get a good grasp on jar lids and bottle tops, open them while holding the lid with a piece of sandpaper, sand side down.

THREE BASIC MIXES FOR QUICK-FIX RECIPES

When you have the spare time, make up batches of the three mixes described here; then on extra-busy days, you can quickly prepare one of the main-course beef dishes, or pancakes and biscuits, or cakes.

GROUND-BEEF MIX*

¼ cup vegetable oil
4 medium onions, peeled and chopped
4 cloves garlic, peeled and finely chopped
4 stalks celery, chopped
2 to 3 carrots, peeled and chopped

5 pounds lean ground beef
1 tablespoon salt
2 teaspoons pepper
3 tablespoons Worcestershire sauce
1 jar (26 ounces) marinara sauce or any other type spaghetti sauce

Divide the oil between two large skillets. Add half the onions, garlic, celery, and carrots to each skillet. Cook over moderate heat for 10 minutes, stirring occasionally. Divide the meat between the two skillets. Break up the meat with a large spoon, then stir and cook until the meat is no longer pink. Divide the salt, pepper, Worcestershire sauce, and marinara sauce between the skillets. Cover and simmer about 20 to 25 minutes. Spoon off all the fat. Cool the mixture thoroughly, then spoon it into seven 1-pint freezer containers, leaving ½-inch space at the top. Seal tightly and label containers. Freeze. Use within 3 months. Makes about 7 pints.

Hamburger-Noodle Skillet

1 package (10 ounces) frozen mixed vegetables
1 pint ground-beef mix, thawed*

2 cups cooked egg noodles
1 can (8 ounces) tomato sauce
1 cup grated Cheddar cheese

To a 10-inch skillet, add the mixed vegetables and cook according to package directions. Stir in the beef mix, cooked noodles, and tomato sauce. Cover and cook over moderate heat for about 10 minutes, stirring occasionally. Add a few tablespoons of water if necessary to prevent the mixture from sticking. Sprinkle the grated cheese evenly over the top. Do not stir. Cover and heat just long enough to melt the cheese. Serve from the skillet. Makes 4 to 6 servings.

Chili Con Carne

1 pint ground-beef mix, thawed*
2 teaspoons or more chili powder

2 cans (15½ ounces each) red kidney beans

Combine ingredients in a medium saucepan. Cover and cook over moderate heat for about 10 minutes. Makes 6 servings.

Speedy Pizza

1 pint ground-beef mix, thawed*
6 English muffins, split
1 cup grated mozzarella or sharp Cheddar cheese

1 teaspoon or more dried oregano
Thinly sliced pepperoni, mushrooms, green peppers, and olives (optional)

In a small saucepan, simmer beef mix for about 5 minutes until heated through. Toast English muffin halves. Spoon meat mixture over the muffins. Sprinkle with the cheese and oregano. Add pepperoni and other toppings, if desired. Broil for about 3 to 5 minutes until cheese is bubbly. Makes 12 individual pizzas.

BISCUIT AND PANCAKE MIX*

6 cups sifted all-purpose flour
2 tablespoons plus
  1½ teaspoons baking powder

1 cup nonfat dry milk
2½ teaspoons salt

In a large mixing bowl, combine the flour, baking powder, dry milk, and salt. Spoon the mixture into a 2-quart glass or plastic container. Cover tightly and store in the refrigerator. Mix will keep for about 1 month. Yield: 7 cups.

Baking Powder Drop Biscuits: Preheat oven to 450° F. In a mixing bowl, stir 2 cups mix* and 1¼ cups heavy cream (or 1 cup heavy cream plus ¼ cup milk) with a fork just enough to moisten the mix. Drop the dough by heaping tablespoons onto a lightly greased baking sheet. Bake for 8 to 10 minutes. Makes about 20 biscuits. Variation: Stir 1 teaspoon of your favorite herb into the mix before adding the cream.

Pancakes: In a mixing bowl, beat 1 egg lightly with a fork, then add 1 cup mix*, ¾ cup cold water, and 2 tablespoons melted butter, margarine, or vegetable oil. Stir just enough to moisten the mix—the batter should be lumpy. Makes about 12 pancakes. Variations: Just before cooking, stir in ½ cup blueberries or chopped apple.

CAKE MIX*

8 cups all-purpose flour
6 cups granulated sugar
¼ cup baking powder

1½ teaspoons salt
1-pound can vegetable shortening (2¼ cups)

In a large bowl, sift together the flour, sugar, baking powder, and salt. Mix well. With a pastry blender, cut in shortening until it resembles very coarse crumbs. Put in a large airtight container. Store in a cool, dry place or in the refrigerator, if you have the space. Use within 10 to 12 weeks. Makes about 16 cups.

Spice Cake

5 cups cake mix*
1¼ teaspoons ground nutmeg
1¼ teaspoons ground cinnamon
½ teaspoon ground cloves

1 cup water
¼ cup butter or margarine
½ cup sour cream or plain yogurt
2 eggs, lightly beaten

Preheat oven to 375° F. Generously grease a 13- by 9- by 2-inch baking pan. In a large bowl, combine cake mix, nutmeg, cinnamon, and cloves. In a small saucepan, combine water and butter or margarine. Bring to a boil. Add to dry ingredients. Mix well. Add sour cream or yogurt, and eggs. Pour into prepared pan. Bake 40 minutes. Cool cake in pan on a rack. Frost cake with your favorite icing.

Chocolate Cake

3⅓ cups cake mix*
9 tablespoons cocoa
1 cup milk

2 eggs, lightly beaten
3 tablespoons butter or margarine, melted

Preheat oven to 375° F. Lightly grease and flour two 8-inch, round pans. Combine cake mix and cocoa in a large bowl. Add ½ cup of milk; beat at medium speed for 2 minutes. Add remaining ½ cup milk, eggs, and melted butter or margarine. Beat 2 more minutes. Pour into prepared pans. Bake 25 minutes. Cool on racks in pans for 10 minutes. Remove cake from pans and cool on racks. Frost cakes with your favorite icing.

Cooking

PANCAKES AND WAFFLES

To make extra-light, airy pancakes, separate the eggs and mix the yolks into the batter first. After everything else has been added, beat the whites until stiff and fold them in at the end.

A different recipe for pancake or waffle syrup: mix ⅓ cup butter, ⅓ cup sugar, and ½ cup frozen orange juice concentrate. Heat, stirring constantly, until the sugar has dissolved.

To keep waffles from sticking, be sure to brush the surface of the waffle iron with vegetable oil after cooking each waffle. Or use a nonstick waffle iron.

MUFFINS

Put a surprise into muffins. Fill only half of each muffin-tin cup with batter. Place in each cup a piece of apple, a piece of canned pineapple, a pitted cooked prune, or any fruit you have on hand. Pour the remainder of the batter on top and bake.

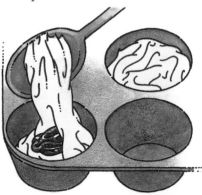

For a deliciously different corn bread, stir cooked onions and green pepper or crumbled, crisp-cooked bacon into the batter before baking the bread.

For a crunchy, sugary crust on muffins, sprinkle white or brown sugar over the batter in the muffin pan before baking.

OTHER BREADS

Crisp, toasted pumpernickel goes well with soup. Buy unsliced pumpernickel bread and put it in the freezer for an hour or more so that you can slice it wafer thin. Spread with unsalted butter and a light sprinkling of Parmesan cheese. Toast at 325°F until crisp.

Place frozen English muffins on a paper towel and thaw uncovered on high in a microwave oven about 30 seconds. They'll be easy to split for toasting.

When preparing peanut butter sandwiches, add some coarsely grated carrots, chopped banana, or drained, crushed pineapple. It's a good way to sneak in a little more nutrition too.

Make great pizzas with leftover French or Italian bread. With a bread knife, slice the loaf in half horizontally; then spoon spaghetti sauce over the halves, add oregano, sliced pepperoni, Parmesan cheese, and top with shredded mozzarella cheese. Bake at 425°F for about 10 to 15 minutes until the cheese melts.

BREAD BAKING

When making bread dough, add water leftover from boiling potatoes to the flour and yeast. It will provide food for the yeast and add flavor.

Add a teaspoon of garlic powder to your flour when making white bread. You'll have a lightly flavored bread that is delicious.

When making bread in a cold kitchen, warm all ingredients, including the flour and the mixing bowl, in a warm oven before mixing. Your dough will rise higher.

Here's a way to prevent bread crusts from cracking. Just before setting the unbaked loaf in the oven, make several shallow, diagonal slashes across its top. Use a single-edge razor blade.

RICE AND PASTA

For more flavorful rice, substitute chicken broth, beef broth, consommé, or undiluted tomato juice for the water.

If you have trouble with gummy rice, cook it like spaghetti. Bring a large pot of salted water to a boil. Add the rice and boil until tender.

EMERGENCY SUBSTITUTIONS

Ingredient	Amount	Use instead:
Baking powder	1 tsp.	¼ tsp. baking soda plus ½ tsp. cream of tartar
Broth, chicken or beef	1 c.	1 bouillon cube or 1 envelope instant broth dissolved in 1 c. boiling water
Buttermilk	1 c.	1 c. plain yogurt or 1 c. whole milk plus 1 T. lemon juice or vinegar (let stand 5 min.)
Cake flour	1 c.	1 c. sifted all-purpose flour less 2 T.
Chocolate, unsweetened	1 square (1 oz.)	3 T. cocoa plus 1 T. butter
Cornstarch (for thickening)	1 T.	2 T. all-purpose flour
Corn syrup, light (not for baking)	1 c.	1¼ c. granulated sugar plus ⅓ c. water
Cracker crumbs, fine	¾ c.	1 c. fine dry bread crumbs
Cream, heavy (not for whipping)	1 c.	¾ c. milk plus ⅓ c. melted butter
Cream, light	1 c.	¾ c. milk plus ¼ c. melted butter
Cream, sour	1 c.	⅞ c. plain yogurt or buttermilk plus 3 T. melted butter
Garlic	1 small clove	1⅛ tsp. garlic powder
Half-and-half	1 c.	⅞ c. milk plus 1½ T. melted butter
Honey	1 c.	1¼ c. granulated sugar plus ¼ c. water
Ketchup or chili sauce	½ c.	½ c. tomato sauce plus 2 T. sugar, 1 T. vinegar, and ⅛ tsp. ground cloves
Lemon juice	1 tsp.	½ tsp. vinegar
Milk, whole	1 c.	½ c. evaporated milk plus ½ c. water, or 1 c. water plus ⅓ c. instant nonfat dry milk powder and 2 tsp. melted butter, or 1 c. skim milk plus 2 tsp. melted butter
Mustard, prepared	1 T.	1 tsp. dried mustard
Onion	1 small	1 T. instant minced onion
Pork, ground	½ lb.	½ lb. mild sausage
Red pepper sauce	3–4 drops	⅛ tsp. cayenne pepper
Tomato paste	1 T.	1 T. ketchup
Vinegar	1 tsp.	2 tsp. lemon juice

c. = cup
T. = tablespoon
tsp. = teaspoon

An easy way to cook spaghetti or linguine is to put the pasta into a large pot of rapidly boiling, salted water. Turn off the heat, cover, and let the spaghetti stand for 15 minutes, linguine for 20 minutes.

Freshly cooked or leftover spaghetti can be pressed over the greased bottom and sides of a pie pan, and filled with any creamed chicken, fish, meat, or vegetables, or with a cheese filling. Bake at 350° F until heated through.

TRICKS WITH EGGS

A tablespoon of sherry does wonders for scrambled eggs and omelets. Beat it into the eggs before you cook them.

A tablespoon of vinegar added to water before poaching eggs helps to keep the whites from spreading.

You can make an egg poacher to keep egg whites from spreading by removing the top and bottom of a tuna can. Place the cutout can in a skillet of simmering water and crack the eggs into it.

When you hard-boil eggs for stuffing, stir them gently for the first 2 minutes. This sets the whites. The yolks will be in the center, leaving a strong wall of white around the yolk that won't break when the eggs are stuffed.

HOW TO MAKE YOGURT

You'll need 1 quart of low-fat milk plus ¼ cup plain store-bought yogurt or 2 tablespoons yogurt culture (available at health food stores).

1. In a heavy saucepan, warm the milk over low heat until it reaches 180° F. (Test with a candy thermometer.) Remove the saucepan from the heat and allow the milk to cool to between 105° F and 110° F. Add the yogurt or yogurt culture and stir until thoroughly mixed.

2. Pour the mixture into a 1-quart jar or several smaller jars. Cover with plastic wrap; set the yogurt to incubate undisturbed in a warm place (between 105° F and 112° F) for 3 to 4 hours or for 7 to 8 hours if using the yogurt culture. Use any one of these incubating methods:

In a gas oven with just the pilot light burning; not a heated oven.

In a warm area with a blanket over the container to prevent drafts.

In an insulated picnic cooler filled with crumpled newspaper.

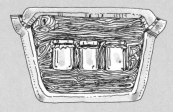

3. As soon as the yogurt retains the impression of a spoon pressed into the surface, it has incubated long enough. Refrigerate for at least 3 hours to firm up the yogurt even more. Save and refrigerate ¼ cup yogurt as a starter for the next batch. Makes 1 quart.

The longer the yogurt incubates, the more sour it will be.

Lumps mean you used too much starter.

For a richer, sweeter yogurt, use whole milk or a mixture of milk and light cream. For a thicker curd, add up to 3 tablespoons of powdered milk to a quart of low-fat milk.

If you don't have time to hard-boil eggs for egg salad sandwiches, scramble them until they're very dry. Cool, then add mayonnaise and the usual seasonings. A touch of curry powder does wonders.

SOUPS

Vegetables added to soup will make a much tastier dish if you sauté them first, preferably in a little butter.

You can make a reasonably good fish chowder from canned tuna. Here's how. Boil and dice some potatoes. Sauté chopped onion, celery, and pieces of bacon together until the vegetables are tender. Then mix all of these with 2 cups of milk and a can of tuna.

If soups, sauces, or stews are too salty, cook them a few minutes with several slices of raw potato to absorb the salt.

An elegant topping for tomato soup or any creamed soup is a dollop of lightly salted whipped cream. If you like, dust the cream with paprika, curry powder, or finely minced chives.

FRUIT

When cooking apple slices, add the sugar at the beginning; this will help the slices to maintain their shape.

To add interest to a fruit plate, spread bananas with sour cream and roll them in toasted coconut.

The next time you have a cookout, put whole bananas, with their skins on, right on the grill. Cook covered at low temperature about 8 minutes, turning once.

JELLY MAKING

If you're a jelly maker, here's news: cooking fruit in a pressure cooker extracts much more juice than top-of-stove cooking. It's a lot faster too.

A piece of string makes it easy to remove the paraffin from a jar of jelly. After pouring the paraffin over the top of the freshly made jelly, place a 5-inch piece of strong kitchen string into the hot paraffin. When you're ready to eat the jelly, lift out the paraffin by the string.

COOKING VEGETABLES

Instead of boiling beets (and losing color and nutrients in the water), try baking them. Wash them thoroughly, and wrap all of them together in one large sheet of aluminum foil. Bake at 400° F for 1½ to 2 hours, depending on their size. They'll be crisp-tender and will have a better flavor.

Some people consider the stalks of broccoli the best part; they're tasty and crunchy. For even cooking, cut the stalks from the florets, then slice the stalks into ½-inch-thick discs or 2-inch sticks. Cook in a small amount of water until they are tender but still crisp—about 4 or 5 minutes.

For cabbage that is even better than steamed or boiled, sauté shredded cabbage and a minced clove of garlic in a few tablespoons of butter for 2 or 3 minutes. Add a small amount of water or chicken broth, cover tightly, and cook until crisp-tender.

A quick topping for cooked cauliflower or broccoli is a can of condensed cheese soup heated with ¼ cup milk.

Looking for a vegetable to serve with a roast? Spread ½-inch-thick eggplant slices with mayonnaise; sprinkle with basil or oregano, bread crumbs, grated Parmesan cheese, and dot with butter. Bake on a cookie sheet at 450° F for about 15 minutes.

Lettuces, especially Boston, leaf lettuce, escarole, or romaine, are good cooked with a small amount of water and minced garlic, if you like, until crisp-tender.

STEAMING VEGETABLES

Steaming is a good way to cook many vegetables because, when properly done, the vegetables retain the most nutrients and flavor. You'll need a large pot, with a tight cover, and a rack or steamer basket to hold the vegetables about ½ inch or so above boiling water. Bring the water to a rolling boil, then lower the heat to just boiling. Lift the lid only when you think the food is done and quickly test the food with a fork. Here are some vegetables that are especially good steamed, with their approximate cooking times:

Vegetables	Approximate cooking times
Artichokes, medium	30–35 min.
Asparagus	8 min.
Beets, medium	40–45 min.
Brussels sprouts	8–10 min.
Broccoli	10–12 min.
Carrots, sliced	20 min.
Cauliflower, florets	6–10 min.
Corn on the cob	6–10 min.
Green beans, whole	20–25 min.
Onions, small white	15 min.
Peas	15 min.
Potatoes, new	20–25 min.
Spinach	5 min.
Squash, summer, sliced	10 min.

For a good low-calorie vegetable, sprinkle large whole mushroom caps with salt and place them, open side up, on a lightly greased cookie sheet in a 350° F oven. Lower the heat to 300° F and bake for 15 minutes.

Mushrooms will gain in flavor and have a better texture if you sauté them in butter before adding them to a stew or braised dish.

Save yourself work: if you're adding onions to a stock that will later be strained and the vegetables discarded, don't bother to peel them. Just wash them and cut them into large chunks. The same is true of garlic.

Out of onions? Use a few teaspoons or so of dried onion-soup mix. It can be a tasty substitute in many dishes.

A baked potato will cook in about half the usual time if you boil it for 5 minutes before you put it in the oven to bake.

To prepare mashed potatoes with excellent flavor, bake Idaho potatoes, peel, and mash with hot milk or light cream, and butter.

The best way to peel a hard-skinned squash, such as acorn or butternut, is— not to peel it! Just cut the squash in sections, scoop out the seeds, and cook. When done, scoop out the pulp, leaving the skin behind.

A treat for pasta lovers is zucchini lasagne. Cut zucchini into thin, lengthwise strips and steam them until crisp-tender. Layer the strips in a casserole dish with spaghetti sauce and grated cheese. Bake uncovered at 350° F.

Put a thin slice or two of Swiss or Gruyère cheese over a cooked vegetable and heat in a 450° F oven until the cheese melts; or put them under the broiler until the cheese browns lightly.

HERBS

A bouquet garni—bay leaf, fresh thyme, and parsley tied together in a bundle—enhances the flavor of soups, stews, and braised dishes. If the herbs are dry, tie them in a piece of cheesecloth so that you can remove them easily before serving the dish.

If you don't have the fresh herbs a recipe calls for, substitute dried ones, using ⅓ the amount of fresh herbs called for. Be sure to crumble the dried herbs between the palms of your hands to release their flavor during cooking.

Before adding dried herbs to a sauce such as mayonnaise, put them in hot water for a moment, then drain. They'll be greener and more flavorful.

A half teaspoon of dried sage simmered with ground pork in homemade or canned tomato sauce makes a flavorful sauce for pasta.

Want to dry herbs from your garden? Place them on a paper towel and heat uncovered on high in a microwave oven for 1 minute.

WHEN YOU COOK WITH HERBS	
Food	**Herb choices**
Beans, green	Basil, coriander, dillweed, savory
Beef	
Boiled	Bay leaf, dillweed, horseradish, rosemary
Hamburgers	Oregano, sage, thyme
Marinades	Bay leaf, coriander, parsley
Pot roast	Basil, rosemary, thyme
Stew	Bay leaf, garlic, parsley, thyme
Beets	Caraway seed, dillweed
Brussels sprouts	Basil, dillweed, rosemary
Cabbage, cauliflower	Caraway seed, dillweed
Carrots	Chervil, mint, rosemary, thyme
Cheese	
Cheese dishes	Chervil, sage, savory
Cottage	Caraway seed, dillweed
Cream	Chives, garlic, rosemary
Chicken	
Creamed dishes	Sage, savory, tarragon
Salad	Dillweed, tarragon
Sautéed, roasted	Cumin, oregano, rosemary
Stuffing	Marjoram, parsley, sage, thyme
Cucumbers	Coriander, dillweed, garlic
Eggs	
Salad	Celery seed, chervil, parsley
Scrambled, omelets	Chives, cumin, dillweed, marjoram
Lamb	
Chops	Basil, oregano, thyme
Roast, stew	Garlic, marjoram, mint, rosemary
Liver	Garlic, rosemary, sage, savory
Mushrooms	Fennel seed, tarragon
Peas	Basil, fennel seed, mint, tarragon
Pork	
Chops	Marjoram, savory
Roast	Garlic, rosemary, sage, thyme
Potatoes	
Boiled	Coriander, dillweed, parsley
Salad	Chives, dillweed, marjoram
Rice	Coriander, cumin, rosemary
Salads	
Mixed fruit	Mint, rose geranium
Tossed	Basil, garlic, parsley, tarragon
Seafood	
Baked, broiled, poached	Chives, dillweed, fennel seed, tarragon
Creamed fish, shellfish	Chives, dillweed, savory, tarragon
Stuffed fish	Marjoram, sage, savory
Squash, summer, zucchini	Basil, chervil, rosemary, savory
Tomato	
Casseroles	Basil, tarragon, thyme
Salad	Basil, coriander, oregano
Sauces	Basil, bay leaf, oregano
Veal	
Chops, roast	Garlic, rosemary, sage
Stew	Basil, tarragon, thyme

SPICES

When making curried dishes, always cook the spices in the butter or oil first. This makes curry, as well as other spiced dishes, much more digestible.

A few grains of nutmeg are a nice addition to creamed spinach and mashed potatoes. Sprinkle nutmeg lightly over custards, rice pudding, and eggnog.

To add color and flavor, mix paprika in the flour for coating fish for deep-frying, or sprinkle it over fried potatoes at the beginning of the cooking period.

SEAFOOD

To tell how long to cook fish, lay the fillet, steak, or whole fish on its side and measure the thickest part. Cook 10 minutes for each inch of thickness. This time applies for all cooking methods.

For a zippy flavor, put a pinch of powdered ginger or a few slices of fresh ginger in the oil in which you sauté fish.

Fish fillets don't need to be turned if they are broiled; they'll break apart if you try to flip them.

Leftover cooked fish can be put through the blender and made into a pâté. Add mayonnaise, herbs, and other flavors. Use for stuffing celery or eggs, or as a canapé spread or for fish cakes.

Do you have a tough time getting a fidgety lobster in the pot? Hold it head down, firmly stroke the back of its head a few times, and it'll stay still temporarily. The fringe benefit? Meat that's more tender and luscious!

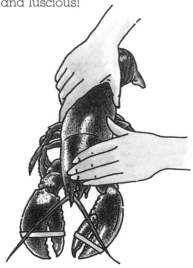

CHICKEN AND TURKEY

A boneless chicken breast will shrink less during cooking if you cut out the white tendon that runs lengthwise through the underside of the meat.

The breast of a large roasting chicken will be more moist if you roast the bird breast-side down for the first 40 or 45 minutes. To finish the roasting, carefully turn the bird breast-side up and baste it with melted butter.

Spoon canned mincemeat into fresh or canned peach halves, sprinkle with brandy, dot with butter, and place in a 350° F oven until hot. Serve with roast chicken or turkey.

TIMETABLE FOR ROASTING CHICKEN

Weight	Temperature	Approx. time*
1½ lb.	400° F	1 hr.
2 lb.	400° F	1 hr. 10 min.
2½ lb.	375° F	1 hr. 15 min.
3 lb.	375° F	1 hr. 30 min.
3½ lb.	375° F	1 hr. 45 min.
4 lb.	375° F	2 hr.
4½ lb.	375° F	2 hr. 15 min.
5 lb.	375° F	2 hr. 30 min.

*Internal temperature should be 185° F. Increase roasting time by 15 minutes if chicken is stuffed.

TIMETABLE FOR ROASTING TURKEY at 325° F

Weight	Stuffed*	Unstuffed*
6–8 lb.	3–3½ hr.	2¼–3¼ hr.
8–12 lb.	3½–4½ hr.	3–4 hr.
12–16 lb.	4½–5½ hr.	3½–4½ hr.
16–20 lb.	5½–6½ hr.	4–5 hr.
20–24 lb.	6½–7 hr.	4½–5½ hr.

*Internal temperature should be 185° F.

If you're poaching a chicken for salad or sandwiches, let the chicken cool in the poaching liquid for an hour before cutting it. It will have more flavor and a velvety texture.

Place your turkey on a bed of celery stalks. They'll serve as a rack for the turkey and keep the bird from sticking. When the turkey is done, you'll have deliciously flavored drippings for gravy. Discard the celery.

For an amazingly good stuffing, use only apples. Peel, core, and stuff the bird with the whole apples. After the turkey is cooked, remove the apples.

You can make an excellent curry with leftover turkey. Use lots of chopped onions.

HAMBURGERS

If you shape hamburgers lightly, without too much pressure, they'll be lighter and juicier.

Form ground beef around a small cube of cheese—any kind—mozzarella, Cheddar, or whatever you have on hand. Cook as you normally do for meatballs. Result: a tasty surprise in the center.

MEAT LOAF

To vary meat loaf, mix in part or all of a package of dried onion-soup mix, depending on the size of the meat loaf. Try grated carrots too. They'll add color and make the meat go further.

Make an "icing" of mashed potatoes to cover the top of your meat loaf. About 15 minutes before the meat loaf is done, spread the mashed potatoes over the surface and lightly brush with melted butter. Return the meat to the oven.

Cook individual meat loaves in muffin tins. They'll be done in less than half the time of a large loaf.

SAUTÉING AND FRYING

When sautéing, always heat the skillet a minute or two before adding the butter or oil. The food will stick less.

When a recipe calls for butter for sautéing, it's best to use half butter and half vegetable oil, then the butter won't burn as easily.

Batter will cling better if you allow the batter-coated food to dry about 30 minutes at room temperature before submerging it in the hot oil.

Add ½ to 1 teaspoon of baking powder to a frying batter for an especially delicate crust. And a tablespoon of sherry or brandy never hurts, particularly for frying fish and seafood.

SAUTÉING, BRAISING, AND DEEP-FRYING

To sauté, quickly brown or cook the food in a small amount of fat. This method is best for tender, thin cuts of meat and for vegetables that cook quickly. To seal in juices and prevent food from sticking to the pan, dry the food or coat it with flour and have it at room temperature. The fat should be very hot before adding the food, and the pan uncrowded.

In braising, the first step is similar to sautéing—brown the food in fat, but over moderate heat. Then add a small amount of liquid, cover, and simmer until the food is tender. The liquid can be broth, wine, or water. Meats cooked by this method are usually those requiring long cooking to tenderize them.

Deep-frying cooks food quickly in a large amount of fat heated to 375° F. A large saucepan or kettle is used to keep the fat from boiling over. Like sautéing, it is best for foods that cook through quickly.

Invert a colander over a skillet when sautéing to keep grease from spattering on you and the stove. The openings in the colander let steam escape, permitting the food to brown.

STEWS AND BRAISED MEATS

When you brown meat in fat, cook only a few pieces at a time and let the meat get deep brown. This improves the flavor. If you crowd the meat in the pan, the meat will steam instead of brown.

Stir a teaspoon or more of paprika into the liquid when you make a pot roast. It adds flavor and color.

Thicken the sauce in a stew or a pot roast this easy way: stir in a handful of bread crumbs when you add the cooking liquid.

TIMETABLE FOR BROILING

Cut	Approx. thickness	Cooking time in minutes Rare	Med.
BEEF			
Rib eye steak	1″	5–6	7–10
	2″	8–10	14–18
Porterhouse or sirloin steak	1″	5–8	6–10
	1½″	8–12	10–15
	2″	12–16	16–20
Tenderloin (filet mignon)	2″	6–8	10–12
LAMB			
Shoulder chops	¾″–1″		7–11
Rib chops	1″		7–11
	1½″		15–19
Loin chops	1″		7–11
	1½″		15–19
FRESH PORK*			
Rib or loin chops	¾″–1½″		30–45
SMOKED PORK*			
Ham slice	½″		10–12
Loin chops	½″–¾″		15–20
* Always cook pork until well done.			

TIMETABLE FOR BRAISING

Cut	Approx. weight or thickness	Approx. total cooking time
BEEF		
Pot roast	3–5 lb.	2½–3½ hr.
Short ribs	Pieces	1½–2½ hr.
Cubes	1″	1–1½ hr.
	2″	1½–2½ hr.
VEAL		
Breast, stuffed	3–4 lb.	1½–2½ hr.
Breast, boneless	2–3 lb.	1½–2½ hr.
Cubes	1″–2″	45–60 min.
PORK		
Chops	¾″–1½″	45–60 min.
Cubes	1″–1¼″	45–60 min.
Spareribs	2–3 lb.	1½ hr.
LAMB		
Shoulder chops	¾″–1″	45–60 min.
Breast, stuffed	2–3 lb.	1½–2 hr.
Breast, rolled	1½–2 lb.	1½–2 hr.
Stew meat	1½″ cubes	1½–2 hr.

CARVING MEAT AND POULTRY

Beef Rib Roast

1. Remove a slice from the large end to form a base for the roast. Slice across the top of the roast.

2. To remove the slice from the bone, cut vertically along the length of the rib's edge.

3. Slide the knife beneath the slice, steady it with a fork, and lift the slice to a platter.

Leg of Lamb

1. Remove 2 or 3 lengthwise slices from the less meaty side of the leg to form a steady base.

2. Turn the leg on its base. Start cutting a few inches in from the end of the shank bone.

3. Carve horizontally along leg bone. Cut off base in one piece, then slice across the grain.

Whole Ham

 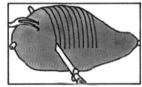 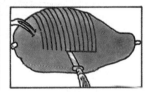

1. Place ham fat side up. Remove 2 or 3 slices from the thin side of the ham to form a base.

2. Turn ham on base. Cut thin slices perpendicular to the leg bone, or lift off in one piece.

3. Cut along leg bone. Remove the base in one piece, then cut across the grain.

Rump Half of Ham

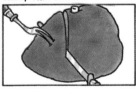  

1. Place ham, cut side down. Cut along the length of the bone and remove the boneless piece.

2. Place the boneless piece cut side down. Carve into thin slices across the grain.

3. Carve the remaining piece by cutting the slices horizontal to the bone.

Turkey or Chicken

1. Begin by removing the drumstick and thigh. Slice the meat from the bones.

2. Cutting close to the body, slice off the wing. Cut the wing in two at the joint.

3. Cut the breast meat in thin downward slices from either side of the breastbone.

ROASTS

Don't add salt to a roast until shortly before the meat is done. Salt coaxes the juices out of meats, and unless you're making soup or stock, you'll want the juices to remain inside.

Remove a roast from the oven when the meat thermometer registers an internal temperature of 5 to 10 degrees below the specified temperature. The meat will continue to cook while it rests before you slice it.

Lamb won't smell as strong while it's cooking and it'll taste milder if you trim off excess fat before broiling, sautéing, or roasting it. To help even more, sprinkle the lamb very lightly with cinnamon.

Roast pork tastes delicious and is juicier when cooked to an internal temperature of 170° F. This is sufficiently high to kill the trichinosis-causing parasites (which die at 137° F), but low enough to ensure that the roast doesn't dry out.

Before a roast is served, brush it lightly with the gravy to give it an attractive glaze.

A good accompaniment to beef or pork dishes is horseradish—yes, horseradish—a teaspoon or more of bottled horseradish mixed with warm or chilled applesauce. Try it with cold leftover meats too.

HAM

If you're going to serve a boiled ham cold, it will be much juicier if you let it cool in the liquid it has simmered in. Cool and freeze the liquid for cooking vegetables and for making split pea soup.

TIMETABLE FOR ROASTING*

(300° F – 325° F Oven Temperature)

Cut	Approx. weight in lb.	Meat therm. reading	Approx. min. per pound**
BEEF			
Rib roast	4–6	140° F (rare)	26–32
		160° F (med.)	34–38
		170° F (well)	40–42
Boneless rump	4–6	150° F–170° F	25–30
Sirloin tip	3½–4	140° F–170° F	35–40
	6–8	140° F–170° F	30–35
VEAL			
Leg	5–8	170° F	25–35
Shoulder, boneless	4–6	170° F	40–45
LAMB			
Leg	7–9	140° F (rare)	15–20
		160° F (med.)	20–25
		170° F (well)	25–30
Leg, shank half	3–4	140° F (rare)	30–35
		160° F (med.)	40–45
		170° F (well)	45–50
Leg, boneless	4–7	140° F (rare)	25–30
		160° F (med.)	30–35
		170° F (well)	35–40
Shoulder, boneless	3½–5	140° F (rare)	30–35
		160° F (med.)	35–40
		170° F (well)	40–45
PORK, FRESH			
Loin, half	5–7	170° F	35–40
Picnic shoulder, boneless	3–5	170° F	35–40
Leg, half (bone in)	7–8	170° F	35–40
PORK, SMOKED			
Ham (cook before eating)			
Whole (bone in)	14–16	160° F	18–20
Half (bone in)	7–8	160° F	22–25
Ham (fully cooked)			
Whole (bone in)	14–16	140° F	15–18
Half (bone in)	7–8	140° F	18–25

*Based on meat taken directly from the refrigerator.
**Roasted meat continues to cook after it has been removed from the oven. In order to avoid overcooking, remove meat from the oven when the internal temperature is 5 to 10 degrees below the temperature at which meat is to be served.

Although a canned ham labeled "ready-to-eat" is safe to eat, the meat should be heated thoroughly in the oven, even if you plan to serve it cold. Heating will greatly improve the flavor.

Remove the skin from a baked ham or boiled tongue as soon as it is cool enough to handle. The task becomes increasingly difficult as the meat cools.

GRAVIES

Try adding a bit of instant coffee powder to a gravy for color. It won't affect the flavor of the gravy.

Lumpy gravy? Buzz in your blender or food processor, beat vigorously with a wire whisk, or push the gravy through a fine sieve.

To obtain a rich brown color when preparing beef stock, brown the bones under a broiler. Then add the bones to the stock and simmer.

To improve the flavor of canned beef or chicken broth, simmer uncovered for 15 or 20 minutes with some chopped onion, carrot, celery, and ¼ cup of red wine.

When a recipe calls for reducing a liquid, here's a foolproof way to measure the amount reduced. Put the handle of a wooden spoon upright in the liquid. Take it out and mark the level of the liquid with a pencil. Check the depth of the liquid periodically with the marked spoon handle.

SAUCES

To thicken a sauce quickly, use a spoon to blend 1 tablespoon of flour with 1 tablespoon of softened butter in a cup. Remove the pan from the heat and beat the mixture, bit by bit, into the hot sauce. Cook, stirring, for 2 or 3 minutes until thickened.

Another method is to dissolve 1 tablespoon of cornstarch or 2 of flour in 2 tablespoons of cold water, stir thoroughly to mix, then add to the sauce. Cook, stirring constantly, over moderate heat for 2 to 3 minutes until thickened.

When preparing a white sauce, pour all the ingredients, including the butter, into the blender or food processor and set it going. When it's thoroughly mixed, pour into a wet, rinsed-out pan and cook over moderate heat, stirring with a whisk, until the sauce has thickened. No lumps and easier than making a regular white sauce.

CAKES

When a recipe calls for the cake pan to be dusted with flour after greasing, sprinkle the pans generously with wheat germ instead. It keeps the cake from sticking and adds nutrients.

Always use unsalted butter for baking. It will make all of your baked goods taste much more professional.

To add an interesting flavor to a white, yellow or chocolate cake, beat 4 tablespoons or more of creamy or chunky peanut butter into the butter-sugar mixture. Beat in the eggs, then proceed with the recipe and bake as directed.

A no-clean-up way to melt chocolate chips or squares: place them in a boilable plastic bag, tie, and set the bag in simmering water. When melted, let the chocolate cool for a moment, cut off a corner of the bag, and squeeze.

Shake nuts, raisins, currants, and other dried fruits with flour before you add them to cake batter and puddings. They won't sink to the bottom of the pan.

Most cakes calling for vanilla extract will taste better if you double the amount of extract.

Sometimes a toothpick is too short to test a cake for doneness, but a piece of uncooked spaghetti works just fine.

Here's a never-fail frosting: in a mixing bowl, beat with an electric mixer 3 ounces softened cream cheese, 2 tablespoons softened butter or margarine, and ½ teaspoon vanilla. Beat until smooth, then gradually beat in 2 cups sifted confectioner's sugar. Covers an 8- or 9-inch round cake.

PIES

Lard, butter, and vegetable shortening can be accurately measured with this replacement method—and the measuring cup is a lot easier to clean. Suppose your recipe calls for ⅓ cup of fat. Fill a measuring cup ⅔ full with water. Then keep adding the fat to it until the water reaches the 1-cup level.

Make piecrust more flavorsome by adding curry powder to the dough for meat or chicken pies. Depending on the filling, cinnamon, chili powder, and ginger are also interesting additions.

A crumb piecrust is less likely to crumble when it's cut if, just before serving, you hold the pie pan for 30 seconds in warm water halfway up the side of the pan.

To add flavor to apple pie, sprinkle a cup of coconut over the apples before adding the top crust.

If you like to serve cheese with apple pie, try baking the cheese in the pie. Spread sharp or extra-sharp grated Cheddar over the bottom of the crust before adding the filling.

For an unusual treat, mix in a ½ teaspoon or so of dill seeds in your apple pie.

Here's an easy crumb topping to take the place of the top crust for a fruit pie. In a small bowl, mix ¾ cup flour, 1 cup white or firmly packed brown sugar, and 1 teaspoon cinnamon. With a fork or pastry blender, cut in 7 tablespoons butter.

If there are "tears" on the meringue topping you've browned in the oven, the sugar probably did not dissolve completely. To avoid this, use small amounts of superfine sugar added a little at a time; whip well between additions.

OTHER DESSERTS

To prevent apple skins from cracking while they bake, remove a ½-inch band from around the center of each apple.

For a treat, pour a little port wine over baked apples just before you take them from the oven.

When the weather's hot, nothing beats chilled, cut-up fruit. Use whatever's in season—melons, grapes, kiwi fruit, peaches, papayas, berries—and always include a citrus fruit—orange or grapefruit—to add tang and juice. Finally, squeeze a lime over all and stir in sugar to taste.

LATTICE-TOP PIE

1. Using a sharp knife or pizza cutter, with a ruler for a guide, cut the crust into ¼-inch strips.

2. Lay down 6 evenly spaced strips over the filling, placing the longer ones in the middle, the shorter ones to the sides.

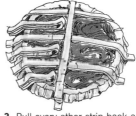

3. Pull every other strip back a little more than halfway. Lay a strip across the center.

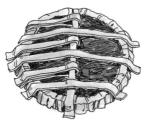

4. Lay the pulled-back strips in their original positions, pulling the alternate strips back over the middle one.

5. Put 2 more perpendicular strips, one at a time, to one side of the middle one, each time pulling back and replacing the alternate strips.

6. Complete the other side. Trim each strip even with the edge of the pan. Gently pinch each strip end into the shell.

Fresh doughnuts without the fuss! Use the dough from a tube of refrigerator biscuits. With the cap from a bottle of cooking oil, cut a hole in the center of each biscuit. Deep-fry in hot oil for 2 to 3 minutes, turning as the doughnuts brown. Drain, cool, and roll in granulated sugar or spread with frosting. Fry the cutout holes too.

To give a fruit cup or fruit salad a boost, add a few slivers of crystalized ginger.

If your vanilla or fruit ice cream accidentally melts, use it as a dessert sauce—on blueberry pie or other fruit pies or on fresh fruit.

To save time when you bake a lot of cookies, cut aluminum foil to fit cookie sheets, place cookies on the foil, then slide onto a cookie sheet and bake. When the cookies are done, slide the foil off and put it on the next sheet of cookies.

COOKING FOR ONE

Buy only what you can use or freeze immediately. Don't hesitate to ask a clerk to divide a wrapped package of meat or fresh produce.

Choose large bags of frozen vegetables rather than small cartons. Use what you need, seal the bag and return the rest to the freezer.

EQUIVALENTS AND YIELDS

Food	Amount	Approximate measure
Apples	1 lb.	3 c. pared, sliced
Bananas	1 lb.	3–4 medium or 1¾ c. mashed
Beans, green, fresh	1 lb.	3 c. uncooked or 2½ c. cooked
Beans, dried	1 lb.	2 c. uncooked or 6 c. cooked
Berries	1 qt.	3½ c.
Bread crumbs, dry	1 slice bread	¼ c.
Bread crumbs, soft	1 slice bread	½ c.
Broccoli	1 lb.	2 c. cooked
Butter	¼ lb.	8 tbsp. or ½ c.
Cabbage	1 lb.	4 c. shredded
Carrots	1 lb.	2½ c. diced
Cheese	¼ lb.	1 c. shredded
Cheese, cottage	½ lb.	1 c.
Chicken, broiler, fryer	3½ lb.	2 c. cooked, diced meat
Chocolate	1 oz.	4 tbsp. grated
Coffee	1 lb.	45 6-oz. c.
Coffee, instant	2 oz.	25 6-oz. c.
Crackers, graham	16	1¼ c. crumbs
Egg whites, large	8	about 1 c.
Flour, all-purpose	1 lb.	4 c. sifted
Lemon	1 med.	2–3 tbsp. juice; 2 tsp. grated rind
Milk, instant, nonfat dry	1 lb.	4 qt.
Mushrooms, fresh	½ lb.	1 c. sliced, cooked
Oatmeal	1 c.	2¼ c. cooked
Onion	1 med.	½ c. chopped
Orange	1 med.	6–8 tbsp. juice; 2–3 tbsp. grated rind
Peach or pear	¼ lb.	½ c. sliced
Peas, dried	1 lb.	2¼ c. uncooked or 5 c. cooked
Pecans, in shell	1 lb.	2¼ c. chopped nuts
Pepper, green	1 large	1 c. diced
Potatoes, 3 medium	1 lb.	2¼ c. cooked or 1¾ c. mashed
Prunes, dried	1 lb.	2½ c. or 4 c. cooked
Raisins	1 lb.	2¾ c.
Rice	½ lb.	1 c. or 3 c. cooked
Spaghetti	1 lb.	6–8 c. cooked
Spinach	1 lb.	1½ c. cooked
Sugar, brown	1 lb.	2¼ c. (firmly packed)
confectioner's	1 lb.	3½ c.
granulated	1 lb.	2 c.
Tea	1 lb.	125 c.

c. = cup

COOKING DURING A POWER OUTAGE

Question: I cook with electricity. What type of equipment can I use when the power goes out?

Answer: A chafing dish is sufficient for low-heat cooking. If you have a fireplace and cast-iron cookware, you might actually enjoy cooking over an open fire. With a reflector oven, available at camping goods stores, you can even do some simple cooking, such as baking biscuits and other quick breads.

A charcoal grill or hibachi can be used safely indoors but only if you place the equipment in a fireplace with a good updraft where the carbon monoxide gases can escape through the chimney. **Caution: Do not use a charcoal grill in an enclosed area. Improper ventilation could be fatal.**

Question: I don't have a fireplace; what shall I do then?

Answer: Your best bet, and actually the most efficient in any case, is a camp stove. Follow manufacturer's instructions carefully when operating it, and cook in a well-ventilated area.

Buy only half a dozen eggs at a time. A cardboard carton of a dozen can usually be broken in half.

Try stir-frying several foods together in one pan, starting with the item requiring the longest cooking time The fast cooking retains more nutrients, and besides, you'll have only one skillet to wash. (You don't need a wok for stir-frying; use any type of large frying pan.)

If you have the freezer space, buy large packages of meat and chicken when they are on special sale. Divide the packages into individual servings, wrap tightly with freezer paper or aluminum foil, and freeze them. Then put the frozen portions into one large plastic bag, and label the bag with the date and contents.

Here's an easy, light dessert: combine ⅓ cup sour cream or plain yogurt, 1 tablespoon confectioner's sugar, and a teaspoon of grated orange rind. Spoon the mixture over a cup of chilled, seedless green grapes.

GLASSWARE

Glasses stuck hopelessly together? Separate fast by filling the top one with cold water and dipping the bottom one in hot water.

Broken glass? Use a dampened paper towel to pick up the slivers.

COOKING UTENSILS

Let your pots and pans clean themselves while you eat. Fill them with hot, sudsy water and let them soak. Later, most will need only a rinse; heavily soiled pots will come clean quickly.

Sprinkle burned saucepans liberally with baking soda, add just enough water to moisten, and let stand for several hours. You can usually lift the burned portion right out. Or soak for 24 hours with 2 tablespoons of dishwasher detergent and a few cups of water.

Spray the outside of an encrusted iron skillet with commercial oven cleaner. An hour or so later, wash with hot, soapy water.

Entertaining Tips & Etiquette

PREPARING TO ENTERTAIN GUESTS

The smaller the party, the more carefully you should choose your guests, because each bears more of the conversational burden. If it's to be a small gathering, avoid inviting opinionated people with widely divergent viewpoints.

It's best not to people a party with one age group, one profession, or one marital status. Shoptalk can be dreary, especially if only one or two persons are outside that experience. Shake the mixture up a bit.

Your dinner party doesn't need an equal number of men and women. Matchmaking is nice but not necessary. If the spouse of a person you know is out of town, it's a kind gesture to ask the one left at home to your dinner party.

PARTY PLANNING

Dinner for close friends might be served buffet style and eaten in the living room. For business associates or acquaintances or for an occasion where someone is being honored, a sit-down meal is more appropriate.

If your house is small or you have many invitations to repay, consider giving parties two days in a row. You'll make the decorations, housecleaning, any borrowed equipment, and some of the food preparation count double.

For large gatherings such as cocktail parties, the rule of thumb is that 25 to 30 percent of those invited will probably decline. So if you want 50 guests, invite 65 to 70. For weddings, special birthdays, or anniversaries, you may lose only 15 percent.

When spacing guests around a table, allow 2½ feet between diners. If your table is small but you have space, set up a card table topped with a round or oval plywood cover. This way you can accommodate six to eight persons.

INVITATIONS

Invitations should be mailed or phoned 3 to 4 weeks in advance for large or formal affairs and about 2 weeks ahead for small parties. Any invitation should include the host's/hostess's name, address of the party, the date and time, the purpose or theme of the party, dress, and any activities, such as swimming or dancing.

Formal invitations, engraved or handwritten on white or off-white paper, are used for such occasions as a cocktail reception, an important lunch, a large dinner party, a formal dance, or a wedding. They are written in the third person—Mr. and Mrs. John Smith request the pleasure of your company.... These invitations may also be engraved in color on contrasting stock; they may have a colored border too.

Looking for a calligrapher to make your formal or informal invitations especially beautiful? Check with your local stationery store. Calligraphers generally charge by the piece; keep in mind that they need plenty of time.

Use R.S.V.P. on all written invitations, indicating you need a firm response. "Regrets Only," with its impersonal request, may not get you an answer at all. Use it only for a large cocktail party.

ADVANCE PREPARATIONS

If you have run out of recipe ideas, look for new ones in reputable cookbooks that feature well-tested recipes. However, it's better not to serve a dish you've never made before. Pretest the recipe first with your family.

Prepare as many dishes ahead of time as possible. Choose recipes that you can make a day or two in advance; keep them refrigerated or frozen, and just reheat them.

When you're cooking in advance, however, remember that dishes to be reheated should be left slightly underdone. Choose no more than one dish that calls for a lot of last-minute attention.

The day before the party, check the weather forecast. If rain or snow is predicted, plan where to store open umbrellas, hats, boots, and wet coats.

Are you sure the directions to your house are clear? Augment your oral or written instructions with visual aids. If the party is during the day, tie brightly colored bandannas or balloons around trees or signposts on your property. At night, hang a lighted lantern on a post at the end of the driveway.

RENTING AND BORROWING

For a large party, save money by renting serving equipment, such as platters, chafing dishes, trays, punch bowls, rather than buying it for onetime use. Or try borrowing from a church or service club.

Rented china, crystal, and flatware won't be as nice as your own. Still, it's better to rent than to borrow fragile items and take a chance that they'll be broken.

If you need many tables and chairs, rent them. If you need only a few, borrow them from friends —and by all means invite them to your party!

In the winter or if rain is predicted, it's a good idea to rent a coatrack if your party is a large one.

Make an accurate list, piece by piece, of whatever you rent or borrow and where it came from. Check off each item before you return it. Be careful of mix-ups, especially of flatware.

HIRING HELP

Here are ways to find a good caterer. Ask a friend who has recently hosted a party. Obtain a business card from a waiter at a catered party. Consult your favorite restaurant for a recommendation (perhaps they'll do the job themselves). And scan the classified section of your local newspaper.

Select a caterer at least a month in advance (6 months ahead during the busy days of November, December, and June).

To compare prices, telephone two or three caterers and ask for an estimate for doing a party for a given number of people with a certain menu. Before choosing, ask the main contenders for two or three references and check them.

Always ask a caterer if you can sample his food ahead of time. It may look beautiful, but the taste may not be to your liking.

To find good waiters and bartenders, keep names and telephone numbers of helpers observed at friends' homes. Ask a local caterer to draw from his roster of part-time staffers. Call a college job-placement office for names of students who have experience waiting or bartending. Call bartending and cooking schools.

Figure on one waiter or waitress to handle 8 to 10 guests at an informal seated dinner, 12 to 16 guests at a buffet. At a formal dinner, count on a minimum of one waiter for each 6 to 8 guests. One bartender can handle about 25 cocktail-party guests.

COCKTAIL PARTIES

If you're having just a few people for drinks, there should be a place for everyone to sit. If it's a large affair, provide just a few chairs and a lot of open space so that people will stand and mix.

Before a large cocktail party, put away prized breakable objects and clear tables of bric-a-brac. That way you limit possible damage and allow places for drinks to be set down. Distribute coasters on all horizontal surfaces.

Open up space by pushing furniture to the walls and taking away small tables and stools that people might trip over. Remove any tables with unattached glass tops.

SETTING UP THE BAR

Figure that a fifth of liquor (26 ounces) will yield 17 jiggers of 1½ ounces each. A liter (34 ounces) will make 22 1½-ounce drinks.

If you plan to have 20 or more people, a bartender will be a great help. One tended bar will handle up to 25 people easily and smoothly. However, self-service for that number will require two or more bars.

Have plenty of cocktail napkins handy. Guests should be given a fresh napkin with each drink and with each hot canapé.

Plan on twice the ice you think you may need. Either make ice cubes ahead of time and store them in plastic bags, or buy bags of ice just before the party. Keep ice for drinks separate from ice for chilling; the latter won't be clean.

EASY HORS D'OEUVRES

Cut circles of bread with a cookie cutter, spread with mayonnaise, top with a cucumber slice and a pimiento sliver or a sprig of dill.

Scoop out the pulp from cherry tomatoes and stuff them with your favorite tuna-fish salad, deviled ham, or guacamole.

To make guacamole, mash 2 ripe avocados and mix with 1 tablespoon lemon juice, 1 teaspoon minced onion, and red pepper flakes and salt to taste.

Spoon cream cheese mixed with a few drops of lemon juice onto crisp endive leaves. Top with red or black lumpfish caviar.

Wrap honeydew melon or cantaloupe balls with paper-thin strips of prosciutto ham or boiled ham. Secure with a toothpick.

Wrap thin slices of smoked salmon around cucumber sticks.

For dipping, cut cooked breast of chicken or turkey into fingers and serve with mayonnaise flavored with curry powder.

Split small cocktail sausages, stuff them with sharp Cheddar cheese, and run them under the broiler until the cheese melts.

PROBLEM DRINKERS

Nonalcoholic beverages should be available for nondrinkers. Offer them also when you take a drink order from a guest who has overimbibed.

Never allow an inebriated person to drive home after your party. You may be held legally responsible if an accident occurs. Call a cab, ask a sober guest to drive your friend home, do it yourself, or offer your spare bedroom. If necessary, take away the car keys.

When entertaining the recovered alcoholic at a dinner where wine is served, have a wineglass in place for your guest. Let your guest decide whether to say "No, thank you" when you pour the wine or to leave the poured glass untouched. Avoid using liquor in the food or dessert unless it's burned off in the cooking.

A PARTY COUNTDOWN

Three to 4 weeks before. Decide on party style and theme. Plan menu. Make guest list. Write or phone invitations. Plan for rentals and extra help.

Two weeks before. Make shopping and cooking schedule. Prepare dishes that can be frozen.

One week before. Plot rearranging of furniture. Plan table decor. Order flowers. Check table linen and candles. Check and buy bar supplies.

Three to 4 days before. Write place cards. Polish silver. Clean house. Shop for all except perishable food.

Two days before. Make and store extra ice. Start cooking all dishes to be served cold or reheated.

One day before. Buy fresh food. Make seating plan. Wash, dry, and store salad greens. Set up extra tables. Select music.

Party day. Give house once-over. Finish cooking. Buy fresh bread. Set table. Arrange flowers. Put out ashtrays. Refrigerate white wine. Prepare closet for storage of guests' coats. Set up bar. Set out serving platters.

One hour before. Open red wine. Stock bar with pitcher of water, ice, lemon slices, utensils. Set out cocktail snacks.

Half an hour before. Relax, freshen your face, and change into your party clothes.

WHEN GUESTS WON'T LEAVE

Having trouble getting guests to leave? Here's one way to move them along: close the bar. If the time is stated on the invitation, stop serving drinks 45 minutes after the hour of the party's ending.

More ideas. Say that you are expected at a friend's house for dinner. Start emptying ashtrays, taking glasses to the kitchen, and tidying the room. Or invite the remaining guests to go out to dinner with you—Dutch treat.

CENTERPIECES

For a striking, inexpensive centerpiece, put wildflowers in a brass jar or a large pitcher. Mix fresh flowers with dried or fabric flowers. Or float a single large bloom (dahlia or rhododendron) in water in a crystal bowl.

Placing a large round mirror on the center of the table under your arrangement will double the effect of your centerpiece.

Decorate with seasonal fruits and vegetables. In the fall, line a dish with maple leaves and fill it with polished apples. In the summer, fill a wicker basket with polished tomatoes, tuck curly parsley or sprigs of fresh basil around the edge, and fill the spaces between the tomatoes with daisies, more parsley, or basil.

No matter how pretty an object is, don't use it on the table if it's unstable. Weigh down flower vases or bowls with stones, marbles, or sand poured into the bottom.

Make your dessert the centerpiece. Put a ring of fresh flowers around a layer cake or surround a giant apple pie with apples and other fruits. For a summertime focal point, hollow out a watermelon and fill it with cut-up fresh fruit.

Will the centerpiece block your guests' views? Measure its height; it should not exceed 15 inches.

SETTING A BUFFET TABLE

If you have the space, place your buffet table in the center of the room, allowing guests to walk around it easily. If space is limited, place the table on one side of the room, but pull it far enough away from the wall so that you can slip behind it and replenish dishes.

If you move the table to the center of the room, tape appliance cords to the floor so that guests won't trip. Make sure you don't overload any circuit by plugging too many small appliances into one outlet.

Set up a separate table for cold drinks, coffee, tea, dessert, and all related glasses, cups, and plates.

ARRANGING A BUFFET TABLE; WHAT TO SERVE

Arrange a buffet table in logical order: dinner plates, rice or noodles, hot main dish (to be spooned on the rice or noodles), vegetables, salad, bread, relishes and condiments, forks and napkins. Place a small table nearby for beverages.

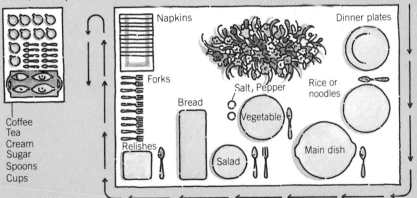

Hot buffet

Beef stew with red wine
Egg noodles
Carrots with ginger
Green salad
French bread
Watermelon boat with
   fresh fruit

Cold buffet

Fish and shrimp mousse
   or ham mousse
Rice and pea salad
Cold sliced beets
   vinaigrette
Herb bread
Glazed strawberry pie

Mixed hot and cold buffet

Cold fried chicken
German potato salad
Zucchini and tomato
   casserole
Corn bread
Carrot cake with cream
   cheese frosting (p.388)

Keep the menu simple, the table uncrowded, and the decorations compact. Leave room beside the main dishes for guests to rest their plates as they help themselves. If you can't manage this for the main dishes, at least do so for a green salad, where two hands are needed for serving.

Here are two tricks for keeping cold foods chilled: freeze water in a deep-dish pie plate, put it in a clear, plastic bag, and place platter of cold food on top. Or freeze water in a ring mold or other molds of interesting shapes; put them on platters with the food around them.

FOODS FOR A BUFFET

The best buffet foods are those that require no cutting, except perhaps with a fork. Casseroles or stews that can be served over rice or noodles are good choices.

Be aware of your guests' dietary needs and preferences. Vegetarians, for instance, probably prefer vegetable stir-fries or casseroles, pastas, grains, and salads.

Diabetics might appreciate fresh vegetables and fruit, cheese, and foods without rich, starchy sauces or sugar. If any guests suffer from high blood pressure, eliminate salt in cooking.

WHEN THE BUFFET BEGINS

If people seem settled in their chairs for the evening, say, "May I get you some dinner?" This will probably get them on their feet.

Arrange chairs so that each guest has a seat and a place to put down plate and glass. Small folding tables and card tables are always handy. It's a good idea to group the seats in threes or more for conversation's sake.

FORMAL MEALS

Try to limit pre-meal cocktails to about 45 minutes, just long enough for everyone to show up.

A formal lunch or dinner may consist of three courses (first course, entrée, and dessert); four courses (first course, entrée, salad served separately, and dessert); or five courses (first course, fish, entrée, salad, and dessert).

If you wish to serve a four- or five-course meal, you'll benefit greatly from extra help.

For a fast, attractive first course, spoon chilled, canned jellied madrilene in avocado halves. Top with a dollop of sour cream or yogurt and a spoonful of red or black lumpfish caviar.

When planning your menu, balance rich foods with light foods, and consider texture and eye appeal. Serve pale food on colored plates, if possible; add color with garnishes (p.400). Avoid serving two or more white or light-colored foods together.

If you're taking the trouble to prepare a formal meal, don't stint on the cost of ingredients. Buy the choicest meat and other foods you can afford. Select fruits and vegetables that are in season—they'll taste better and cost less.

For a formal lunch, you can use place mats or an organdy or lace tablecloth. If your table will be crowded with dishes, a tablecloth looks better. The napkins may be of damask, but reserve your damask tablecloth for dinners only.

For a formal dinner, the centerpiece is usually flowers. Candles should always be included and should burn either above or below the eye level.

PLACE CARDS AND MENU CARDS

It's helpful to use place cards for a dinner of eight or more guests. If you know your guests well, you can make a seating diagram and refer to it privately before calling your guests to the table.

SETTING A FORMAL TABLE: WHAT TO SERVE

A. Napkin
B. Fish fork
C. Dinner fork
D. Salad fork
E. First-course soup and liner plate
F. Dinner or service plate
G. Dinner knife
H. Fish knife
I. Soupspoon
J. Bread-and-butter plate
K. Butter knife
L. Dessertspoon and fork
M. Place card
N. Water goblet
O. Red wine
P. White wine

A three-course dinner

Marinated shrimp with dill
Roast rack of lamb
Buttered spinach
Mushroom caps stuffed with herbed wild rice
Chocolate-mocha mousse

A four-course dinner

Cold cucumber soup
Filet mignon with sauce béarnaise
Lemon-buttered asparagus
Sautéed potatoes
Endive and watercress salad
Fresh strawberries with raspberry sauce

A five-course dinner

Beef consommé with lemon slices
Scallops in the shell
Roast chicken with natural gravy
Baked rice and onions
Broccoli florets
Romaine and arugula salad
Open-face apple tart

Menu cards are a delightful way to provide guests with a memento of special occasions. The cards should be 5 inches by 7 inches and either handwritten or typed. On each card, write the date, the foods, and the wine or wines. Make one for each guest.

DINNER MAY 2
Artichokes with
Mustard Vinaigrette
~
Roast Leg of Lamb
Eggplant, Tomato,
Z   ni C   role

John   Jane

SERVING THE FOOD

To serve a formal meal without help, fill each guest's plate in the kitchen, restaurant style, and carry it to the table. A well-coached teenage offspring might do the serving and clearing.

Remember to serve the guests' plates or serving dishes from the left and remove the empty plates from the right.

Another good choice is to let your guests help themselves to the entrée and vegetables from a buffet or sideboard and then take their plates to the table.

GARNISHES: THE FINAL TOUCH

Here are some suggestions for delicious and decorative garnishes. Float lemon slices, cucumber rounds, or snipped chives on light or clear soups. Add spiced apples to cold roast beef platters. Top seafood casseroles or skillet dishes with cherry tomatoes. Sprinkle desserts with toasted coconut, chopped nuts, or grated citrus peel.

Parsley or watercress nosegay. Wash and dry parsley; bundle together several sprigs. Secure with a pimiento strip. For any main-dish platter.

Tomato rose. Starting at the smooth end, peel a ¾-inch-wide strip in a spiral. Roll from stem end, skin side out. For meat or poultry platters.

Citrus twists. Slice thin; cut from edge to center. Twist into a bow. For meat or seafood platters or desserts.

Carrot curl. Cut peeled carrot thin with a vegetable parer. Roll up and fasten with wooden picks; chill in ice water. Drain and remove picks. For appetizer trays or salads.

Pickle or zucchini fan. Make thin cuts from the top to ¼ inch from the bottom. Spread slices to form fan. For meat, poultry, seafood platters.

Bacon curl. Cook bacon slices until limp. Cool, roll up and fasten with wooden picks. Cook until crisp; drain, remove picks. For egg dishes, pasta, poultry, or vegetable salads.

To keep from constantly getting up from the table to serve guests, bring the appetizer to the living room. Collect dirty plates and take them to the kitchen before guests sit down at the table.

Serve dessert on plates stacked in front of you; pass them from person to person. Or use a rolling tea cart to hold the dessert. Later it can move soiled dishes to the kitchen.

A good way to get people up from the table is to serve coffee in the living room from a tray set up ahead of time with cups and saucers, sugar bowl, and creamer. First, be sure that cocktail glasses and snacks have been cleared away and ashtrays emptied.

SPECIAL TYPES OF PARTIES

When planning a potluck dinner, set the tone of the meal by providing the main-course dish yourself. Ask your friends to bring dishes that will complement your entrée. Find out specifically what these dishes are and tactfully choose those you think best.

Planning a barbecue for 50? You'll need 17½ pounds of ground beef for hamburgers and 70 buns (for 4-ounce burgers); or 10 pounds of hot dogs (100 buns); 2 gallons of baked beans; 6 quarts of potato salad; 10 pounds of coleslaw.

For nighttime outdoor parties, illuminate garden paths and the driveway with candlelight. Place candles in glass tumblers filled halfway with sand or stones. Or outline the branches of trees and bushes with small, white lights.

Make an adult's birthday party special. Have a horoscope made up for the guest and read it aloud. Show home movies featuring special events in the person's life, such as a graduation or wedding. Plan a party around an activity the person especially enjoys— hiking, bowling, dancing.

For an important event—a wedding, a 50th birthday, or a special anniversary—have the party videotaped. You can have the work done by professionals (see under "Video–Production" in the Yellow Pages), or you can rent the necessary equipment from your local video store and have a family member record the celebration.

If you're asking a family for lunch and a swim in your pool, designate an arrival and departure time; otherwise, the youngsters will persuade their parents to come early and stay forever.

LIVE ENTERTAINMENT

Looking for entertainers for your party? Musicians may be found through a local college, a music school, or the entertainment classifieds of your local paper.

Other types of entertainment: magicians, palm or tarot readers, handwriting experts, mimes, caricaturists, clowns. Try to see your entertainers before you hire them to be sure their performances are in line with your tastes.

CHILDREN'S PARTIES

Consult your child before issuing invitations to the party. Some children prefer guests of the same sex; others want both sexes.

A good rule of thumb is to invite as many guests as the birthday child is old. For example, one baby guest for a first birthday, two children for a 2-year-old, and three for a 3-year old.

PRESCHOOL CHILDREN

To minimize mess, serve little children precut foods such as chicken or peanut-butter-and-jelly sandwiches in bite-sized pieces. For older kids stick to favorites: hamburgers, hot dogs, ice cream.

For kids under 5, a party is a novel experience. They'll be content to play with the host's or hostess's toys, sing songs, have a piece of birthday cake, and receive party favors. Keep the entertainment short and simple.

With colored felt-tip pen or crayon, write each child's name on the front of a shopping bag for carrying home the favors. Or let the kids do the writing themselves.

Ask an older brother or sister to jot down what gifts were received and from whom. If the birthday child is old enough to write, suggest short thank-you notes.

CHILDREN'S PARTY GAMES

For preschoolers, play each game for a short time only. Announce the games in a definite way; don't ask "Shall we play...?" One negative can sour a suggestion.

Be sympathetic toward a shy child who may choose to watch rather than participate in the game.

Pin the Nose on the Celebrity. Instead of using a donkey and a tail, pin up a poster of a favorite TV personality or cartoon character. Make funny-looking paper noses (one for each child). Blindfold one child at a time, turn him around two or three times, and send him off toward the poster while the others watch.

Hide the Thimble. Here's one for preschool and early elementary kids. While one child leaves the room, the others hide a thimble. The child is called back to find it. The others clap their hands quietly when the searcher is far from the thimble, louder when he's close to it.

Memory Game. For children who are able to write, assemble 10 to 20 household items on a card table. Give the youngsters 3 to 5 minutes to look over the table and memorize the items. Then cover the table with a sheet. Ask the children to write down as many items as they can recall. Make sure you select objects they can spell easily.

Simon Says. This old standby works well for all ages. Choose one player to be Simon. He tells the others to do certain actions, such as "jump," "clap your hands," "scratch your ear," sometimes including the words "Simon says," sometimes omitting them. Only "Simon says" commands should be obeyed and all those forgetting this instruction are "out." The winner is the last person left besides Simon.

To facilitate cleanup, spread the Sunday funny papers under a preschooler's party table.

A good way to control the length of the party is to offer to drive all the youngsters home.

SCHOOL-AGE CHILDREN'S PARTIES

Children love to get mail, so it's nice to send invitations. Ask a birthday child who's old enough to help make and address them.

Here are some themes for school-agers: treasure hunt; a cast-off party (the day before a child with a broken leg has the cast removed); a winter carnival with ice skating or snow sculpture.

Any entertainment for children of elementary school age—clowns, puppets, magicians—should be carefully planned. If the children are too young to understand a magic act, they'll be restless; if too old, they'll be bored.

Be sure the entertainer you hire for the party understands the differences between a child of 6 and an 11-year-old.

TEENAGE PARTIES

Open parties to which anyone can come may be invitations to trouble. Help your teen make up the list of guests who will behave responsibly. Make the rule "No uninvited guests" and stick to it.

To some teenagers, "partying" means using drugs and alcohol. If your teenager wants to give a party, make it clear that these substances are not allowed.

If your teen thinks it's a good idea, ask a college student whom you both know and respect to bring a date and act as chaperone and "bouncer" at the party—for a fee. Ask the student to keep an eye out for drugs and alcohol and notify you if things get rowdy.

Plan to be at home throughout the party, whether a chaperone is there or not. Greet the guests and appear once or twice during the evening, but don't embarrass a teenager by joining the party.

Try to keep young teenagers busy. Provide games such as Scrabble, backgammon, Trivial Pursuit, or involve guests in setting the table and preparing the food.

Table tennis is a good indoor game for teens. If you don't have a table, borrow a tabletop for the night and put it on your dining room table with a thick blanket or other padding underneath.

A VCR and a popular movie or two provide entertainment without making demands for social interaction.

If you have close neighbors, you might suggest that your teenager tell them about the party and ask them to call if they're disturbed by the music or noise. A consulted neighbor may be a little more tolerant if the music gets too loud.

CHAPTER SIX

A MORE BEAUTIFUL HOME

Make your home more attractive—change the color scheme, repaint, panel, or hang new wall coverings; investigate new lighting and flooring alternatives. Keep your home looking great by maintaining all your furnishings in tip-top condition.

types of window coverings; selecting the best carpet fiber; wall-to-wall carpeting and area rugs; carpet colors and patterns; furnishing basics; determining quality in furniture; furniture on a budget; picture hanging made easy; arranging pictures; special hints on framing; working magic with mirrors; displaying your special collections.

Decorating Made Easy
Page 405

Before beginning to decorate; making a basic plan; free decorator services; deciding on a color scheme; working wonders with color; how to set up a floor plan; placing furniture in a room; wall and ceiling preparation; patching plasterboard and plaster; brushes, rollers, and other painting tools; selecting paint; determining how much paint you'll need; special painting techniques; tips on painting walls, ceilings, and windows; successful stenciling; wall-covering choices; removing the old wall coverings; hanging prepasted wall covering; repairing damaged wall coverings; how to panel walls; tips on ceilings; flooring alternatives; lighting hints; a lighting glossary; window treatments; dealing with problem windows;

Taking Care of the Furnishings
Page 431

Glass and dinnerware; how to mend broken porcelain and cracks in pottery; taking care of silverware; keeping metals clean and shiny; how to remove dents from metal; caring for mirrors and pictures; fixing a wobbly picture frame; patching a gilt frame; caring for mar-

ble and leather; cleaning other furnishings; caring for wooden furniture; choosing and using furniture polishing products; treating spots and stains on wood; scratches, burns, and blisters; repairing a burn; fixing scratches in wood; minor furniture repairs; repairing loose chair joints; patching damaged or missing veneer; preparing to refinish; sanding hints; stripping furniture; choosing and applying a new finish; varnishing; special refinishing problems; preparing to refinish a wood floor; sanding and touching up; using sealants; refinishing tools and procedures; painting floors; hints on slipcovering; caring for and shampooing upholstered furniture; choosing fabric; repairing torn upholstery; getting ready to reupholster; stuffing, padding, springs, and webbing.

Decorating Made Easy

BEFORE YOU BEGIN

Why should you decide to decorate—or redecorate? Perhaps because your lifestyle has changed: you've just got a big raise; your children have left home; you're just recently widowed or divorced. Or maybe because you're just plain tired of looking at the same surroundings day after day.

Take stock of what you have, what you want to keep, and what to give away. Be ruthless. Redecorating is a time for eliminating. Don't keep Aunt Sarah's bulky old sideboard purely out of sentiment. Space is too valuable today.

Before you begin decorating, call a family meeting and get everyone's opinions. As much as possible, each family member should agree on the new color schemes, furnishings, and how much to spend. This way, no one person gets blamed for a mistake.

THE BASIC PLAN

For continuity and a sense of spaciousness, maintain basically the same color scheme throughout, varying only the accent colors from room to room. Also, it's best to stick to one style, whether traditional, contemporary, or transitional (a blend of the two).

The only exceptions to this are the family bedrooms and bathrooms. As personal space, they can depart from the style and color scheme of the overall theme.

For a small room, choose pale colors and light-scaled furniture and accessories. See-through pieces, such as armchairs with open arms or cane seats and backs, will give an illusion of greater space.

You can make a large room more intimate with highly varied textures and dominant patterns for rugs, draperies, and upholstery. Big sprawling seating arrangements, large paintings, and area rugs also pull a room together.

DECORATOR SERVICES FOR FREE

Depending on the extent of the changes you intend to make and the time and energy you're willing to invest, you don't necessarily have to pay for the services of an interior designer when you need decorating advice. Sources of free advice include paint stores, wallpaper outlets, fabric shops, and picture framers. And often you can get good solid information for free from decorators in furniture stores or in home furnishings departments.

Bring with you a floor plan and a photograph of the room or rooms you plan to decorate, including any furniture you expect to keep. It's also a good idea to bring magazine clippings of rooms (identifying the specific features that appeal to you), furniture, and fabrics (or swatches) that you like to give the decorator an idea of your tastes. With these in hand, the professional will assist you in making selections.

Take home samples (as large as possible) whenever you can. Scale, size, and color are dramatically different in a department store setting as opposed to your home. When you make your final decision, the decorator can order what you need from the store's stock or from catalogs.

DECIDING ON A COLOR SCHEME

It's not hard to choose a new color scheme for your home. Just think of the colors that most please you or recall a favorite painting, fabric, or rug. The key is to choose colors that harmonize and that you enjoy.

If all else fails, you're bound to be successful if you refer to a color wheel containing the 12 base colors. Using this simple tool, you can arrive at a variety of color schemes, one of which will be right for you.

The monochromatic scheme: A range of tints (the base color lightened by white) and shades (the base color deepened by black) of a single color on the wheel.

The analogous (or related) scheme: Two or more adjoining colors on the wheel.

The complementary scheme: Opposite hues on the color wheel.

The adjacent complementary scheme: The two opposite colors on the wheel, plus a third accent color, that's right or left of either of the two.

The triad complementary scheme: Three colors equidistant on the wheel.

The split complementary scheme: One color plus the two colors that flank its opposite color.

Establishing the basic color scheme is a big step forward, but important planning still lies ahead. The next step is to allocate the scheme colors to the various parts of your home. Use the lighter tone in the scheme for the background—that is, the walls, ceilings, and floors. The other scheme colors can appear in the upholstery, draperies, and accessories.

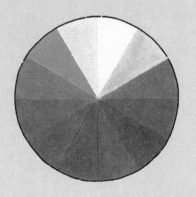

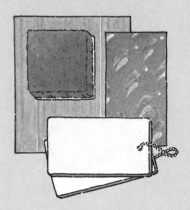

WORKING WONDERS WITH COLOR

Remember, color is your least expensive decorating tool. And it can do any number of things. For example, you can "heighten" a too-low ceiling with a light color, or you can "bring down" a too-high ceiling by painting it a shade darker than the walls. Another way to "lower" a ceiling is by continuing its color along the top 8 to 12 inches of wall, creating a "frieze."

Select a dominant color for every room. After you've decided on it, choose other colors to harmonize.

To make a room look smaller, paint the ceiling and walls different colors. The walls will appear closer to each other with deeper-toned or warm colors such as red, yellow, and brown.

You can visually enlarge a small room with expanses of mirrors and with lighter-toned colors such as pale blue or green.

Shorten a long narrow room by painting one end a darker tone than the side walls.

Widen a narrow room by painting one side wall a lighter shade than the other and using lighting to brighten that side wall even more.

Use color, pattern, and texture to demarcate areas of a room: set a conversation section apart with upholstery and wallpaper of the same design. Highlight a dining area in a dual-purpose room with a change in carpet and a lighter or darker wall color.

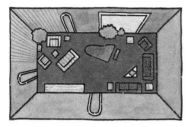

SETTING UP A FLOOR PLAN

An excellent way to establish a floor plan is on graph paper, allowing each ¼ inch on the paper to equal 1 foot in the actual room. Draw the room to scale and indicate the exact size and location of all doors, windows, radiators, air conditioners, and door swings.

Measure each piece of furniture in the room. Carefully plot the measurements on construction paper or on heavy cardboard, using the same scale that you used for the floor plan. Label and cut out the drawings; then move them around the floor plan until you get an arrangement that uses your space and furniture to best advantage.

With your graph-paper plan in hand, you'll be able to note areas of waste space where you could

place a storage piece or build a closet, a bookcase, or display shelves for a collection of glass or china. (For more storage ideas, see pp. 35–69.)

ARRANGING A ROOM

Distribute your furniture carefully. Place the largest pieces—an armoire or a large cabinet, for instance—on the longest wall. To save space, keep all large units parallel to walls and avoid placing a piece diagonally.

Avoid a jumbled look by keeping all the taller furniture at about the same height. The tops of chests, cabinets, and bookcases should maintain more or less the same line around the room.

Plan a room in groupings. In a large living room there can be a primary seating area with sofa and armchairs at one end and secondary seating, such as a love seat and light-scaled chairs, at the other.

Relate the scale of furniture in groupings. Avoid tall wing chairs next to a low sofa, and side tables that are higher than the arms of a sofa or a chair.

Keep traffic lanes open. Allow for easy access from one area of the room to another. Don't use a huge shin-buster of a coffee table in front of a long sofa—two small movable tables are a much better solution.

Remember that it's better to have too little than too much in a room. Not only is a lot of bulky furniture dangerous for traffic, it gives a cluttered appearance and detracts from other furniture.

PREPARING WALLS AND CEILINGS

Proper preparation is the key to a professional-looking and long-lasting paint or wall-covering job. Take time to check for and fill all cracks and holes. If the plaster is so severely cracked and gouged that the entire wall needs renewing, hire a professional plasterer.

If you plan to paper the room, you can nail plasterboard over the old plaster, attaching it to the existing studs behind (p.49).

Before beginning to paint, fix all protruding wall nails. If you discover any, remove them with pliers and replace each with a larger nail. If this doesn't work, drive another nail 1½ inches above or below the popped nail. Using a nail set, drive in the popped nail.

Fill in behind a big hole in plaster with wadded-up newspaper. Apply patching mixture in layers, working in from all sides. When the patch has dried, sand until smooth.

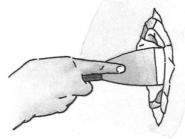

An old paintbrush makes an excellent duster to rid moldings of sanding dust before you begin to paint.

Match a patch to a textured surface; while the patch is still wet, texture the area with a sponge.

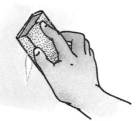

Before painting or wallpapering, remove all nails and picture hangers and all hardware from

PATCHING PLASTERBOARD OR PLASTER

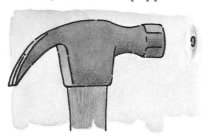

1. Remove loose plaster. Scrape out plaster from the back of the crack or hole until the back is wider than the front surface. Dampen the surface with a wet paintbrush.

2. Mix a small amount of patching compound, following package directions, or use premixed compound. Fill small cracks and holes, then smooth the surface with a medium-width putty knife. Fill a large crack or hole gradually in several steps.

3. Even out the surface with a damp sponge. After the patch has dried, sand it with a sheet of sandpaper wrapped around a sanding block (p.443). Brush away all dust from sanding. Wipe with a damp cloth before painting.

doors and windows (or cover with masking tape). Turn off the power to all circuits in the room (p. 163). Remove electrical fixtures and switch and outlet cover plates. (For light while working, run a cord from another room.)

Immediately before decorating, remove dirt, oil, grease, rust, and flaking paint by washing the walls and ceiling with a solution of half chlorine bleach and half water. At the same time, you'll be eliminating mold and mildew.

Rub protective cream into your hands and arms before beginning work. Paint and paste will come off much easier when you wash up (with soap and warm water) after you've finished the job.

If you're using solvents or solvent-thinned paints, be sure all pilot lights and fires are out before you begin. When using any type of paint or coating, be sure there's plenty of fresh air and ventilation in your working area.

Paint woodwork before wallpapering but after painting a room.

PAINT BRUSHUP

To test a brush before buying it, slap the bristles against the palm of your hand. If it fails to spring back into shape and bristles fall out, select a better grade brush.

CLEANING BRUSHES AND ROLLERS

Brushes. Clean brushes right after you've finished painting. Place them on newspaper and, wearing rubber gloves, squeeze out as much excess paint as possible. Wash those used with latex, or water-base, paint in warm water, adding a bit of dishwashing detergent; work the paint out of the bristles with your fingers; rinse until there's no hint of pigment. Soak brushes used with alkyd, or oil-base, paint in the recommended solvent until it becomes discolored; replace with fresh solvent and soak again; wash with detergent and warm water; then rinse well.

To expel excess water from a brush, twirl the handle rapidly between the palms of your hands, then place the brush in its plastic cover (with the flap open) to retain its shape, and hang it from its handle while drying. To store a brush after cleaning, wrap it in wax paper or kraft paper and seal with a rubber band.

If you're going to use a brush the next

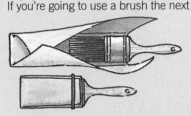

day, you can store it overnight without cleaning by suspending it in water (if you're using latex paint) or solvent (if you're using alkyd). The bristles must not touch the bottom of the container. Dry thoroughly before beginning work.

Rollers. Clean rollers as soon as possible after use. First, roll out excess paint on several layers of newspaper. Wearing rubber gloves, remove latex paint from a roller with warm water, working the nap between your fingers. Immerse a roller used with alkyd paint in the recommended solvent. Wearing rubber gloves, work the fluid into the nap with your fingers; then wash in detergent and warm water and rinse well.

Wring the excess water from the roller, then rub with a clean, absorbent cloth. Upend the roller on newspaper to dry.

You can reuse a roller used with alkyd paint the next day if it's kept damp in paint thinner.

409

One way to judge the quality of a paintbrush is to examine its bristles for split ends known as "flags." These enable the brush to retain more paint and spread it more uniformly. On good brushes, at least half of the bristles are flagged.

Use natural-bristle brushes for alkyd, or oil-base, paints; synthetic-bristle brushes for latex, or water-base, paints.

For painting large areas, buy a flat 3- to 5-inch brush; for woodwork and other trim, a 1- to 2-inch brush is best.

ROLLERS

Rollers are available up to 15 inches in length—the larger the roller, the faster you'll cover your wall space. There are also smaller rollers, 2 to 3 inches wide, that are handy for trim.

Pick the roller with the correct pile for the job. The general rule is the smoother the surface, the thinner the pile. The proper roller will hold the paint, instead of allowing it to dribble down as you work.

Like brushes, roller covers also vary in quality. Poor-quality ones will frequently mat or shed fibers.

Three complete revolutions of the roller in the tray usually loads the roller properly.

Take the roller off its holder immediately after use. It may be impossible to remove once the paint has dried.

OTHER TOOLS

Before you buy a bargain package of tray, roller, and brush combined, check the quality of similar items priced separately. Then decide if the bargain package compromises on quality.

A heavy-duty metal tray is best. A lightweight tray may not hold firm to the ladder and may not keep its shape, causing uneven absorption of the paint.

SELECTING A PAINT FOR INDOOR USE

Interior paints may seem to come in a bewildering variety, but in reality there are only two types: latex (water base) and alkyd (oil base). Both are available in a variety of finishes. The most expensive isn't necessarily the best; ask a reputable paint store which brands have the best covering ability, and watch for sales.

Latex, or water-base, paints apply easily with a brush or roller. The cleanup is easy (water and soap); they aren't flammable and have only a mild odor. Latex paints are appropriate for walls, ceilings, and trim in any situation where moisture isn't a problem.

Alkyd, or oil-base, paints apply well with a brush or roller, but they need turpentine or mineral spirits for cleanup. They're longer lasting and more washable than latex paints, and so are often chosen for areas, such as kitchens and bathrooms, where frequent cleaning is necessary. Alkyd paints have a strong odor during application, but it generally disappears after a few days.

To prevent paint buildup—and to make cleanup a lot easier—line the tray with aluminum foil before adding paint or buy disposable plastic tray liners.

Painting pads apply paint smoothly and quickly, but skill is required to use them, since they tend to cause streaks and produce lap marks. Pads do work well, however, on flush doors, wide, flat trim, baseboards, and similar surfaces.

If you open paint cans with a screwdriver, make sure it's an old or a cheap one that you don't need for driving screws. A damaged screwdriver blade can mar screw slots.

BEFORE PAINTING

Cover glass and areas adjacent to where you're painting with masking tape. When you remove the tape, you'll have a neat edge.

Instead of drop cloths to protect floors, lay down newspaper, shingle fashion, with 6 inches of overlap between sheets. Tape edges to the baseboards to hold them in place.

HOW MUCH PAINT DO YOU NEED?

To figure out the amount of paint you'll need for a specific area, multiply the number of feet around the room by the height from the baseboard to the ceiling. Don't forget to deduct the square footage of anything that you don't intend to paint, such as door openings or windows.

Count on 1 gallon of paint covering 450 square feet of wall, slightly more if you're covering fresh plasterboard. When in doubt, it's better to overestimate because it may be difficult to match colors exactly with another batch of paint. Most paint stores will take back unopened cans of standard colors.

PAINTING TECHNIQUES

When you need a prime coat (usually white) and you've chosen a dark finish color, add a bit of the finish paint to the primer. The final coat will cover much better.

When painting in corners, stroke with the flat part of the brush. Painting with the side causes fingering and a less neat job.

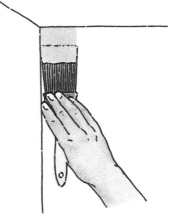

Spray-painting saves time, but it requires practice to avoid misting and unequal paint distribution. Hold the spray gun at a right angle to the surface, 6 to 10 inches away, and move the nozzle parallel to the wall or other surface. **Caution:** When spray-painting, open doors and windows and wear a spray-paint respirator.

After the paint has dried, remove spills with a single-edge razor blade in a holder.

Spots of latex paint despite your care in masking stained wood trim? Even after paint has dried, you can remove it with scouring powder on a damp sponge. Be gentle in order not to harm the wood, and wipe off all residue with a clean damp sponge.

AROUND THE ROOM

Paint the ceiling first. To prevent one section from drying before you paint the next, work across the width of the ceiling rather than the length. Paint in slightly overlapping strips about 2 feet wide.

When painting walls, begin at the upper left-hand corner if you're right-handed, and the upper right-hand corner if you're left-handed; work down toward the floor.

Before painting floor molding, put wide masking tape along the floor to protect it from paint.

When painting windows, tape along the edges of the glass, then paint the various parts in the order shown below.

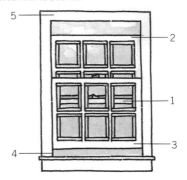

After painting a sash window, leave both halves open to dry and insert matchsticks between the sashes and frame to prevent them from sticking together.

Leftover paint? Dispose of it by wrapping it tightly and placing it in the garbage. Or donate it to someone who needs paint.

PAINTING WALLS

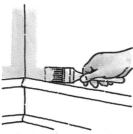

1. Brush a narrow strip of paint where the walls meet the ceiling, in the corners where the walls meet, around the door and window frames, and along the baseboards. This is called "cutting in."

2. Work in 3-foot-square areas. Roll several zigzag strokes, pushing the roller upward on the first stroke and increasing the pressure to spread the paint evenly. Smooth out zigzags with horizontal strokes.

3. For an even paint job, after loading your roller, stroke toward the wet paint rather than away from it. Blend your strokes from the wet paint area into the previously applied layer.

STEPS TO SUCCESSFUL STENCILING

Although you can buy stencil patterns and complete stencil kits, it's much more rewarding, and not too difficult, to create your own designs and cut your own stencils. Materials are available in office- or art-supply stores.

You can stencil almost any wall, as long as its surface is dull, porous, and fairly smooth. Before you begin to stencil, paint the wall with flat latex or alkyd paint.

After cutting the stencils, make a few trial runs. Tape the design to a sheet of white paper (freezer wrap works well) and practice. Repeat until you get a feel for the process.

1. With a wax pencil, trace your design on a sheet of clear acetate. Repeat the design on several sheets of acetate so that you have a separate stencil for each color in your design.

2. Protect your work surface with a large piece of cardboard. Then, holding a very sharp artist's knife like a pencil, cut out the design on each of the acetates. Use your free hand to turn the stencil so that the knife is always cutting in the same direction. Don't lift the knife until the shape has been completely cut out.

3. To compute how many times to repeat the design, measure the stencil and the area you're applying it to. Divide the stencil's measurement into the area; if there's a remainder, use it for spacing between repeats of the design.

4. Hold the acetate in place and lightly mark the wall at the stencil's corners.

5. Place the stencil of the color you plan to use most at the starting point. Tape it to the wall.

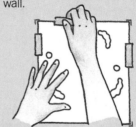

6. Work with one color at a time. With a tiny amount of stencil paint on the stenciling brush, work up and down, keeping the brush perpendicular to the stencil.

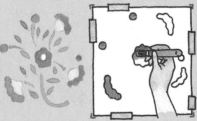

7. Untape the acetate and carefully lift it straight up; wipe off any wet paint. Tape the second-color acetate's into position and stencil as before. Continue with the other stencils, filling in all the cut-out areas.

8. Beginning with the first-color stencil, repeat the pattern on the adjacent space until you have covered the area you plan to stencil.

9. If you want to make the wall washable and to preserve the stenciling longer, apply a coat of polyurethane varnish with a smooth roller.

SETTING OUT TO COVER WALLS

Keep in mind the space that you're decorating. Vertical stripes will give an appearance of greater height. Small patterns are best in small areas, large patterns in large ones. A boldly patterned paper will dominate a room, detracting from the furniture and accessories. (Or, on the other hand, it will make less-than-wonderful pieces less conspicuous).

Order all the wall coverings that you expect to need at the same time so that they'll all be from the same color run. Just to be on the safe side, check the lot numbers on all the rolls before you unwrap them.

Unroll and inspect the entire length of each roll of wall covering before cutting it. Return damaged rolls to the paint and wallpaper store.

Never use newspapers to cover a pasting table; the ink is likely to soil the wall covering. Instead, cover the table with plastic tablecloths or wrapping paper.

REMOVING OLD WALL COVERINGS

Strip old covering from the wall if possible; however, if it's in fairly good condition and firmly stuck to the wall, you can leave it on. You can't paper over with vinyl, foil, or plastic papers, however.

If it's strippable or if it's vinyl wallpaper, simply grasp a corner and peel it off. Wash the walls with warm water, then scrape off any remaining glue with a putty knife.

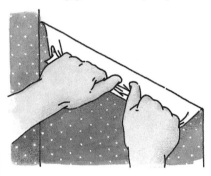

Wallpaper should peel off in sheets if you use a solution of equal parts of vinegar and hot water. Apply with a sponge until the paper is wet but not dripping. (For the best results, apply the solution at least twice.)

WALL-COVERING CHOICES

Type	Best use	Comments
Cork	Family rooms; children's rooms	Deadens sound. Hang over lining paper. Vacuum to clean
Fabric	Special effects; low-traffic areas	Expensive; does not wear well. Hang over lining paper. Dry-cleanable
Foil	Highlighting small areas	Expensive; not durable. Difficult to hang; use lining paper. Avoid sunlight, which may cause glare. Wash to clean
Papers (plain, vinyl-coated, cloth-backed)	Low- to medium-traffic areas; dining rooms; living rooms; adult bedrooms	Prepasted paper easiest to hang. Only vinyl-coated washable
Textured coverings (burlap, grasscloth, silk)	Living rooms; dining rooms; single wall as accent	Hang over lining paper. Dry-cleanable
Vinyl	High-traffic areas; kitchens; bathrooms; playrooms	Most durable. Prepasted vinyl easiest to hang; wash to clean

HANGING PREPASTED WALL COVERING

1. Measure width of wall covering; mark this width, less 1 inch, from the top corner to the right of where you plan to begin work; mark same width at bottom; snap a weighted string colored with chalk, or a plumb line, between these two points.

2. With plumb line, measure from ceiling to baseboard here and in several places around the room. After determining the maximum wall height, add 3 or 4 inches and use this measurement to cut each strip of wall covering. Cut two strips.

3. Place a water tray at the base of the wall. Roll the first strip, pattern side in, into the water for 30 seconds. Then slowly draw it through and onto a flat work surface. Fold the strip pasted side to pasted side and leave it that way for 3 minutes.

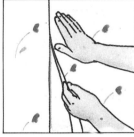

4. Line up this strip to the left of first plumb line and around corner. Let strip overlap ceiling and baseboard. Smooth wall covering with a brush or sponge; move any air pockets to the edge and out. Sponge off excess paste with clean water; dry with a soft cloth.

5. As you continue hanging, move to the right around the room. Do not overlap the strips; just butt their edges. Make sure that the strips are tight against each other and the wall by smoothing them with a brush or sponge.

6. At each corner, wrap the strip around to the next wall. Drop a new plumb line and hang the next strip against it, overlapping corner again to cover previous strip's edge. With a utility knife, cut through both layers where they overlap; remove surplus strips and smooth.

7. Work around the room, hanging wall covering across doors and windows. Cut away excess, leaving 2 inches overlap all around. Make diagonal cuts at corners, then smooth wall covering into edge of frame with a putty knife; trim with a sharp, razor-edged knife.

8. When the wall covering has been on the wall for 10 minutes, roll the seams lightly with a seam roller. However, if the wall covering is embossed or foil, just tap the seams down with the tip of the smoothing brush.

9. After the walls are covered, trim the overlap at the ceiling and baseboard with a sharp razor-edged knife. Hold a broad putty knife against the wall as shown to ensure a straight line.

A MORE BEAUTIFUL HOME · DECORATING MADE EASY

415

Two fast ways to strip wallpaper: Rent a wallpaper steamer or buy wallpaper-removing liquid. Both will soften the paper so that you can scrape it off easily with a wide putty knife. Then wash the walls with a washing soda solution, rinse, and allow to dry.

Caution: Use wallpaper-removing liquid only in well-ventilated areas, following the manufacturer's instructions to the letter.

HANGING HINTS

If you're a beginner, get some practice by hanging a medium-weight lining paper on the wall before attempting the final covering. An added bonus: this extra step improves the finished job.

Papering a problem wall? Buy heavily embossed or textured wallpaper or hang a heavy-duty lining fabric that is specifically designed for walls of this kind.

Before wallpapering over dark or bright paint, apply a 1-inch stripe of white paint along the top of the wall. If the wallpaper fails to align exactly with the edge of the ceiling, the white stripe will mask the original wall color.

To ensure smooth coverage when installing metal foil, apply two coats of absolutely lump-free adhesive to the wall, not to the foil. Use a short-pile paint roller for spreading; brush marks would show through the foil's delicate surface.

Save yourself a lot of measuring time. When taking down old vinyl paper, number each strip from left to right or vice versa. As you cut the new paper, use the numbered strips as a pattern, making sure

both papers are lying completely flat. (This works only if the old and new papers are the same width.)

Guard against mildew. Spray an antibacterial agent on the damp, pasted side of wallpaper before hanging it.

For a better looking job, take your time—you don't have to finish the project in one day. Wall-covering paste dries slowly, so check each newly hung strip for seam match and bubbles and adjust a strip if necessary.

REPAIRING DAMAGED WALL COVERINGS

To remedy tears or loose edges, apply the appropriate wall-covering paste to both the wall and the back of the covering. Press in place, smooth with a seam roller, and wipe away any excess paste.

Here's how to patch a small damaged area: Paste a new piece of wall covering larger than the hole over the damaged area, matching the pattern exactly. Let the patch set for an hour, then cut through both layers with a razor knife. Clean the area and repaste the top piece. Wait approximately 15 minutes, then roll the fitted edges smooth.

WALL PANELING

Paneling hides uneven plaster, old wallpaper, and masonry. It permanently solves a decorating problem and, once installed, requires little further upkeep.

Installed vertically, panels increase the apparent height of an area; arranged horizontally, they seem to lengthen it.

Panels placed diagonally adjacent to a wall of mirrors create the simultaneous illusion of width and height.

How many standard 4- by 8-foot panels will you need? If your ceiling height is 8 feet, just measure each wall's width and divide by four.

Store wooden paneling or boards in the room where they're to be used for 7 to 10 days before installing them. This allows them to adjust to the room's humidity and reduces shrinkage and expansion after installation. Place spacers between each sheet of paneling so that room air can circulate.

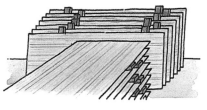

If you run out of colored nails to match the paneling, use some of your old, plain finishing nails. Drive the nails below the surface with a nail set, and fill in the holes with a colored wax stick.

BEFORE YOU PANEL

Consider the following factors before you decide to panel a room.
1. The size of the room will diminish by the thickness of the panel, plus that of the furring strips (if used). If paneling is a dark color or a wood tone, the room will also appear to "shrink."
2. Electrical outlets and wall switches will have to be moved forward to the paneling's surface. (Hardware is available for doing this.)
3. Heating and air-conditioning registers will need extension collars. (Ask a heating contractor to make them.) If there are electric baseboard heaters, the power will have to be turned off and the heaters removed.
4. Door and window frames, baseboards, and ceiling moldings will have to be repositioned.

CEILING SECRETS

An old trick that adds height to a room is mirrors, especially when applied to a dark ceiling. Buy inexpensive, easy-to-install mirror tiles and secure them with the recommended adhesive.

Create a constellation on the ceiling of a child's bedroom. Buy reflective vinyl and cut it into star shapes; arrange them on the ceiling in the configuration of the Big Dipper or some other group of stars. When the lights are out at night, it will seem just like sleeping outdoors. An extra bonus: the stars will function as a night light. (You can also buy constellation kits.)

A skylight dramatically increases the sense of extra space and lets in five times more light than a window the same size, transforming a dark room into a brightly lit living area.

Ventilating skylights (those that open) allow odors, smoke, and heat to be exhausted to the outdoors. An added plus: skylights save on electricity bills.

Hide exposed plumbing, wiring, or joists with a dropped ceiling, a suspended metal grid in which acoustical panels rest.

CEILING TILES

For a neat-looking job, always make border tiles on facing sides of the room the same width.

Apply tiles with adhesive or cement only if the ceiling is sound and even. If a ceiling has exposed joists, cracked plaster, or an uneven surface, nail furring strips to the ceiling before applying tiles.

Don't cover the entire tile with adhesive or cement. Just place a daub in each corner (about 1 inch from the edges) and a single daub in the middle.

When stapling tiles to furring strips, place three staples on one edge of the tile and staple corners only on the other edge. (This will allow for the tiles to shrink and swell as the humidity changes in the room.)

FLOORING ALTERNATIVES

Don't make any decisions about new flooring before considering whether you can revitalize the old in any way. Wood floors may only need polishing or, at most, sanding down and sealing with polyurethane or tung oil for a brand-new look.

If your wood floors are in such poor condition that they can't be revived by sanding, staining, or bleaching, they may still be rescued by paint, which can cover a multitude of pits and blemishes.

Before you decide on a new floor covering, consider what kind of wear and tear the room will have. Wood floors work well in living rooms and more formal areas. For hard-wear areas like the family room, kitchen, bathroom, and children's rooms, your best choice is probably resilient flooring, preferably in a dark pattern that won't show the dirt.

To give extra character to a stained floor, try stenciling a border. (The method for stenciling floors is basically the same as for walls; see p.413.) Or paint a checkerboard pattern or an "area rug" on it.

Tough, durable, and washable, deck paint gives a thick coating to heavy-traffic areas, such as stairs and entryways. Deck paint's main drawback is its limited color range.

For longer wear, finish off a painted surface with several coats of polyurethane; to postpone repainting, give your floor a coat of polyurethane every year or so.

COMMON TYPES OF FLOORING

Type	Description	Surface	Installation
Ceramic tile	Diverse sizes, shapes, colors	Durable. Waterproof; stain resistant but susceptible to scratching. Hard underfoot; slippery when wet	Lay on concrete subfloor or wooden subfloor with rubber-based floor-tile adhesive
Hardwood	Oak, maple, teak, among others; many finishes available. Parquet, plank, or strip. Warm, natural look; ages well	Durable, but can warp or split. Water resistant when properly sealed. Comfortable underfoot	Nail over plywood subfloor. Parquet available with self adhering backing. Or secure with recommended adhesive
Quarry tile	Natural look. Various sizes and shapes	Durable. Water and stain resistant. Hard underfoot	Lay on concrete subfloor or wooden subfloor with rubber-based floor-tile adhesive
Resilient flooring (linoleum, sheet vinyl, vinyl tile, vinyl asphalt tile)	Diverse shapes, sizes (both sheet and tile), and patterns. High- or low-gloss finish	Durable; thickness governs length of wear. Water and stain resistant but may show scuffs and scratches. Comfortable underfoot	Unless old floor is in above-average condition, remove it. If resilient flooring is self adhering, peel off backing and lay over smooth, clean flooring. Or lay over subfloor with recommended adhesive
Softwood	Spruce, fir, or pine; tongue-and-groove boards most common	Porous; easily distressed. Comfortable underfoot	Staple or nail through tongues to plywood subfloor or lay in recommended adhesive

LIGHTING UP

The average-size room usually needs four or five light sources. In a room where light is "absorbed" by dark-colored walls and upholstery, you may need more lamps or higher wattage bulbs.

To achieve harmony in a room, the tops of table and floor lamps should be at the same level, and all shades should be similar in style and fabric.

A table lamp should be no more than 1½ times the height of the table. The diameter of the shade should be no wider than that of the tabletop.

If you're using a floor lamp as a reading light, place it slightly behind you either to the left or the right of your shoulder. With a table lamp, line up the base with your shoulder twenty inches to the left or right of the center of the book. The bottom of the lampshade should be above eye level; a lower one restricts the light that falls on the book.

If you're left-handed, place the light source to your right; if right-handed, position the light on your left side—this way your arms or hands won't cast shadows.

Make TV viewing easier on the eyes—use a dimmed downlight or a table lamp with a three-way bulb on its lowest setting. (Place lamps carefully so that they aren't reflected in the TV screen.)

Worried about choosing the right size of chandelier for your dining room? A good rule of thumb is that its diagonal in inches should equal the diagonal of the room in feet.

Some decorators feel that when it comes to chandeliers it's better to overscale than to underscale. For example, a large chandelier may give a small dining room or a narrow hall just the extra glamour that it needs.

Choose lampshades according to the effect you want to create. An opaque shade, which produces a strong pattern of up and down light, is more decorative than practical. If you want cheerful diffuse light that you can read by, select a shade of light-diffusing fabric, plastic, or paper.

Avoid narrow-topped shades—the heat the confined bulbs beneath generate can cause premature deterioration of their fabric.

MOOD LIGHTING

Install dimmers for flexible mood lighting. Bright lights stimulate activity; dim lights are more conducive to relaxation. Just follow the easy instuctions on the dimmer switch package.

To create a warm, intimate atmosphere, substitute small pools of light for general lighting.

Pink bulbs warm up a room, making its light much more flattering than white light. Blue and green bulbs are cool, making a room seem more serene.

A GLOSSARY OF LIGHTING TERMS

Accent lighting emphasizes specific details in a room, such as paintings or decorative objects.

General lighting provides background light in a room.

Local, or task, lighting illuminates a specific area for a specific activity, such as reading or cooking.

General lighting — recessed floodlights

Task lighting — fluorescent bulbs

Fluorescent bulbs provide cool light; they generally last 4 to 5 years. Some are now available that provide warm light.

Incandescent bulbs give a golden light; bulb life averages 750 to 1,000 hours.

Low-voltage bulbs furnish a precise beam for floodlighting or highlighting.

Baffles are panels that conceal bulbs for indirect lighting.

Cornice lighting casts light downward over a wall.

Dimmer switches permit a variety of lighting levels at the turn of a knob; they save energy when operated at a low level.

Downlights cast pools of light on surfaces below them; their fixtures may be semi-recessed or mounted on the ceiling.

Spotlights are used for directional and accent lighting; they can be mounted straight onto the ceiling, set into it, or attached to a track.

Track lighting provides flexibility in directing beams of light and consists of one or more fixtures mounted on a metal track connected to a single electrical outlet. The track can be surface-mounted or recessed in or on a ceiling or above the baseboard.

Uplights accent objects above them; the soft, diffuse light comes from canister-type lighting fixtures placed on the floor.

Valance lighting, or cove lighting, provides a wash of light downward over draperies and upward over a ceiling by means of a bulb-concealing shield mounted just below the ceiling.

Valance lighting

Track lighting

Uplighting

Wall washers direct beams of light at the wall, expanding the feeling of space in a room; they can be recessed, surface-mounted, or on a track.

Ceiling-mounted fixtures usually refer to fixtures dropped from the ceiling on a wire; they provide good overall light but generally need to be used with accent lights.

Floor lamps furnish general or local light depending on their shape and shade.

Pendant fixtures give light according to their shades. The larger the shade, the subtler the light cast.

Table lamps provide concentrated areas of light.

Wall sconces are best used as directional lights to bounce light off the ceiling or walls or to light an object or a surface.

WINDOW TREATMENTS

If you're planning new window treatments, consider what your home looks like from the outside. All windows seen from the same angle should appear similar in style and color.

The best decorated window is usually the least decorated. Remember, the primary function of a window is to admit light and air.

When a window provides a beautiful view, don't hide it with heavy draperies or undercurtains. Hang simple draperies in quiet colors and think of the window as framing the view like a picture.

In planning a window treatment, consider the kind of light the room gets. If the windows face north, aim to admit as much light as possible; if they face south or west, you may want to cut back on the amount of sun the room receives.

PROBLEM WINDOWS

When you need the light but the view outside is dreary, suspend plants from the ceiling in front of the window. Or stretch glass shelves across the panes and show off a collection of glasses or old bottles through which the light can shine.

When French doors or casement windows open into a room, use extra-wide drapery rods so that you can draw the draperies clear at each side before opening the doors or windows. Or place shades over the frames so that the doors or windows can open freely.

Get the most light from the small high windows usually found in basements. Miniblinds or translucent window shades that can be raised by day and closed at night are a good solution.

Two tiny windows on one wall? If they're relatively close together, treat them as a single unit by spanning them with one set of venetian blinds or a single window shade.

Minimize a bulky air conditioner with this clever window treatment: Hang two sets of louvered shutters, one over the window and another over the air conditioner. To admit cooled air, you need only fold the shutters open or adjust their louvers.

Make the most of a short, high window with a café curtain that hangs below the windowsill. Pull back the curtain above to admit light and air.

Dormer windows look their best with a blind or shade fitted inside the frame.

WINDOW MAGIC

"Resize" a single, average-size window. Attach a valance or cornice on the wall above the window frame to add height. Or hang draperies across the width of the wall; closed at night, the draperies will seem to conceal a wall of windows.

Hang narrow columns of ceiling-to-floor draperies to make a too low room appear higher.

BRIGHT IDEAS

Add light to a windowless wall. Surround mirror panels with moldings, and you'll gain a feeling of depth and openness.

Make a "window" on a windowless wall by hanging a mirror directly facing a real window. If a window is in a corner, place a mirror opposite it.

WINDOW COVERINGS

How do draperies differ from curtains? Generally, draperies are made of heavier fabric, are lined, and are hung from hooks. Curtains are usually of a lightweight fabric, are unlined, and have a casing, or pocket, for the rod.

Draperies can correct architectural flaws as well as capitalize on advantages. For example, you can compensate for skimpy moldings and oddly located or strangely shaped windows with draperies and undercurtains that tie a whole wall area together.

For adequate fullness, all curtains and draperies (except straight flat panels) should measure at least double the width of the area to be covered. Sheer curtains should be triple the width.

Doubtful about spending the extra money to line your new draperies? Consider this: Linings give more privacy, more protection for the drapery fabric against sun damage, more insulation against heat and cold, and a more pleasing appearance from the outside.

Shoji-type translucent panels are a terrific way to regulate light and maintain privacy in a room. Slide the panels back and forth to restrict or expand a view and to control the amount of light in the room.

WALL-TO-WALL CARPETING

Density is one of the keys to durability in a carpet. The closer the tufts, the better the wear. Use the "grin test" to determine closeness: Bend a corner of the carpet over your finger and see how much of the backing shows. In a high-quality carpet the visible backing, or "grin," will be minimal.

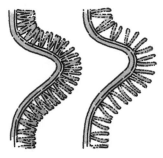

To conserve energy (and also deaden sound), choose wall-to-wall carpeting with very dense, deep pile and thick padding that incorporates many pockets of air.

If floors are in bad condition, it may be cheaper to carpet them wall-to-wall than to refurbish them. Mask any unevenness with padding.

For easy turning (to distribute wear) and cleaning, have carpeting cut to your room's exact dimensions (minus 2 to 3 inches) and bound on the edges. It will look like wall-to-wall carpeting, but you'll be able to clean it better and more cheaply. For security, place padding beneath it or anchor corners with special carpet tape.

When buying carpeting, remember that a medium color will look better longer; a dark color won't show the dirt but will show the lint; a light shade, on the other hand, will appear dirty sooner, but you won't be able to see the lint.

WHICH IS THE BEST CARPET FIBER?

No carpet fiber is perfect; each has different characteristics. Make your selection according to the intended use, appearance, and your budget. Compare each fiber's characteristics and choose the one that's most appropriate for your needs.

Fiber	Characteristics	Advantages and Disadvantages
Acrylic	Natural looking; of the man-made fibers, most wool-like in appearance and feel. Moderately expensive	Moderately durable. Resists water-soluble stains but susceptible to oily stains. Resists moisture and mildew
Nylon	Wide range of clear colors. Considered to be the strongest rug fiber. Wide price range	Very durable. Built-in ability to conceal and resist soil; resists water-soluble stains. Unaffected by mildew. Resists shedding and pilling. May generate static unless brand has built-in static control
Olefin	Excellent color fastness; limited range of colors. Used indoors (especially in kitchens) and outdoors. Relatively inexpensive	Very durable. Resists permanent soil and stains. Resists moisture and mildew. Naturally resistant to static
Polyester	Wide range of colors; soft, lustrous, and luxurious. Relatively inexpensive	Moderately durable. Resists water-soluble stains but susceptible to oily stains. Needs frequent cleaning
Wool	Wide range of colors and textures; soft and luxurious appearance. Most expensive	Very durable. Crush resistant. Resists soiling but resists staining to a lesser degree

Patterned carpets are extremely practical because they don't show dirt as readily as plain carpets. Abstract patterns are especially useful for disguising irregularly shaped rooms.

If you're planning to carpet your stairs, be sure to select a high-quality product with a dense pile. Avoid shags and loose pile that can snare a high heel.

For a look of formal richness, select wall-to-wall plush carpeting; for a natural look, try sisal squares wall-to-wall or a room-size shag rug.

Why do you need padding? Unless a carpet is foam backed, padding protects the underside so that it won't wear out. The carpet will feel softer to walk on; and it won't slip from beneath your feet as you hurry to answer the telephone.

You needn't spend a lot of money on padding. Just buy foam rubber in sheets from wholesale foam-rubber outlets and cut it to the size of your carpet.

AREA RUGS

If you'd just as soon have no installation costs and you like the idea of being able to turn a rug in order to distribute its wear, consider an area rug. Also, if you anticipate moving and want to take your floor coverings along, area rugs are unquestionably the best choice.

An area rug in a color that blends with the surrounding floor makes a room appear larger. Conversely, a contrasting rug color makes a room seem smaller, more intimate.

Add a patterned area rug over plain wall-to-wall carpet for a luxurious effect. Because an area rug may "travel," place an old wool blanket or a muslin sheet (cut to size) beneath it.

For a particularly dramatic decorative effect, set an area rug into your wall-to-wall carpeting; a professional carpet installer can seam it in. Use the cutout remnant with its edges bound as an area rug in the kids' playroom or in the basement.

In a large living room, area rugs are a good way to define groupings of furniture—for conversation, games, fireside chats.

Prevent the "postage stamp" look—don't use too small a rug in a large room.

Avoid oddly shaped area rugs in a symmetrical room. They'll give a jumbled, disturbing effect.

COLOR AND PATTERN

As part of a room's background, carpet color can do remarkable things. A carpet the same color as the walls or a lighter shade can make the room seem larger. A sharply contrasting color concentrates attention on the furniture and lessens focus on the walls.

Patterns should fit the size of a room: A dominant carpet pattern suits a large room, whereas a small overall design is more appropriate for a modest-size room.

For a small room, a patterned wall-to-wall carpet and a coordinated patterned paper on the walls and ceiling can, amazingly, make the space seem much larger.

If you have patterned wallpaper, lots of pictures on the walls, or collections on shelves, avoid a patterned floor covering.

FURNISHING BASICS

Choosing your style of furniture, like choosing your style of clothes, is largely a matter of personal taste. If you know what your lifestyle is—whether it's formal or casual—you can easily decide what style of furniture best goes with it and select accordingly.

Low-luster woods—such as pine, maple, and birch—and light finishes suggest a casual style of living; fine, highly polished woods—such as mahogany, cherry, and walnut—and dark finishes seem more formal.

If, like most people, you have furnishings of different styles or periods, you can still mix them to give visual unity to a room. Match modern and period pieces that have simplicity of line, similarity of scale, or the same type and finish of wood. Or, use fabric coverings in complementary colors or with similar designs to provide an appropriate visual link.

You can alter the character of a chair or a sofa by changing its padding and fabric. Plump cushions, curved lines, and soft textures suggest a warmer, more relaxed atmosphere than do flat cushions, straight lines, and slick smooth surfaces.

QUALITY IN FURNITURE: QUESTIONS TO CONSIDER

Do the materials in the piece of furniture appear to be of good quality?

Is the finish durable, smooth, and evenly applied? Does the wood graining match across all doors and drawers?

Does the piece stand squarely?

Are the joints firm and tight—and put together with screws, not nails? (A screw has a notch in its head; a nail has none.) Do globs of glue show around the joints? (A sign of sloppy workmanship.)

Do movable parts such as drawers fit well and operate easily?

Do the drawers have dust panels between them?

Is the wood inside the drawers and on the back and under the piece smoothly sanded and finished?

Is the hardware heavy, solid, and securely attached?

If upholstered, is the piece covered with a closely woven fabric? Do the patterns match all around? Are the seams straight? Is the welting firmly sewn in place and the skirt lined for extra body?

Is a chair or sofa comfortable to sit in?

What can you learn about the parts that you can't see?

Built-in furniture, such as window seats and wall units, takes up less space than free-floating pieces. An added bonus: The space beneath can be used for storage. You need only hinge the seat so that it can be lifted, or put shelves beneath the wall units, and you have immediately doubled the usefulness of the piece.

When selecting fabric for reupholstering, choose light colors for an airy spacious look, earthy colors to suggest the outdoors, and medium to dark colors and small patterns for a cozy feeling.

Before you buy a piece of furniture, write down its dimensions, then measure the wall and floor space at its intended location to make sure that it fits. Try to "see" the piece in its intended spot.

If you're bewitched by an extra-large piece of furniture and you live in an apartment, measure before buying to make sure that it will fit into your building's elevator. In a house, check that it will go through the doorways.

FURNITURE ON A BUDGET

A handpainted canvas drop cloth, a designer sheet, or any other printed fabric will transform an old chair. Drape the cloth over the chair and cut it to fit, allowing 2 inches extra for the hem. Make small buttonholes in the fabric and sew buttons onto the chair to keep the cover in place.

A piece of glass (¼- to ½- inch thick) makes a stylish coffee table. Support it with terra-cotta urns, blocks of beautifully grained and polished wood, or a pair of wine racks—the possibilities are nearly endless.

Prevent scratching a glass-topped table by attaching nonskid rubber washers to the top of its supports.

A plywood box (p.64), sealed and painted any color you like, makes an attractive plant stand, TV table, or sculpture pedestal.

Make an ottoman to go with your favorite easy chair from a plywood box (p.64). Attach glides or casters at the bottom corners; staple cotton batting to the wood; then tack on upholstery fabric, making box pleats at the corners.

Use an old 6½-foot-long paneled door as an alternative to a store-bought headboard for your king-size bed. Attach L-brackets to the wall at each stud (p.49), rest the door on the L-brackets, and screw the top and bottom to the studs. Position the L-brackets so that the door's edge is below the mattress.

NINETEENTH-CENTURY THOUGHTS ON DECORATING

Having duly arranged for the physical necessities of a healthful and comfortable home, we next approach the important subject of *beauty* in reference to the decoration of houses. For while the aesthetic element must be subordinate to the requirements of physical existence...it yet holds a place of great significance among the influences which make home happy and attractive, which give it a constant and wholesome power over the young, and contributes much to the education of the entire household in refinement, intellectual development, and moral sensibility.

An excerpt from *The American Woman's Home*, by Catherine E. Beecher and Harriet Beecher Stowe, published in 1869.

PICTURE PERFECT

There are two fundamental points to remember when hanging art: A large picture should not be any bigger than the furniture (either a single piece or a grouping) beneath it; a small picture should not be hung in isolation on a large wall.

The basic rule for positioning a picture: Hang it so that the eye of the viewer looks into the main area of interest. (In living and dining areas, remember that the viewer is usually seated, while in hallways and foyers, the viewer is standing.)

Pictures need not always be hung singly. Cluster several pictures of various sizes or design an arrangement made up solely of similar-size pictures.

Vertical arrangements of pictures will make a room seem higher, just as horizontal ones will make an area appear wider.

To create an attractive picture arrangement for a large wall area, cut paper templates the same size as the pictures you plan to hang. Move the templates around on the wall (attaching them with masking tape) until you arrive at a pleasing composition. Mark the pictures' positions lightly with a pencil.

A small, low-ceilinged room will seem larger if you hang pictures about 4 inches lower than the average eye level. This works best when the furniture stands away from the wall and you aren't visually measuring the picture placement against a sofa or a chest.

HANGING PICTURES AND MIRRORS

Hardware stores and frame shops sell picture hooks in packages that indicate the maximum weight that each hook will hold; so before hanging a picture or mirror, find out its weight. If it weighs less than 5 pounds, simply nail on a saw-tooth hanger. If the picture or mirror weighs more than 5 pounds, attach two screw eyes and braided picture wire. If the frame is extra-heavy, put two screw eyes on each side and use two picture hooks. Nail the hooks into studs (p.49).

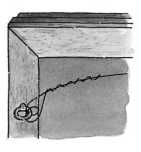

1. Screw in each screw eye one-third of the way down from the top of the frame. Cut the wire 8 inches longer than the frame's width. Slip one end through a screw eye, pull it out 4 inches, slip it through again, then twist the short end tightly around the main wire. Repeat with the other screw eye.

2. Pull the wire taut toward the top center of the frame; measure from the uppermost point of the taut wire to the frame's top. Have someone hold the frame at its intended position on the wall. Mark the midpoint of the frame's top; from there measure down to where the hook should meet the taut wire and mark the spot.

3. Crisscross masking tape over the marked point. Place the hook (with the nail in place) flat against the wall and hit the nail head firmly, with the hammer in line with the direction of the nail. Continue to drive the nail until the hanger fits just snugly against the wall—don't beat it into the wall.

A random assortment of pictures will work well together if they share a predominant color: all sepia tints or black and white photographs, perhaps. Another way to unify them is to use identical mats and frames.

Instead of hanging a painting on a wall, display it on an easel. It's a clever way of filling a corner and of making a painting or print look like a masterpiece.

FRAME-UP

A great way to show off needlework or a canvas painting is in a floater frame. After mounting the cloth on a wood support, screw the frame and support together.

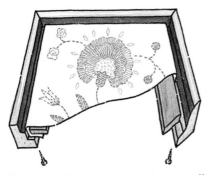

You don't have to spend a small fortune for a custom frame. Instead, buy a framing kit sold in frame shops and art supply stores. You'll get a sheet of glass or plastic, a frame or metal clamps, hardware, plus instructions for putting it together.

A fragile-looking picture needs a frame about ½ inch wide, a medium picture can use a frame up to 2 inches wide, and a large, strong one needs a bold, wider frame.

Glass protects and adds depth to watercolors, pastels, and prints. Buy picture glass rather than window glass; it's thinner and clearer. Nonglare glass is available, but it tends to dim pale colors and fuzz delicate lines.

For protecting artwork, clear acrylic is a lightweight alternative to picture glass.

Artwork is expensive. Take the time and the money to mat it properly; either go to a professional or buy materials from an art supply store and do it yourself.

Don't use a mat of the same width as the frame or the art. Let your eye be your guide, but remember, a mat too narrow for its setting will appear unnecessary, and one too wide will monopolize attention.

MIRROR MAGIC

Mirrors widen and heighten space; they intensify lighting; they give off a shine that complements contemporary interiors—and they mask all wall defects.

Position a mirror so that a person of average height looks directly into it. However, if you plan to use the mirror primarily for decorative effect—for example, over a mantel—its height is less critical.

Want to bring some sunshine into a dark and dreary room? Mirror the window reveals (the sides of the window between the wall and the frame) to reflect the light outside and to bring some glimpses of the outdoors inside. For a professional-looking job, have a glazier custom-cut the glass.

Make a small dining room look twice its size by mirroring an entire wall. For the best effect, place your dining table directly against the mirrored wall. This way, your table will look twice as long.

DISPLAYING COLLECTIONS

Show off your special treasures in a brilliant display case; install mirrors all around a wall niche and fit it with glass shelves.

Properly lit and starkly displayed against a mirror or a bare wall, an interesting shape such as a bird decoy, an old clock, or a candelabrum can be shown off as though it were a piece of sculpture.

To add a personal note to a child's room, attach a strip of molding and hang his collection of baseball hats or cowboy hats from it. Also, suspending a collection of kites from the ceiling is colorful, decorative, and inexpensive.

A blank wall can become a focus of interest if you hang on it small objects with interesting silhouettes—for example, a collection of hinges, locks, and keys.

Put your plants on display by creating a garden area in your living room. Just lay ceramic tiles down over a sheet of plastic right on the carpet or hardwood floor; the tiles will add a look of style *and* protect the floor from dirt and water stains.

Taking Care of the Furnishings

GLASSWARE AND DINNERWARE

To scrape food particles off fine plates before washing them, use a sponge, paper towel, or rubber spatula. Abrasive utensils, such as knives and forks, can damage delicate finishes.

Rinsing dinnerware soon after use prevents stains and makes washing easier. Rinse with cold water to remove milk, eggs, and starches, and moderately hot water for all other foods.

Make glasses sparkle by adding a few drops of laundry bluing or ammonia to the suds. Rinse thoroughly. (To separate two glasses stuck together, see p.391.)

Reduce the risk of chipping or breaking delicate items: Use a dishpan and a drying rack made of plastic or rubber. Also, place a rubber collar around the faucet and a rubber mat or thick towel on the floor of the sink.

To prevent coffee or tea from staining china, rinse cups in a solution of 1 part 30 percent hydrogen peroxide to 3 parts water containing a drop of clear ammonia. Rinse again with clear water.

In addition to saving you time and energy, a dishwasher offers one other advantage: The high temperature of its water sanitizes dinnerware. For tips on loading and maintaining a dishwasher, see pp.142–145.

MENDING CRACKS IN POTTERY

1. Using a cotton swab dipped in soapy water, clean the area around the crack. Place the object in an oven set at 125° F and remove it after 30 minutes.

2. Mix a slow-drying epoxy glue. Force the glue into the crack with a toothpick so that the crack absorbs as much of the glue mixture as possible.

3. When the crack is full, remove any excess glue with a cotton swab dipped in alcohol or nail polish remover. Let the object cool before using.

Although most dinnerware and glassware today is dishwasher-safe, items that are old, finely crafted, or made of delicate materials should be carefully hand-washed. This includes glued or repaired pieces, cut or etched glass, antique or hand-decorated china, and any item containing gold, silver, ivory, or wood.

To remove stubborn stains from glassware, fill the vessel with water, add 1 teaspoon of ammonia, and let it stand overnight. If that doesn't work, rub the stain with baking soda, but don't use abrasive cleansers or scouring pads.

Dry glasses with a linen towel to keep them lint-free. For a less expensive substitute, try a cotton-linen blend with at least 25 percent linen.

Store seldom used china in plastic bags or in quilted, zippered cases made especially for this purpose. You won't have to wash them before that special occasion.

To prevent unglazed footings on china plates from scratching delicate finishes, insert paper plates between stacked dishes.

MENDING CHINA AND PORCELAIN

If a cup or plate has a clean break, you can easily repair it by matching the edges exactly and supporting the pieces while the glue sets. To adjust the pieces, use a slow-drying epoxy glue (p.192). Don't try to repair dinnerware with complicated or jagged breaks.

First clean and dry the broken surfaces and edges thoroughly. Then fit the pieces together dry to determine the best order of assembly. Using a matchstick or a small spatula, apply a very thin coat of glue along one edge of the break. Join and brace the pieces, then wipe off any excess glue with a cotton swab dipped in the appropriate solvent. Clamp and support the glued piece, using one of the following methods.

For a plate broken in two, anchor the larger piece in a basin filled with sand, balancing it so that the piece you attach will stand without support. Hold the smaller piece in place with two pinch-type clothespins.

For a plate broken into several pieces, pack soft modeling clay around the bottom of the unbroken segment. After the mold has set, shift it to the broken side. Then fit the pieces into the mold.

For a broken cup handle, wrap vertical and horizontal strips of masking tape around the cup. Leave the tape in place until the glue has set. Then remove the tape carefully.

Smooth tiny chips in glassware by rubbing them with fine, wet emery paper. If the glass is valuable or the chip is large, have the item repaired by a professional.

SILVERWARE

Fine silverware should be used frequently, not packed away for special occasions. Constant wear actually enhances the beauty of a solid silver piece by giving it a deep, mellow patina.

As soon as silver flatware has been cleared from the table, wash it in hot sudsy water and rinse it in clear hot water. This is especially important for items that have been in contact with salt, eggs, olives, mustard, vinegar, fruit juices, or cooked vegetables.

To prevent water-spotting, don't allow silverware to air-dry. Dry items with a lint-free towel.

Although most silverware is dishwasher-safe, there are two exceptions: antique silverware and oxidized silverware. Hot water can loosen hollow handles on the former and dissolve the decorative pattern applied to the latter.

Dip polishes will remove tarnish from silver, but they'll also remove any oxidized pattern. For oxidized silver, use a commercial cream or paste polish instead.

To polish silver, gently rub the item lengthwise with a soft, dry cloth. Clean crevices with a cotton swab or a natural-bristle brush. Wash and rinse the item, then buff it with a soft cloth.

Because the outer layer of a silver-plated item is soft and thin, avoid rubbing it harshly and polishing it frequently. Or use a dip polish.

To remove tarnish from a small piece of silver, try this: Cover the bottom of a heatproof glass container with a piece of aluminum foil, shiny side up. Place the tarnished item in the container. Add 1 heaping tablespoon of baking soda, then pour in enough boiling water to cover the item. The tarnish will collect on the foil. Remove the piece, rinse it thoroughly, and polish it with a soft cloth.

To clean tarnish from the edges of fork prongs, rub them with a string coated with silver polish.

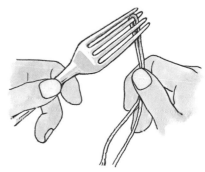

If you're tired of polishing large or intricate silver pieces, such as vases, trophies, or candelabras, have them lacquered by a jeweler so that they won't tarnish. Silver flatware and serving trays, however, should not be lacquered.

Because silver is tarnished by sulfur compounds in the air, wrap it in tarnish-inhibiting fabric or in tarnishproof tissue paper.

Keep rubber bands and plastic food wrap away from silverware. They can stain or corrode even those items covered with several layers of tissue or cloth.

Silver pieces displayed in cabinets will tarnish less quickly if you store an open container of tarnish-retarding compound with them.

Spoon bowl dented? Place it over a curved, oval surface, such as a darning egg, and gently hammer it into shape with a rubber mallet.

CLEANING AND POLISHING METALS

Choose a polish designed especially for the metal that needs cleaning. Otherwise you could damage an item's finish.

An old cotton sock makes an ideal polishing cloth. Use one side to apply polish, the other side to buff.

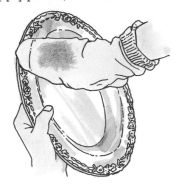

Be sure to wipe away or rinse off all traces of polish after an item has been cleaned. Any residue that remains will only hasten tarnishing.

BRASS

Outdoor brasses will stay nice and bright if you apply a thin coat of paste wax after polishing them. For indoor brasses, use lemon oil.

Here's a homemade polish you can use on slightly tarnished brass. Combine equal parts of salt, flour, and vinegar in a small bowl. Rub the paste on the object with a soft cloth. Because salt is corrosive, be sure to rinse the piece thoroughly before buffing it.

REMOVING DENTS FROM METAL

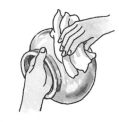

1. Using a jackknife and a rasp, shape the end of a short length of wood to fit the curve of the damaged item.

2. Holding the wood in a vise, gently press and rub the dented area against the shaped end until the surface is smooth.

3. Mix a paste of denatured alcohol and whiting powder, available at jewelry supply stores. Rub it on the repaired item with a soft cloth. Rinse and dry.

KEEPING METALS SHINY AND SPOTLESS

Metal	Regular cleaning	Removing corrosion
Brass, bronze	For lacquered objects, wash in lukewarm sudsy water, rinse, and dry; buff with a soft cloth For bright finishes, wash in hot sudsy water and rinse; apply brass polish with a soft cloth or brush; let polish dry thoroughly, then buff with a soft cloth For dull finishes, mix finely powdered pumice and linseed oil to form a heavy cream; apply with a soft cloth and rub surface vigorously; wipe off excess, then polish with a soft cloth	Rub with a piece of lemon dipped in hot vinegar and salt; wash and rinse; if this fails, use a commercial brass polish
Chrome	Wipe with a damp cloth soaked in warm sudsy water; rinse; buff with a clean soft cloth	Rub with fine scouring powder; if this fails, rub with extra-fine (000) steel wool
Copper	For lacquered objects, wash in lukewarm sudsy water, rinse, and dry; buff with a soft cloth For unlacquered objects, apply copper polish with a soft cloth; wash in hot sudsy water, rinse thoroughly, and dry	Rub with a piece of lemon dipped in hot vinegar and salt; wash and rinse; if this fails, use a commercial copper polish
Iron	For wrought iron, wipe with a damp cloth	Rub with kerosene, then scour with extra-fine (000) steel wool; if this fails, use a coarser grade of steel wool
Pewter	For bright finishes, mix whiting powder and denatured alcohol to form a paste; apply with a soft cloth and rub gently; when dry, polish with a clean soft cloth; wash, rinse thoroughly; wipe dry For dull finishes, mix finely powdered pumice and vegetable oil to form a paste; apply with a soft cloth and rub gently; wash thoroughly, rinse, and wipe dry	Rub with extra-fine (000) steel wool dipped in vegetable oil

MIRRORS

Remove paint splatters from a mirror by rubbing the spots with extremely fine (0000) steel wool. Or use a razor blade in a holder.

To remove dirt from mirrors, use liquid glass cleaner. If the surface is badly soiled, wipe it with a warm solution of tea, water, and detergent. Or use a mixture of 2 tablespoons vinegar, ammonia, or denatured alcohol and 1 quart water.

Don't allow cleaning solutions to come in contact with the rear or edges of a mirror. They can discolor the reflective backing.

To disguise a worn spot in the reflective backing of a mirror, tape a piece of aluminum foil to the back.

Want to prevent the bathroom mirror from fogging? Before taking a bath or a shower, trail a soapy finger across the surface a few times. Then shine it with a cloth.

PICTURES

Avoid hanging pictures, particularly oil paintings, in direct sunlight or near heat sources. (For other hints on hanging pictures, see p.428.)

Because watercolors and photographs can't be cleaned, they should be framed so that they remain dust-free. Cover the face with glass and the entire back of the frame with brown paper. Use a narrow mat to prevent the glass from touching the picture.

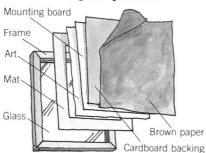

Mounting board
Frame
Art
Mat
Glass
Brown paper
Cardboard backing

Glass-covered photos, prints, and paintings should be cleaned very carefully, especially if they are valuable. Any cleaning solution that drips behind the glass could cause permanent damage.

For valuable art, use matboard and backing made of all-rag, acid-free material. Other materials may cause chemical stains. If you notice such a stain, remount the picture immediately to prevent further damage.

If you're certain that an oil painting isn't valuable, you may want to brighten its dulled surface with a furniture cream wax. Valuable paintings should be left alone, except for an occasional dusting with a spotless cloth.

When a picture needs dusting, take it off the wall so that you can clean its front, back, and frame. Dust the wall behind the picture to prevent dark outlines from forming.

To clean a wooden picture frame, wipe it with a soft cloth dipped in warm, soapy water and wrung almost dry. Dry the frame with a clean cloth; polish if desired.

Brighten a grimy gilt frame by cleaning it with rubbing alcohol and a cotton ball. Use a cotton swab to clean crevices.

FIXING A WOBBLY PICTURE FRAME

1. Remove the paper backing from the frame, then pull out the brads with pliers. Lift out the cardboard backing, mounting board, picture, mat, and glass.

2. Separate the weak corner (or corners) and remove the nails. Remove old glue with a vinegar solution. Refill nail holes with plastic wood; let dry.

3. Apply yellow glue to the ends of both pieces of molding, then put them in a right-angle clamp. While the glue is wet, tap veneer brads into both moldings.

PATCHING A GILT FRAME

Before repairing gold leaf, you'll need to purchase the following materials at an art supply store: a book of gold leaves, a gilder's brush, and a round sable brush.

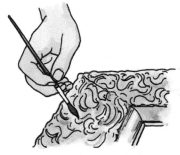

1. In a glass measuring cup, mix 1 part denatured alcohol to 3 parts distilled water. Using a single stroke, apply the solution to the worn spot with a round sable brush.

2. When the area is tacky, then rub petroleum jelly on your wrist. Slide a thin knife beneath a gold-leaf sheet and pick up the leaf by its edge with the gilder's brush. Lay the leaf on the tacky area.

3. Tamp the leaf lightly with a ball of cotton. After 12 hours, polish the surface very gently with a cotton swab. For an antique appearance, apply a coat of glaze of contrasting color, then gently wipe some of it off.

MARBLE

Removing a marble tabletop? Lift and carry it in a vertical position. Otherwise it could break under its own weight.

Marble is very easily stained and scarred. Protect tabletops by placing coasters under drinking glasses; dressers by laying plastic under cosmetics; and floors by using throw rugs in heavy traffic areas.

To clean streaked or dirty marble, wipe it with a damp sponge and buff dry. For stubborn dirt, use dry borax and a damp cloth; then rinse with warm water and buff dry.

To remove stubborn stains from marble, try one of the following pastes. Mix whiting with acetone for grease or oil stains; hydrogen peroxide and a few drops of ammonia for food stains; or liquid rust remover for rust stains. Apply to the stain, cover with plastic wrap, and seal with masking tape. Let the acetone and peroxide mixtures stand overnight; the rust paste, a few hours. Then sponge off the mixture and buff the area.

If removing a stain dulls the surface of marble, wet the area with water and sprinkle it with marble-polishing powder (tin oxide). Rub with a thick cloth, then buff.

Smooth away surface scratches on marble with superfine sandpaper. Polish the spot with tin oxide, then buff with a chamois.

LEATHER

To prevent damage to leather, keep it away from heat sources and out of direct sunlight. Avoid storing leather in damp areas.

Time to clean your leather chair or sofa? First remove wax buildup with a mixture of ¼ cup vinegar and ½ cup water. Then wash the piece with water and saddle soap, available at a hardware or a shoe repair shop. Rub briskly with a soft cloth to restore the shine.

OTHER FURNISHINGS

To remove rust from unpainted metal furniture, scrub it with a cloth dipped in turpentine. (For advice on how to clean and polish specific metals, see pp. 433–435.)

Without adequate moisture, wicker furniture may crack or split. Keep wicker well away from a fireplace, stove, or radiator. If a piece becomes brittle, drench it with water. Bring wicker furniture indoors during freezing weather.

Because vinyl can be hardened by oil, avoid oil-base cleaners or polishes. Remove body oil by washing with a damp cloth sprinkled with baking soda or vinegar. Then clean with a solution of water and mild dishwashing liquid.

WOOD FURNITURE

If you dust your wood furniture often with a slightly dampened lint-free cloth containing a small amount of furniture polish, you won't have to polish as frequently.

No matter which type of polish you choose, apply it sparingly. The real secret to a good shine is more rubbing, not more polish.

Avoid switching back and forth from a polish containing oil to one containing wax. Applying both kinds to the same surface could cause blotches or smudges.

FURNITURE POLISHING PRODUCTS

Choose a polish that matches your furniture's finish rather than its wood. Follow the directions on the furniture tag or in the care booklet. If neither is available, buy a product recommended for wooden furniture. Test a small amount on an inconspicuous area; if you're satisfied with the results, proceed according to the directions.

Product	Application	Results
Liquid polish	Apply with a soft cloth; buff lightly with a clean, soft cloth while wet	High luster; little protection
Paste wax	Apply sparingly with a soft cloth; buff vigorously with a clean, soft cloth when dry	High luster; moderate protection; slight yellowing
Cream polish	Apply with a soft cloth; buff with a clean, soft cloth when dry	Moderate luster; moderate protection
Spray wax	Spray on; buff with a clean, soft cloth while wet	Moderate luster; little protection
Dusting spray	Spray on; wipe off with a clean, soft cloth	Prevents dust from scattering; no protection
Scratch-cover liquid polish	Apply with a soft cloth; wipe off with a clean, soft cloth	Conceals blemishes; no protection
Oil finish	Apply with a soft cloth; dry with a clean, soft cloth	High luster; no protection

To remove wax buildup from furniture, wipe the surface with a soft cloth dampened with synthetic turpentine or mineral spirits. Or clean the area with liquid polish.

SPOTS AND STAINS ON WOOD

To remove water stains from wood, lay a thick blotter over the spot and press it with a warm iron until the stain is gone. If that doesn't work, rub lemon oil into the area and let it set overnight. Wipe off the excess the following morning.

Left untreated, alcohol can dissolve wood finishes. Clean up spills from drinks, medicines, and cosmetics immediately. Then rub the spot with a cloth moistened with lemon oil. Treat dried stains as you would light burns (see hint in next column).

Because milk products can damage wood finishes, wipe up spills promptly. Rub stains with a damp cloth dipped in ammonia or with a finger dipped in silver polish or wet cigarette ashes. Then wipe with a dry cloth.

Forgot to protect your mahogany table with coasters? Glass rings will disappear if you rub them with mayonnaise and white toothpaste. Wipe the area dry, then polish the entire surface.

MARRED WOOD SURFACES

To darken a scratch, rub it gently with the meat of a walnut. Rub the kernel of the nut directly into the scratch to avoid darkening the surrounding wood.

Hide scratches on mahogany or dark cherry by rubbing them with a cotton swab dipped in iodine. For unshellacked maple and light cherry, dilute the iodine by 50 percent with denatured alcohol.

For scratches in oiled finishes, rub in the direction of the grain with fine (0) steel wool and lightweight mineral oil or boiled linseed oil. Let the oil soak in, then wipe the area dry with a clean cloth.

Here's how to remove a light burn from the surface of finished wood. Form a thin paste by mixing finely powdered pumice (available from woodworking suppliers) with linseed oil. Using a soft cloth, rub the paste with the grain. Repeat until the burn disappears.

REPAIRING A DEEP BURN IN WOOD

1. Gently sand or scrape away the blackened wood with a single-edge razor blade or a utility knife. Heat the blade of a small, finely pointed knife or a curved grapefruit knife over the sootless flame of a spirit lamp or over an electric-stove burner.

2. Using a tinted wax or shellac stick that matches the lightest grain in the wood, hold the stick against the heated blade. Guide the wax into the depression as it melts. Fill the hole so that it's slightly higher than the surrounding area.

3. When the wax has cooled, scrape off any excess with a razor blade. To match the grain, paint darker streaks across the patch with a fine-tipped artist's brush. Seal the patch with clear polyurethane or an acrylic varnish spray.

FIXING WOOD SCRATCHES

A minor scratch can often be disguised with furniture oil or polish, or with a scratch-cover liquid polish. If that doesn't work, rub the area with a retouch crayon, available at woodworking suppliers and hardware stores. For a more professional look, follow one of the methods described below. Afterward, buff the area with extra-fine (000) steel wool, then wax or polish the surface.

If a scratch is in the finish only, clean the area thoroughly. To test the finish, place a drop of denatured alcohol and a drop of lacquer thinner on a hidden spot. Using a fine-tipped brush, apply whichever solvent softens the finish. Brush the solvent diagonally across the scratch and blend in the surrounding finish.

If a scratch penetrates the wood, clean the area with alcohol or lacquer thinner (use whichever one is *not* the solvent for that particular finish). Hold a tinted wax stick or shellac stick against the heated blade of a knife, and guide the filler into the depression as it melts. Smooth the filler with the heated blade. Let the filler cool, then repeat if necessary.

To remove a blister from veneer, cover the area with a damp cloth and press the cloth lightly with a warm iron. Place a heavy weight on the spot for several days. If this fails, cut through the blister in the direction of the grain. Lift the edges, scrape out the old adhesive, and apply white glue to both surfaces. Weight the spot for 24 hours.

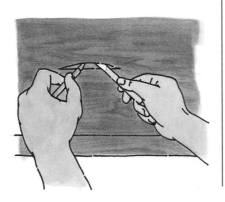

Fine cracks all over a wood surface may be due to excessive heat or insufficient humidity. To improve the piece's appearance, apply a furniture refinisher or a wax polish that matches the wood finish. If cracking is extensive, the entire surface should be stripped and refinished.

If wood is slightly dented, remove the finish over the damaged area with an appropriate solvent. Lay a damp cloth over the area and press the tip of a hot iron against the cloth for a few seconds. After the surface dries, sand and refinish the area.

MINOR FURNITURE REPAIRS

A wooden drawer may stick if it's overfilled or if high humidity has swollen the wood. If the problem persists even after you remove some of the contents or wait for drier weather, try this. Lightly sand the wooden runners, then lubricate them with wax or soap. Or lubricate the metal slides with a small amount of grease.

To fix a split drawer bottom, glue a canvas strip along the underside of the split. Use white glue.

Do drawers wobble when they're opened and closed? Glue triangular wooden blocks where the tops of the supports form right angles with the sides of the dresser.

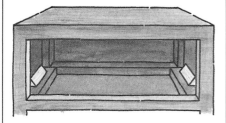

Furniture leg wobbly? Reinforce it with a metal mending plate or corner brace. Drill pilot holes first to prevent the screws from splitting the wood.

If a chair or table wobbles, place the piece where it will be used and rock it to determine which leg is short. Push thin pieces of cardboard under the short leg until the item is steady. Measure the combined thickness of the cardboard pieces, then cut that amount off an appropriate size dowel. Sand the end of the short leg, then glue the dowel cutoff in place.

To tighten a cane seat that has sagged, wet the unlacquered side with a damp sponge dipped in water. Let it dry overnight.

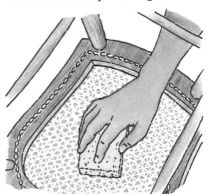

REPAIRING LOOSE CHAIR JOINTS

If a joint is shaky, try to reinforce it without disassembling the chair. Pull the joint apart slightly and scratch off old glue with a knife. Then squirt in white glue, wiggling the joint to work the glue into the wood. If a socket is enlarged, jam matchsticks or toothpicks into the fresh glue around its edges. If the joint is still weak after the glue has dried, you'll have to disassemble the chair to repair the joint.

1. Remove any nails, screws, or braces, then tap the joint apart with a mallet or a padded hammer. Separate the two pieces and scrape away the old glue.

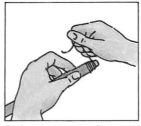

2. If a dowel or tenon fits loosely into its socket or mortise, wrap thread around it to fatten it. Or insert a new dowel or tenon large enough to provide a snug fit.

3. Reglue the joint. Tighten a rope around the legs, tourniquet style, to apply even pressure during the drying period. Protect the wood with padding.

PATCHING DAMAGED OR MISSING VENEER

1. At a woodworking supply house or a craft store, buy a piece of veneer that matches the grain direction and type of the original surface as closely as possible. Tape tracing paper over the damaged area, leaving one edge untaped. Trace the outline of the break.

2. Slip the veneer patch under the tracing paper and align the grain with the original. Hold the piece firmly in place. Using a utility knife, cut through the new and old veneer, just outside the traced line. Remove the tracing paper and the patch, then clean out the old veneer and glue.

3. Test fit the patch. Wipe the underside of the patch with veneer glue. Apply a thin layer of veneer glue to the wood base. Press the patch into place carefully. Cover it with wax paper and a wood block, then clamp. Let the patch dry overnight. Strip and refinish the entire surface.

BEFORE REFINISHING

Refinishing may not be necessary for a dull-looking piece of furniture. You may be able to rejuvenate it just by removing wax build-up. A tung oil-base preserver will clean, polish, and restore the finish in one step. Test it on a hidden area before applying.

If you've never tackled a refinishing job before, start with something small, such as a picture frame or a footstool. Photograph the item first so that later you can see how well you did.

Cover the floor of your work area with layers of newspaper. As each top layer gets messy, remove a few sheets and discard them.

Unscrew handles and other hardware. If they're coated with paint or finish, immerse them in paint remover. Scrape off the softened paint with steel wool or a stiff brush. Wash, apply polish, and store in a labeled container.

Here's a test to determine whether paint remover or furniture refinisher is right for your project. Moisten a cotton ball with nail polish remover and touch it to the furniture. If the cotton ball sticks, use refinisher; if it doesn't, use paint remover.

For vertical surfaces, a semipaste stripper is better than a liquid. Because semipaste doesn't run, evaporate, or dry quickly, it requires only one application; a liquid must be reapplied several times.

SANDING

If a surface feels smooth, sand it with fine paper; otherwise start with medium and then switch to fine. Finish with very fine paper. Sand with the grain, but avoid oversanding. Wipe off the residue as you work.

Aside from convenience, there's another good reason to use a sanding block: Sanding with your hand against the paper can result in uneven surfaces and rounded edges. Glue a thin layer of felt or sponge rubber to one side of a block of wood (3 x 5 x ¾ inches is a good size). Wrap a layer of sandpaper around the block. Hold the block tightly to prevent the sheet of sandpaper from shifting around as you work.

To sand inside grooved surfaces, such as moldings, make a sanding stick. For rounded crevices, wrap sandpaper around the cutoff of a dowel that's slightly narrower than the groove. Move the piece back and forth along the groove. For angular crevices, use a piece of scrap that fits into the groove.

The best way to remove dust after sanding is with a tack cloth. To make one, dip a piece of cheesecloth into a mixture of equal parts varnish and turpentine. Wring the cloth nearly dry and store it in an airtight jar. Several times a year, sprinkle the cloth with turpentine.

STRIPPING A PIECE OF FURNITURE

Caution: When removing paint or varnish with a caustic stripper, work in a well-ventilated area, away from any open flame. Don't smoke. Wear safety goggles and cotton-lined neoprene gloves. Keep children and pets away from the work area. Store scrapings in a disposable can.

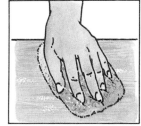

1. Remove knobs, hinges, handles, and other hardware. Apply a thick layer of paint remover or stripper with an old, clean paint brush. Brush with the grain in one direction only.

2. When the finish bubbles, scrape it off with a blunt-edged, round-cornered putty knife. Be careful not to gouge the softened wood beneath. For crevices, use a stiff toothbrush.

3. After the entire surface has been scraped clean, look for any dark or glossy patches. Recoat these missed spots with stripper or paint remover, then scrub them with steel wool.

443

APPLYING A NEW FINISH

Want to stain wood before adding a surface finish? Coat the end grain with thinned shellac first. Otherwise the end grain will absorb more stain and appear darker than the rest of the wood.

Open-pore woods, such as oak, hickory, and ash, should be treated with filler paste after an old finish has been removed and be-fore a new one is applied. First thin the paste to the consistency of thick paint according to the manufacturer's directions. Brush it on with the grain, let it set for 5 to 10 minutes, then wipe it off across the grain with burlap. Polish with the grain, using a clean cotton cloth. Wait 24 hours before refinishing.

Before applying a furniture stain, test the color on an inconspicuous spot or on a similar piece of scrap wood. For a true test, apply a coat of the final finish over the stain.

To give bare wood a warm, golden tone once required many coats of finish, each laboriously rubbed in. Now you can do it with two to four coats of clear resin-type penetrating finish, often sold as Danish oil or natural finish. Just wipe it on with a clean cloth or brush, wait a few minutes while it soaks in, then wipe off the excess with a clean cloth. Repeat after 24 hours.

CHOOSING THE RIGHT WOOD FINISH

Finish	Surface	Application	Solvent	Comments
Lacquer	Matte to highly glossy	Brush (natural bristle only) or spray; 2 or 3 coats recommended; allow 5 hr. between coats, 24 hr. before last coat	Lacquer thinner	Dries clear; darkens wood least; provides good water resistance; for best results, apply in dust-free surroundings
Penetrating resin	Clear	Pour on; spread with rag or brush; 1 or 2 coats recommended; allow 12 hr. between coats	Turpentine or mineral spirits	Darkens wood most; provides fair water resistance
Shellac	Semiglossy	Brush (natural bristle only); 3 or more coats recommended; allow 3 hr. after first coat, 4 hr. after second, 5 hr. after third, and so on	Denatured alcohol	Dries clear; darkens wood slightly; provides poor water resistance; for best results, apply in dust-free surroundings
Tung oil; tung-oil varnish	Matte to semi-glossy	Spread with rag; rub vigorously enough to generate heat; 1 or 2 coats recommended; allow 24 hr. or more between coats	Turpentine or mineral spirits	Darkens wood slightly; provides good water resistance
Varnish (poly-urethane or oil-base)	Glossy, semi-glossy, or satin	Brush or spray; 3 coats recommended; allow 24 hr. between coats of oil-base, 12 hr. between coats of poly-urethane	Turpentine or mineral spirits	Dries clear to dark brown; provides fair water resistance; for best results, apply in dust-free surroundings

If the furniture in your children's rooms is old or inexpensive, finish it with a colorful alkyd enamel paint rather than a clear finish. It'll not only look more attractive, but hold up better to cleaning and abuse.

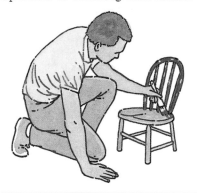

VARNISHING

The key to protecting varnish from specks is to work in an area that's as dust-free as possible. Choose a clean, low-traffic room; vacuum it thoroughly the day before so that dust settles overnight.

To keep varnish smooth, avoid patting the brush against the side of the container and wiping it across the rim. The former creates air bubbles; the latter causes a lumpy buildup.

If dust sticks to the brush and ends up in the varnish, strain the varnish through a nylon stocking or several layers of cheesecloth into a clean container.

For the final coat over varnish or shellac, use a paste wax. Apply it with a soft clean cloth, rub vigorously, then remove any excess with a clean cloth.

SPECIAL REFINISHING PROBLEMS

For pieces with intricate carvings or rough textures, such as wicker, spray-painting is your best bet. Practice on a piece of cardboard to refine your technique. Keep the can in motion once you push the button; release the button before you finish each stroke.

Here's how to spray-paint a piece of furniture without messing up the surrounding area. Place the item inside a large appliance box with the front cut off. Spray in from the outside.

You won't have to sand between coats of finish if you allow each coat to dry for the optimum time (p.444). However, if the previous coat has dried longer, sand with fine sandpaper to give the surface some bite for the next layer.

PREPARING TO REFINISH A WOOD FLOOR

Refinishing a floor takes about a week: a day to prepare the space and gather materials and tools, another to sand, and several more to apply finish and allow drying time between coats. Save time by asking someone to help you.

Rent a drum-type floor sander for a thorough job on main surfaces and an edger for edges and corners; manually sand areas that the machine can't reach. Stock up on sandpaper, and make sure you have the right tools for attaching the paper to the sander. Have the salesperson show you how to operate the machine and how to change the sandpaper.

Before you start sanding, remove any carpet staples from the floor and repair damaged or loose flooring. Drive protruding nailheads below the surface with a nail set, then fill the holes with wood putty.

Nail set

Before sanding edges and corners, remove such obstacles as radiator covers and floor molding. Number the molding sections and their places on the wall so that you'll know where to put them when you're through.

SANDING

Sanding floors sends dust in every direction; the sander's dust bag can't catch it all. Remove all portable items from the room; cover permanent fixtures as well as doorways and air vents with plastic sheeting. Remove the curtains. If you can't do this, pin them up and wrap them in plastic. Seal closets with masking tape.

Sanding dust is a highly flammable substance. Don't smoke or strike matches while sanding. Be sure pilot lights on nearby appliances are turned off.

Sanding dust can irritate your eyes and respiratory system. Wear goggles and a respirator mask while sanding. Wear earplugs to cut down on the noise.

Using an industrial drum floor sander is like walking a headstrong dog. Your job is to let it pull you, but not as fast as it can. Always keep the machine moving or the sander will "eat down" into the floor and leave an uneven surface. Wearing work gloves will ease the pressure on your hands.

Respirator mask

Dust bag

Drum-type floor sander

Generally, wood floors need three grades of sandpaper: coarse for the first pass, followed by medium and fine. If your floor is in bad shape, start with an extra-coarse grade of paper.

For "seamless" sanding, overlap the area you have just sanded as you move to an unsanded section. Sand floor edges immediately after drum sanding an area. Saving all the edges until last may result in a visible meeting line.

Dust bag   Edger

After each sanding, damp mop the floor to remove dust and raise the grain. When finished sanding, sweep, then vacuum thoroughly. (Save sanding dust for crack filler.) Damp mop and finish by wiping with a tack cloth (p. 443). Wear thick socks or white-soled sneakers to avoid marking the floor.

TOUCHING UP

Fill floor cracks with putty that's been mixed with stain sealer and sawdust to give it the same color as your floor.

If your floorboards are stained or too dark for your taste, try rubbing household bleach on them. After 15 minutes, rinse the bleach off with a solution of half water, half vinegar. For a truly blond floor, try industrial-strength bleach.

SEALANTS

If you want floors to be only slightly darker, apply a sealant of any type. If you want the finish to have a much darker tone, apply wood stain before the sealant.

You need three coats when you use polyurethane. Thin the first coat with one part mineral spirits to four parts polyurethane; this acts as a sealer. Let each coat dry 24 hours before recoating; observe ventilation precautions on container. In between coats, buff with a rented floor-polishing machine equipped with superfine steel wool; clean with a tack cloth.

Things to consider when choosing a finish: Penetrating sealants are easier to use for touching up or reapplying. If you're dealing with surface coatings, such as polyurethane, varnish, or lacquer, you must sand them before recoating.

TOOLS AND PROCEDURES

Use a long-handled roller to apply sealer or varnish on the main surface of the floor; use a small brush for edges and corners. Inexpensive foam rubber rollers are best; just throw them away instead of cleaning them between coats.

447

Allow the floor finish to cure for a few days before replacing the room's furnishings. It needs time to toughen. Lift furniture to replace it in the room; or move heavy pieces on old blankets or drop cloths.

Enhance and prolong your floor's beauty: 3 days after the finish has dried, apply paste wax; buff the floor with an electric polisher. Repeat with a second coat.

PAINTING FLOORS

Generally, wall and woodwork paints aren't durable enough for floors. However, they can be used for low-traffic surfaces such as the edges of partially carpeted stairs. For high-traffic surfaces, use paint designated for wood floors.

High-traffic surfaces need a highly durable finish. Use porch or floor and deck paint as the container's instructions direct.

Before painting, remove old wax with fine steel wool and a commercial wax remover or turpentine. Turn off nearby pilot lights, keep the room well ventilated, and don't smoke while working.

SLIPCOVERS

You'll have an easier time making slipcovers if you choose a fabric with a plain design or texture. (Striped materials must be kept straight; those with bold patterns require matching.) Look for fabric that's preshrunk, washable, colorfast, and stain resistant.

A little confused about how to lay out slipcover pieces for cutting? Place all the lengthwise measurements (top to bottom or, for cushions or seats, back to front) on the fabric's length; all widthwise measurements (side to side) on the fabric's width.

If your slipcover won't have a skirt, you can still make it fit as smoothly as upholstery. Add a small flap to turn under the seat's bottom and line it with Velcro; attach corresponding strips to the seat's underside. Cut notches between the flaps to let the legs protrude.

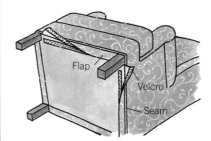

Avoid slipcover sag. Gently poke the fabric into the crannies of an armchair or sofa with the end of a wooden yardstick.

If the fabric label on your slipcovers says they're washable, follow the washing and drying instructions, but replace them on the furniture while they're still slightly damp and pliable. This avoids shrinkage and resulting problems with fit.

MAINTAINING UPHOLSTERED FURNITURE

Give upholstered furniture a good vacuuming weekly: Run the upholstery attachment's nozzle slowly over all surfaces and crannies. (For more on furniture care, see pp. 98-99.)

Are your cushions dank from humid weather? Air them outdoors on a dry, breezy day. Place them in the shade (to avoid fading) on a clean surface for several hours. Turn them over at least once.

When wet-cleaning fitted upholstery, don't over-wet it. This can cause some foam fillings to deteriorate. Dry cleaning solvents can have the same effect if overused.

Use a hand hair dryer to speed up the drying of upholstery fabric. To avoid scorching, don't hold it too close to the fabric.

CHOOSING COVER FABRIC

Here's a test for wearability when choosing upholstery fabric: Pull the fabric lengthwise and crosswise, then release it. Threads that shift out of place and stay there indicate poor quality; those that spring back are preferable. A tight, flat weave usually wears better than a loose one.

Consider fabric-backed vinyl covering for heavily used furnishings in a sun-room or porch. It resists household chemicals, food stains, and dirt; it also withstands long exposure to sun without fading.

When measuring a piece for fabric, first measure between the two widest points. Then add—on all sides—¾-inch for seams and for tacking to exposed wood, plus 2 inches for hand gripping while tacking. For tacking fabric under the frame, add four inches more.

A YEARLY SHAMPOO FOR UPHOLSTERED FURNITURE

You'll need a whisk broom or a vacuum cleaner with an upholstery attachment, a rubber or plastic scraper, 2 tablespoons soap flakes and 2 tablespoons ammonia in 1 quart hot water, a pan of warm water, soft cloths, and paper towels. (To clean leather or vinyl, see p. 438.)

1. Brush or vacuum the furniture well. After the cleaning solution has jelled, whisk it until a mass of suds forms. Rub suds into a small, hidden area of the fabric. Let dry. If it fades, discolors, or shrinks, have the job done professionally; if not, proceed to the next step.

2. With a suds covered cloth, gently rub the suds on a small area. When the suds become soiled, scrape them off with a scraper. Wipe the scraper clean on paper towels.

3. Wet a cloth in rinse water, wring well, then wipe sudsy area (dampen the fabric only slightly). Repeat steps, overlapping the previously cleaned areas. Change suds, rinse water, and cloths when they get dirty. Dry with an electric fan.

PREPARING TO REUPHOLSTER

Remove all visible tacks or staples with a stripping tool and a mallet (p. 450). Take the covering off piece by piece; remove the stitches, then press the material flat and use it as a pattern for cutting new fabric. (You can pattern a slipcover the same way.)

As you dismantle stuffing or padding, make sure you write down, sketch, or photograph the position of each piece of material as well as its layered sequence prior to doing the actual stripping. By doing this you'll be able to reassemble them correctly. Remove only damaged stuffing and padding.

When you run your hand across a pile or napped fabric, it either smooths down or stands up. An upholstery cover should be cut so that on the sides (or vertical surfaces) the nap smooths down toward the floor; on top it should smooth toward the front. If you cut pieces going the wrong way, the finished cover will appear to have different tones.

To help keep the padding in place, cover it with muslin before tacking on the outer cover. Then, before cutting the new cover, pin the old pieces of fabric onto the muslin; check for shape changes. You may have to add or subtract an inch here or there to accommodate contour changes before cutting the new cover.

Use gimp or braid to mask tacks and raw edges where the covering is attached to the frame. Glue the braid or fasten it with decorative, roundhead brass tacks.

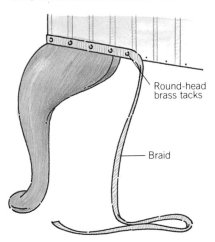

Round-head brass tacks

Braid

REPAIRING TORN UPHOLSTERY

Tacks

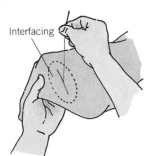

Interfacing

1. If possible, remove the damaged fabric from the furniture piece (if not, see step 3). Press the torn section flat. Cut out a piece of heavy iron-on or denim patch interfacing that overlaps the tear.

2. Place the patch material or interfacing centrally under the tear, fusible side up, and press it fast. Use a dry muslin cloth between the hot iron and the upholstery. Using fabric-matching thread, slip stitch across the line of the tear in small, neat stitches.

3. Replace the repaired fabric on the piece of furniture. If you can't remove the fabric, slip the interfacing under the tear, pull the tear together with a few slip stitches, then iron.

Look for upholstery tools in craft stores. Tacks, decorative nails, gimp and other braids, and webbing are sold in upholstery departments of large stores. Some small upholsterers will supply materials for stuffing and padding.

STUFFING AND PADDING

Traditionally, upholstered furniture was stuffed with horsehair. Now that this product is scarce and costly, Algerian fiber (palm grass), cotton, or curled hair (an animal mixture) is usually substituted. However, if your original stuffing is horsehair and it's salvageable, hand wash it in soapy water and rinse well. Comb out as it dries.

Foam rubber and polyurethane are good for padding because they're nonallergenic, washable, and mildewproof. Foam is easier to work with; although slightly more expensive than other padding, it gives comfortable, uniform support and resumes its shape.

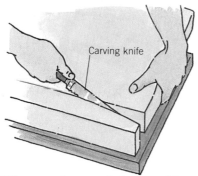

Carving knife

When working with foam rubber, sprinkle powdered soapstone or talcum across the surface of the working area to prevent the padding from sticking and gripping.

All paddings emit toxic fumes if they catch fire, and polyurethane can be extremely dangerous in this respect. If you have some concerns about fire in your home, it is advisable to cover polyurethane padding with fire-resistant fabrics.

Foam and polyurethane padding need air flow. To ventilate closed-base chairs, drill holes in the base at regular intervals.

SPRINGS AND WEBBING

Has a spring come loose from your chair's webbing? Compress the spring and sew it to the webbing using a curved needle and stitching twine. Secure the spring at three points and tie off the first and last stitches.

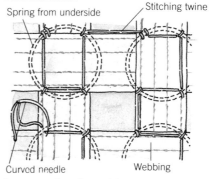

Spring from underside

Stitching twine

Curved needle

Webbing

Is your chair's webbing too worn to hold the springs? Support them with ½-inch plywood slats. Strip off the worn webbing and screw a 2-inch-wide slat across each row of springs. Cut slats slightly shorter than the width of the chair's bottom so that they won't show. Tie the springs to their slats with heavy twine.

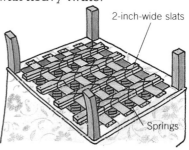

2-inch-wide slats

Springs

Index

460

The editors are grateful to the following for information and guidance:

Agriculture Canada
American Apparel
  Manufacturers Association
American Council for an Energy
  Efficient Economy
American Ladder Institute
American Textile Manufacturers
  Institute
American Wool Council
APC Corporation
Armour-Dial Company
Association of Home Appliance
  Manufacturers
Borden Chemical, Borden, Inc.
Broan Mfg. Co., Inc.
Canada Safety Council
Canadian Hardwood
  Plywood Assn.
Canadian Home Builders Assn.
Canadian Medical Assn.
Canadian Standards Assn.
The Carpet and Rug Institute
Clorox Co.

Con Edison
Energy, Mines and Resources
  Canada
General Electric Company
Georgia-Pacific Corporation
Gold Seal Co.
Good Housekeeping Institute
The Handy Hint Journal
Health and Welfare Canada
Hill's Pet Products Inc.
Home Center Institute/National
  Retail Hardware Association
Hydro-Québec
International Fabricare Institute
International Linen Promotion
  Commission
International Silk
  Association-U.S.A.
International Wool Secretariat
Johnson Wax
Lever Brothers Company
The Maytag Company
National Broiler Council

National Paint & Coatings Assn.
National Research Council of
  Canada
National Turkey Federation
Neighborhood Cleaners Assn.
New York State Energy Office
Ontario Ministry of the
  Environment
Ontario Ministry of Housing
W.H. Perron Co.
Porcelain Enamel Institute
The Procter & Gamble Company
Revenue Canada
St. John Ambulance
Sears Roebuck and Co.
The Soap and Detergent Assn.
Texize, Division of Morton
  Norwich
U.S. Department of Agriculture
The Wallcovering Information
  Bureau
Western Wood Products Assn.
Whirlpool Corporation

Acknowledgments

Acropolis Books Ltd. PARENT TRICKS-OF-THE-TRADE by Kathleen Touw and illustrated by Loel Barr, copyright © 1981 by Acropolis Books Ltd. COLOR ME BEAUTIFUL by Carole Jackson, copyright © 1980 by Acropolis Books Ltd. Reprinted by permission. *Addison-Wesley Publishing Company* TAKE CARE OF YOURSELF by D.M. Vickery & J.F. Fries, copyright © 1985 Addison-Wesley Publishing Company. Reprinted by permission. *American Apparel Manufacturers Association* CONSUMER CARE GUIDE FOR APPAREL. Reprinted by permission. *Arbor House Publishing Co.* HINTS FROM HELOISE, copyright © 1980 by King Features Syndicate, Inc. HELOISE'S BEAUTY BOOK, copyright © 1985 by King Features Syndicate, Inc. Reprinted by permission. *Atheneum Publishers, Inc.* FEAST WITHOUT FUSS by Pamela Harlech, copyright © 1977 by Pamela Harlech. Reprinted by permission. *Avon Books* SEW SUCCESSFUL by Claire B. Shaeffer, copyright © 1984 by Claire B. Shaeffer. Reprinted by permission of Dominick Abel Literary Agency. *Charles C. Thomas, Publisher* SUBURBAN BURGLARY by George Rengart & John Wasilchick, copyright © 1985 by Charles C. Thomas, Publisher. *Chronicle Books* CUTTING-UP IN THE KITCHEN by Merle Ellis, copyright © 1975 by Merle Ellis. Reprinted by permission. *Church & Dwight Co., Inc.* ARM & HAMMER BAKING SODA GREAT IDEAS CLINIC. ARM & HAMMER is a trademark of Church & Dwight Co., Inc. Reprinted by permission. *Coats & Clark Inc.* BUTTONS, SNAPS, HOOKS AND EYES, copyright © 1983 by Coats & Clark Inc. MENDING, copyright © 1978 by Coats & Clark Inc. Reprinted by permission. *The Countryman Press* HOMEOWNER'S GUIDE TO LANDSCAPE DESIGN by Timothy Michel, copyright © 1983 by The Countryman Press. Reprinted by permission. *Crown Publishers, Inc.* CRIME STOPPERS by Wesley Cox, copyright © 1983 by Wesley Cox. Reprinted by permission. *Dell Publishing Co., Inc.* SMART SHOPPING WITH COUPONS & REFUNDS by Bronnie Storch Kupris, copyright © 1980 by Bronnie Storch Kupris. CATS: BREEDS, CARE, AND BEHAVIOR by Shirlee A. Kalstone, copyright © 1983 by Shirlee A. Kalstone, Dell Publishing Co., Inc. and Sanford Greenburger Associates Inc. TIPS FOR TODDLERS by Brooke McKamy Beebe, copyright © 1983 by Brooke McKamy Beebe. Reprinted by permission. *Dodd, Mead & Company, Inc.* EVERYTHING YOU WANTED TO KNOW ABOUT COSMETICS by Toni Stabile, copyright © 1984 by Toni Stabile. Reprinted by permission of Dodd, Mead & Company, Inc., and Toni Stabile. *Dorling Kindersley Ltd.* COLOR RIGHT DRESS RIGHT by Liz E. London and Anne H. Adams, copyright © 1985 by Dorling Kindersley Ltd, London, text copyright © 1985 by Liz E. London and Anne H. Adams. Reprinted by permission of Liz E. London and Anne H. Adams. *Doubleday & Co., Inc.* TRAINING YOU TO TRAIN YOUR DOG by Blanche Saunders, copyright © 1946 by United Specialists, Inc. MARY ELLEN PINKHAM'S 1000 NEW HELPFUL HINTS, copyright © 1983 by Mary Ellen Pinkham. SYLVIA PORTER'S NEW MONEY BOOK FOR THE 80's, copyright © 1975, 1979 by Sylvia Porter. THE AMY VANDERBILT COMPLETE BOOK OF ETIQUETTE: A GUIDE TO CONTEMPORARY LIVING. Revised and expanded by Letitia Baldridge, copyright © 1978 by Curtis B. Kellar and Lincoln G. Clark, Executors of the Estate of Amy Vanderbilt Kellar and Doubleday & Company, Inc. THE FURNITURE DOCTOR by George Grotz, copyright © 1962 by George Grotz. THE INDOOR CAT by Patricia Curtis, copyright © 1981 by Patricia Curtis. Reprinted by permission. *E.P. Dutton Company, Inc.* TIME MANAGEMENT MADE EASY by Peter A. Turla and Kathleen L. Hawkins, copyright © 1984 by Peter A. Turla and Kathleen L. Hawkins. Reprinted by permission. *The East Woods Press* INTERIOR FINISH AND CARPENTRY: SOME TRICKS OF THE TRADE, by Bob Syvanen, copyright © 1982 by Bob Syvanen. Reprinted by permission. *Encyclopaedia Britannica, Inc.* 1980 MEDICAL AND HEALTH ANNUAL, copyright © 1979 by Encyclopaedia Britannica, Inc. Reprinted by permission. *Facts on File Publications* HELPFUL HINTS FOR BETTER LIVING by Hap Hatton and Laura Torber, copyright © 1984 by Hap Hatton and Laura Torber. Reprinted by permission. *Gaines Foods, Inc.* FEEDING YOUR DOG RIGHT, copyright © 1982 by General Foods Corporation. Reprinted by permission. *Globe Mini Mag* SEWING TRICKS, copyright © 1984 by Globe Mini Mag. Reprinted by permission of Globe Mini Mag and Deutsch, Levy & Engel. *Harcourt Brace Jovanovich, Inc.* THE I HATE TO HOUSEKEEP BOOK by Peg Bracken, copyright © 1962 by Peg Bracken. Reprinted by permission Harper & Row, Publishers, Inc. THE AIDA GREY BEAUTY BOOK by Aida Grey and Kathie Gordon, copyright © 1979 by Aida Grey and Kathie Gordon. Reprinted by permission. *Henry Holt and Company, Inc.* KITCHEN WISDOM by Frieda Arkin, copyright © 1977 by Frieda Arkin. Reprinted by permission of Henry Holt and Company, and Severn House Publishers Ltd. MORE KITCHEN WISDOM, by Frieda Arkin, copyright © 1982 by Frieda Arkin. Reprinted by permission of Henry Holt and Company. *Holt, Rinehart and Winston* PERSONAL & FAMILY SAFETY & CRIME PREVENTION by Nancy Z. Olson, copyright © 1980 by Preventive Medicine Institute/Strang Clinic. Reprinted by permission. *Home Magazine Ltd.*, May, 1983 issue. Reprinted by permission. *Houghton Mifflin Company* TAYLOR'S ENCYCLOPEDIA OF GARDENING, copyright © 1961 by Norman Taylor. Reprinted by permission. *Jonathan David Publishers, Inc.* THE HOUSEHOLD BOOK OF HINTS AND TIPS by Diane Raintree, copyright © 1979 by Jonathan David Publishers, Inc. Reprinted by permission. *Little, Brown and Company* MARSHALL LOEB'S 1986 MONEY GUIDE, copyright © 1985 by Marshall Loeb Enterprises, Inc. FAST AND LOW by Joan Stillman, copyright © 1985 by Joan Stillman. Reprinted by permission. *Macmillan Publishing Company* THE PRUNING MANUAL, Based on THE PRUNING MANUAL by L.H. Bailey by E.P. Christopher, copyright © 1954, 1982 by E.P. Christopher. TREES FOR AMERICAN GARDENS by Donald Wyman, copyright © 1965 by Donald Wyman. SHRUBS AND VINES FOR AMERICAN GARDENS, copyright © 1949 by Donald Wyman. THE GOOD DOG BOOK by Mordecai Seigal, copyright © 1977 by Mordecai Siegal. HOWARD HILLMAN'S KITCHEN SECRETS by Howard Hillman, copyright © 1985 by Howard Hillman. Reprinted by permission. UPHOLSTERING by James E. Brumbough, copyright © 1986 by Macmillan Publishing Co. *The Maytag Company* MAYTAG GAS COOKING APPLIANCE SERVICE MANUAL, MAYTAG ELECTRIC COOKING PRODUCTS SERVICE MANUAL, copyright © 1982 by The Maytag Company. MAYTAG ENCYCLOPEDIA OF HOME LAUNDRY, copyright © 1973 by The Maytag Company. Reprinted by permission. *McGraw-Hill Book Company* THE MEAT BOARD MEAT BOOK by Barbara Bloch, copyright © 1977 by National Live Stock & Meat Board and The Benjamin Company, Inc. Reprinted by permission of The Benjamin Company, Inc. HOW TO RESTORE AND REPAIR PRACTICALLY EVERYTHING by Lorraine Johnson, copyright © 1984 by Lorraine Johnson. Reprinted by permission. *William Morrow & Company, Inc.* 20001 HINTS FOR WORKING MOTHERS by Gloria Gilbert Mayer, copyright © 1983 by Gloria Gilbert Mayer. Reprinted by permission. *Necessary Trading Company.* NECESSARY CATALOGUE, Volume 3, copyright © 1983 by Necessary Trading Company. Reprinted by permission. *Nitty Gritty Productions* HOUSEHOLD HINTS by Anna Cope, copyright © 1980 by Nitty Gritty Productions. Reprinted by permission. *101 Productions* WORKING FAMILY'S GUIDE by Sheila Kennedy and Susan Seidman, copyright © 1980 by Sheila Kennedy and Susan Seidman. Reprinted by permission. *W.W. Norton & Company, Inc.* GETTING ORGANIZED, The Easy Way to Put Your Life in Order by Stephanie Winston, copyright © 1978 by Stephanie Winston. HOME FREE, The No-Nonsense Guide to House Care, by Ann Guilfoylo, copyright © 1984 by Ann Guilfoyle. JANE BRODY'S NUTRITION BOOK, copyright © 1981 by Jane E. Brody. JANE BRODY'S GOOD FOOD BOOK, copyright © 1985 by Jane E. Brody. Reprinted by permission. *Orbis Book Publishing Corporation Ltd.* THE CAT CARE QUESTION AND ANSWER BOOK, copyright © 1981 by Orbis Publishing Corporation Ltd. *Oxmoor House* ®HOME PAINT BOOK by Richard V. Nunn, copyright © 1975 by Oxmoor House ®. Reproduced by permission. *Penguin Books Ltd.* THE NATIONAL TRUST MANUAL OF HOUSEKEEPING by Hermione Sandwith and Sheila Stainton (Allen Lane in association with the National Trust, 1984), copyright © 1984 by The National Trust. *Prentice-Hall, Inc.* BUILT-INS, STORAGE AND SPACE-MAKING by Allen D. Bragdon, copyright © 1983 by Allen D. Bragdon. CARING FOR YOUR AGING PARENTS by Robert R. Cadmus, M.D., copyright © 1984 by Prentice Hall, Inc. SUPER HANDYMAN'S ENCYCLOPEDIA OF HOME REPAIR HINTS by Al Carrell, copyright © 1971 by King Features Syndicate, Inc. LOOKING AFTER YOUR DOG by John and Mary Holmes, copyright © 1981 by John and Mary Holmes. SPEED SEWING by Janice S. Saunders, copyright © 1982 by Van Nostrand Reinhold Company, Inc. Reprinted by permission. *The Putnam Publishing Group* A BASIC GUIDE TO DOG